Housing and Interior Design

10th Edition

Evelyn L. Lewis, Ed.D.
Professor Emerita, Home Economics
Northern Arizona University
Flagstaff, Arizona

Carolyn S. Turner, Ph.D., CFCS
Professor Emerita, Department of Family and Consumer Sciences
North Carolina Agricultural and Technical State University
Greensboro, North Carolina

Publisher
The Goodheart-Willcox Company, Inc.
Tinley Park, Illinois
www.g-w.com

Library of Congress Catalog Card Number 2010016997

ISBN 978-1-60525-337-4

2 3 4 5 6 7 8 9 10 – 12 – 17 16 15 14 13 12

The Goodheart-Willcox Company, Inc. Brand Disclaimer: Brand names, company names, and illustrations for products and services included in this text are provided for educational purposes only and do not represent or imply endorsement or recommendation by the author or the publisher.

The Goodheart-Willcox Company, Inc. Safety Notice: The reader is expressly advised to carefully read, understand, and apply all safety precautions and warnings described in this book or that might also be indicated in undertaking the activities and exercises described herein to minimize risk of personal injury or injury to others. Common sense and good judgment should also be exercised and applied to help avoid all potential hazards. The reader should always refer to the appropriate manufacturer's technical information, directions, and recommendations; then proceed with care to follow specific equipment operating instructions. The reader should understand these notices and cautions are not exhaustive.

The publisher makes no warranty or representation whatsoever, either expressed or implied, including but not limited to equipment, procedures, and applications described or referred to herein, their quality, performance, merchantability, or fitness for a particular purpose. The publisher assumes no responsibility for any changes, errors, or omissions in this book. The publisher specifically disclaims any liability whatsoever, including any direct, indirect, incidental, consequential, special, or exemplary damages resulting, in whole or in part, from the reader's use or reliance upon the information, instructions, procedures, warnings, cautions, applications or other matter contained in this book. The publisher assumes no responsibility for the activities of the reader.

The Goodheart-Willcox Company, Inc. Internet Disclaimer: The Internet resources and listings in this Goodheart-Willcox Publisher product are provided solely as a convenience to you. These resources and listings were reviewed at the time of publication to provide you with accurate, safe, and appropriate information. Goodheart-Willcox Publisher has no control over the referenced Web sites and, due to the dynamic nature of the Internet, is not responsible or liable for the content, products, or performance of links to other Web sites or resources. Goodheart-Willcox Publisher makes no representation, either expressed or implied, regarding the content of these Web sites, and such references do not constitute an endorsement or recommendation of the information or content presented. It is your responsibility to take all protective measures to guard against inappropriate content, viruses, or other destructive elements.

Library of Congress Cataloging-in-Publication Data

Lewis, Evelyn L.
    Housing and interior design / Evelyn L. Lewis, Carolyn S. Turner. -- 10th ed.
      p. cm.
    Previous eds. under title: Housing decisions.
Includes index.
    ISBN 978-1-60525-337-4
    1. Housing. 2. Dwellings. 3. Interior decoration. 4. House furnishings. I. Turner, Carolyn S. II. Lewis,
Evelyn L. Housing decisions. III. Title.
    TX301.L46 2012
    645--dc22

                                               2010016997

Photography Credits

Page 6, 15, 274–275 Calico Corners—Calico Home Stores; Page 16, 538–539 Trex Company, Inc.

Introduction

With a new look and a new title, this edition of *Housing and Interior Design* encourages you to develop foundational knowledge and skills relating to career pathways in housing and interior design. Chapter topics will lead you through many concepts and issues home owners and interior designers face when selecting and designing living spaces. With a strong emphasis on universal and green or sustainable design, this text offers you many practical ways to put the *design process* into practice.

Through this text, you will learn how to identify and evaluate the wide array of housing and design options to fill human needs. Hundreds of beautiful photos effectively illustrate design concepts you can adapt to fit various structures. The charts and illustrations help demonstrate and clarify important text information about such topics as architectural design, furniture design, and design technology and trends.

With a focus on professional practices and career success, the *Housing and Interior Design* text includes a number of elements that can help you on your career journey. The *Career Focus* features highlight related housing and interior design careers with a bright job outlook. In the chapter review, the *Design Practice* activities offer you a wealth of practical ways to develop your design creation and presentation skills. Because involvement with student and professional organizations is key to career success, the FCCLA activities at the end of every chapter reinforce teamwork, workplace skills, and community involvement.

About the Authors

Dr. Evelyn L. Lewis, Professor Emerita, taught 37 years in primary, secondary, and higher education. She developed curricula for the Arizona Department of Education and prepared training programs for Coconino County career education. Lewis also served Flagstaff's Habitat for Humanity as a volunteer.

Dr. Carolyn S. Turner is Professor Emerita, Department of Family and Consumer Sciences, North Carolina Agricultural and Technical State University, Greensboro, North Carolina. Dr. Turner has taught housing and resource management at the college level. She has also conducted research on housing for populations with special needs, residential energy efficiency, and renewable energy applications. Turner served on the board of directors as a national officer of the American Association of Family and Consumer Sciences. She is past president of the national Housing Education and Research Association and the North Carolina Association of Family and Consumer Sciences. Turner has also served on the States Energy Advisory Board for the U. S. Department of Energy and an Executive Advisory Board for the U. S. Department of Homeland Security.

Acknowledgments

The authors and Goodheart-Willcox Publisher would like to thank the following professionals who provided valuable input to this edition of *Housing and Interior Design*:

Contributing Authors

Judith Brinkley-Berry, ASID
Judith Brinkley-Berry Interior Design
Hilton Head Island, South Carolina

Madge Megliola, ASID
Madge Megliola Interiors
Greensboro, North Carolina

Technical Reviewers

Jennifer Blanchard Belk, IIDA, IDEC, LEED AP
Assistant Professor, Interior Design Program
Winthrop University
Rock Hill, South Carolina

Mark Baker, ASLA
Partner, Wood + Partners, Inc.,
Land Planning, Landscape Architecture, Community Planning, Resort Development and Urban Design Services
Hilton Head Island, South Carolina

Dr. JoAnn Emmel
Associate Professor
Department of Apparel, Housing and Resource Management
Virginia Polytechnic and State University
Blacksburg, Virginia

Rebecca Ewing, CMG
Rebecca Ewing, Color and Design
Decatur, Georgia

Lora Getterman
Lora Getterman Interiors
Greensboro, North Carolina

J. Terry Keane, AIA
Hilton Head Island, South Carolina

J. Edward Pinckney, FASLA
President, Edward Pinckney/ Associates, Ltd.
Landscape Architecture, Land Planning and Urban Design
Bluffton, South Carolina

Gary Upchurch
Landscape Designer/Project Director
New Garden Landscaping and
    Nursery
Greensboro, North Carolina

Dr. Jane E. Walker
Associate Professor
Department of Family and Consumer
    Sciences
North Carolina Agriculture and
    Technical State University
Greensboro, North Carolina

Allen Ward, PE
President, Ward Edwards, Engineering,
    Planning, Science and Surveying
Specializing in Building Healthy
    Communities
Bluffton and Beaufort, South Carolina;
    Savannah, Georgia

Instructor Reviewers

Jaylie I.L. Beckenhauer, Ph.D., CFCS
Department of Family and Consumer
    Sciences
Baylor University
Waco, Texas

Carol Diane Boudreaux
Family and Consumer Sciences
    Instructor
Aldine High School
Houston, Texas

Sandra Bryson
Family and Consumer Sciences
    Instructor
Oakland High School
Murfreesboro, Tennessee

Serina Gay
Family and Consumer Sciences
    Instructor
GIVE Center West
Norcross, Georgia

Nicole Minshew
Housing Instructor
Autauga County Technology Center
Prattville, Alabama

Brittany Reinking
Family and Consumer Sciences
    Instructor
Lawrence Central High School
Indianapolis, Indiana

Susannah Turner-Harvell
Greensboro, North Carolina

Group 3, Architectural and
Interior Design, Hilton Head
Island, South Carolina.
Photography courtesy of
John McManus.

Welcome to
Housing and Interior Design

The purpose of *Housing and Interior Design* is to help you succeed in mastering the concepts in this textbook. Read further to discover key elements that will help lead you on the path to career success.

Chapter Titles introduce the topics covered in each part of your text.

Chapter Objectives provide a framework for concepts and skills you will learn from studying the chapter.

Terms to Learn appear in bold type in the text where they are defined.

Reading with Purpose strategies help you engage with chapter content and enhance your reading skills.

The Inside Story

PART 4

10 Using the Elements of Design
11 Using Color Effectively
12 Using the Principles of Design
13 Textiles for Environments
14 Creating Interior Backgrounds
15 Furniture Styles and Construction
16 Arranging and Selecting Furniture
17 Window Treatments, Lighting, and Accessories
18 Selecting Appliances and Electronics
19 Planning and Presenting Interior Designs

CHAPTER 10

Using the Elements of Design

Terms to Learn

visual imagery
design
function
construction
aesthetics
line
horizontal lines
vertical lines
diagonal lines
curved line
form
realistic form
abstract form
geometric form
free form
space
mass
high mass
low mass
texture
tactile texture
visual texture

Chapter Objectives

After studying this chapter, you will be able to

- summarize the characteristics of good design.
- evaluate the use of the elements of design in residential and commercial interiors.
- analyze the psychological impact of the elements of design on people.
- analyze the effects the elements of design have on aesthetics and function.

Reading with Purpose

Before reading the chapter, make a list of five things you already know about the elements of design. Leaf through the pages of the chapter and note the heading topics. Predict five things you will learn about using the elements of design.

Calico Corners—Calico Home Stores

More Interior Design Emphasis

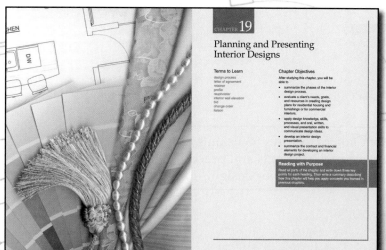

New!

A full chapter covers the *Design Process* for creating interior designs and making design presentations.

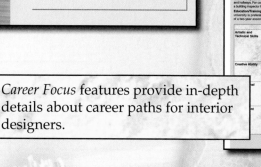

Career Focus features provide in-depth details about career paths for interior designers.

FCCLA activities in every chapter focus on ways to use your housing and interior design skills.

FCCLA

Family, Career and Community Leaders of America (FCCLA) is a national career and technical student organization that promotes personal growth and leadership development through Family and Consumer Sciences education. Through various programs—including *STAR Events, Career Connections, Leaders at Work, Dynamic Leadership,* and *Community Service*—FCCLA helps young women and men develop life skills necessary for success at home and in the workplace. Projects developed through various FCCLA programs can help you

- develop and apply academic and communication skills

- enhance leadership, decision-making, and problem-solving skills

- establish positive work-related attitudes and habits

The FCCLA activities in this text suggest ways to develop projects for community activities and competitive events. For additional information about FCCLA, visit www.fcclainc.org.

Informative Features

GREEN CHOICES

Let the Environment Work for You!

The famous American architect, Frank Lloyd Wright, led the way in placing housing on land that takes advantage of the natural environment. (Review 2-16.)

Housing that takes advantage of the natural environment is "green" because the house will cost less to heat and cool. Also, there will be fewer disturbances to the natural environment by the construction process. Specifically, home buyers and builders can select or build houses with the following "green" ideas in mind:

- Use natural sunlight as much as possible to heat interior spaces (place most lived in areas on southern side of the home)
- Place rooms that produce heat on the northern side of the home (kitchen, bathrooms, utility rooms)
- Chose landscaping that blocks northern winds from reaching the house (large trees/bushes that keep their leaves all year)
- Build levels of the house to match the natural slope of the land

These strategies can reduce energy costs. They also add to the thermal comfort and views of the home.

Green Choices features focus on *green* and *sustainable* concepts and practices for housing and interior design.

and permit others. Housing is more than a response to the physical environment. It is a setting for the development of the members of the household.

A positive behavioral environment is desirable for the growth and development of all household members. Housing that is safe and adequate contributes to such positive behavior, 2-18. However, when housing is substandard, it can produce a behavioral environment that has a negative effect on household members. For instance, psychological distress due to substandard housing may influence drug addiction, alcoholism, violence, and other negative behaviors among household members.

Interaction of the Environments

Each type of environment affects the other two, causing a chain reaction. One example is a community that has no open space. Houses in this community

2-17
The people who live in this beach house have easy access to the ocean plus a beautiful view.

Group 3, Architectural and Interior Design, Hilton Head Island, South Carolina. Photography provided as a courtesy of John McManus, Savannah, Georgia.

CAREER FOCUS

Interior Designer—Schools

Can you imagine yourself as the interior designer for a school in your community? If you can, you may want to consider a career as civic contract designer who designs schools.

Interests/Skills Are you interested in developing the youth of the next generation? Do you believe design can affect relationships between teachers and their students? Have you thought about better ways to navigate the crowded hallways between classes or how to make the cafeteria more functional for students and staff? Project organization and time management skills are essential for civic designers. Designers must be able to convey their thoughts and ideas so others understand them. For example, effective communication about design plans between designers, architects, and school board members helps improve the quality of education.

Career Snapshot: Designers must educate themselves about any special requirements. They need to know the age group for whom they are designing. Educational buildings age rapidly and constantly need to be brought up to current codes and standards. For these types of projects, designers need experience with designing existing spaces. Current trends point the way to eco-friendly design and using sustainable products that promote a healthy environment. As a result, designers must constantly update their education.

Education/Training: Completion of a bachelor's or master's degree is preferred. Classes include business management, lighting, textiles, and CADD. To specialize in designing spaces for schools additional courses in psychology of learning, education, and ergonomics are essential. Continuing education is a career-long requirement.

Licensing/Examinations: Approximately one half of the states require interior designers to be licensed. The National Council for Interior Design Accreditation administers an examination that interior designers must pass in order to obtain a license and to be competitive.

Professional Association: The American Society of Interior Designers (ASID) (www.asid.org), The International Interior Design Association (IIDA) (www.iida.org)

Job Outlook: Jobs are expected to be in demand through 2018. Outlook will be especially good for designers who specialize in ergonomic design or sustainable design. Also, because of the large number of aging schools, the job market will be strong for designers with knowledge of the special needs of this sector.

Source: Information from the Occupational Outlook Handbook (www.bls.gov/OCO) and the Occupational Information Network (O*NET) (www.online.onetcenter.org)

©2005 Image by Greg Loffin–The Loffin Group/ LS3P ASSOCIATED, LTD. Knightdale High School, Knightdale, North Carolina.

Career Focus profiles numerous careers in the housing and interior design career pathways that relate to the *Architecture & Construction* and *Arts, A/V Technology, & Communications* career clusters.

somewhat like a bird's-eye view, that shows the size and arrangement of rooms, hallways, doors, windows, and storage areas on one floor of a home. In 7-5 you can see the symbols used in the floor plan.

When discussing plan views and describing houses, the term *square footage* is often used. This is a measurement of house size that refers to the amount of living space in the home. You will use the room dimensions that appear on the floor plan to determine square footage.

Elevation Views

Exterior elevations are architectural drawings that show the outside views of the house. A set of drawings usually includes four exterior elevations showing all four sides of the house. If the building is simple, there may be only the front elevation and one side elevation.

7-5
Understanding an architectural drawing is a matter of knowing what the symbols mean.

Bloodgood Sharp Buster Architects & Planners, Inc.

MATH MATTERS

Determining Square Footage of a Home

Often a house plan or description refers to the total square feet in a home. Square footage is used to compare homes in terms of size. The higher the square footage, the larger the home will be.

Square footage is the total amount of living space (area) in the home. You can determine the total living space by adding together the square footage space from rooms. The dimensions of each room appear on the floor plan. Note that closets, storage space, and garages do not count toward the square footage of a house. Once you find the dimensions on the floor plan, use the following formula to determine the square footage for each room:

$$Area = Length \times Width$$

If a room is 12 feet long and 10 feet wide, the square footage will be the following:

$$A = 12 \text{ ft.} \times 10 \text{ ft.}$$
$$A = 120 \text{ sq. ft.}$$

To calculate the total square footage of a home, complete the calculation for each room and add them together.

Math Matters features help reinforce relevant math concepts.

Link to Science & Technology focuses on topics—ranging from telecommuting to nanotechnology in household products—that influence housing and interior design.

Health/Safety features focus on health and safety topics for the home and workplace.

Link to Social Studies & Culture features highlight such key topics as anthropometrics (human scale) and color psychology.

Chapter Review

Summary provides an overview of important chapter content.

Review the Facts helps you recall important chapter concepts.

Think Critically activities challenge you to use your critical thinking skills to respond to key topics of concern in housing and interior design today.

Community Links activities relate chapter content to situations and locations in your community.

Academic Connections activities strengthen your academic skills in core areas, such as writing, reading, math, science, and social studies.

Technology Applications activities help you apply today's technology to important housing and interior design concepts.

Design Practice activities provide hands-on practice for developing design skills that can lead to careers in housing and interior design.

FCCLA activities link key chapter content to related FCCLA programs and activities.

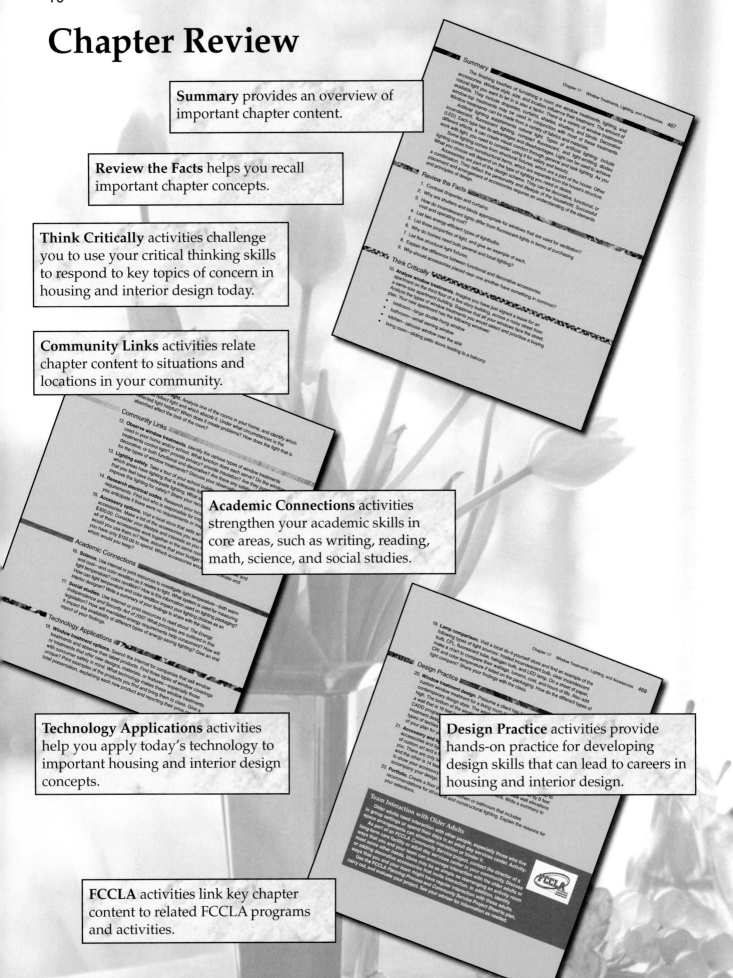

Appendices

Appendix A—Housing and Related Legislation—highlights major legislation impacting housing and interior design.

696

APPENDIX **A**

Housing and Related Legislation

Few items affect housing as much as government policy. Even the cost of housing is affected by government controls. Also, the federal government provides supervision and regulation to assure safety in environmental areas. These also affect housing and its occupants, particularly hazardous materials (such as lead-based paint), air and water quality, and conservation of natural resources. Several of the most significant actions that occurred at the federal level are listed here.

1901

The Tenement House Act was passed to improve conditions in tenement houses. It applied to houses already constructed and set standards for building new ones.

1918

The U.S. Housing Corporation was established to provide housing for veterans of war.

1932

The President's Conference on Home Building and Home Ownership discussed the national decline in building and the shrinking availability of mortgage credit. As a result of the Conference, the Federal Home Loan Bank Act of 1932 was passed. This Act established 12 district Federal Home Loan Banks as the framework of a reserve credit organization for home-

Appendix C—ASID Code of Ethics and Professional Conduct—outlines the professional responsibilities of members of the American Society of Interior Designers (ASID).

706

APPENDIX **B**

Entrepreneurship

Entrepreneurs are people who start and run their own business. Like most careers, entrepreneurship has both advantages and disadvantages. There are many issues to research when you are starting your own business. Consider all aspects carefully before deciding that entrepreneurship is for you.

Advantages and Disadvantages of Entrepreneurship

Many people become entrepreneurs so they can be their own boss. They enjoy being able to make all the decisions and work whatever hours they choose.

Some people start a business for the satisfaction of working with subjects they understand or enjoy. Starting a business may also provide a sense of accomplishment. However, many people become entrepreneurs for monetary reasons. If a business is successful, the owner can make a sizable profit.

Chief among the disadvantages to becoming an entrepreneur is the hard work. At first, you may have to work nonstop just to get the business started. During this period, very little money—if any—is coming in. You may have to put most of your savings into your business, since affordable loans for starting a business are rare. If the

Appendix B—Entrepreneurship—provides an overview of the requirements for starting a business of your own.

719

APPENDIX **C**

ASID Code of Ethics and Professional Conduct

1.0   PREAMBLE

Members of the American Society of Interior Designers are required to conduct their professional practice in a manner that will inspire the respect of clients, suppliers of goods and services to the profession and fellow professional designers, as well as the general public. It is the individual responsibility of every member of ASID to uphold this code and bylaws of the Society.

2.0   RESPONSIBILITY TO THE PUBLIC

2.1 Members shall comply with all existing laws, regulations and codes governing business procedures and the practice of interior design as established by the state or other jurisdiction in which they practice.

2.2 Members shall not seal or sign drawings, specifications or other interior design documents except where the member or the member's firm has prepared, supervised or professionally reviewed and approved such documents, as allowed by applicable laws, rules and regulations.

2.3 Members shall at all times consider the health, safety and welfare of the public

722

APPENDIX **D**

Related Careers

In addition to interior design careers, a number of other careers relate to and are necessary components to providing attractive housing for people from all walks of life. The following passages include a number of careers that fall into the *Architecture & Construction* and the *Arts, Audio/Video Technology, & Communications* career clusters. To complete more in-depth career research, use the following career Web sites:
* O*Net (www.onetcenter.org)
* CareerOneStop (www.careeronestop.org)
* U.S. Bureau of Labor Statistics, *Occupational Outlook Handbook* (www.bls.gov/OOH)

Architectural Drafters

Career Description: Architectural drafters help prepare architectural designs and plans for buildings following the specifications an architect provides. Tasks include, but are not limited to, analyzing building codes, planning interior room arrangements, and preparing rough and detailed scale plans. These drafters must have excellent communication, critical-thinking, math, and problem-solving skills. Many of these positions focus on green and sustainable design.

Technical Skills: Architectural drafters must be able to use CADD software and equipment and traditional drafting equipment, graphics- and photo-imaging software, and project management software.

Education/Training: Most positions require an associate's degree and related on-the-job experience.

Job Outlook: Employment growth for drafters is expected to increase through 2018. However, growth for architectural drafters is expected to be about as fast as average in this same period.

Model Makers

Career Description: With knowledge about blueprints and drawings, model makers are able to construct scale-size mock-ups of buildings and structures. Ability to use woodworking tools to cut shapes and patterns is essential along with strong math (algebra, geometry, calculus), critical-thinking, and problem-solving skills. Model makers must have good finger dexterity to make precise movements and manipulate small objects.

Technical Skills: Model makers must know how to use design tools and techniques and know how to apply principles of engineering science and technology.

Education/Training: Positions may require vocational training, on-the-job training, or an associate's degree.

Job Outlook: Job growth for model makers will have little or no change through 2018.

APPENDIX **E**

Practical Math Review

Math skills are essential to the housing or interior design professional's success on the job. For example, a designer or builder uses computational skills when taking measurements or creating a bid. When a designer works from a set of plans, math is used to obtain distances or to extrapolate actual dimensions.

Could you calculate the areas of ceilings or walls, or estimate the amount of wall covering or fabric a job requires? Could you estimate how much paint is needed to cover a structure's exterior or a room's walls? What if the area to be covered is not rectangular, but a triangular- or circular-shaped space? What if measurements are given in meters instead of feet?

You learned many of these skills throughout this text. This appendix reviews some basic mathematical operations a housing and interior design professional may use.

Place Values of

are the thousands position, the ten-thousands position, and so forth.

Example
2, 542, 908

8 has a place value of *ones*
0 has a place value of *tens*
9 has a place value of *hundreds*
2 has a place value of *thousands*
4 has a place value of *ten-thousands*
5 has a place value of *hundred-thousands*
2 has a place value of *millions*

Addition

Addition is the combining of at least two numbers to result in a new figure, or *sum*. When adding, align numbers by place value. For instance, line up the numbers that are in the ones column beneath each other.

the next digit to the left that is in the hundreds position. Moving left, there

1205
+2237
4241

Adapted with permission from *Painting & Decorating* by E. Keith Blankenbaker. Available through Goodheart-Willcox Publisher (www.g-w.com).

Appendix E—Practical Math Review—offers a quick review of basic math concepts.

Appendix D—Related Careers—highlights additional careers in the housing and interior design career pathways.

Brief Contents

Contents

Chapter 19

Planning and Presenting Interior Designs........502

Part 5 A Safe and Attractive Environment

Chapter 20

The Outdoor Living Space and Environment.......538

Chapter 21

Home Safety and Security...............568

Chapter 22

Maintaining a Home....596

CAREER FOCUS

GREEN CHOICES

MATH MATTERS

LINK TO SOCIAL STUDIES & CULTURE

LINK TO SCIENCE & TECHNOLOGY

HEALTH/SAFETY

Housing for You

CHAPTER 1

Housing and Human Needs

Terms to Learn

housing
house
home
near environment
needs
physical needs
archeologist
adobe
yurt
psychological needs
esteem
self-esteem
self-actualization
beauty
self-expression
creativity
values
family
roles
lifestyle
household
life cycle
quality of life
human ecology
sustainable design
green design

Chapter Objectives

After studying this chapter, you will be able to

- assess how housing helps people meet their needs.

- analyze factors that affect housing choices, including values, space, costs, roles, and lifestyle.

- summarize how housing needs change over the life span.

- examine ways housing affects quality of life.

- summarize human ecology and the move toward green and sustainable design.

Reading with Purpose

Rewrite each chapter objective as a question. As you read, look for the answers to each question. Write the answers in your own words.

Housing, good or poor, has a deep and lasting effect on all people. Winston Churchill once said, "We shape our buildings, and then they shape us." This is especially true of the buildings in which people live. First people find shelter to satisfy their needs, and then this shelter affects the way they feel and behave.

Housing, as this text uses the word, means any dwelling that provides shelter. It refers to what is within and near the shelter, such as furnishings, neighborhood, and community. A **house** is any building that serves as living quarters for one or more families. In contrast, a **home** is any place a person lives. The relationship between people and their housing will be the focus throughout this text.

People and Their Housing

Housing is your **near environment**, a small and distinct part of the total environment in which you live. Housing includes your dwelling place, the furnishings in the space, your neighborhood, and your immediate community. Your *total environment* includes all your interactions with people and buildings as well as different geographical areas outside your dwelling place, neighborhood, and local community. Although housing is just one part of your total environment, it is a very important part, 1-1. It has great impact on how you live and develop as a person.

Whether you live alone or with others, you interact with your housing. Housing affects your actions, and in turn, your actions affect your housing. For example, if you live in a small apartment, you will not easily host large parties. You will not have enough room, and your neighbors might complain about the noise. However, if you want to host large parties, you might choose to live in a large house that is set apart from other houses.

You can also view interaction with housing on a smaller scale. Suppose you choose to decorate a room in your house with many fragile and expensive accessories. This gives a feeling of formality and elegance. You would not want to exercise in this room. However, if exercise is important to your lifestyle, you could furnish the room differently. You could adapt your housing to match your way of life.

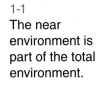

1-1
The near environment is part of the total environment.

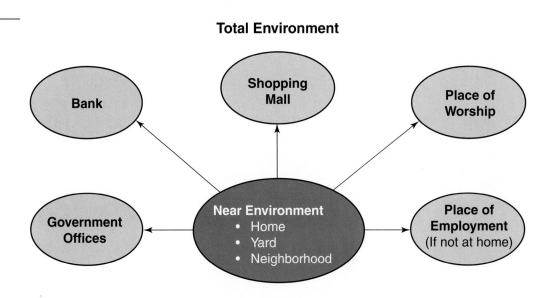

Meeting Needs Through Housing

Everything around you affects well-being. Your near environment, in the form of housing, helps you meet your needs. **Needs** are the basic requirements that people must fill in order to live. All people have physical, psychological, and other needs. They share the need for shelter in which to eat, sleep, and carry on daily living activities.

A director of a shelter for the homeless observed that human needs were arranged in the following order: soup, soap, and salvation. When people came to him for help, their basic needs had not yet been satisfied. They were hungry and could think only of food. Once they had eaten, their next concern was to be comfortable. Only when the people's most basic needs were met could they think of their psychological needs.

Psychologist Abraham Maslow prioritized human needs as shown in 1-2. According to Maslow, as each type of need is met, you progress up the pyramid to the next level. You must meet basic physical needs first. When they are satisfied, you can think about such other needs as security, love, esteem, and self-actualization.

Physical Needs

Physical needs are the most basic human needs. They have priority over other needs because they are essential for survival. Physical needs include shelter, food, water, and rest. Basic or primary needs are other words for physical needs.

Shelter

The need for shelter and protection from the weather has always been met by a dwelling of some type. The findings of archeologists show this is true. **Archeologists** are social scientists who study ancient cultures by unearthing dwelling places of past civilizations. Their findings reveal how ancient structures were made and used, and how they met the need for shelter.

Such natural settings as caves and overhanging cliffs are examples of the earliest dwellings, 1-3A and 1-3B. Later,

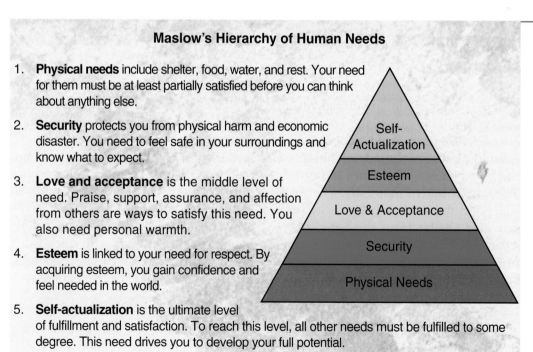

Maslow's Hierarchy of Human Needs

1. **Physical needs** include shelter, food, water, and rest. Your need for them must be at least partially satisfied before you can think about anything else.

2. **Security** protects you from physical harm and economic disaster. You need to feel safe in your surroundings and know what to expect.

3. **Love and acceptance** is the middle level of need. Praise, support, assurance, and affection from others are ways to satisfy this need. You also need personal warmth.

4. **Esteem** is linked to your need for respect. By acquiring esteem, you gain confidence and feel needed in the world.

5. **Self-actualization** is the ultimate level of fulfillment and satisfaction. To reach this level, all other needs must be fulfilled to some degree. This need drives you to develop your full potential.

Pyramid levels (bottom to top): Physical Needs, Security, Love & Acceptance, Esteem, Self-Actualization

1-2
Physical needs are the most basic needs and, therefore, the first step of the pyramid.

1-3

The Qumran Caves (A) are located near the Dead Sea. You can see the entrances to caves that were used for shelter by shepherds over 2,000 years ago. The large cliff dwelling called Montezuma Castle (B) is located in central Arizona. It gave shelter to Native American farmers who lived there probably over 1,000 years ago. Adobe (C) is still used in housing today to help keep houses cool in warm climates. The housing of the Apache (D) is a clue to their way of life. Their summer house is being constructed, while their sturdier house in the background is occupied during winters.

(D) Western Ways Features

A

B

C

D

people built crude dwellings from readily available materials. The Pueblo Native Americans used **adobe**, which is building material made of sun-dried earth and straw. They also used rafters made from native materials. The thick walls and flat roofs, as shown in 1-3C, provided shelter from the hot climate. Apache Native Americans built houses from tree branches, 1-3D. Cooling breezes circulating through the branches and protection from the scorching sun are key features of Apache homes.

Some tribes throughout the world, called *nomads*, periodically move their residences depending on weather, available farmland, and other factors. Today nomadic tribes in Kazakhstan, Central Asia, still use tents or huts such as the *yurt*, 1-4. A **yurt** is a portable hut made of several layers of felt covered with canvas. People use these huts in summer as they move to more fertile growing areas. In winter, the occupants live in permanent huts with thick walls to stay warm in severely cold temperatures, which stay below 0°F for long periods.

Food and Water

In the past, people located their housing near sources of food and water. They stored food and a small supply

1-4
A yurt is a portable hut made of several layers of felt covered with canvas. It can be taken down in about 20 minutes and folded to fit on the back of a camel or horse.

Photo by Carolyn S. Turner

of water in their dwellings while they prepared and ate their food outside.

Today, areas within dwellings are set aside for storing, preparing, and eating food, 1-5. However, people still like to prepare food and eat outside. Some house designs keep this in mind. Food preparation areas are sometimes located in enclosed patios to make outside eating easier.

Rest

A basic human need is rest—a period of inactivity that allows recovery and growth. Rest can take the form of sleep or relaxing. Rest helps people overcome fatigue and restore energy to the body. The amount of sleep each person needs varies but most adults sleep seven and one-half to eight hours at night. Rest and relaxation are as important as sleep. After strenuous work, complete rest may be necessary. At other times, people need relaxation or a change of pace. Any activity different from the usual routine can be relaxing. Pleasurable and relaxing activities help a person shed tension and remain robust.

Areas within dwellings are designated for sleep, generally the bedrooms. These areas or others can also provide space for relaxation. Shared common areas, such as family rooms, offer space for group relaxation. Hobby areas and other rooms promote individual relaxation.

Psychological Needs

Once basic physical needs are met, people strive to meet the psychological needs. These needs are higher on Maslow's hierarchy of human needs. **Psychological needs** relate to the mind and feelings that people must meet in order to live a satisfying life.

Security

Housing provides security from the outside world. It offers protection from physical danger and the unknown. It helps you feel safe and protected.

1-5

Today's modern kitchen has developed from a simple area for stockpiling food and water to a comfortable room for storing and preparing food and eating meals.

Photography Courtesy of Bosch Home Appliances

Living in a dwelling that is well built and located in an area free from crime can help you feel secure.

Love and Acceptance

Housing affects your feelings of being loved and acceptance. If you have your own bedroom or private place, you know others care about you. They accept you as a person who has needs. When you receive task assignments, it is because of your acceptance as part of a group and you have responsibilities as part of that group.

Esteem

You need to feel **esteem**, or the respect, admiration, and high regard of others. Your housing tells other people something about you and can help you gain esteem. A home that is clean, neat, and attractive will gain the approval and respect of others.

You also need self-esteem. **Self-esteem** is awareness and appreciation of your own worth. When you have self-esteem, you think well of yourself and are satisfied with your own roles

and skills, 1-6. Living in a pleasant, satisfying home can help you gain self-esteem.

Self-Actualization

When you meet the need for **self-actualization**, you are developing to your full potential as a person. You are doing what you do best. If your talent is sports, you will be trying to increase your strength, stamina, and athletic skills. If your talent is building furniture, each piece will be of higher quality than the previous one.

For self-actualizing people, housing is more than a place to live. It is the place where each person can progress toward becoming all that he or she is capable of being. Striving toward self-actualization is often a lifelong process.

Other Needs Met Through Housing

Recognizing the levels of human needs as described by Maslow can help you understand how important needs are in relation to housing. Beauty, self-expression, and creativity are also important needs. You can achieve these needs through your housing decisions.

Beauty

Beauty is the quality or qualities that give pleasure to the senses. Your concept of beauty is unique. What is beautiful to you may not be beautiful to someone else. In fact, the same objects may not appear beautiful to you as you mature. An appreciation of beauty develops over time as exposure to it increases. Beautiful surroundings, such as those in 1-7, can make you feel content and relaxed.

Self-Expression

Showing your true personality and taste is **self-expression**. Self-expression is evident when you choose colors to decorate your home or the home of someone else. Those colors are often a clue to your personality. For instance, if you have an outgoing, vibrant personality, you might show it by using bright, bold colors inside your home. If you have a quiet, subdued personality, you might show it by using pale, soft colors, 1-8. Furnishings can also help you express yourself.

Creativity

Creativity is the ability to use imaginative skill to make something new. Combining two or more things or ideas into a new whole that has beauty or value is another way to describe creativity. You show creativity when you express your ideas to others.

Your housing provides opportunities for you to express your creativity. Primitive people exhibited creativity when they painted pictures on the walls of their cave dwellings. Today, people still use painting to express their creativity. Likewise, some people enjoy gardening and working with flowers. They express their creativity by designing beautiful gardens or making floral arrangements

1-6
Being able to maintain your home and its furnishings contributes to a feeling of self-esteem.

1-7
Beauty in a room can help you feel happy, content, and peaceful.

Brown Jordan
International Company,
Designs by Rich Frinier

to display around the house, 1-9. Creative people look to many sources of inspiration, including nature, music, books, and other creative people.

Factors Affecting Housing Choices

There are many factors that influence choices in housing. These include values, family relationships, space needs, costs, roles, and lifestyle.

1-8
What does the use of bright, bold colors tell you about the personalities of the people who live here?

J. Banks Design Group

Values

Values are strong beliefs or ideas about what is important. They can be views, events, people, places, or objects you prize highly. When you choose something freely and take action on that choice, you are acting on a value. This gives meaning to your life and enhances your growth.

All the values you hold—such as family, friendship, money, status,

1-9
This woman, who enjoys gardening, created this space to arrange fresh-cut flowers and repot plants.

religion, and independence—form your value system. Your value system is different from anyone else's. You form your value system as a result of experiences you have. The people you know and the activities in which you participate all influence your value system.

Whenever you decide between two or more choices, you use your value system. The choice you make depends on which items you desire most. Suppose you have a choice between sharing an apartment with a friend and living alone. If money is not an issue, your decision depends on how highly you value privacy versus interactions with others.

If you share a home with others, you will find that some of your values differ from theirs. The values that household members have in common will control the thinking and actions of the group. Shared values influence your housing decisions.

How Needs and Values Relate

Your needs and values are closely related. For example, you need a place to sleep. A cot can satisfy this need. However, the cot may not meet your value for comfort. If you have a choice, your value for comfort may cause you to choose a bed with a mattress instead of the cot.

You may also need space in your bedroom for activities other than sleeping. Your values determine whether you choose a large or small bed for the room. While the large bed may provide more comfort, the smaller bed will use less floor space. Some people may want to devote a corner of a bedroom to a play area, desk, or exercise equipment, 1-10.

Space

People have spatial needs. While too much space can make people feel lonely, they need a certain amount of space around them to avoid feeling crowded. They create invisible boundaries around themselves. Others can sense those boundaries and, therefore, know whether they have permission to enter.

Hobbies and activities can influence the need for space. For example, people who like to garden need space for a garden. People who enjoy spending time with friends need space for entertaining.

The way people use space also influences the amount they need. In places where you cannot add or remove space, the right furnishings can make the space seem larger or smaller. For example, reducing the number of furniture pieces in a crowded room can make it more spacious and airy. Likewise, by adding furniture a large room can become warm and cozy.

Privacy

People need privacy to maintain good mental health. Sometimes they need to be completely alone, where others cannot see or hear what they are doing. Sometimes, too, they want to avoid seeing and hearing what others are doing. They may want to think, daydream, create, read, or study without being disturbed, 1-11.

Since the need for privacy varies among people, it can be satisfied in a number of ways. One of the most extreme ways is to live alone in a dwelling that is set apart from other dwellings. Another way is to have a private room or some other private place where people can enter only when invited.

Some people may not have the opportunity to live alone or have their own private place. However, they can still meet their need for privacy. Doing a task alone—such as mowing the lawn or driving a car—provides some privacy. A chair that is set apart from other furnishings in a room can

1-10
This bed allows part of the room to be used for other activities.

Photo Courtesy of JELD-WEN Windows and Doors

create a sense of privacy. Also, solitary activities that require concentration, such as woodworking or piano playing, can free people from interacting with others. Even the sound of a TV or music playing gives some degree of privacy. It isolates a person from sounds made by others.

Family Relationships

If people believe the well-being of their family is important, they consider this factor when making housing decisions. Families that value such relationships make decisions to benefit all family members, not just some. A **family** is two or more people living together who are related by birth, marriage, or adoption.

When concern for family relationships is an important value, several

1-11
This area provides privacy for a teen to work on the computer.

Costs

For most people, the cost of housing is an important factor in making housing decisions. Whether people rent or buy housing, it costs money. Additional expenses include the furnishings and equipment that go into a dwelling plus the bills for repair and maintenance. Utilities, such as electricity, gas, and water, also cost money.

When money is very limited, people choose dwellings that provide just enough space for their needs. They buy only the furnishings and equipment they can afford. They save money by conserving energy, as in turning off lights in empty rooms and setting thermostats at moderate temperatures. People can also maintain their homes well since maintenance bills nearly always cost less than repair and replacement costs. These owners do their own home repairs whenever possible.

Roles

Roles are patterns of behavior that people display in their homes, the workplace, and their communities. Usually each person has more than one role. An adult female, for example, may have the roles of a wife, mother, teacher, and hospital volunteer. An adult male may be a husband, father, grandfather, carpenter, and neighborhood soccer coach. You currently balance the roles of a student and son (or daughter). Perhaps you are also a brother (or sister) and even a part-time worker.

The roles people have can affect the type of housing they choose and how the housing is used. To fulfill the role of student, a home needs a quiet area for studying. If young children live in a home, they need space to play with toys and each other. People involved in sports and hobbies need room for their supplies and equipment.

1-12
An eating area next to the food preparation center allows family members to spend more time together.

areas of the house can be designed for group living. For example, family members may use a great room for family activities. A large eat-in kitchen may be desirable so family members can cook and eat together, as in 1-12. Families may also have an outside area for group recreation.

The role of a wage earner can also impact housing choices. A lawyer may work from home, needing an office for working with a seating area for greeting clients. A professional tailor needs space for storing supplies, cutting fabric, and sewing garments, as well as space for clients trying on and modeling their finished clothing. People whose work involves entertaining at home have other requirements to address before the housing meets their needs. Ideally, housing should meet the needs of all its members in all their roles, 1-13.

Lifestyle

A **lifestyle** is a living pattern or way of life. Together, all the various roles of the occupants make up the lifestyle of a residence. How you live influences the type of housing you choose to enhance your way of life.

When thinking of lifestyles and their influences on housing choices, consider everyday activities in the home. The following questions can help identify activities related to lifestyle:

- Are members involved with hobbies that need space, such as furniture refinishing or indoor gardening?

- What type of entertaining, if any, occurs in the home—both inside and outside?

- Do any adults work from home and need a high-tech office?

- Are the occupants retired, traveling frequently, and not spending much time at home?

The answers to these and other related lifestyle questions determine the type of housing selected. For example, people who love the outdoors seek housing with a view of nature or a private patio or garden. Those who spend little time at home often prefer a maintenance-free residence close to major thoroughfares so they can travel quickly to their various

commitments. Retirees may choose a retirement community with a convenient central dining room plus on-site recreation and grooming services, 1-14.

Income also influences lifestyle. Higher incomes allow people to spend more money on their homes. Consider the example of those who enjoy swimming. They can use a local recreation center to enjoy their favorite form of exercise, but if they can afford it, many install a pool at home. Depending on their income, installation of a new pool may be aboveground, in-ground, or perhaps inside as part of a new wing built onto the home. Income greatly affects the degree to which people add comforts and conveniences to a home to address their lifestyles.

1-13
A home office is becoming a common feature of many residences since greater numbers of people are working from their homes.

Photography Courtesy of Pottery Barn

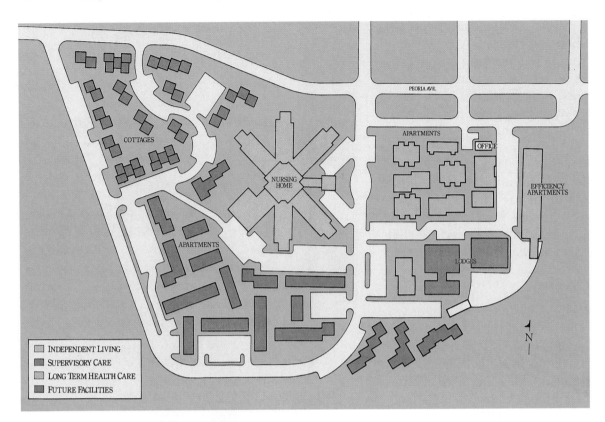

Map legend:
- INDEPENDENT LIVING
- SUPERVISORY CARE
- LONG TERM HEALTH CARE
- FUTURE FACILITIES

Housing Needs Through the Life Span

On almost a daily basis, you can be sure of change. Life situations and circumstances cause change and affect the way you live. They relate to every aspect of your life. They set the stage for the way you interact with other people and with your housing.

In group housing, people are generally not relatives. Retirement complexes and college residence halls, 1-15, are some common examples. The occupants live in separate units within the group dwelling. In contrast, people in residential dwellings are often relatives.

Households

The most common residential dwelling is a household. A **household** includes all people who occupy a dwelling. The household size can vary, but most households contain families. The following describes the five basic family structures:

- **Nuclear family.** This family includes couples and their children. The children are either born into the family or adopted. None of the children are from a previous marriage, 1-16.

- **Single-parent family.** These families consist of a child (or children) and only one parent, often because a parent has died or left home. Other single-parent families consist of a never-married adult with one or more children.

- **Stepfamily.** This family consists of parents, one or both of whom have been married before. The family also includes one or more children from a previous marriage.

- **Childless family.** These families consist of a couple who have not had

LINK TO SOCIAL STUDIES & CULTURE

The Changing American Household

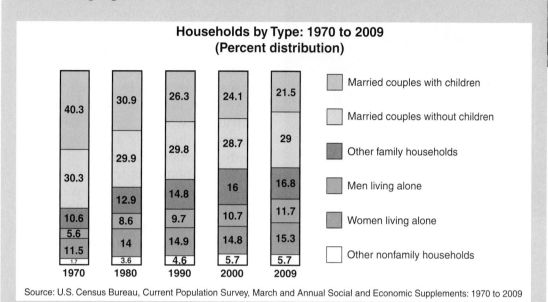

Households by Type: 1970 to 2009
(Percent distribution)

	1970	1980	1990	2000	2009
Married couples with children	40.3	30.9	26.3	24.1	21.5
Married couples without children	30.3	29.9	29.8	28.7	29
Other family households	10.6	12.9	14.8	16	16.8
Men living alone	5.6	8.6	9.7	10.7	11.7
Women living alone	11.5	14	14.9	14.8	15.3
Other nonfamily households	1.7	3.6	4.6	5.7	5.7

Source: U.S. Census Bureau, Current Population Survey, March and Annual Social and Economic Supplements: 1970 to 2009

According to the U.S. Census Bureau, the composition of U.S. households changed between 1970 and 2009. The most significant changes include

- **Reduction of family households.** Family households—two or more members related by birth, marriage, or adoption—accounted about 67 percent of households instead of 81 percent.

- **Reduction of married-couple households.** The share of married-couple-with-children households decreased from 40 percent to just over 20 percent of households.

- **Increase in nonfamily households.** The proportion of nonfamily households—mostly people who live alone—increased from about 19 to 33 percent of households.

The Census Bureau cites many reasons for these changes. For example, the roles of men and women have changed. More women are working and living on their own. People are marrying and having children later or not at all. Also, people are living longer due to technological innovations. The baby-boom generation—those born between 1946 and 1964, who make up almost 40 percent of the adult population—is moving into retirement.

Changes in the composition of U.S. households bring changes in the housing market. For example, after their children grow up and leave home, many baby boomers choose to downsize into smaller homes and condominiums. Older adults generally prefer single-level homes or buildings with elevators since climbing stairs can be difficult.

1-15
A residence hall offers group housing to students pursuing an education.

North Carolina A&T State University

Photo by Charles E. Watkins, University Photographer

1-16
The nuclear family is the first image that comes to mind when people picture a typical family.

children, parents, and grandparents. Variations can include aunts, uncles, or cousins as well as their children, 1-17. A second type of extended family consists of members from the same generation, such as brothers, sisters, and cousins.

The smallest household is a *single-person household*, which consists of one person living alone in a dwelling. That person may be someone who has never married or whose marriage has ended because of the loss of a spouse through death, desertion, or divorce.

Throughout this text, you will see how your household affects your housing decisions. In turn, you will also learn how the decisions you make concerning your housing affect your household.

Life Cycles

Life cycles are another way to view your housing needs. A **life cycle** is a series of stages through which an individual or family passes during its lifetime. In each stage, there are new opportunities and new challenges to face. You develop new needs and values and prioritize them according to what is most important to you. These changes relate to your housing.

Individual Life Cycle

Each person follows a pattern of development, or an individual life cycle. It is divided according to age groups into the following four stages:

- infancy
- childhood
- youth
- adulthood

Each stage can be divided into substages, as in 1-18. In what stage do you belong? Do you have siblings in other stages?

children. For some couples this is a temporary condition, delaying the arrival of children until their finances improve. For others, it is a permanent condition. The couple is unable to have children or chooses to remain childless, for whatever reason.

- **Extended family.** There are two basic types of extended families, which form by adding one or more relatives to a household already identified. One type consists of several generations of a family, such as

Family Life Cycle

Just as you have a place in an individual life cycle, your family has its place in the family life cycle. A family life cycle has six stages, 1-19. One or more substages may exist within each stage.

- **Beginning stage.** This is the early period of a marriage when a couple is without children. The husband and wife make adjustments to married life and to each other, 1-20.

- **Childbearing stage.** This is the time when a family is growing. It includes the childbearing periods and the years of caring for preschoolers. Depending on the household lifestyle and working arrangements, the family may need child care. If so, the design of the early childhood environment should meet the developmental needs of the child.

- **Parenting stage.** During this stage, the children are in school. This stage includes the years of caring for school-age children and teens.

- **Launching stage.** Children become adults and leave their parents' homes during this time. They may leave to go to college, take a job, or get married.

- **Midyears stage.** During this time span, the children leave home and the parents retire. When all the children leave home, the couple is again alone.

- **Aging stage.** This stage begins with retirement. Usually, at some point in this stage, one spouse lives alone after the death of the other. As people live longer, the length of this stage increases.

In some cases, the family fits the description of two life cycle stages. For example, when a family has both a preschool child and a school-age child, the family is in overlapping stages. Other families may have gaps between the stages or substages. An example is a family in which the mother is pregnant and the children are teens.

1-17
Some families are extended in more than one direction.

Individual Life Cycle			
Infancy Stage	**Childhood Stage**	**Youth Stage**	**Adulthood Stage**
• Newborn, birth to 1 month old • Infant, 1 month to 1 year old	• Early childhood, 1 to 6 years old • Middle childhood, 6 to 8 years old • Late childhood, 9 to 12 years old	• Preteen • Early teen • Middle teen • Late teen	• Young adult • Mature adult • Aging adult

1-18
This chart divides the individual life cycle into substages.

1-19
The family life cycle includes both stages and substages.

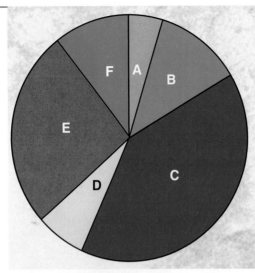

Family Life Cycle

A. **Beginning Stage:** Married couple without children.
B. **Childbearing Stage:** Couple with child(ren) up to 2½ years old; couple with child(ren) 2½ to 6 years old.
C. **Parenting Stage:** Couple with child(ren) 6 to 13 years old.
D. **Launching Stage:** Couple with child(ren) leaving home; couple with child(ren) living away from home.
E. **Midyears Stage:** Couple before retirement, but after all children left home.
F. **Aging Stage:** Couple during retirement until death of both spouses.

1-20
These newlyweds are entering the beginning stage of their own family's life cycle.

Courtesy of Trina Olson Photography

Life Cycles and Housing Needs

As you move from one stage or substage of a life cycle to another, your housing needs change. When planning housing, consider what stage or substage of the life cycles you are in. If you think about both your present and future needs, your housing can help you live the kind of life you desire.

One example of a need that changes as a person moves through the life cycles is the need for space. During the infancy, a baby takes no more space than a small crib. As that baby grows, he or she needs more sleeping space. From the childhood stage through the youth stage, children often sleep in twin or bunk beds, 1-21. As adults, people prefer more spacious beds that provide greater comfort.

The need for space also changes throughout a family's life cycle. In the beginning stage, a young married couple may not need very much space. However, once they enter the childbearing stage, their space needs increase. During this stage, the number, ages, sexes, and activities of their children will affect their space needs.

With the addition of new members, families require more space. As each member grows, he or she requires even more space. Teens need space for studying and entertaining friends. They also need space to store sports equipment, computer equipment, clothes, and personal belongings.

When family members leave home during the launching stage, they take

MATH MATTERS

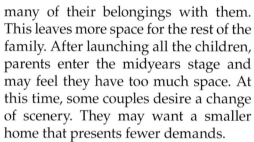

Fraction/Decimal Conversions

How much of your class is female? male? These questions are asking for proportion, which is the relation of one part to the whole. Proportion is often expressed in fractions.

If 21 out of 28 students in your class are girls, you can represent that with the fraction $^{21}/_{28}$. You can convert fractions to decimal numbers by dividing the fraction's numerator (top number) by the denominator (bottom number).

Ex: $^{21}/_{28} = 0.75$

You can convert a decimal number to a fraction. The fraction's numerator is simply the decimal number minus the decimal point. The fraction's denominator is the place value of the right-most number.

Ex: $0.75 = ^{75}/_{100}$

many of their belongings with them. This leaves more space for the rest of the family. After launching all the children, parents enter the midyears stage and may feel they have too much space. At this time, some couples desire a change of scenery. They may want a smaller home that presents fewer demands.

Other couples, however, prefer to stay in their present homes. They may not want to leave behind the memories linked to their family's home. They may also want to have plenty of room when their children and grandchildren come to visit.

Housing and Quality of Life

Quality of life is the degree of satisfaction a person obtains from life. Housing is "good" when it provides people with satisfying surroundings that can improve their quality of life.

Personal Quality of Life

Quality of life is important to you as an individual. Just as you are unique,

1-21
When a child outgrows a crib, he or she may sleep in a trundle bed. This also provides space for playmates to spend the night.

your concept of the quality of life is unique. Your idea of an improved quality of life may not appeal to someone else. Your housing environment helps you meet your needs and values. It also adds satisfaction to your life and, therefore, improves the quality of your life.

Quality of life is also important to the other members of your household. Your household, whether it is your family or some other group, is one part of your

1-22
The values of the people who live in this home are obvious in the furnishings used in this room.

Group 3, Architectural and Interior Design, Hilton Head Island, South Carolina. Photography courtesy of John McManus, Savannah, Georgia

1-23
Due to the efforts of community volunteers, a family was able to move into a newly constructed house.

Habitat for Humanity® International

life situation. The members play a part in shaping your attitudes and values. In turn, the combined needs and values of the members determine the type of housing environment in which you live. See 1-22. If all the members show concern about the well-being of the group as a whole, this action enhances the quality of life for everyone.

Quality of Life for Society

The future of a society depends on individuals and groups who work to make life better for everyone. Some of the work is social in nature. That means groups of people must cooperate to reach a common goal, 1-23. This goal is to improve the quality of life for society. All people cannot make equal contributions toward any given goal. One example is the plight of people who are homeless. They do not have the resources to secure housing for themselves. In such cases, groups of people work together to make housing available for people without homes.

People must also work together and use their resources of time, money, and energy to maintain and support beautiful surroundings. Examples of such surroundings are well-kept buildings and natural landscapes. These surroundings satisfy the needs and desires of many people in society.

Human Ecology

Human ecology, the study of people and their environment, is the focus of considerable research. People are concerned about the problems caused by pollutants entering streams, lakes, and underground water supplies. Generating electricity and burning fuel for heat and power add harmful elements to the air.

Instead of wishing for the good old days to return, people must move forward to find solutions for today's problems. Noise and air pollution, traffic congestion, and the waste of natural resources are just some of these problems. Solving them will improve housing and the quality of life for society.

GREEN CHOICES

What Does "Green" Mean?

"Green" refers to making choices about various aspects of housing and interiors that are environmentally friendly. This means making choices to incorporate sound environmental principles of building, materials and energy use. The basic intent of green choices is to have low negative-environmental impact on air quality, soil quality, or use of natural resources. Environmentally friendly choices include

- using less water
- using less energy
- using nontoxic materials and substances
- choosing materials that can be recycled or have been recycled
- recycling and reusing items

These choices range from such small items as cleaning supplies to all aspects of buildings. Specifically, "green" choices affect consumers and the fields of architecture, landscape architecture, urban design, urban planning, engineering, graphic design, industrial design, and interior design.

Many terms are used when referring to green choices including: environmentally friendly, green design, eco-design, design for the environment, eco-friendly, and sustainable design.

(NOTE: Throughout this text, *Green Choices* features offer ideas and ways to incorporate green concepts for housing consumers and people in the housing and interiors professions.)

Green and Sustainable Design

A major trend in today's society is the movement toward *green design* and *sustainable design*. Both forms of design encourage the use of sound environmental principles in structures, materials, and energy use to have *low* or *no* environmental impact. A distinction between green and sustainable design is the degree of impact on the environment. **Sustainable design** strives to have *no* impact on the environment. In contrast, **green design** attempts to have *low* environmental impact. It is a subset of sustainable design. For example, the use of green products and approaches is actually a part of sustainable design. Many other terms refer to environmentally sensitive design, including "eco-design" and "design for the environment." Every time you make a choice to use green or sustainable design options, you make a choice to preserve the environment and improve the quality of life for future generations.

CAREER FOCUS

Interior Designer—Early Childhood Facilities

Can you imagine a career as an interior designer of early childhood development facilities? If you can, read more about the following details.

Interests/Skills: If you share some of following interests and skills, you may want to consider becoming an interior designer who specializes in designing early childhood development centers. Do your interests include an enjoyment of artistic and creative projects? Do you feel design takes a major roll in children's growth and development? In addition, do environments for children interest you? Are your communication skills strong—especially with listening, writing, and speaking? Do you pay attention to details and have a strong background in art? Planning and organizing are essential skills for completing a project.

Career Snapshot: Along with researching and understanding the special needs of the children and adults who use the space, interior designers in this field also need additional training in working with civic contract projects. Designers work closely with a center's director. Together they make sure that all building and interior codes and all classroom needs are met when making design decisions for the project. For example, napping, teaching, circulation, and storage spaces need to fit together and meet certain health and safety standards. Creating a play area where children come to learn and interact requires attention to the details.

Education/Training: Completion of a bachelor's degree is preferred. To specialize in designing spaces for early childhood development, take additional courses in childhood development and psychology.

Licensing/Examinations: Approximately one-half of the states require interior designers to be licensed. The National Council for Interior Design Qualification (NCIDQ) administers an examination that interior designers must pass in order to obtain a license and be competitive in their careers.

Professional Associations: The American Society of Interior Designers (ASID) (www.asid.org) and the International Interior Design Association (IIDA) (www.iida.org)

Job Outlook: As long as the population keeps growing, there will be a need for early childhood development centers. Designers who pave a career path to specialize in this particular field will thrive.

Sources: Information from the Occupational Outlook Handbook (www.bls.gov/OCO) and the Occupational Information Network (O*NET) (www.online.onetcenter.org)

©2007 Image by Warren Lieb/LS3P ASSOCIATED, LTD. Children's Center at Carolina Park, Mount Pleasant, South Carolina.

Summary

People interact with their housing. Their housing affects them, and they affect their housing. Housing helps satisfy people's physical and psychological needs and can help them move toward self-actualization. Beauty, self-expression, and creativity are other needs people meet through housing.

Each person's housing reflects the lifestyle he or she has chosen. Needs and values are closely related. However, the needs and values of people and living units vary as they move through the life cycles.

Housing affects the quality of life for both individuals and society. The study of human ecology can help improve housing and the quality of life for society. As often as possible, choosing green and sustainable design options in housing helps improve the quality of life for individuals and society.

Review the Facts

1. What is housing?
2. Distinguish between the near environment and total environment.
3. Identify three physical needs people have.
4. What are four psychological needs that people have?
5. Given the chance, how would you change your housing to better meet your need for self-actualization?
6. Give an example of how housing can help you meet each of the following needs: (A) self-expression; (B) creativity.
7. How does a person form his or her value system?
8. Describe five ways to achieve privacy.
9. How do space and privacy relate?
10. Provide an example of an extended family that is not a stepfamily.
11. List the four stages of the individual life cycle.
12. Give an example of the way housing needs change as a family moves from one stage of the life cycle to another.
13. Explain how a couple in the beginning stage of the family life cycle differs from a couple in the aging stage.
14. How does housing help individuals and society meet quality-of-life needs?
15. How can decisions about green and sustainable design enhance quality of life?

Think Critically

16. **Draw conclusions.** Suppose a family's lifestyle involves some members using their home to do work for their jobs. Draw conclusions about what changes might have to be made to the interior of the home if one or more family members begin (or already are) working from home.
17. **Assess needs.** What needs and values are met by housing? Make a personal assessment and list your needs and values in order of priority.

18. **Analyze space.** Analyze and describe how the use of a spare bedroom may change depending on whether the living unit includes the following: small children, teens, people with hobbies, a person working at home, or retirees.

19. **Analyze behavior.** In teams, brainstorm actions or behaviors that may be useful for enhancing creativity for interior designers. Share your teams ideas with the class.

Community Links

20. **Household descriptions.** Identify 10 households in your community that you know well. (Note: Keep family names private.) For each, identify the type of household it is. Also, write a one-sentence description of each member, identifying gender, approximate age, and relationship to the family.

21. **Forecast household needs.** Consider your household members and examine your home's interior space. In the last five years, has the size of your household changed? If so, how? Did the change result in more or less space per person? In comparison, do you have more or less personal privacy today than five years ago? Forecast your household's need for space five years from now. What possible changes in the household may occur in the next five years that will increase the amount of space per person? that will decrease the space per person?

22. **Lifestyle interview.** Interview an older adult and ask him or her to describe changes in his or her housing over the years. Ask how the person's lifestyle and housing impact each other. Is ability to *age-in-place* important to this older adult? Why? If possible, ask the older adult's permission to audio-record the interview and share it with the class.

23. **Prevent homelessness.** Does your community have homeless people? Investigate what the town (city) and local charitable organizations are doing to handle this problem. What actions do these organizations take to prevent it? Summarize your findings in a one-page report.

Academic Connections

24. **Writing.** In your own words, write a brief summary of the chapter content in 15 sentences or less. Save your summary for future reference.

25. **Social studies.** Imagine a full day in the life of a homeless person. Look for a Web site that tries to convey that experience and examine the information it provides. What facts about homeless people surprise you? How many children and youth are homeless? How does homelessness affect their learning? Look for facts about homeless youth and make a printout of a fact that surprised you. What options exist for preventing homelessness or meeting the needs of homeless people? Share your findings with the class.

Technology Applications

26. **Internet research.** Use the Internet to research cliff dwellings. Determine who built them and why they were built. Find out how many different sites containing cliff dwellings exist in Colorado. How many households do these cliff villages contain? Why did the people build their homes in the cliffs? Present a brief report to the class.

27. **Electronic presentation.** Use a digital camera to photograph examples of housing in your community that address a household's psychological needs. Take separate pictures to demonstrate examples of housing that meet the following four needs: security, love/acceptance, esteem, and self-actualization. Use presentation software to display your examples to the class. Describe why the housing example in each picture meets a particular need.

Design Practice

28. **Design for privacy.** Obtain permission to rearrange furniture in a part of your home, or the home of someone else you know, to provide more privacy. How did the new furniture arrangement lead to more privacy? How did household members react to the change? Report your actions and results to the class.

29. **Portfolio.** Building a quality portfolio about your design experience is essential to having a successful career in housing and interior design. Along with the design examples you will create throughout this course, you will also need to include writing samples that showcase your ability to communicate well in writing. In one page or less, write a goal statement about your future career as an interior designer. Why do you want to pursue this career? What aspects of this career ignite your passion for housing and interior design? Use word-processing software to create your goal statement. Save a copy of the document for your portfolio.

30. **Portfolio.** Create a storyboard that reflects housing appropriate for a family progressing through the six stages of the family life cycle. Use photos or images from the Internet, magazines, or other sources to show the stages. Assume the following details about the family:
    Beginning—The couples live on one partner's earnings while the earnings of the other go toward savings and paying of college loans.
    Childbearing—The family has one full-time wage earner working outside the home, one part-time wage earner working from home, and two children under age four.
    Parenting—The family has enough savings for a down payment on a moderately priced home, the part-time wage earner is now working full-time outside the home, and all family members are very active in sports.
    Midyears—The couple frequently entertains children and grandchildren on weekends and travels as much as possible.
    Aging—One partner lives alone after the death of another.

Leadership, Housing, and Human Needs

What do community service and your feelings and attitudes about "home" have in common? Both begin in the heart—with those things you value most. Take a look around your community. What housing-related concerns do you see? Are there people living in homeless shelters or unsafe housing? Are there needs that you could help meet?

Take the lead in planning and implementing an FCCLA *Community Service* project that focuses on meeting the needs of those who live in homeless shelters or unsafe housing. For example, consider collecting grooming and personal-hygiene items and donating them to your local homeless shelter.

Use the FCCLA *Planning Process* and related documents to plan, implement, and evaluate your project. See your adviser for information as needed.

CHAPTER 2

Influences on Housing

Terms to Learn

agrarian
density
row houses
tenement houses
architect
substandard
census
tract houses
new town
new urbanism
subdivision
culture
hogan
demographics
baby boomers
disability
dual-career family
telecommuting
Sunbelt
environment
climate
topography
resources
housing market
gross domestic product (GDP)
technology
high tech
computer-aided drafting and design
   (CADD)
building codes
zoning regulation
infrastructure

Chapter Objectives

After studying this chapter, you will be able to

- relate historical events to housing.

- summarize various cultures and housing characteristics.

- determine the relationship between societal changes and housing.

- analyze concerns about environmental aspects of housing.

- compare and contrast the effects of economy and housing on each other.

- assess the impact of technology on housing.

- summarize the role of government in housing decisions.

Reading with Purpose

Predict what you think will be covered in this chapter. Make a list of your predictions. After reading the chapter, decide if your predictions were correct. If they were not correct, explain why.

Housing changes occur according to the needs and desires of those who occupy it. Housing also changes because of outside influences. These include historical, cultural, societal, environmental, economic, technological, and governmental influences.

Historical Influences on Housing

The story of housing in the United States began before the first European settlers established the colonies. There is a sharp contrast between the houses of today and those of early North America.

Early Shelter

Early humans lived in caves that provided a degree of safety and protection from the weather and wild animals. These caves helped people meet the basic need for shelter—a place to sleep and rest.

Another form of early shelter was a dugout—a large hole dug in the earth. Dugouts were warm in cold weather and cool in warm weather. Sometimes a dome-shaped covering was added to the dugout to make it roomier. Typical materials for such coverings were animal skins, mud and bark, or mud and branches.

Housing of Native Americans

Some early Native American cliff dwellers often used a crude rock overhang or cliff for housing (review 1-2). The overhangs or cliffs were modified for housing by adding an enclosure. The enclosure gave warmth, privacy, and security to the cliff dwellers. Living in cliffs gave these Native Americans the ability to see great distances—an added advantage to their security.

Native Americans occupied North America before European settlers began to arrive. The materials used for their housing depended on what was available in the section of the country in which they lived. Some lived in huts that were constructed from a framework of poles with coverings of thatch, hides, or mud over the framework. Others lived in tepees and wigwams. Some Native Americans lived in permanent dwellings constructed of adobe. See 2-1 for the different types of Native American dwellings and their locations.

Housing of the Colonists

The first English settlement in North America was established in 1585 on the island of Roanoke in North Carolina. The first shelters used by the European settlers were copied after Native American dwellings. Other houses were built of sod. Dirt floors were common.

The early colonists built their own houses. Sometimes they built them with the help of many neighbors, an event called a *house-raising*. Because many people helped with the work, a house could be built in a short amount of time. The quality of these early dwellings was limited due to the lack of skills, tools, and materials.

After settling in North America, the colonists attempted to copy the houses from their homelands. However, the styles had to be adapted to the available materials. Some housing styles of the colonists' homelands did not suit the climate of the new land and consequently were not copied. For instance, the thatched roof, commonly used in England, was not suited to the cold New England climate, 2-2.

The abundance of trees in the eastern forests made the log cabin convenient to build. It is believed that the first *log cabins* were built about 1640 by Swedish and Finnish colonists. They began as one-room structures with

Native American Housing

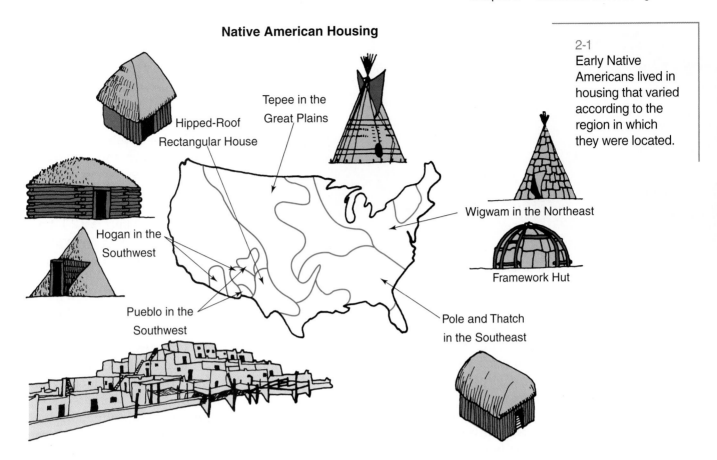

Hipped-Roof Rectangular House

Tepee in the Great Plains

Hogan in the Southwest

Pueblo in the Southwest

Wigwam in the Northeast

Framework Hut

Pole and Thatch in the Southeast

2-1
Early Native Americans lived in housing that varied according to the region in which they were located.

fireplaces for heating and cooking, 2-3. The chimneys were located on the outside of the cabins.

Later, the log cabin was built in a variety of styles. Rooms were often added as families grew larger. Some log cabins were built with three rooms—an entryway, kitchen, and sleeping room. Others were two stories tall. The kitchens in these log cabins were large, so food could be both processed and prepared in the house. Sleeping rooms were small and sometimes located in a loft. If a small log cabin was replaced by a larger dwelling, the small cabin was sometimes used for storage.

The log cabin spread from the Northeast into the South and onto the western frontier. It became a symbol of the early United States.

Most housing in early settlements could be found in group settings. Security was the key reason for building

2-2
The thatched roof, which is not appropriate for cold climates, is very common in warmer climates.

2-3
A typical log cabin looked similar to this.

Housing of the 1700s and 1800s

Throughout the 1700s and 1800s, many people moved west to settle on large plots of land. They lived on their land in a variety of dwellings. Farmhouses ranged in design and construction from sod houses to log cabins to ranch houses. At the same time, construction of large plantation houses was happening in the South, 2-4.

In the late 1700s, most North America settlers were **agrarian**, or people who earned their living from the land. By 1890, the rural population had decreased as a result of the Industrial Revolution (1750–1850). The Industrial Revolution brought major changes to the economy and society through the use of new machines and efficient production of goods. The demand for workers grew out of changes in mass production due to use of such machines. Along with immigrants, rural people began moving to the cities looking for jobs. With an increasing birth rate, the cities grew. This increased the demand for housing in the urban areas.

houses close together. Generally square or rectangular in form, many houses had one or two rooms and a fireplace. When other rooms were added around the main room, it became known as the *great room*.

As the country became settled, more people with building skills arrived. They helped build houses and taught others their skills. When logs were cut into lumber, it became a common building material. Other houses also appeared that were built of stone or brick.

2-4
Plantation houses were common dwellings for large landowners of the South.

Urban Housing

The housing in cities was built close together and crowded with inhabitants, causing a high density. **Density** is the number of people in a given area. Early urban dwellings included row houses and tenements.

The first row houses were built in the 1820s. **Row houses** are a continuous group of dwellings linked by common sidewalls. Many of them were built to house factory workers, 2-5. Two-story row houses sometimes housed as many as six families at a time.

Eventually, row houses with fewer common walls evolved into dwellings for one family. Two-family dwellings, called *duplexes*, were built. Multifamily housing was built for four or six families.

Most houses were frame houses in various designs. A number of **tenement houses**, or early apartments, were built before housing regulations existed. The first tenement houses appeared in New York City around 1840 to house immigrants. Most were built on city lots measuring 25 by 100 feet. A typical tenement house was a five-story building, measuring 25 by 25 feet. Next to each dwelling was another 25-foot-square building.

The typical tenement house had as many as 116 two-room apartments. The outdoor toilets were located on the land between the buildings. Conditions were very poor, earning the landlords the title of *slumlords*.

By 1890, government regulations required that each room in a new tenement house have a window. Each apartment was to have running water and a kitchen sink. Community toilets were to be located in the stairway area connecting the floors.

The tenement houses and row houses were the forerunners of modern apartments. Some apartments first appeared during the housing shortage caused by the Industrial Revolution. At the

2-5
Many employees of The Pullman Palace Car Company lived in these row houses in the late 1800s.

Historic Pullman Foundation

same time, mansions were built for the wealthy, 2-6.

Changes in Housing

Many changes were taking place in housing and the housing industry in the 1700s and 1800s. There were new inventions, machinery, and technology.

Wood- and coal-burning stoves appeared in houses. Steam-heating systems were installed. Oil and gas lamps replaced candles. Iceboxes (early refrigeration units) were available. Water supplies, plumbing, and sanitation facilities were improved. Some houses had indoor toilets and bathtubs. However, only people with high incomes could afford to take advantage of these new developments. Rural areas were slow to adopt the improvements.

Machinery, craftspeople, and architects were all important in the housing industry. An **architect** is a person who designs buildings and supervises

2-6
Mansions, such as the Alva Vanderbilt Marble House shown here, were often built for wealthy businesspeople in the late 1800s.

their construction. They got ideas from designs used in buildings from other countries. Machinery, such as electric saws, helped the buildings go up rapidly. People skilled in various crafts—such as carpenters, plumbers, and electricians—contributed high-quality work. No single housing style dominated the scene.

Housing in the 1900s

During the early 1900s, the number of immigrants to the United States increased dramatically and many moved to the cities. A housing boom in the early 1900s began to meet this need for housing.

Then, during World War I (1914–1918), almost no housing was built except by the federal government. This caused a housing shortage. House ownership declined. Housing was overcrowded. There was a shortage of materials and, as a result, structures fell into disrepair. After World War I, about one-third of the population was living in substandard housing. **Substandard** means the houses are not up to the quality living standards that are best for people. For example, substandard conditions

often included inadequate light from windows (and sometimes no windows), unheated spaces, limited access to working plumbing for water, and unsanitary means of handling human waste. These homes were often unsound structures with leaky roofs and holes in the floors. During this time, only a half-hearted housing reform was taking place.

By the time of the Great Depression in 1929, more than half the U.S. population lived in cities. However, the building of houses had slowed down. People of all income levels struggled to meet their housing needs. Private enterprise as well as the government soon saw the need for housing reform and began to lay the foundation for change.

The first census of housing in the United States was taken in 1940. A **census** is an official count of the population by the government. The census supported what the people knew—the housing needs of people at all income levels had not been met. The impact of the increased population, World War I, and the Great Depression had left housing conditions in a neglected state.

Solutions to Housing Shortages

In response to housing shortages, factory-produced units emerged as a major type of American housing. Depending on the type, units were produced to various levels of completion and delivered to a housing site. The advantage of factory-built housing involved the savings in cost as well as in construction time.

Houses that are conventionally built on-site generally take more time to complete. This is because weather-related delays often prolong construction and coordination of many different tradespeople. When factory-building housing on an assembly line, coordination is easier and takes less time to complete. While some units are finished

2-7
Some manufactured homes must be moved in sections and joined on-site.

Schult Homes

at the factory, others come in parts that need to be put together. All involve a certain amount of labor when being placed on the site. Full descriptions of these housing types are in Chapter 4.

Factory-built housing units helped with the housing shortage by serving as year-round housing for many people, including defense workers, factory employees, and military personnel. Housing units on wheels provided an affordable solution for home ownership since the cost was considerably less than a conventional house built on a foundation at a housing site. Today, factory-built housing is one of the fastest growing types of affordable housing in the United States, 2-7.

Following World War II, housing construction resumed. Along with this construction came the appearance of **tract houses** which are groups of similarly designed houses built on a tract of land. These tract houses, or "cookie cutter" houses, all looked alike. They were moderate in size and built to meet the needs of the moderate-income family. The owners of tract houses have adapted them to fit their needs. For example, many have added room extensions and garages. Others have personalized the homes with new exterior materials and colors.

Improvements in Urban Housing

Throughout this period, several new housing ideas emerged to improve housing. Two of these included new towns and subdivisions. A **new town** is an urban development consisting of a small to midsize city with a broad range of housing and planned industrial, commercial, educational, and recreational facilities, 2-8. It covers up to 6,000 acres. The number of residents ranges from 10,000 to 60,000. The industrial facilities provide employment opportunities. A new town is designed to appeal to people of all ages, economic levels, races, educational backgrounds, and religious beliefs.

The idea for new towns dates back to the early 1900s, but it was 1960 before the idea started to gain attention. New towns are carefully planned from the beginning and are usually constructed in an undeveloped area. Because of their structure, they promote the orderly growth of areas with fast-growth

RESTON
MASTER PLAN

- Single Family
- Townhomes
- Apartments/Condominiums
- Parks/Open Space/Tennis/Pools
- Community Use/Schools/Churches/ Child Care
- Lakes
- Town Center District
- Town Center Urban Core Office/Retail/Hotels/Residential
- Business and R & D
- Village Centers/Convenience Retail

2-8
A master plan was used when developing the planned community of Reston, Virginia.

Courtesy of Reston Land Corporation

to communities that are planned to encourage pedestrian traffic, place more emphasis on the environment, and are sustainable. *Sustainable* means producing most of the energy needed and/or using minimum natural resources. In communities built on the new urbanism concept, everything is within walking distance of home. These developments are mixed-use, which means shops, offices, apartments, and single-family homes are included in one planned area. Another name for new urbanism communities is *live/work communities*. As a characteristic of these communities, a housing unit is often located above a commercial shop, such as a jewelry store or an insurance office.

A **subdivision** is the division of a tract of land into two or more parcels that make it easier to sell and develop. This division involves laying out a parcel of raw land into lots, blocks, streets, and public areas. As a result, the density and types of buildings are controlled. The focus of a subdivision is on the division of land for various purposes. There is a distinct difference between a subdivision and a planned development. A subdivision is the planning and development of the land itself. Once the division of land occurs, it needs further organization before construction can begin on it. In contrast, a planned development has a master plan showing how to use land for various purposes.

Subdivisions are often created from undeveloped land by private investors called *developers*. Developers must obtain permission to create a subdivision from local government officials, who must consider many factors. One such factor is the impact the new subdivision will have on the amount of traffic it will add to area roads. Other considerations include the potential overcrowding of schools and excess strain on such government services as police and fire protection, a fresh-water supply, waste

potential. The early 1970s saw the beginnings of about 15 new towns. By 1990, at least 60 new towns were in progress in the United States.

A new town is an example of planned development. A planned development is the design and implementation of a community, city, or neighborhood with a master plan. A master plan includes more than one primary type of zoning area (housing, commercial, and industrial). New towns, planned communities, planned cities, and planned neighborhoods are all examples of planned developments.

Since the early 1990s a newer version of new town, or *new urbanism*, has gained popularity. **New urbanism** refers pick-up, and sewage treatment. In setting up subdivisions, land surveyors play an important role in making sure the lots and roads are properly laid out and that property lines are correct. See the end of this chapter for more information about the duties of a land surveyor.

A well-thought-out design for a subdivision may include areas that can be developed for recreational facilities as pools, tennis courts, basketball courts, hiking trails, bike paths, and man-made lakes for boating and fishing. New roads are included in the plan and possibly a new school, too. A well-designed subdivision may also include easy access to shopping centers and medical offices.

Adequate housing for everyone has never fully been achieved in the United States and remains one of the nation's greatest challenges, 2-9. Ideally, the housing supply will someday meet the needs of a growing, diverse U.S. population. This includes people with special needs—such as older adults or those with physical or mental limitations—singles, first-time home owners, and people of all cultures, races, and income levels.

Cultural Influences on Housing

The beliefs, social customs, and traits of a group of people form their **culture**. A group's culture influences its housing choices, and the housing becomes part of the culture. The following examples illustrate how housing influences culture.

The Navajo, a Native American tribe of the North-American Southwest, lived in **hogans**, which were buildings made of logs and mud. The windows faced west and a single door faced east. The placement of the door had religious significance. The Navajo believed that the door must face east so the spirit guardians could enter. The tradition exists today, even though the type of housing for many Navajos has changed. Homes built by the Crow, a Native American tribe of the Northwest, also have doors facing east.

2-9
House by house, Habitat for Humanity International is helping meet one of the greatest needs in the United States— adequate housing for all people.

Steffan Hacker/Habitat for Humanity® International

The cultures of Native American tribes in North America closely entwined the environment with their religious beliefs. They typically viewed the land and water as common property to which everyone must show respect and use wisely. With the arrival of European settlers in North America, came contrasting views. These settlers saw the opportunity for private ownership of the land and water.

Before regions in the South and Southwest became states, people from Spain settled them. The Spaniards built missions with whitewashed walls and red-tiled roofs. The style of the Spanish missions greatly influenced the local architecture. In the early 1900s, there was a revival of Hispanic heritage including architecture. Along with preservation of the old missions, came construction of houses and other buildings following details of early Spanish architecture, 2-10. Throughout the nation and the South

and Southwest today, much architecture shows Hispanic influence.

With the arrival of the Pilgrims at Plymouth Rock in the winter of 1620, the need for shelter was immediate. They duplicated the housing of the Native Americans. After the winter was over, they began to duplicate the English cottages of their homeland. They used wood, which was abundantly available and the traditional building material of their homeland. The first cottages were often crude and made of timber—large, squared-off pieces of wood. They had dirt floors, few windows, and chimneys built of sticks and heavy clay. As better materials and skills became available, the cottages more closely resembled the cottages in England.

As other cultures came to North America from Europe, they also contributed their styles of housing to the American landscape. As mentioned earlier, the Swedish log cabin became a popular form of housing. The Dutch Colonial, Pennsylvania Dutch (German) Colonial, French Normandy, and Italianate housing styles are other examples of European influences on American housing. (You will learn more about these influences in Chapter 6.)

Throughout history, houses have been strong indicators of culture. Housing reflects the heritage as well as traditional skills and materials of the builders. As cultures change, the changes are evident in the housing.

New Immigrants

Each year, the United States welcomes thousands of legal immigrants from all over the world. Now, as in the past, these immigrants bring their dreams and expectations for a better life as they adapt to their new homeland. Finding housing that reflects their cultural preferences and personal values is part of that dream.

Many immigrants, for example, are members of large extended families that

2-10
Spanish missions, such as this one, influence architecture even today.

need extra space in housing for sleeping quarters. Other immigrants may want to have a large yard where they can grow a vegetable or fruit garden, just as they did in their homelands.

Low wages and limited knowledge of the English language can be barriers to finding decent, safe, and affordable housing. Too many new immigrants live in conditions that are substandard and unsafe, jeopardizing their families' desires for better living. To help find suitable housing that reflects their culture in a way that meets housing codes and regulations, new immigrants need simple housing information provided in their own languages.

Not all immigrants fall into the category of low-paid laborers, however. Many new immigrants are skilled workers and professionals such as doctors and lawyers. Others are workers with advanced degrees or exceptional abilities, including university teachers and skilled musicians. Even the majority of low-paid immigrants are eventually able to improve their living conditions and save enough money to buy a home. Acquiring a home, personalizing it, and becoming a part of a community is a desire shared by foreign-born and native-born citizens alike, 2-11.

Societal Influences on Housing

Signs of societal change are everywhere. You can see them in the growth of the cities and the movement of people to new jobs and locations. You can also see them in relationships and lifestyles. Many of these changes affect housing.

Household Size

The U. S. Census Bureau collects data to provide information on **demographics**—statistical facts about the human population. Demographic information helps

2-11
About 67 percent of foreign-born citizens are home owners, which is about the same percent of U.S.-born citizens who own homes.

society plan for future needs and understand trends that affect those needs. Demographic information includes such characteristics of individuals as age, income, race, gender, and the relationship of people living in a household.

One important social change that influences housing is the average number of people living in a household. Since the first U.S. Census in 1790, the average number has gradually decreased. This first census showed that most households had between three and seven members. In 1900, the majority had two to five members. The 2000 U.S. census and recent statistics show that only one or two people live in most households today.

Household Composition

The decrease in the number of household members is not the only change evident in households. Their composition has also changed. In 1940, for example, married couples headed 75 percent of all households, and 7 percent were single-person households. By 2009, the number of nonfamily (mostly single people) households increased dramatically, accounting for more than 30 percent of the total. Households headed by married couples, however, decreased to just over 20 percent.

In the past, married couples were more likely than single people to own their own homes. This has changed, however, due in part to an increase in the number of singles. For example, the 2000 U.S. census counted 81 million single people over 19 years of age. In 2007, there were 100 million unmarried adults, representing an increase of more than eight million singles in five years. The increase is due to many reasons, such as the tendency to postpone marriage until careers are established and the steady increase in the nation's divorce rate. Recent census figures show that women and men are marrying later than ever before. The percentage of people marrying in their 20s continues to decline.

Some singles choose to live with roommates and share housing costs, while others prefer to live alone, 2-12. Many singles are renters and live in apartments. Others are home owners living in a variety of housing types.

Some singles live with their parents. Never-married singles or single-again adults may return to live with their parents after living on their own for a while. The combined living arrangement may last for a short or extended period.

An Older Population

The continual aging of the population is another change in society that affects housing. The median age of the U.S. population is 36.5 years, reflecting the ever-growing number of people in higher age categories. Median means the arithmetic average.

According to the most recent U.S. census estimates, the two age categories showing the fastest growth are 45-to-49-year-olds and 50-to-54-year-olds. Their members are part of the large segment of the adult population referred to as **baby boomers**. They get their name from the period after World War II called the *baby boom*, which includes births from 1946 through 1964. Since this group is so large, the housing they need as they age is placing high demands on society.

Already the housing needs of older adults are large and growing. Recent U.S. census information indicates about 35 million people are age 65 or older, accounting for 12 percent of the population. By 2020, the U.S. census projections show the number of people age 65 or older will increase to 55 million, accounting for 16 percent of the total population. The majority of older persons live with a spouse. Among those who live alone, most are women.

Housing needs for older adults differ from those of the general population. Many older people lose some of their physical abilities as they age. They may have a partial loss of hearing or sight. Some are more sensitive to heat and cold. They may no longer be able to use stairs. Many older people live in housing that presents limits or barriers to taking full advantage of their homes.

2-12
Singles who want extra space to pursue a hobby or a business may prefer to live alone rather than share housing with a roommate.

Housing that is adapted or designed to fit the needs of older adults helps them live in their homes longer, thus remaining independent, 2-13.

As a result of the aging population, housing and related services for the older adults are a national concern. Retirement centers, assisted living arrangements, and personal health assistance will need to expand to meet the changing population demands.

People with Special Needs

Many people have physical, sensory, or mental disabilities that limit their activities. A **disability** is an impairment or limit to a person's ability to carry out daily living activities. For example, such disabilities may interfere with a person's ability to walk, lift, hear, or see. These physical limitations may be temporary or permanent. As a result, an individual will have special housing needs. His or her housing must not restrict the ability to carry out day-to-day activities.

When housing limits a person's daily activities, housing professionals must give consideration to ways to build or adapt housing to meet specific needs. Guidelines for meeting these needs will follow in later chapters.

Finding Affordable Housing

Many people live in inadequate housing. In general, housing is inadequate if the occupants pay more than 30 percent of their income for housing or if the housing itself is substandard in some way. Some people with inadequate housing may live on social security benefits or other housing assistance, which provide minimum resources. Some become homeless as a result of unemployment and loss of income.

Inadequate housing has many effects on society. Substandard dwellings become overcrowded, which results in a lack of privacy and increased family conflict.

2-13
Compact, one-story houses are ideal for senior citizens.

It also contributes to the spread of disease.

The middle-income group is the largest in the United States. Most jobs provide middle-income salaries, and most housing and furniture designs have middle-income families in mind. However, today's middle-income individuals and families sometimes have difficulty buying houses. This is because they have excess debt (usually credit-card payments) and incomes that are not rising as fast as housing costs. Often times, they have not saved enough money for a down payment.

In the recent past, families were advised to spend no more than two and one-half times their annual income to purchase a house. Today, the average house in the United States is more costly. The average family spends at least one-third of its income on housing. Some of those who purchase houses may pay up to four times their annual income for an average house. These increases in the cost of housing make single-family homes unaffordable for many.

Since the housing costs have risen faster than income, middle-income families must decide how to balance their housing and lifestyle needs.

2-14
Many families today choose to live in low-maintenance apartments such as these.

Copyright Kavanagh Homes

Instead of buying a single-family house, for example, they may choose to buy a home in a multifamily unit or simply rent an apartment, 2-14.

Changing Roles

Today, many women work outside the home. Some are working to support themselves. Others are working to support their families, which might include children or older relatives. Many women own their own houses.

When both adults in a family have employment outside the home, they have a **dual-career family**. This common situation is necessary for many families because income does not keep up with the cost of living. While dual-career families may have more income, they may have less time for household tasks. They may desire more convenient housing and timesaving devices.

Planning for Leisure Time

People today are spending more time at various types of work—balancing their jobs with home tasks, child care, and sometimes parent care responsibilities. This often leaves little time for relaxation and recreation. Consequently, many individuals and families must make time for leisure and use that time wisely.

How you choose to use your leisure time affects your housing decisions. Many people choose housing with low-maintenance requirements to spend less time on upkeep. Others may enjoy decorating or fixing up their homes, and view these as leisure or recreational activities.

Some people specifically choose housing that provides opportunities for leisure activities. The house may have a special room, such as an exercise or hobby area. It may be near a golf course, tennis court, or swimming pool. A large backyard may be the place a home owner wants to spend leisure time with family and friends.

Working at Home

Due to technological and other changes in the workplace, the number of people working from their homes is increasing. These individuals may have their own businesses in their homes or may be employees working as telecommuters. **Telecommuting** is working at home or another site through an electronic link to a computer network at a central office. In addition, fax machines, e-mail, and the Internet make working at home easier.

The use of the home as the workplace requires creating a work area that is both functional and convenient. This has implications for the design or redesign of the home environment. You will learn more about how to design a workspace that successfully meets the specific needs of a telecommuter in following chapters.

Working at home not only presents challenges for designing the workspace, but also for dealing with distractions that interfere with the work routine. Persons working at home need to develop strategies to deal effectively with difficulties that may arise in family relationships, completion of household tasks, and focusing their job requirements.

A Mobile Society

In a mobile society, people often travel from one location to another. The average vehicle owner travels 15,000 miles a year. Some travel with their portable dwellings, 2-15. The average household moves every four years, which can exceed 17 moves in a lifetime.

Sometimes people move to change from renting to home ownership or vice versa. The main reason for so much movement is to relocate for employment reasons. Other reasons for moving include retirement, a better climate, the desire for larger (or smaller) housing, or the preference for a quieter (or livelier) neighborhood.

Population shifts in the United States are the result of a mobile society. Before 1970, there was a slow, continuing westward movement. People also moved toward large bodies of water such as the oceans, Great Lakes, and Gulf of Mexico. After 1970, people began moving to the Sunbelt. The **Sunbelt** includes the southern and southwestern regions of the United States.

Environmental Influences on Housing

Your **environment** is the total of all conditions, objects, places, and people that are around you. People adapt to their environments in the housing they design and build. They are also able to manipulate their environments through their housing decisions.

The Natural Environment

Nature provides the *natural environment*. Land, water, trees, and solar energy are elements of the natural environment. The natural environment also includes **climate**, which is the combination of weather conditions in a region over a period of years such as temperature, wind velocity, and precipitation. The altitude and distribution of the land and water help produce the climate.

Shelter varies according to the climate in which it is located. For instance, in areas where it snows or rains often, roofs are sloped to shed snow and rain. In warm, dry areas, roofs may be flat and accessible so people can sleep

2-15
Many people use motorized recreational vehicles as a home for traveling around the country.

Photography Courtesy of GoRVing.com

on the cooler rooftops at night. In cold regions, houses may have smaller doors and fewer windows.

While people want protection from nature, they do not want to be closed off from it. Large windows can frame views of the outdoors while providing protection from the elements. On mild days, patios, swimming pools, and decks provide great opportunities for outdoor living.

A region's **topography**, or the arrangement of physical features of the land, and its climate influence the location and design of dwellings. Houses with locations and designs that harmonize with the natural setting and climate are more likely to be efficient. For example, placing a house on a location to take advantage of the sun and wind exposure can reduce the amount of energy necessary to heat and cool the interior space and add to occupant comfort.

During the 1950s, integrating houses with the natural environment was explored. Architects designed houses to fit various natural environments. One of the most influential architects concerned with the environment was Frank Lloyd

Wright. He broke away from traditional housing designs, saying people should have the courage to follow nature. He used natural settings and many native building materials. For example, Figure 2-16 shows *Fallingwater*—a home Wright designed. Located in Pennsylvania's Laurel Highlands about 90 miles from Pittsburgh, Fallingwater was built over a waterfall between 1936 and 1939. Wright positioned houses to take advantage of natural sunlight and prevailing breezes. He also located them so they had a great deal of privacy. Design for much of today's housing takes advantage of the natural environment.

The Constructed Environment

The *constructed environment* includes the natural environment after changes from human effort. A constructed environment is created when a dwelling is built, landscaped, and heated and/or cooled to control the indoor climate.

Together, natural and constructed environments can provide pleasing surroundings. Highways through the mountains make the beautiful scenery accessible to people. Dwellings located along beaches allow people to enjoy a view of the ocean, 2-17.

The Behavioral Environment

Housing creates an environment for people to interact with one another. This interaction is called the *behavioral environment*. Human qualities, such as intelligence, talent, and energy, are part of this environment. Feelings, such as happiness, loneliness, love, and anger, are another part of it.

The behavioral environment overlaps with the natural and constructed environments. It is found wherever people interact—in child care centers, schools, shopping centers, neighborhoods, and houses.

Housing fosters social behavior. It may restrict certain types of behavior

2-16

Frank Lloyd Wright designed this building to visually blend into its hillside environment.

Courtesy of The Frank Lloyd Wright Foundation

GREEN CHOICES

Let the Environment Work for You!

The famous American architect, Frank Lloyd Wright, led the way in placing housing on land that takes advantage of the natural environment. (Review 2-16.)

Housing that takes advantage of the natural environment is "green" because the house will cost less to heat and cool. Also, there will be fewer disturbances to the natural environment by the construction process. Specifically, home buyers and builders can select or build houses with the following "green" ideas in mind:

- Use natural sunlight as much as possible to heat interior spaces (place most lived in areas on southern side of the home)

- Place rooms that produce heat on the northern side of the home (kitchen, bathrooms, utility rooms)

- Chose landscaping that blocks northern winds from reaching the house (large trees/bushes that keep their leaves all year)

- Build levels of the house to match the natural slope of the land

These strategies can reduce energy costs. They also add to the thermal comfort and views of the home.

and permit others. Housing is more than a response to the physical environment. It is a setting for the development of the members of the household.

A positive behavioral environment is desirable for the growth and development of all household members. Housing that is safe and adequate contributes to such positive behavior, 2-18. However, when housing is substandard, it can produce a behavioral environment that has a negative effect on household members. For instance, psychological distress due to substandard housing may influence drug addiction, alcoholism, violence, and other negative behaviors among household members.

Interaction of the Environments

Each type of environment affects the other two, causing a chain reaction. One example is a community that has no open space. Houses in this community

2-17

The people who live in this beach house have easy access to the ocean plus a beautiful view.

Group 3, Architectural and Interior Design, Hilton Head Island, South Carolina. Photography provided as a courtesy of John McManus, Savannah, Georgia.

2-18
Many of a person's fondest memories are often linked to the social experiences he or she enjoyed at home.

crowded. They do not have the space they need or the natural beauty they want. Because their environments are not controlled, all their needs and wants cannot be met. Individuals in such an environment cannot move toward self-actualization.

Economic Influences on Housing

The economic influences on housing involve the production and consumption of goods and services related to housing. These influences include the interaction among consumers, businesses, and government in meeting housing needs.

People make economic decisions every day. Their decisions concern how they use their resources to meet their goals. **Resources** are objects, qualities, and personal strengths that can be used to reach a goal. One resource people have is money, or purchasing power. They will need that resource to achieve the goal of paying for housing.

Houses are expensive and costs keep rising. According to the National Association of Realtors, the median price of existing homes was $52,200 in 1980. By 1990, the median price rose to $95,500. In 2000, the median price of an existing home was $139,000. By 2007, the National Association of Realtors reported the median housing cost of existing homes was $221,900. However, recent reports from this same group indicate that during the housing crisis of 2008–2009 housing prices dropped dramatically. For example, the median price of existing single-family houses dropped to $186,000 in 2008 and to $173,000 in 2009.

are built close together, covering most of the land. No land is set aside to preserve part of the natural environment.

The behavioral environment in this community can be full of conflict because the constructed and natural environments are not satisfying to the residents. People are simply too

GREEN CHOICES

What Is Sustainability?

A special term used in referring to "going green" is *sustainability*. Sustainability means meeting the needs of the present without compromising the ability of future generations to meet their own needs. Consequently, sustainability should have no impact environmentally, socially, and economically. It is the ultimate goal of going green. Sustainable designs create the following:

- **No negative environmental impact.** This means no use of resources except for what is generated in the structure. For example, zero-energy buildings show this concept. These buildings actually generate their own energy from solar or other renewable energy sources.

- **No negative social impact.** This means the design does not cause problems in communities by interfering with the daily living or lifestyles of people in communities.

- **No economic impact.** The design does not contribute to economic losses in communities. For example, taking wood for buildings from forests could remove opportunities for local farmers and others to make a living. This would have a negative economic impact.

How Housing Affects the Economy

One way to measure the economy is to determine the number of families that can afford to buy a median-priced home in their area. High mortgage rates and high unemployment affect the ability of households to purchase housing. According to the U. S. Census Bureau, 52 percent of the total population in 1984 could afford to purchase median-priced homes in their area. By 1995, only 48 percent could afford to buy them. As a result of the economic conditions of 2008–2009, many potential home buyers had reduced incomes and could not buy homes. Although the estimated percentage of buyers who could afford the median-priced existing single-family homes decreased during this period, the affordability is expected to increase slowly from 2009 over the next few years. This is due to the drop in housing prices and housing loan interest rates.

Another measure of the economy is the number of *housing starts*, or new houses being built in a given year. In an average year, the housing starts should number around two million which would meet the demand for new housing. When the economy is up, that number may be reached. When the economy is down, the number of housing starts may fall short of expectations.

How the Economy Affects Housing

The economy affects, and is affected by, the production of houses. Many nationally produced goods and services relate to the housing industry. Employment goes up and down in relation to the condition of the housing industry, 2-19. The housing industry employs planners, developers, builders, material suppliers, tradespeople, and financial experts. There are millions of enterprises involved in this industry.

2-19
Construction workers have plenty of employment opportunities when demand for housing is strong.

The housing industry depends on the housing market. The **housing market** is the transfer of dwellings from the producers to the consumers. The strength of the housing market depends on supply and demand. This is the number of existing houses versus the number needed by the population. The housing market changes considerably from year to year since it follows the general pattern of economic prosperity and decline. War, recession, depression, inflation, and economic uncertainty all negatively impact the housing market.

Housing is traditionally the first major sector of the economy to rebound after an economic slump. Growth in the housing industry has a positive impact on the **gross domestic product (GDP)**, which is the value of all goods and services produced within a country during a given time period. The GDP is the most accurate indicator of the health of a nation's economy.

Home loan interest rates and tax advantages affect growth in the housing industry. Interest rates on home loans and inflation seem to increase at the same time. When rates for home loans are low, demand for housing is

so high that enough housing may not be available to meet the demand. When rates are high, fewer households invest in new housing.

The federal tax advantages to owning a home include the opportunity to deduct home-loan interest and real estate taxes from your taxable income. Also, home owners are not required to pay taxes on any profits they make from selling their homes, provided they meet a few easy conditions. Finally, those who move because of a job change may have yet another tax advantage.

Technological Influences on Housing

Technology is the practical application of knowledge. Knowledge of tools, materials, and processes allows people to adapt to their environments. Technology changes over time as new and better ways of meeting human needs are discovered.

Early Technology

Technology began with the early cave dwellers. Caves met the housing needs of the day because they were dry and secure, and maintained a moderate temperature. However, caves were in short supply and often located far from food and water.

When people evolved from hunting and gathering food to farming, living in caves became less desirable. People then used technology to build dwellings. They constructed their houses with naturally occurring materials, such as logs, sticks, bark, rocks, leaves, grass, mud, and snow. These houses were temporary, lasting only two or three years. They were quickly abandoned if the household wanted to move or better housing became available. The

LINK TO SOCIAL STUDIES & CULTURE

Economics: The Laws of Supply and Demand

The U.S. has an economic system in which businesses are privately owned and operated with limited government regulation. Businesses compete with one another for sales and profits and people generally make their own decisions about what to buy and sell.

In other economic systems, the prices of goods and services, including housing, may be set by the government. However, in the market economy of the U.S., prices are determined by *supply and demand*.

- *Supply* is the quantity of a product or service businesses are willing to provide. According to the *law of supply*, the higher the price at which something can be sold, the more of it businesses want to produce.

- *Demand* is the quantity of a product or service consumers are willing to buy. According to the *law of demand*, the higher the price of something, the less of it consumers want to buy.

When demand is greater than supply, price rises. This is why airfares are highest during the holidays. More people want to fly then so airlines can charge a premium. Likewise, when supply is greater than demand, price falls. In the months after the holidays, the same seats on the same planes cost less. Airlines lower their prices to entice people to fly.

Supply and demand help set prices in the housing market as well. Supply is the number of existing homes for sale and demand is the number of homes sought by home buyers at a given time. For example, a home for sale near the seashore or other desirable area may cost $400,000 or more. In a less desirable area, the same home would sell for substantially less.

---

main shortcoming of these dwellings was the quality of materials used, not the design.

Over time, technology improved natural materials and new techniques replaced the old. Logs were made into wood planks and stones were chipped into blocks. Animal hides became coverings for windows and doors. Later, methods for developing bricks, tiles, pipes, glass, and cement enhanced the quality of homes.

Industrialization

The Industrial Revolution had a dramatic technological impact on housing. Goods were mass-produced and the railroad system moved them effi-

ciently. Farmers and factories used the railroads to ship their products, which included ready-made housing materials. These ready-made houses became popular because they could be shipped in sections. Between 1908 and 1944, Sears, Roebuck & Company shipped 100,000 mail-order houses. These were "kit" houses ordered from a catalog. All the parts needed for the construction were delivered to the site. Today, some "kit" houses or factory-made houses are available for delivery.

Industrialization changed housing in many ways. Today, many parts of houses, such as doors and windows already in frames, come from the factory ready to install. Factory-produced climate-control units, such as heat pumps, air conditioners, and furnaces, have replaced fireplaces and simple fans. Replacement of hand tools with such laborsaving devices as electric saws and automatic power nailers, made completing such labor-intensive tasks as sawing wood and nailing house frames easier.

The pace of change is increasing faster than ever, fueled by nonstop scientific discoveries. Change is occurring so rapidly that sometimes equipment becomes outdated before it is fully utilized.

High Tech

The latest technology, or **high tech**, continues to be a growing influence on housing decisions. Homes often may include media rooms or home theaters complete with large screens and high-tech sound systems, 2-20. Household members extensively use home computers for connecting to the Internet and for creating documents. People can even use computers to select and locate housing through virtual tours of homes on the Web.

Computer technology is the basis for many of the high-tech items found throughout the home. You probably do not even think about the simple computer systems you use, such as a touch-tone telephone or touch-pad microwave oven. Computer technology is the reason they operate as they do,

and this is true for many other household items. Computerized systems, for example, allow central control of energy management, entertaining, and security systems, and promote convenience in living.

Many energy-saving and other features on today's appliances result from technology advances. Ranges now have safety locks to protect children and others from unauthorized use. Voice-activated commands assist blind individuals in using appliances. The future may allow the home owner to order groceries from a flat-panel computer on the refrigerator door. Appliances may soon be Web-connected to the appliance manufacturer, who can diagnose any problems that may arise.

Advances in technology continue to improve building design, assembly systems, and construction materials. For example, treated materials such as wood shingles and asphalt are now made to last at least a half century. Today's factory-built housing offers higher quality materials, too.

Many architects and interior designers use **computer-aided drafting and design (CADD)**, which is software and hardware that creates designs with a computer. CADD is useful in creating housing interiors and house plans. With CADD, designers can quickly adjust plans to conserve materials and improve a building's structure and energy efficiency. They can also more easily make adjustments based on client needs and desires. Consumer versions of CADD are also available for individuals who wish to use their computers to explore possible home modifications or decorating plans, 2-21.

While technology can solve some problems, it sometimes causes others. One example is a freeway system in a large city that helps people drive quickly and easily between home and

2-20
More and more homes are being designed to include media rooms and home theaters.

work. However, with increased traffic, pollution often develops and decreases air quality.

Governmental Influences on Housing

Government at all levels—federal, state, and local—influences housing decisions. This influence began early in U.S. history and continues today.

Legislation

Laws regulating housing began during colonial times. Some laws prohibited the building of houses on the village green, which was often set aside for government buildings and places of worship. Other laws helped control the spread of fire between adjacent houses. Fireplaces used to cook food and provide heat were often inferior. They caught fire easily and soon the whole house burned. The fire would often spread to other dwellings, and sometimes a single fire would wipe out a whole settlement. In 1649, the British ordered that houses be built of brick or stone and the roofs be made of slate or tile to help prevent the spread of fire.

2-21
Several brands of computer software in the consumer market can simplify house planning and design.

LINK TO SCIENCE & TECHNOLOGY

Telecommuting Technology

People who telecommute or run home-based businesses usually rely on the Internet to do their jobs. Using a high-speed Internet connection, or big broadband, enables computer users to send and receive large files, photos, and streaming video, and to perform other business functions. Unfortunately, the U.S. lags behind other industrialized nations in providing big broadband to consumers at affordable prices.

If you plan to telecommute, consider big broadband availability before renting or buying a home. Find out which companies provide Internet service in the area and how that service is delivered. You'll get the fastest speeds if your home is hooked up to a fiber optic network, which is not available in all communities. Fiber optics technology uses narrow glass strands to carry data at the speed of a laser light beam. Telephone and cable companies are replacing their older copper wires and cables with fiber optic cables.

Also ask about upload and download speeds and under what conditions and price you can achieve optimal speeds. Many companies charge more for their highest-speed connections.

Over the years, the government has played an increasingly stronger role in safeguarding people and their housing. In the late 1800s, Congress began enacting laws and allocating money for housing. Laws were also introduced at the turn of the twentieth century to control the use of land, prevent overcrowding, and encourage beautification.

Since the 1930s, the federal government has stepped up its efforts to improve housing conditions in the United States. Efforts were made to rebuild the slum areas. The Federal Housing Administration (FHA), an agency that still exists today, was the result of the Housing Act of 1934. With the passage of the Housing Act of 1937, came the creation of the public-housing program with the objective of providing decent, sanitary housing for families with limited incomes.

Subsequent legislation continued to provide housing programs for families with limited incomes and older citizens. This led to building even more tract houses and numerous apartments and townhouses. In 1965, the *U.S. Department of Housing and Urban Development (HUD)* was formed. This is a cabinet-level, policy-making body whose mission is to promote a decent, safe, and sanitary home, and suitable living environment for every American.

Due to an economic downturn beginning in 2007, the federal government passed several stimulus packages to offset related economic problems. Sections of the stimulus packages were to assist individuals and families in making payments on their housing loans. These packages included special sections and assistance for renters, home owners, and first-time home buyers.

In 2008, Congress passed and the president signed into law the *Housing and Economic Recovery Act of 2008.* The economic conditions of the United States and its households led to extensive foreclosures on homes throughout the nation. This law provides ways to offset these conditions and to encourage activity in the housing market. The act includes a tax credit and increased loan limits to assist first-time home buyers.

In 2009, Congress passed and the president signed into law the *American Recovery and Reinvestment Act of 2009.* This law has many provisions affecting housing. For example, it includes provisions for first-time home buyer assistance, rental assistance, and construction incentives for housing for people with limited incomes.

Congress continues to pass housing legislation and allocate money for housing programs. Appendix A summarizes important national laws that impact housing.

States also pass laws that relate to housing, which must conform to federal legislation. The federal government is delegating more and more responsibility for regulating housing in the states.

City or county governments may establish local housing-related ordinances. These regulations must also conform to both federal and state laws. Most local housing legislation falls into one of the following categories:

- standards for quality construction
- control of land and density
- funding for housing
- housing for people in need
- environmental protection

Standards for Quality Construction

Much of the housing legislation sets minimum standards of quality for various areas. Standards are set for land use and dwelling construction. They are also set to control density and separate residences from industry. Other standards are set to protect human health.

Standards include building codes. **Building codes** establish minimum standards for materials and construction methods. There are codes for plumbing, heating, ventilation, and electrical systems, 2-22. Placement of stairways and exits are also included in the codes. The codes help assure healthy, safe, and sanitary conditions. Some standards also relate to appearance. They indicate roof styles or maximum height. Local and state governments formulate and enforce such codes. The latest edition of the *International Building Code* is the most widely adopted model building code in the world. It sets minimum standards for building construction.

Standards become part of the building code only after formal adoption by a broad range of industry experts. Standards help ensure the safety, health, and integrity of materials, products, and services for consumers. Organizations such as the American National Standards Institute (ANSI) and the American Society for Testing and Materials (ASTM) promote and facilitate standards development.

Some housing codes determine the use, occupancy, and maintenance of buildings. One reason is to prevent overcrowding. Another is to guarantee that major alterations made to a dwelling meet required standards. Enforcement of these codes may be poor in some communities, sometimes because of too few inspection officials. Also, some people resist inspections that will result in exposure of their code breaking, which often involves a fine and/or penalties.

Control of Land and Density

A **zoning regulation** is a government requirement that controls land use. It specifies and permits the type of buildings and activities in a certain area. For example, such regulations may dictate land for residential, commercial, or industrial use. In a residential zone, only residential dwellings can be built. Commercial zones limit structures to stores and office buildings, 2-23. In industrial zones, only construction of

2-22
Building codes require qualified electricians to install the electrical systems. The same is true for the heating, cooling, and plumbing systems.

factories and other industrial businesses can occur. Sometimes regulations may only permit one type of dwelling within a residential area. Many communities restrict the location of manufactured housing and multifamily dwellings to specific areas. Zoning laws may also specify the minimum size of dwellings in an area.

Zoning regulations also control density. Controlling density reduces the risk of fire and keeps traffic and pollution manageable. It also restricts excessive noise and lighting. Density restrictions also limit lot size and the placement of a building on a lot.

Government controls at all levels tend to increase the cost of housing. However, the intention of building and zoning controls is to serve the best interests of the public.

Funding for Housing

Funding is another example of govern-ment involvement in housing. Several government agencies are charged with buying and selling home loans. The government assures some loans, which

2-23
The land under this sign is zoned for commercial purposes only.

Seaboard Properties, Hilton Head Island, S.C.

means it stands behind the lender if home owners do not meet their obligations. The government helps special groups—such as older people, people with disabilities, veterans, families with limited incomes, and first-time home owners—acquire funding. Most of these financial organizations are a part of HUD.

Housing for People in Need

Various forms of government assistance are available to help people who cannot afford housing. HUD provides rent supplements to individuals and families with low incomes. HUD also builds public housing for those unable to fully pay for satisfactory housing. The federal government also gives support to private programs created to help the homeless.

Local governments may donate existing houses that need rehabilitation or may assist with the infrastructure. **Infrastructure** is the underlying foundation or basic framework. In housing, the term often refers to installation of the sewer, water, gas, and electrical lines to make housing liveable.

In recent years, the number of homeless people has increased dramatically. Current estimations indicate there are between 500,000 and seven million homeless people in the United States. A large percentage of homeless people are members of families with children

and war veterans. Many are newly and temporarily homeless, having suddenly lost a job or the ability to work. Others are chronically homeless, having accepted their homeless condition as a way of life. In addition, the number of homeless people in rural and suburban areas rose dramatically in 2007 and beyond.

People who become homeless do not fit any one description. However, all people experiencing homelessness have basic needs, including adequate incomes, affordable housing, and health care. Some homeless people may need special services, such as mental health or drug-abuse treatment, to have adequate housing. Preventing homelessness requires meeting all their needs.

Many people have benefited from government housing assistance. However, there never seems to be enough assistance to accommodate everyone who needs it. Since government assistance cannot meet the total housing-assistance needs in American society, various community partnerships have formed to help meet the housing needs of limited-resource families.

An important example is *Habitat for Humanity*. This is a partnership formed to help eliminate homelessness and substandard housing, not only in the United States, but also in other countries. Habitat for Humanity relies on volunteers for a number of tasks, including the providing of labor to actually build houses, 2-24. The future home owners must make a generous hands-on donation of labor or similar resources, called "sweat equity," to help produce their own housing. They make a down payment and have low monthly payments. The money goes into a revolving fund to help others obtain housing through the program. Hundreds of volunteers from civic clubs, religious groups, professional organizations, student groups, and institutions regularly join forces with Habitat for Humanity to build housing structures and a true sense of community.

2-24
These college students spent their spring break as volunteers building new homes for families without adequate housing.

Habitat for Humanity®
International

Environmental Protection

Concern for the environment has led to a number of environmental protection laws. In addition, creation of such government agencies as the *U.S. Environmental Protection Agency (EPA)* and the *U.S. Consumer Product Safety Commission (CPSC)* helps foster a positive natural environment. They support research and provide information to consumers so the housing environment, and the total environment, will be safe and protected. The agencies have telephone hotlines to assist consumers with problems concerning the environment.

The job of the *Environmental Protection Agency (EPA)* is to safeguard the natural environment, including the air, water, and land upon which life depends. Consequently, the agency focuses on the natural environment as well as the quality of air and water within housing, 2-25. EPA also assists with voluntary pollution-prevention programs and energy-conservation methods.

The *Consumer Product Safety Commission (CPSC)* has jurisdiction over more than 15,000 consumer products used in and around the constructed environment. The agency's focus is to save lives and keep families safe by reducing the risk of injuries and deaths associated with consumer products. Examples of products the commission tests include cleaning supplies, small and large household equipment (such as toasters and dishwashers), lamps, and outdoor play equipment. The CPSC has the authority to recall unsafe products or require their repair. The agency also investigates product complaints linked to injuries and deaths and issues safety guidelines and consumer education.

2-25
Safeguarding the natural environment will allow people to enjoy the beauty of nature for generations to come.

CAREER FOCUS

Land Surveyor

Can you imagine yourself as a land surveyor? If you can, read more about this interesting career.

Interests/Skills: If you share any of the following interests, you may want to pursue a course of study that would lead to a career as a land surveyor. Do you enjoy searching for facts and mentally working out problems? Do you like to start up and carry out projects? Are you a decision maker and a risk taker? Do you like to work outside and appreciate plants and animals? Land surveyors must have good math skills and should be able to see objects, distances, sizes, and other forms in their minds. Surveyors also have to be able to work with people and to work as part of a team. Learning to lead others is another important skill.

Career Snapshot: Surveyors measure and draw the appearance of the earth's surface. Surveyors do different types of work—some measure land, air space, and water areas. For example, some may define air space for airports while others measure construction and mineral sites. They describe land location, its features, and its size. Surveyors might lead survey projects and also study legal records. They look for previous property boundaries and record the results of the survey. Surveyors put these facts in legal documents about property. Surveyors check their facts and create drawings and maps of what an area looks like. They also write reports.

Education/Training: Most surveyors have a bachelor's degree in surveying or a related field.

Licensing/Examinations: All 50 States and all U.S. territories license surveyors.

Professional Associations: The National Society of Professional Surveyors (NSPS), (www.nspsmo.org) and the American Association of Geodetic Surveying (AAGS), (www.aagsmo.org).

Job Outlook: Surveyors should have favorable job prospects. These occupations should experience much faster than average employment growth. As technologies become more complex, opportunities will be best for surveyors who have a bachelor's degree and strong technical skills.

Source: Occupational Information Network (O*NET) (www.online.onetcenter.org) and the Occupational Outlook Handbook, Bureau of Labor Statistics (www.bls.gov).

Summary

Many forces work together to influence housing. Some forces, such as history, culture, and society, involve people. Other forces, such as the environment, economy, technology, and government, involve conditions. All are interrelated.

The cultural development of housing in North America began when settlers arrived from all over the world to join the Native Americans. They brought their unique cultures with them, which influenced their housing.

Historical events such as the Industrial Revolution, Great Depression, and World Wars I and II impacted how people were housed. Societal events—such as changes in household needs, wants, and lifestyles—affected housing designs.

The Industrial Revolution, population increases, and economic crises all caused housing shortages. To ease the shortages, use of technology and government agencies helped develop new solutions for affordable housing.

Housing is a part of the constructed, natural, and behavioral environments. Each type of environment impacts the other two. The government passes legislation that establishes building standards, zoning regulations, and environmental protection. It makes sure all three environments work well together and provides funding for affordable housing for many people.

Review the Facts

1. Identify three types of early Native American dwellings.
2. Describe the housing of the first European settlers.
3. Why is the log cabin the symbol of the early United States?
4. What was the main cause of the population shift from rural to urban areas in the late 1700s?
5. Identify two housing problems created by the population shift.
6. Contrast row houses and tenements.
7. What three historical events resulted in substandard housing?
8. Summarize the principles behind the concept of new urbanism.
9. Name an example of how culture influenced housing.
10. What are three factors regarding households that can influence housing?
11. Name two reasons many older adults have special housing needs.
12. Why are many middle-income families choosing to live in multifamily housing instead of single-family houses?
13. How can leisure time affect housing decisions?
14. Contrast a constructed environment with the natural environment.
15. What effect does housing growth have on the GDP?
16. What determines the strength of the housing industry?
17. List two ways that CADD is used to improve housing.
18. Summarize two responsibilities of HUD.

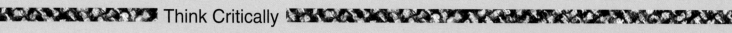

Think Critically

19. **Analyze options.** Not all people have incomes sufficient to meet their housing needs adequately. In your opinion, should all, part, or none of their housing costs be paid (subsidized) by government sources? If the government is involved, what selection process should be used to determine who is eligible to receive assistance?

20. **Draw conclusions.** What could happen to housing if building regulations were suddenly eliminated—allowing anything to be built in any way? In what instances (if any) could the resulting housing be better? In what instances could it be worse? Draw conclusions and share your opinions with the class.

21. **Predict technology.** Working with two or three classmates, predict what new technology will be used in houses in 20 years. List your ideas with as much detail as possible and share them with the class.

Community Links

22. **Research.** Identify a local problem that involves the environment. Research how this problem could be solved and which government agencies could help you.

23. **Oral-history interview.** Conduct an oral-history interview with one or more older members of your community about what housing was like when they were growing up. Where did they grow up? Ask them how housing has changed and improved over time. Share your findings with the class.

24. **Housing promotions.** Obtain brochures from different housing developers and house builders. List the advantages they give for the types of houses they promote. Explain how the advantages relate to the natural, constructed, and behavioral environments.

25. **Investigate building codes.** Suppose you want to add a three-season room off the back of your house. Use Internet or print resources to research information on local building codes to determine what building code requirements are necessary for this project. How do the local building codes expand on the International Building Code? Write a summary of your findings to share with the class.

Academic Connections

26. **Writing.** Identify a style of housing in your community that appears in this chapter. Research the housing style and determine its country of origin. Then write a short essay describing how the style has influenced housing in the United States.

27. **Social studies.** Locate and read a biography or autobiography about an Early American settler. What was life like for this individual? What shelter options did this person have? How did these options impact daily living? Give an oral book report to share with the class.

Technology Applications

28. **Research technology.** Search the Internet for new technologies in housing. Choose one that interests you and determine the following: What are the benefits of using the technology? What are some possible disadvantages with using this technology? In your opinion, is the technology likely to be used in almost all houses? Why or why not?

29. **Investigate paint.** Investigate the harmful health effects that lead-based paint poses to humans. Check out the Web sites for the National Safety Council or the U.S. Consumer Product Safety Commission for your research. Determine where it is generally found and how it can be removed safely. What groups of people are identified as most affected by lead-based paint? Use presentation software to create an informative news bulletin or brochure.

30. **Electronic presentation.** Choose a topic from the chapter and use images and presentation software to show how the topic has influenced housing. Obtain the images off the Internet or take pictures with a digital camera. Add appropriate captions to the photos. Possible topics include: household composition, life expectancy, government influences, and technological advances. Share your presentation with the class.

Design Practice

31. **Designing for older adults.** Presume that you and your design team have taken on the challenge of redesigning living space for an older adult with moderate mobility problems who still manages all self-care activities. Modifications to the living space will make daily-care activities easier for the older adult. Use Internet or print resources as needed to complete the following:

- Write a 300 word proposal indicating design modifications—especially to the living area, kitchen, and bath—that will enable the older adult to better provide self-care.

- Locate photo examples for your proposed modifications to use with presentation software. Obtain facts that support your modifications for the space.

- Share your presentation with your client (the class).

32. **Portfolio.** Walk around your neighborhood and look for ways people have altered the natural environment for housing purposes. Use a digital camera to photographically record the changes you find. Assess how the constructed environment influenced the alterations to the natural environment and write a short summary of your assessment. Create a digital presentation to save on a CD or other storage device, or create a storyboard to share your findings. Save your presentation for your portfolio.

Active Citizens Influence Housing

As communities look for ways to improve housing for citizens and protect the environment, opportunities exist for people to take action. How can you get involved? Start by attending one or more meetings of your city council or county board. What housing related issues are facing your community? Is your community supporting a recycling program or other environmentally friendly practices? On what level can citizens become involved?

Once you have answers to these questions and more, plan and implement an FCCLA *Power of One* project involving a community housing issue. Use the FCCLA *Planning Process* as a guide. Then evaluate your project. See your adviser for information as needed.

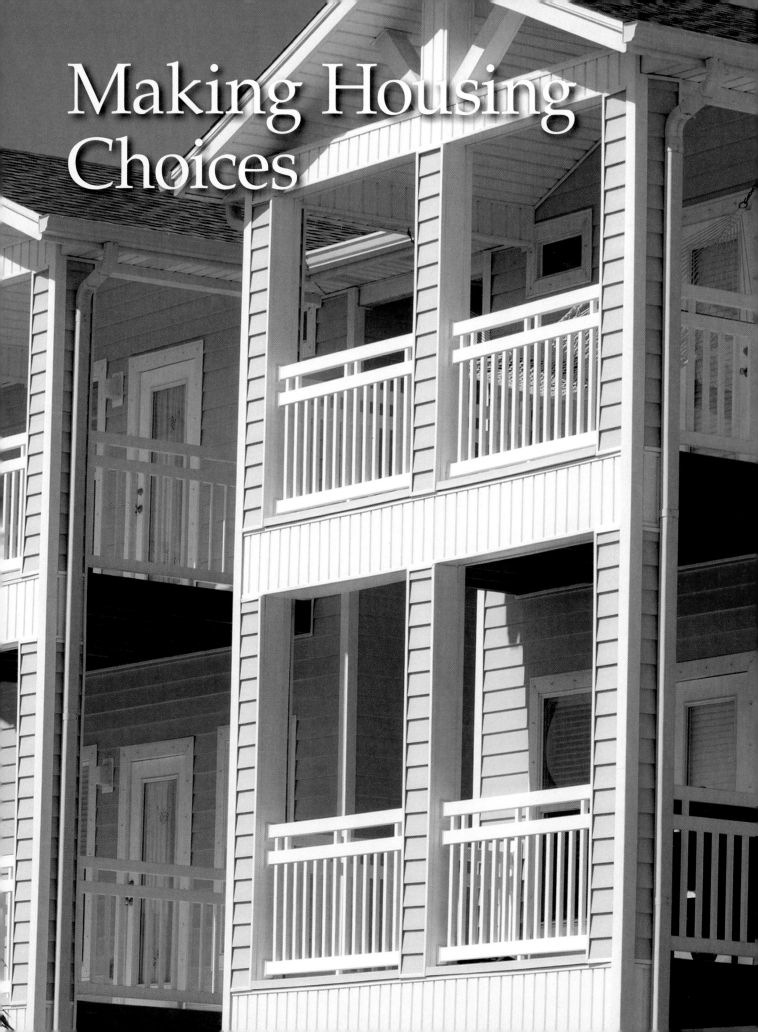

Making Housing Choices

CHAPTER 3

Using Decision-Making Skills

Terms to Learn

rational decision
impulse decision
habitual behavior
central-satellite decision
chain decision
human resources
nonhuman resources
implement

Chapter Objectives

After studying this chapter, you will be able to

- summarize the different types of decisions.

- identify human and nonhuman resources.

- summarize the steps of the decision-making process.

- demonstrate how to make wise decisions.

Reading with Purpose

Find the terms list at the beginning of the chapter. Write what you think each term means. Then look the terms up in the glossary and write the textbook definition.

In the first two chapters of this textbook, you read that many decisions affect housing. These decisions relate to your needs, values, life situations, lifestyle, and environmental and governmental influences. Because these factors are constantly changing, you continually face making new decisions. By making these decisions wisely, you and other members of your household will have the chance to grow and develop to full potential. It is important to develop good decision-making skills so you are able to enhance your life and your housing. These skills will also be necessary in any career path you choose to follow whether it is as an interior designer or other housing career.

Types of Decisions

All decisions are not alike. Learning to recognize the different types of decisions will help you develop decision-making skills.

Decisions can be classified into two groups, 3-1. One group consists of those decisions that vary according to the thought and care used in making them. The other group of decisions consists of interrelated decisions and is based on their relationship to other decisions.

Decisions Made with Thought and Care

The three types of decisions separated according to the amount of thought and care used are rational, impulse, and habitual behavior. Suppose you have your own bedroom and you want to place an upholstered chair in it. If you shop until you find a chair that looks good with what you already have in your room, you are making a rational decision. A **rational decision** is one based on reasoning. However, if you buy the first chair you find appealing without thinking about how it would look in your room, your decision is an impulse decision. An **impulse decision** is one that is made quickly, with little thought of the possible consequences.

Habitual behavior, in contrast, is an action that is done as a matter of routine without thought. It does not call for you to make a decision unless there is a new factor in the situation. For instance, turning on the faucet in your bathroom to brush your teeth is a habit. You do not need to make a decision unless water fails to flow from the faucet.

3-1
Decisions are classified by the amount of thought devoted to them or by their relationships to other decisions.

Types of Decisions	
Based on the Degree of Thought Involved	
Rational Decisions	Choices are made only after looking at problems carefully. Consequences are considered.
Impulse Decisions	Choices are made quickly, with little thought given to possible outcomes.
Habitual Behavior	An action results instinctively. Decisions are involved only when new situations arise.
Based on Relationships	
Central-Satellite Decisions	A major decision is surrounded by related but independent decisions.
Chain Decisions	One decision creates other choices that must be made to complete the action.

Interrelated Decisions

Central-satellite decisions and chain decisions are examples of decisions that can be described according to their relationship to other decisions.

Central-Satellite Decisions

A **central-satellite decision** is a group of decisions consisting of a major decision that is surrounded by related but independent decisions. See 3-2 for an illustration of the concept of central-satellite decisions.

Chain Decisions

Chain decisions are a sequence of decisions in which one decision triggers others. All decisions in the chain must be made to complete an action. Figure 3-3 shows a diagram of a chain decision relating to housing.

The following housing-related case shows one example of making interrelated decisions. Suppose a home owner needs to decide what to do about the many patches of dead grass in the yard. Right after planting the grass, the backyard looked very attractive. Now children and pets use the yard constantly as a playground. Neighborhood children walking back and forth to school also use a part of it as a path. This heavy traffic is preventing the grass from growing.

Suppose the owner decides to keep the grass and protect it from heavy use. In this case, the decision to keep the grass becomes a central decision. The owner will need to make satellite decisions. Perhaps moving play activities

Central-Satellite Decisions

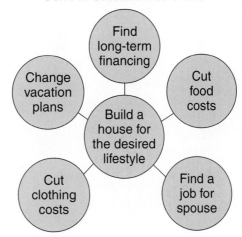

3-2
The central decision is to build a house; the others are satellite decisions. They relate to the central decision, but they are not dependent on it.

to a patio since they are better suited to hard-surface areas is one decision, 3-4. Creating a place for pets to run and play is another. The owner might establish traffic barriers or convert areas that receive high traffic to natural areas. Adding stepping-stones to the landscape plan is yet another decision. Careful placement of lawn furniture, shrubs, or flowers could force people to walk around the grassy area instead of through it.

As an alternative, the owner may choose to remove the grass and replace it with a hardier variety instead. The new variety would withstand the traffic and still look attractive. It would also require less care.

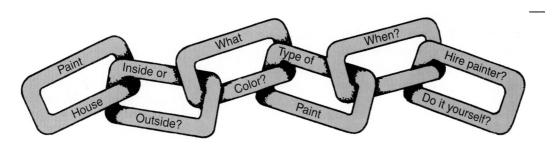

3-3
In chain decisions, you need to make additional decisions to complete the action of the first decision.

3-4
Placing steppingstones through the grassy area of a garden is part of a chain decision in seeking ways to protect the grass from heavy use.

Resources for Housing Decisions

As you learned in Chapter 2, resources are material objects, qualities, or personal strengths you can use to reach a goal. You need resources to carry out any type of decision you make. Resources are available to you in many forms.

Human Resources

Human resources are resources available from people. They include ability, knowledge, attitude, energy, and health, 3-5.

You may have many resources that help you make housing decisions. For instance, if you have the ability to make house repairs, you have skill as a human resource. If you are willing to learn how to make house repairs, you have intelligence as human resource. When these resources are developed and used, decisions can be made and results can be achieved.

If you are a person with a high energy level, you may spend time after school and on weekends doing extra projects to improve your housing. If you have a low energy level, you may choose to hire someone to perform maintenance tasks to keep your house in shape.

If you have good health, that resource will enable you to use other human resources to an advantage. For example, when you are healthy you are likely to be motivated to use your knowledge and skills. You might decide to remodel your kitchen. If you have poor health, you are likely to postpone the project or hire someone to do it for you.

Nonhuman Resources

Nonhuman resources are resources that are not directly supplied by people. They include money, property, time, and community resources, 3-6.

The decision to replace the dead grass is the first decision in a chain. The second link is deciding which variety of grass to plant. The next decision is to determine where you will buy the grass. Other links include deciding whether you will plant it yourself or have someone else do it, when to plant it, and how to pay for it. The owner must make each of these decisions before replacing the grass.

Inventory of Human Resources

Person	Physical health	Energy	Knowledge and information	Ability or skill	Attitude	Other (specify)
Husband/Father:						
Wife/Mother:						
Teens:						
Children:						
Others:						

3-5
Make an inventory of the human resources in your household by preparing a chart similar to this. Rate members on a scale of 1 to 5, with 5 being the highest rating.

Money

Consider the use of the nonhuman resource of money in housing. Everyone has some housing expenses. You need money to buy or rent a place to live. You need additional money for furnishings, equipment, utilities, and repairs. You must decide what you can afford to spend for these items. The following factors will determine the amount to spend:

- income
- savings
- lifestyle
- possessions

3-6
Books, land, buildings, money, and tools are examples of nonhuman resources.

Cliff Snider.

Property

The property you acquire and the way you use it relate to your housing decisions. Property resources include such items as land, buildings, and furnishings. The choices you have made and the property you already possess partly determine the amount you can afford for housing. Perhaps you are willing to live in a less expensive apartment so you can have new furniture. If you choose a more expensive apartment, the furniture or some other housing feature may need to wait. You may decide to reupholster or repair older furniture rather than replace it.

Time

Time is also a nonhuman resource. How you use time is what counts most. You have 24 hours a day, 365 days a year, just as everyone else has. Time is the only resource all people have in equal amounts. Other resources come in different quantities for different people.

Community Resources

People often take community resources for granted, but these resources can play an important part in your housing decisions. You may base the decision of where you will live on the quality of the community resources available. For example, you may want to have a good public library in your community. This will help you do your homework, prepare for a career, and even find a job. You can also use library resources for recreation.

A city park with a playground and a picnic area is another community resource. If you know that a park is nearby, you may choose housing with a yard smaller than originally planned.

Some community schools and recreation departments offer special classes for self-improvement. By taking advantage of these classes, you can learn such skills as furniture refinishing, upholstering, remodeling, and home maintenance. As interest in do-it-yourself projects increases, many home-improvements stores are also teaching classes on home maintenance as well as some television programming.

Other community resources include hospitals, fire stations, police departments, shopping centers, and sports facilities, 3-7. What community resources are available where you live?

Using Resources

You will have different quantities of resources at different times in your life. For instance, today you may have more energy than you will 30 years from now. In the future, you may have more money to spend than you have now.

Some people have little of both money and energy. To make their resources meet their needs, they must know how to use their knowledge and abilities to save money and energy.

You can choose which resources to spend and which to save. Suppose that you own a house that needs painting. You could paint it yourself. This would take a lot of time that you may prefer

3-7
A community pool and picnic shelter is a valuable entertainment resource.

spending in some other way. You may decide to hire someone else to paint the house, such as a professional painter or experienced friend.

Some of your human resources decrease as you use them, namely time and energy. Others increase with use, such as your abilities and knowledge. You will seldom use only one resource at a time since all are closely related. To develop a new skill, you will need a good attitude, knowledge, energy, health, and time.

The Decision-Making Process

To make a wise decision, you must first understand the question, problem, or issue involved. Knowing that, you can then reach a satisfactory answer or solution by following the steps in the decision-making process, 3-8.

Steps in Decision Making

The first step in the decision-making process involves *identifying the challenge*. It focuses on defining the question or challenge accurately. This is the most important step. If you cannot properly identify the real issue, all the work that follows may be in vain.

Steps in the Decision-Making Process
1. Identify the challenge.
2. List possible solutions.
3. Make a decision.
4. Take action.
5. Evaluate results.

3-8
Following these steps carefully will help you make good decisions.

The second step involves *exploring possible answers or solutions*. You look for various ways to address the issue and list each possible option. While exploring your options, you would answer the following questions:

- What is the likely outcome of each possible approach?
- Will any approach provide lasting satisfaction to those involved?
- What other decisions must you make first?

During the second step, you must also examine your resources since they will affect which decisions you can make. Suppose you plan a backyard get-together with friends. If storms arrive, you must have the resource of sufficient indoor space to use. Without it, you do not have all the resources you need for the get-together.

Sometimes you cannot consider an option because of limitations imposed by others. Suppose a student decides to use the money earned mowing lawns to buy a pet rabbit. However, if her family will not allow a pet rabbit at home, she cannot make that decision. She must reconsider her options and make a different decision.

The third step involves *making a decision by choosing which of the recommendations on your list is best*. If one option does not clearly stand out as the best choice, you probably need to repeat one or both of the earlier steps. Then, the best option should be clear, 3-9.

The fourth step involves *taking action to implement your decision*. **Implement** means to put thoughts into action. You will need to devise an action plan to fully implement your decision. Before taking action, you will need to plan exactly what to do as well as *when, where, how, and with whom* to do it.

3-9
Shopping for items to fill a specific need forces you to go through the steps of the decision-making process.

The fifth step is to *evaluate the results of your decision*. Did everything go as planned? Was the problem or challenge satisfactorily addressed? Did something totally unexpected occur? If so, you may need to plan a new course of action or repeat part or all of the decision-making process.

That last step will *provide ideas on how to improve your decision making next time*. If you are not pleased with the results, ask yourself the following questions: Did I define the problem clearly? Did I think of all possible alternatives? Did I implement my decision in the most desirable way? How could I have made a better decision in this case? How could I have implemented the decision with a better plan of action? See 3-10.

GREEN CHOICES

Choose a LEED Certified Home

LEED stands for *Leadership in Energy and Environmental Design*. A LEED certified home means that the structure meets the guidelines to be a green and sustainable building. The U.S. Green Building Council sets the guidelines and ratings. The Council has a rating system with four levels that certify that a house is environmentally responsible. The four levels include the following: Certified, Silver, Gold, and Platinum (highest).

The LEED certification means that a home's features promote such green and sustainable design, construction, and operations practices as the following:

- Innovation and design—highest standard for "green" performance
- Environmentally responsible within the larger community
- Sustainable sites—minimal impact of the home on the land
- Water efficiency—indoor and out
- Energy efficient—in the structure and heating and cooling design
- Materials and resources—efficient use of materials, use environmentally preferred materials, and produce less waste in construction
- Indoor environmental quality (IAQ)—reduce the creation of and exposure to pollutants
- Home owner education—how to use and maintain the green features
- Third-party verification—someone other than the builder has certified the green parts of the home.

3-10
This couple is carefully deciding what option will be best for their family.

Going Through the Steps

One way to learn about the decision-making process is to consider a housing-related problem and think through the steps needed to make a decision about it. For example, imagine that your grandmother who lives in Maine is coming to spend a winter at your family's home in Arizona. She needs to spend the winter in a milder climate and cannot afford to pay rent.

As a result of this visit, the housing needs and desires of every family member is likely to change. How will the family meet its new needs and values? How will your grandmother meet her needs and values? To answer these questions, go through the decision-making steps.

Step One: Identify the Challenge.

State the basic question or problem. In this case, the question is as follows: Where in your family's house will grandmother stay in order to address the needs and values of the new, larger household?

Step Two: List Possible Solutions.

Look for ways to solve the problem or answer the challenge. You need to find a comfortable place in your home for grandmother while making sure the others remain comfortable, too. Suppose all the options available to your family are as follows:

- Have grandmother use the living room sofa.

- Turn the storeroom into a new bedroom, move all the stored items elsewhere, and buy new furniture and bedding.

- Let grandmother use someone's room for the winter and have that person crowd into another member's room.

- Give her the combination office/guest room and move the computer and file cabinet to a corner of the living room.

GREEN CHOICES

LEED Accredited Architects and Interior Designers

When you decide to build a home or design the interior of a home with green or sustainable design, a first step is to choose architects and/or interior designers who have the designation of LEED Accredited Professional (LEED AP).

An architect or interior designer who has the LEED AP has passed an exam given by the Green Building Certification Institute, a division of the U.S. Green Building Council. Passing the exam indicates that the architects or interior designers have knowledge of the LEED rating systems that allows them to facilitate the integrated-design process and streamline LEED certification for their projects.

The first option might work if grandmother's stay were only for a weekend. However, complete disruption of family life would occur if the living room became someone's bedroom for an entire winter. The second option needs the purchase of furniture and bedding—requiring money that the family does not have. The third option would make life uncomfortable for the members who would need to vacate one bedroom and crowd into another. The fourth option seems the best choice for grandmother's comfort as well as the comfort of others. Can you think of other options?

All family members should thoroughly discuss grandmother's living arrangements. Because the decision affects the entire family, everyone should have input into the decision. In this case, Steps 2 and 3 require input from all household members.

Step Three: Make a Decision.

Suppose your family decides that grandmother will occupy the guest room. While this option is not perfect, it causes the fewest problems. For example, family members can keep their own rooms. They will not be disrupted if grandmother wakes and sleeps around a different schedule. Also, family members will still have access to the computer.

Step Four: Take Action.

Turning the idea into a reality will require the cooperation of all family members. Perhaps the whole family would spend a week with grandmother, help her pack, and drive her to Arizona. Maybe just one or two family members would handle these tasks. Perhaps relatives living in Maine could help grandmother pack and arrange her travel.

In Arizona, everyone would need to make small adjustments to blend another person into the family routine. This is the only way to achieve greater satisfaction for all.

Step Five: Evaluate the Results.

Evaluating a major change, such as adding a relative to the household, requires more than a day or two. After a week, the family may be able to judge whether everything is proceeding as planned. If everyone wants grandmother to stay when spring arrives, that would mean the visit was more successful than planned, 3-11.

Going through the decision-making process takes time and thought. It helps you make rational and wise decisions. The decisions related to grandmother's move—such as when she will move, how she will move, and what items she will bring—are rational and chain decisions.

The decisions your family makes fit the classification of a central-satellite decision. The central decision is that grandmother is coming to stay with the family for the winter. The other decisions are satellite decisions.

When choosing housing, you must make many different types of decisions. For example, you will need to decide the location, method of financing, type of house, and interior and exterior design. The skills learned in this chapter will help you make these decisions.

3-11
Having an older relative move into the house can be a pleasant experience for all when family members express possible problems and address them before the move.

CAREER FOCUS

Interior Designer—Hotels/Vacation Lodges

Can you imagine yourself as the interior designer of a hotel or vacation lodge where families spend their vacations? If you can, you'll want to read the following about this exciting career.

Interests/Skills: Do your interests include a love of or desire to travel? Do you share the value that it is important for families and individuals to have safe and fun places to tour and spend their vacation time? Skills include a talent for researching information and understanding details. The ability to work well with a team is essential. Strong math, communication, and computer skills along with an understanding of mechanical systems are critical.

Career Snapshot: Making a profit in hotel or vacation lodges is a challenge. That is why interior design is so important and must leave a lasting impression on visiting guests. Hospitality designers have special training in designing such commercial buildings. Many factors enter into the design process. First, designers must identify the people who will be using the space. Second, they must consider the location for the hotel or vacation lodge. The look and feel of the décor should speak to the surrounding environments. For example, mountain resorts might have a more rustic feel than a vacation resort at the beach. As a designer, you would work with and listen closely to the owner of the proposed resort. In order to create a design that meets all client requirements, cooperation of the entire team is essential. For a resort business to be successful, the design must be one that people enjoy and to which they want to return.

Education/Training: Completion of a bachelor's or master's degree is preferred. Classes include business management, lighting, computer technology, color theory, textiles, and CADD. Additional courses in culinary arts and psychology make the designer more competitive in the job market.

Licensing/Examinations: About one-half of the states require licensing of interior designers. The National Council for Interior Design Qualification (NCIDQ) administers an examination that interior designers must pass in order to obtain a license and to be competitive in their careers.

Professional Association: The American Society of Interior Designers (ASID) (www.asid.org); The International Interior Design Association (IIDA) (www.iida.org)

Job Outlook: The hospitality landscape is constantly changing with many older hotels renovated into new hip designs. Your hotel cannot afford to lose out to the competition as the look and feel of a luxury hotel is something that many travelers have come to expect.

Source: Information from the Occupational Outlook Handbook (www.bls.gov/OCO) and the Occupational Information Network (O*NET) (www.online.onetcenter.org)

Summary

There are three types of decisions that are grouped according to the amount of thought or care used. They are rational, impulse, and habitual. Other types of decisions, such as central-satellite and chain decisions, are grouped according to the relationships between decisions.

You use resources as you make decisions. Human resources—such as ability, knowledge, attitude, energy, and health—are factors in making decisions. Nonhuman resources, such as money, property, time, and community resources, also affect decisions.

If you follow the logical steps of the decision-making process, you are more likely to make wise decisions. The problems or challenges will be identified as well as possible alternatives. You will not know if you have made the best decision until after you evaluate results.

Review the Facts

1. Describe a rational decision.

2. What is the difference between an impulse decision and habitual behavior?

3. Contrast central-satellite and chain decisions.

4. What is the difference between human and nonhuman resources? Give an example of each.

5. Name five community resources.

6. What one resource is the same for everyone?

7. What are three resources that people possess in different quantities during their lives?

8. Give an example of how your use of resources, both human and nonhuman, can change over time.

9. Summarize the five basic steps in the decision-making process. Give an example demonstrating how to make a wise decision using each step of the process.

Think Critically

10. **Evaluate decisions.** Evaluate a recent decision that you made in terms of the success of its outcome. What could have been done differently to yield more successful results? What lesson did you learn to help you improve future decision making?

11. **Analyze decisions.** Read the following case study and complete the suggested activities. Andy and Noelle are both students at a community college. They plan to marry in June. Both have part-time jobs, will continue in school after the wedding, and graduate after another year. Andy plans to work in an auto repair and welding shop. Noelle wants to continue her job in the college library. In four or five years, they plan to start a family. They want two children. Noelle likes music and wants a piano. Andy likes to fish and play golf.

    A.   Identify a major housing decision this couple will face.

    B.   What resources will be available to them? What are the alternatives they may consider? What are the possible outcomes of each alternative? What other related decisions will they need to make?

    C.   Which alternative would you choose as a solution? Give reasons for your choice.

12. **Analyze behavior.** Select a favorite TV series and video-record one of the shows. Listen carefully to the plot and note all the decisions made by the characters in the program. Then analyze each decision made and label the behavior as rational, impulsive, or habitual.

Community Links

13. **Debate.** Take a pro or con position on the following statement: rational decisions give more satisfaction than impulse decisions. Prepare to defend your position in a debate with a classmate having the opposing view. Use common examples seen in the community to support your position.

14. **Household decisions.** Divide a sheet of paper into three columns. Label the first column *Decision*, the second column *Type of Decision*, and the third column *Degree of Satisfaction*. In the first column, list three housing decisions that have been made by members of your household. In the second column, identify whether the decision was rational, impulsive, or habitual behavior. In the last column, write + + if a great deal of satisfaction resulted from the decision, + if some satisfaction resulted, and − if no satisfaction resulted.

Academic Connections

15. **Reading.** Read the classified ads in the newspaper or online to learn current purchasing and rental costs of housing in the area. Share your findings with the class.

16. **Writing.** Join two or three students to write and present a skit showing how some resources decrease while others increase at the same time. Video-record the script. Play the recording for the class, but first give a brief introduction. Then answer any questions your classmates have after your presentation.

Technology Applications

17. **Internet research.** Search the Internet for a real estate Web site that allows you to select an apartment to rent in your area or in a city of interest to you. Consider your college or career plans for the year after high school and search for housing in that area. What type of housing would you need? Select a type of housing that appeals to you and determine what it costs. How does its cost compare to similar housing units in the area? Make a printout of the information you find to share with the class.

18. **Evaluate software.** Use Internet resources to locate free software available for interior design. If possible (and with permission from your teacher or parents), download the software and work with its design features. Draw conclusions about the usefulness of the software for interior design applications.

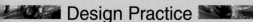 Design Practice

19. **Design decision.** Assume your new clients desire to build a new home for their expanding family. They have two preteen children and are soon expecting a baby. They desire a master bedroom with a sitting area and private bath; however, a full bath for the children is important, too. Space efficiency and green design are very important to your clients. Use Internet or print resources to locate floor plan examples for your clients. Narrow your choices to three. Use the decision-making process to determine why each floor plan would be a great choice for your clients. With two of your classmates acting as your clients, role-play a discussion of options with your client. Present each floor plan and justify the reasons why each would benefit the client.

20. **Portfolio.** Presume that you want to pursue an interior design career after high school. Your dilemma concerns where you want to go to school to get your four-year degree in interior design. Search the Internet for three accredited colleges or universities of interest to you. Use the decision-making process to choose which school to attend. Use a computer with word-processing software to record your decisions and actions for each step of the process. Save a copy of your decision for your portfolio.

Taking the Lead—Parliamentary Procedure Training

Learning to use parliamentary procedure takes training and practice. Volunteer to lead your FCCLA chapter (and perhaps other student organizations in your school) in learning how to conduct a successful meeting through parliamentary procedure. This is an orderly system of conducting business that protects the rights of group members. Discuss the impact of following or not following this procedure on the effectiveness of an organization. How might failure to use parliamentary procedure impact making decisions? Use the information and activities in the FCCLA *Chapter Handbook* to guide your training.

Once you feel confident with using parliamentary procedure, have your adviser and an officer of a local organization evaluate your ability to conduct a business meeting.

CHAPTER 4

Choosing a Place to Live

Terms to Learn

region
community
neighborhood
physical neighborhood
planned neighborhood
site
landscaping
orientation
minimum property standards (MPS)
public zone
service zone
private zone
multifamily house
cooperative
condominium
condops
single-family house
attached houses
freestanding houses
contractor
owner-built housing
factory-built housing
site-built house
modular housing
manufactured housing
mobile homes
panelized housing
precut housing
kit house
universal design (UD)
assisted-living facility
graduated-care facility
reverse mortgage
Fair Housing Act

Chapter Objectives

After studying this chapter, you will be able to

- assess factors about region, community, and neighborhood that people should consider when choosing housing.

- evaluate and describe different types of available housing.

- identify decisions involved in choosing a site and house.

- summarize the principles of universal design (UD).

- examine universal design housing features that meet the needs of all people, including those special needs.

Reading with Purpose

Read the review questions at the end of the chapter *before* you read the chapter. Keep these questions in mind as you read to help determine which information is most important.

You will have many decisions to make when finding a place to live. Some of these decisions will concern the location and type of dwelling to choose. Other decisions will concern choosing a design that meets the needs of all people, including those with special needs.

Location

When choosing a place to live, you will need to carefully consider the following about the location, 4-1:

- the region or area of the world, country, or state
- the community—rural, suburb, or city

- neighborhood or section of the community
- composition of the population
- the site or lot within the neighborhood

Region

A **region** is a specific part of the world, country, or state in which you live. The reasons for choosing to live in a certain region vary. You may like the scenery. Perhaps the climate is important to you, 4-2. You may want to be close to family members or friends. Employment may also lead you to a certain region. Jobs are usually easier to find in regions with large cities. Figure 4-3 lists several items to consider when choosing a region in which to live. Which describes your ideal region?

Community

A region is divided into communities. A **community** may be a large city, small village, or rural area.

Cities are high-density areas. Many people live close together. If you enjoy living in close proximity to other people, you are a *contact* person. You may enjoy an urban lifestyle.

Rural areas and the outskirts of towns and cities are low-density areas.

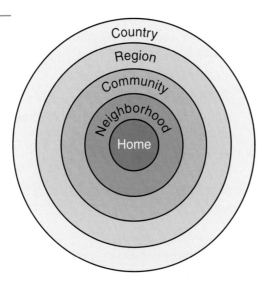

4-1
Selecting a location in which to live involves considering the country, region, community, neighborhood, and the actual home.

4-2
Some people choose a place to live that is close to the sports activities they enjoy. For example, they may prefer living where they can spend most of the year (A) playing at the beach, (B) hiking, or (C) snow skiing.

A

B

C

Choosing a Region	
Considerations	**Range of Choices**
General Climate	Hot to Cold
	Dry to Wet/humid
	Constant temperature to Varying temperature
Topography (mountains, lakes, prairies)	Flat to Mountainous
	Desert to Forest
	Low altitude to High altitude
Cost of Living	Low to High

4-3
These are some of the choices that will influence your selection of a region in which to live.

If you enjoy a less populated area and reduced contact with other people, you are a *noncontact* person. You may prefer a more secluded community.

Specific groups of people often want or require certain types of communities. For instance, older people who no longer work, yet desire the companionship of peers with like interests and values, want the freedom and activities retirement communities have to offer. Planning for university communities must meet the needs of large groups of students and professors. Some businesses develop special communities for employees and their families.

Before choosing a community, you should consider more than just its size and social aspects. You should study the number and type of services a community offers. For instance, what stores are in the community? Does the school have a reputation for high academic standards? Does your religious group have a meeting place? Are there high-quality medical facilities? Will you have adequate fire and police protection? Are resources available for self-improvement? What recreational facilities does the community offer? Are jobs easy to find? If some of these services are not available in the community, how far away are they? What type of public transportation is available?

The chart in 4-4 can serve as a guide for evaluating a community. Which factors apply to your present community? Which would you want in your ideal community?

Neighborhood

While regions are divided into communities, communities are divided into neighborhoods. A **neighborhood** consists of a group of houses and people. The buildings in any one neighborhood are usually similar in age, design, and cost. The people in a neighborhood usually have some similarities, too.

Physical Neighborhood

The usage of land and buildings determines the **physical neighborhood.** Some neighborhoods are all residential, with homes occupied by people. Commercial neighborhoods include stores and businesses. A shopping center is a kind of commercial neighborhood. Industrial neighborhoods include businesses, factories, warehouses, and industrial plants.

Some neighborhoods combine residential, commercial, and industrial buildings. For instance, when houses surround a local grocery, the neighborhood is a combination of residential and commercial buildings.

4-4
When you look for the ideal community, these factors are considered.

Choosing a Community	
Considerations	**Range of Choices**
Type	Rural to Urban/suburban
	Residential to Industrial/commercial
Size	Farm to Ranch
	Village/town to City/metropolis
Population Density	Uncrowded to Crowded
Cost of Living	Low to High
Employment Opportunities	Few to Many
	Little variety to Varied
	Low-paying to High-paying
	Seasonal to Steady
Public Facilities and Services	Few to Many

GREEN CHOICES

Consider a Live/Work Community

When considering a place to live, a "green" decision is a live/work community. This is part of the *New Urbanism* movement that began in the 1990s. A live/work community combines where you live with where you work. Often the living quarters are located on the second floor of a building while a business is located on the first floor.

Most live/work communities involve self-contained neighborhoods that have restaurants, laundering services, grocery stores, and other commercial options within walking distance of home. The advantages of a live/work community are the following:

- lower gasoline costs without the need to drive to work

- convenient location of services

- neighborhood activities that create a sense of community and belonging

Zoning Regulations and Other Restrictions

Zoning regulations control land use in certain areas, as you read in Chapter 2. A neighborhood may include zones for residential, commercial, or industrial use, or a combination of uses.

Housing *developers* subdivide land and make such improvements as streets and street lighting before building structures. Developers can set additional limits, called restrictions. These restrictions may control the design and construction of the buildings in an area. They may also limit the type and number of animals that residents can keep in a neighborhood. In 4-5, you can see a set of restrictions drawn up for a subdivision.

Declaration of Restrictions for Swiss Manor Subdivision

1. All of said lots in Swiss Manor Subdivision shall be known and designated as residential lots and shall not be used for any business purposes whatsoever.
2. No structure whatsoever other than one private dwelling, together with a private garage or carport for not more than three cars, shall be erected, placed, or allowed to remain on any of the lots.
3. No dwelling house shall be erected which contains less than 1,200 feet of livable space, exclusive of attached garage, porches, patios, and breezeways. No residence shall be built which exceeds the height of 2½ stories or 30 feet from the curb level. All structures on said lots shall be of new construction and no building shall be moved from any other location onto any of said lots.
4. There shall be no trailer houses or homes built around or incorporating trailer homes. All camper trailers, campers, or boats shall be stored behind the dwelling house or within the garage.
5. There shall be no unused automobiles, machinery, or equipment allowed on theses premises outside of enclosed garages. All driveways or parking areas used for parking vehicles shall be constructed of concrete.
6. All clotheslines, equipment, service yards, woodpiles, or storage piles shall be kept screened by adequate planting or fencing to conceal them from views of neighboring lots or streets. All rubbish, trash, or garbage shall be removed from the lots and shall not be allowed to accumulate thereon. All yards shall be kept mowed and all weeds shall be cut. Garbage and refuse containers may be brought to the street not more than 12 hours before collection time and must be removed within 12 hours after collection time.
7. No animals, livestock, or poultry of any kind shall be raised, bred, or kept on any lot, except for dogs, cats, and other household pets that may be kept, provided they are not kept, bred, or maintained for commercial purposes, and so long as applicable laws on restraining or controlling animals are observed.
8. No lot may be subdivided or a portion sold unless it becomes a part of the adjacent property.
9. No solid wall, hedge, or fence over 2½ feet high shall be constructed or maintained past the front wall line of the house. No side or rear fence shall be constructed more than 6 feet in height.
10. All utility lines must be brought underground to the dwelling house.

4-5
This is a partial list of typical restrictions for a subdivision. Its purpose is to assure all owners maintain a similar style of living.

After a community government designates a parcel of land as a subdivision, planning begins on how to use the land. A **planned neighborhood** is usually in an area with zoning restrictions. In such neighborhoods, developers organize the subdivision and make decisions about the size and layout of individual lots before constructing dwellings. This creates the shape of the neighborhood. Figure 4-6 shows three ways to arrange lots.

All houses built in a planned neighborhood must fit into the overall community plan. Some planned neighborhoods

4-6
There are several ways to arrange lots, including (A) the traditional "gridiron" arrangement, with all lots the same size and shape; (B) the contour arrangement, with the shape of streets and lots adding variety and interest to the neighborhood; and (C) the cluster layout, with houses placed together in groups to discourage traffic from nonresidents.

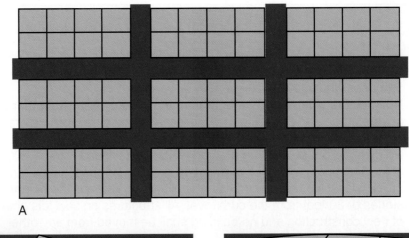

A

B

C

have single-family houses. Some have only apartment buildings. Others include more than one type of housing with the types grouped together. A recent development in planned communities relates to *live/work communities*. These communities often combine living space and work space.

Communities sometimes control the quality of construction and the types of design in a planned neighborhood. This assures buildings in the neighborhood will not deteriorate because of poor quality materials or workmanship.

Many planned neighborhoods include recreational facilities. Nearby parks and playgrounds offer locations that are convenient to people living in the neighborhood, 4-7. Clubhouses include places for meetings and social activities. *Urban planners* help develop these neighborhoods and areas within a city. See the end of this chapter for more

information about a career as an urban planner.

Population Composition

The people who live in any neighborhood may be quite varied. When this happens, the neighborhood is *heterogeneous*. If the residents are very similar to each other, the neighborhood is *homogeneous*. Some neighborhoods or whole communities have residents of similar age, ethnic background, income level, or occupation. These patterns occur in both rural and urban settings.

Another factor associated with the people in a neighborhood is population density. A low-density neighborhood has more space for each person than a high-density neighborhood. Smaller houses, smaller lots, and more people in less space create high-density neighborhoods. Apartment buildings and manufactured-housing parks also fit in the high-density category.

Which kind of neighborhood would you choose? What are your reasons for making that choice? The factors listed in 4-8 can help you make a decision.

Site

A location within a neighborhood is a site, or lot. A **site** is the piece of land on which the dwelling is built. It extends to the property lines.

Each site has its own characteristics—size, shape, contour (hills and curves), and soil type. What kind of site would be your ideal? Would you like to have your house on a hill or on flat land? What kind of view would you like? Would you like to be close to your neighbors, or would you prefer to have more privacy? Consider these characteristics before you choose a site for your house. See 4-9.

If you are buying a house that someone else built, or if you are renting an apartment, you should look carefully at the placement of the house on the site. It will have a great effect on your near environment. It will determine the views, the amount of sunlight, and the amount of protection from wind you will have.

If you are building a house, you can choose the site and the type of house you want. You can place the house where you want it on the site. This gives you

4-8
Which of these factors are important to you in selecting an ideal neighborhood?

Choosing the Neighborhood	
Considerations	**Range of Choices**
Physical Appearance	Zoned to Not Zoned
	Strictly residential dwellings to some commercial and/or industrial buildings
Organization of Lots	Attractive to Unattractive
	Planned to Unplanned
	Low street traffic to High traffic area
	No park/play areas to Many park/play areas
Type of Structures	Single-family to Multifamily
	Low spread to High spread
Location in Community	Edge to Center
Population Composition (age, income, occupation, educational level, interests, religious beliefs)	Homogeneous (similar) to Heterogeneous (varied)
Residents	Mostly singles to Mostly Families
	No friends/acquaintances to Many friends/acquaintances
Prevailing Values (views/beliefs that seem to dominate the thinking and actions of people)	Very different from own values to Similar to own values

4-9
Before you select a site, consider all your choices.

Choosing the Site	
Considerations	**Range of Choices**
Location in Neighborhood	Edge to Center
Orientation to Environment (view, sun, water, wind)	Does not use natural features well to Uses natural features well
Physical Qualities	Tiny to Large Size
	Rectangular to Irregular shape
	Flat land to Steep slopes
	Sandy soil to Dense clay
	No obstructions to Many large trees and/or rocks that must be removed

the chance to make the house and site work together to form a satisfying near environment for you.

When you plan your site, you will encounter restraints, or obstacles. Some will be natural restraints. Others will be legal restraints.

Natural Restraints

Natural restraints are those that come from nature. To gain the maximum advantage from the site, it is important to consider the topography. *Topography* is the configuration of a surface including its natural and manufactured features showing their relative positions and elevations. One kind of natural restraint is the topography of a site.

- Flat sites make the job of mowing grass easy, 4-10. Flat lawns are also good places for children's games and lawn furniture.

- Hilly sites are more difficult to maintain, but they are often attractive. Some houses, such as split-level houses, look best on hilly sites.

- Sites with extremely steep slopes have some disadvantages. A house built at the top of a slope may be difficult to reach, especially in icy weather. Also, soil may wash away and cause land erosion.

Landscaping is altering the topography and adding decorative plantings to change the appearance of a site, 4-11. For instance, building small hills for such plantings makes the site more attractive. You will learn more about landscaping in Chapter 20.

Soil and water can be natural restraints. Soil conditions affect both the site and the house. Poorly drained soil freezes and expands. This can cause sidewalks and driveways to crack and bulge. Plants have difficulty growing in shallow or nonporous topsoil. High water levels can cause swampy yards, wet basements, and poor plant growth.

4-10
The topography of this site is very flat, which makes yard maintenance easy.

Orientation can be a restraint or an advantage. **Orientation** refers to placing a structure on a site in consideration of the location of the sun, prevailing winds, water sources, and scenic view. Houses with southern and western exposures receive more sunlight than houses with northern and eastern exposures. In colder regions, houses often have large amounts of glass on the south and west sides of the dwelling. The glass allows sunlight to bring light and warmth into the dwellings.

4-11
In this landscape plan, brick and stone were used to create terraces and to take advantage of the lot.

Photography Courtesy of Ed Pinckney

4-12
The sun shines on the south side of a house at different angles depending on the time of the year. By knowing this, architects can plan proper roof overhangs.

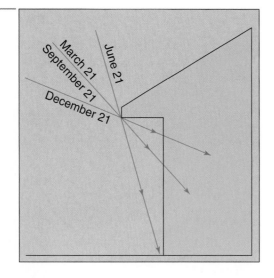

Because of the earth's changing position in relation to the sun, more sunlight reaches the earth during the summer. See 4-12. Some houses may need protection from the intense summer sun. Trees shade some houses. Built-in features, such as roof overhangs, can also provide shade. The width of the overhang on a roof affects the amount of sunlight that enters a building. Wider overhangs block out more sunlight.

Orientation to the wind is another natural restraint. Locating houses on the land to protect them from strong winds is essential in some regions. Windbreaks provide some of this protection. Trees and shrubs are natural windbreaks. Walls and stone or wood fences are also windbreaks. The placement of a garage on the north side of a house will usually eliminate drafts from cold winter winds and reduce home-heating costs.

In most regions, the general direction of the wind links to the season of the year. Consider this factor when planning for protection from the wind. The illustration in 4-13 shows a house that is well oriented to both the sun and wind.

Orientation to scenery is also a consideration. A pleasant view is desirable, but nature does not always provide one. If necessary, you can create a nice view through landscaping. Landscapers use gardens, shrubs, trees, and decorative elements to change the scenery.

4-13
Orientation to sun and wind are important factors to consider when deciding the ideal location for a dwelling on a site.

Cliff Snider

Orientation to Sun and Wind

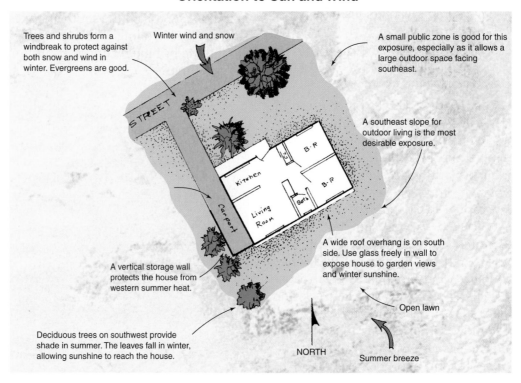

Legal Restraints

Federal, state, or local laws establish the legal restraints that affect a site. They are set for your protection.

Minimum property standards (MPS) are standards set by the Federal Housing Administration (FHA). These standards regulate the size of lots. MPS vary according to the shape and location of a site. In some cases, the minimum lot size is 65 feet wide and 130 feet long. Look at 4-14 to see a plan for a lot that meets these MPS.

The local government or the developer may set higher standards than the MPS. State and local authorities also establish limits and standards for the quality of construction, water supplies, and disposal of wastes. Do you have a housing authority office in your community? If so, what legal restraints does it enforce?

Zones Within the Site

The part of the site that is not the actual dwelling is divided into three zones—public zone, service zone, and private zone.

The **public zone** is the part of the site people can see from the street or road. It is usually in front of the house. If the house is on a corner lot, the public zone is L-shaped. It includes the front and side of the lot closest to the street. Since people see the public zone more often than any other part of the site, they want to make it attractive. They seldom use it for activities.

If the house is as far forward on the lot as the law permits, the public zone is small. Many people want small public zones because they are easier to maintain.

The **service zone** is the part of the site that household members use for necessary activities. It includes sidewalks, driveways, and storage areas for such items as trash, tools, lawn equipment, firewood, and cars. Others can usually see at least part of the service zone. However,

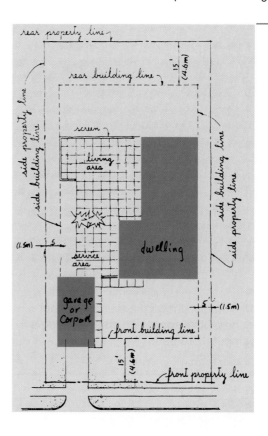

4-14
This plan meets the MPS for a rectangular lot in the middle of a block.

Federal Housing Administration

many people choose to screen as much of it as possible from view.

In this zone, convenience is most important. The outdoor service area should directly connect to the indoor service area, which includes kitchen and laundry areas. It is important for the service zone to be accessible from the street since deliveries are usually made in the service zone.

The **private zone** is the part of the site hidden from public view. It provides space for recreation and relaxation, 4-15. Shrubs, hedges, screens, fences, or walls can separate private zones from public zones.

Some households want a large private zone. They may want a place for yard accessories, such as outdoor furniture and barbecue equipment, yard games, or a swimming pool. Other households prefer a small private zone that requires little upkeep. Some want all the available space inside the house and do not

4-15
This image, showing a swimming pool in the private zone, was created using a computer program.

Courtesy of Software by Chief Architect

want an outdoor private zone. Figure 4-16 shows the placement of a house on the site to provide all three zones—public, service, and private.

Types of Housing

After choosing a region, community, neighborhood, and site, your next decision is to choose a form of housing. As you learned earlier, a *house* is any building that serves as living quarters for one or more families. A *home* is any place a person lives. The two major groups of houses are multifamily and single-family. Within each group are several variations.

GREEN CHOICES

Urban Designer's Role in Green and Sustainable Design

Urban designers, working together with architects, have a major role in promoting green and sustainable design by examining ways a developing city can impact the environment. Specifically, urban designers follow these principles in creating green and sustainable communities:

- **Design on a human scale.** Place housing, shops, and cultural resources close together so that residents can walk among these areas.
- **Provide choices.** Arrange for different options in housing, shopping, recreation, transportation, and employment.
- **Encourage mixed-use development.** Integrating different land uses like living and shopping areas in the same building.
- **Preserve urban centers.** Restoring, revitalizing, and infilling neighborhoods and buildings to avoid new building and unnecessary expansion.
- **Vary transportation options.** Giving people the option of walking, biking, and using public transportation.
- **Build vibrant public spaces.** Citizens need welcoming, well-defined public places to stimulate face-to-face interaction, collectively celebrate and mourn, encourage civic participation, admire public art, and gather for public events.
- **Create a neighborhood identity.** A "sense of place" gives neighborhoods a unique character, enhances the walking environment, and creates pride in the community.
- **Protect environmental resources.** A well-designed balance of nature and development.
- **Conserve landscapes.** Open space, farms, and wildlife habitat are essential for environmental, recreational, and cultural reasons.

Source: Information is from AIA Communities by Design—Envision Create and Sustain (www.aia.org/)

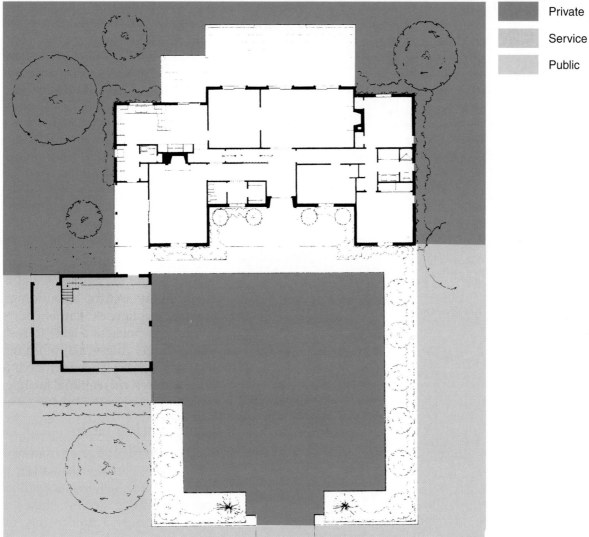

Private

Service

Public

4-16
The house at the top has a huge private zone. How do the sizes of the public and service zones compare?

Home Planners, Inc.

A

B

4-17

(A) Cityfront Place is a series of high-rise buildings in Chicago where several hundred families live. (B) Low-spread apartment buildings require larger lots per household than high-rise buildings.

(A) Cityfront Place, photographer David Clifton

Multifamily Houses

A **multifamily house** is a structure that provides housing for more than one household. Each household within the dwelling has its own distinct living quarters.

Today, lifestyles are changing, and the demand for multifamily housing is increasing. In the past, single people, young married couples, and retired people were the primary residents of this type of housing. Now, others are turning to multifamily housing, too. This type of housing is usually less costly and easier to maintain than single-family houses.

Some multifamily housing is in *high-rise buildings*. Other multifamily housing is in low-rise buildings, 4-17. Those in *low-rise* buildings may be *duplexes* (two households), *triplexes* (three households), or *quadraplexes* (four households).

Rentals

Rental apartments range from garden apartments to penthouses. Penthouses are suites located at the top of apartment buildings. *Garden apartments* are one-story units with landscaped grounds. Rentals also vary in the number and type of facilities offered. An *efficiency apartment* has one main room, a small kitchen area, and a bathroom. Many apartment buildings have laundry appliances, tennis courts, and swimming pools available to residents. Some large, high-rise buildings are like small cities. They include business offices, stores, recreational facilities, and parking space.

Cooperative Units

The word **cooperative** refers to a type of ownership in which people buy shares of stock in a nonprofit housing corporation. These shares entitle them to occupy a unit in the cooperative building. When people move into a cooperative unit, or co-op, they "buy" their apartment by purchasing shares of stock in the corporation. If a resident wants a larger unit, he or she purchases more stock. Residents have an absolute right to occupy the unit for as long as they own the stock.

Although residents do not own their units, they own an undivided interest in the entire property. They have a voice in how the corporation operates and even get the chance to select their neighbors. When people want to buy shares in the corporation and move into the building, the members of the corporation vote on admitting them.

An advantage of living in a co-op is that neighbors meet regularly and work together to create a pleasant housing environment for all residents. A disadvantage is that anyone who disagrees with the majority on an issue must accept and live with the decision.

Condominium Units

A **condominium** is a type of ownership in which the buyer owns individual living space and *also* has an undivided interest in the common areas and facilities of the multiunit project. In comparison to co-ops, buyers purchase condominium units as separate dwellings. At the same time, the buyers receive a portion of the common areas. They share the ownership of the site, parking areas, recreational facilities, hallways, and lobbies with the other condominium owners.

Although condominium owners own their units, they must answer to the desires of the entire group of owners for certain items. For instance, the appearance of the outside of their units and their yards may be under the control of the group's management.

Some experimentation is occurring with **condops**, which are a blend of condominium and cooperative units. With condops, the buyers own their individual living spaces—just like condominium

4-18
This multifamily unit could be rentals, co-ops, or condos. There is no way to know by looking at exteriors.

ownership. However, ownership of the common areas and facilities are cooperative ownership.

Remember, the terms *cooperative* and *condominium* refer to a type of ownership, not a building design. When you look at a multifamily dwelling, you cannot tell if it is a rental, cooperative, or condominium, 4-18.

Single-Family Houses

In spite of the rising trend for multifamily dwellings, the **single-family house** is still popular. These dwellings house one family. People can rent or own single-family houses.

Attached Houses

Some single-family houses are **attached houses**. Each unit holds one household but shares common walls with the houses on each side. End units, however, have only one shared wall. Townhouses and *row houses* are names for these houses. A *townhouse* is a unit that has at least two floors.

Usually, these houses share entire sidewalls, but there are variations. The designs of the attached dwellings are often alike.

The owners of an attached, single-family house possess the dwelling itself and the land on which it is located. They have their own entrance and yard area.

Freestanding Houses

When single-family houses stand alone, without connections to another unit, they are **freestanding houses**. They vary in size, design, color, features, and cost.

The most individualistic type of house is *custom-designed* and *custom-built* by an architect and a contractor. This kind of house is a dream house. It is often expensive and takes a long time to plan and build.

When custom-designing a house, an architect considers the needs, values, and life situations of the household. He or she then designs a house to "fit" that household's needs and desires.

A **contractor** is a person who contracts, or agrees, to supply certain materials or do certain work for a specific fee. With a custom-built house, a contractor arranges for all the tradespeople to do their various jobs efficiently and on schedule. He or she builds the house according to the architect's plans and owner's wishes. The general contractor is responsible for completing the construction of the house. He or she may arrange with one or more subcontractors to complete certain parts of the construction. A subcontractor can either be an individual or can be a firm.

Some houses are custom-built from stock plans. In these cases, people go to a contractor and look at house plans. They choose the plan they want and the contractor builds a house for them on their site. They also incorporate any adjustments or individualized treatments the owner desires. For example, the owner may want larger windows with different locations than the plan indicates, 4-19.

Owner-built housing is for people with lots of spare time, energy, and building skills. This type of house can be less expensive than a custom-built house. There is less investment in money and more investment in such resources as time and energy. Sometimes the owner hires a contractor to construct the house shell while the owner does the interior work. In other cases, the owner builds the entire house, often with volunteer help from friends. Building codes usually require qualified experts to handle some parts of the project, such as electricians and plumbers.

In contrast, developers sometimes build entire neighborhoods at once, creating *tract houses*. They build these houses before selling them. Repeating one or two sets of plans throughout the development saves money on construction costs. Tract houses lack individuality because there are few variations. However, they are less expensive to buy than custom-built houses.

Factory-built housing is housing constructed in a plant and moved to a site. Some units are fully finished in the plant, while others arrive in parts that are joined at the site, 4-20. All involve some labor for placement on the lot. The advantages of factory-built housing include decreased cost and/or completion time in making a home available. You often cannot tell a site-built house from a factory-built house. A

4-19
This home's exterior looks like the stock plan, but many changes were made to the inside. The kitchen area was doubled and an office was added to the first floor.

site-built house is built on a lot, piece by piece on a foundation, using few factory-built structural components. Five types of factory-built housing in use today include

- modular
- manufactured/mobile
- panelized
- precut
- kit

Modular housing is factory-built in a coordinated series of modules. The wall, floor, ceiling, and roof panels are combined in boxes (or modules) complete with windows, doors, plumbing, and wiring before delivery to the site. When the modules arrive at the housing site, workers place them on the foundation and join them together. These housing units are built to meet local building codes and standards.

Both **manufactured housing** and **mobile homes** are single-family dwellings that are completely built in a factory. The completed housing units are moved with attached wheels to a lot or housing site. Units built before 1976 are called mobile homes, while those built later are called manufactured housing. Early units first appeared as travel trailers in the 1920s and 1930s, and evolved into house trailers in the 1930s and 1940s.

Manufactured houses are built to federal standards called the HUD Code because the U.S. Department of Housing and Urban Development (HUD) administers it. A manufactured or mobile home is one solution to affordable home ownership since cost is considerably below that for a conventional, site-built house. See 4-21.

Manufactured housing is available in many sizes. Smaller homes come in single units called single-sectional housing. Larger homes come in two or more units, either double-sectional or multi-sectional, that are joined at the site. Because these housing units are

pulled across highways to their sites, their length and width are limited by transportation requirements.

Although manufactured houses and mobile homes have wheels for moving, less than five percent ever move from their original sites. Each state has laws that movers must follow when moving one of these homes. Some local governments have additional rules, such as zoning regulations that prohibit the placement of these homes in certain areas.

The owners can move single-sectional homes as long as they follow all laws. Larger homes must be moved in parts from the factory to the site. A company specializing in moving manufactured or mobile homes

4-20
This modular home was assembled on site by connecting the parts (modules).

Photography Courtesy of Palm Harbor Homes

4-21
When in place and landscaped, a manufactured home is difficult to distinguish from a site-built home.

Photography Courtesy of Palm Harbor Homes

handles the job. Once joined together, double-sectional and multi-sectional units are usually fixed permanently to their sites.

Panelized housing involves panels of walls, floors, ceilings, or roofs that people can order separately and have assembled at the housing site. The units are usually complete with windows, doors, plumbing, and wiring.

Precut housing refers to housing components that are cut to exact size in the factory and delivered to the building site. A crew then assembles lumber, finish materials, and other components at the site. See 4-22.

A **kit house** is a type of factory-built housing. Kit houses are shipped to the site in unassembled parts or as a finished shell from the factory. The interior is then completed according to the buyer's wishes.

A kit house is less costly than most other types of factory-built housing. Several factors, such as the size and style of the house, influence the total cost. Another cost factor is the delivery cost, which is based on the distance from the factory to the site. Finally, the cost of a kit house is influenced by whether all the materials and labor for the house are purchased with the kit or separately.

More Decisions

Other items to consider when choosing a dwelling include the house's condition (if it is not new), price, size, design features, and appearance on the site. The chart in 4-23 can guide you as you make decisions about a house.

Universal Design for Housing

In recent years, housing has become a much-discussed issue. Government officials, builders, housing developers, and the general public expressed a growing need for safe, decent, affordable housing for all people. Initially, groups of people with special requirements were the focus, such as older adults, people of all ages who have disabilities, and households with children. Today, many housing designs utilize *universal design* to accommodate the needs of all people. **Universal design (UD)** is a design concept that focuses on making living environments, and the products used to create them, without special adaptations. Its focus is to make housing more usable by all people, even those with physical impairments, for little to no extra cost.

Ronald Mace at the Center for Universal Design at North Carolina State University developed the concept of universal design. Mace realized that, through careful design, products and environments could be usable by more people at little or no extra cost. Mace named the design concept *universal* since it simplified living for practically everyone.

The universal design concept targets the needs of all people, regardless of age, physical characteristics, or ability. By contrast, *accessible* or *adaptable design* benefits only certain people, such as persons with mobility limitations.

When universal design principles are used, every building and product within is developed to provide greater usefulness to as many people as possible, 4-24. That includes every faucet, light fixture,

4-22
Many modern-day log homes are precut housing.

Velux-America, Inc.

Choosing the Dwelling	
Considerations	**Range of Choices**
Type of Ownership	Rental to Buyer (cooperative, condominium, or private dwelling)
Type of Dwelling	Low spread to High rise
	Multifamily to Single family
	Old to Newly built
	Owner-built versus contractor-built
	Stock plans versus custom design
	Site-built versus factory-built (modular, manufactured/mobile, panelized, precut, or kit housing)
Landscaping	Dwelling looks out of place to Site harmonizes with dwelling
	No landscaping to Attractive use of landscaping elements
Size of Outside Zones (public, service, and private)	Small to Large
Structural Quality	Substandard/deteriorated quality to High Quality
Size of Dwelling	Cramped to Spacious
Price	Affordable to Expensive

4-23
Many options are possible when choosing a home.

The Principles of Universal Design

1. **Equitable Use:** The design is useful and marketable to people with diverse abilities.
2. **Flexibility in Use:** The design accommodates a wide range of individual preferences and abilities.
3. **Simple and Intuitive Use:** Use of the design is easy to understand, regardless of the user's experience, knowledge, languages, skills, or current concentration level.
4. **Perceptible Information:** The design communicates necessary information effectively to the user, regardless of ambient conditions or the user's sensory abilities.
5. **Tolerance for Error:** The design minimizes hazards and the adverse consequences of accidental or unintended actions.
6. **Low Physical Effort:** The design can be used efficiently and comfortably and with a minimum of fatigue.
7. **Size and Space for Approach and Use:** Appropriate size and space is provided for approach, reach, manipulation, and use regardless of user's body size, posture, or mobility.

4-24
The *Principles of Universal Design* were developed by The Center for Universal Design in collaboration with researchers and professionals across the United States.

Copyright ©1997 North Carolina State University, The Center for Universal Design (www.design.ncsu.edu/cud)

shower stall, public telephone, entrance, and all other implements people use in everyday life. The principles of universal design also apply to the spaces everyone uses for daily activities.

Many universal design features are structural and must be built into the house. Other are nonstructural features are items that are easy to add to existing housing. Some universal design features are regularly built in homes of today, especially by request of the occupants.

Benefits of Universal Design to All Users

The benefits of universal design to people with physical limitations are obvious. However, the benefits to others may not be as apparent. Here are some examples of how universal design benefits people who do not have physical limitations. These benefits focus on four areas: entrances, the kitchen, bathrooms, and the general interior.

Entrances

Level and accessible entrances

- are easier to enter with groceries and packages
- pose fewer hazards when wet or icy
- are easier to repair and maintain than steps
- are easier to clear of snow, ice, and leaves
- provide more convenience for moving furniture, appliances, baby strollers, and bicycles in and out

Covered entries

- provide less damage to the door's finish from the weather
- offer sheltered space for receiving a package delivery or waiting for a school bus

Full-length side window at entry door

- increases the natural light in the foyer
- allows everyone to see who is at the door before opening it

Kitchen

Knee space under sink and cooktop

- provides a space to store a serving cart or recycling bins
- allows people to work while sitting on a stool

Lever-type water controls

- permit easier adjustment of water temperature and volume
- can be operated with use of a single hand or elbow
- have fewer parts than other types of controls, so are less costly to repair
- are easier to keep clean because of few crevices

Variable-height work surfaces

- make it easier to designate counter space for different functions
- allow family members of all heights to help with meal preparation

Contrasting borders on countertops

- makes it easier to repair damaged edges without repairing the entire countertop
- reduces the likelihood of spills because the ends of counters are easier to see

Pull-out shelves in cabinets

- make it possible to reach items stored in the back without stretching, 4-25
- permit easier maneuvering of large items in and out of the cabinet

Pantry cabinet with full-length shelves

- provides storage that can be reached from all heights
- offers the maximum storage per square foot of floor space

Bathrooms

Adjustable-height showerhead

- can be adjusted to suit the height of different users
- makes it possible to avoid wetting a bandage, cast, hairdo, or anything else that should remain dry
- can be used for massaging one's back, rinsing hair, and washing the dog

Grab bars in tub or shower

- can double as a towel bar when hung horizontally

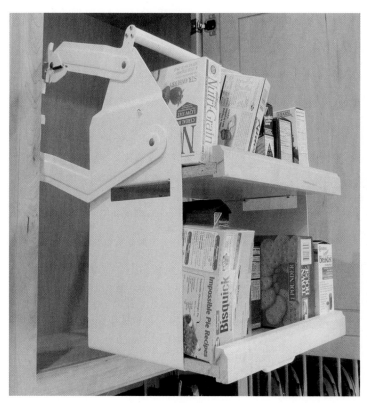

A

B

- make it easier and safer to enter and exit a tub or shower

Over-sink mirror extending down to backsplash

- allows children and seated adults to have a view of the mirror while using the sink

- reduces water damage to the wall behind the sink

- makes it easier to clean behind the faucet

- makes the room seem more spacious

The General Interior

Minimum door opening of 32 inches

- improves circulation throughout the house, especially when guests are visiting

- reduces damage to the door frame when moving furniture or equipment through doorways

Lever-style door handles

- are easier for everyone to use

- permit owners to open the doors with just an elbow or knee when hands are filled

- add an elegant touch, as in 4-26, at little or no extra cost

Adjustable-height closet rods

- make closets usable by children

- increase storage by creating room for a second-tier closet rod or other types of organizers

- tailor closets to individual wardrobe needs

Tall windows placed low on the wall

- provide a good view for everyone, especially children and seated adults

- add more natural light and elegance to the room

- are easier for a child to open

4-25
Pull-down shelves (A) and roll-out trays in base cabinets (B) are handy for everyone, especially those with reach limitations.

(A) Universal Design Home of the Future, AARP
(B) Kraftmaid

4-26
Lever handles come in many styles from plain to elegant, like the one shown here.

Kwikset Corporation

4-27
Electrical outlets that are raised to 18 inches off the floor are much easier to use in both a standing and seated position.

Muscular Dystrophy Association

- require less reaching to open, close, and lock (24 to 36 inches from the floor)

Electrical receptacles 18 inches from the floor

- are easier to find than those low to the floor and are easier to reach without bending

- are located conveniently for electric cords to be removed correctly—by grasping the plug, not pulling on the cord, 4-27

These and other universal design features are generally standard features in all types of new housing. However, considerations can also be made for the special needs of older adults, people who have disabilities, and families with children.

Needs of Older Adults

Many people look forward to retirement. They may plan to enjoy activities they could not pursue much in the past, such as golfing, fishing, traveling, or volunteering. Their retirement plans will likely affect their housing decisions. They may want housing that requires less maintenance or that will be secure while they are away. The situations vary with each older adult, as do their housing choices.

Most adults over age 50—according to a recent AARP study—prefer to stay in their homes as they age. The concept of *aging-in-place* identifies a need for older adults to remain independent and live safely and comfortably in their homes. Having familiar surroundings, community services, and built-in social network are all important to aging well. In order to meet aging-in-place needs, it is important to understand the challenges of aging that influence ability to live successfully.

As people age, their energy levels often decrease. Perhaps their health declines and they find their houses difficult to maintain. This makes it hard for older people who prefer to *age-in-place,* or stay in their present houses. They need housing that permits easy cleanup and requires little maintenance. Adding universal design features to an existing home or moving to a home designed with such features can make housing more accessible and condusive to aging-in-place.

With universal design, older adults can remain independent even when aging reduces their mobility. For example, adding a no-step entrance with a wider doorway and nonslip floors are universal design changes that benefit everyone. However, they would especially benefit a person with a broken leg using crutches. Even more so, the changes would benefit those in wheelchairs or with permanent impairment from aging.

Some older adults find that living in their old neighborhoods is no longer convenient. They may be far from shopping areas and community centers where they can be with their peers. If they have difficulty driving, they may not want to leave home often. This can lead to loneliness, especially if they live alone.

When older adults can no longer live alone due to loneliness or health problems, they usually change housing. They may become a part of another household. They may live with a son, daughter, or someone who can help care for them. They may choose to become part of larger group quarters, such as a senior-living community. They may instead choose a retirement home or an assisted-living facility, 4-28.

- **Assisted-living facilities** serve those who need daily living assistance but not constant care. Meals, laundry service, and household cleanup are the most common services these facilities provide.

- **Graduated-care facilities** offer more than one level of care. Older adults may move from individual apartments with no care, to assisted living, or to a nursing-home unit as their needs change. Facilities with good design and optimal administrative services offer comfortable living.

For older adults who choose to live on their own, the cost of house ownership can be high. Some may find they are "house rich and cash poor" because their savings went to acquire their houses. With time, their houses may need repair. With limits on income, older adults may not have money for maintenance, repairs, utilities, or taxes. In this case, they would not have extra money to adapt their houses to meet their special needs.

Measures have been taken to assist older adults. Some states allow reverse

4-28
Senior-living communities often include assisted-living facilities.

Chambrel at Roswell, Georgia, an Oxford Senior Living Community

reverse mortgage cost will be attached to the dwelling. Also, older adults should only consider reverse mortgages if their income is such that they cannot pay bills and plan on living in their homes until death. If older adults take out reverse mortgages and later move, they may end with less money than if they had sold the house originally.

Needs of People with Disabilities

There are many people with disabilities in the United States. They include children, older adults, and adults who work and live on their own or with their families. The types of disabilities vary. Some people have a vision or hearing loss. Many have difficulty moving and must use wheelchairs, crutches, or walkers. Others may have learning or developmental disabilities.

People with disabilities need housing to meet their needs. They may be unable to live independently in housing built in the past. Appropriate housing can assist people who have disabilities with their daily living. For example, the bathroom in 4-29 has been adapted to meet the needs of a person in a wheelchair.

The **Fair Housing Act** of 1988 gives people with disabilities greater freedom to choose a place to live that meets their needs. The Act forbids discrimination in housing and requires multiunits to be accessible to people with disabilities. The law requires accessible entrances, wider doors, and easier installation of grab bars around toilets and bathtubs. Although the law does not address every aspect of making multiunits fully accessible, definite improvements were made. As a result, the law helps provide housing that is safer and easier for everyone to use. (See "Appendix A, Housing and Related Legislation" for additional information.)

If you or a member of your household has a disability, consider

4-29
The smooth floor, space around the sink, toilet, and bathtub, and the convenient grab bars make this bathroom accessible to everyone in the household.

Photo Courtesy of Kohler

mortgages. A **reverse mortgage** enables older people to convert the money tied up in their houses into income. They receive a monthly payment as long as they live in the dwelling. When they no longer live in the house, the mortgage company assumes ownership of the dwelling. Reverse mortgages can help older home owners stay in their houses.

There are some disadvantages with reverse mortgages. Although the older adult can pass the house on to heirs, the

- a ground-level dwelling
- a building with a minimum 5-foot by 5-foot level entryway or landing that permits entry doors to open easily
- wide interior doorways and hallways
- good lighting for people with low vision
- audio and visual smoke detectors and carbon monoxide detectors
- housing along or near public transportation lines
- housing near shopping areas

When people with disabilities have housing that meets their needs, they can live more independently. If you should build a home someday, you can incorporate features of universal design to extend the house's usage for all conditions of life.

Needs of Families with Children

Children develop physically, mentally, emotionally, and socially. No matter how old they are, they need to live in a safe and healthy housing environment that promotes positive development.

A housing choice that fits the needs and desires of a couple without children may not be satisfactory when a child arrives. Children need room to grow as they learn to crawl and walk. As they grow older, they need additional space for activities, 4-30. An outdoor play area that is protected from street traffic is desirable. This gives children a place to move around and play safely.

The community in which children grow can influence their development. When choosing a place to live, look for communities and neighborhoods that will foster healthy growth and development. Look for good schools, safe neighborhoods, park programs, and recreational facilities.

Often children have pets, which also require special considerations. If you rent a house, you may find that the owner wants neither children nor pets. However, antidiscrimination laws prevent landlords from refusing to rent apartments to families with children. The same is not true for pets.

4-30
This outdoor play area in front of the house offers the children in this family a space to grow and develop.

CAREER FOCUS

Urban Planner

Can you imagine yourself as an urban planner? If you can, review the following information about this exciting career.

Interests/Skills: Do you enjoy problem solving and decision making? Do you have the desire to contribute to improving the living conditions of the population and you think it important the communities meet the total needs of all of its members regardless of age and physical abilities? Do you share an interest in creating communities that are both green and sustainable? Urban planners have these skills: complex problem solving, active listening, critical thinking, time management, judgment and decision making, and computer.

Career Snapshot: City or urban planners figure out the best way to use the land in cities and neighborhoods. They report on the best location for houses, stores, and parks. They try to solve a lot of problems. These include such things as traffic problems and increases in air pollution. Planners need to plan where people should drive their cars and where they can park. Planners make new plans when more people move into a community. They might tell community leaders when they need new schools or roads. Planners also are concerned about saving trees and wetlands. They try to find safe places for getting rid of trash.

Education/Training: Job prospects will be best for those with a master's degree and strong computer skills. Bachelor's degree holders may find positions, but advancement opportunities are limited.

Licensing/Examinations: Most states do not require licensing; however certification from the American Institute of Certified Planners is recommended. New Jersey is the only state that requires planners to be licensed, although Michigan requires registration to use the title "community planner."

Professional Associations: American Planning Association (APA), (www.planning.org)

Job Outlook: Faster than average employment growth is projected for urban and regional planners. Most new jobs will be in affluent, rapidly expanding communities. Job prospects will be best for those with a master's degree and strong computer skills.

Sources: Occupational Information Network (O*NET) (www.online.onetcenter.org) and the Occupational Outlook Handbook, Bureau of Labor Statistics (www.bls.gov)

Summary

When choosing a place to live, you need to examine its location. Considerations include the region, neighborhood, site, and zone within the site. You also need to consider the restraints, natural and legal, of the location.

There are many different housing choices. Multifamily houses include apartments, cooperatives, and condominiums. Single-family houses may be attached or freestanding. They can also be owner-built, built by contractors or developers, or a type of factory-built housing. You can either rent or buy housing.

Universal design features in housing help make housing accessible to all people. If an older adult or someone with a disability is part of your household, you will need to consider his or her special needs when making housing decisions. If there are children, their needs must also be considered. You want to choose housing that promotes their development.

Review the Facts

1. What are five major factors about location to consider when choosing housing?
2. Name three reasons for living in a certain region.
3. Contrast residential, commercial, and industrial neighborhoods.
4. What are two natural restraints that affect sites?
5. What legal restraints affect housing sites? Why?
6. Summarize how the FHA relates to the MPS.
7. Describe the three zones within a site.
8. Contrast the ownership differences among rentals, cooperative units, and condominium units.
9. How do attached houses and freestanding houses differ?
10. What are the roles of the architect and contractor in custom housing?
11. How does a tract house differ from a house custom-built from stock plans?
12. Name the five types of factory-built houses.
13. What is the purpose of universal design?
14. Name one benefit of universal design for each of the following areas of a home: entrance, kitchen, bathroom, and general interior.
15. Identify three groups of people who have special housing needs. How do universal-design features help meet these needs?
16. What key housing features are important for families with children?

Think Critically

17. **Analyze trends.** One trend in housing is to build the total housing or various parts in a factory and move them to the housing site. Analyze the possibility of this trend continuing. Do you think it will ever be predominant? Why or why not?
18. **Assess adaptations.** Visit a house that is for sale. Assess the features that need to be adapted for a person with a mobility disability or an older adult who desires to age-in-place. Create a list to discuss with the class.

19. **Summarize details.** Summarize the principles of universal design. Give an example of each of these principles at work.

Community Links

20. **Zoning regulations.** Use Internet or library resources to look up the zoning regulations and building codes of your community. Find out what the requirements are for local housing.

21. **Community features.** Contact your local chamber of commerce office and obtain the literature it provides to new or prospective area residents. What features of the area might appeal to different types of residents, such as older adults, people with disabilities, families with children, and single persons? Summarize your findings in a short written report.

22. **Community survey.** Survey 10 people in your community and ask what they like about living there. Also find out what they dislike. Select individuals of both genders and different ages to get a range of responses. Using a computer, create a chart or spreadsheet to display the information to your class. Keep the identities of the surveyed individuals confidential.

Academic Connections

23. **Writing.** Review the information about reverse mortgages on the Federal Housing Administration Web site (www.mortgageloanplace.com/). Write a summary of your findings to share with the class.

24. **Social studies.** Use Internet or print resources to research the link between universal design (UD) and the *Americans with Disabilities Act (ADA)*. What role does universal design play in developing barrier-free environments for people with limitations and disabilities? How does the ADA law link to universal design? Present your findings to the class in an oral report.

Technology Applications

25. **Electronic presentation.** Choose a region beyond your community where you would enjoy living. Locate the Web site for the area's chamber of commerce and find out more about the community. What would be the advantages and disadvantages of living there? Use presentation software to create a report to share with the class.

26. **Internet research.** Use reliable Internet resources—such as the AARP and National Association of Home Builders (NAHB) Web sites—to research the requirements for becoming a *Certified Aging-in-Place Specialist*. Write a summary or prepare an electronic presentation of your findings to share with the class.

27. **Video report.** With a classmate, use the Internet to research information about one of the following topics:
    A. housing for older adults who desire to age-in-place
    B. housing for people (either adults or children) with disabilities
    C. housing for children

    With a digital video camera, create a news report about your topic. Consider doing an "on the scene" report at a housing site for your topic. Share your news video with the class.

Design Practice

28. **CADD practice.** Using a CADD software package, draw a dwelling on a site showing the three zones within the site. Print a copy of your drawing or burn a copy to a CD-ROM.

29. **Portfolio.** Put a copy of your CADD drawing from item 28 in your portfolio along with a written description identifying why you positioned the zones in the manner you did on the site.

Citizens in the Know—Universal Design

Alone or with a team, prepare an FCCLA *Illustrated Talk* STAR Event on the topic of *universal design* in housing. From a citizen's view, investigate the use of universal design in your community. What are the pros and cons of this type of design in housing? How does it impact the lives of those who inhabit these structures? How could it make a difference to you?

Use a digital camera to take photos of one or more dwellings (interior and exterior) that utilize universal design in your community. Be sure to obtain written permission to take and use the photographs. Follow the presentation requirements in the *STAR Events Manual*. See your adviser for information as needed.

Then give your presentation at several school or community events. Step up to the challenge and give your presentation at your FCCLA state competition.

CHAPTER 5

Acquiring Housing

Terms to Learn

down payment
interest
installment buying
finance charge
security deposit
lease
lessor
lessee
assign
sublet
breach of contract
eviction
principal
equity
foreclosure
gross income
housing-to-income ratio
debt-to-income ratio
credit history
bid
mortgage
amortize
conventional mortgage
private mortgage insurance (PMI)
adjustable rate mortgage (ARM)
FHA-insured mortgage
VA-guaranteed mortgage
preapproval
earnest money
agreement of sale
points
home inspection
appraisal
abstract of title
title
deed
closing costs
declaration of ownership
bill of lading

Chapter Objectives

After studying this chapter, you will be able to

- assess the advantages and disadvantages of renting and buying housing.

- contrast the impact of needs and wants on housing costs.

- identify items to check before signing a lease.

- define legal and financial terms related to acquiring housing.

- summarize the home-buying process.

- contrast buying condominium units with cooperative units.

- compare the different ways to move.

Reading with Purpose

Take two-column notes as you read the chapter. Fold a sheet of paper in half lengthwise. On the left side of the paper, write the main ideas. On the right side, write subtopics and detailed information. After reading the chapter, use the notes to study. Fold the paper in half so you only see the main ideas. Quiz yourself on the subtopics and details.

At some time, you will need to decide how to spend money for housing. You will need to use rational decision making to choose between renting and purchasing a house as well as to make other related choices. Your choices will depend on your lifestyle, stage of the life cycle, and other life situations. Finally, you will need to make decisions regarding the various moving options possible.

Acquiring a Place to Live

People make many decisions in the process of acquiring a place to live. *Process* refers to the method used to accomplish a task. These decisions are part of a process beginning with the decision to rent or buy housing, followed by a determination of how to pay for the housing choice and moving. Additional decisions are required later for operating the unit as well as replacing and adapting it through time, 5-1.

In thinking about the process of acquiring housing, can you describe how your family acquired the housing in which you live? Was it purchased or rented? If purchased, was it new or pre-owned? Was the housing built for a previous owner or for your family?

After choosing to either rent or buy, additional decisions in the process are needed to operate and maintain the housing. You need to make arrangements to have the water, electricity, and/or gas turned on. You need to arrange to move your belongings to your house. You also need to repair or replace parts of the dwelling from time to time. It may involve something as simple as replacing a worn seal in a leaky water faucet or as complex as adding a second floor.

You will need to decide how to pay for these housing expenses. You can pay for them in the following ways:

* Pay the full amount now with cash, a check, transfer of funds from another account, or by debit card. (A *debit card* is similar to a credit card but immediately releases money from your account when you use it.)

* Postpone payment by using a credit card. (Use caution when using this form of payment.)

* Pay part of the total now, or make a **down payment**, to secure a purchase. You then pay the remainder in regular installments.

Human and Nonhuman Costs

When considering housing costs, it is important to recognize the many factors that affect them. Cost is the amount of human and nonhuman resources used

---

5-1
When acquiring housing, you will want to consider all available choices.

The Process of Acquisition				
Possession Choices		**Financing Choices**		
• **Own**—Buy, Build, Own to Rent • **Rent**—Privately Owned, Publicly Owned, Company Owned		• **Cash**—Currency, Check • **Loan Terms**—Short-term, Long-term • **Sources of Financing**—Current Income, Savings, Private Loan, Commercial Loan, Government Loan		
Operating Choices		**Replacement Choices**		**Adaption Choices**
• Furnish • Maintain • Repair		• Sell • Trade • Abandon		• Remodel • Refinish • Redecorate

to achieve something. The money you spend for rent or house payments, utilities, and home maintenance is part of your housing costs. The other resources you must spend, such as time, energy, and skills for running the household, are other forms of housing costs.

For example, consider what is involved in adding plumbing to a house. First, you need to pay for materials. Additional costs involve the time and energy you would spend installing the new plumbing. If you do not have the necessary skill to install it yourself, or cannot spend the time and energy necessary, you would need to pay for the labor of an expert, 5-2.

Usually the cost of materials for a house is far lower than the human costs involved. Human costs can involve planning the work, ordering materials, and delivering them plus handling their installation, maintenance, and repair.

Needs, Wants, and Housing Costs

When considering the costs associated with acquiring housing, it is important to know the difference between your housing needs and wants. Needs are basic necessities, while *wants* are things you desire. Wants almost always cost more than needs. Sometimes people have wants that cost far more than they can afford on their current incomes.

An example is a couple of first-time home buyers who want the home of their dreams. In reality, they only need adequate shelter that protects them from the elements. As they search for housing, they will likely find that what they want is not what they can afford. They must examine their priorities and identify which of their preferences they can afford. It is a good idea to determine in advance the amount to spend for housing, and then refuse to go over that amount.

Costs Involved in Payment Methods

When you pay cash for an item, such as a lamp, you know its exact cost. However, when you pay by check, debit card, credit card, or automatic transfer of funds, you may have some banking costs. Some banks charge for checks and for providing various banking services.

Sometimes people use credit cards to make a purchase. A *credit card* is an extension of money to the cardholder based on an agreement to repay. The cost of using a credit card varies. Some companies charge an annual fee, while others are free. If you make only the minimum payment by the bill's deadline, the company will add interest to the rest of the amount you owe. **Interest** is the price you pay for the use of someone else's money. By law, the credit card company must tell you exactly how much interest it will charge you. You can avoid paying interest by paying

5-2
This new home owner had the time and energy to paint her home. She is using these personal resources rather than money resources to hire a professional painter.

the entire amount of the bill by the due date. To determine the cost of a credit card, ask the following questions:

- How much is the annual fee?
- What is the interest rate?
- Is this an introductory interest rate?
- What may cause the interest rate to increase?
- Do interest charges begin at the time of purchase?

Installment buying is the process of buying something by making a series of payments during a given length of time, 5-3. Installment buying often costs more to use than most other methods. This is because a person, company, or bank is *financing*, or providing credit to you. The lender has paid your bill and is willing to wait for you to repay the amount. In addition to the original cost of the merchandise, you must pay extra for the privilege of using the lender's money.

This extra amount, or **finance charge**, includes the interest and any other service fee. The finance charge is stated as an annual percentage rate (APR) of the amount borrowed. You can pay back the money you borrow over a short or long period of time. The longer you take the more interest you will pay. Most home owners purchase houses with *long-term financing*. You can take up to 40 years to pay back the money you borrow for a house. However, with long-term financing, the total interest you eventually pay

may far exceed the cost of the dwelling itself.

It is important to know all the costs associated with any housing consideration and figure them into the purchase decision. For instance, it may be better to wait to buy a lamp with cash rather than pay extra for credit card fees. However, few people could ever afford to buy a house if they had to save all the money needed to make a cash purchase. For them, paying some extra interest each month is the only way to afford such a costly purchase.

Deciding to Rent or Buy

The first decision in selecting housing is whether to rent or buy. There are advantages and disadvantages to both. Figure 5-4 outlines some of the major considerations in renting versus buying. It is important to remember, however, that if you choose to buy a house you will begin to examine your finances immediately. All these considerations will become clearer as you read the chapter.

A Place to Rent

About one-third of all people in the United States rent their housing. The majority of these are single people, young married couples, and older adults. Many are people who have very mobile lifestyles.

Renters usually pay for their housing in monthly installments. When they first move into a building, the owner or building manager usually requests a security deposit in addition to the first month's rent. The **security deposit** is a payment that ensures the owner against financial loss caused by the renter. For example, the renter may damage the property or fail to pay the rent. The amount of the security deposit commonly includes one month's rent and may include an additional amount.

5-3
Whenever you consider spreading the cost of a purchase over time, find out about the extra charges you may encounter, such as interest rates and fees.

Renting Versus Buying	
Renting Advantages	**Renting Disadvantages**
• Rent is usually less than a mortgage • Down payment is lower • Total housing costs are clearer • Greater mobility—renters can move more easily • Few maintenance responsibilities; no repair responsibilities	• No tax benefit • No equity build-up in property • Rent can increase frequently • Little control of living space (e.g., having pets, decorating living space) • Eviction possibility
Buying Advantages	**Buying Disadvantages**
• Usually a good investment for increasing wealth • Equity builds; potential for selling at a profit • Tax benefits—ability to deduct mortgage interest and property taxes on federal income tax • Greater stability and sense of security • Greater control—more choice in space arrangement and decorating	• Monthly mortgage and housing expenses usually cost more • Payment on some types of mortgages can increase • Responsibility for property taxes, maintenance, and repairs • Less mobility since homes usually can't be sold quickly • Possibility of equity loss due to foreclosure for failure to pay • Cash is tied up in house

5-4
To make a wise decision about where to live, you need to consider the advantages and disadvantages of both renting and buying.

Renting has a number of advantages. Renters have more freedom to move as they desire. They do not need to worry about the value of property going up or down or about buying and selling. They have a clear idea of what housing will cost them. There are no hidden costs, such as roof repairs, that often come with ownership. Since renters do not own the dwelling, they do not need to budget money for maintenance and repairs. These are the responsibilities of the building's owner.

Although rentals can be many types of housing, the most common are multifamily dwellings. Renters usually occupy duplexes, triplexes, and apartment buildings. People can rent single-family houses and vacation houses, too.

As a renter, examine a rental unit closely before you move into it. Many community governments and rental agencies have helpful *rental inspection guides.* These guides outline the basic features of apartments and other rentals in a checklist form. You can use these guides to evaluate each rental unit and to compare several units. In addition to items on your checklist, ask the unit owner the following questions:

• What is the rent per month? How and when is it to be paid? Is a security deposit required? If so, how much is it? Under what conditions will it be returned?

• Does the lease allow rent increases if real estate taxes or other expenses rise for the lessor?

• What are the expenses/fees besides rent? (These may include utilities, storage space, parking space, air conditioning, TV connections, use of recreational areas, installation of special appliances, and late rent fees.)

- Is loud noise prohibited at certain hours?

Be sure to obtain a complete answer to each question—and make sure you are happy with these answers. You want your housing to bring you satisfaction, not frustration.

The Written Lease

Rental agreements can be on a month-to-month basis or for a specific length of time, such as one year. An oral agreement is possible, but a written agreement between renter and owner is preferable, 5-5.

A **lease** is a legal document spelling out the conditions of the rental agreement. It lists the rights and responsibilities of both the property owner, or **lessor**, and the **lessee**, who agrees to pay rent for a place to live. Other names for lessor and lessee are *landlord* and *renter*, respectively.

Always read a written lease carefully. It should include the following information:

- **Location.** The lease should clearly state the location of dwelling—address and specific apartment number.

5-5
The lease clearly states the responsibilities of the lessor and the lessee. If you choose to rent, be sure to read the lease carefully.

- **Rental amount.** What is cost of rent? When and where should it be paid? It should also include the penalties, if any, for late payment.

- **Security deposit.** The lease should state whether a security deposit is required and the amount of deposit. It should also identify the conditions that must be met before it is returned and when it will be returned.

- **Lease period.** The date of occupation and length of lease should be part of the lease. It should also include a statement on lease renewal—when to renew or give notice of nonrenewal. The document should also indicate what happens if you must leave before the lease expires. Can you assign or sublet the lease?

- **Appliances, furnishings, services, and amenities.** The lease should include a statement about what appliances, furnishings, services, and amenities (pool, work-out room, laundry facilities) are included in the rent. Are there cable TV and telephone hookups? What items may cost extra? Who is responsible for such items as shoveling snow, cutting the lawn, or painting the walls?

- **Utilities.** The lease should state who is responsible for paying utilities such as water, electricity, and gas, and recycling and waste pick-up. (If you are responsible for payment, ask to see a record of previous billings.)

- **Upkeep, maintenance, and repairs.** The lease should clearly state who is responsible for specific upkeep, maintenance, and repairs. What can either party do if one or the other fails to carry out their responsibilities? An entry clause allowing the landlord to enter the apartment for specific reasons (with notice) or in an emergency is also part of the lease.

- **Legal issues.** The lease should outline what legal remedies are available if either party breaks the lease in some way (landlord failing to make repairs; renter failing to pay rent on time). What legal actions are available to resolve disagreements? Who pays the legal fees?

- **Conditions of use.** Can you keep pets? Are there any parking restrictions? Can you paint, hang wallpaper, or decorate the dwelling? In addition, can you have a roommate? The lease should also outline any specific costs involved with any conditions of use. For example, landlords who allow pets may charge an additional fee, or security deposit, to cover any pet damage.

- **Special clauses.** The lease should include a clause stating the final inspection of the premises will be made in the renter's presence. It should also state that the lease cannot be changed without the written approval of both landlord and renter.

- **Signatures.** Both the renter(s) and landlord should sign the lease agreement.

If the renter does not like one or more of the provisions in the lease, he or she should try to have them removed from the lease. Similarly, if the renter desires additional provisions in the lease, he or she should request to have them written and added to the original lease. Such provisions might include necessary repairs, additional furniture, or the installation of appliances. The lease should include a specific date and time by which the landlord will make all changes.

Leases vary greatly. Be sure you are aware of any special restrictions in a lease before you sign it. Sometimes the words in a lease are hard to understand. Assistance for renters is often available from a renter's association in the community or state. A member of the renter's association will be glad to explain the unfamiliar terms. Do not sign a lease until you understand everything in it.

Assigning or Subletting a Lease

If you have signed a lease, but you wish to move out early, you have the following three options:
- continue rent payments until the lease expires
- assign the lease
- sublet the lease

To **assign** the lease, you transfer the entire unexpired portion of the lease to someone else. After the assignment is transacted, you can no longer be held responsible for the lease.

To **sublet** the lease, you transfer part interest in the property to someone else. For instance, you could turn over your apartment to another person for a period of time. Both you and the other person would be responsible to the landlord for all terms of the lease.

If you do not prefer any of these options, talk with the landlord to see if other options exist, 5-6. Most states have laws to protect renters. Usually, renters can pay to get out of the lease—sometimes three or six months rent. Become familiar with the laws of your state before talking to the landlord.

Responsibilities and Rights of Renting

Both landlords and renters have responsibilities and rights in the rental relationship. The lease agreement states these responsibilities. Two legal consequences can occur when there is a violation of the responsibilities of the lease—breach of contract and eviction.

5-6
If you have signed a lease and need to move for some reason, be sure to talk with your landlord about your options.

Breach of Contract

Landlords and renters are sometimes unable to fulfill promises. When this happens there is a **breach of contract**. This is a legal term for failure to meet all terms of a contract or agreement. If you cannot keep your agreement, you should try to work it out with your landlord. You should be aware that a landlord could file a lawsuit against you for breach of contract. Responding to lawsuits is costly and time-consuming.

The most common breach of contract on the part of the renter is failure to pay rent. For example, if you lose your job, you may not be able to pay the rent on schedule. Make arrangements with your landlord, if possible, to allow for a late rent payment.

A landlord may also be guilty of breach of contract. If there is failure to provide water or a means of heating your dwelling, a contract violation occurs. Major repairs are usually the responsibility of the owner. If your dwelling needs such repairs, you should give written notice to your landlord. If he or she does not make the repairs, you will have grounds for breach of contract.

Eviction

If a renter fails to live up to his or her responsibilities, the landlord can evict the renter. **Eviction** is a legal procedure that forces a renter to leave the property before the rental agreement expires. Landlords may begin a court action leading to eviction only after a renter fails to live up to his or her responsibilities.

The eviction process varies from state to state. However, nearly all states require that the renter receive a warning before eviction. The warning is a written legal notice.

Renter's Insurance

As a renter, you need to have insurance to protect against the loss of your personal property due to theft, fire, natural disasters, or other causes. Rental insurance also offers some liability protection. For example, suppose your friend comes to visit. He or she slips on the floor and breaks an ankle. Your rental insurance may include payment for medical expenses of a nonresident. This helps protect you against unexpected loss.

You can obtain renter's insurance for a reasonable price. In some cases, college students can obtain a rider on their parents' home owner's policy. It provides a sense of security in event of loss of personal property, 5-7.

A Place to Buy

About two-thirds of the people in the United States own their own houses. Instead of renting, they prefer to stay in one place for several years and buy a house. House ownership has many advantages. It provides a sense of freedom. For example, home owners know they have a place to live. Eviction is not likely unless they fall behind in their house payments. Also, they can make decisions about their housing and do not need to depend on another person such as an apartment owner.

Financial advantages also exist with house ownership. A house can be a hedge against inflation, which means it probably will increase in value at a higher rate than the rate of inflation. People who pay rent must make higher payments for the same housing as inflation rises. Depending on the condition of the economy, houses tend to increase in value over time.

As the value of your house increases, and you make payments on the **principal** (the original sum you borrowed) of the home loan, you build up equity. **Equity** is the money value of a house beyond what you owe on it. Renters are not able to build equity in their housing. Homeowners can gain from equity if they sell or refinance their houses.

House ownership also offers a tax advantage. The federal government permits deductions for annual real estate taxes on a house and the interest paid on the home loan. Some states allow these deductions, too.

Although there are many attractions to home ownership, it is not for everyone. Buying a house is a complex, time-consuming, and costly process that brings many ongoing responsibilities.

One possible drawback to home ownership is the potential strain on finances. Usually, you can expect to pay more monthly for your housing than you did for rent, at least for the first several years. Even if your house payments are less than you paid previously in rent, you must pay property taxes, home owner's insurance, utilities, and maintenance expenses.

Another possible drawback to home ownership is the potential for foreclosure on the home. **Foreclosure** is a legal proceeding in which a lending firm takes possession of the property. This occurs when the borrower fails to make monthly house payments on a timely

5-7
Renter's insurance helps protect you against loss of your personal property due to such causes as fire and theft.

basis or does not fulfill the agreements related to the loan. The agency that lent the money to buy the home may take the property and sell it, 5-8.

Home owners tend to have less mobility than renters. The owner of a house cannot simply move away and stop making the house payment. He or she must fulfill the terms of the loan contract and pay all real estate taxes. These responsibilities continue until a new owner buys the property. If a person is expecting a transfer within the next year or two, this might not be a good time to buy a house.

Handling maintenance and repairs is a necessary part of owning a single-family house. Some home owners prefer to avoid maintenance requirements, such as mowing the grass, by owning a condominium unit. Condominium owners pay a monthly fee for routine upkeep of the entire property.

When people decide to seek home ownership, a number of people, agencies, and organizations are available to assist them. Each of the many participants in the home-buying process offers different services. See 5-9 for a listing of the primary participants and services they provide. If you decide to buy a house,

Dealing with Foreclosure

Suppose you secure a home loan and buy a house. It will probably be the largest purchase you ever make. You agree to make monthly payments for many years, often decades. What happens if you lost your job or became ill and cannot make your house payments?

Legally, the lender could foreclose on your loan and take possession of the property. To recover the money you borrowed but cannot repay, the lender could then sell the property.

It is extremely important to notify your lender about problems that prevent you from making payments on time. If possible, make a personal visit to the lender to try to agree on an alternative payment plan until your situation improves. The possibility of losing your home is at stake. You may ask for an extension of time. Know your financial situation and be prepared to answer these questions:

- Why did you miss your payments?
- From where are you currently getting income?
- When will you begin payments again?
- When can you pay the payments you missed?

5-8
Notify your lender if a personal situation arises that could cause you to lose your home. In some cases, foreclosure can be avoided.

you will work with these professionals on your journey to home ownership.

Examine Your Finances

Buying the right house is not a simple task. You want a house that makes you feel comfortable and happy. However, it must also be one that you can afford.

The ability to afford home ownership begins with a realistic assessment of your finances—your income, the size of your savings account, and your debts. Most people do not have the cash to buy a house outright and must borrow a substantial amount of money. The financial institution you choose will make the ultimate decision about your ability to buy a house.

Moneylenders want to deal with responsible borrowers who will pay them back. They carefully screen applicants to avoid future home foreclosures. They will determine how much you can afford for a house while still meeting your other financial obligations. Lenders examine how high your monthly house payments can go and, therefore, how much they can safely lend you.

There are three general guidelines for determining the price range of a house you can afford. One is a general rule for estimating house affordability. The other two lending agencies use to determine how much of your income can go toward a house purchase. These guidelines provide a fairly clear picture of what house price is best for you.

Estimating What You Can Afford

One way to quickly determine the price range you can afford in buying a home is to use a simple rule. Multiply

People Involved in the Home-Buying Process	
Title	**Service Provided**
Appraiser	• A qualified professional who is certified to evaluate real estate property and determine the fair market value.
Attorney (lawyer)	• A person legally appointed or empowered to act on behalf of another—giving legal advice and providing court representation. He or she reviews real estate sale documents and may make arrangements for the title search, funds disbursement, and legal transfer of ownership.
Borrower (mortgagor)	• A person who borrows money to buy a home. • This person pledges to repay the money with interest and maintain hazard insurance on the property.
Government Program Representatives	• First-time home buyer programs vary from one community to the next. A local Housing and Urban Development (HUD) office is a good place to search for programs in your area. • State and local government agencies may offer some assistance with the down payment and extra tax credits through special housing programs.
Home Buyer Counselor	• A person who provides education and assistance to first-time home buyers with all aspects of the home-buying process. HUD funds many home-counseling programs.
Home Inspector	• A professional who evaluates a home for structural defects, such as problems with the roof, wiring, plumbing, or heating and cooling systems. Some states require a separate termite inspector to evaluate the home for insect damage.
Homeowner's Insurance Representative	• A person who provides hazard insurance to protect the home owner and the lender against physical damage (from fire, wind, and vandalism) and other liabilities to a property.
Lender (mortgagee)	• An institution or person that lends mortgage money and uses the property as security for debt payment.
Loan Servicer	• An institution or person that actually collects mortgage payments. The original lender may not provide service for a mortgage.
Mortgage Insurer	• An institution that insures the lender against loss in case the borrower defaults on the loan. This *private mortgage insurance* (PMI) is usually a requirement when home buyers have a down payment that is less than 20 percent of the appraised value.
Real Estate Professional (broker or agent)	• A person licensed to negotiate and complete the sale of real estate. • The broker or agent may be an *exclusive buyer agent* (one who works only with buyers) or a *seller's agent* (one who works only with sellers). Some brokers or agents do both.
Title Company Representative	• A person who arranges for a title search, disbursement of funds, and legal transfer of property ownership.

5-9
A number of persons providing various services are involved in the home-buying process.

two-and-one-half times your annual **gross income**, or income before deductions. This provides a general idea of the maximum house price you can afford. If you have an annual income of $50,000, for example, you should be able to afford up to $125,000 for a place to live.

Remember, though, this rule for measuring house affordability provides just a "ballpark" figure. A lender will take into account the other debts and responsibilities the buyer has that may make it difficult to repay a loan. Consequently, a person with many debts may not receive approval for a loan to acquire housing valued at two-and-one-half times his or her gross income.

Estimating How Much Money You Can Borrow

For most home loans, the buyer must make a down payment that cannot be part of the loan. This is usually at least 5 percent of the cost of the home, but may vary depending on the loan requirements. Obtaining a loan from a lending institution then pays the unpaid balance on the home.

Your earnings and existing debt will determine the loan size you can obtain. Most lenders use a computer program to determine the eligibility for a loan. The program includes the applicant's income, debts, and other financial

MATH MATTERS

Meeting Lender Guidelines

Suppose a couple wants to buy a house. They have an annual combined income of $75,000 with gross-monthly pay of $6,250. The potential house payment is $825 monthly. The other monthly housing-related costs total $700—which covers property taxes, home owner's insurance, utilities, repairs, and maintenance. The couple owes $600 monthly on long-term debts (those taking over 10 months to pay) for two car loans, college education costs, and a dining room set. Would this couple meet approval guidelines to obtain a loan for the house?

To answer this question, the couple must meet two ratios. They include

Housing-to-Income Ratio (must be 28% or less)

To calculate the housing-to-income ratio, use the following formula:

Total Housing Costs ÷ Gross Income = (result) × 100 = Housing-to-Income Ratio
$1,525 ÷ $6,250 = 0.244 × 100 = 24% (rounded) Housing-to-Income Ratio

Conclusion: The couple's housing-to-income ratio is 24%. They meet this guideline.

Debt-to-Income Ratio (must be 36% or less)

To calculate the debt-to-income ratio, first add together the total housing costs and long-term debt. Then use the following formula:

Total Debt ÷ Gross Income = (result) × 100 = Debt-to-Income Ratio
$2,125 ÷ $6,250 = 0.34 × 100 = 34% Debt-to-Income Ratio

Conclusion: The couple's debt-to-income ratio is 34%. Couple meets this guideline.

Because the couple meets both ratios, the couple will likely get approval for a house loan with a monthly house payment of $825. In addition to these guidelines, the couple will also need to have a good credit history in order to get approval for a home loan.

factors. Some lenders use two guidelines or ratios to determine the size loan that an applicant can afford. A good way to determine if you qualify for a loan is to calculate the following two ratios:

- **Housing-to-income ratio.** Your monthly housing costs should total no more than 28 percent of your gross monthly income. These housing costs include the house payment, property taxes, insurance, utilities (such as gas, water, and electricity), repairs, maintenance, and a cooperative or condominium fee, if applicable. To obtain your **housing-to-income ratio,** divide your total housing costs by your gross income. Then multiply your decimal result by 100 to obtain the percentage.

- **Debt-to-income ratio.** This second guideline compares total monthly debt to total monthly income. Your monthly housing costs plus other long-term debts should total no more than 36 percent of your monthly gross income. *Long-term debts* are those debts that will take 10 or more months to repay. To obtain your **debt-to-income ratio,** divide your total debt (debt + housing costs) by your gross income. Then multiply the decimal result by 100 to obtain the percentage.

If you can meet these ratios, you will probably qualify for a loan. These ratios may vary slightly depending on the specific type of loan. See the math feature that shows how to meet and calculate these ratios. Other factors also enter into the decision to receive a loan to buy housing. A major factor is the credit history of the potential buyer.

The **credit history** of a person includes the past payment record and a profile of outstanding debts. The credit history includes a person's credit score. A *credit score* is a complex mathematical calculation that evaluates the information in a person's credit history. Lenders use this information to determine whether a person qualifies for a particular form of credit.

Three consumer-reporting companies keep and monitor a person's credit history. The Federal Trade Commission (FTC) requires each of the nationwide consumer-reporting companies—Equifax, Experian, and TransUnion—to provide a free copy of a person's credit report, at his or her request, once every 12 months. A person can obtain a copy of his or her credit report through the following Web site: www.annualcreditreport.com.

The credit reports include the past payment record as well as a profile of outstanding debts. The credit history gives a bank or other lending agencies information about whether a person is likely to repay a loan. People are considered "high risk" if their credit history indicates frequent late payments and high debt.

Decisions to Buy or Build

Once you know how much you can afford to spend for a house, you will want to decide whether to buy a newly built house, a pre-owned house, or build a new one. All options have their advantages and disadvantages. Home buyers will need to weigh these options as they make a decision.

Buying a New House

If you want a new house, but do not want to build it, you can buy a recently built home, 5-10. This process requires much less time than buying land and having a house built on it.

When a reputable builder builds the house, the builder will guarantee workmanship for a period of time, usually one to two years after completion. Some top builders guarantee their work for five to ten years. Be sure to get the guarantee in writing for your protection.

Buying a new house has some unique advantages. One is that you can

5-10
Sometimes contractors build houses that are ready for sale. What traditional features do you find in this new home?

Photo courtesy of Palm Harbor Homes

5-11
A pre-owned house may include mature landscaping that does not come with new homes.

Photo Courtesy of JELD-WEN Windows and Doors

move in right after closing the deal, or after settling all legal and financial matters. Another advantage is you can see the finished product before you buy. If you are a person who cannot visualize a finished house by studying the plans, you may prefer a new house already built.

Buying a Pre-Owned House

For various reasons, many buyers choose previously occupied houses. The same amount of space usually costs less in a pre-owned house rather than a new one. Often you can see how previous owners made use of the space, 5-11. When you look at furnished rooms, you can get a better idea of how much usable space exists. This can help you visualize how your furniture will fit into the same

space. Another bonus is that taxes in established communities are not likely to increase as rapidly as those in new areas.

In addition, some items that usually do not come with a new house may be included with a pre-owned one. The previous owner usually leaves the window coverings and their hardware. The lot may have mature trees and shrubs. Fences, walls, and screens may have been added. These are costly in time, money, and effort if you add them yourself.

While you may find that some pre-owned houses are bargains, others are not. No house is perfect. You need to know the flaws before you buy. If you do not find out about the shortcomings until after you move in, it can be a shock. The shock becomes greater when you realize how much they cost to fix.

Before you sign a contract agreeing to buy a pre-owned house, you should check carefully. Look for serious defects, such as the following:

- A cracked foundation indicating that the house will probably sag or shift, which will weaken the structure.

- Rotten or sagging roofs, walls, or supports are signs of major construction defects or poor care. All are costly to repair.

- Insect damage may be serious enough to require major repairs. It may also mean defects exist that are not visible to the inexperienced observer.

You can repair less serious conditions if you want to spend the time, money, and effort. Perhaps a window is broken, the roof needs repair, or the structure needs painting. Walls, ceilings, or floors may show slight damage, or the electrical wiring may be inadequate. The yard may appear shabby, needing major landscaping work.

GREEN CHOICES

Consumer Responsibility in Green and Sustainable Design

Whether choosing to rent or buy a place to live, consumers should consider the many choices and how their choices affect the environment. Consumers should be wise shoppers and know the "green" factors to look for in housing. The following "green" factors should guide their decisions:

- Does the house have a "green" or "sustainable" certification or designation? This means the unit is more environmentally friendly.

- To what extent does the house use the natural environment to reduce energy cost? For example, is there use of the natural sunlight or landscaping that shades the southern side of the house in summer?

- Do the appliances have ENERGY STAR® ratings? This means they use 30 percent less energy than the standard appliances.

- How does the house rate in its "carbon footprint" as compared to the average house? (Check www.epa.gov for a carbon-footprint calculator). This will determine the number of pounds of carbon dioxide the house might emit into the atmosphere.

These are just a few items to consider. "Green" decisions not only affect the environment but also benefit the consumer with reduced utility costs.

To learn about the home ahead of time, you should have a home inspection. Lenders will also require an appraisal. You will learn more about home inspections and appraisals later in this chapter.

Building a House

If you choose to build a house, there are several ways to accomplish it. First you may choose to work with an architect to build a custom-designed house. Another option is to choose from a number of standard house designs. If you choose the second option, you can have an architect or contractor make additional changes to the plans to fit your needs. As a consumer, you need to especially be aware of the green or sustainable aspects of the home's design.

If building a house is your choice, you will need to buy a lot (a portion of land) and then build the house. This involves four steps, accomplished in the following order:

1. **Location.** Choose a region, community, neighborhood, and site. Finding the right location may take weeks or months.

2. **House plan.** Find a house plan you like that fits the site and your lifestyle. The plan may be custom-designed by an architect or chosen from stock plans, 5-12. Changes can be made to either set of plans. In addition, you can include elements of green or sustainable design into the plans.

5-12
An architect or contractor can help you choose a house plan that best meets your housing needs.

3. **Select the contractor.** Check the reputation and character of each contractor you are considering by obtaining a list of references of recently completed jobs. Let each contractor examine your plans, the list of materials for the house, and their type and quality of the materials. When you have narrowed your choices to a few contractors, you should ask each for a **bid**, or the fee each would charge to build the house. The bid should include the cost for both materials and labor. You also need to find out when work can start and how long the job will take. Ask about the method and timing of payments. Once the work is in progress, you generally pay builders or contractors by installments.

4. **Financing.** Obtain enough money to pay for the house. If you do not have enough cash, you must borrow more money. When you apply for a loan, you must provide the appraised value of the dwelling. You can estimate the home's value by using the information given in your house plans. Generally, financing a new home happens in two parts. The first loan will be for construction of the house. After the house is finished, you can receive a long-term loan.

The Home-Buying Process

Once potential home buyers examine their finances and determine whether to buy a new or pre-owned house, the home-buying process begins in earnest. There are several parts in this process, the first of which is selecting a mortgage lender, type of mortgage, and gaining preapproval for a loan. Because of recent changes in the U.S. economy, many real estate agents require home buyers to have preapproval before shopping for a home. After home buyers gain preapproval and search for a house, the remaining parts of the process occur at the same time. For example, after acceptance of an offer on a house occurs, such activities as inspections, the survey, title search, appraisal, and obtaining home owner's insurance occur while the lender finalizes the mortgage loan.

Mortgage Selection and Preapproval

A **mortgage** is a pledge of property that a borrower gives to a lender as security for a loan with which to buy the property. The borrower agrees to gradually **amortize**, or pay off, the loan (the principal with interest) in monthly installments for a given number of years. If he or she fails to pay, the lender can repossess the home. The lender is usually a bank, savings bank, credit union, or mortgage company. The seller may also be the lender.

GREEN CHOICES

Choose an ENERGY STAR Qualified Home

When selecting a new house that has green and sustainable features or certification, choose an eco-friendly program to guide your decision making. Such a program assures you that there are green components in a home. For example, the US Environmental Protection Agency (EPA) sets the guidelines for the *ENERGY STAR® Qualified Home* program. The guidelines state these homes are 20 to 30 percent more energy efficient than the standard home. Home features that lead to lower energy demand and reduced air pollution include

- properly installed insulation
- high-performance windows
- tight construction and ducts
- efficient heating and cooling equipment
- efficient products (appliances, lighting)
- third-party verification (independent rating)

Because mortgage loans can vary between lenders and from state to state, it is wise for potential home buyers to examine all their loan options. What type of mortgage loan best meets the home buyer's needs? Here are some examples of the most common types of home mortgages.

Types of Mortgages

For many years, the standard home mortgage has been a long-term, fixed-rate loan. This means that the mortgage was usually written for a specific period of time with the interest rate and monthly payments constant. Several mortgage options exist for borrowers today. They include conventional fixed-rate mortgages, adjustable-rate mortgages (ARM), and government-backed loans that are FHA-insured or VA-guaranteed.

Conventional Mortgage. A two-party contract between a borrower and a lender is a **conventional mortgage**. A conventional loan is a long-term, fixed-rate loan. The typical term lengths for conventional loans are 15, 20, and 30 years, although some lenders may write mortgages for 10 or 40 years. The down payment on a conventional loan may vary from five to 20 percent, with many lenders requiring the latter. When the home buyer does not have a 20 percent down payment, the lender may require the home buyer to purchase **private mortgage insurance (PMI)**—insurance that protects the lender if the borrower fails to pay. The government does not insure this type of mortgage.

Adjustable Rate Mortgage. With an **adjustable rate mortgage (ARM)**, the interest rate is adjusted up or down periodically according to a national interest rate index. Depending on interest rate changes, monthly payments may increase or decrease. Initially, some lenders offer these loans at a lower interest rate than fixed-rate mortgages. However, some of these mortgages have rate caps. This means the interest rate will never exceed a certain rate regardless of the national interest rate index.

FHA-Insured Mortgage. A three-party contract that involves the borrower, a lender, and the Federal Housing Administration (FHA) is an **FHA-insured mortgage**. This government agency is part of the U.S. Department of Housing and Urban Development (HUD). FHA does not make loans, but it insures the lender against the borrower's possible default. Anyone can apply for an FHA-insured loan by going to an approved lending institution. In comparison to conventional loans, a home buyer can often secure an FHA-insured loan with a smaller down payment.

VA-Guaranteed Mortgage. A three-party loan involving the borrower (who is a veteran of the U.S. Armed Forces), a lending firm, and the Veterans Administration (VA) is a **VA-guaranteed mortgage**. These mortgages generally cost less than the other types of common, fixed-rate mortgages. Veterans may apply for a VA-guaranteed loan at a lending institution. The lender submits the applications to a VA office for approval. Congress sets the eligibility requirements. The VA does not require a down payment, but the lender may. The veteran and the lender decide the size of the down payment and the length of the repayment period.

Other alternative house-financing options are presented in 5-13. One type of financing is available to limited-income, first-time home buyers who are taking a home buyer education and counseling program. The program counselors help these buyers secure financing after they attend buyer education classes, reduce personal debts, and maintain good credit ratings. To find out more about housing counseling programs, visit the U.S. Department of Housing and Urban Development Web site at www.hud.gov.

House financing alternatives vary from state to state and lender to lender. Research all the options to find the method of financing that is best for you.

5-13
Many alternative home-financing options exist to meet the varying needs of buyers and sellers.

Alternative Home-Financing Options	
Type	**Description**
Balloon Mortgage	Monthly payments based on a fixed interest rate, usually short term. Payments may cover interest only, with principal due in full at term's end.
Assumable Mortgage	Buyer takes over seller's original, below-market interest rate mortgage.
Land Contract (or contract for deed)	Seller retains original mortgage. No transfer of title until loan is fully paid. Equal monthly payments based on below-market interest rate with any unpaid principal due at loan's end.
Rent with Option to Buy	Renter pays an option fee for the right to purchase property at specified time and agreed-upon price. Rent may or may not be applied to sales price.
Secondary Financing (or second mortgage)	Financing the buyer secures to reduce the amount of funds required for down payment and/or closing costs.
Biweekly Mortgage	With this type of mortgage, instead of making a monthly payment the home owner makes a payment every two weeks. This results in making an extra mortgage payment per year, leading to a slightly shorter mortgage term.

LINK TO SOCIAL STUDIES & CULTURE

The Housing Bubble Burst

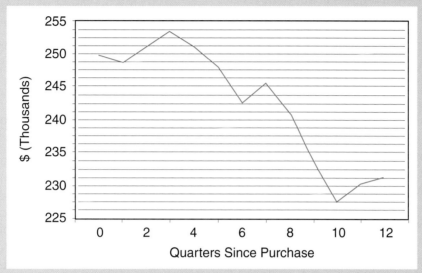

Source: HPI (House Price Index) Calculator, Federal Housing Finance Agency, www.fhfa.gov

Suppose you purchased a single-family house in Illinois for $250,000 during the housing bubble in the third quarter of 2006. Three years later, it would only be worth about $231,300.

Buying a home has long been part of the American dream. Generations of Americans put their savings into a home and were rewarded with an asset that grew slowly but steadily in value over the years. For many people, purchasing real estate was a sure and safe way to create wealth.

In the mid 1990s, home values skyrocketed in many parts of the U.S. and around the world. The boom in housing markets—especially in California, Florida, Arizona, and Nevada—was fueled by many factors. Historically low Interest rates decreased the cost of borrowing. Low unemployment increased the pool of prospective home buyers.

Perhaps the most important factor was psychological—people believed that housing prices would continue to climb steeply indefinitely. This belief led people, businesses, and investors to take unwise financial risks. For example, many home buyers bought homes that were priced too high. To pay for their homes, they took out loans they did not understand and could not afford. Many financial institutions relaxed lending requirements—sometimes waiving customary requirements for down payments and borrowers' proof of employment—which allowed many more people to qualify for loans.

A market developed in mortgage-backed securities. After making loans to home buyers, many financial institutions sold them to other financial institutions and investors. Large numbers of mortgages were packaged and then bought and sold like stocks and bonds.

An asset "bubble" forms when excess demand drives up the value of assets. Like most bubbles, the housing market bubble eventually burst. By 2005, the rate at which home prices rose began to level off and decline. By 2007, house prices began to fall around the country. Interest rates rose. A growing number of home owners could not pay their mortgages and lost their homes. By the end of 2009, almost one in four borrowers were *underwater,* or owed more on their mortgages than the properties were worth. Housing markets across the U.S. became clogged with foreclosed homes that drove down the value of all homes.

Shopping for a Mortgage Lender

Because so many mortgage options exist today, it is best to compare at least three different lenders about their mortgage options and interest rates. Also, consider getting information from different types of lenders, including commercial banks, credit unions, online lenders, and mortgage companies.

Dealing with reputable companies is essential because mortgage applications require so much personal information. This is especially true for online lenders. Look for a lender that is financially stable with a strong reputation for providing quality customer service. If questions arise about the financial health of any lending institution, you can check with the regulatory agency in your state that deals with banks and other lending institutions. Also, lenders who try to push you to use just one lender are cause for suspicion—they may not have your best interests in mind.

Comparing the same information for each lender—the loan amount, the interest rate, the length of the loan, and the type of loan—helps you make sound decisions. Some of this information is available in the real estate sections of your local newspaper. You can obtain other information about fees and costs directly from the lenders. In addition, ask each lender about the following:

- What is the down payment requirement for each loan? Will the lender require private mortgage insurance (PMI) if your down payment is less than the requirement?

- Is the interest rate fixed or adjustable? Also ask about the loan's APR.

- Do the loan costs involve **points**, or fees paid to the lender for the loan (usually one point equals one percent of the loan)?

As you shop for a mortgage and mortgage lender, do not be afraid to negotiate the best deal. This includes making lenders or brokers compete with each other for your business. Smart consumers take time to shop for a mortgage and gather all the facts before making a final decision. Arming yourself with the right information can help you avoid becoming a victim of predatory lenders—those who, for example, knowingly lend more than a customer can afford or charge higher interest rates to borrowers based on personal characteristics other than credit history. To find further information on fair lending laws, visit the U.S. Department of Housing and Urban Development (HUD) Web site (www.hud.gov/), 5-14.

5-14
Fair lending laws help prevent discrimination against potential home buyers.

Fair Lending Laws Protect Consumers	
Laws	**Key Provisions**
The Equal Credit Opportunity Act	• Prohibits lenders from discriminating against credit applications in any part of the credit transaction based on race, color, religion, national origin, sex, marital status, age, or whether part of an applicant's income comes from a public assistance program.
The Fair Housing Act	• Prohibits discrimination in residential real estate transactions based on race, color, religion, sex, handicap, family status, or national origin.

Obtaining Preapproval for a Loan

Although you can shop for a home and then apply for a mortgage, it is to your advantage (and often a requirement) to seek preapproval for a loan first. **Preapproval**, means that the home buyer has gone through a preliminary approval process in which the lender verifies employment and checks tax records, bank references, and the borrower's credit history. The lender gives then gives the buyer a *preapproval letter* indicating commitment. Preapproval gives the buyer a definite amount to spend on housing. It also gives the buyer negotiating power with sellers because it shows the buyer has serious intentions. Once a home buyer finds a house, he or she will need to finish the approval process to meet other requirements and conditions of the lender.

Searching for a Home

When you know what type of house you want and can afford, it is time to go shopping. You can locate a home through real estate firms, the Internet, and the real estate section of newspapers. Also, you can learn about homes for sale through word-of-mouth. Finally, you can drive through neighborhoods looking for sale signs.

Using a Real Estate Firm

Real estate firms are in the business of selling land and buildings. They often advertise properties in free shopping guides, in the real estate section of newspapers, and on the Internet, 5-15. Most real estate firms are part of a larger network called the *multiple listing service* (MLS). This service provides a combined list of all area houses for sale by network real estate firms.

Real estate agents, who are members of the National Association of Realtors, are called *realtors*. Realtors can give you

Rachel Sanchez Real Estate

200 E. Main Street

OPEN HOUSE
Saturday and Sunday
April 22-23, 1-4 p.m.
$189,900

Remodeled, updated, and delightful! 4-bedroom brick ranch with fireplace, 2½ baths, utility room, 2½-car garage, and sunroom off master bedroom. Great layout. Quiet location plus a bonus— 160-ft. lake frontage on South Lake. Get your fishing pole ready! Take Rt. 50 to Western. Turn west at 3rd Street, north at Walnut, and east at Main Street. Signs are posted.

5-15
Advertisements in local newspapers can help you find real estate firms.

information about the community and neighborhood that you are considering. They can screen out places that would not appeal to you. Sometimes they can help you get financing.

Realtors charge a commission, or fee, for their services. The commission ranges from 5 percent to 10 percent of the selling price. The seller usually pays the real estate fee. However, the seller may raise the price of the house to cover this cost.

It is important to hire a real estate agent that represents you, the buyer, and not the seller. This person is also known as the "buyer's agent."

Locating Homes for Sale

As well as working with a realtor, you can also find homes for sale on your own. Several options exist and can save you time during the search process. They include the following:

Internet Shopping. Many realtors offer Internet home-shopping sites that include floor plans plus inside and outside photos of housing for sale. You can search for housing by specifying such options as the number of bedrooms, the geographic area, and price range. Detailed information about the homes you select will include property taxes and the location of schools. Some sites offer *virtual tours* that allow you to "walk" through or see 360-degree views of each room. Prospective buyers can use this information to narrow down choices before spending time to actually visit different units.

Newspapers. As well as newspaper listings by real estate firms, you may find homes for sale by owner. This means that you buy directly from the owner. It also means that the price of the house is not inflated to cover the fees the seller must pay to a real estate agent.

Word-of-Mouth. When shopping for a house, tell friends and acquaintances that you are looking for a home to buy. They may know about certain houses that you would like. They may even know about some houses that will be up for sale in the near future.

For Sale Signs. In general, driving or walking past houses you like is a good way to become familiar with a neighborhood. You may find places with *For Sale* signs that are easy to overlook in real estate ads, 5-16. You may also find a model house on display or find houses that are not advertised anywhere else. As you look at houses and talk with people, keep a written record about each dwelling. Note the price and the location.

Get the name and address of the owner. Write down the features of each house—number and size of the rooms, lot size, condition of the structure, and your reactions to it.

Shopping on your own without a real estate agent takes a great deal of time and knowledge. If you do not have knowledge about real estate deals, the mistakes you might make could be much more costly than any money you might save.

Making an Offer—The Sales Contract

When you find a house that you like in your price range, it is time to make a formal offer on the property. Your real estate agent can give you information about prices of comparable homes that are for sale or have sold in your area. With this information in mind, you can make an *offer to purchase* to the seller. When you make the offer, you will include a check for the earnest money. **Earnest money** is a deposit, or sum of money you pay to show that you are serious about buying the house. The money is held in trust until the closing of the deal. When the deal goes through, the earnest money is applied toward the payment of the total price. If you cannot get a loan, the money is refunded. You may lose the earnest money if you back out of the agreement for other reasons.

The **agreement of sale** (also known as *offer to purchase, contract of purchase, purchase agreement,* or *sales agreement*) gives a detailed description of the property and its legal location and all specific terms and conditions of the real estate sale. It includes the total purchase price, the amount of the down payment, and the possession date of property. In addition, it states that the seller must have clear title to the property in order to complete the sale, 5-17.

5-16
Walking through a neighborhood and identifying additional "for sale" signs, increases your options and helps you get to know the neighborhood.

The agreement of sale will also spell out any specific contingencies, or terms and conditions of the sale. For instance, an owner may agree to leave the draperies, carpeting, range, and refrigerator in the house. The agreement will list such items. This way, you know exactly what you are buying. Other specific terms the document should explain include how the payment of property taxes will be divided and who bears the risk of loss to the property. Loss may occur as a result of fire, wind, and other disasters during completion of the deal.

When the buyer and seller agree to a negotiated price for the house, both sign the agreement of sale making the document legal and binding. Read all of the fine print before signing it. At this time, the buyer moves forward with securing financing and home owner's insurance and having a survey, appraisal, and title search.

Finalizing the Financing

If you have gone through the preapproval process for a mortgage before your home search, the final approval

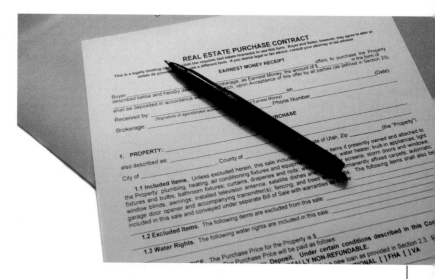

of the loan generally moves swiftly. At this point, the lender provides the buyer with a *lock-in* on the interest rate—a written agreement guaranteeing the interest rate. You will need to present the sales contract to the lender and complete an application and any other documentation the lender requires. If you do not have preapproval, you will need to find a lender and apply for a loan. When applying for a loan, the lender will require

5-17
Making an offer on a home involves completing an agreement of sale. Many experts recommend that home buyers consult a lawyer about real estate transactions before signing any documents.

MATH MATTERS

Calculating Price per Square Foot

Before making an offer to buy a home, home buyers evaluate a seller's asking price. Is the price fair or is the seller asking for too much? Home buyers can compare the home's price to that of a comparable home in the same neighborhood that recently sold. The calculation of price per square foot enables buyer to make a comparison.

For example, home A, which has 1,500 square feet of living space, has an asking price of $200,000. In the same neighborhood, a comparable home, home B, recently sold for $230,000. Home B has 2,200 square feet of living space. Calculate the price per square foot of each home.

(House A) $200,000 ÷ 1,500 = $133.33 per square foot
(House B) $230,000 ÷ 2,200 = $104.55 per square foot

House A has a much higher price per square foot than House B. House A is probably priced too high.

MATH MATTERS

Calculating Finance Charges

Over the life of a loan, finance charges often total more than the principal, or the loan amount itself. Finance charges increase with the annual percentage rate (APR), the amount borrowed, and the length of the repayment period. Given this information, you can calculate the finance charge.

For example, the finance charge on a $165,000 30-year mortgage with a 6 percent APR and a monthly payment of $989 is calculated as follows:

- Calculate how many payments must be made over the 30-year life of the mortgage. There are 360 months in 30 years.

- Calculate the total amount of all payments made over the life of the mortgage. If $989 is paid per month for 360 months, the amount equals $356,040.

To calculate total finance charges paid, subtract the amount borrowed from the total payments made over the life of the loan. For example:

$356,040 - $165,000 = $191,040 (total finance charges paid over 30 years)

- tax documentation for the previous two years with W-2s

- two or more paycheck stubs

- debt information

- several recent bank statements

- proof of other assets or income (for example, life insurance policies with cash value)

- the address and property description you want to buy

- a copy of the signed agreement of sale

Obtaining Home Owner's Insurance

While your home loan is in progress, you will need to find home owner's (hazard) insurance. Home owner's insurance helps protect your investment and can save you from financial loss. Most mortgage holders require the home buyer to protect the house from loss with insurance against fire and other hazards. The lender will also want to be listed as the mortgage holder on the property. At the time of closing, the lender will require documentation that an insurance policy is paid in full for one year.

When looking for insurance, be sure to find a licensed company and agent, 5-18. Know what coverage you need and comparison shop for your policy. Talk with relatives and friends about companies and agents they like and find reliable and helpful. You can also contact your state's department of insurance to obtain information about companies and agents licensed in your area.

You will want to make sure that you purchase enough insurance to rebuild the home at replacement construction costs—not the current value of the home. Demolition and debris removal can add to the cost of rebuilding. You also want to purchase enough insurance to replace your personal belongings. You can insure your personal items for *actual cash value* (with depreciation) or *replacement cost* (without depreciation). Insurance agents or company representatives can help you determine how much insurance you need. To find an affordable policy that covers your needs, be sure to obtain estimates from several providers before making your choice. Remember, insurance is expensive and you need to make the best possible decision.

Although types of policies can vary from state-to-state, basic insurance coverage includes property and personal liability coverage.

- **Property coverage.** This insurance pays for physical damage to your house, personal property (furnishings, clothes, etc.), garage, and other detached items such as a garden shed or fence. Perils that cause sudden and accidental damage to your home and property include fire, wind, vandalism, and theft. Your policy will spell out the specific details about items it covers. In addition, your policy may cover living expenses (such as motel and restaurant costs) that occur if you must leave your home temporarily for repairs.

- **Personal liability coverage.** If another person has an accident on your property, this insurance pays for bodily injuries. It will pay for a person's medical expenses for the accidental injury up to the limit of medical coverage you buy. In addition, liability coverage generally pays for damage to another's property for which you or a family member is responsible.

Home owner's insurance *does not* cover every type of property loss. When evaluating insurance policies, it is important to look at the *exclusions*—items policies do not cover. Most policies do not cover such catastrophic events as flood, earthquake, war, or nuclear disaster, 5-19. Additional exclusions may include: property covered by other policies (cars, boats), damage due to wear and tear on the property, damage from sewer backup

or sump-pump overflow, and other hazards such as injuries by pets.

For some exclusions, home owners can buy additional insurance options—or *endorsements*—to meet their needs. For example, if home owners live in earthquake- or flood-prone areas they can buy additional protection for their property. They can buy separate flood insurance through the National Flood Insurance Program (www.floodsmart.gov) and from private insurance carriers.

5-18
Meeting with an insurance agent to acquire home owner's hazard insurance is a step along the path of the home-buying process.

5-19
Be sure to find out what types of property losses home owner's insurance does not cover. Natural disasters such as flooding require that home owner's purchase additional property protection.

Obtaining a Home Inspection

A **home inspection** is an evaluation of construction and present condition of the house. The inspection will reveal if any defects exist that impact the value of the home and ultimately the sales price. Some states also require inspections for termites or mold. If the inspections identify any problems with the property, the buyer can renegotiate the terms and conditions of the sale with the seller (if agreeable) or in most cases back out of the deal.

A home inspector works for the home buyer. Therefore, the home buyer arranges for and pays for the home inspections at the time they occur. When selecting an inspector, obtain referrals and possibly have multiple inspections. Most states license or certify inspectors to make home inspections.

Having a Survey, Appraisal, and Title Search

Many mortgage lenders (and home buyers) require a professional survey of the property. The result of a survey will be a map showing the property lines and indicating where the house, driveway, garage, and other features such as fences are located. This assures the mortgage lender and home buyer that the building is actually located on the land identified in the legal description.

In addition to a survey, lenders require a house appraisal before you buy it (whether the house is pre-owned or new). An **appraisal** is an expert estimate of the quality and value of the property given by a licensed appraiser. The appraiser tours the property and researches properties with comparable sales data in the area. The appraiser then sends a report to the lender about the property value. See the end of this chapter to learn more about a career as a real estate appraiser.

Title and Deed

Before purchasing a house, the buyer must be sure the seller is the legal owner. A lawyer or title insurance company reviews an **abstract of title**, which is a copy of all public records concerning the property. The abstract reveals the true legal owner and any debts, or liens, which are held on the property. This is important since the buyer becomes responsible for any such debts when he or she becomes the owner of the property. Lenders require the buyer to purchase title insurance for protection against financial loss caused by errors in the abstract of title.

When the sale closes, the title passes to the new owner. The **title** is a document that gives proof of the rights of ownership and possession of a particular property. A **deed** is the legal document that shows the transfer of title from one person to another, 5-20. The deed describes the property being sold. It is signed and witnessed according to the laws of the state in which the property is located. The following types of deeds indicate transfer property:

5-20
A general warranty deed transfers the title of the property to the new owners and guarantees the title is clear of any claims.

- **General warranty deed.** This type of deed transfers the title of the property to the buyer. It guarantees that the title is clear of any claims against it. If any mortgage, tax, or title claims are made against the property, the buyer may hold the seller liable for them. This type of deed offers the greatest legal protection to the buyer.

- **Special warranty deed.** This deed also transfers the title to the buyer. However, it guarantees that during the time the seller held the title to the property, the seller did nothing that would, or will in the future, impair the buyer's title.

- **Quitclaim deed.** This legal document transfers whatever interest the seller has in the property without providing a guarantee or warranty of title. By accepting such a deed, the buyer assumes all legal and financial risks for the property.

Closing the Sale of a Home

Before a real estate sale is final, payment of fees and charges for settling the legal and financial matters—or **closing costs**—must occur. These closing costs can amount to several thousand dollars. The buyers should receive a *good faith estimate* from the lender of all closing costs several days prior to closing. Buyers should come to the closing table with enough money to pay for them, 5-21. Buyers can pay closing costs with cash or a cashier's check. Closing costs may include

- recording fees for the deed and mortgage.
- attorney's fee or fee to a title company.
- abstract of title and title insurance.
- appraisal fee.
- survey charge.
- origination fee. This fee is paid to the lender for processing the loan. It usually is one percent of the mortgage loan.
- escrow fees. These are funds paid to an escrow agent to hold until a specified event occurs. After the event has occurred, the funds are released to designated people. In practice, this often means that when the homeowner makes mortgage payments, he or she pays an additional sum that is placed in a trust fund. This extra money is used to pay other expenses, such as taxes, insurance premiums, and special assessments.
- points. This refers to a type of interest paid to offset interest lost by the lender. One point equals one percent of the mortgage loan.

5-21
Home buyers should come to the closing table with enough money (either cash or cashier's check) to pay the closing costs for their real estate deal.

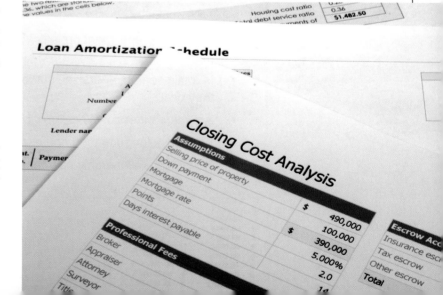

- miscellaneous fees. Other costs include flood insurance, termite inspection, a credit report, tax services, the underwriter's charge, and application fees.

The seller also has some closing costs. They may include the real estate commission and his or her share of the year's taxes, insurance, and any special assessments. Both the buyer and seller pay the taxes, insurance, and special assessments for the portion of the year they own the property. The seller's closing costs may actually be higher than those of the buyer. He or she may raise the price of the house to cover them.

After you have lived in your new home a while, you may notice that mortgage interest rates are lower or you may desire to do some home remodeling. Because of these factors, you may decide to refinance your mortgage. Making the decision to refinance requires weighing many options and re-evaluating your financial situation. See 5-22 for more information on refinancing.

Special Ownership Considerations

The home-buying process is much the same for all types of housing. Several types of home ownership, however, require special considerations on the part of the buyer. These include condominium and cooperative ownership.

Condominium Ownership

Buying a condominium unit is similar to buying any other house. You will need to choose a location you like and a unit you can afford. You must decide between a new and pre-owned unit. You will probably work with either a real estate agent or developer. You will sign an agreement of sale, make a down payment, secure a mortgage, pay closing costs, and sign a deed.

Condominium owners have the same financial advantages conventional home owners have. They are investing in real estate and can take advantage

---

5-22
Some home owner's choose to refinance their mortgages for a number of reasons after a period of time.

Refinancing a Mortgage
Reasons to Refinance
• Lower monthly payments
• Take advantage of lower interest rates (one percent or more below your rate)
• Make home improvements
Actions to Take
• Shop for the best rate—begin with your current lender to possibly eliminate some costs (such as closing costs)
• Ask questions before making a decision to refinance. Get the answers to the following questions:
• Is there a prepayment penalty? Will paying off the old mortgage early cost more?
• Is a title search, appraisal, survey, or inspection required? How much will they cost?
• Are there other costs?
• Who pays the recording and escrow fees?
• How much will monthly payments change?
• How many months will it take to recover the cost of refinancing?

of certain income tax deductions. They also build equity in their property.

Condominium units are usually less costly to build than freestanding, single-family houses. However, because of the extras you buy, the price may be high. Extras may include access to such recreational facilities as a clubhouse, swimming pool, and tennis courts, 5-23.

Approach the purchase of a condominium unit with care. First, be sure to read the **declaration of ownership**. It contains the conditions and restrictions of the sale, ownership, and use of the property within a particular group of condominium units. Check to see that you can sell your unit at any time and that you are liable for only the mortgage and taxes for your unit. Then find out who controls the management of the units.

Lastly, get a detailed breakdown of your monthly payments. Besides mortgage payments and taxes, you must pay utilities, insurance, and maintenance fees. Maintenance fees are used for the repair and maintenance of the common areas of the complex. They vary widely and are usually subject to change. Check to see that the fee seems reasonable.

Cooperative Ownership

Buying a cooperative unit is different from buying a house. The first step, finding a unit, may be the most difficult one. Although the concept of cooperative dwellings is increasing, most exist in large urban areas.

The legal and financial aspects of cooperative housing are unique. When a corporation buys an entire building or a lot to begin a cooperative housing project, it secures a mortgage on the property. When you move into a cooperative building, you *cannot* get a traditional mortgage. This is because you are buying stock, not real estate.

In some cases, you will need to pay the full price of the stock in cash. However, you will not pay closing costs, since you are dealing directly with the corporation.

5-23
A swimming pool may be part of the common-use area when a condominium unit is the buyer's choice.

In other cases, you can obtain a *share loan* from a lender to buy shares (or stock) in a cooperative unit. Not all banks and lenders offer share loans because they can be complicated, so the buyer will need to shop around to find a lender. With a share loan, you not only make monthly payments to your lender, but you also make monthly payments to the housing cooperative to cover property taxes, maintenance, and management fees.

The tax advantages of living in a cooperative unit differ from those for other types of house ownership. In a cooperative situation, the corporation owns the building. It pays real estate taxes and makes the mortgage payments. As a stockholder, you can deduct from your income tax a certain portion of what the corporation pays in real estate taxes and mortgage interest.

As mentioned earlier, when you live in a cooperative dwelling you will pay a monthly fee. This money helps pay for maintenance and taxes. It also helps pay the corporation's mortgage payments on the property. If some residents fail to pay this fee for any length of time, the corporation might be unable to make mortgage payments and, therefore, face the possibility of foreclosure. Because of this risk, check the financial stability of the cooperative corporation before you buy any stock.

Moving to a New Home

Sometimes a household moves from one house to another within the same neighborhood or community. Many families expect such short moves as they end one stage of the life cycle and enter another. Changes in lifestyle, occupation, socioeconomic status, or other life situations—such as buying a home—also cause people to move.

A long-distance move is a bigger job and has a greater emotional impact than a move across town. Relocating family and possessions is likely to cause stress. You can reduce the amount of stress by taking the right steps before moving day.

No matter how far you are moving, it is a good idea to get rid of household items you no longer need or want.

People often find they have paid to move items that they discard shortly after the move. You may consider selling, and then later replacing, heavy items such as old refrigerators that add to moving costs. If you decide to sell and replace goods, consider renting them at your new home. This gives you a chance to look around for the best deals.

Another way to eliminate the amount of belongings you move is to have a yard or garage sale. You can also give unwanted items to charity or recycle them. Items you give to charity are good for an income tax deduction if you get a receipt.

Moving expenses may also qualify as an income tax deduction. If you move because of a job change or transfer and live at least 50 miles farther from work, you may qualify. You must be working full time and make the move within one year of starting the new job.

Use the moving expense checklist in 5-24 to be sure you have all the records

---

5-24

A moving-expense checklist helps when you move. Some items may be tax deductible.

Moving Expense Checklist

Keep the following records pertaining to your move in your possession at all times. Put them in a place you can easily access.

House-Hunting Trip Receipts
- Transportation costs (air, bus, train, automobile)
- Meals
- Lodging

Residence Replacement Records
- Advertising expense
- Real estate commissions
- Attorney fees
- Appraisal fees
- Mortgage expenses (title fees, points, escrow fees)
- State transfer taxes
- Lease settlement costs

Mover's Documents
- Bill of lading
- Inventory
- Packing and unpacking certificates
- Weight certificates

Receipts for Temporary Living Quarters
- Lodging
- Meals

you need to claim a tax deduction. Be sure you have the correct forms from the Internal Revenue Service (IRS) to claim your deductions.

Once you decide to move, you need to decide how to do it. You have two alternatives: moving yourself or hiring a moving company.

Moving Yourself

About two-thirds of all moves are do-it-yourself efforts. If you do not own a truck or trailer, you can rent one and move yourself. There are many good reasons for tackling the job on your own. First, the cost is about one-third of what a professional mover charges. Second, you can move on your own schedule. Third, you and your goods arrive at the same time.

In comparison, realize what you save in money will cost you in time and energy. You will do all the packing, loading, unloading, and unpacking yourself. Family and friends can help if the move is only a short distance. They can also help with packing and loading for a long move.

Before you begin the moving process, plan ahead. Make arrangements with a rental firm early to assure the equipment you need is available when you need it. Also, before you reserve a truck or trailer, estimate the amount of items you will be moving. This will help you choose the correct-size truck or trailer. The rental firm can help you with this. You can also rent supplies, such as furniture pads and dollies, or purchase moving cartons and other materials.

As you rent moving equipment, check on liability and damage insurance for it. Find out the cost of insuring your belongings. Sometimes your home owner's or renter's policy covers your goods. If not, you may buy supplemental insurance to cover them. Get a written estimate from the insurance company and ask if there will be additional charges.

You can begin packing early. As you pack, take an inventory of your household items. An inventory will help you check the arrival of your belongings at your new house. It will also provide information you may need to collect insurance if you lose or damage any of your goods, 5-25. If this seems like too much to do, consider the money you will save by moving yourself.

Hiring a Moving Company

If you choose to hire a moving company, you will also need to plan ahead for the move. Thousands of moving companies exist in the United States. To decide which one to hire, you can ask your friends, neighbors, or business associates who have moved

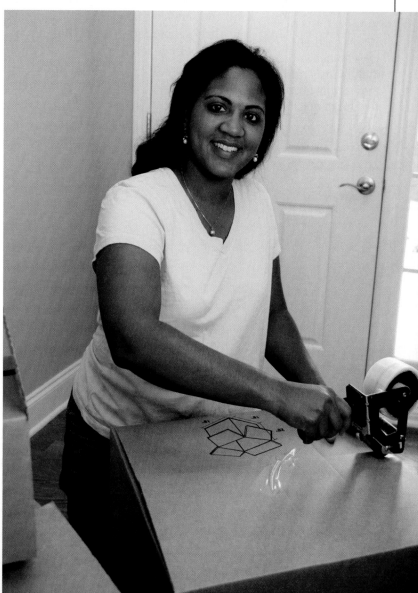

5-25
Many people choose to pack their unbreakable items and find it worth the expense to hire professionals to pack their breakable household items.

recently about a dependable carrier. If you are moving for a job, the relocation manager of your company and a reliable real estate agent can also be valuable resources. Choose only licensed movers and obtain at least three written estimates to compare.

After choosing a moving company, you need to ask about insurance. Be sure to read the fine print and ask about additional costs. Also, ask about discounted moves, which offer a lower cost for moving during the off-peak season. Most people move between May 15 and September 30—the peak season. If you move during an off-peak season, be sure the cost is the only item that changes.

The next step is deciding how much, if any, of the packing and unpacking you will do. The cost of the packing boxes and the service of packing and unpacking are not included in the actual moving expense. However, the extra cost can be worth it. Packing takes time and it can be hard work. Also, if you pack items

yourself and damage occurs during the move, it will be harder to file a claim with the moving company. It is a good idea to photograph expensive pieces to prove their condition and value.

When you are moving with children, you need to make special considerations. Moving may be traumatic for them. It is helpful to involve children in the move as much as possible, 5-26. Tell them about the move early and let them decide what to pack. Give them a floor plan of their new bedrooms so they can have fun deciding where to put their furniture.

It is best to move when it is most convenient for all family members. For instance, children usually do not like to change schools, especially during the school year. When the children arrive at their new schools, make the change as easy as possible by having their records already there.

When the moving van arrives at the new house, be sure the dwelling is ready for occupancy. Clean or paint ahead of time since both are difficult to do in a house filled with moving cartons. Decide how you want your furniture arranged and supervise its placement. Be sure items that were taken apart are reassembled.

As your belongings are unloaded from the van, check for damaged or missing items. List any of these items on the driver's copy and your copy of the **bill of lading**, which is a receipt listing the goods shipped.

If you file a claim for damaged or missing items, first list the lost items. Then make a list of damaged items and estimate the cost to repair them. Interstate movers are required by law to acknowledge and respond to your claim.

Moving can be difficult. Therefore, it is important to weigh the advantages and disadvantages of the different ways to move. This will help you decide whether to move yourself or hire a moving company.

5-26
When children take an active part in the family move, they adjust better and more quickly.

CAREER FOCUS

Real Estate Appraiser

Can you imagine yourself as a real estate appraiser? If you share some of the following interests you may want to consider a career as a real estate appraiser.

Interests/Skills: Do you have a good eye and mind for detail? Do you enjoy doing computer research and comparing prices of one item to another? Are you interested in laws, regulations and standards? Appraisers and assessors must possess good analytical skills, mathematical skills, and the ability to pay attention to detail. They must also work well with people and alone. Since they will work with the public, politeness is a must, along with the ability to listen and thoroughly answer any questions about their work.

Career Snapshot: Real estate appraisers estimate the value of property for a variety of purposes. They often specialize in appraising certain types of real estate such as residential buildings or commercial properties. However, they may also estimate the value of any type of real estate, ranging from farmland to a major shopping center.

Education/Training: The requirements to become a fully qualified appraiser are complex and vary by state and, sometimes, by the value or type of property. Currently, no formal degree requirements exist to become an appraiser. However, starting in 2008 all appraisers who need a license will be required to have a bachelor's degree or the equivalent in credit hours. Most practicing appraisers have at least a bachelor's degree, sometimes in a related field such as economics, finance, or real estate. Obtaining on-the-job training is also an essential part of becoming a fully qualified appraiser and is required for obtaining a license or certification. In the past, many appraisers obtained experience working in financial institutions or real estate offices. However, the current trend is for candidates to get their initial experience in the office of an independent fee appraiser.

Licensing/Examinations: Federal law requires that any appraiser involved in a federally related transaction with a loan amount of $250,000 or more must have a state-issued license or certification. Licensing requirements vary by state, but they typically include specific training requirements, a period of work as a trainee, and passing one or more examinations. Many states require any practicing appraiser to obtain a license or certification, regardless of transaction value.

Professional Associations: American Society of Appraisers (ASA) (www.appraisers.org), National Association of Independent Fee Appraisers (NAIFA) (www.naifa.com), National Association of Real Estate Appraisers (NAREA) (www.narea-assoc.org), and Appraisal Institute (AI) (www.appraisalinstitute.org).

Job Outlook: Employment of appraisers and assessors of real estate is expected to grow faster than average for all occupations. Job opportunities should be favorable for those who meet licensing qualifications and have several years of experience.

Sources: Occupational Information Network (O*NET) (www.online.onetcenter.org); Occupational Outlook Handbook of the Bureau of Labor Statistics (www.bls.gov)

Summary

When acquiring a house there are various processes and costs involved. You must determine how much you will spend and how you will finance your house.

You may decide to rent your housing. Any type of dwelling can be rented, but the most common types are multifamily dwellings. Carefully inspect the dwelling you choose before you sign a lease. It is also important to know about assigning or subletting, breach of contract, and eviction.

If you decide to buy, it is important to know how much you can spend. There are several methods to help you determine this. Before shopping for a home, it is wise to evaluate different types of mortgage loans and lenders. Obtaining preapproval for a mortgage before you shop helps you identify what you can spend and helps show sellers you are serious about buying. It also makes the home buying process move more swiftly. Then decide which you want to do: buy a new house already built, buy a pre-owned house, or build a new house.

Once you have decided what type of house you want, shop for one that is right for you. You may use a real estate agent or shop on your own. After you find the house, follow the procedure for purchasing a house. This includes making an offer; securing financing; acquiring home owner's insurance; having a home inspection, survey, appraisal, and title search; and paying the closing costs. If you should need to refinance your house, you will need to go through many of the same steps again.

Instead of buying a single-family dwelling, you may choose to buy a condominium unit or shares in a cooperative. When choosing a condominium unit, carefully read the declaration of ownership and understand what maintenance fees are required. When choosing a cooperative unit, understand the unique legal and financial aspects of the corporation and make sure it is financially stable.

After choosing a place to live or buying a home, you must decide how to move to it. The move may be short or cross-country. You can move your own belongings or hire a moving company. Both options have advantages and disadvantages. After you make your decision, there are certain steps you need to take to ensure a smooth move.

Review the Facts

1. List four advantages of renting a house.
2. How do needs and wants impact housing costs?
3. Name eight items a written lease should include.
4. Contrast assigning and subletting an apartment.
5. What happens if a renter fails to pay the rent?
6. What is a general way to determine the cost of a house that a person or family can afford?
7. As the new owner of a mortgaged house, which of the following items should you consider when figuring your monthly housing costs: (A) income tax; (B) mortgage loan payments; (C) house insurance payments; (D) heating bill; (E) car payments; (F) real estate taxes; (G) maintenance allowance
8. Compare and contrast the following types of mortgages: conventional, fixed-rate, and adjustable rate.
9. Name five items included in an agreement of sale.

10. What information will an appraiser give you?

11. Why should the buyer of a house purchase title insurance?

12. How are the terms title and deed related?

13. How do condominium and cooperative ownership differ?

14. What are the advantages of moving yourself versus hiring a professional mover?

Think Critically

15. **Predict outcomes.** Suppose someone broke into your apartment and stole your computer and an expensive personal media player you borrowed from a friend. Predict the costs you could recover from the theft. What might you recover without insurance?

16. **Draw conclusions.** When home inspectors evaluate a home that is about to be purchased, perhaps there are problems in the foundation, heating system, or windows. Draw conclusions about whether or not you think the new owner should fix the items. Give evidence to support your conclusions.

17. **Analyze pros and cons.** Ask the manager of a condominium complex for a copy of the declaration of ownership for the units. Examine it closely. Analyze the pros and cons of condominium ownership. Summarize your findings for the class.

Community Links

18. **Analyze a lease.** Visit an apartment building and ask the landlord for a copy of the lease used. Does it include all the important points listed in this chapter? Does it include any additional restrictions?

19. **Assess mortgage costs.** Find a classified ad in your local newspaper offering a house for sale. Investigate the monthly cost of buying it using three different types of loans. Compare and contrast the loans for the interest rate, monthly payment, duration of the loan, and any conditions or restrictions. Share your findings with the class.

20. **Determine moving risk.** When moving from one place to another, one way to save money is to have friends help you move. Would you accept the risk of possible damage to furniture or the new home due to accidents caused by your friends? What could you do to help prevent any damage?

21. **Investigate endorsements.** Use Internet or print resources to investigate various endorsements for home owner's insurance policies. Find out what types of endorsements are available. What are the costs? Compare rates for several different insurance companies.

Technology Applications

22. **Real estate research.** Use the Internet to check out houses available by various real estate companies. Select a geographic area, number of bedrooms, and a price range on a home-finder Web site. How many choices did you find? What types of information can be learned about an individual house?

23. **Mortgage calculations.** Find a mortgage calculator on the Internet and enter a house purchase price, down payment amount, and interest rate. Then enter a higher interest rate and identify the monthly payment cost. How does the monthly payment change when the interest rate increases? Is it better to have a low interest rate or a high interest rate in terms of being able to pay for the home?

24. **Research moving companies.** Search the Internet to locate at least two moving companies that serve the local area. What services do they provide? How are the costs calculated? Make a chart showing the services provided and the costs per company. Enter the data into a table created with a word processing program to share with your class. Which company would you choose and why?

Academic Connections

25. **Writing.** Along with Internet resources and class information, use a computer with word-processing software to develop a chart showing the advantages and disadvantages of buying each of the following types of housing:

    A. pre-owned house

    B. newly built house ready for occupancy

    C. new house yet to be custom-built

26. **Math.** Determine the *housing-to-income ratio* and the *debt-to-income ratio* for the following situation. Suppose you and a sibling decide to buy a house. Your combined monthly gross income is $5,500. The proposed monthly mortgage payment for the house you like is $695. Other monthly related housing costs are $500. You pay $200 per month in credit card debt and your sibling's college loan payment is $150.00 per month. Will you and your sibling be able to borrow money for a mortgage based on your housing-to-income and debt-to-income ratios? What other factor(s) may determine your eligibility for a mortgage?

27. **Math.** Suppose you want to purchase a house that costs $92,000. Your mortgage lender requires a 20 (.20) percent down payment. How much money will you need to have for the down payment? Use the following formula:

    Percent down payment × House price = Down payment

Design Practice

28. **Create a virtual home tour.** Presume your design firm has been hired to create a Web design for a local real estate company's virtual home tours. As part of the analysis process for your design plan, you and your team take a virtual tour on a competing realtor's Web site. Is the tour realistic—prompting interested buyers to contact the company? With your team mates, put together a Web site plan for virtual home tours that is attractive and engaging. Share your plan with the class.

29. **Portfolio.** Develop a plan for selecting and renting an apartment. Include guidelines for conducting a search, reviewing your housing options, reviewing your housing rights and responsibilities, and examining required contracts. Save a copy of your plan in your class portfolio.

Take the Lead in Financing Your Future

Although it may be a while before you are ready to rent or buy your own place, it is not too soon to start preparing financially. Through the FCCLA *Financial Fitness* peer education program, plan and carry out a project related to the *Financing Your Future* unit. What do you need to know to become a wise financial manager and a savvy consumer? How can this help you when it is time to rent or buy a place of your own?

Use the FCCLA *Planning Process* and other related documentation to develop, carry out, and evaluate your innovative project. See your adviser for information as needed. Check out the application requirements to receive FCCLA national recognition for outstanding *Financial Fitness* projects.

PART 3

From the Ground Up

CHAPTER 6

The Evolution of Exteriors

Terms to Learn

traditional
folk
classic
Early English
half-timbered
Tidewater South
New England
Cape Cod
symmetrical
dormer
Saltbox
Garrison
Spanish
stucco
asymmetrical
Scandinavian
log cabin
gable roof
German
pent roof
Dutch Colonial
gambrel roof
French Normandy
French Plantation
French Manor
Mansard roof
French Provincial
Georgian
hip roof
Federal
Adam style
Early Classical Revival
Greek Revival
Southern Colonial
Victorian
Modern style
Prairie style

Arts and Crafts
bungalow
International style
ranch
Contemporary style
earth-sheltered

Chapter Objectives

After studying this chapter, you will be able to

- summarize the development of exterior architectural styles throughout history, including Traditional (both folk and classic), Modern, and Contemporary house styles.

- compare and contrast historical architectural and housing styles.

- summarize the value of historical preservation.

Reading with Purpose

As you read this chapter, write a letter to yourself. Imagine that you will receive this letter in a few years when you are working at your future job as an interior designer. What key chapter points will be important to remember from this chapter? In the letter, list these points.

The evolution of housing exteriors is usually grouped into a number of styles and time periods. The greatest influences on these styles include geographical location and the historical and economic events during the era in which they were built.

To better understand period housing styles, it is important to note that while each time period and style has specific characteristics some overlapping does exist. Because of this, dates for periods and styles are approximate. For example, in different regions of the country certain design styles could exist at the same time. In addition, not all designs in a certain style or specific era would be identical. The individual architects and builders brought their own personal creativity to their designs. The architectural history of housing was and still is an ongoing process.

Housing in North America began with the Native Americans. They developed a wide variety of housing styles prior to the arrival of foreign explorers and settlers. The styles included hogans, pueblos, teepees, wigwams, pole-and-thatch structures, and others. When immigrant settlers arrived in North America, they brought with them the styles that existed in their homelands. Over time, these styles evolved into new types of housing that have become known as traditional styles.

Traditional Houses

Traditional houses reflect the experiences and traditions of past eras. These designs have adapted and changed over time to meet the needs of their inhabitants. Many house designs in use today were actually created in previous time eras of North American history. Each style has distinct characteristics and features that set it apart from the others.

The two categories of Traditional style design are folk and classic. **Folk** style originates from the common experiences of a group of people, such as common values and concerns. **Classic** style refers to the use of formal architectural elements that have been recognized over time for their enduring design excellence. Various renditions of folk and classic styles appear in many periods of architectural history.

Traditional Folk Houses

The styles of traditional folk houses varied from region to region. In some cold areas such as the Midwest, houses had to withstand heavy snowfalls. In warm climates such as the Southeast, orientation to the cooling breeze was important. In windy locations such as the coastal Northeast, housing needed to withstand heavy gusts.

Besides the effects of climate and geographical location, the style of traditional folk housing was based on the ethnic experiences and lifestyles of the inhabitants. These housing styles were also shaped by the natural resources available to construct them. Styles described as Native American, Early English, Spanish, Scandinavian, German, Dutch, and French are types of traditional folk houses.

Native American

The many different styles of Native-American housing have influenced today's housing. Early settlers sometimes copied the eight-sided mud and log hogans of the Navajo or the wood frame structures of the Seminole. See Chapter 2 to review the widely varied styles of Native-American housing.

The Pueblo in New Mexico still live in apartment-type adobe dwellings, 6-1. The basic design of these adobe dwellings repeats in housing throughout the country, especially the Southwest. Characteristics of Pueblo housing include boxlike construction, flat roofs, and projecting roof beams.

Early English

An architectural style built by English settlers in North America beginning in the early 1600s is **Early English**. Several distinct housing types evolved from this traditional folk architecture. These types include Tidewater South and the New England styles known as Cape Cod, Saltbox, and Garrison.

The first successful English settlement in North America was established in 1607 in Jamestown, Virginia. Archaeologists think these early English settlers used the *mud-and-stud method* of building. Early records trace this technique back to Lincolnshire County along the east coast of England. In this building technique, the frame of the house was constructed from upright forked logs with cross beams. The walls were filled with mud and clay and the roof was thatched with leaves, tree bark, or bundles of reeds and straw. This technique was later refined and referred to as half-timbered construction. In **half-timbered** houses, the wood frame of the house actually formed part of the outside wall, 6-2. Brick or plaster was used to fill the spaces between the beams.

Tidewater South. Settlements continued to grow in the low-lying coastal lands called Tidewater areas. An architectural style built by early English settlers in the southern coastal regions of what is now the United States is **Tidewater South**, 6-3. The construction style of these homes was simple: a one-room wooden building with a wood or stone chimney at one end. As families grew, house additions were built. The first addition was another room, often built as large as the first. It was added next to the wall with the chimney. Many rural farmhouses throughout the South had similar plans. Covered porches were also added to these simple plans to increase the amount of living area and to provide shelter from the hot sun.

6-1
The Pueblo live in these adobe dwellings.

New England. Plymouth, Massachusetts was the second successful English settlement in 1620. By 1640, a number of small English settlements were established along the eastern area of North America. This region of North America is known as **New England** and now includes the states of Maine, New Hampshire, Vermont, Massachusetts, Connecticut, and Rhode Island.

Early seventeenth century English settlers in northern New England commonly built two-story houses. They were constructed of heavy timber frames. In timber framing—or post-and-beam construction—large pieces of wood are joined together with woodworking joints (mortise-and-tenon joints), or with wooden pegs, braces, or trusses.

6-2
This thatch-roof house in the re-created 1610–1614 colonial fort at Jamestown Settlement History Museum in Williamsburg, VA, is an example of half-timbered construction.

Photo Courtesy of the Jamestown-Yorktown Foundation

6-3
The Tidewater South architectural style was commonly built by English settlers along the southern coastal regions of the United States.

Metal nails were used sparingly because of their expense.

Timber frame construction was the construction method for all frame houses in seventeenth and eighteenth century America because of the abundance of wood. The house exteriors were covered with shingles, unpainted clapboards, or other wooden siding. A *clapboard* is a board that has one edge thicker than the other and is typically used for exterior horizontal siding. When applied, the board above laps over the thinner edge of the one below.

This application is also know as bevel siding or lap siding.

The Cape Cod style grew out of variations on the one-story house design. As a family grew, rooms were added to the basic plan.

- **Cape Cod**. The **Cape Cod** is a small, symmetrical, one or one-and-one-half story house with a steep gable roof and side gables. A design is **symmetrical** when objects on both sides of a center point are identical, 6-4A. The Cape Cod style has a central entrance and a central chimney with several fireplaces. The eave (lower edge) line of the roof overhangs the exterior wall just above the first floor windows. The windows are multi-paned and usually have shutters. Originally, the siding was made of shingles or unpainted clapboards.

The loft area of the Cape Cod is usually expanded and made into finished bedrooms. Openings are then cut in the roof for dormers. **Dormers** are structures with windows that project through a sloping roof in the second story. They add light, space, and ventilation to the second story.

GREEN CHOICES

Reusing Old Buildings

Old buildings often outlive their original purposes. A way of reusing an old building is called "adaptive reuse." This process adapts old buildings for new uses. An example of adaptive reuse is converting an old post office to a retail center with many shops.

When the building has historic features, the adaptive reuse retains these features through historic preservation techniques. Adaptive reuse has the following advantages:

- **Environmental sustainability.** Historic preservation is really "recycling" on a grand scale and is an effective tool for protecting environmental resources.

- **Economic sustainability.** Reusing old buildings supports the economy of the local community.

- **Social sustainability.** Historic preservation protects and celebrates the social and cultural resources that will enrich communities and their citizen's lives for generations to come.

Information Courtesy of the National Trust for Historic Preservation www.PreservationNation.org

A—Cape Cod

B—Saltbox

C—Garrison

6-4
(A) The Cape Cod is a one-and-a-half-story house with a gable roof and central entrance. (B) A saltbox house has narrow wood siding and windows without shutters. (C) This Garrison style house, which was originally owned by Paul Revere, features an overhanging second story.

(C) Massachusetts Office of Travel & Tourism

- **Saltbox**. Another type home built by the English settlers in the New England area was the Saltbox house. The **Saltbox** is a variation of the Cape Cod, 6-4B. The earliest saltbox houses were created when a lean-to addition was built on the rear of the house. The Saltbox house takes its name from the shape of the wooden box in which salt was kept at that time.

In saltbox construction, the house has two or two-and-one-half stories in the front but just one story in the back. It is characterized by a long, steep-pitched gable roof that slopes down from the front to the back. Other typical features are large windows with small panes of glass, and a large central chimney.

- **Garrison**. A later design built by the English settlers in New England was the **Garrison** house, which is named after early garrisons, or forts. Like the old forts, Garrisons have an overhanging second story, 6-4C. The overhang allows extra space on the second floor without widening the foundation. It also has a supporting effect, which prevents the second-story floor from sagging in the middle. This supporting effect is created when beams extending out from the first floor support the second floor. The farther the beams extend out, the greater is the support in the center.

The overhang is always on the front of the house and sometimes extends to the sides and rear. Carved drops or pendants below the overhang provide ornamentation. Other characteristics of the Garrison house are symmetrical design, a steep gable roof, and windows that have small panes of glass. Originally, the siding was made of wood shingles or unpainted clapboards.

Spanish

The first Europeans to establish colonies in North America were Spaniards. These colonies were mostly in Florida and the Southwest beginning in the 1500s. Florida's Spanish-colonial city of St. Augustine was begun in 1565, making it the oldest continuing permanent European settlement. Between 1565 and 1821, Florida was mostly under Spanish control.

A large portion of what is now the southwestern United States was under Spanish, then Mexican, control from the seventeenth to the mid-nineteenth century. Spanish Texas gained its independence from Mexico in 1836.

The **Spanish** style developed in these areas where the climate was warm and dry. Early Spanish style was characterized by one-story structures with flat or low-pitched red tile roofs. The houses were masonry construction of adobe brick or stone covered in stucco. **Stucco** is a type of plaster applied to the exterior walls of a house. The interior was usually simple with earthen floors, beamed ceilings, and whitewashed plaster walls.

The overall design of Spanish-style housing is **asymmetrical**. This means that one side of the center point is different from the other. During the seventeenth century, Spanish settlers in California and parts of the southwest built more elaborate styles. A Spanish-style house is pictured in 6-5. Specific features include courtyards, enclosed patios, wrought iron exterior decor, and arched windows and doors. This style of housing is still widely used today in the Southwest.

Scandinavian

Immigrants from Sweden, Finland, Norway, and Denmark were known as **Scandinavians**. Of this group of immigrants, the Swedish settlers are credited with introducing the log cabin to North

6-5

This house includes many of the traits of the traditional Spanish style house.

America in the early 1700s. The **log cabin** originally was a one-room, rectangular house about 10 feet wide and 12 to 20 feet long.

Typical log cabins were built on a stone or rock foundation to keep the logs above the ground. The logs were squared off and notches were cut on the top and bottom of each end. The logs were then stacked with the notched ends fitted together in the corners. *Chinking*—a filling of sticks and wood chips—was used to fill the gaps between the logs and was then covered with a layer of mud to fill the remaining spaces. A door opening and at least one window were then cut into the house. The fireplace was built of stone, and the floor was dirt or gravel that had been raked smooth.

The log cabin had a gable roof. A **gable roof** comes to a high point in the center and slopes on both sides, 6-6. A gable is a triangle formed by a sloping roof.

Log cabins were a popular style for the North American midlands and frontier, where timber was a readily available resource as a building material. They are still popular today in many areas as either a primary residence or as a second home used for vacations. Many companies specializing in manufactured log cabins offer a wide range of floor plans and price ranges. They meet the need that many home owners have for a rustic style that depicts a simpler lifestyle.

German

The majority of early **German** settlers, who traveled from the region called Germany today, arrived in North America in the late seventeenth century. They primarily settled in what is now southeastern Pennsylvania. They built large, durable homes of wood and fieldstone for warmth. The entry led to the kitchen on the first floor. The fireplace was in the center of the first floor with

a family room for entertaining located on the opposite side of the fireplace. If the home was large enough, there would be a number of small bedrooms behind the family room. The houses were constructed with gable roofs. Some also had small roof ledges between the first and second floors called **pent roofs**, 6-7.

Dutch

Dutch settlers founded settlements in North America as early as 1614 in what is now known as Albany, New York. A later settlement began in 1626 in New Amsterdam, which became New York City. The first Dutch houses were

6-6
The original log cabins looked very similar to this one.

6-7
Germans who settled in Pennsylvania built houses similar to this. Many had a pent roof—a small ledge between the first and second floor.

Photography Courtesy of Bradley S. DeForest of the Skippack Historical Society

one-story structures of brick in urban areas, or stone in rural areas. One of the most important characteristics was the front door, which was divided in half horizontally. This style became known as the *Dutch door*. However, it was the later Dutch design that left the most long-lasting mark on architecture.

The later style is known today as Dutch Colonial. **Dutch Colonial** is a housing style with a gambrel roof. A **gambrel roof** is a roof with a lower steeper slope and an upper less-steep slope on both of its sides. Sometimes the lower portion extends over an open porch, which is known as the *Dutch kick*. Houses of this style were often built of fieldstone or brick, and in some cases wood. Other characteristics of the Dutch Colonial are dormers, a central entrance, an off-center chimney, and windows with small panes, 6-8.

Dutch Colonial homes were most commonly built in northern states such as New York and Delaware. The Dutch did not bring this style from their homeland, but created it after settling in North America.

French

During the colonial period, French settlements formed in the 1700s along the St. Lawrence River, Great Lakes, and Mississippi River. Early French homes were built in the **French Normandy** style, which was brought to North America by the Huguenots. These homes were one-story structures with many narrow door and window openings. The roofs were steeply pitched and either hipped or side-gabled. The walls were stucco, which was usually applied over a half-timbered frame. Porches were added in settlements located in warmer regions. Also, houses in the South were constructed on posts one story above ground. This provided better air circulation in the humid environment and protected the house from floods. The Southern adaptation of this design is known as the **French Plantation** house.

A distinctive style evolved in New Orleans known as the *Louisiana French* style. The most outstanding characteristics of this style include balconies with elaborate ironwork railings and white stucco walls. The structures were built on raised brick or stone basements to protect them from flooding.

Even after Louisiana became the eighteenth state in the Union in 1812, the French influence continued to impact American architecture in many ways. One example, the **French Manor**, is a symmetrically styled home with wings on each side and a Mansard roof on the main part of the house, 6-9. A **Mansard roof** is a variation of the gambrel roof. Its designer was a French architect named Francois Mansard. When used on detached single-family dwellings, the roof continues all around the house. Dormers often project from the steeply pitched part of the roof. When used on commercial buildings, the Mansard roof may be used only on one or two sides.

French influence is also seen in the house style called **French Provincial**. This style originated in New Orleans and became popular all over the country. It has a delicate, dignified appearance and is usually symmetrical. The windows are a dominant part of the design. The tops of the windows break into the eave line. A French-Provincial house can be as tall as two-and-a-half stories.

6-8
This home has features that are typically original to Dutch Colonial homes such as a *gambrel* roof that flares at the bottom.

Classic Traditional Houses

As the early settlements flourished and colonies and states were formed, prosperity brought change and improvement to housing. The quality of building materials improved and the growth of trade brought new information to the settlers. Architects and house plans from Europe became available. Growing prosperity fostered interest in refined taste (cultivated and genteel) and classic style. Classic traditional homes include the following time periods and styles: Georgian, Federal, Greek Revival, Southern Colonial, and Victorian.

Georgian

The **Georgian** style (1690 to 1800) was adapted from English architecture. It is called Georgian because it was popular during the era when Kings George I, II, and III ruled England.

Georgian houses have simple exterior lines, dignified appearances, and symmetry. The centrally located front doors have windows with small panes of glass, and either gable or **hip roofs**—roofs with sloping ends and sides. A flat area with a *balustrade*, or railing sometimes tops hip roofs. This area is called a captain's or widow's walk. Georgian houses usually have a tall chimney at each end of the roof, and most have some ornamentation under the eaves. A distinctive type of eave ornamentation, known as *dentil molding*, is still popular today. As a trim board with square, toothlike blocks, this ornamentation is sometimes mislabeled as "dental" molding, 6-10.

As the Georgian style developed, it became more elaborate. Additional ornamentation was given to doors and windows. The front door was often highlighted with a decorative crown over the top and flattened columns, or *pilasters*, on each side. The style also changed according to the region in which it was built.

6-9
French Manor houses are noted for their stately appearance and *Mansard* roofs.

Wood was used in New England, and stone in the Mid-Atlantic region. In the South, brick was used and a wing was added to each side of the main house.

Federal

Following the American Revolution (1775 to 1783), interest grew in developing distinctly American styles and symbols. National pride was strong and Americans adopted a new style of architecture that reflected confidence in their newly won independence. The style was named in honor of the Federal form of government in the United States. Federal-style architecture became popular between 1780 and 1840. A house built in the **Federal** style has a boxlike shape, is symmetrical, and at least two stories

6-10
Georgian houses have simple, dignified lines with ornamentation—or dentil molding—often found under the eaves.

MATH MATTERS

Symmetry

Objects are often described as being *symmetrical* or *asymmetrical*. An object is symmetrical if a line drawn through it divides it into two matching halves. The dividing line is called the *line of symmetry*.

An object may have one or more lines of symmetry. For example, a rectangle has two lines of symmetry. A circle has an infinite number of lines of symmetry since any line drawn through the center creates a line of symmetry.

An object is asymmetrical if it has 0 lines of symmetry; no two halves match. Your hand is asymmetrical; you cannot draw a line that will result in two matching halves.

Symmetry creates balance. Architects and interior designers often incorporate symmetry in their work. For example, the exterior of a Georgian home exhibits symmetry. You can also achieve symmetry by placing matching chairs on both sides of an entryway.

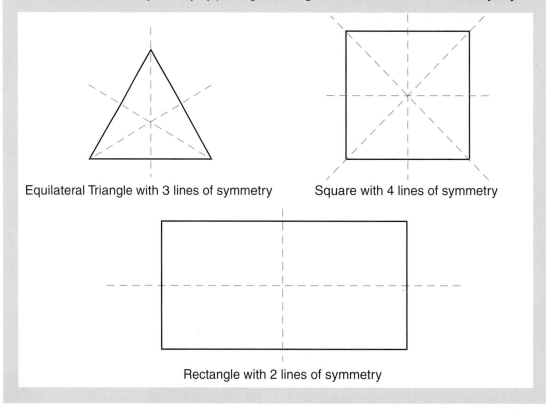

Equilateral Triangle with 3 lines of symmetry

Square with 4 lines of symmetry

Rectangle with 2 lines of symmetry

high. Sometimes a small portico was added to the main entrance. A *portico* is an open space covered with a roof that is supported by columns. Federal-style houses also had *pediments*, which are architectural rooflike decorations that are usually found over a portico, window, or door. The pediments can be segmental or triangular, 6-11. During the Federal period, two important architectural styles emerged, Adam style and Early Classical Revival.

Adam Style. The **Adam style** of architecture was named after the design work of two Scottish brothers, Robert and James Adam. These talented team-

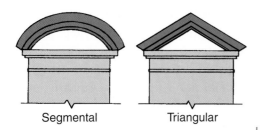

Segmental   Triangular

6-11

Pediments are used over doors and windows to add interest to a design.

mates were architects, interior designers, and furniture designers. Their work was based on plans for Italian houses and palaces. The Adam style continued the symmetry of the Georgian style. The types of graceful details that were added to the Georgian style architecture included swags, garland, urns, and other refined motifs. The main identifying feature of the Adam style is a fanlight over the front entrance, 6-12. Other characteristics include *Palladian windows* (windows with a large center section and two side sections, usually arched), circular or elliptical windows, recessed arches, and oval-shaped rooms. The most famous oval-shaped room in this style is the Oval Office of the President of the United States in Washington, D.C.

Early Classical Revival. During the Federal period, architecture evolved using the classical details of Greek and Italian design, which became known as **Early Classical Revival**. One of the best examples of this architectural style is *Monticello* (meaning "little mountain" in Italian), the home Thomas Jefferson designed and built for himself, 6-13. He began construction in 1769. Because of the influence of Roman architecture, the architectural style of his home is classified as *Roman Neoclassicism*. (*Neoclassicism* refers to an adaptation or revival of classical details.) Monticello has a large portico on its west front with columns

and a triangular pediment gable. Jefferson added the dome in 1800 after being influenced by the French architecture he saw while traveling in France. Jefferson was the founder of the University of Virginia in Charlottesville, Virginia and designed the original campus.

In addition to these major contributions, Jefferson was the principal author of the *Declaration of Independence* and third President of the United States. He was also an inventor and renowned political leader.

Greek Revival

Greek Revival (1825 to 1860) is another style of classic traditional design. It developed during a period that embraced, and carefully duplicated, the formal

6-12

The gabled pediment over the door is an example of the Federal influence.

6-13

Monticello—the home built by Thomas Jefferson—is found in Charlottesville, Virginia. It is an example of Early Classic Revival architecture.

Photography by the Thomas Jefferson Foundation/Monticello

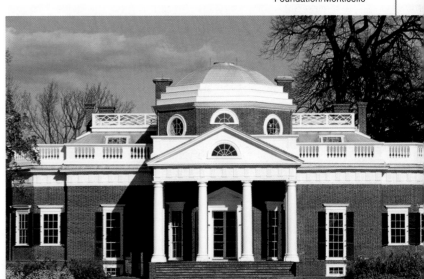

6-14
A Greek Revival house is characterized by a two-story portico supported by Greek columns with a large triangular pediment.

6-15
The design of this Southern Colonial evolved from the Greek Revival style.

Oak Alley Plantation, Louisiana Office of Tourism

elements found in ancient Greek architecture.

One characteristic of a house in the Greek Revival style is the two-story entry porch across the entire front of the structure. This structure is supported by Greek columns. Another key characteristic is a large triangular gable with a pediment, 6-14. These houses are also symmetrical with bold moldings and heavy *cornices* (molded and projecting horizontal members that crown architectural elements such as columns). Houses of this style are large and impressive. Some government buildings are designed in the Greek Revival style.

Southern Colonial

An offshoot of the Greek Revival style developed in the 1800s is the Southern Colonial. The **Southern Colonial** is a large, two- or three-story brick or frame house of symmetrical design, 6-15. Two-story columns extend across the entire front, covered by an extension of the roof. The roof style is hip or gable. Dormers, shutters, and a belvedere are often included. A *belvedere* is a small room on the roof of a house used as a lookout.

Victorian

Following the Civil War, growing industrialization greatly influenced architecture of the **Victorian** period—a time during the reign of Queen Victoria of England (1837 to 1901). House styles of the Victorian period, Figure 6-16, include the following:

- Italianate
- Gothic Revival (wood and masonry)
- American Second Empire (Mansard style)
- Stick style (also called Carpenter Gothic)
- Richardsonian Romanesque
- Eastlake Victorian
- Queen Anne

The main feature of all Victorian housing styles is the abundance of decorative trim. Other characteristics include high porches, roofs with steep gables, tall windows, high ceilings, dark stairways, long halls, and *turrets*, which are small towers. Not every Victorian house had every feature, but a strong combination of these elements came to be associated with the haunted-house stereotype in horror movies.

As the style developed, owners tried to outdo one another in the amount of decorative trim on their houses. Machine-made trim became a sign of prosperity and high style. Quantity

A—Italianate

B—Gothic Revival

C—Romanesque

D—Queen Anne

E—Gingerbread

6-16

These homes show some of the varied features of Victorian homes, including a turret (small tower) with much decorative trim.

became more important than quality. Scrolls and other decorative trim made from wood appeared under eaves and around windows and doors. This came to be known as *gingerbread*.

Modern Houses

The housing designs developed in the United States from the early 1900s into the 1980s are classified as the **Modern style**. Compared to the other housing styles discussed so far, these are quite new. Modern styles include the Prairie style, Arts and Crafts, Bungalow, International style, and the ranch and split-level. All are very popular and their use will likely continue in the future.

Prairie Style

Frank Lloyd Wright, who is one of the most noted architects of modern times, designed the Prairie style house. Wright is considered the greatest figure in modern American architecture. He designed a series of Prairie style houses between 1893 and 1920 that were very different from the traditional architecture built before this period, 6-17.

Prairie style houses have strong horizontal lines, low-pitched roofs, and overhanging eaves. Wright believed that a house should strongly relate to its environment, or setting. He liked to create the illusion that the house had actually evolved from the site. Prairie style homes were constructed of wood, stone, plaster, and materials found in nature. Earth-tone colors were used to emphasize the link between the man-built structure and its natural setting.

Previous architectural styles used walls to divide interior space into boxlike rooms. Wright reduced the number of walls to allow one room to flow into another, creating an open floor plan. In addition, this style allowed interior space to visually flow outdoors through porches, terraces, and windows. His flexible use of space greatly influenced the design work of European architects.

Arts and Crafts

Arts and Crafts style, or *Craftsman*, houses were built between 1905 and 1930. This popular style had its roots in the Arts and Crafts Movement of the 1880s. It celebrated use of natural materials worked by hand. Simple, nature-inspired colors and patterns were often used for interior fabrics and wall coverings. As a response to the over-abundance of machine-made gingerbread and other architectural excesses of the Victorian era, English designers such as John Ruskin and William Morris and many others began this movement. In the United States, two brothers from California—Charles Sumner Greene and Henry Mather Greene—designed houses during the Arts and Crafts Movement. They were widely praised for creating the "ultimate" bungalow—a larger, sprawling version of the earlier bungalow.

6-17
The many porches, terraces, and windows of this house designed by Frank Lloyd Wright are characteristic of the Prairie style.

Larry G. Morris

6-18
Bungalows typically have low-pitched roofs and covered porches as is characteristically found in this California bungalow.

The name "Craftsman" came from the title of a popular magazine published between 1901 and 1916 by Gustav Stickley—the famous furniture designer. At that time, a true *Craftsman*-style house was built strictly according to plans published by Stickley. Gradually, other magazines, mail-order houses, and builders began to publish plans with their own Craftsman-like details, modifying and often diluting the true Craftsman style.

Characteristics of a Craftsman-style house include a low-pitched roof, wide eaves with triangular brackets, exposed roof rafters, and wood, stone, or stucco siding. Craftsman houses feature stone porch supports with thick, square or round columns and exterior chimneys made of stone. The floor plans are open, with few hallways. These structures use beamed ceilings and many windows. Some windows feature stained glass or leaded-glass designs.

Bungalow

Built between 1905 and 1930, the bungalow style house expressed the simple and economical ideals of the Arts and Crafts Movement. A **bungalow** is one and a half stories with a low-pitched roof, horizontal shape, and a covered front porch. Sometimes the porch is enclosed. The bungalow is usually made of wood or brick. The shingled roof extends beyond the walls. Windows are set high to allow the placement of furniture beneath them. Most of the living spaces are on the ground floor. The floor plan features a living room at the center and connecting rooms without hallways. The design of the floor plan is very efficient with such features as built-in cabinets, shelves, and seats. The *California Bungalow* is similar in design, but larger, 6-18.

International Style

The most dramatic architectural style of the Modern movement is the **International style**. It is a style of architecture and furniture design that began in the 1900s, influenced strongly by Bauhaus. Bauhaus was the German state school of design that merged art and technology. It focused on emphasizing the simplicity of design and eliminating unnecessary elements.

International style is a blend of ideas from four leading architects of the early twentieth century:

LINK TO SOCIAL STUDIES & CULTURE

Asian Origins of American Bungalows

Home designers often blend elements of different cultures in their work. The history of the bungalow illustrates how a home, considered by many as the essence of American design, reflects influences from other parts of the world. Bungalow-style homes line the streets of American cities from Los Angeles to Chicago. Although there are regional variations in style, a bungalow is generally a one- or one-and-a-half-story home with a low-pitched roof.

The bungalow originated in a tropical region that is now eastern India and Bangladesh. These early bungalows were thatched-roof huts suited to the climate. They were designed to minimize heat buildup and take advantage of cooling breezes. By the early 1800s, the British controlled India. When British soldiers and merchants settled in the area, they lived in single-family homes that incorporated elements of the Indian huts. The huts, called "bangla" or "banggolo," spread across India and then to the U.S. and Europe.

In the early 1900s, California architects Charles and Henry Greene popularized the bungalow. The Greene brothers, leaders in the Arts and Crafts movement, added Japanese features to their bungalows. For example, interior and exterior spaces were designed to flow into one another. This created an open and airy feel. One of the Greene brothers' masterpieces, the David B. Gamble House, completed in 1909 in Pasadena, California, reflects such Japanese influences.

6-19
This home is an example of the International style of architecture.

American Plywood Association

- Frank Lloyd Wright, American architect
- Walter Gropius, a German architect and founder of the Bauhaus School
- Ludwig Mies van der Rohe, another famous German architect and director of the Bauhaus School
- Le Corbusier, a famous French architect

Geometric shapes and large expanses of glass windows were the foremost features of U.S. houses built in the International style. Emerging technology fostered the use of new building materials and opened new ways of thinking about space, form, and beauty. With this form of construction, flat rooftops were possible and rooftop gardens became commonplace. Many of these houses were constructed of reinforced white concrete. The exteriors of the houses had little or no ornamentation, 6-19.

Ranch

A **ranch** house is a one-story structure that may have a basement. It has a low-pitched roof with a wide overhang. Large windows and sliding glass doors that open onto a patio are common, 6-21. The use of building materials and energy-saving features vary according to each region. For instance, light-colored siding and paint are used to reflect the heat in warm climates. Brick is another common exterior siding choice.

The ranch style began in the West. The informal lifestyle, large plots of land, and generally warm climate made the ranch style ideal for the region. Ranch style homes have since become popular throughout the country.

Ranch houses vary considerably in size. Small ranch houses may be relatively inexpensive to build, while larger sizes can be expensive. This is due to the large foundations and costly roof areas. Larger ranch style houses are less energy efficient than more compact house plans. One-story ranch houses are easy to maneuver through and maintain. Modified ranch structures are regaining popularity as older adults seek homes with all rooms on one level in an effort to eliminate climbing stairs. One-story ranch houses are also a good choice for incorporating universal design.

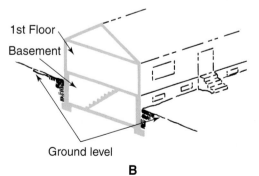

6-20
Ranch-style houses began in the West on farms and ranches where space was plentiful. Now they are found in many communities.

There are many variations of the ranch style. One is the *hillside ranch*. As its name implies, the house is built on a hill. It has a basement that is partly exposed, allowing use of natural light and the possibility of an exterior entry. This style of basement is also known as a "walkout" basement. Depending on the layout of the lot, the exposed part of the basement may be anything from a living area to a garage.

Another variation is the *raised ranch*, or split-entry, 6-21. It is like a ranch, except the upper half of the basement is aboveground. This allows light to enter the basement through windows. The

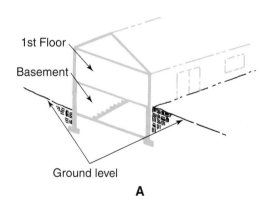

A

B

6-21
(A) Part of the basement of a hillside ranch is aboveground level. (B) Since the top part of the basement of a raised ranch is aboveground, the basement can be used as a living space.

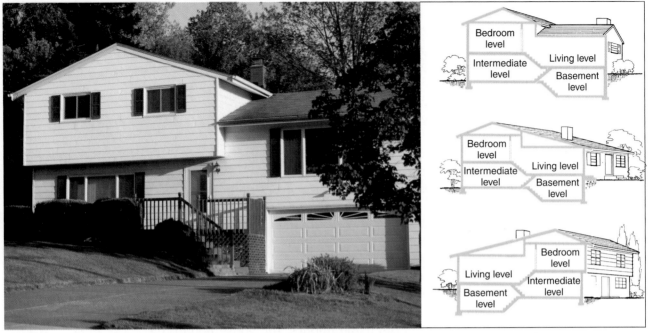

A

B

6-22
(A) Split-level houses are designed to adapt to sloped sites.
(B) Changing the arrangement of levels in a split-level house also changes its outside appearance.

basement living area can be very pleasant if it is well insulated and waterproof. A disadvantage is that stairs must be climbed to get anywhere in the house. This can be a problem for small children, people with disabilities, and older people.

Split-Level

A split-level house has either three or four levels. The levels can be arranged in many ways, 6-22. The split-level was developed for sloping lots, although it is occasionally built on flat lots.

One advantage of a split-level house is that traffic into the social, quiet, and service areas can be separated easily. Also, there are few stairs to climb to get from one level to another. However, getting from one level to another always requires climbing stairs. Again, the stairs may present a problem for individuals who are less physically agile.

Contemporary Houses

Contemporary styles are the current or latest house designs being constructed today. Many of the styles reflect design features from the traditional styles, both folk and classic. In some cases, current contemporary designs actually combine design features from several traditional architectural styles. However, there are some commonly recognized characteristics of contemporary houses. These include a wide variation in ceiling heights, very tall windows with large glass panes, open floor plans, and unusual use of shapes and spaces. The exterior architecture often reflects these elements through such features as rooflines and tall windows.

Some contemporary housing designs may seem surprising or even controversial when compared to the traditional styles of the past. Other contemporary houses may combine both traditional and modern elements in their plans, 6-23. The successful blending of unrelated styles and features requires careful planning to coordinate and harmonize their impact. Because of this, it is not as easy to classify and describe Contemporary-style houses as it is the purely traditional or purely modern styles. Contemporary designs may also vary widely from one to another in shape, material usage, and details. Many convey a custom or distinctive one-of-a-kind design. The exterior may be brick, siding, stucco, stone, concrete, or a combination of these materials.

Roof styles used in contemporary houses can also vary widely. While most of these styles are used in traditional houses, they can also be used in unique ways for contemporary housing, 6-24.

Although contemporary houses do not easily fit into categories, there are two distinct types that do. They are solar houses and earth-sheltered houses.

Solar Houses

Solar energy is energy derived from the sun. Today, many house designs utilize solar energy. They can use either active solar heating systems or passive solar heating systems, 6-25A.

Houses with *active solar* heating systems use special equipment, such as panels installed in the roof of the build-

6-23
This contemporary house utilizes the classic features of a gambrel roof.

Photo Courtesy of JELD-WEN Windows

ing, to capture the sun's energy. Then fans and pumps move heated air or liquid from the panels to a storage area or wherever heat is needed.

Passive solar heating systems have no working parts. Instead, they include any design feature or construction material that makes maximum use of the sun for heating. A passive solar house might include large areas of windows on the home's southern side. Reinforced, concrete-pipe columns or dark-colored walls may absorb heat from the sun and gradually transfer it inside.

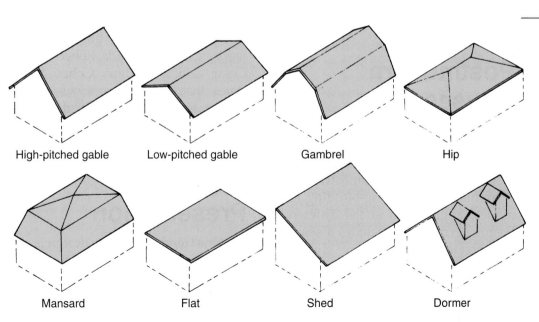

High-pitched gable   Low-pitched gable   Gambrel   Hip

Mansard   Flat   Shed   Dormer

6-24
Roof styles have a great effect on the exterior design of buildings.

A

B

6-25
(A) This house has both active and passive solar heating systems.
(B) This earth-sheltered house is partially covered with soil. The soil helps insulate it from the desert heat.

(B) Concept 2000, Hermann J. Fraunhoffer

Earth-Sheltered Houses

Another type of contemporary housing is earth-sheltered housing. **Earth-sheltered** houses are partially covered with soil. They are energy-efficient since the soil is a natural insulation and helps protect the house from weather elements and climate extremes, 6-25B. Some earth-sheltered houses are designed to be partly underground. Other dwellings are built into a hill or have soil compacted against the sides of the building.

A number of earth-sheltered houses are powered in part by solar energy. They may utilize active or passive solar heating systems or both.

Postmodern Houses

Postmodernism is a view about the architectural style of housing that began in the 1970s and continues today. This view often deviates from strict rules of architecture by using building techniques, angles, and styles differently. Postmodern design includes a sense of rebellion to the "less is more" simplicity of modern architecture. In addition, it includes a sense that anything in design is acceptable.

Some features of postmodernism include residential designs filled with absurd humor or wit. Some architectural critics say that if the "wit" feature is absent from postmodern design, it may just be modern or some other design style. Unexpected and playful elements are essential in the postmodern design, 6-26.

Postmodern homes are all unique. The diversity of design also includes some blending of previous styles including traditional, contemporary, and newly invented forms. Details may be exaggerated. Postmodern houses can be bizarre or shocking.

Architects leading this era of postmodern design include Robert Venturi, Cesar Pelli, and Frank Gehry. Venturi states that although previous architectural styles are easily identified by consistent characteristics, postmodernism is characterized by its diversity in features.

Historic Preservation

One trend in housing design is actually a step back in time. Nationally, there is a growing concern for restoring and preserving older buildings and houses.

6-26
This example of postmodern design can be seen at the *Massachusetts Institute of Technology* in Cambridge, Massachusetts.

Increasingly, various agencies, local governments, and private organizations are identifying properties that represent architectural value and importance. One such group is the *National Trust for Historical Preservation*. This group identifies such structures and grants them landmark status. Once they become landmarks, these buildings cannot undergo destruction or significant alteration. A person who helps restore these buildings is an *historical preservationist*.

Restoration work follows careful guidelines to insure that materials, colors, and designs are true to the original era of a building's construction. In this way, society preserves the best of its past for future generations to experience, 6-27.

6-27
As a designated national historic landmark, the preservation of *Beacon Hill* makes this neighborhood one of the most desirable neighborhoods in Boston.

CAREER FOCUS

Historic Preservationist

Can you imagine yourself as an historic preservationist? If you share some of the following talents, interests, and skills, you may consider exploring a career as an architect or interior designer who specializes in historic preservation.

Talents/Skills: Do you have a love of studying architectural styles in history? Are drawing and sketching a major part of your hobbies? Do you share the value of historical buildings with others and believe that older buildings should be given new life through *adaptive reuse*? Do you believe it is important for future generations to understand the evolution of such buildings? Skills necessary for this important career include excellent computer knowledge and ability. Exceptional research and organizational skills along with strong presentation and communication skills are necessary to work with others.

Career Snapshot: Historic preservationists usually have an architecture or interior design background. They choose to specialize in the adaptive reuse of old buildings and commonly work in an architectural or design preservation firm. Historic preservationists also work with local governments and community groups. They help identify buildings with historic significance and are often consulted on the true historic value of a structure. Historic preservationists need to be salespeople, too. It can be difficult to educate and convince others of a structure's importance to the community. The history and style of a building are most important, but the use of materials and applications must also have proven value. For example, paint colors must be authentic to the time period a building was constructed.

Rhonda Hull Interiors; Rhonda Hull, Allied ASID; ASID Historical Renovation Merit Award 2007; Harper House Hickory History Center. Photography by Bob Huffman, Hickory, North Carolina.

Education/Training: A five-year bachelor's degree is most often required. A master's degree or postgraduate studies are preferred. Courses of study include the history of architecture, history, art, art history, specific courses in the techniques and research for historic preservation, architecture, and computer programs.

Examination/License: All states require architects to be licensed. Architects must pass all divisions of the Architect Registration Examination. Many states require interior designers to be licensed or registered. Interior designers must pass the National Council of Interior Design Qualification (NCIDQ) exam to receive licensure.

Professional Associations: Membership in the National Trust for Historic Preservation (www.PreservationNation.org), the American Society of Interior Designers (ASID) (www.asid.org), and the International Interior Design Association (IIDA) (www.iida.org) is ideal.

Job Outlook: Current trends for green and sustainable architecture are positive for historic preservationists. Skills in adaptive reuse design methods and techniques to repair and maintain buildings that already exist are valuable.

Summary

There are many varieties of exterior housing styles in the United States. They evolved from the housing styles of the Native Americans and of the settlers who brought styles from their homelands.

Traditional folk styles include those from Native Americans, Spanish, Scandinavians, Dutch, Germans, French, and English. During colonial times, other styles unique to the United States began to evolve. They include the Cape Cod, Saltbox, and Garrison styles. Later, the classic traditional styles of Georgian, Federal, Adam, Early Classical Revival, Greek Revival, Southern Colonial, and Victorian were developed.

During the twentieth century, modern and contemporary housing was designed to fit and take advantage of the environment and changing lifestyles. Modern houses include the Prairie Style, the bungalow, the International Style, the ranch and its variations, and different versions of the split-level.

Contemporary housing covers the styles of homes that are built today. Two categories of contemporary design are the solar house and the earth-sheltered house. Contemporary homes may use traditional or modern styles, or can be a unique, distinctive one-of-a-kind design. Postmodernism is a recent approach to housing design that often combines features of past housing with a new look that sometimes has a jarring effect on the viewer.

As housing styles continue to evolve to meet changing trends and lifestyles, preserving the best of the past for future generations is desirable. Historical preservation saves outstanding examples of past architectural styles from demolition or significant alteration.

Review the Facts

1. Red tile roofs, enclosed patios, and arch-shaped windows and doors are characteristics of which style of traditional housing?
2. Contrast the meaning of *folk* and *classic* styles of traditional architecture.
3. What are the characteristics of a Tidewater South home?
4. Compare and contrast the following styles: Cape Cod, Saltbox, and Garrison.
5. Name two features typical of the Spanish style.
6. How were log cabins built?
7. What are the similarities and differences between the Dutch Colonial and the French Manor house styles?
8. Identify three features of a Georgian-style house.
9. What two architectural styles emerged from the Federal period?
10. What is the difference between a *portico* and a *pediment?*
11. How can you identify Greek Revival style architecture?
12. Identify four characteristics of Victorian houses.
13. Who designed the Prairie style house?
14. What two features were characteristic of houses built in the International style in the United States?
15. Name one advantage and one disadvantage of the ranch house.
16. What kind of lot is best suited to the split-level house style?

17, Contrast the following roof styles: gable, gambrel, and hip.

18. Solar and earth-sheltered houses are two energy-efficient examples of the _____ housing style.

Think Critically

19. **Draw conclusions.** As many older homes and buildings face destruction in the modern world, many people are striving to preserve the heritage of these older structures. Draw conclusions about why is there growing concern to restore and preserve these older buildings.

20. **Form a hypothesis.** Review the styles of architecture from the 1700s to the present time. How are architectural features similar and different throughout the ages? What features appear again and again? Form a hypothesis about why certain architectural features are presently popular. What does this say about people and culture?

Community Links

21. **Walking tour.** Take a walking tour of one of the oldest residential areas of your community. What styles of architecture do you see? If possible, take a few digital photos of the various architectural styles (be sure to ask permission of the owners). Then examine the historical records of your community to find out when it was first settled. Who were the earliest inhabitants? Which of the houses in your photos can you track down? Prepare a photo essay and summarize your findings for the class.

22. **Real estate research.** Use Internet or print resources to examine the classified ads about real estate in your local community. Using the information and pictures in the ads, compile a price list of different styles of homes that are currently on the market. What styles do the ads mention? What are their descriptions? What architectural trends can you identify in the ads? Are older homes more expensive because of historical significance? Are certain styles of homes priced below the market average? Is there a style of house that reflects the greatest value?

Academic Connections

23. **Writing.** Imagine you and your family were among the early settlers in North America. Pick a style of Folk architecture and write a story that describes the lifestyle you and your family might have experienced living in the house. Think in terms of cooking, sleeping, bathing, working, learning, enjoying recreation, and conducting other aspects of daily life. You may wish to illustrate your story. Share your story with the class.

24. **History.** Choose an architect to research, such as Thomas Jefferson, Frank Lloyd Wright, Robert and James Adams, William Morris, Walter Gropius, Ludwig Mies van der Rohe, Robert Venturi, or Frank Gehry. Write a one-page report summarizing the architectural influence of the architect. Include photos or drawings of this architect's work that represent his/her style. To where would your class need to travel to find the closest example of a building designed by this architect?

Technology Applications

25. **Log cabin technology.** From the early Swedish immigrants to modern time, the log cabin remains a house style appealing to many in the U.S. culture. Trace the roots of the log cabin from its earliest beginnings to present time. How has the technology (the practical application of knowledge in a particular area) for building log cabins changed over the years? What role does computer-aided drafting and design (CADD) and computer-aided manufacturing (CAM) play in building modern-day log cabins? Use presentation software to share your findings with the class.

26. **Earth-sheltered house technology.** For many generations, people have used the soil to help protect their homes from severe climate conditions. Investigate ways that computer technology has improved the way people build earth-sheltered structures. How is beauty combined with form and function in such houses? How does 3-D modeling help improve such designs?

Design Practice

27. **House design.** Imagine you are an architect designing housing in the year 2030. Create an exterior design that you think would reflect future design trends. Does your design relate to any previous historical styles or time periods? What features of exterior design, if any, do you think are classic and will be repeated in the future? How does your design relate to changes of lifestyle for future generations?

28. **Portfolio.** Presume you are a contractor who is selecting photos, drawings, and descriptions of the house styles your company builds for a new Web site. Determine the styles of homes that your business will offer. If the styles are part of a planned housing development or subdivision, describe it as well. Put together a storyboard of your offerings in preparation for meeting with a Web designer.

Citizenship and Historical Preservation

Check out your community's Web site or the telephone directory to find out about a historical preservation group in your area. Alone or with your team, attend a meeting of this group to learn more about the group's activities with historic preservation. What needs does the organization have? How can youth get involved?

Report your findings to your FCCLA chapter. Determine if and how your team might work with this organization to help preserve historic buildings in your community. Then use the FCCLA *Planning Process* to plan, carry out, and evaluate your project. Use your project for an FCCLA *Illustrated Talk* STAR Event or a project for *Leaders at Work*. See your adviser for information as needed.

CHAPTER 7

Understanding House Plans

Terms to Learn

architectural drawings
schematic drawings
presentation-drawings
construction drawings
schedule
specifications
Building Information Model (BIM)
print
alphabet of lines
symbols
plan view
floor plan
exterior elevations
elevation view
section view
detail view
rendering
model
isometric drawing
private area
multipurpose room
work area
work triangle
social area
alcove
traffic patterns
built-in storage
common-use storage

Chapter Objectives

After studying this chapter, you will be able to

- interpret architectural drawings.
- describe how computers can assist in understanding house plans.
- organize space by grouping rooms according to function.
- plan safe and convenient traffic patterns.
- evaluate storage needs and space.
- summarize ways to modify housing for people with physical disabilities.

Reading with Purpose

Arrange a study session to read the chapter with a classmate. After you read each passage independently, stop and tell each other what you think the main points are in the passage. Continue with each passage until you finish the chapter.

The design and construction of a house involves many people working together. These people include the owner, architect, designer, contractor, banker, and various tradespeople. These people and many others form the design and construction team. Members of the team communicate through house plans. If you are buying or building a house, it is important that you, as a member of the team, be able to interpret the house plans.

Architectural Drawings for a House

Important to the development of house plans are the architectural drawings. **Architectural drawings** contain information about the size, shape, and location of all parts of the house, 7-1. They vary in complexity and depth of information presented according to their intended use. Architectural drawings include the following:

- **schematic drawings**—freehand sketches of a proposed plan the designer uses in refining a design

- **presentation drawings**—refined drawings or renderings to use for publication or for showing the design to a client

- **construction drawings**—drawings with detailed instructions to the builder to obtain necessary permits and erect the structure

This universal language of the construction industry uses lines, symbols, views, and notes to convey ideas. To ensure that everyone understands architectural drawings, standard rules of drafting determine the types of lines, symbols, and views, and the location of dimensions. These rules give meaning to each set of architectural drawings.

Architectural drawings are drawn in proportion to actual size. For instance, if a drawing is *half size*, it is one-half as large as the actual object. When an architectural drawing is either smaller or larger than the actual object, it is *drawn to scale*. Drawings for a house are normally drawn at a scale of ¼″ = 1′. This means that one-fourth inch on the drawing equals one-foot on the house. The scale for each drawing is indicated in a note. Sometimes a designer uses a graphic scale, such as a person or vehicle, to visually depict the scale. A designer uses a graphic scale when the size of the final print is unknown, such as for presentation drawings.

Architectural drawings cannot convey all information about a house. For example, it is hard to show texture or represent paint color on the drawings. However,

7-1
The architect has provided both a floor plan and a rendering so his clients can visualize how their new home will look.

© Charles M. Hill, AIA

wall texture and paint color are important to finishing a house. A **schedule** is an organized chart of detailed notes in a ruled enclosure, 7-2. Designers and contractors use schedules to describe large quantities of information in the drawings. Construction drawings define many items by schedules of repetitive or similar items. A typical construction drawing includes schedules for such details as doors and windows, electrical fixtures, plumbing fixtures, door hardware, and finishes. Other information for design and construction relates primarily to construction-quality standards called specifications or *specs*. The **specifications** tell the types and quality of materials to use and give directions for their use.

Prints of Architectural Drawings

In the past, drafters in architects' or contractors' offices used manual drafting machines and instruments to create most architectural drawings. Today drafters use *computer-aided drafting and design (CADD)* software to create most drawings. Many CADD programs are available both for the novice and professional. These programs range from simple home-plan design software to very sophisticated professional CADD programs requiring extensive training.

One of the newest tools available to architects, designers, and builders is the **Building Information Model (BIM)**. BIM is an approach to building that embraces every stage of a building's lifecycle: design, construction, maintenance, and sometimes demolition. Some software programs that utilize BIM, help architects, designers, and builders design buildings that are green and sustainable. Before construction begins, software using BIM can evaluate "virtual

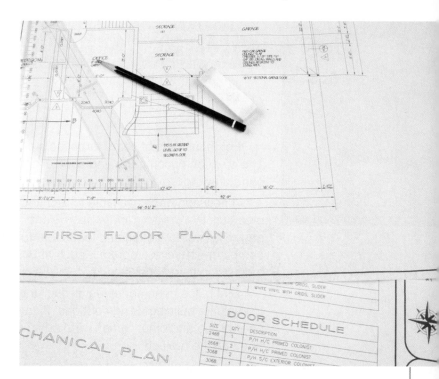

materials" that have the same properties as real materials (for example, concrete and lumber). Once a "virtual building" is built, the design and building team can analyze the building for structural integrity and environmental impact.

Using BIM and compatible software allows architects, designers, and builders to collaborate more easily. Some software even offers a video-conferencing feature to allow team members in different areas to view plans simultaneously.

When the drafter completes a set of architectural drawings, he or she makes copies for all members of the construction team. A **print** is a copy of a drawing. In the past, a reproduction of a drawing consisted of white lines on a dark blue background. Consequently, the term *blueprint* came into being.

Although some designers reproduce the drawings by the *diazo process*, which creates prints that have dark blue lines on a light blue background, many commonly use engineering

7-2
Because a floor plan cannot show all details, *schedules* are used to provide specifics about such items as doors and windows.

GREEN CHOICES

Architect's Responsibilities for Green and Sustainable Design

For thousands of years, architects planned buildings using hand-drawn plans. The creation of computer and special software programs streamlined the timely job of hand drawing, saving both time and money.

A new approach available to architects and all professionals involved in a building project is the *Building Information Model (BIM)*. This approach provides consistent and reliable information and leads to improved building performance. Several computer-software programs, such as Autodesk® Revit for example, incorporate BIM to assist in this process.

BIM helps bring about faster decision making, better documentation, and a way to evaluate building design options. It can also predict how the building will perform in energy use and other "green" and sustainable areas before the first piece of work is done on the project!

Here's what BIM and a computer program can do:

- **Provide many 3D views at all project stages.** This can help the client and designers work together better in producing the final design. For example, a well-built BIM model can show you the before, during, and after stages of construction, in 3D, and from any angle.

- **Improve the design coordination.** One of the biggest pushes with BIM is to get architects, engineers, and construction firms talking to each other by using compatible software to share their ideas.

- **Analyze the impact of green designs.** For example, BIM models are made using "virtual materials." Imagine you are developing plans for a skyscraper. You can choose the materials (for example, steel used in beams and exact type of concrete). The computer software that uses BIM can then analyze both soundness of the structure and impact on the environment.

Use of BIM and the software program that uses it will see more frequent use in the future. Architects using BIM can increase the quality of design and have a positive impact on the environment.

copiers. Engineering copiers or large-format copiers are similar to office photocopiers and handle the heavier and much larger sheets of paper for copying these drawings. Publishing drawings to the Internet is also becoming more popular. This allows the construction team to access and simultaneously view the latest set of construction documents.

Alphabet of Lines

To understand the architectural drawings, you must first understand the lines used on the drawings. Seven different lines, called the **alphabet of lines**, are commonly used on architectural drawings. They allow the drafter to communicate ideas clearly and accurately.

somewhat like a bird's-eye view, that shows the size and arrangement of rooms, hallways, doors, windows, and storage areas on one floor of a home. In 7-5 you can see the symbols used in the floor plan.

When discussing plan views and describing houses, the term *square footage* is often used. This is a measurement of house size that refers to the amount of living space in the home. You will use the room dimensions that appear on the floor plan to determine square footage.

Elevation Views

Exterior elevations are architectural drawings that show the outside views of the house. A set of drawings usually includes four exterior elevations showing all four sides of the house. If the building is simple, there may be only the front elevation and one side elevation.

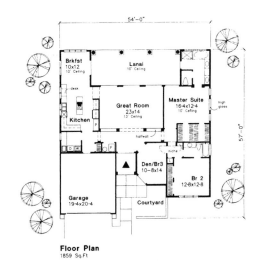

Floor Plan
1859 Sq.Ft

7-5

Understanding an architectural drawing is a matter of knowing what the symbols mean.

Bloodgood Sharp Buster Architects & Planners, Inc.

MATH MATTERS

Determining Square Footage of a Home

Often a house plan or description refers to the total square feet in a home. Square footage is used to compare homes in terms of size. The higher the square footage, the larger the home will be.

Square footage is the total amount of living space (area) in the home. You can determine the total living space by adding together the square footage space from all rooms. The dimensions of each room appear on the floor plan. Note that closets, other storage space, and garages do not count toward the square footage of a house. Once you find the dimensions on the floor plan, use the following formula to determine the square footage for each room:

Area = Length × Width

If a room is 12 feet long and 10 feet wide, the square footage will be the following:

A = 12 ft. × 10 ft.
A = 120 sq. ft.

To calculate the total square footage of a home, complete the calculation for each room and add them together.

Interior elevation drawings may show cabinetry or other special areas.

An **elevation view** shows the finished exterior appearance of a given side of the house. Elevations usually show height dimensions. These views help people visualize the completed house. By studying both the floor plan and the elevation views, you can envision the completed structure, 7-6.

Section Views and Detail Views

To show how individual structural parts of the house fit together, section and detail views are used. For instance, the drafter may want to show the inside of the house. When a view is taken from an imaginary cut through a part of a house, such as a wall, it is called a **section view**. Therefore, the plan view is a horizontal slice through the house and the section view is a vertical slice. See the example in 7-7. (Notice that 7-5, 7-6, and 7-7 are various views of the same house. Figure 7-7 views an interior slice of Figure 7-6 at the line marked B-B.)

A **detail view** is usually an enlargement of some construction feature. The detail drawing often uses a larger scale than other drawings. It shows the details of a small part of the house. See 7-8 for a house and garage detail.

Renderings and Models

To help clients better visualize a finished house, architectural firms frequently produce a rendering. A **rendering** is a presentation drawing—usually with color, texture, and shadows—that shows a realistic view of the completed house. Refer back to the top of 7-1.

Some architectural firms also develop a model to show all sides of the new house. A **model** is a three-dimensional miniature of a design. A client can view it from different angles and in various lighting conditions to get more realistic views of the house.

Producing renderings and models by hand is very costly in terms of time and materials. It also requires considerable artistic skill. These views usually

7-6
The main feature of this house is the great room in the center.

Bloodgood Sharp Buster Architects & Planners, Inc.

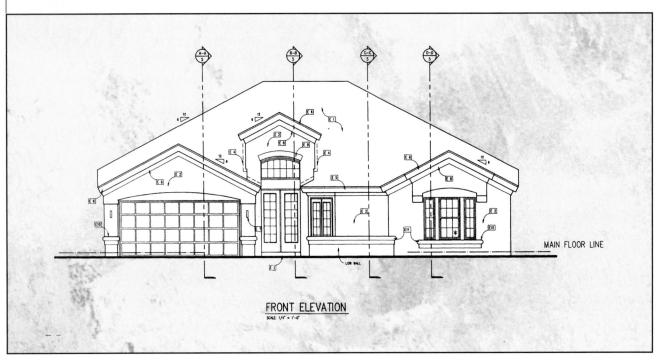

FRONT ELEVATION
SCALE: 1/4" = 1'-0"

MAIN FLOOR LINE

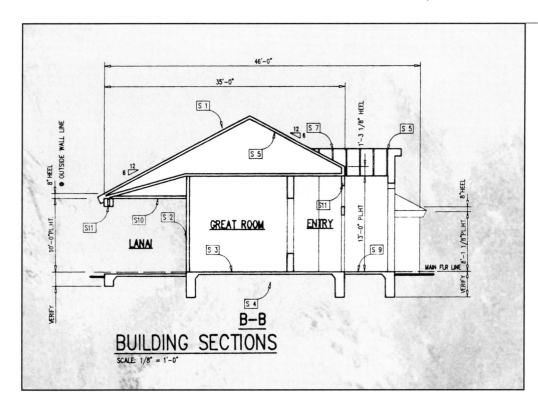

7-7

This section view shows that the ceiling in the great room is higher than the lanai's ceiling.

Bloodgood Sharp Buster Architects & Planners, Inc.

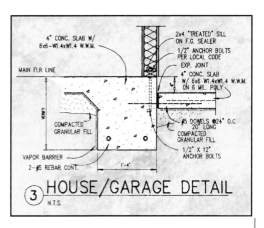

7-8

This detail view shows how the outside wall is fastened to the garage floor.

Bloodgood Sharp Buster Architects & Planners, Inc.

incorporate landscaping plans and other aspects of the completed house.

Today, architects have a choice in producing renderings and models. Depending on the requirements of the project, they may use CADD. The computer creates very realistic views of the house under various lighting conditions, 7-9. Saving time and accuracy is the biggest advantages of using computers to create housing views.

Some architectural firms use CADD to allow the client to view the structure from many different angles before finalizing the plan. The customer can virtually "walk through" the space and determine if the building's layout meets expectations. If not, the designer can easily make adjustments to the plan, and produce different versions of the plan quickly. CADD brings the plan to life for the client. It also helps architects and builders avoid costly mistakes and verify that the final design meets client expectations.

An **isometric drawing** illustrates a space or product in three dimensions (width + length + height) at the same time. The resulting image is an overhead view showing depth perception at 30-degree

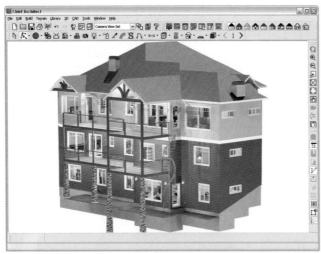

A   **B**

7-9
The rendering of this house was created by using computer-aided drafting and design (CADD). The rendering shows realistic views of the house under various lighting conditions at different times of the day.

Courtesy of Software by Chief Architect

angles, 7-10. It combines information from a plan drawing (width + length) and an elevation drawing (width + height). Designers may use this image to visually communicate the written information in specification documents. It is a valuable tool for ensuring quality construction, fabrication, and installation.

For presentation to a client, however, isometric drawings have their limits. This is because of the distortion in the overhead images. A better use of the designer's time is to prepare perspective drawings to show clients realistic eye-level views of space.

The Space Within

Once you understand the drawings for the house, you need to consider the space within. The division of space within the house is one of the most basic concerns in housing.

When planning how to use the space within a house, the designer must give consideration to the activities, habits, lifestyles, and life situations of the occupants. Then the designer divides the interior space into areas according to the intended use of each. Optimal space

divisions should satisfy the needs and preferences of the occupants.

Grouping by Functional Zones

As you look at floor plans, you will notice that certain rooms of a house are usually located next to one another. This is because certain rooms serve similar purposes, or *functions*. Grouping rooms together by functional zone is an efficient way to organize space. Three zones encompass most of the space within a house: a *private area*, *work area*, and *social area*.

The Private Area

The **private area** in most houses consists of bedrooms and bathrooms. These rooms provide space for sleeping, resting, grooming, and dressing. The private area of a house offers the best setting for rest and relaxation. It is usually a comfortable and quiet place.

Because sleep and rest are basic needs, they should be among the first to consider when planning the use of space. In some homes, each person has a separate room. In other homes, this is not possible or desirable. The important

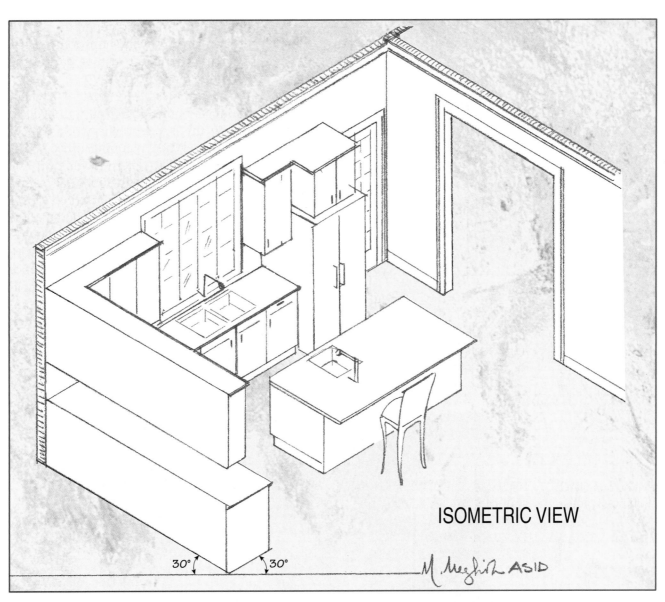

ISOMETRIC VIEW

30°   30°

M. Megliola ASID

7-10
An isometric
drawing shows a
three-dimensional,
birds-eye-view
of a space at
30-degree angles.

Madge Megliola, ASID

goal is to ensure the comfort of each person and put his or her spatial needs ahead of group needs.

Dressing and grooming are other activities that take place in the private area, 7-11. They require privacy and space for storing clothes and grooming supplies. Both bedrooms and bathrooms help fulfill these spatial needs, 7-12.

Some bedrooms may provide space for other activities, such as reading, studying, watching TV, listening to music, and working on hobbies. When this is true, the rooms become **multipurpose rooms**. Household members use them during active periods of the day as well as sleeping hours.

The Work Area

Some rooms in a home are set aside for the work area. The **work area** includes all parts of the house needed to maintain and service the other areas. Sometimes the work area overlaps with the service zone outside the house. Rooms in the work area vary from house to house. The kitchen, laundry area, utility

7-11

The shaded area of this floor plan represents the private area.

© Charles M. Hill, AIA

room, and garage are generally part of the work area. A workshop, home office, or sewing room may also be part of the work area, 7-13.

If your lifestyle or that of a client requires a home office, you will need to include this space in the work area of the home. When planning office space, the first step is to determine its purpose. Is it for occasional use, such as paying bills and organizing household documents? Will people use the home office frequently, perhaps by children doing homework or adults bringing work home from the office? Will the office receive daily use, perhaps by a household member working from home or telecommuting? Knowing how inhabitants will use the home office helps to determine its location.

7-12

This bathroom is part of the private area of the house.

Photography Courtesy of Kohler

7-13
The shaded kitchen and utility room represent the work area.

© Charles M. Hill, AIA

The actual space available in the dwelling also affects the location of a home office. Plans for some home offices require a corner of the kitchen or in an alcove. For daily use, a home office generally requires much more space, such as a separate room. However, few households can afford to give that much space to a home office. Instead, most plans for home offices utilize a spare bedroom, the basement, or attic space, 7-14.

After the workspace for the home office is determined on the floor plan, attention can later turn to the next steps. These include selecting and arranging furniture, securing the lighting, and getting the necessary equipment. You will learn more about these topics in Chapters 16 through 18.

In most homes, the kitchen often receives more use than any other room in the work area. It has the following three primary areas of activity:

- food preparation and storage center (associated with the refrigerator)

- cleanup center (associated with the sink and dishwasher)

- cooking and serving center (associated with the range and oven)

The imaginary line that connects these three centers forms a **work triangle**. Anyone preparing a meal in a kitchen will walk along the lines of the triangle several times before the meal is ready. In a well-designed kitchen, the total length of all sides of the work triangle does not exceed 22 feet. Figure 7-15 shows six basic kitchen designs and summarizes the advantages and disadvantages of each.

7-14
This home office is an attractive, functional space.

Photography Courtesy of **Pottery Barn**

Peninsula Layout

Corridor Layout

L-Shaped Layout

U-Shaped Layout

One-Wall Layout

Island Layout

Advantages and Disadvantages of Kitchen Layouts		
Kitchen Layout	**Advantages**	**Disadvantages**
Peninsula	Adds a countertop to use as either extra work space or as eating space with chairs or stools	May hinder movement into and out of the kitchen work area
L-Shaped	Allows traffic flow into the kitchen without entering the work triangle; the work areas on the two adjoining walls use square footage efficiently	Offers less countertop work space than other kitchen designs
U-Shaped	Uses space efficiently in work areas; allows traffic into the kitchen without entering the work triangle	Depending on door location, traffic may enter the work triangle and interfere with task completion
Corridor	Can use space efficiently	Any traffic entering the room will cross the work triangle
One-Wall	Uses space most efficiently; can be easily added into other rooms	Limits countertop work area
Island	Allows for ample countertop area for activities that do not enter the work triangle	May require more square footage than other designs

7-15
The distance around the work triangle in each of these kitchen designs is less than 22 feet.

LINK TO SOCIAL STUDIES & CULTURE

Anthropometrics

What factors influence building codes for such parts of a structure as minimum doorway height, depth of a kitchen cabinet, or the height at which a handrail is attached along a stairway? To answer this question, a designer must not only know building codes, but must also understand the bodily dimensions of the average person who will enter the doorway, store items in the cabinet, and use the handrail. Measurements of height, weight, and arm reach are some of the data available from researchers in anthropometry. *Anthropometry* is the scientific study of human body measurements on a comparative basis.

Researchers working for the government, universities, and businesses usually collect this data. One of the largest databases of anthropometric data, collected by the U.S. military, is based on men and women in the U.S. armed services. The U.S. government also collected data on children. Designers and manufacturers use data averages to create building materials, appliances, and home furnishings to fit the general population.

Design professionals can access much of this data in tables or on the Internet free of charge. However, there are some limits to this data. For example, data from measurements of healthy young adults may have less usefulness to someone designing housing for older adults or people with disabilities. Also, data collected decades ago may not reflect the changes in average weight and size of populations over time. It does not reflect changing demographics.

Anthropometric data is expensive to collect. Some businesses sell it. New technology is revolutionizing how to collect and use this data. For example, designers can take their own measurements of virtual bodies scanned by researchers using 3-D body scans. The types of measurements that can be collected in this way are limitless.

The Social Area

Members of a household spend much of their time in the social area of the house. The **social area** provides space for daily living, entertaining, and recreation. It includes entrances, dining rooms, living rooms, and family rooms, 7-16.

An entry or entrance is a place where household members identify and greet guests. It is here that guests remove outerwear and place it in nearby coat closets. Entries also help direct the movement of people throughout the house. If a dwelling has more than

7-16
The shaded portion represents the social area.

one entrance, each may have a slightly different purpose. However, each is still part of the social area.

Some houses have separate dining rooms for eating meals and entertaining guests. If a dining room does not get regular use, the cost of having a separate dining room may be too great. In that case, household members may prefer to eat close to where the food is prepared. This can be in the kitchen at a special counter or a separate table. During mild weather, household members often enjoy eating outdoors. When special events are on TV, many families like to eat meals in the family room or living room.

Living rooms provide space for family activities as well as for entertaining guests. If a dwelling has both a living room and a family room, the family room is often more casual. It offers space for recreational activities and relaxation, 7-17.

7-17
This living room offers space for family activities and entertaining guests.

Photography Courtesy of Karastan

Separating Areas and Rooms

There are several ways to separate the private, work, and social areas. One way is to locate different areas on different ends or levels of the house. For instance, the private area may be upstairs, while the social and work areas are on the ground floor. Hallways are another way to separate areas. Besides physically separating areas, hall space also acts as a buffer zone for noise. A hallway between the private and social areas makes it possible for some people to rest or sleep, while others are entertaining guests, dining, or watching TV. Hallways near work areas help reduce the volume of noise from appliances and tools that reach the quiet and social areas.

Hallways range from 36 inches to more than 48 inches wide. Very short halls use a 36-inch width. In contrast, a 42-inch width is customary in very long halls or in halls where wheelchairs are in regular use. A 46-inch width is the most common width used.

Walls usually separate individual rooms. However, some dwellings have large open areas with divisions into separate areas. For example, **alcoves** (small recessed sections of a room), varied ceiling heights, and balconies sometimes separate spaces for different functions. Screens, freestanding storage units, and careful arrangement of furniture can also separate space according to function. Even when there are no walls dividing a room, you can see that the room design provides for different activities.

An advantage of not separating areas with walls is a large, open area where people can enjoy more than one activity at a time. For instance, the kitchen may be open to the family room or living room. The open space allows those preparing food to take part in other activities, such as conversing with family members or entertaining guests.

Room Relationships

The nearness of and connections between various rooms is important to convenience and ease of use. For example, kitchens should be close to the dining room to make food service faster and more efficient. A garage or parking area should be close to the kitchen to make carrying in groceries easier. Bathrooms should be close to the bedrooms for convenience. Outdoor living areas should be close to the social areas to allow guests to enter the house without going through the work or private areas. Considering how to use the space and its closeness to related activities will improve the functionality of the living space, 7-18.

Types of Circulation Activities

There are four types of circulation, or movement, activities that impact living space: family, guest, work, and service. These circulation activities have specific considerations.

- **Family.** Family members should be able to move freely between living areas without having to pass through a bedroom to get to another part of the house. High-frequency routes are short and direct.

- **Guest.** Guest circulation provides access to a coat closet, living room, and dining room without have to walk through the work areas or private areas of a home. There should also be a bath close by for guests.

7-18
This casual living and dining room are part of the social area of the home.

- **Work.** To meet this circulation need, the kitchen should be located near the service entrance and have easy access to basement, garage, and laundry/utility areas.

- **Service.** This type of circulation refers to movement of persons into and out of the home including repairmen and service people. Service circulation also includes taking garbage out and bringing in groceries.

Traffic Patterns

Have you ever been in a traffic jam after leaving a football game or concert? Often the police relieve the congestion by directing traffic and creating alternate routes.

Traffic planning also helps reduce or prevent congestion throughout a house. It relates to the types of circulation activities that occur throughout the home. When organization of a space is effective, people move easily within a room, from room to room, or to the outdoors. **Traffic patterns** are the paths they follow.

Traffic patterns require enough space for people to move about freely. However, it is wasteful to use more space than is needed. As a rule, traffic patterns should be about 40 inches wide.

The design of traffic patterns should allow people to move throughout a house without disturbing other activities. For example, major traffic patterns should avoid the private area of a home so it can remain quiet. Work areas are unsafe if people frequently walk through them. To avoid accidents, traffic patterns should lead to work areas, but not through them. Also, traffic patterns should not be located through social areas, since this can interrupt conversation, study, and TV viewing.

The easiest way to evaluate traffic patterns is to study floor plans. Look at the examples in 7-19. Do the traffic patterns use the following guidelines for safety and convenience? Traffic patterns should

- be convenient and direct

- provide adequate space without wasting it

- provide easy access from the entrances to other parts of the house

- separate traffic to the work area from traffic to the private and social areas

- avoid cutting through the middle of rooms

- avoid interfering with a good furniture arrangement or interrupting activities within a room

- avoid interfering with privacy in areas of the house where privacy is expected

- avoid cutting through a kitchen, work area, or any other hazardous area

- give the kitchen easy access to all areas of the home

7-19

The open floor plan of this home permits traffic to flow smoothly in many directions.

© Charles M. Hill, AIA

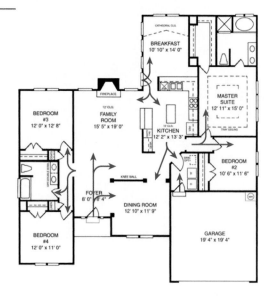

- provide a direct access from the service entrance to a cleanup area
- provide access from a service entrance to the private area without going through the social area
- provide direct access from utility area to the outside service zone
- provide direct access from the main entrance to social areas without going through work or private areas

Space for Doors

Outside doors and doors between rooms also help determine the flow of traffic. Other doors within a room may conceal storage. It is important that the space in front of these doors remain free. Blocked doors will stop traffic and cut off access to stored items.

Not only should the space immediately in front of doors be free, but there should also be space for doors to swing and stand open. Figure 7-20 shows the space requirements that different types of doors need to swing open. People also need space to go through the doors or to use storage areas.

Survey the Storage Space

It is important to have plenty of storage space scattered throughout a house. When looking at house plans, look at what storage space is available. Make sure there is enough space to store all your belongings. Check to see if the storage space is located in convenient places. If you plan to use some rooms for more than one activity, make sure they have the storage space you need. For instance, you may plan to use the dining room as both a study area and a place to eat. In this case, you will need space to store paper, pens, and reference books as well as dishes and table linens.

Looking at floor plans can help you evaluate the storage space of a home. A floor plan, such as the one in 7-21, shows the location of built-in storage units. **Built-in storage** includes shelves and drawers that are built into a housing unit. You cannot sell, replace, or move built-in storage like pieces of furniture.

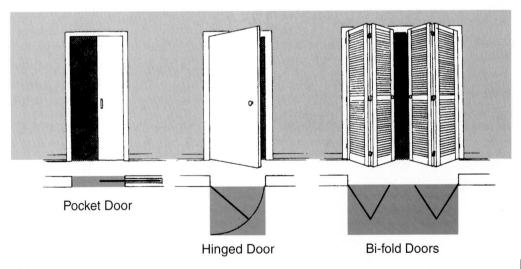

Pocket Door

Hinged Door

Bi-fold Doors

7-20
The colored areas show the amount of space that must be kept clear around each type of door.

7-21

This floor plan shows the location of closets, a pantry, and kitchen cabinets, which are all forms of built-in storage.

© Charles M. Hill, AIA

7-22

Baskets under tables can be used in addition to built-in storage to hold household items.

Photography Courtesy of Pottery Barn

A section view will show the number of shelves and drawers in the storage unit. Floor plans also show how much floor space is available for additional storage, such as shelves and bookcases.

Planning for Storage

If you plan to build a house or have one built for you, you will need to plan for storage. First, you need to determine the storage needs of each member of your household. A rule-of-thumb to follow is to devote 10 percent of the floor space to storage. Then you need to plan for **common-use storage**, which is storage used by all who live in a house. It includes the storage near the entrance where household members keep outerwear and storage for food, tools, and other items for sharing.

You can add to the amount of built-in storage available in a dwelling with storage units and storage furniture. Storage furniture includes desks, chests, armoires, and dressers, 7-22. You can move storage furniture to other locations in the house and take it with you when you leave. You may need to disassemble some units.

Built-in storage, storage units, and storage furniture also have advantages. Because you cannot take built-in storage with you when you move, you will not have the cost of moving it. Also, a home increases in value if it includes built-in storage.

Evaluating the Floor Plan

When considering a floor plan on paper, on a computer screen, or by walking through a home, evaluate the layout carefully. Ask yourself the questions in 7-23. By answering these questions, you can identify any areas that may present future problems.

Evaluating a Floor Plan

Answering "yes" to the following questions indicate a well-designed floor plan. Any "no" answers may indicate a need to modify the floor plan.

- Would all members of your household have enough space to satisfy their needs?
- Are rooms grouped according to function?
- Are private areas away from public view and traffic?
- If a multipurpose room exists, can it be used for all the intended purposes?
- Are eating areas close to the kitchen?
- Is space provided for entertaining as well as day-to-day living?
- Are the entrances conveniently located?
- Are the traffic patterns safe and convenient?
- Is storage adequate and convenient?
- Is the house free of barriers?

7-23
Can you think of other questions you would ask yourself when evaluating a floor plan?

No floor plan is perfect for everyone so your ideal plan may present problems to someone else. A plan that fits your immediate lifestyle needs may not work as your lifestyle changes. You can solve problems in a floor plan by making changes to the construction of the space or by *adapting the space*. When you adapt a space, you use it for something other than the original purpose. Sometimes, too, using interior design treatments may help solve floor-plan problems.

Housing Modifications for People with Special Needs

Housing should provide convenience, safety, and accessibility for all members of the household. This includes people with special needs, including physical limitations.

Houses for people with physical limitations can be attractive and affordable. By spending approximately two percent above the base cost on a new house, builders can incorporate universal design features to make it barrier free. Also, you can modify the exterior and interior of existing features at a reasonable cost to meet the needs of people with physical limitations. For example, modifications in a kitchen can make the cooking and cleanup areas more accessible to household members with limited reach.

Exteriors

The exteriors of houses for people with physical limitations should be as safe and accessible as possible. When building or choosing a house, keep the following points in mind:

- Choose flat lots for easy access.
- Plan the entrance to face south, so ice and snow on sidewalks and the driveway will melt faster.
- Utilize nonskid surfaces, such as textured asphalt or concrete for sidewalks, driveways, and garage floors. (Keep oil and debris off these surfaces.)
- Make driveways and garages wide enough to park cars and to move in and around wheelchairs.
- Use garage door openers that automatically light garages.
- Install ramps with handrails for easy access to the house.
- Make sidewalks, ramps, and entries wide enough for wheelchairs to move easily. To allow for enough

7-24
Instead of installing storage cabinets under this sink and cooktop, the space was left open to accommodate a wheelchair.

Barrier Free Environments, Inc., Raleigh, NC

room on each side of a wheelchair, sidewalks should be four or five feet wide and entries should be three feet wide.

- Make thresholds as level as possible to prevent stumbling.
- Consider push-button or automatically operated doors because they are the easiest to use.
- Equip doors with levers or handles, which are easier to grasp and turn than conventional knobs.
- Install effective lighting outdoors and at entry areas.

Interiors

Since people spend most of their time inside, safety and accessibility are important, 7-24. When choosing housing that eliminates barriers for people with physical limitations, some key features are very important. Barrier-free homes should include the following:

- Stairs with an easy rise (not too steep) and steady handrails, thin enough to grip securely.
- Floors and stairs with wood or hard-surface coverings for easy mobility. If carpet is used, it should have a low pile.
- Floor plans accommodate use of a walker or wheelchair.
- Open traffic lanes lead directly to specific areas.
- Halls at least four feet wide to permit a wheelchair to turn into a room.
- Rooms with adequate turnaround space for wheelchairs (usually five square feet).
- Doors that swing both ways or fold for ease of use, with doorways that are at least 32 inches wide.

- Storage space, equipment, and appliances are within easy reach.

- Electrical outlets are 24 inches to 36 inches off the floor and switches no higher than 48 inches.

- Trays and drawers that pull out for ease of use instead of traditional shelves, 7-25.

- Lavatories and toilets mounted at heights for easy access.

- Showers or bathtubs with doors for easy access.

- Grab bars conveniently located at toilets and bathtubs or showers.

- Lever handles, rather than knobs, for easy grasp and use.

- A home elevator or staircase-lift if the living quarters are on more than one level of the house.

If house modifications cannot make life easier for a person with physical limitations, household members must make a decision. Can that person live in the home comfortably, or should members find another house? This is an important question to answer and should include input from all household members.

7-25
Pull-out storage is convenient for everyone, especially people with disabilities.

CAREER FOCUS

Architect

Is the design of buildings—old and new—fascinating to you? Do you ever wonder what it might be like to design such buildings? If you do, a career as an architect might be for you.

Interests/Skills: Do your interests include working with lines and patterns and having freedom to develop your own designs? Do you like to solve problems by researching facts and information? Do you enjoy interacting with people? Skills include a strong background in math and working with computers. Effective organizational skills, attention to details, along with active listening skills are a must. Strong communication skills in both writing and speech are also essential.

Career Snapshot: Architects plan and design structures, such as private residences, office buildings, factories, theaters and airports. The buildings they design have to be safe, economical, and must suit the needs of the people who use them. They work on computer programs to help them accomplish this. They prepare many contracts and documents. Architects also supervise the construction of the building or structure to make certain that their design plans are followed. Architects spend a great deal of time explaining their ideas to clients and others. Successful architects must be able to communicate well and get others to "buy-in-on" their ideas.

Education/Training: A 5-year bachelor's degree is most common. Most programs have a design studio in which students apply classroom learnings to real projects. They create drawings and 3D models of their designs.

Licensing/Examinations: Licensing requires a professional degree in architecture and at least 3 years of practical work training. In addition, a person must pass all divisions of the Architect Registration Examination.

Professional Association: American Institute of Architects (AIA) (www.aia.org/).

Job Outlook: Jobs are expected to be in demand in the foreseeable future. Outlook will also be good for architects with knowledge of "green" and sustainable design.

Source: Information from the Occupational Outlook Handbook (www.bls.gov/OCO/) and Occupational Information Network (www.online.onetcenter.org).

Summary

Architectural drawings contain information about the size, shape, and location of all parts of the house. They are drawn to scale. Then prints are made, accompanied by schedules and specifications. To understand architectural drawings, it helps to be familiar with the special lines and symbols used. Architectural drawings usually include several views of the house.

After the drawings are evaluated, the actual space within a house needs to be considered. Rooms are usually grouped by function, room relationship, and circulation activities. Space is divided into three different areas—for privacy, work, and socializing. Levels, hallways, walls, screens, freestanding storage units, and furniture arrangements separate these areas.

Planned traffic patterns help reduce and prevent traffic congestion and provide enough space for opening doors. Organizing space to provide plenty of storage is also important. This can be done with built-in storage, storage units, and storage furniture.

The exterior and interior space of a house sometimes needs to be modified to meet the needs of a household member who has a physical disability. If a house is convenient, safe, and accessible for people with physical disabilities, it will meet the needs of any occupant.

Review the Facts

1. What does an architectural drawing contain?
2. Contrast *schematic*, *presentation*, and *construction* drawings.
3. When is an architectural drawing drawn to scale?
4. Why do designers and contractors use schedules in architectural drawings?
5. What shows the arrangement of rooms, halls, and doors on one floor of a house?
6. How do elevation views differ from section, detail, and isometric views?
7. What are the three functional zones that divide the space of a house?
8. In a well-designed kitchen, what is the maximum length around a work triangle?
9. What are the six basic kitchen designs? Give an advantage and disadvantage of each.
10. How does considering the use of a space and its closeness to related activities improve functionality? Give an example.
11. Name four types of circulation activities.
12. List five guidelines for functional traffic patterns.
13. Name one advantage of each: built-in storage and storage furniture.
14. Give two examples of how housing exteriors can be modified for people with physical limitations.
15. Describe three features of a house interior that is free of barriers for people with physical limitations.

Think Critically

16. **Analyze traffic patterns.** Suppose you analyze the traffic patterns in a home you plan to buy and see potential problems between the private and social areas. Otherwise, the house is very pleasing and convenient to use. Would you buy the house with the idea of changing the traffic patterns later, or would you keep looking for a better floor plan? Give the reasons to support your choice.

17. **Draw conclusions.** Housing should be adaptable to meet the needs of changes in life circumstances and the family life cycle. Imagine having a home with flexible features such as movable walls and adjustable kitchen countertops. Draw conclusions about why you think this *is* or *is not* a good idea.

Community Links

18. **Model home tour.** Visit a model home in a new subdivision or a nearby housing complex and do the following:
    A. Walk through the home and answer the questions in Figure 7-23.
    B. Compare the impression of the house you get from studying the floor plan to the actual experience of touring the house. Were some aspects of the house not conveyed clearly in the floor plan?
    C. Identify aspects of the floor plan that you would like to change.

19. **Identify accessibility.** Locate either an apartment or home that has features specifically designed for people who need a walker or wheelchair to get around. Describe these features. What other features would make the housing more usable to these occupants?

Academic Connections

20. **Reading.** Answer the following questions by examining and reading the details in Figure 7-5: (A) How many windows are in the house? (B) Where is the furnace located? (C) The house has approximately how many square feet? (D) How many bathrooms does the house have? (E) What type of layout exists in the kitchen?

21. **Writing.** Use Internet or print resources to investigate further information about the Building Information Model (BIM). If possible, interview an architect or builder who uses BIM. What are the best features of this process? Write a brief report and share your findings with the class.

Technology Applications

22. **Floor plans.** Locate a floor plan on the Internet that you like and print a copy. Use the floor plan to do each of the following:
    A. Shade the quiet, social, and work areas with different-colored pencils. Determine if the areas are divided appropriately and justify your decision.
    B. Trace the traffic patterns, and check them with the guidelines listed in this chapter. Explain if they are safe and convenient.
    C. Identify which storage is for individual use and which is for common use.
    D. Indicate how the living space could be modified for people with physical disabilities, if this became necessary.

23. **Create a flyer.** Using a desktop publishing program, develop a flyer that shows safety issues in housing plans. Develop a list of safety considerations for adults and children in the following areas of a floor plan: the home's entrances, traffic patterns in kitchens, and placement of interior doors.

24. **Anthropometrics.** Use Internet or print resources to investigate ways that anthropometric measurements are used in house design. Locate images that help support your findings to share with the class.

Design Practice

25. **Draw a floor plan.** Suppose you have been hired to create a floor plan that has safe and convenient traffic patterns for a person who uses a wheelchair. Use a computer with a CADD program to draw a floor plan that includes three bedrooms, one bathroom, a kitchen, dining room, and living room. Evaluate it according to the questions in Figure 7-23. Make changes in the plan as needed to improve the design. Print a copy of the plan and present your design to the class.

26. **Portfolio.** Using one of the house exteriors from the portfolio activity in Chapter 6, create an interior floor plan on graph paper that includes built-in storage. Apply the symbols and lines discussed in this chapter.

Leading the Way on Housing Tours

Many communities sponsor a yearly "Parade of Homes" for either historic or well-designed homes. Consider volunteering as a tour guide for this community event. Work alongside community organizers and architects to learn as much as you can about the homes, their floor plans, and architectural details. Some historical data about the inhabitants of these homes will add interest to the tour.

Use the FCCLA *Planning Process* to plan, carry out, and evaluate your tour guide experience for this community event. Your project can work as an FCCLA *Interpersonal Communications* STAR Event or a project for *Leaders at Work.* See your adviser for information as needed.

CHAPTER 8

House Construction

Terms to Learn

foundation
footing
concrete
foundation wall
frost line
moisture barrier
sill plate
pressure preservative treated (PT)
anchor bolt
joist
girder
subflooring
plywood sheet
oriented strand board (OSB)
stud
bearing wall
nonbearing wall
header
autoclaved aerated concrete (AAC)
insulated concrete forms (ICF)
rafter
ridge board
truss rafter
masonry
siding
brick
natural stone
veneer wall
pattern bond
shingle
flashing
gutter
downspout

Chapter Objectives

After studying this chapter, you will be able to

- summarize house construction including the parts of the foundation and frame of a house.

- compare the advantages and disadvantages of different types of materials used for exterior construction.

- distinguish between basic types of windows and different types of doors used in houses.

- summarize how computer applications can assist the house construction process.

Reading with Purpose

As you read this chapter, take notes in presentation software. Make one slide for each of the main headings. List three to four main points on each slide. Use your finished presentation to study for tests.

When buying a pre-owned house or building a new one, it is helpful to understand basic house construction. Familiarity with housing construction helps you make good decisions when selecting a place to live. Poor decisions, however, can result in poor investments and/or expensive repair costs.

The Foundation and Frame

The foundation and frame are the basic structure of the house. Understanding how they are constructed is the first step in making an informed housing decision. When buying a pre-owned house, you may be able to inspect the foundation and frame for defects and needed repairs. When building a house, you will be able to observe the construction and make sure it is done correctly.

The Foundation

The **foundation** is the underlying base of the house. There are three types of foundation construction. Houses may be constructed with a basement, a crawl space with a pier foundation, or a slab-on-grade foundation. The foundation consists of foundation walls and the footing. The **footing** is the very bottom of the foundation, 8-1. Footings are usually made from **concrete** which is a strong and durable hard building material consisting of cement, sand, and gravel with water.

For added strength, a system of horizontal bars—or rebar—reinforces the footings. The concrete and steel footings should be strong enough to support the rest of the foundation and the house it will support. The footings need to be the correct width and thickness to support the weight of the foundation and house.

Foundation walls support the load of the house between the footing and the floor. They form an enclosure for basements or crawl spaces. Concrete or concrete block are the most common foundation-wall materials. Some *permanent wood foundations* (PWF) utilize pressure-treated lumber. The thickness of the foundation wall varies from 6 to 10

8-1
The footing is a wide concrete base that supports the foundation and the rest of the house. The footings for both the slab-on-grade and basement must be below the frostline to prevent damage to the foundation.

Modern Carpentry by Wagner and Smith, Goodheart-Willcox

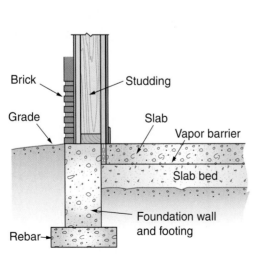

A—Slab-on-Grade

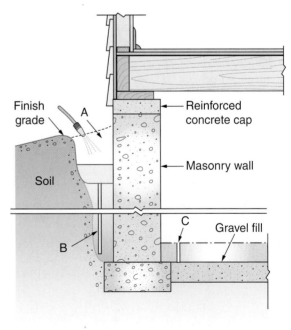

B—Footing and Foundation Wall for Basement

inches with 8 inches being the most common thickness. Local building codes normally control wall thickness and reinforcement requirements.

Footings are placed on undisturbed, compacted soil below the frost line. The **frost line** is the depth to which frost penetrates soil in the area. If the footing is above the frost line, the soil under it freezes and expands. This expansion causes the foundation to crack until the soil is compact again. It also causes cracks to appear in the foundation wall. In extreme cases, cracks will appear on inside walls. This cracking and settling will continue for years. During this time, the cracks will continue to expand and lengthen. The local building code may specify how deep the foundation must be according to soil conditions and the depth to which the ground freezes.

Most foundations settle evenly as the house adjusts to the ground. The foundation and walls may show hairline cracks, which are cracks less than ⅛-inch wide. Cracks greater than ⅛ inch are excessive. The builder is required to surface patch these cracks.

Stress cracks differ from hairline cracks and are signs of possible structural problems. They are usually wider at one end than the other. Stress cracks can occur when the footing settles more at one point, and the foundation pulls apart from underneath. They can also indicate that one side of the house is settling more than the other.

Stress-crack repair depends on the extent of the damage and usually requires leveling the house and reinforcing the footing. This is a costly procedure. Unless the purchase price of the house is low enough to cover the cost of this problem, the prospective buyer should not purchase a house with this problem.

When looking at a pre-owned house, make sure that the foundation walls are straight and square at the corners. They should not have major stress cracks.

A house with a *slab-on-grade* foundation has no basement or crawl space, 8-2. This type of construction is particularly useful when building ranch style homes in areas in which the ground does not freeze. The earth beneath the slab must be very hard and compact. Before pouring the slab, the contractor first grades or levels the ground at the site. Usually, some fill material is brought in to raise the foundation above the existing grade. The contractor then spreads the filler, which is usually gravel or stone. This allows any groundwater to dissipate without causing damage to the slab. A **moisture barrier**, or a sheet of 6- to 10-millimeter polyethylene (pahl-ee-EH-thuh-leen)—a type of plastic—is then spread across the filler. Parts of the heating and plumbing systems are actually put in place before pouring the slab. Concrete is poured over the moisture barrier, forming a slab that is about 4 inches thick. The slab has a turned-down footing that totals approximately 16 inches in depth. Rebar reinforcements strengthen the concrete slab and discourage cracking.

The Frame

The frame of the house is the skeleton around which the builder constructs the rest of the house. It consists of joists, studs, and rafters fastened together to support the house and its contents, 8-3. When

8-2
This brick ranch style house is built on a slab-on-grade foundation.

LINK TO SCIENCE & TECHNOLOGY

Designing for Disaster: Earthquakes

The number of earthquakes in the United States during 2009 was 4,123, according to the U.S. Geological Survey (USGS). The USGS is the federal agency that records and reports U.S. earthquake activity. Fortunately, most earthquakes are mild and cause little or no damage. However, they can be extremely destructive and lethal. In 2008 for example, an earthquake in Sichuan, China, caused more than 5 million buildings to collapse and killed an estimated 87,587 people. In 2010, another earthquake killed multitudes of people in Haiti. Many lost their lives in their homes, schools, and other buildings by falling debris.

An earthquake is a sudden and sometimes violent shaking of the earth's crust or outer layer. The crust consists of large jigsawlike pieces called *tectonic plates*. These plates float on a layer of rock melted by the high temperatures and pressure deep inside the earth. The plates are in constant motion, usually moving only a few centimeters a year. However, volcanic action or a sudden release of energy along points of stress between and within the plates can cause intense shaking or earthquakes.

The goal for design and construction in earthquake-prone areas is to minimize damage to homes and other structures and to prevent deaths. Designers and builders use such resources as the following:

- **International Residential Code (IRC).** In the United States, this is the principal building code for residential construction. It includes recommendations by the *National Earthquake Hazards Reduction Program* (NEHRP).

- **Homebuilders' Guide to Earthquake-Resistant Design and Construction.** This document, published by the Federal Emergency Management Agency (FEMA), offers construction guidance and provides supplemental information to the IRC. This guide also presents some "above code recommendations" and low-cost construction measures to increase building performance and functionality during and after an earthquake.

For more information about the theory of plate tectonics and earthquakes, go to the U.S. Geological Survey's Web site at http://www.usgs.gov/. Use the key words *plate tectonics* and *earthquakes*.

8-3
The framing members of the house provide the skeletal structure.

assembled and covered with sheet materials, they form floors, walls, and roof surfaces.

Floor Frame

After completing the foundation walls, construction of the floor frame occurs. First, the builder places a sill sealer and sometimes a termite shield on top of the foundation walls. Next, the installation of the first piece of lumber, or **sill plate**, occurs. When the sill plate comes in contact with masonry, it must consist of pressure preservative treated (PT) lumber. Note that the process for creating **pressure preservative treated (PT)** lumber forces chemical preservatives into the cellular structure of the wood under pressure. This process preserves the wood from mold, mildew, termites, and other insects.

The sill plates support the outside walls of the house. **Anchor bolts** secure the sill plate to the foundation walls. Local building codes will determine the spacing between the anchor bolts to meet uplift requirements to withstand tornadoes and hurricanes. Anchor bolts are set into the concrete of the foundation walls before the concrete hardens.

If the foundation wall consists of concrete block, the top two cores (or layers) of the blocks are first filled with *mortar*—a mixture of sand, cement, and water. Then the builder embeds anchor bolts into the mortar to bolt down the sill plate.

The floor frame is built on top of the sill plate or on top of wall frames when a second or third floor is desired. It consists of joists, girders, and subflooring. **Joists** are lightweight horizontal support members. Header joists and rim joists form the perimeter of the floor framing. The ends of the floor joists are nailed to the header joists at 16- to 24-inch intervals. In some homes, a wood or steel girder supports the joists. A **girder** is a large horizontal member in the floor that takes the load of joists. It supports the load of the floor joists and the weight of the floor or roof above it. Girders may be solid lumber, built-up lumber (often three wooden planks fastened together with nails or screws), engineered wood (layers of wood secured with strong adhesives), or steel beams.

Subflooring covers the floor-framing members. **Subflooring** consists of a covering of plywood or oriented strand board (OSB) sheets directly glued and nailed to the floor joists. **Plywood sheets** are layers of thin wood veneers that have been glued and pressed together. **Oriented strand board (OSB)** is made by layering wood chips and fiber in a cross-hatch pattern and gluing them together to form a sheet. The better the construction of the floor frame, the less likely it is to develop problems. Squeaky floors usually indicate problems with floor-framing construction. Because normal vibrations over a period of time may loosen the subflooring, some houses develop floor squeaks, especially in heavy traffic areas. Refer to 8-4 to see the components of a floor frame and wall frame.

Wall Frame

The wall frame is built on top of the floor frame. Lumber that is 2-inches by 4-inches or 2-inches by 6-inches forms the vertical framing members, or **studs**, and the plates, or the horizontal framing members. Wall frames have a single *sole plate* on the bottom and a double *top plate* that supports the ceiling joists and roof members. Exterior and interior walls are generally built by laying them flat on the subfloor. The builder then raises and nails them into position on the floor frame.

Wall frames are either bearing or nonload bearing. A **bearing wall** supports some weight from the ceiling or roof of the structure. A **nonbearing wall** does not support any weight from the structure beyond its own weight. Exterior frame walls are usually bearing walls. Interior frame walls are called *partitions* to distinguish them from exterior walls. While some main partitions are also bearing walls, most interior partitions are nonbearing.

Headers are small, built-up beams that carry the load of the structure over door and window openings. For a 6-inch-thick outside wall, headers are made from 2-inch by 10-inch lumber

8-4

The floor and wall framing consists of joists, studs, girders, plates, headers, and subflooring.

Modern Carpentry by Wagner and Smith, Goodheart-Willcox

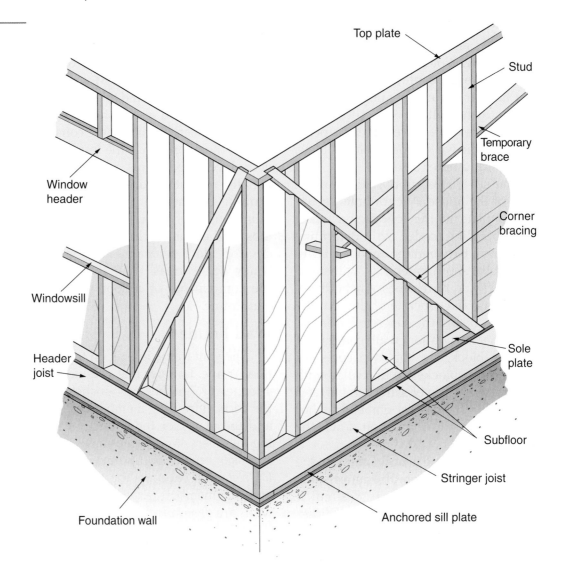

Top plate

Stud

Temporary brace

Window header

Corner bracing

Windowsill

Header joist

Sole plate

Subfloor

Foundation wall

Stringer joist

Anchored sill plate

on edge with a piece of ½-inch thick plywood between them. This forms a header that is 3½ inches thick. (See Chapter 14 for a discussion on finishes for interior walls.)

Cracks, waves, or buckles in these wall frames indicate shifting of the wood frame or an incorrectly installed wall covering. Also, stains on the wall covering may indicate moisture from a leaky roof or leaks around windows and doors. It is important to correct any such area to prevent the growth of mold in the structure.

Alternatives to traditional wood wall framing for the exterior walls of houses include the use of autoclaved

aerated concrete (AAC), insulated concrete forms (ICF), and metal framing systems.

Autoclaved aerated concrete (AAC) block construction involves mixing sand, fly ash, cement, and water, with aluminum powder—an expansion agent. The mixture is cast into a mold and then cut into blocks. It cures under pressure and heat for 8 to 12 hours at the manufacturing plant. The builder assembles the finished blocks at the job site to create the framing system of the house. The result is an ultralightweight concrete building material that is energy efficient, very strong, sound absorbent, and not harmful to the environment. AAC systems have been used in Europe for many years and have gained acceptance in the U.S. market.

AAC masonry block construction has many advantages over traditional wood framing. Because it is noncombustible, home owners can reduce the cost of their home owner's insurance. It also resists termite or insect attack. In addition, it is a low-maintenance product and cannot rot as wood does and builders can use traditional hand tools to work with it. You can expect to see more homes in the future built with this material.

Insulated concrete forms (ICF) consist of rigid polystyrene (plastic) foam forms with internal plastic for ties. These forms stack together like building blocks. Reinforcing steel is put into the ICF during the stacking process. Concrete is poured into the open middle forming a reinforced concrete wall with insulation on the face. Exterior finishes, such as stucco or wood, can be used to cover this system. Traditional materials can be used to cover interior walls.

Contractors may also use metal framing systems very much like wood framing; however, they fasten metal framing together with screws. An advantage of these systems is that they are fireproof and rot resistant. The cost of alternative framing systems depends on several factors. These factors include the location in which you are building and the training of the workforce in your area.

Roof Frame

The roof frame consists of a series of beams, or **rafters**, that support the weight of the roof. They extend from the exterior walls to the ridge, 8-5. The **ridge board** is the horizontal member at which the two slopes of the roof meet. It is the highest point of the roof frame.

In modern houses, most roof framing utilizes truss rafters. A **truss rafter**

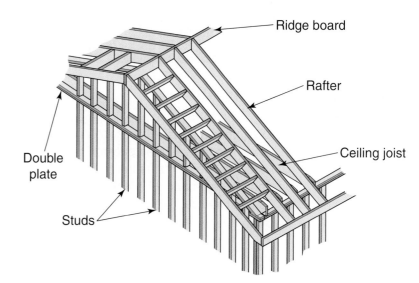

Roof and Ceiling Frame

is a group of members forming a rigid-triangular framework for the roof. They are assembled at a factory and delivered to the job site. The builder then attaches them directly to the double top plate. Truss rafters usually span the distance between exterior walls.

As you evaluate the frame of the house, remember to look for stress cracks and hairline cracks. If you notice a sagging ceiling, it could indicate use of the wrong size or type of lumber. New houses will not show problems until they have settled. Pre-owned houses have had time to settle and probably will not crack further unless remodeling or more construction takes place.

8-5
The roof and ceiling framing consists of plates, joists, rafters, and the ridge board.

Modern Carpentry by Wagner and Smith, Goodheart-Willcox

Materials Used for Exterior Construction

After the foundation and frame are built, the exterior walls and the roof coverings are put in place. The materials used for exterior construction vary. The first layer applied is the sheathing. It may be wood, nail-base fiberboard, OSB, or plywood that is nailed to the

MATH MATTERS

Polygons

A polygon is a plane figure bounded by straight lines on three or more sides. Polygons are classified by the number of sides and the angles they contain. For example, a five-sided polygon is a pentagon. An angle is where two sides meet. There are five angles inside the pentagon. A regular polygon is one in which all sides are of equal length and all interior angles are equal. You can use a formula to calculate the size of an interior angle of a regular polygon. If x is the number of sides, the size of each interior angle is (x-2) × 180° ÷ x.

Regular Polygons		
Name	**Number of Sides**	**Number and Size of Interior Angles**
triangle	3	3, 60°
quadrilateral	4	4, 90°
pentagon	5	5, 108°
hexagon	6	6, 120°
heptagon	7	7, 128.57°
octagon	8	8, 135°
nonagon	9	9, 140°
decagon	10	10, 144°

studs. The sheathing is then usually covered with a thin plastic sheet called *house wrap* or a water-resistant paper called *building paper*. It is important for house wrap or building paper to form a water-resistant membrane but remain permeable enough to allow water vapor to pass through it.

Next is the siding application. The most common types of siding are wood, aluminum, vinyl, pressed wood (OSB or fiberboard), or fiber-cement siding. Other siding materials include **masonry**—a hard building material, such as brick, concrete block, stucco, and natural stone, bonded together with mortar. The selection of materials depends on their availability in the area, the cost of the materials, and the preference of the homeowners. Siding materials present different advantages and challenges.

Wood Siding

Siding is the material forming the exposed surface of outside walls of a house. It is applied in strips, as shown in 8-6. Wood is a common material used. Wood siding is milled from cedar, redwood, pine, and cypress. It is suitable for a wide variety of exterior styles. Sustainable or green wood siding materials come from forests in which the highest ethical, social, and environmental practices are used in forest management.

Wood has some distinct advantages as a siding material. It has a relatively low cost and is an excellent nonconductor of heat. It is also easy to cut and assemble. The ease of working with and fastening wood together with simple tools provides flexibility without extensive redesigning. Wood does, however, expand and contract with changes in temperature or humidity.

With wood siding, routine inspections for rot and pest invasion (such as termites or carpenter ants) must occur to check for damage. Another disadvantage of wood is the maintenance cost of frequent painting or staining. Some parts of the country have climates that require painting every four years. However, periodic painting does give home owners the flexibility of changing house colors as they see fit.

When inspecting the exterior siding of a house, look for putty marks covered with paint. This may indicate poor siding application or repair. Also, a house that has siding covered up with putty and paint may have other problems that have been disguised.

Plywood siding is another type of wood siding. It can be applied horizontally or vertically. It covers large areas and saves installation time. Plywood siding must also be painted or stained, then sealed. It is also susceptible to termite damage and climatic changes.

Manufactured Siding

Siding materials also make use of such products as aluminum, vinyl, pressed wood, and fiber-cement products. These different materials have varying advantages and disadvantages.

The advantages of *aluminum siding* are its durability and lack of need for repainting. It often has weather- and corrosion-resistant finishes. However, it does dent, as often occurs in hailstorms, and may conduct electricity.

Vinyl siding is also durable and does not conduct electricity. It can expand and contract with changes in the temperature and humidity, but it is not the most sustainable of products. Like aluminum, it does not require painting. However, it, too, will show dents.

Pressed wood siding is made from *oriented strand board (OSB)* or primed fiberboard. As you know, OSB is made by layering wood chips and fiber in

8-6
Fiber-cement siding is being applied to the side of this new house.

a crosshatch pattern. Fiberboard has similar construction but uses longer strands of fiber. Both products are easy to paint, but cannot be stained. They are less expensive than plywood siding. Special surface treatments are available, such as brushed, texture-embossed, and V-grooves.

Fiber-cement siding is made from a calcium-silicate material that is evenly dispersed with reinforcing fibers. It is dimensionally stable, and resists moisture, mold and mildew development, and pests. It will not burn and has a zero smoke-development rating. It is less expensive than brick, but has all the benefits. Fiber cement siding can be

GREEN CHOICES

Forest Stewardship Council (FSC)

Why is the Forest Stewardship Council (FSC) considered green? This international, nonprofit Council is *green* because it promotes responsible forestry standards. The FSC certification provides a label certifying that certain wood products for use in building houses and furniture come from forests that are managed to meet the needs of present and future generations.

As you know, forests provide clean water and fresh air. Preserving forests is an important factor in making sure the world is sustainable through protection of its natural resources. However, in many forests, certain timbering practices still contribute to habitat destruction, water pollution, and more.

The FSC label certifies the wood products come from forest timbering that supports the highest social and environmental principles of conservation of natural forests. In order for a company or organization to earn the right to use the FSC label, it must first comply with all applicable FSC requirements. Also, the FSC labeled wood products meet the requirements of the Green Building Council's certified LEED program.

Source: www.fscus.org

©1996 Forest Stewardship Council A.C. The use of this logo is the mark of responsible forestry. FSC

ordered with a factory-primed finish. It does require painting, but holds paint two to three times longer than wood.

Masonry Siding

Construction of the exterior wall sometimes utilizes brick, clay tile, concrete block, natural stone, or exterior stucco. As you learned earlier, stucco is a type of plaster, 8-7. **Brick** is a block molded from moist clay and hardened with heat. **Natural stone** is hardened earth or mineral matter.

Builders sometimes use a brick veneer wall to create the look of a masonry wall. A **veneer wall** is a nonsupporting wall. House wrap covers the sheathing on the wall frame and thin sheet-metal ties secure the veneer wall to the sheathing. Note there is about a

1-inch space between the veneer and sheathing to allow any moisture to flow to the bottom of the structure and out weepholes located in the bottom of the veneer. Masonry construction is porous by nature so control of water in the wall design is very important. In many areas of the country, usage of masonry veneer walls is common.

Masonry products have distinct advantages. The products are strong, durable, and usually inexpensive to maintain. Also, they generally last a long time. The disadvantage of masonry products is the initial cost. They are usually hand-laid, which is one reason for their expense.

Masonry materials are available in a wide range of sizes, colors, and textures to produce different architectural effects. The **pattern bond**, or the pattern formed by masonry units and the mortar joints on the face of the wall, can create other interesting effects. By varying the bonds and the depth and shape of mortar joints between units, additional depth dimensions and shadows add to the masonry wall.

When you examine a masonry house, you need to look for cracks or bows in the walls. Hairline cracks in the joints are normal expansion cracks. However, larger cracks can break bricks as they continue up or down the wall.

Roofing Materials

Common roofing materials include asphalt, fiberglass, vinyl, wood, tile, slate, concrete, and metal. These materials provide color and texture that make the exterior of the house more attractive. However, they must also provide a protective, watertight covering to keep out rain and snow. If the roof leaks, damage to the house structure and its contents can happen.

Most houses have sloping roofs with a covering of shingles. **Shingles** are thin pieces of building material that lay in overlapping rows on roofs. Asphalt shingles are the most common roofing material. In warmer regions, usage of shingles that combine asphalt and fiberglass help keep the house cooler. Asphalt shingles range in price from inexpensive to more costly depending on the composition, warranty, and quality of the product, 8-8. Vinyl shingles are similar to asphalt shingles and come in a variety of textures and colors. Shingle color is a consideration factor depending on the climate. Dark roof colors tend to absorb heat and light colors tend to reflect heat.

Wood shingles as well as *shakes*—which are a thicker, less uniform shingle—are more costly than asphalt shingles. Treatment with fire-retardant and decay-resistant chemicals is important for durability. Shingles and shakes

are popular because of their natural colors. Usage of these shingles is most common where cedar, redwood, and cypress trees grow.

In parts of the country with hot sun and little snowfall, clay or fiberglass tile, slate, and concrete roofing materials are often used. These materials are heavy and require proper roof design and structure to support the extra weight, 8-9. Also, they are expensive. Clay or fiberglass tile, slate, and concrete roofing materials are very durable and will last the lifetime of the house.

Metal roofing material is also available. Sheets of metal roofing are obtainable in aluminum, zinc-plated steel, terneplate (a lead-tin coating on steel), and stainless steel. Copper may be used on an entire roof or as an accent to a small area. The price of metal roofing varies depending on the quality. Metal roofing materials are more costly than asphalt and vinyl shingles, but not as expensive as tile.

The application of most roofing materials occurs in the same manner. First the builder covers the roof frame with sheathing. Then an application of a heavy building paper or roofing felt helps keep out a limited amount of

8-7
Stucco homes have remained popular throughout the years.

Group 3, Architectural and Interior Design, Hilton Head Island, SC. Photography provided as a courtesy of John McManus, Savannah, GA.

8-8
Many roofs are covered with asphalt or asphalt and fiberglass shingles.

8-9
Roof tiles weigh about ten pounds each. This heavy load requires stronger rafters and other framing members to support the total weight of the roof.

rain. After installation of a metal *drip edge* along the eaves, the builder applies a starter strip of shingles along the roof bottom and then fastens the rest of the shingles in straight lines. When complete, a shingled roof should have a uniform appearance in the pattern of application.

When inspecting an existing roof, it is important to ask about reasons for every roof repair. A change in shingle color may indicate patching instead of reroofing. Problems that lead to patching usually resurface at a later date. In addition, it is important to pay close attention to the materials used for flashing and their installation. **Flashing** is a water-resistant sheet metal used to help keep the roof watertight. It is used in valleys—the junctions that form where two sloping roofs meet at an angle. It is also used where a roof meets a vertical surface such as a wall or chimney. If the flashing is a substandard material or installed incorrectly, leaks can occur.

Give special attention to inspecting flat areas of the roof. These areas should have a covering that consists of a buildup of layers of roofing felt and asphalt or a membrane product such as heavy rubber sheeting. If the sheeting is used, it should have few or no seams. Inspect such flat areas on a roof carefully because they are very prone to leaks. All flat areas must be sloped to drain areas that collect standing water to help prevent leaks.

The remaining components of a roof system are the gutters and downspouts. A **gutter** is a horizontal open trough located under the perimeter of the roof to channel away water. A **downspout** is a vertical pipe that connects the gutter system to the ground to carry rainwater away from the home's foundation. The construction of gutters and downspouts uses aluminum or vinyl materials. The color is baked onto aluminum, but exists throughout vinyl. The advantage of both materials is that they do not require painting. Aluminum has one additional advantage over vinyl—gutter extrusion can actually happen on site for a seamless installation.

GREEN CHOICES

Builder Responsibilities for Green and Sustainable Design

Builders are important players in creating houses that have a positive impact on the environment. A good source of builder information on green and sustainable design is the *Model Home Building Guidelines* from the National Home Builders Association (NAHB). Many local home-builders associations across the nation are developing programs that use these guidelines.

Builders with concerns for the environment can obtain these guidelines and use them in their construction projects. Also, builders can acquire the *Certified Green Professional Designation* from the NAHB by attending 24 hours of special training and continuing education every two years.

Builders can follow green design principles by doing the following:

- Use the natural environment in lot preparation to enhance the home's long-term performance.

- Use advanced framing techniques to get the most from building materials.

- Focus on the best ways to handle waste from construction.

- Build more energy efficient structures and incorporate more energy efficient mechanical systems, appliances, and lighting into a home.

- Use ways to reduce indoor and outdoor water usage.

- Control moisture, ventilation, and other issues to create a more comfortable and healthier indoor living environment.

- Inform the homeowner on green aspects of the home and how to best operate and maintain the home.

Source: National Home Builders Association (NAHB)

Windows and Doors

When people first built dwellings, a window was an opening that provided ventilation. A door was an opening for entry and security. In the past, windows and doors did not fit houses well and allowed heat to escape from houses. They also provided very little insulation. Over time, many new types of windows and doors were developed. They were built to prevent air from escaping and to provide better insulation, 8-10. Today a wide range of styles, shapes, and special options are available for both windows and doors.

Windows

Windows have many uses in a house. From the interior, they provide natural light, air circulation, and a view. They can also serve as a point of emphasis in a room or as a part of the background. On the exterior, their size, shape, and placement affect the appearance of the house. In addition, some windows have built-in features or special coatings that conserve energy, are UV resistant, and prevent heat transference. Also, high-impact glass panes add protection from breakage by flying objects during

8-10
The installer is checking to be sure the rough opening is the correct size for the window installation. Note the waterproof house wrap on this structure.

Photography Courtesy of JELD-WEN Windows and Doors

in modern insulated windows are an overlay on a large sheet of glass. They no longer separate or support small panes of glass.

- **Stool.** The stool is the horizontal trim member located on the bottom of the interior window frame.

- **Apron.** The apron is a strip of decorative interior trim that is below the stool.

Originally, window frames were made from either wood or aluminum. Today, windows are often clad (covered) with aluminum or vinyl for low maintenance or are made from vinyl extrusions. As a result of strict local and national energy codes, more energy-efficient materials are used in the construction of window units.

storms or high winds. These windows are more costly because of the additional features. However, certain regions of the country, such as coastal areas, are adopting building codes that require these windows in new construction.

Windows have many parts, 8-11. These parts include the following:

- **Frame.** The frame is the perimeter of the window that fits into the window opening and is nailed or screwed into place. The sides of the frame are called *jambs*. The top of the window frame is the *header* and the bottom of the window frame is the *sill*.

- **Pane.** The pane is the window glass.

- **Sash.** The sash is the framework that holds the glass in the window. The sash swings or slides open. *Muntins* are vertical and horizontal dividers that separate different panes of glass in a window. Originally made of wood, these muntins divide the pane of glass into smaller sections. Muntins

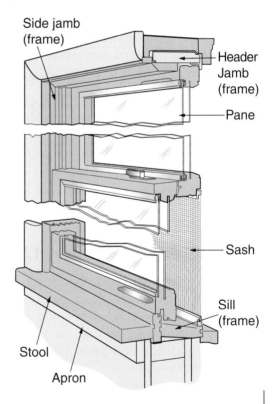

8-11
The five main parts of a window are the frame, sash, pane, stool, and apron.

Pella Corp.

There are three basic types of windows: sliding, swinging, and fixed windows. All other window styles are based on these three. The type chosen for a house depends on the exterior style of the house, building codes, and personal preference. A traditional design, such as a Southern Colonial or French Provincial, looks best with a sliding window with muntins. A contemporary house may feature large expanses of fixed windows.

Sliding Windows

Sliding windows can operate either vertically or horizontally. A *double-hung window* is a vertical sliding window, as shown in 8-12. It provides an opening of about one-half the size of the window.

Horizontal-sliding windows have two or three sashes. Two-sash windows have one sash that slides and the other that stays fixed, 8-13. On a three-sash window, the center sash is fixed and the two outside sashes slide toward the center. Screens are mounted on the outside.

Swinging Windows

There are four types of swinging windows. They are casement, awning, hopper, and jalousie windows, 8-14. *Casement windows* open and close with a crank and swing outward. Usually the entire window area can be opened for ventilation, 8-15.

Awning windows swing outward at the bottom and are hinged at the top. This provides protection from rain. A similar window is the *hopper window*. It is hinged at the bottom to allow the top of the sash to swing inward.

Jalousie windows are a series of horizontal, adjustable glass slats fastened into a metal frame. They open and close with a crank and are used where ventilation is needed. Screens and storm windows are located on the interior.

8-12
The windows in this bathroom are double-hung sliding.

Photography Courtesy of JELD-WEN Windows and Doors

Fixed Windows

Fixed windows admit light and provide a view. However, they do not open. They come in many shapes and sizes, including rectangular, oval, half-round, round, and arched, 8-16. Glass blocks are

8-13
One sash is operable in this two-sash, horizontal-sliding window.

Photography Courtesy of JELD-WEN Windows and Doors

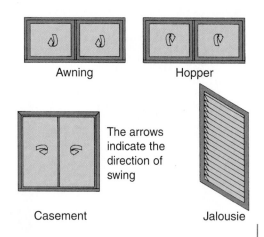

Awning   Hopper

Casement   Jalousie

The arrows indicate the direction of swing

8-14
Awning, hopper, casement, and jalousie windows swing out to provide excellent ventilation.

8-16
This fixed window unit creates a dramatic focal point in the room.

Image Courtesy of Anderson Corporation

fixed windows that provide light while preserving visual privacy, 8-17.

Combination Windows

Fixed windows used with other types of windows are called *combination windows*. For example, hopper windows are often used above a fixed window. A large fixed window can have a casement window on either side.

A *bay window* is a combination window that projects outward from the exterior wall of the house. It often has a large fixed window in the center and double-hung windows on both sides.

Skylights and Clerestory Windows

Using skylights and clerestory windows helps let light into areas that get little or no natural light. They can also offer additional light to give a room an airy appearance, 8-18. *Skylights* are normally located in the ceiling or roof. They are usually square or rectangular and come in various sizes. *Light tubes* are an economical and energy efficient form of skylight. They have a small clear plastic dome on the roof and a shiny metal tube that connects to a lens with a light diffuser in the ceiling. Placement of clerestory windows is generally high on an outside wall. They can be standard or custom-made windows.

Doors

Doors provide access, protection, safety, and privacy. They also provide a barrier against sound, extreme temperatures, and light. Exterior doors are made from wood or wood covered with metal or vinyl. Interior doors are made from wood, metal, or wood covered with vinyl.

8-15
These dormer windows are casement style. The curve of the windows adds interest.

Photography Courtesy of JELD-WEN Windows and Doors

8-17
Glass-block windows admit light but provide privacy.

8-18
The half-round clerestory window and skylights play an important part in the interior design of this house.
Velux-America, Inc.

Operation of Doors

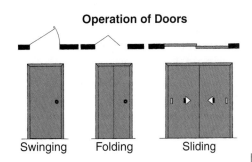

Swinging   Folding   Sliding

8-19
Doors operate in three different ways—by swinging, folding, or sliding.

Doors are often classified by their method of operation, 8-19. *Swinging doors* operate on hinges and usually swing open in one direction. Enough room needs to be left for the door to swing open and close. *Sliding doors* are set on a track and open or close by gliding on the track. When open, a *folding door* folds into a multisection stack. Classification of doors also occurs by their method of construction and assembly, 8-20.

Stile and Rail Doors

Stile and rail doors consist of stiles (solid vertical members), rails (solid horizontal members), and panels (that fill the space between stiles and rails). The panels may be decorative or glass. They may be raised or flat. Raised panels are cut from solid wood, and flat panels are usually cut from plywood. The number of panel combinations is limitless.

Construction of Doors

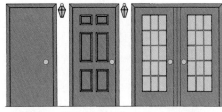

Flush   Stile and rail   Framed glass (French)

8-20
Doors can be constructed in many different ways, including these three methods.

Flush Doors

Construction of flush doors requires covering a framework core with wood or other material, such as metal or vinyl. There are two basic types of cores—solid and hollow. A *solid-core door* consists of tightly fitted blocks of wood covered with veneer. Some doors utilize particleboard as the core. These doors are heavy and are used mainly for exterior doors and for interior doors where sound control is a consideration. A *hollow-core door* has a heavier outside frame combined with wood strips, stiff cardboard, or paper honeycomb as the core. This type of door is lightweight and is used mainly as an interior door.

Framed-Glass Doors

These stile and rail doors have glass panels. The glass may be single pane or insulating glass. French doors are framed-glass doors with the glass divided with muntins into small sections. Installation of *French doors* is usually in pairs, 8-21. Sliding glass doors are another example of a framed-glass door. They often take the place of windows in small or medium-sized houses.

8-21
These dramatic French doors create both a division and a transition between spaces.

Photography Courtesy of JELD-WEN Windows and Doors

Computer Applications in Construction

Most architects, engineers, building contractors, and interior designers use a computer to assist them with decisions related to house construction. Computer applications usually speed the process of designing houses and help to assure the accuracy of the designs. Another advantage of using a computer is the realistic view it provides of the final product—the house. Since most people cannot visualize how a finished house will look from architectural plans, seeing a lifelike picture can avoid disappointed clients.

House designers use the computer in three basic ways. One way is to analyze the strength and appropriateness of planned materials. They also use a computer to select construction components and manage the building process.

Analyzing Components of Construction

The designer of a house must assure the structural integrity of the design. For instance, the design of the steep roof on the home in Figure 8-22 helps prevent the build-up of snow. Besides providing the support needed under normal conditions, the house design will also withstand heavy snowfalls of several feet at a time.

Specialized computer software can analyze the planned materials and structural supports. It can also examine the stress these materials will undergo as a result of conditions in the geographic area, such as high heat and humidity. Computer programs also allow the designer to "test" various designs and materials to assure the safety and effectiveness of the structure before it is built. See 8-23 for an example of using a computer to analyze structural components.

Selecting Components of Construction

Housing components that are available in a wide variety of choices, such as windows, are best selected with the help of a computer. Housing designers and builders, for example, can view various window options and different placement combinations by using the Internet or special CD-ROMs. The Internet has become the primary resource for such material selections.

Often CD-ROMs provide product photos, price charts, sizing charts, design templates, and order forms. Window companies, cabinet manufacturers, and providers of other construction components make CD-ROMs available. You can also obtain the most up-to-date information about these companies by going online to their Web sites.

Managing the Construction

Computers can assist the designer and builder in developing plans that identify the sequence of steps required to construct the house. To ensure house completion in a timely and cost-effective manner, computers can develop a timetable for the project.

8-22
The builder of this house used special windows with insulated glass. The roof was engineered to withstand heavy snow.

Photography Courtesy of JELD-WEN Windows and Doors

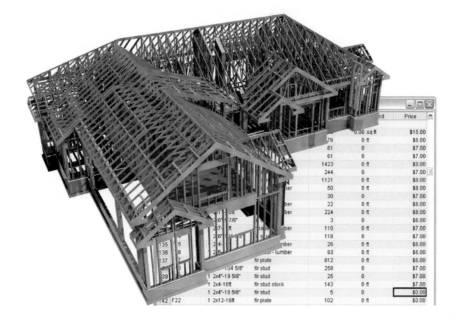

8-23
This image clearly shows the structural parts of the frame. The designer can identify and solve problems before construction begins.

Courtesy of Software by Chief Architect

CAREER FOCUS

Building Inspector

Can you imagine yourself as a building inspector?

Interests/Skills: If you share some of the following interests you may wish to explore the possibility of becoming a building inspector. Are you fascinated with buildings and how they are constructed? Are you interested in how things work in a building, such as the electrical, mechanical, plumbing, and HVAC systems? Do you enjoy working on construction projects such as building and working with your hands?

Career Snapshot: Building inspectors determine the structural soundness of buildings. It is also their job to be certain that the structures are safe and meet all local building codes, regulations, and specifications. Their inspections may be general in nature or may be limited to such specific areas as the footings, foundation, framing, electrical, and plumbing.

Education/Training: Most employers require at least a high school diploma or the equivalent, even for workers with considerable experience. More often, employers look for people who have studied engineering or architecture. A growing number of construction and building inspectors enter the occupation with a bachelor's degree.

Licensing/Examinations: Many states and local jurisdictions require some type of license or certification for employment as a construction and building inspector. Requirements vary by state or local municipality.

Professional Associations: National Association of Home Inspectors (NAHI) (www.nahi.org), American Institute of Inspectors (AII) (www.inspection.org), American Society of Home Inspectors (ASHI) (www.ashi.org), National Association of Certified Home Inspectors (NACHI) (www.nachi.org)

Job Outlook: Inspectors should experience faster than average employment growth. Job opportunities in construction and building inspection should be best for highly experienced supervisors and construction craft workers who have some college education, engineering or architectural training, or certification as inspectors or plan examiners.

Sources: Occupational Information Network (O*NET) (www.online.onetcenter.org) and the Occupational Outlook Handbook, Bureau of Labor Statistics (www.bls.gov)

Summary

Understanding house construction helps house buyers make good decisions. The foundation and the frame are the basic structure of the house. The foundation supports the frame structure above it. It needs to be constructed correctly to prevent uneven settling.

Once the foundation and frame are built, the exterior walls and the roof are added. A variety of materials are used.

Windows and doors complete the basic construction of the house. The three main types of windows are sliding, swinging, and fixed. Other windows are variations of these three types or combinations of them.

Doors are classified by their method of operation—swinging, sliding, or folding. They are also classified by the method of construction used to make them. With the help of the computer, designers and builders can work more efficiently.

Review the Facts

1. What are footings? Why do footings need to be placed on undisturbed, compact soil below the frost line?

2. What structural problems might cause stress cracks?

3. Identify the three main parts of the frame that work together to support the house and its contents.

4. What are three advantages of wood siding?

5. Contrast the advantages and disadvantages of each of the four types of manufactured siding discussed in the chapter.

6. What are five types of roofing materials?

7. For each of the following, identify whether the window is fixed, sliding, or swinging: (A) jalousie; (B) double-hung; (C) awning; (D) half-round; (E) horizontal-sliding; (F) casement; (G) hopper.

8. How is an interior door construction different from an exterior door?

9. Contrast a solid-core with hollow-core door.

10. What are three benefits of computer applications in construction?

Think Critically

11. **Assess buildings.** Presume you have been hired by the local government as a building inspector. Develop a house evaluation form that will help you inspect buildings and assess them for problems. Use additional Internet or print resources to help develop your evaluation. Share your results with the class.

12. **Analyze information.** Assume your client is building a home in the northwest region of the United States. Sustainable design and construction is an important factor for your client. Use Internet or print resources to locate information on the best window and siding options for this region. Analyze which options support your client's value for sustainable design and construction. Write a summary outlining the best options.

Community Links

13. **Construction observation.** Observe a house under construction and identify as many of the structural components discussed in this chapter as you can. If possible, take photographs of the house under construction. Report your findings to the class.

14. **Assess replacement costs.** Make a list of the door and window sizes in one room of your house. Take this list to a building supply company and obtain costs for replacing these windows and doors with energy-efficient units. Compare the costs of two manufacturers. Also find out the labor cost for installing them. Share your findings with the class. As an alternative, use the Web sites of two building supply companies to do your comparison.

15. **Consumer awareness.** Review the Web site for your state's attorney general regarding information about problems with new home construction or remodeling that home owners report. Also, check the cautionary information to home owners that these offices provide. Use the information and desktop publishing software to create a consumer flyer noting a list of brief steps to help home owners avoid potential problems when building or remodeling.

Academic Connections

16. **Math.** Imagine you are a contractor hired by a family to build their new home. The house plan they have selected contains a total of 1,800 square feet of heated space. Your clients want a rough estimate of how much it will cost to build this plan before they proceed with contract discussion. How would you determine this? Contact a number of builders in your community, and ask them what the building costs currently are per square foot of space. Find the average and multiply it by 1,800 square feet. What is your estimate?

17. **Science.** Use the Internet to examine information about the process for creating pressure-treated lumber and engineered wood beams. What environmental and safety factors are involved in the manufacture of this lumber? Is it sustainable? Why or why not? Write a summary of your findings.

Technology Applications

18. **Software evaluation.** Determine if your school has housing design software similar to what is used in the housing industry. If so, explore the program(s) and determine how the software can assist a builder. Print out a drawing from the computer and present it to the class along with a summary of your findings.

19. **Electronic presentation.** Locate a major window manufacturer on the Internet. Identify photos of various window styles, shapes, and special options to share with the class. Copy and insert the photos into presentation software and share your presentation with the class. Be sure to credit the window manufacturer in your presentation.

20. **Internet research.** Search the Internet using the key term *house construction* to find a site containing photos of houses under construction. Identify the various stages of construction.

Design Practice

21. **Frame design.** Use a CADD software program to draft the footing and foundation design for a home. Apply local building codes and guidelines for house construction in your area. Print a copy of your design to keep in your portfolio.

22. **Portfolio.** Choose a house design discussed in Chapter 6. Then draw the foundation and frame of the house using a ¼ inch to 1 foot scale. Label each part. Then select the types of windows and doors you would suggest for it. Include drawings, Internet or magazine photos, or pictures from sales brochures to illustrate your selections. Write a summary about your proposal. Keep your project in your portfolio for future reference.

Teaming Up with Habitat for Humanity®

As an FCCLA chapter, team up with *Habitat for Humanity* to help build or renovate a home in your community. To be a member of the building team, Habitat requires that you be 16 years old. If you are under 16, there are other ways you can share your leadership skills. Check out the Habitat for Humanity Web site (www.habitat.org) to find out more about Habitat's *Youth Programs*.

Then join forces with your team members and a Habitat construction-team leader to plan and carry out your FCCLA *Community Service* project. Use the FCCLA *Planning Process* and other documentation as a guide. See your adviser for information as needed.

CHAPTER 9

The Systems Within

Terms to Learn

system
electricity
electric current
conductor
circuit
ampere (amp)
voltage
watts
fossil fuel
conduit
service drop
meter
service entrance panel
overcurrent protection devices
fuse
circuit breaker
ground fault circuit interrupter (GFCI)
home generators
septic tank
vent stack
soil stack
trap
composting toilet
HVAC
forced warm-air system
duct
thermostat
hydronic heating systems
electric radiant-heating systems
central heat-pump system
fireplace insert
insulation
R-value
weather stripping

Chapter Objectives

After studying this chapter, you will be able to

- summarize the parts of the electrical system.

- distinguish between the use of natural gas and liquid propane gas in households.

- summarize the functions of the two main parts of the plumbing system.

- compare and contrast the different types of heating systems.

- summarize how cooling systems work.

- analyze ways to conserve household energy.

Reading with Purpose

Find an article on http://news.google.com that relates to the topic covered in this chapter. Print the article and read it before reading the chapter. As you read the chapter, highlight passages in the news article that relate to the text.

Photography Courtesy of Kohler

Almost every house has systems within it to make it physically comfortable. A **system** is an interacting or interdependent group of items forming a unified whole. The systems in a house—or *mechanical systems*—control the interior temperature and relative humidity, and provide electricity, gas, and water to the house.

Basic housing considerations regarding the interior systems may include the following questions: Will I have gas or electric appliances, or both? How can I make the house more energy efficient? How much insulation do I really need? What window type is best for the climate? What new technologies do today's houses use? These questions will be easier to answer after studying this chapter.

Electrical Systems

Almost all houses in the United States have electrical power. Electricity provides energy for lighting and the operation of appliances. It also powers the operation of most of the systems within the house, 9-1.

Around your house, perhaps you have noticed words like *watts, volts,* or *amperes (amps)* on electrical appliances or even lightbulbs. Knowledge of basic electricity will help you understand these terms and how the electrical system functions.

Electrical Terms

Electricity is the movement of electrons along a conductor. Another name for electricity is **electric current**. The **conductor** allows the flow of electricity and is usually a wire. This movement takes place at about the speed of light. A **circuit** forms when electrons follow a path from the source of electricity to the device and back to the source. The circuit is composed of a delivery wire and a return wire.

The greater the number of electrons passing a given point in a circuit, the greater is the current. The measure of the amount of electricity passing through a conductor per unit of time is the **ampere (amp)**. For example, a 100-watt incandescent lightbulb requires almost one ampere (0.83 amp) of current to make it work properly.

Voltage is a measure of the pressure used to push the electrical current along a conductor. This pressure is present in wiring circuits whether electricity is in use or not.

The electrical utility company delivers electricity to your house at a voltage that will operate your lighting, electrical appliances, and other electrical equipment. Lighting and most small appliances require 110 volts. Larger appliances—such as an electric kitchen range, electric water heater, electric clothes dryer, and furnace—require 220 volts.

The amount of electrical power used is measured in **watts**. When operating a device, watts tell consumers how much electrical power the device will use. For example, the usage of one watt of power occurs when one ampere lights a 100-watt incandescent lightbulb in a circuit with a force of one volt. The following equation helps show this concept:

$$watts = amperes \times volts.$$

9-1
Electricity provides the capacity to watch TV in a well-lighted room.

Electrical Power Generation

Electrical power comes from a variety of sources. Power plants usually generate electrical current by converting the energy from falling water, atomic fission, or burning fossil fuels into electricity. A **fossil fuel** is a fuel that forms in the earth from plant or animal remains. Fossil fuels include natural gas, propane, gasoline, coal, charcoal, and wood. Burning of these energy sources produces steam that turns turbines in generators to produce electricity.

Another form of electrical power generation comes from the wind. How does this renewable source of energy produce electricity? Modern-day wind turbines (similar to the old-style windmills) capture wind energy. The large blades of the wind turbines rotate as wind flows over them. While rotating, the blades move a drive shaft that runs an electric generator to make electricity. You will learn more about using wind as an energy source in Chapter 23.

Power plants transmit electricity at high voltages in wires held high by steel towers. When the electricity reaches the community, a transformer reduces the voltage and increases the current. Distribution of electricity occurs throughout a neighborhood via wires on poles or buried underground in a conduit. A **conduit** is a metal or plastic pipe that surrounds and protects the wires.

Before the electricity reaches your house, another transformer lowers the voltage even further. A three-wire line from the transformer provides both 110 and 220 voltages for the house.

Electricity in the House

At the house, the electric company installs a service drop. A **service drop** contains the wires connecting the utility pole transformer to the point of entry to the customer's house, 9-2. The wires can also run underground to the house through a *service lateral*. In both instances, the three wires run to the electric meter for the house. The **meter** monitors electrical usage. A power company representative periodically checks the meter to determine power usage for the house. In some locations, the power company uses computerized technology to read the meter from a central office.

The **service entrance panel** is a large metal box that receives power from the electric company's service drop or service lateral. It divides the power into individual circuits. These circuits provide electricity to each room or combination of rooms in the house, 9-3. An **overcurrent protection device**

9-2
Electricity travels from the power plant to your house through conductors that carry the electric current.

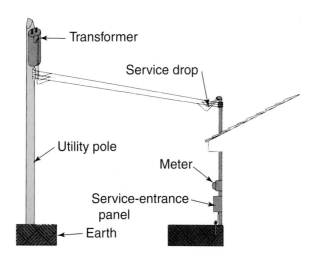

- Transformer
- Service drop
- Utility pole
- Meter
- Service-entrance panel
- Earth

Aboveground

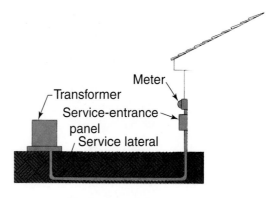

- Meter
- Transformer
- Service-entrance panel
- Service lateral

Underground

9-3
A circuit carries electricity from the service entrance panel to the electrical devices in your home.

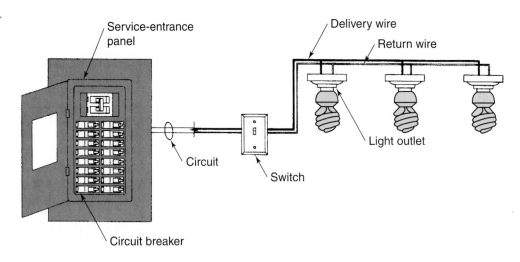

Service-entrance panel

Delivery wire

Return wire

Light outlet

Circuit

Switch

Circuit breaker

LINK TO SCIENCE & TECHNOLOGY

GFCIs for Household Use

There are three types of GFCIs available for household use. They include the following:

- **Circuit breaker GFCI.** Installation of this special circuit breaker is in the electrical service panel and replaces ordinary circuit breakers. They are much more sensitive to abnormal electrical conditions.

- **Receptacle GFCI.** This type of GFCI replaces a standard receptacle near the kitchen or bathroom sink. Test and reset buttons are in the middle of the receptacle. Although available for use in any house, houses that have a service entrance panel with fuses must use receptacle GFCIs.

- **Portable GFCI.** The most common type of portable GFCI combines an extension cord with a GFCI. You might use a portable GFCI for computers or other appliances where installation of GFCI receptacles is not practical.

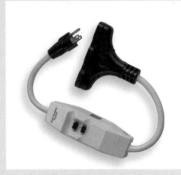

Coleman Cable, Inc.

Photograph Courtesy of Siemens Industry, Inc.

protects each circuit by stopping the excessive flow of electrical current in the circuit. This situation occurs when appliances or other electrical items on a circuit draw too much current. Most large electrical appliances—such as refrigerators or dishwashers—require their own circuit (or dedicated circuit). This means no other appliances should be on this circuit.

Two types of overcurrent protective devices exist: a fuse and a circuit breaker. A **fuse** is a device that includes a wire or strip of fusible metal that melts and interrupts a circuit when an electrical-current overload occurs. A **circuit breaker** is a switch that automatically trips and interrupts the flow of electrical current in event of an abnormal condition. If trouble develops on one circuit, only that circuit will be out of operation when the fuse blows or circuit breaker trips. Usage of fuses mainly occurs in older houses, while newer houses utilize circuit breakers.

In addition to fuses and circuit breakers, **ground fault circuit interrupters (GFCIs)** are special electrical devices that stop the flow of electrical current in a circuit as a safety precaution. (A "ground fault" is an unintentional electrical path between a current source and a grounded surface.) GFCIs help protect people from burns or electrical-shock injuries that are severe or fatal. The *National Electrical Code* requires installation of GFCIs in kitchens, bathrooms, new garages, and other areas where water may be present.

Electricians install the wiring inside the house from the service entrance panel to the points of electrical power use. Wiring installation happens while the wall framing is open and accessible. An electrical code authority must inspect the wiring installation while it is still visible.

Deciding where to place electrical outlets and other electrical connections requires advance planning of each room's use. The electrician will need to know the placement of such specific items as the range, refrigerator, furnace, and water heater. Knowing furniture placement is very useful, too. Furniture placement helps determine where connections for phones, TVs, and computers go. As a general guideline, each room should have at least three outlets (receptacles). Also, no point along the base of a wall should be more than 6 feet from an outlet.

With greater use of computers, electronic communications, and home automation, homes need integrated wiring schemes (or *structured cabling*) to be able to use electricity-dependent technologies. Existing homes may need rewiring or additional wiring. Often both options are expensive. However, in new or remodeled homes, installation of the integrated wiring can easily occur during the construction process. This is an affordable way to prepare for present and future electrical needs. In addition, more and more technology supports wireless applications that do not require additional hard-wired connections.

Integrated wiring includes threading coaxial cabling and telephone connections through a central plastic pipe extending vertically to all floors. The purpose of wiring in this manner is to integrate, or join, all the systems in the home. This integration offers occupants additional convenience in home entertainment, safety, communications, and home management.

- **Entertainment.** For entertainment options, occupants can program from one location the same video and audio selections throughout the house. Although integration of TVs and other entertainment systems is convenient, occupants can also operate them separately.

9-4
This illustration shows how a home generator works (A). It comes on automatically when there is electric utility failure and provides seamless electricity for the home. The home occupants do not need to worry when the utility power goes off because this home generator provides the necessary back-up electricity (B).

Illustration and Photography Courtesy of Kohler

- **Safety.** Integrated systems enhance safety because occupants can view visitors on TV before answering the door. Likewise, they can monitor strangers near the house. They can also control and monitor smoke and carbon monoxide detectors for exit strategies in event of smoke, fire, or carbon monoxide.

- **Communication.** Improved communication of information results as family members send messages to all computers and monitors in the home. The home computer can also link to a variety of home services, including banking and shopping.

- **Home management.** Integrated wiring makes installation and repair of home systems easier. For appliance maintenance, a manufacturer can monitor the equipment through the computer to alert the owner of what steps to take for a repair. The computer lets occupants control and monitor activities and systems in the home, including lighting and room temperatures.

In response to electric power outages that result from severe weather or other causes, some homes now have back-up generators, or **home generators**. These home generators can turn on automatically to create electricity when the electric power fails. Power sources for home generators include natural and propane gas. See 9-4.

Gas as an Energy Source

Many houses use gas as an additional source of energy. It is a popular fuel for cooking, heating water, and heating the air. Gas fuels include natural gas,

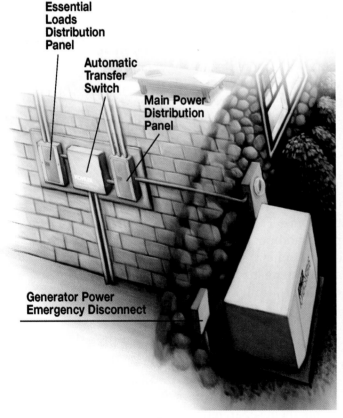

Essential Loads Distribution Panel

Automatic Transfer Switch

Main Power Distribution Panel

Generator Power Emergency Disconnect

A

B

which is piped from a gas main to your house, and liquid propane gas, which is delivered in pressurized tanks to your house.

Natural Gas

Natural gas comes from wells in the ground. From the gas fields, high-pressure pumps force the gas through large pipelines to communities, 9-5. After reducing the pressure, the gas company distributes the gas throughout the community in pipes called *gas mains*. To furnish gas to your house, the gas company taps the main and lays an underground pipe to your house. The company then places a gas meter where the line enters your house. Like an electric meter, it records the amount of fuel usage.

In the house, the plumber installs branch lines to all gas-burning appliances. Branch lines consist of black pipe and fittings. Usage of a pipe-thread compound prevents the leakage of natural gas on all fittings. The plumber checks the system for leaks before it is used.

Liquid Propane Gas

Propane is a colorless, odorless gas. Houses that normally do not have access to a natural gas line use propane as fuel. Oil refineries produce propane from natural gas, crude oil, or oil refinery gases. Gas supply companies then deliver the *liquid propane gas* (LG or LPG) in tanker trucks to each house as needed. Storage of LPG must be in large, pressurized metal tanks on concrete pads near the house, but not next to it. Then the gas line from the house connects to the tank. LPG has about twice the heating value of natural gas per cubic foot. However, with the delivery cost and storage requirements, it is normally more expensive than natural gas.

9-5
Natural gas is transported in large pipes to communities where it is distributed to houses through gas mains.

Plumbing Systems

The plumbing system in a house provides water to the house and removes waterborne waste from it. (As you know, the gas lines are also part of the plumbing system.) A water supply system provides sufficient hot and cold water so fixtures and appliances can function properly. A wastewater removal system removes waste and used water, depositing them into a sewer line or private septic tank.

Water Supply System

Water flows under pressure to your house from a community water main or a private well or system. It enters the house through a pipe called the *building main*. Inside the house, the water may pass through a water softener, filter, or another treatment device. It then flows to separate cold and hot water mains. The hot water main starts at the water heater. Hot and cold water-branch lines travel throughout the house to each fixture or appliance that needs water.

Piping for the water supply system is located in the floor, walls, or ceiling of a house. Water lines are usually made of ½- or ⅜-inch-diameter pipes of copper, plastic, or galvanized steel, 9-6. Copper water pipes are the most popular but are expensive. Various types of plastic are also used. They include the following:

- PEX (cross-linked polyethylene), which is commonly used because it is economical, easy to install, and flexible in a large range of temperatures.

- CPVC (chlorinated polyvinyl chloride) is also widely used and is very economical.

Because of serious failure issues, PVC (polyvinyl chloride) water pipe is *not* used for water lines. Local codes may restrict the use of certain types of pipe.

The lines are usually under a pressure of 45 to 60 pounds per square inch (psi).

Installation of a shutoff valve at the water meter in a convenient place near or in the building is necessary to turn the water off to the house. Additional shut-offs on each branch line next to fixtures or appliances make it possible to repair separate parts of the system without shutting off the water for the entire house. A leak in the main water line requires closing the valve at the meter.

Wastewater Removal System

In the house, waterborne waste comes mainly from bathrooms, kitchens, and laundry areas. Since it tends to decompose quickly, removal of waste should happen before it causes odors or becomes hazardous to human health.

Waste disposal pipes are completely separate from the water supply system. They are much larger (generally 1½ to 4 inches in diameter) than water supply lines and are not pressurized. Instead, they rely on gravity to remove waste. The number and type of plumbing fixtures that discharge into the line determine the size of wastewater piping. Piping such as plastic, cast iron, copper, and brass alloy are used. Local codes specify the types and sizes of pipes required in the area.

As the wastewater leaves the house, it moves either to the community sewer lines or a private septic tank. When connected to a community sewer line, wastewater goes through a treatment system. Then it usually is recycled and used for industrial and irrigation purposes.

When community sewer lines are unavailable, homes use septic tanks to dispose of wastewater. A **septic tank** is an underground tank that decomposes waste through the action of bacteria. The wastewater flows into the tank where

9-6
The small metal pipes are the hot and cold water lines. The large white pipes are the waste disposal pipe and vent stack.

Lowden, Lowden and Co.

bacteria dissolve much of what settles to the bottom. The liquid wastewater at the top of the tank flows into a system of perforated underground pipes called a *drainfield*. There, wastewater disperses into the soil.

Removal of gases that result from wastewater removal system must also occur. A **vent stack** is a vertical pipe that extends through the roof to release gases and odors outdoors. It connects to the drain lines or soil stack that carries the wastewater. The **soil stack** is the main vertical pipe that receives waste matter from all plumbing fixtures. In the use of a combination waste and vent (CWV), the vent also acts as the soil stack. The pipe channels the water and waste to drain down and away from the house. Every house has at least one soil stack for each toilet.

Each plumbing fixture has a **trap**—a bend in the pipe within or just below a fixture that catches and holds a quantity of water. This pocket of water prevents sewage gases from seeping back into the house. Installation of a trap is necessary at each fixture unless the fixture has a built-in trap, as in a toilet. Notice the trap under the sink in 9-7.

In remote cabins or isolated cottages, sometimes a water source and sewage system for installing a toilet is not available.

9-7
The trap under this sink catches and holds a pocket of water that prevents sewage gas from backing into the house.

GREEN CHOICES

Conserving Water in the Kitchen

When it comes to saving water in the kitchen, a few small steps can make a big difference. Consider these tips for reducing your water consumption every day.

- Capture running water while waiting for the temperature to change. Use the excess to water plants.

- When washing dishes by hand, use as little water as possible. Use only the required amount of dish liquid and put the dishes in a rack to rinse them all together and reduce rinse water. Use short bursts instead of letting the water run when rinsing. When using the dishwasher, use appropriate water and energy efficient settings.

- Keep a container of drinking water in the refrigerator. With cold drinking water on hand, you will waste less than you would while waiting for the temperature change for each glass of water.

- Do not defrost frozen food with running water. Use the microwave or defrost in the refrigerator.

- When cooking, use only the amount of water required. This reduces the amount of water wasted when straining.

Information courtesy of the Kohler Company. www.kohler.com/conservation

9-8
The surfaces of plumbing fixtures are extremely durable and stain resistant.

Photo Courtesy of Pottery Barn

Installing a toilet in places such as basements, workshops, and garages may also be difficult. In these cases, one option is a composting toilet. A **composting toilet** is a self-contained, stand-alone toilet. These units require no water or external plumbing. The system operates like a garden compost pile, transforming waste into a stable end product.

9-9
Kitchen sinks can be plain or quite fancy, as this beautiful design shows.

Photography Courtesy of Kohler

Plumbing Fixtures

A plumbing fixture is a device that connects to the plumbing system. Plumbing fixtures include kitchen sinks, lavatories, toilets, and bathtubs. Modern plumbing fixtures are made from a variety of materials. They include enameled cast iron, enameled steel, stainless steel, fiberglass, and plastics. These materials are durable, corrosion-resistant, nonabsorbent, and have smooth, easy-to-clean surfaces, 9-8. Industrial designers often design these fixtures.

Plumbing fixtures have a variety of characteristics and purposes, including the following:

- **Kitchen sink.** A kitchen sink is a flat-bottomed plumbing fixture used for food preparation and cleanup. Sinks are available in a large variety of sizes and shapes. The most common is the double-compartment sink installed in a cabinet countertop, 9-9.

- **Lavatory.** A *lavatory* is a plumbing fixture designed for washing hands and faces in bathrooms. Lavatories come in a variety of colors, sizes, and shapes. They are available in wall-hung, countertop, and pedestal models.

- **Toilet.** A toilet is a water-flushed plumbing fixture designed to receive human waste. Toilets are usually made of a ceramic material called porcelain. They are installed directly on the floor or suspended from the wall.

- **Bathtub.** A bathtub is a fixed tub that holds water for bathing. It comes in a variety of shapes, but the most common is rectangular. Overhead installation of showerheads is common in many bathtubs. In addition, separate showering units are available.

GREEN CHOICES

Conserving Water in the Bathroom

When it comes to saving water in the bathroom, a few small steps can make a big difference. Consider these tips for reducing your water consumption every day.

- Turn off the faucet while brushing your teeth, and rinse out the sink when you are done.

- Capture shower/bath water while waiting for water to change temperatures: Use this excess water for watering plants.

- Do not wait for the water to get hot before filling the tub for a bath. Put in the plug and adjust the water temperature as the tub fills.

- Do not use the toilet as a garbage can: Only flush the toilet when disposing of sanitary waste.

- Turn off the water while shaving: Fill the bottom of the sink with a few inches of water to rinse your razor.

Bathrooms and kitchens are two of the busiest rooms in the home. Over one-fourth of the water used in an average home is flushed down the toilet. When you are building or if it is time to remodel, consider using water-conserving products and technologies to help reduce wastewater and decrease your water bill.

Information courtesy of the Kohler Company. www.kohler.com/conservation

Heating Systems

Heating a house may occur by using one of four conventional heating systems. They are forced warm-air, hydronic, electric radiant, and central heat-pump systems. Nonconventional heating systems—such as solar heat, fireplaces, and stoves—can also heat a house. **HVAC** (heating, ventilating, and air-conditioning) is a common term that refers to systems that condition the living space for thermal comfort.

Conventional Heating Systems

Conventional heating systems may use electricity, gas, oil, or coal as fuel. However, the use of coal is rare in newly built houses. The choice of which energy source to use is based on availability and the cost of fuel and operation. Environmental concerns also influence the fuel choice.

Forced Warm-Air System

In the **forced warm-air system**, the furnace heats and delivers the air to the rooms through supply ducts. A **duct** is a large round tube or rectangular boxlike structure that delivers heated (and air-conditioned) air to distant rooms or spaces. Ducts are located beneath floors and along ceilings, 9-10. They connect the heating (or cooling) system to vents in or near the floor or ceiling. The heating unit consists of a heater (and/or cooler) and a blower section that connects to the duct system.

A furnace uses gas, oil, or electricity to heat the air. A blower moves the

9-10
In a forced warm-air system, supply ducts are located under the floor and in the attic.

heated air through the supply ducts to the living quarters. A separate set of ducts, or air return, carries the cool air from each room back to the furnace. This periodic movement of warm air into cold spaces continues until rooms reach the desired temperature.

The indoor temperature is controlled in the living area with a thermostat that is wired to the furnace. A **thermostat** is a device for regulating room temperature. Furnace filters trap dust to prevent blowing it throughout the house. Forced warm-air systems are very common because they are economical and easy to install. However, some people dislike the sound and feel of the rapid air movement they cause.

Hydronic Heating System

Circulating hot water systems are called **hydronic heating systems**. Water heats in a boiler to a preset temperature, usually 180°F to 210°F. When the water reaches the proper temperature, a pump circulates it through pipes to radiators, 9-11. As the water cools, it returns to the boiler for reheating. Radiators are located throughout the living areas, usually along the outside walls to reduce cold air drafts and increase comfort.

A *radiant-hydronic heating system* circulates hot water through copper or plastic tubing embedded in a coil or grid pattern in a concrete floor, wood floor, or plaster ceiling. As the water circulates, heat radiates from the floor or ceiling into the room. Usage of this system is common in mild climates and also as a backup heating system.

Hydronic heating is a quiet, clean, and efficient type of system that does not create drafts. However, it takes longer to raise a room's temperature to a comfortable level. Also, if installed in a concrete floor that cracks for any reason, repairs are costly. Hydronic heating systems normally don't provide for cooling, air filtration, humidification, or dehumidification.

Electric Radiant-Heating System

Electric radiant-heating systems use resistance wiring to produce heat in the wire. The placement of wires may be in the ceiling, floor, or baseboards. The heat moves from the wiring through the air molecules since heat travels from hot to cooler objects. Individual thermostats control the temperature in each room.

This type of heating system allows complete freedom in furniture and drapery placement. There is no introduction of air, no radiator usage, and air movement from the system is almost nonexistent. Disadvantages of the electric radiant-heating system include the high cost of electrical energy and the installation costs. Installation of this type of system generally occurs during house construction.

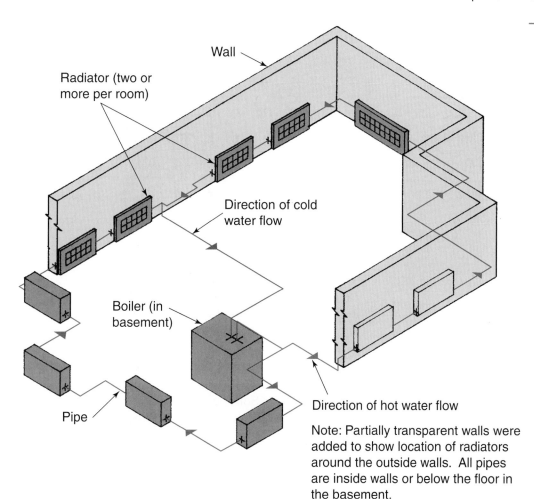

Wall

Radiator (two or
more per room)

Direction of cold
water flow

Boiler (in
basement)

Pipe

Direction of hot water flow

Note: Partially transparent walls were
added to show location of radiators
around the outside walls. All pipes
are inside walls or below the floor in
the basement.

9-11
Hot water is
pumped from
the boiler to
the radiators
in individual
rooms. Cool
water is returned
to the boiler for
reheating.

Central Heat-Pump System

A **central heat-pump system** is an electric refrigeration unit used to either heat or cool the house. It removes heat from the outside air or ground in cold weather. In warm weather, it removes heat from the air in the house. The heat pump consists of liquid refrigerant, a compressor, and heat exchangers. A fan circulates the heated or cooled air through the house, 9-12.

A central heat-pump system is most efficient in areas with moderate to mild winter climates, where temperatures stay above 20°F. It usually costs more than other heating systems. However, it costs less than buying both a heating system and an air-conditioning unit.

Solar Heating Systems

Solar heating systems use energy from the sun to provide heating and sometimes hot water for a house. A house that uses a solar heating system often has a backup heating system such as a stove to compensate for long periods of cloudy weather. The two main types of solar heating systems are active and passive. Both systems consist of a collector and a storage area.

Active Systems

Active systems have solar collector panels on the roof of the house. This type of system requires pumps, fans, or other devices to move the heat from the collectors to a storage area or the space requiring heat.

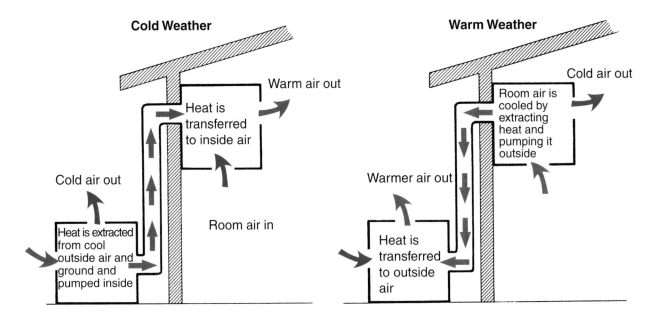

Cold Weather

Warm air out

Heat is transferred to inside air

Cold air out

Room air in

Heat is extracted from cool outside air and ground and pumped inside

Warm Weather

Cold air out

Room air is cooled by extracting heat and pumping it outside

Warmer air out

Heat is transferred to outside air

9-12
In cold weather, the heat pump absorbs heat from the air and ground outside and pumps it inside. In warm weather, the heat pump absorbs heat from the air inside the house and pumps it outside.

Passive Systems

Passive systems have no solar panels. Instead, they rely on the construction materials to collect and store the sun's heat. Windows, doorways, greenhouses, or skylights act as solar collectors. Walls and floors made from masonry materials such as concrete, concrete block, brick, stone, and adobe absorb the heat and act as the storage areas. Water-storage walls or tanks also store heat effectively.

Fireplaces and Stoves

Fireplaces and stoves are sources of heat as well as focal points. They differ from models of the past because they are safer, cleaner, and more efficient. However, wood-burning fireplaces and stoves still require cutting, splitting, and stacking of firewood. Moving wood indoors can leave debris on the floor. Also, after prolonged use, most stoves and fireplaces produce a light film of smoke residue in the room.

Fireplaces

Careful design and construction of fireplaces is necessary for them to operate correctly and prevent heat loss when not in use. Most fireplaces today have a single opening, or *face*, in the front. Some also have two or three openings. Contemporary houses often use metal, freestanding fireplaces.

Traditional fireplaces are made from masonry, while newer models are often made from metal. Metal fireplaces may have a covering of brick or other materials so they look like solid masonry. Many of these new units are wood burning. However, some use electricity or gas to give the appearance of a log fire.

A fireplace consists of a hearth, firebox, damper, smoke shelf, chimney, and flue, 9-13. The hearth is the flat area where you build the fire, and the apron is in front of the fire area. The firebox is the combustion chamber. Firebrick—which is made from fire-resistant clay—lines the firebox. A damper is a metal device that closes off the airflow when the fireplace is not in use. The smoke shelf is where the smoke collects before going up the chimney. The smoke shelf also prevents outside air currents from forcing smoke back into the room. The flue carries smoke outdoors and creates a draft for the fire. Special tiles or metal liners that resist high temperatures line

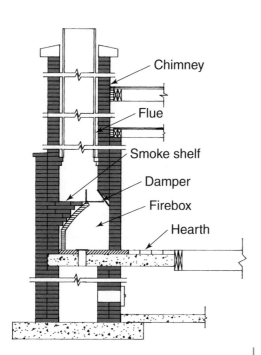

9-13
Each part of the fireplace plays an important role in the efficient burning of wood and removal of smoke.

Chimney

Flue

Smoke shelf

Damper

Firebox

Hearth

9-14
This beautiful fireplace design was created by using quality wall and decorative tile.

the flue. The chimney pipes the smoke out of the house, 9-14.

A **fireplace insert** is a metal device that fits into an existing fireplace and attaches to the chimney liner. The fireplace may be made of masonry or factory-built. A fireplace insert transforms a drafty fireplace into a more energy-efficient heat source. The insert draws the room's air into the fireplace, circulates it around a heat exchanger, and returns it to the room. Heat-detecting sensors on the insert automatically shut off the blower when the room reaches a desired temperature. This can reduce heating costs since fireplaces with inserts normally have efficiency ratings near 70 percent. Fireplaces without inserts have an efficiency rating of 15 to 35 percent.

Stoves

Stoves usually produce more heat than fireplaces. They generally use coal or wood to generate heat. There are two main types of stoves. *Radiant stoves* produce heat that radiates through the room to cooler objects. The surfaces of these stoves are extremely hot. You must keep flammable materials away from them.

In *circulating stoves*, a compartment separates the main fire area from the outside of the stove. Air circulates into and out of the compartment, transferring heat into the room. Sometimes a fan helps the air move through the compartment. A thermostat controls the level of heat entering the room. These stoves are safer than radiant stoves because they produce less smoke and their exposed surfaces are cooler.

Stoves are more efficient and clean burning because of standards established by the U.S. Environmental Protection Agency (EPA). One standard limits the amount of smoke released per hour through the chimney. Another requires stoves to produce more heat per unit of fuel used. These two standards help to assure a cleaner and safer environment.

Another type of stove is the *pellet stove*, 9-15. It burns waste wood or other organic materials such as agricultural waste. The waste materials are compressed into pellets resembling

9-15
A pellet stove is a highly efficient and functional heating unit.

Vermont Castings

rabbit food. One ton of pellets will generate about 17 million British thermal units (Btu) of heat. A wood-burning stove generates about 8 to 10 million Btu per cord of firewood. The pellet-stove hopper (a receptacle that holds pellets) may hold 35 to 130 pounds of pellets—enough to heat a home about a day. These stoves usually burn a handful of pellets at a time. This results in high combustion efficiency, which means less ash and no visible smoke. Instead of the conventional chimney, a pellet stove requires a vent.

Cooling Systems

Cooling systems provide cool, clean, moisture-free air during hot, humid weather. Usage of a central air conditioner is the most frequent cooling system in houses. Room air conditioners are also used for cooling certain rooms. The most common cooling system is the compressor-cycle system. It uses a compressed refrigerant to absorb heat, which cools the air. The refrigerant absorbs heat as it passes through an evaporator coil and changes from a liquid to a gas. The gas passes through the compressor, where it is pressurized. The hot, pressurized gas passes through the condenser coil, where it gives up heat and changes back to a liquid. Moving through the liquid line, it passes through a metering device into the evaporator coil to begin the cycle again, 9-16.

When a cooling a room, moisture in the air condenses on the fins of the condenser and drains away. This process dehumidifies the air and increases the comfort level. The cooler air moves to various parts of the living space through a system of ducts. A blower or air handler usually moves the air through the heating system's ducts.

In a central air-conditioning system, the compressor and the condenser unit are placed outside the building while the air handler is located inside the house. With a room air conditioner, all components are contained in one unit. A part of this unit extends outside through a window or wall opening.

Conserving Energy

Housing consumes about one-fifth of all the energy usage in the United States. Efforts to improve the energy-efficient construction of houses are underway. The U.S. Department of Energy (DOE) has the goal of

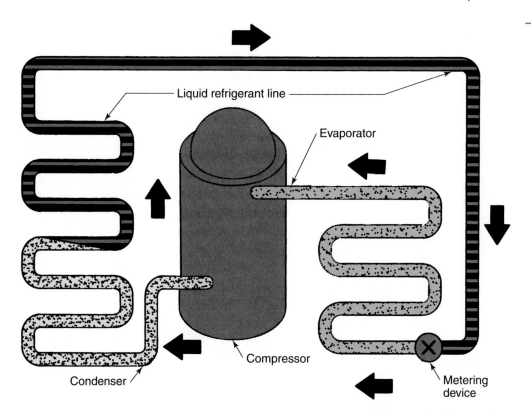

Liquid refrigerant line

Evaporator

Compressor

Condenser

Metering device

9-16
This diagram shows the path the refrigerant takes as it moves through the compressor-cycle system of air conditioning.

GREEN CHOICES

Engineer Responsibilities for Green and Sustainable Design

During the building process, architects begin by creating a design. Then engineers add equipment and systems for heating, cooling, electricity, plumbing, and other parts of the structure. In the past, lack of communication between architects and engineers led to such problems as buildings that were not durable, comfortable, energy efficient and were expensive to operate.

Now engineers collaborate with the architects and other industry members in the initial planning stage of the building. This collaboration is possible because of the BIM (Building Information Model), and the software programs that utilize the BIM.

Mechanical, electrical, and plumbing systems (MEP systems) represent one-third of the building cost. Well-engineered MEP systems are vital for the longevity and sustainability of the buildings.

Responsibilities of engineers for green and sustainable design include the following:

- keeping up-to-date on energy efficiency and environmental principles in heating, ventilating, and air-conditioning equipment and design
- choosing new, innovative, and high-performance products from the lighting industries that reduce the amount of energy used for lighting
- selecting plumbing fixtures that can reduce water usage by 30 percent or more
- including rainwater-collection systems for irrigation or toilet flushing while at the same time reducing storm water runoff

reducing household energy consumption of both new and existing houses. Energy codes, as part of state building codes, can accomplish this goal by requiring improved construction materials and techniques. Thus, building-code authorities are promoting the inclusion of energy codes in state building codes to accomplish this goal. The National Association of Home Builders (NAHB) is a leader in this effort. The ultimate in energy efficiency are the zero-energy-use homes, which is part of the push for sustainability and green housing you will learn about in Chapter 23.

In addition, ENERGY STAR®—a joint program of the EPA and DOE—informs consumers about how to save money and protect the environment by choosing the most energy-efficient housing, materials, and appliances on the market. Consumers can achieve the greatest energy savings by choosing products with the ENERGY STAR label. For example, in 2008 Americans were able to save $19 billion on their utility bills by choosing household products with the ENERGY STAR rating. See Chapter 18 for more information about the Energy Star program and household appliances.

Controlling room temperature through heating and cooling systems accounts for most of the energy used in a home. Heating water is the next greatest energy user. Together, space conditioning and hot water systems account for over two-thirds of the energy used in homes.

There are many ways to use less energy at home and thus reduce energy bills. However, a major focus of saving energy should be improving the air-tightness of the building and installing energy-efficient equipment. The remainder of this chapter examines ways to save energy with insulation, energy-efficient windows and doors, and computerized energy management.

Sealing and Insulation

Air leakage is one of the largest wastes of energy in houses. A first step in reducing air leakage is to seal a house with building wrap and by properly applying weather stripping and sealant on windows. The next step to conserving home-energy usage is to surround the living space with proper insulation during house construction. **Insulation** is a material that restricts the flow of air between a house's interior and the outdoors. Insulation has millions of tiny air pockets that resist the flow of heat through it. Insulation materials keep heated air indoors in winter and outdoors in summer. How well a material insulates is measured by its **R-value**. The greater the R-value, the more resistant the material is to the movement of heat, 9-17.

Insulation is made from a variety of materials that differ in efficiency, quality, and safety. These materials include fibrous glass, rock wool, cellulose, urethane, and polystyrene. Insulation is available in blanket, board, loose-fill, and spray foam forms. Each has different uses and shapes and meets different requirements.

- *Blanket insulation* comes in long rolls, or *batts*, which are shorter rolls usually 4 to 8 feet long. Both rolls and batts come in 16- to 24-inch widths and in various thicknesses. The thicker the insulation is, the shorter the roll. Common usage of blanket insulation occurs in floors, walls, and around pipes and ducts, 9-18.

- *Foam board insulation* is made from rigid-foamed plastics. It is available in sheets 1½-inches to 4-inches thick. It is usually 2 by 4 feet or 4 by 8 feet in size. Foam board insulation is higher in R-value per inch of thickness than other forms of insulation. However, foam board insulation also tends to be more expensive. It

R-Values of Common Insulation Materials	
Note: The higher the R-value, the better the material blocks transfer of heat per one inch of thickness. Values are averages.	
Insulation Material	**R-Value per Inch**
Batts or Blankets	
• Fiberglass	• 2.9–3.8
• Rock Wool	• 3.7
Loose Fill (poured in)	
• Fiberglass	• 2.2–2.7
• Rock Wool	• 3.0–3.3
• Cellulosic Fiber	• 3.2–3.8
Foam Board	
• Molded Expanded Polystyrene	• 3.8–4.4
• Extruded Expanded Polystyrene	• 5.0
• Polyisocyanurate and Polyurethane	• 5.6–8.0
Spray Foam	
• Open-Cell Polyurethane (permeable)	• 3.6
• Closed-Cell Polyurethane (nonpermeable)	• 6.5

9-17
This chart compares the R-values of common insulating materials.

Source: U.S. Department of Energy

is used between concrete and earth, around foundation walls, and on one side of the footing. It is also used on the outside of studs as sheathing.

• *Loose fill* is used in spaces where other types of insulation are difficult to install. It may also be used in attics, inside frame walls, in cores of concrete block, and as filler between other types of insulation. It comes in bags and may be poured or blown into place, 9-19. Loose fill insulation tends to compact over time and looses some of its insulating quality.

• *Spray foam insulation* is becoming more commonplace and is very effective at both insulating and sealing a house. Spray foam comes in both permeable and impermeable types. Note that the permeable type allows moisture vapor to pass through while impermeable does not. Advanced designers and builders now insulate the entire envelope of a house, from the underside to

9-18
Blanket insulation is used here to insulate a wall.

Lowden, Lowden and Co.

9-19
Here, recycled cellulose insulation is being blown into the attic area. It is excellent for sound control, fire protection, and energy savings.

U.S. Green Fiber, Cocoon Insulation

Having insulation of the proper R-value is very important for promoting energy efficiency and occupant comfort. Equally important is the proper installation of insulation. Consumers should use skillful installers from companies with a reputation for doing high-quality work.

Targeted Air Sealing

A major way to control energy use in a residence is to block conditioned air from leaving the living area. The top of the building should receive first priority, followed by the bottom of the building. Give attention to any leakage from the ducts in forced warm-air heating systems and target walls, windows, and doors last. A special test can help identify air leakage from the home, 9-21. Designers can then develop an appropriate strategy and design to reduce energy loss.

Windows and Doors

Heat loss around windows and doors and through glass panes is an energy problem. Adding weather stripping to windows and doors helps prevent drafts and heat transfer. **Weather stripping** is a strip of material that covers the edges of a window or door to prevent moisture and air from entering the house.

Another way to conserve energy is to install storm windows over single-pane glass windows. The air space between the windows acts as an insulator.

Windows that have double or triple the insulation value of single-pane windows are available. Window ratings assist the consumer in evaluating the expected energy performance of specific types of windows.

Many types of energy-efficient windows contain two or three gas-filled insulating chambers that block almost all the sun's ultraviolet rays. They provide more daylight with less winter heat loss and less

the roof to the crawl space or basement. This allows greater efficiency with the HVAC systems in semi-conditioned spaces.

Installing more insulation usually slows the escape of heated air in winter and cooled air in summer. This helps to lower energy use, which lowers heating and cooling bills. Some areas of the country need insulation to combat intensely hot summers, extremely cold winters, or a mix of both.

Both heating and air conditioning contribute to the recommended R-values shown in Figure 9-20. These figures reflect national, state, and local recommendations. To use the information, look at the map and find the zone that covers your area. Then read the various R-values shown for that zone to determine your insulation needs.

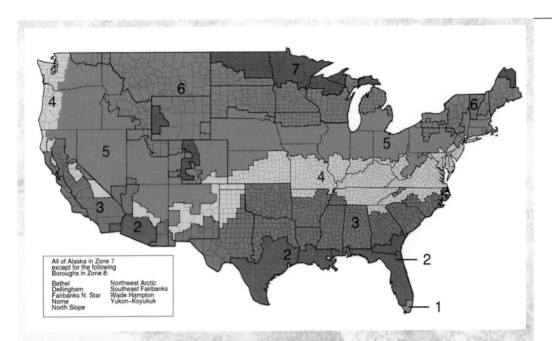

9-20
The different
heating zones
in the states are
numbered 1 to 8.
The chart shows
the R-values
recommended for
house insulation in
each zone.

U.S. Department of
Energy

Recommended R-Values for Zones						
Zone	Heating System	Attic	Cathedral Ceiling	Walls		Floor
				Cavity	Insulation Sheathing	
1	All	R30–R49	R22–R38	R13–R15	None	R13
2	Gas, Oil, Heat Pump, Electric Furnace	R-30–R-60	R22–R38	R13–R15	None	R13
						R19–R25
3	Gas, Oil, Heat Pump, Electric Furnace	R-30–R-60	R22–R38	R13–R15	None	R25
					R2.5–R5	
4	Gas, Oil, Heat Pump, Electric Furnace	R-30–R-60	R22–R38	R13–R15	R2.5–R6	R25–R30
					R5–R6	
5	Gas, Oil, Heat Pump, Electric Furnace	R-30–R-60	R22–R38	R13–R15	R2.5–R6	R25–R30
			R30–R60	R13–R21	R5–R6	
6	All	R49–R60	R30–R60	R13–R21	R5–R6	R25–R30
7	All	R49–R60	R30–R60	R13–R21	R5–R6	R25–R30
8	All	R49–R60	R30–R60	R13–R21	R5–R6	R25–R30

9-21
Trained heating and cooling technicians use a blower-door test to check air leakage in a home.

Advanced Energy, Raleigh, North Carolina

Energy Conservation Through Computer Power

An inexpensive device for controlling heating and cooling levels is a programmable thermostat, which uses a computer chip. You can set programmable units to automatically adjust temperatures around your personal schedule—a comfortable setting when you're home and an energy-saving setting when you're away. Most climate controls can be set to change temperatures four times during a 24-hour period—when you wake, leave for work, return home, and go to bed. A programmable thermostat is inexpensive and generally pays for itself in a short period of time.

More powerful comfort controls resemble a thermostat, but do so much more. These controls can reduce energy use 20 to 40 percent by monitoring items that operate electronically, 9-23. Electronic items include appliances as well as communications, HVAC, and electronic equipment. Computerized controls can manage the lighting, interior climate, and maintenance systems in the following ways:

- turn lights on and off automatically as people enter and leave rooms

- roll shades up and down automatically to admit sun or block cold air

- adjust heating, ventilation, and air-conditioning systems to outdoor weather conditions

- adjust the interior temperature according to activities in the house

- report maintenance and equipment problems automatically so total climate comfort and maximum use of equipment are maintained

- monitor the climate-control system for dirty filters to maximize the efficiency of this system

The most advanced comfort-control centers provide all the features

summer heat gain. Very energy-efficient windows are available, including *low-emission glass* (low-e) and other window technologies, 9-22. Consumers can also add a film to windows to control excessive heat transfer and damaging rays. Frequent exposure to sun rays can fade and/or weaken fibers and wood finishes.

The need for energy efficiency is not limited to windows. Sliding patio doors feature the same double- and triple-pane window systems. Door construction has evolved so that many attractive doors are also extremely durable and energy-efficient.

MATH MATTERS

Calculating Percentages and Energy Savings

Home owners can save a substantial amount of money by making their homes energy efficient. How much can they save? By plugging a zip code into the federal government's Home Energy Saver calculator, you can find out. The calculator estimates the annual energy costs for two homes in a zip code—an average home and an energy efficient one. Use the calculator to find the estimates for two homes in your zip code.

For example, home owner A with an average home in Riverside, Illinois, paid about $1615 in energy costs in 2009. How much money did home owner B save by having an energy efficient home? For the same time and place, home owner B paid $969, or $646 less than home owner A.

With these estimates, you can calculate home owner B's savings in terms of percent. Divide the amount that home owner B saved by the total amount that home owner A paid:

$$646 \div 1615 = 0.40$$

Convert the decimal number into a percentage by multiplying the decimal by 100 and adding the percent sign (%):

$$0.40 \times 100 = 40\%$$

Home owner B, therefore, enjoyed a 40% savings in average energy costs that year. The Home Energy Saver calculator at http://hes.lbl.gov also allows users to input detailed facts about their homes to calculate more accurate estimates.

9-22
This remodeling contractor is installing quality windows that provide energy efficiency and reduce the harmful effects of ultraviolet rays on interior furnishings.

Photography Courtesy of JELD-WEN Windows and Doors

9-23
Besides regulating the home's lighting, this center also manages home security and messages.

Image Courtesy of Honeywell International

discussed previously with additional conveniences. Occupants can regulate their home's system from anywhere inside or outside the building. Since the control system links wirelessly to the Internet, home owners can make adjustments to their settings from anywhere they can access the Internet, 9-24.

Conserving Water

The quality and availability of water is increasingly becoming an important environmental issue. Some areas of the country have severe rainfall shortages that affect how people use water in their homes.

When selecting plumbing components for homes, such as faucets and toilets, people should consider the many products on the market that reduce the use of water. These include low-flow showerheads and water-efficient faucets.

To assist consumers and professionals in making choices about water-efficient products, the United States Environmental Protection Agency (EPA) has developed a program and label called WaterSense®. Products showing this label undergo independent, third party testing. This assures consumers these products meet the EPA's criteria to use at least 20 percent less water than conventional models while still performing well, 9-25.

9-24
New technology allows a home owner to control a home's systems from any location that has access to the Internet.

Image Courtesy of Honeywell International

9-25
The EPA provides this WaterSense™ label to help consumers identify products that use water efficiently.

Image Courtesy of the Environmental Protection Agency

CAREER FOCUS

Industrial Designer

Can you imagine yourself as an industrial designer? Read more about this interesting and challenging career.

Interests/Skills If you share some of the following interests you may want to consider a career as an industrial designer. You are artistic, realistic and enterprising. You enjoy working with forms, designs, and patterns in a way that requires self-expression. You enjoy practical, hands-on problems and solutions. You appreciate plants, animals, and real-world materials like wood, tools, and machinery. You like to start up and carry out projects. Industrial designers have these skills: creativity, artistic ability, detail-orientation, problem-solving, communication, and computer skills.

Career Snapshot: Industrial designers are engineers who combine the fields of art, business, and engineering to design the products people use every day. In fact, these designers are responsible for the style, function, quality, and safety of almost every manufactured good. Usually designers specialize in one particular product category, such as automobiles and other transportation vehicles, appliances, technology goods, medical equipment, furniture, toys, tools and construction equipment, or housewares.

Education/Training: A bachelor's degree is required for most entry-level commercial and industrial design positions. Many designers also pursue a master's degree to increase their employment opportunities.

Licensing/Examinations: none

Professional Association: Industrial Designers Society of America, (IDSA) (www.idsa.org)

Job Outlook: Employment of designers is expected to grow about as fast as the average for all occupations through the year 2018. Competition for jobs is expected; those with strong backgrounds in engineering and computer-aided drafting and design and extensive business expertise will have the best prospects.

Sources: Occupational Information Network (O*NET) (www.online.onetcenter.org) and the Occupational Outlook Handbook, Bureau of Labor Statistics (www.bls.gov)

Photography Courtesy of Kohler

Summary

The systems within a house provide electricity, gas, and water to the house to make it more comfortable. As you choose or evaluate systems for your house, you will have several options.

Electricity provides energy for operating lights, appliances, and most of the systems within the house. Understanding the basic electrical terms—conductor, electric current, circuit, ampere, voltage, and watt—and how electricity works will help you use electricity wisely.

Gas is another source of energy for the home. It can be in the form of natural gas, which reaches the house from a gas main. Liquid propane gas, which is delivered to the house in pressurized tanks, is another option.

The plumbing system brings water to and through the house via the water supply system. Waterborne waste is removed from the house through the wastewater removal system.

The four types of conventional heating systems used to heat houses are the forced warm-air, hydronic, electric radiant, and central heat-pump systems. Nonconventional heating systems include solar heat, fireplaces, and stoves. Central air conditioners and room air conditioners provide cool, clean, dehumidified air during hot, humid weather.

When choosing systems for your house, look for those that conserve energy. Use the proper insulation to keep the house warm in cold weather and cool in warm weather. Energy-efficient windows and doors also provide insulation. Computer systems can help conserve energy in your home by controlling lighting and interior climate, and by maintaining the systems.

Review the Facts

1. What is electricity? What role do conductors and circuits play in electricity?
2. Contrast *ampere, voltage,* and *watt.*
3. What is the function of the service entrance panel?
4. Explain the differences between a *fuse, circuit breaker,* and *GFCI.*
5. What is the benefit of an integrated wiring scheme?
6. What are the key differences between natural gas and liquid propane gas (LPG)?
7. Why are gas lines checked before they are used?
8. Describe how the water supply system functions.
9. How does the waste removal system function?
10. Name four common plumbing fixtures.
11. List advantages and disadvantages of the four types of conventional heating systems.
12. Why might someone choose a radiant-heating system instead of a forced warm-air heating system?
13. Describe a fireplace, wood stove, and pellet stove. Explain which you would choose for a new house.
14. What is the most common cooling system? Briefly explain how it works.
15. Contrast *blanket, foam board, loose fill,* and *spray foam* forms of insulation.

16. Identify three ways to save energy with windows and doors.

17. How can a personal computer help conserve energy in a house?

18. Why is conserving water important?

Think Critically

19. **Compare and contrast.** Suppose you bought a house with an elaborate computerized program to manage its systems. Make a list of what home systems you would like to control with the computer. Compare and contrast the advantages and disadvantages of using such a computerized system.

20. **Predict outcomes.** In your lifetime, to what extent do you believe the United States can totally become reliant on domestic energy sources rather than foreign energy sources? Predict what new or renewable energy sources are needed for such independence.

Community Links

21. **Identify overcurrent devices.** Determine the type of overcurrent protection devices you have in your house and where they are located. Summarize what to do when a fuse blows or a circuit breaker trips.

22. **Plumbing identification.** Create a floor plan of your home. Locate the water shutoff valves for each water-using fixture in your house and mark their locations on the floor plan. Post your floor plan in a place that family members can easily find.

23. **Analyze ads.** Locate Internet or print ads for windows and doors that claim to be energy efficient. Then use reliable Internet or print resources to determine characteristics consumers should look for in energy-efficient windows. Display the ads on a bulletin board or with presentation software for others to compare. How can you tell if the information the ads claim is true?

Academic Connections

24. **Writing.** Use Internet or print resources to research the cost of installing a computer system to conserve energy use by the systems in a house. Write a brief report and share your findings to the class.

25. **Math.** Survey your classmates to determine all the types of heating systems used in their homes. Create a pie chart to show the systems and the percentage used by classmates. Which types of heating systems are used most frequently? Which, if any, are not used? Summarize your results and share your findings with the class.

26. **Science.** Composting toilet systems are one option for homes located in remote areas. Use Internet and print resources to locate information about how these systems work. What scientific facts support such systems for remote areas? Use presentation software to summarize your findings with the class. What is your initial reaction to this type of waste management? What questions do you have that are not answered in the information provided by companies selling these toilets?

Technology Applications

27. **Investigate new technologies.** New technologies for use in home construction are always under development and in the media. Search the Internet for five examples of household equipment or computer programs that relate to this chapter. Obtain photos if available. Use desktop publishing software to develop a brochure to share with your classmates. Analyze what needs these new technologies meet in a home. To extend this activity, investigate ways these new technologies are also used in commercial construction.

28. **Home energy audit.** Use the "Home Energy Audit" Web site (http://hes.lbl.gov/) to complete an online energy audit for your home. Write a summary about your findings to share with the class.

29. **Determine airtightness.** Use the "Energy Savers" Web site (www.energysavers.gov/) to locate information on the *blower door tests* that professional home energy auditors use to determine the airtightness of a home. What information do consumers need to know about quality blower door tests? Use the Web site link to locate reliable energy auditors in your area. If possible, contact a local energy auditor about observing a blower door test. Summarize your findings for the class using presentation software.

30. **Household emissions calculator.** If possible, use the *Household Emissions Calculator* on the Environmental Protection Agency Web site (www.epa.gov/) and complete the process. How does your household compare to that of the average U.S. household? What might you do to help lower the carbon emissions of your household? Write a summary of your findings.

Design Practice

31. **Designing for energy efficiency.** Presume you have a client who has hired you to create a house renovation plan to maximize the energy efficiency of the home. The 1200 square foot home was built in the late 1960s. It has single-pane windows, a 25-year-old furnace in the unfinished walk-out basement, and no attic insulation. The client desires to finish off the basement to create a family room. Create a plan that includes a list of features and products you would recommend to maximize the energy efficiency of this home. Identify your rationale for choosing each product. Share your plan with the class.

32. **Portfolio.** Continue working on the home you chose for the Chapter 8 portfolio project. Create plans for the electrical, gas, plumbing, and heating and cooling systems of the home. Keep a copy of your plan in your portfolio.

Leadership in Using Alternative Energy

As citizens look to the future, finding and using alternative energy systems to heat and cool their homes is important to creating a sustainable environment. What alternative energy forms interest you most? Perhaps geothermal systems come to mind.

Use the FCCLA *Planning Process* to plan and carry out an FCCLA STAR Event *Illustrated Talk* on using alternative energy systems in the home. Use the FCCLA *STAR Events Manual* on the Internet (www.fcclainc.org) for details on developing your project. See your adviser for information as needed.

PART 4

The Inside Story

CHAPTER 10

Using the Elements of Design

Terms to Learn

visual imagery
design
function
construction
aesthetics
line
horizontal lines
vertical lines
diagonal lines
curved line
form
realistic form
abstract form
geometric form
free form
space
mass
high mass
low mass
texture
tactile texture
visual texture

Chapter Objectives

After studying this chapter, you will be able to

- summarize the characteristics of good design.

- evaluate the use of the elements of design in residential and commercial interiors.

- analyze the psychological impact of the elements of design on people.

- analyze the effects the elements of design have on aesthetics and function.

Reading with Purpose

Before reading the chapter, make a list of five things you already know about the elements of design. Leaf through the pages of the chapter and note the heading topics. Predict five things you will learn about using the elements of design.

Communication takes place in many ways. It can be verbal or nonverbal. Verbal forms of communication include expressing yourself by talking, writing a letter, or singing a song. Nonverbal communication includes using sign language or body language such as a smile, a grimace, a shrug of the shoulders, or making a "high five" sign. In order for people to understand each other, they must understand the language. For example, the sender and the receiver must both know the sign for "high five" and its meaning.

Visual imagery is a type of *nonverbal communication*. It is the language of sight. When you see an item of clothing, a piece of furniture, or an unusual object, you see a visual image. This image communicates a feeling to you. Look at 10-1 and 10-2. Each room's visual image communicates a certain personality or mood and can have a psychological impact on the room's occupants. Design is the basis for this visual image. Understanding and creating good design requires knowing design characteristics and the elements of design.

The word *design* has many meanings. Interior designers refer to **design** as the entire process used to develop a specific project. The project might be an object, room, or building. Design also refers to the product or result of the process.

Design Characteristics

Design has three characteristics: function, construction, and aesthetics. Designers use all three guidelines in creating and evaluating any design.

The first characteristic is **function**, or how a design works. A design's function includes usefulness, convenience, and organization. Good design makes a product or room better or easier to use. It considers the needs of people

10-1
What does this room communicate to you?

10-2
How does the visual image of this room differ from that in Figure 10-1?

using the item. Good functional design also accommodates the ages, sizes, and physical abilities of the users. Successful functional design provides easy access for all people and eliminates barriers.

The second characteristic of design is **construction**. Construction includes materials and structure. *Materials* are the different kinds of fabrics, woods, metals, plastics, or stones used to build a product or room. Choosing appropriate materials is necessary to support the room's function. When selecting materials, consider design function, quality, initial cost, maintenance, environmental implications, and long-term costs such as repair and replacement. Materials also need to meet industry standards, government codes, and regulations.

Structure refers to how the materials are assembled. Products need to be safe, durable, and well made. The assembly method must also be appropriate for the intended use of the product or space. Like materials, structures must meet industry standards, government codes, and regulations.

The third characteristic of design is **aesthetics**, or beauty, which is a pleasing appearance or effect. Because each person has his or her own personal taste, aesthetics or what is beautiful is difficult to define. However, good aesthetic design is pleasing to many people. It may stimulate an emotion or communicate a message, such as excitement or relaxation, humor or serious, 10-3. Personalized design reflects the aesthetics a person wants to express in a room.

Designers must consider function, construction, and aesthetics to create a successful design. For example, a room that is aesthetically pleasing but does not function well and is poorly constructed is not good design.

10-3
This room's pleasing casual appearance communicates a feeling of relaxation.

Elements of Design

Successful designers use tools to create designs. These tools—or the elements of design—include line, form, space, mass, texture, and color. Because color involves such a detailed discussion, you will read about it separately in Chapter 11. All the elements of design are necessary to describe, plan, and evaluate housing interiors.

Line

A **line** is the most basic element of design. It forms when two dots are connected. Lines connect the edges or outlines of objects and areas. They also show direction and cause the eyes to move from one point to another. For example, a line can cause you to look from objects on one end of a shelf to objects at the other end.

10-4
Horizontal lines can make a room feel more relaxing and informal.

Photo Courtesy of JELD-WEN Windows and Doors

10-5
These columns give the front of this house the feeling of height, strength, dignity, and stability.

Photo Courtesy of JELD-WEN Windows and Doors

Types of Lines

The two major types of lines are straight and curved lines. The different types of lines create varying emotional responses.

Straight lines can be horizontal, vertical, or diagonal. **Horizontal lines** are parallel to the ground, 10-4. They often direct your eyes across. Horizontal lines communicate feelings of peace, relaxation, calmness, and restfulness. For example, horizontal lines are associated with a sunset on the horizon, which suggests the end of a day and time for rest. This is the same feeling you get when sleeping in a horizontal position.

Many home furnishings utilize horizontal lines. You can see them in fireplace mantels, bookcases, long sofas, shelving, fabrics, or wallcoverings that embellish a room.

Vertical lines are perpendicular to the ground. They cause your eyes to move up and down. This movement suggests height, strength, dignity, formality, permanence, and stability.

In 10-5, notice how the columns visually communicate height. This is because the vertical lines direct your eyes upward. A feeling of strength is also communicated since the columns support the porch roof. Because the columns stand straight and tall, they communicate a feeling of dignity. Vertical lines that rest on the ground convey stability.

Vertical lines appear in many home furnishings. Look for vertical lines in window treatments, striped wallpaper, and decorative trims that carry your eyes upward. Grandfather clocks, highboys, armoires, and tall mirrors have vertical lines.

Lines that angle between horizontal and vertical lines are **diagonal lines**. They communicate different levels of activity, ranging from a low- to high-level of energy, 10-6. The level depends upon the degree of the angle and total number of angles. For example, the symbol for a bolt of lighting has several sharp diagonal lines. This symbol communicates action, excitement, and sometimes agitation. Use of diagonal furniture placement in floor plans not only brings movement, interest, and excitement, but can also enhance conversational areas.

In home furnishings, diagonal lines create a feeling of transition from one level to another. They appear in rooflines, cathedral ceilings, staircases, lampshades, and various fabrics and paintings.

MATH MATTERS

Estimating Perimeter

Perimeter is the distance around a building, room, or other closed space. You need the perimeter of a room if you are installing baseboards and ceiling moldings, or painting the walls.

To calculate perimeter of a quadrilateral or four-sided room, measure each side and add the measurements together. If a room is square, you can estimate its perimeter by measuring one side and multiplying that number by 4. If the room is rectangular in shape, estimate perimeter by adding one short and one long side together, and doubling the sum.

The perimeter of a circle is called the *circumference*. Given the diameter or radius of a circle, you can calculate the circumference. The *diameter* is the line that bisects the circle into two symmetrical parts. The *radius* is a straight line from the center point of a circle to its outer edge; radius is half the diameter.

Circumference = d × π, where *d* is diameter

Circumference = 2 × π × r, where *r* is radius

The symbol π, called *pi*, is approximately equal to 3.141592. It can be rounded to 3.14.

Example: What is the circumference of a circle with a diameter of 8 feet?

Circumference is 8 × π or 8 × 3.14, which equals 25.12 feet

10-6

The diagonal lines in carpeting and rugs create interest and movement.

Photo Courtesy of Karastan

Curved lines are the second major type of line. A **curved line** is part of a circle. If you completely extend and connect a perfectly curved line, it becomes a circle. You can also modify the curved line and extend it to form an oval. Curved lines can also take a free-form shape and range from slightly curvy to very curvy.

The different degrees of curves in lines communicate different ideas. Generally, curved lines seem softer than straight lines. A circle or oval reflects organization, eternity, and uniformity. Slightly curved, free-form lines have a natural, soothing and flowing movement. They communicate softness, freedom, and openness, 10-7.

Using Lines in Housing and Interior Decisions

Applying different types of lines to specific interior design situations can result in different effects. For example, a

10-7
The curved lines of the doorway and these accessories convey a calm, organized feeling. The curved lines in their decorative patterns are flowing and active.

Photo Courtesy of JELD-WEN Windows and Doors

10-8
Combining horizontal, vertical, diagonal, and curved lines can be very pleasing to the eyes.

Photo Courtesy of JELD-WEN Windows and Doors

draw the eyes upward. Horizontal lines in the bed make the space appear wider. Diagonal lines in the carpet create a feeling of movement as you enter the room and move toward the outdoor entry. Finally, curved lines of the bed and window help soften the many straight lines in the room.

Form

Form is the physical shape of objects. It outlines the edges of a three-dimensional object and contains volume and mass. Form also has height, width, and depth. Form can have a great psychological impact on the feelings individuals have when they enter a room or area.

Types of Form

There are four different types of form: realistic, abstract, geometric, and free form. When a form looks very much like the real thing, it has **realistic form**. Realistic form communicates a lifelike, traditional, and familiar feeling, 10-9. For example, a common chair has realistic form because of its specific form. It is easily recognizable as a chair.

Abstract form rearranges or stylizes a recognizable object. The abstract item has traits that look like the real item, but altered. Abstract form communicates a contemporary, changing, creative, and artistic feeling.

Geometric form uses squares, rectangles, circles, and other geometric figures to create form. It communicates organization, order, planning, and a tailored look. You can find geometric forms in home furnishings, such as square tables, round lampshades, and various shapes of pillows.

Free form is random and flowing. You can find it in nature—in plants, stones, and wood. It does not have geometric design. Free form communicates a sense of freedom. Free form is untraditional, unfamiliar, and different from realistic form.

space can appear larger, smaller, calmer, or busier just by using different types of lines. Repeating straight lines or curved lines can create a strong, intense statement. To create a more subtle and diverse look, combine various types of lines.

Observe the use of various straight, diagonal, and curved lines in 10-8. The vertical lines of the windows and doors

10-9
The floral image on this ceramic tile kitchen wall is an example of realistic form.

Using Form in Housing and Interior Design Decisions

There are three guidelines to follow to help use form wisely in housing design. They include

- Form follows function.

- Related forms are more agreeable than unrelated forms.

- A gradual change in form smoothly directs the eyes.

With the first guideline, consider the function of an object first in developing the design concept. Then choose the form. For instance, chairs for a family room should have a form that lets people sit comfortably and relax. If chairs have seats that slanted to one side or legs that are too tall, they will not be comfortable. The unusual form would not function well as a chair.

According to the second guideline, your eyes feel comfortable looking at similar forms. For instance, square forms dominate the room in 10-10. The use of such forms throughout this room gives it a crisp, organized look.

The third guideline means seeing an abrupt change in form or too many different forms together may be unpleasant and confusing. When forms change, your eyes work harder to follow the different shapes. However, sometimes a change in form can cause excitement.

Space

Space refers to the area around a form, such as the area around a table. It also refers to the area inside a form, such as the area inside a room. When discussing space, consider these two closely related factors: the size of the space and its arrangement.

Size of the Space

Height, length, and width often define the size of interior space. The size affects who will use the space and how they will use it. For example, a bedroom that is 10 by 12 feet is probably too small for two teenagers who each need a bed, dresser, desk, and chair. However, the same size bedroom is adequate for two small children who only need beds and one shared dresser.

The size of a space can also communicate positive or negative feelings. For example, a large space can communicate feelings of openness, grandeur, or

10-10
The related square forms used in this bath create a pleasing look.

Southface Energy Institute, Atlanta, Georgia

LINK TO SOCIAL STUDIES & CULTURE

Proxemics

If you are like most people, you maintain a bubble of personal space around yourself. When someone breaches that bubble—as when a stranger brushes against you—you are uncomfortable and may even back away. Researchers in the field of *proxemics* study this social-distancing behavior. Among other things, they measure the physical distances people maintain between themselves and others. A person's distance requirements vary by situation and by relationship. For example, close friends and family members are usually allowed to get closer than strangers. Strangers crowded into an elevator tolerate the situation because they know it is temporary. They maintain social distance by avoiding eye contact.

The father of proxemics, anthropologist Edward T. Hall, found that the size of each person's bubble of space depends on cultural background. For example, South Americans generally tolerate more physical closeness than North Americans. People in many South American countries are accustomed to people, even strangers, moving very close to them during a conversation. That same interaction would probably require more distance between two North Americans or two Japanese people.

Designers apply proxemics in their work. When interior designers create a conversation area in a living room, for example, they must consider how far apart to place the seating. If the arrangement of furniture forces people to sit too close, they will be uncomfortable. If furniture is placed too far apart, people will also feel uneasy. They may be unable to hear one another or miss important nonverbal clues such as facial expressions. As a result, the general rule is to place chairs within 10 to 12 feet of each other.

---

freedom, 10-11. However, a large space such as a sports arena may make you feel small, lost, or overwhelmed.

Small spaces can make you feel cozy, intimate, or comfortable. However, adding more people and furnishings to a small room might feel very crowded.

Arrangement of the Space

When using space in design, you first need to evaluate the space and decide what design effects you want to achieve. You can achieve various effects by arranging the space differently. For example, you can arrange space to make large spaces look smaller and small spaces look larger.

To open and expand spaces, you can expand a window area, use mirrors, or remove walls. To create the feeling of cozy quarters, designers can divide the space into separate areas. For example, using area rugs, clustering furniture, or even building a kitchen island can physically and visually divide space. See 10-12. You must be careful, however, because poor divisions of space can create an unorganized or confused feeling. You will learn more about arranging space in Chapter 19.

Mass

Mass is the amount of pattern or objects in a space. It also refers to how crowded or empty a space appears. A space can have high mass or low mass.

High Mass

High mass refers to a space that is visually crowded. Fabrics with a high-mass design have a lot of pattern or lines. A room with high mass has many items in it and

10-11
This cathedral ceiling creates an open and visually expanding space.

may look congested. High-mass rooms may reflect a full, crowded, or cluttered feeling, 10-13. High mass may communicate an impression of formality and weightiness.

Low Mass

Low mass refers to a space that is simple and sparse. It is the opposite of high mass. Low-mass designs use only the most essential furnishings. Low mass communicates clean and airy feelings. The traditional design styles called *Minimalism* and *Shaker* reflect low mass. The room in 10-14 is an example.

Using Mass in Housing and Interior Design Decisions

Designers can use either high mass or low mass to create a strong design statement. Blending high and low mass can create variety in a room design. For

example, placing a low-mass design above a high-mass design creates a very open feeling in the room. The two extremes may complement each other.

Texture

Texture refers to the way a surface feels or appears to feel. There are two kinds of texture: tactile and visual texture.

Tactile Texture

Tactile texture is the way a surface feels to the touch. You can see and feel tactile texture. For example, think of yourself standing next to a stone wall. You can see the ridges and crevices in the stone with your eyes, and you can feel its coolness and roughness with

10-12
These furnishings and their arrangement create a cozy setting in this open, expansive space.

10-13
The use of high mass evident in the patterned fabric, wallcovering, and dark heavy furniture gives this room a formal feeling.

Visual texture

Visual texture is texture that you see, but cannot feel. You can find it in scenic wallcoverings or pattern design in fabric. A plaid pattern in a fabric has visual texture although the tactile texture of the fabric could still be smooth to the touch. You can also find visual texture in photography. For instance, in a photograph of a stone fireplace, you can visually see the texture. However, you cannot feel the coolness and roughness, as you do with actual stone. Instead, you only feel the smoothness of the photo.

Using Texture in Housing and Interior Design Decisions

You can use specific textures to communicate different feelings in a room. For example, rough surfaces, such as textured plaster or paint treatments, can create a more casual feeling. Smooth surfaces, such as glass, polished wood, or brass, may communicate an elegant feeling. Polished stone or marble can communicate both elegance and strength. Terms used to describe the roughness or smoothness of texture include *nubby, crinkled, quilted, ribbed, uneven,* and *even.* Terms that describe the hardness and softness of texture include *rigid, crisp, harsh, flexible,* and *limp.*

The use of textures can affect the visual size of a room. Heavy or rough textures absorb more light than smooth textures. They do not reflect light throughout the room, so the room looks smaller. In contrast, smooth surfaces make small rooms look larger. The light reflects off the smooth surface, creating the illusion of a larger space.

You can create variety by using both visual and tactile textures. When a designer uses more than one texture in a room, the room looks more interesting, 10-15. However, too many kinds of texture in one room may be a distraction.

your hand. A stone wall has tactile texture.

There are many tactile textures used in design. For instance, a surface might feel bumpy, rough, soft, smooth, grainy, porous, or hard. When selecting items for the home, you should consider the way they feel. For example, some fabrics may be too rough and uncomfortable to use in upholstery. Tactile textures can also be functional, such as those used in slip-resistant flooring.

Using visual and tactile textures creates interest in a room. What texture do you find most pleasing in this photograph?

Photography Courtesy of Karastan

CAREER FOCUS

Interior Designer—Community Libraries

Can you imagine yourself as the interior designer of a community library? If you can, read more about this interesting career.

Interests/Skills: Do you have a strong desire to improve the quality of life in your community? Do you love books and learning? Have you ever wondered what could be done to reduce the noise volume in a library? Or perhaps, you noted the lighting is not adequate and have wondered how it could be improved. You may have thought the space could be rearranged so that the room functioned better for the staff and the public. Designers who work with library design must have knowledge of construction and design and know how libraries must function. In addition, their marketing skills for library design can bring all ages together and compete with the modern bookstore/coffee shops. Superior writing, speaking, and active listening skills, are critical for interior designers to communicate ideas to other people. Strong math skills and computer skills are a necessity.

Career Snapshot: Library interior design requires detailed preparation before plans are drawn. The needs of the library patrons must be considered when planning the design. Designers must be aware of the atmosphere library personnel want to convey to the visitors. Because many bookstores feature nice comfortable chairs and coffee services, visitors are enticed to stay longer. To compete effectively, modern libraries need to be equally enticing. Designers must work closely with librarians and architects to understand how to plan the space. The library needs to function for members of all ages and abilities. Special areas for small children, meeting rooms for public use by local clubs and groups, and efficient and comfortable staff work areas are important design considerations. Designers need to advise clients on such factors as space planning, use of furnishings and equipment, and color coordination. As in all areas of interior design, they must demonstrate and apply the principles of universal design and meet all local building and fire codes. Since funding for most libraries comes from local tax dollars, it is very important for designers to keep costs down without compromising quality or safety.

©2004 Image by Rick Alexander/LS3P ASSOCIATED, LTD. Bluffton Library, Bluffton, South Carolina.

Education/Training: Completion of a bachelor's or master's degree is preferred. Classes include business management, lighting, computer technology, color theory, textiles, and CADD. Additional courses in library science and psychology help make the designer more competitive in the job market.

Licensing/Examinations: Approximately one-half of the states require interior designers to be licensed. The National Council for Interior Design Qualification (NCIDQ) administers an examination that interior designers must pass in order to obtain a license and to be competitive in their careers.

Professional Association: The American Society of Interior Designers (ASID) (www.asid.org), The International Interior Design Association (IIDA) (www.iida.org).

Job Outlook: Job growth is expected to be faster than average through 2018. Outlook will be especially good for designers who specialize in ergonomic design, or green and sustainable design.

Source: Information from the Occupational Outlook Handbook (www.bls.gov/OCO) and the Occupational Information Network (O*NET) (www.online.onetcenter.org).

Summary

Visual imagery is the language of sight. It communicates different feelings. Understanding visual imagery is based on knowing the design characteristics and elements of design.

The three characteristics of design—function, construction, and aesthetics—are used as guidelines in creating and evaluating design. The tools used to create good design are color, line, form, space, mass, and texture.

Using different types of straight and curved lines can create different emotions in a room. They can be used together in different combinations to create various effects. The four types of form and the three guidelines for using form can inspire countless design ideas. When using space, the area inside and around a form, you need to consider its size and arrangement. You can use high mass or low mass to create a strong design statement. You can also use both types together to create variety in a room. Tactile and visual texture can be used to communicate different feelings, affect the visual size, and create variety.

Review the Facts

1. How does visual imagery relate to room design?

2. Contrast the three characteristics of design: function, construction, and aesthetics. Why are all three important to good design?

3. Describe the different types of lines. What feeling does each communicate?

4. Identify the type of form described by each of the following: (A) lifelike, normal, and traditional; (B) random and flowing; (C) organized, ordered, planned, and tailored; (D) rearranged or stylized

5. List three guidelines for using form in design.

6. Why are related forms more agreeable than unrelated forms?

7. How can you use space to create a cozy feeling in a room?

8. Give an example of an object with high mass and one with low mass.

9. Contrast tactile and visual texture. Give an example of how you might use each in a room.

Think Critically

10. **Draw conclusions.** The elements of design in a dwelling can have a psychological impact on its occupants. Draw conclusions about how each element of design might psychologically impact the occupants of a home. Give examples to support your conclusions.

11. **Predict outcomes.** For each of the three characteristics of design—function, construction, and aesthetics—predict some possible outcomes of poor design.

12. **Make generalizations.** Select any room in your school and evaluate whether form follows function. Make a list of five generalizations about the items in the room that address the room's function. Make a separate list of five generalizations of items that address form. What recommendations would you make to improve both the form and function of the space?

Community Links

13. **Evaluate design.** Choose a room in your school, home, or a community building and evaluate how well each element of design is used and its impact on the users. On a sheet of paper, rate each element on a scale of 1 to 5:1 = very poor and 5 = very good. Identify at least one reason to support your rating of each element. Total the score and share your evaluation with your classmates.

14. **Identify elements of design.** Use Internet or print resources to locate at least four pictures of rooms in a house, each illustrating several elements of design discussed in the chapter. Mount the pictures on separate sheets of paper and label the design element shown in each. As an alternative, use digital pictures with presentation software to show your room pictures and the elements of design used in each.

15. **Texture collage.** Choose a word that describes a texture. Write the word in the middle of a large sheet of poster board or construction paper. Locate examples of this texture—such as pieces of fabric, wood, or stone as well as pictures representing the word—and mount your examples on the poster board. Share your texture collage with the class and explain why each artifact is an example of the texture. Identify ways each texture can be used in a room design.

Academic Connections

16. **Writing.** Think about an attractive and inviting room you have recently seen. How did the elements of design impact your feelings about the room? Write a short description identifying how each element of design was used in the room.

17. **Reading.** Locate an article about the elements of design in a popular magazine such as *This Old House, Architectural Digest,* or *Country Living.* Read the article. Write a short summary identifying at least five additional concepts you learned about the elements of design. How do these concepts relate to what you already know about the elements of design? Be sure to note the name of the article, the writer, and date of publication, and magazine title on your summary page.

Technology Applications

18. **Evaluate size and space.** Search the Internet for the term *interior design* and find a site that provides useful ideas dealing with a room's size and space. What interior design techniques are recommended for changing the perception of a room's size and space? What design choices can make a room appear smaller? appear larger? How does mass influence the space? Print out copies of the design examples to show the class, and identify the product or service offered by the Web site sponsor.

19. **Video presentation.** Select a favorite photo in the text outside this chapter. Use a video camera or digital camera with a video-clip option to develop a short video presentation about your photo selection. In your video, identify the photo you selected and summarize how the room's line, form, mass, space, and texture convey good interior design. Share your video with the class.

Design Practice

20. **Community design.** Suppose you are a professional architect who is hired by your community to design a new building for the city's art collection. The design must incorporate examples of as many different lines as possible. Try to include horizontal, vertical, diagonal, and curved, including circular, oval, curvy, and complex free-form. Either by hand or with CADD software, draw the interior and exterior of a building that meets these requirements.

21. **Portfolio.** Create a digital storyboard with presentation software to show beautiful room interiors. Each image should clearly show all elements of design. Label the elements of design in each image. Share your presentation with the class and save a copy for your portfolio.

Leadership in the Workplace

To learn more about interior design careers—specifically the use of the elements of design—complete an FCCLA *Power of One* unit called *Working on Working*. Contact an interior designer in your community. Make arrangements to job-shadow him or her for a day. Focus on how the designer uses the elements of design in daily work. How does working knowledge of the elements of design help the designer lead clients effectively in planning interiors?

Use the FCCLA *Planning Process* and the *Working on Working* unit activities to plan, carry out, and evaluate your project. See your adviser for information as needed.

CHAPTER 11

Using Color Effectively

Terms to Learn

color
color spectrum
color wheel
primary colors
secondary colors
tertiary colors
hue
value
tint
shade
tone
intensity
complement
pigment
warm colors
cool colors
color harmony
monochromatic color harmony
complementary color harmony
split-complementary color harmony
double-complementary color harmony
analogous color harmony
triadic color harmony
neutral color harmonies
color scheme

Chapter Objectives

After studying this chapter, you will be able to

- analyze the psychological impact and meaning of different colors.

- summarize how color influences human behavior.

- analyze and describe the relationships between colors on the color wheel.

- evaluate the use of color harmonies in planning interior designs.

Reading with Purpose

On a separate sheet of paper, write down the main headings from this chapter. Leave space for note-taking under each heading. As you read the chapter, write down three key points you learn from each section. Then answer the following: How does this information relate to what I already know about color?

In the previous chapter, you learned about the elements of design—line, form, space, mass, and texture. In this chapter, you will learn about another element of design—color. Color is likely the most important element of design. Deciding what color to use is usually the first decision made when designing a room. It is one of the first things others notice about your design. Color sets the mood in a room and leaves a lasting impression with most people.

Understanding Color

Color is an element or property of light. It can help you create certain moods in your home by communicating excitement, calmness, mystery, or other sensations and emotions. When you understand the effects of color, you can use it to make your personal living space attractive and satisfying, 11-1.

The Psychology of Color

Each color has certain psychological effects on people and can evoke certain feelings. Factors that can influence peoples' reactions to color include age, gender, culture, and life experiences.

Although there is no single specific system for identifying ways all people respond to color, some of the effects for each of the following colors may include:

- *Red* is associated with power, danger, fire, strength, and passion. It is bold, aggressive, exciting, and warm. It demands attention. Red can make you feel energetic. However, too much red in a room can be overpowering.

- *Orange* is hopeful, cheerful, warm, and less aggressive than red. It expresses courage and hospitality. It can make a room feel energetic and friendly.

- *Yellow* is friendly, happy, and warm. It is associated with sympathy, sunlight, prosperity, cowardice, and wisdom. Yellow rooms are cheerful, light, and airy. However, pure yellow draws attention due to its brightness, so take care when using it in large amounts.

- *Green* is the color of nature. Consequently, it is refreshing, friendly, cool, and peaceful. Additional meanings include hope, good luck, and envy. Green mixes well with other colors and looks especially good next to white.

- *Blue* is cool, quiet, and reserved. It is associated with tranquility, serenity, and formality. Blue can be soothing and peaceful. It can be especially pleasing when used with white. However, too much blue in a room can be depressing.

- *Violet* is a royal color. It is dignified and dramatic. It works well with most other colors.

- *Black* is sophisticated and mysterious. It is associated with wisdom, evil, and death. Small amounts of black help ground a room, or may add a timeless, classic elegance. When used in large quantities, however, black may be oppressive.

11-1
The combination of colors used in this child's room creates a cheerful space.

Photography Courtesy of Calico Corners—Calico Home Stores

LINK TO SOCIAL STUDIES & CULTURE

Color Psychology at Work

Color is a vital tool for interior designers because it impacts how people feel. Vibrant colors, especially oranges and reds, enliven the seating areas of many fast-food restaurants. They tend to stimulate customers' appetites.

Designers working for clients in various industries use color to achieve other goals. For example, designers of airplane interiors avoid using large expanses of fast-food reds and oranges. Their goal is not to stimulate appetites, but to create a relaxing environment for passengers. Neutrals and muted shades often work well. In hospital rooms, color is used to create spaces that do not raise anxiety or trigger depression among ill or injured people.

In residential settings, designers often use the color blue in bedrooms because it has a calming and peaceful effect.

- *White* is fresh, peaceful, and pure. It is associated with youth, innocence, and faith. White can make rooms look crisper and livelier.

People feel most comfortable when colors in their surroundings reflect their personalities. For instance, outgoing people might choose bright red or yellow for the main color in a room. Shy people might feel awkward in a red room. Instead, they might prefer a room that features a soft blue or green.

When making color decisions for your home or the home of a client, consider the preferences of each family member. No single color will satisfy everyone. However, the color and design of the social area of the home should make all members feel as comfortable as possible. Use individual color preferences in personalized sleeping areas and other private work or play spaces.

The Color Spectrum

The **color spectrum** is the full range of all existing colors. A beam of white light produces *spectral colors* as it passes through a prism. Although limitless in number, more than 10 million colors have been identified in the color spectrum. Each distinct color derives from a few basic colors. The rainbow in 11-2 is the ideal example in nature of how sunlight can separate into a continuous band of colors, or a *spectrum*. In the case of a rainbow, the raindrops themselves serve as tiny prisms separating the light.

The variety of colors possible in nature is virtually limitless. Paint manufacturers have translated the spectrum into several hundreds of different paint colors, 11-3.

11-2
The water droplets in a rainbow separate light into its many colors.

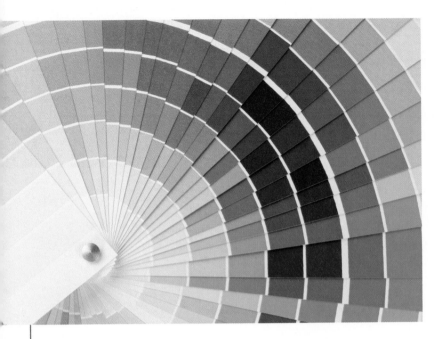

11-3
This fan of different paint colors represents a portion of the many colors that exist in nature.

The Color Wheel

Color relationships are easy to understand when you learn a few basic principles. The standard color wheel is the tool used to best illustrate these principles. The **color wheel**, 11-4, is the most commonly used tool to understand the basis of all color relationships. It is made of three concentric rings: an outer, middle, and inner ring. The middle ring of the color wheel consists of three types of colors: primary, secondary, and tertiary.

Yellow, red, and blue are the **primary colors**. They are the basic colors and you cannot create them by mixing other colors. However, mixing, lightening, or darkening the primary colors can make all other colors.

Orange, green, and violet are the **secondary colors**. Mixing equal amounts of two primary colors produces these colors. Orange is a mixture of red and yellow. Green is a mixture of yellow and blue. Violet is a mixture of blue and red. Look again at the color wheel. Notice each secondary color is located halfway between the two primary colors used to make it.

The other colors in the middle ring of the color wheel—yellow-green, blue-green, blue-violet, red-violet, red-orange, and yellow-orange—are the **tertiary colors,** or the third level of colors. Another name for the tertiary colors is *intermediate colors*. The names of tertiary colors reflect the names of the two colors used to make them—an equal mixture of a primary color with a secondary color adjacent to it on the color wheel. Note that their names always have the primary color listed first. For example, blue-green is correct but not "green-blue."

The lightest color on the color wheel is yellow and it is always at the top of the wheel for that reason. Violet is the darkest color on the color wheel. It is directly opposite from yellow at the bottom of the wheel.

Color Characteristics

Each color has three characteristics: hue, value, and intensity. Various tools illustrate these characteristics. For example, the color wheel shows hues and some values. Separate scales, such as the *color rendering index* (CRI), show color values more completely as well as color intensity. You will learn more about the color rendering index in Chapter 17.

Hue

A **hue**, or color name, is the color in its purest form, with no added black, gray, or white. It is the one characteristic that makes a color unique. It is what makes red different from blue and green different from yellow. It is the specific, individual nature of each color.

Value

The **value** of a hue is the relative lightness or darkness of a hue. The middle ring of the color wheel shows the normal values of hues. The normal values of some hues are lighter than the

LINK TO SCIENCE & TECHNOLOGY

Visible Light and the Electromagnetic Spectrum

Light is a form of energy called *electromagnetic radiation*. It travels through space as oscillating waves. From crest to trough, these waves range in size from large as a building to small as a microscopic particle. *Wavelength* is the distance between the crests of two adjoining waves. *Frequency* is the rate at which a wave oscillates or fluctuates and is measured in hertz. The chart shows the electromagnetic spectrum arranged according to wavelength and frequency in hertz. As the length of a wave increases, its frequency decreases.

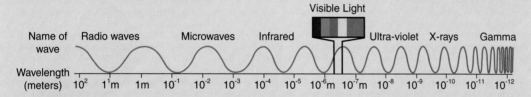

Visible light makes up a small part of the electromagnetic spectrum and it's the only part you can see. Visible light consists of the colors you see in a rainbow—red, orange, yellow, green, blue, and violet. These colors form the basis for the color wheel interior designers use for creating color schemes.

The spectrum also includes other forms of energy you encounter every day: infrared, radio waves, microwaves, X-rays, gamma rays, and ultraviolet rays. Many consumer electronics products utilize the electromagnetic spectrum. Can you identify a few of them?

normal values of others. For instance, yellow has the lightest normal value of any color in the middle ring of the wheel. As you move away from yellow on the color wheel, the normal values of hues become darker. Violet has the darkest normal value.

Adding white to a hue makes its lighter. The addition of white to a hue produces a **tint**. For instance, pink is a tint of red. Adding white to red creates pink. Adding white to blue creates baby blue, a tint of blue. Peach is a tint of orange. Lavender is a tint of violet. The innermost ring of the color wheel shows the tints. Lighter tints require the addition of more white.

You can make the value of a hue darker by adding black. The addition of black to a hue produces a **shade**. For instance, burgundy is a shade of red. Adding black to red creates this shade. Navy blue is a shade of blue and is created by adding black to blue. Darker shades require the addition of more black. The outer ring of the color wheel shows the shades. Refer again to the color wheel to identify the normal value of hues, tints, and shades.

Adding gray softens the value of a hue, which produces a **tone**. Rose is a tone of red. Wedgwood blue is a tone of blue, created by adding gray to blue. Note that adding light gray to a hue causes confusion with a tint. Likewise, adding dark gray to a hue can cause confusion with a shade. However, there is a difference. Medium grays, of course, are the easiest to recognize as tones when mixed with hues.

Outer ring = shades of hues

Middle ring = normal values of hues

Inner circle = tints of hues

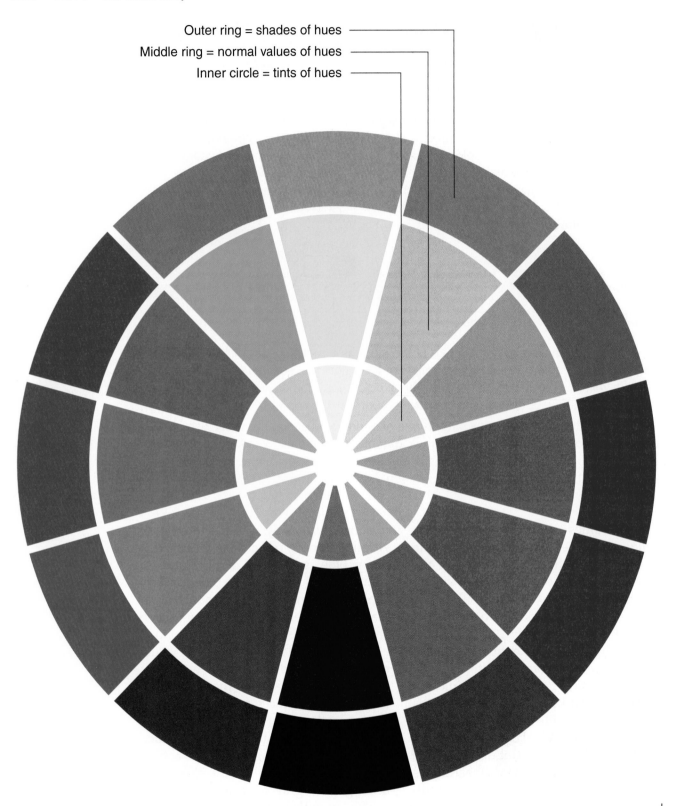

11-4
The arrangement in a color wheel provides a basis for all color relationships.

Figure 11-5 pictures a *value scale*. The left column shows the range of tints obtained by adding greater amounts of white to the blue color. The right column shows the range of shades obtained by adding greater amounts of black to the blue.

Intensity

Intensity refers to the brightness or dullness of a hue. The middle ring of the color wheel shows the normal intensity of each hue.

One way to dull a hue, or lower its intensity, is to add some of its complement. The **complement** of a hue is the hue opposite it on the color wheel. For instance, blue is the complement of orange. To lower the intensity of orange, you add varying amounts of blue, as shown in 11-6. To lower the intensity of red, you add small amounts of its complement, green. Examples of high-intensity colors include hot pink and fire-engine red. Smoky blue and rust are examples of low-intensity colors. Another way to lower the intensity of a hue is to add gray, making the color a tone.

Neutrals

Although neutrals are not really colors, they are usually classified as colors when discussing design. Black, white, and gray are neutrals. Black is the combination of all colors when it exists as a pigment. A **pigment** is a coloring agent used in paint and printed materials. In contrast to black, white used as a pigment has no color. Gray is a combination of black and white. Brown and its tints and shades are also neutrals. Combining equal amounts of complementary colors forms a brown color.

By adding a neutral color to a hue, the value of the hue changes to either a tint or a shade. This makes the hue less intense. With any of these changes, neutralization of the hue occurs. Neutralized hues blend better with other colors.

11-5
Values for the color blue, ranging from tints to shades, are shown on this value scale.

11-6
Adding blue to orange reduces the intensity of orange, making it a duller color.

Warm and Cool Colors

Colors can be classified as either warm or cool. Although the actual temperature may be the same throughout an entire home, some rooms may seem cooler or warmer due to the usage of certain colors in decorating.

Warm colors include yellow, orange, red, and the colors near them on the color wheel, with red being the warmest. They are called warm colors because they remind us of fire and the sun.

Warm colors are the *advancing colors*. Warm-colored objects appear closer to you. Warm-colored walls look closer together. For example, a room painted red, yellow, or orange appears smaller than its actual size.

Warm colors attract your attention. They can make you feel happy, energetic, and full of excitement. Research shows the color red actually stimulates the nervous system and can increase blood pressure, heartbeats, and breathing rate. Many advertisements use warm colors to make you notice them. Restaurants use warm colors to increase your appetite. Locker rooms use them to generate excitement. Warm colors in homes make household members feel lively and cheerful. An overuse of warm colors, however, may make people feel nervous or tense, especially if they are full-intensity colors.

Cool colors are opposite the warm colors on the color wheel. These include blue, green, violet, and the colors near them. They are cool colors because they remind people of water, grass, and trees.

Cool colors are *receding colors*. They make objects seem smaller and walls seem farther away than they really are. Decorating a small room in cool colors can make it appear larger than actuality.

Cool colors are quiet and restful. Hospitals often use them to help patients relax and feel calm. They are also popular for bedrooms. With overuse, however, cool colors may make people feel depressed.

Warm and cool colors create different moods that make people feel differently, 11-7. For example, workers in an office complained their lunchroom was always cold. When the employer changed the light blue room to orange, the complaints stopped even though the temperature never changed.

Color Harmonies

The surest and easiest way to achieve success when using color is to follow one of the standard color harmonies. A **color harmony** is a pleasing combination of colors based on their respective positions on the color wheel. There are seven basic color harmonies: monochromatic,

11-7
By comparing these two living rooms, you can sense the warmth created by the use of yellow and red (A) and the feeling of coolness generated by the use of green and blue (B).

A

B

GREEN CHOICES

Avoid Greenwashing

Are "green" products always "green?" Some companies and agencies may be less than truthful about the "green" aspects of their products and services. These companies and agencies realize that more consumers are looking for green products and are easily influenced by terms relating to green features. They may use terms that mislead consumers and professionals about the "green" features of their products. Some environmental product claims are false while others are misleading. The term for this deceptive way of doing business is *greenwashing*.

An example of greenwashing involves low- or zero-volatile organic compound (VOC) paints. Because they are less toxic to humans and the environment, these paints are catching on quickly with consumers. Several reliable paint suppliers produce these paints. Other companies are putting "green" on the labels, but their paint may actually be neither low- or zero-VOCs products.

Before buying any green products, check a number of Web sites that provide information on the validity of products that indicate green features. A few of the Web sites include the following:

www.greenbiz.com
www.edcmag.com
www.greenguard.org

complementary, split-complementary, double-complementary, analogous, triadic, and neutral. Established color harmonies bring colors together in combinations that are very satisfying to the eyes.

Monochromatic Color Harmony

A **monochromatic color harmony** is the simplest color harmony. It uses a single hue from the standard color wheel. The hue selected for the monochromatic color harmony in 11-8 is green.

You can achieve variation in a monochromatic color harmony by changing the value and/or intensity of the hue. For example, you could use light blue, gray blue, and navy blue—a tint, a tone, and a shade of the same hue. A paint fan deck will usually show five to seven values of the same hue. To add

interest to the color scheme, use accents of neutral colors. Using a monochromatic color harmony can make a room appear larger. It can also unify the furnishings and accessories used in the space. The monochromatic color scheme is the most restful of all, because it has the least contrast or drama.

Complementary Color Harmony

Selecting two colors that are directly opposite each other on the standard color wheel creates a **complementary color harmony**. Complementary colors are sometimes called contrasting colors because they make each other look brighter and more intense. For example, when using blue next to orange, the blue looks bluer, and the orange looks stronger. A complementary color harmony can make a room look bright and dramatic.

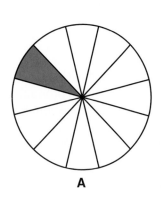

A

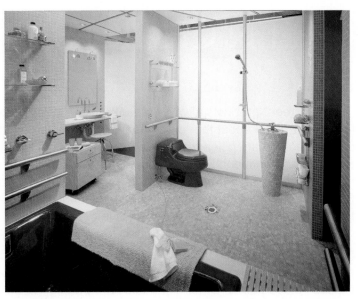

B

11-8
Green is the basis for this monochromatic color harmony.

Photography Courtesy of Kohler

Although such a sharp contrast is fine for some rooms, most rooms are more comfortable with less contrast. Varying the values and intensities of the colors can do this along with varying the amounts of the colors, 11-9. The more one color dominates the other, the less noticeable the contrast.

Split-Complementary Color Harmony

Using one hue with the two hues adjacent to its complement creates a **split-complementary color harmony**. For example, if you choose the blue hue first, you would look directly across the color wheel to find orange, its complement. You would then select the colors on both sides of orange to establish your split-complementary color harmony. The resulting color harmony uses blue, yellow-orange, and red-orange, 11-10. With this color selection, blue will likely be the dominant color, while yellow-orange and red-orange provide lively contrast.

Double-Complementary Color Harmony

Selecting two colors and their complements from the standard color wheel creates a **double-complementary color harmony**. In this way, you use four colors to create the color harmony. One example of a double-complementary color harmony results from pairing red and green with violet and yellow, 11-11. As long as each pair is composed of complementary colors, you may use any combination of pairs.

Analogous Color Harmony

Selecting related hues from the standard color wheel creates an **analogous color harmony**. These are hues that are next to each other on the color wheel. In an analogous color harmony, usually three to five hues are used. Since they are related, they blend together well. One color seems to merge into another. Even when the colors in an analogous

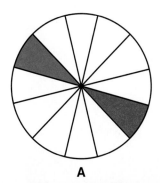

A

B

11-9

Shades of green and red are used in this contemporary bedroom to create a complementary color harmony.

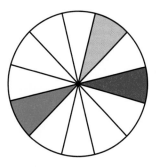

11-10

A split-complementary color harmony uses a main color with the colors on both sides of its complement.

color harmony are all warm, the room will be more restful than one that uses colors from both sides of the color wheel. Figure 11-12 shows an example of an analogous color harmony.

An analogous color harmony will look best if you choose one color as the dominant color and use smaller amounts of the others to add interest and variety. You may also want to use a tiny amount of an unrelated color as an accent.

Triadic Color Harmony

A **triadic color harmony** uses any three colors that are equally distant from each other on the standard color wheel. The triadic color harmony will follow a pattern of using every fourth color on the color wheel. For example, yellow, blue, and red—the primary colors—form a triadic color harmony, 11-13. The secondary colors—green, orange, and violet—also create a triadic color harmony. The two other possible color combinations are: yellow-orange, red-violet, and blue-green; or red-orange, blue-violet, and yellow-green. Designers use great care and skill to achieve pleasing triadic harmonies. Changing values and intensities can lessen the sharp contrasts.

11-11
A double-complementary color harmony is made of two sets of complementary color schemes.

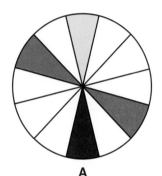

A

B

11-12
An analogous color harmony using yellow, yellow-orange, orange, red-orange, and red, gives this room a vibrant appearance.

Neutral Color Harmony

Although black and white are not hues on the standard color wheel, they are the basis for **neutral color harmonies**. Combinations of black, white, and gray create neutral color harmonies. Brown, tan, and beige can also be used. Sometimes adding small amounts of other colors to neutral color schemes gives the room more interest, 11-14.

Using Color Harmonies

Now that you have learned about color and the color harmonies, you can begin to use this information to create interior design color schemes for a home. A **color scheme** is the combination of colors selected for the design

A

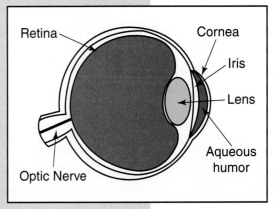

B

11-13
Triadic color harmonies are often used in children's bedrooms.

LINK TO SCIENCE & TECHNOLOGY

The Anatomy of Color

Objects absorb and reflect light. The color that you see depends on the wavelength and frequency of the reflected waves. Red has the longest wavelength; violet has the shortest.

Humans have *trichromatic color vision*. The key part of the eye responsible for color vision is the retina. This area, at the back of the eye, contains millions of light-sensitive nerve cells called rod and cone cells. *Rod cells* enable you to see in low light. *Cone cells* enable you to see color and detail.

The *tri* in trichromatic refers to the three types of cone cells. Each type is sensitive to waves of a different part of the visible light spectrum. "Blue cone cells" react to the shorter waves on the blue end of the color spectrum. "Red cone cells" react to longer waves on the red end of the spectrum. "Green cone cells" react to medium-length waves in the green spectrum.

When light enters the eyes and hits the retina, it stimulates the cone cells and sends electronic impulses to the brain. The signals from the cone cells are transmitted to the brain. In a complex process that researchers are still trying to understand, the human brain collects and processes this and other information to produce a color image.

Retina   Cornea   Iris   Lens   Aqueous humor   Optic Nerve

11-14
Combinations of black, gray, and white create neutral color schemes. Small splashes of accent colors can add interest.

11-15
Colors found in nature were the inspiration for the earthy color scheme in this bedroom.

of a room or house. When designing a room, choose colors that you like seeing together. The chosen colors probably look good together because they conform to an established color harmony.

A well-planned color scheme will use color harmonies to blend and unify the design of the home as you transition from one room to another. It will also consider the function of the room. As you will see, even if you love red, it may be a poor choice for a bedroom because of its intensity. By following important guidelines, you can create a color scheme that will enhance the near environment and increase the enjoyment of a home, 11-15.

Choosing the Right Colors

The color harmonies you choose for the color scheme of a home depend on several factors. They include what mood

or style a person wants, the lifestyle of the family members, the function or the way the occupants will use the room, the items in the room, and the room's location.

Moods and Styles

You can create a variety of moods in a room through the use of color. For example, you may want a room to feel restful, or you may want it to appear exciting. Choosing cool colors that have similar values will create a restful mood in the room, such as in 11-16. Choosing warm colors with contrasting values will make the room feel exciting.

You can also choose colors that will create a certain style in a room. Different styles, such as southwestern or country, often suggest the use of specific colors. You can use these colors in different color harmonies to achieve the style you want.

In a southwestern-style room, for example, you may choose warm desert colors, such as rust, sunset orange, brick, and sand. In a country-style room, you may choose low-intensity shades of reds, blues, oranges, and yellows.

Lifestyles

Some people have active lifestyles while others lead quieter lives. The colors you choose depend on the lifestyles of household members. For instance, with small children, give consideration to darker colors and shades that do not show dirt easily. In contrast, a household of adults may choose lighter colors for the walls and upholstery because upkeep is less of a concern.

The colors you choose for each room also depend upon how they are used. Primary and secondary colors of normal intensity are fine for a child's room, such as in 11-17. If you use the same hues in an adult's bedroom, however, softer tints or tones at lower intensity levels are preferable.

11-16
By using a CADD program, you can test how a paint color will look in a room to see the warmth or coolness it creates.

Courtesy of Software by Chief Architect

Function of the Room

While teens may sleep, study, and socialize in their bedrooms, most adults use their bedrooms for rest and relaxation. In this case, cooler colors and less drama are more conducive to good sleep. A den or family room where everyone meets and socializes is often more appropriate in warm colors. For a writer or an accountant that works alone from home, the home office may be best in cool colors. In contrast, a salesperson who talks on the phone most of the day may perform best in warm colors. When choosing colors and color schemes, give thoughtful attention to colors that support the function and purpose of a room.

Items in the Room

Another way to choose color harmonies is to consider the usage of all items in the room plan. For instance, plans for a room may include an area rug, couch, or favorite picture. To create a color scheme around any of these items, you need to select one color used in the object. This color becomes the base, or main color. After choosing the base color, use your knowledge of color harmonies, values, and intensities to pick colors to go with it, 11-18.

You also need to consider the type of lighting used in the room. The colors you select must work well during both day and night. This means you must view the intended colors during daylight hours in natural light and at night under the influence of artificial light. Always make your final color selections in the actual room and under

11-17
The use of primary and secondary colors in this child's room give the room a feeling of fun and excitement.

Photography Courtesy of JELD-WEN Windows and Doors

11-18
A neutral base color and harmony in this room provide a backdrop for the existing art collection.

the lighting conditions where you will use them. Many people experience disasters after selecting a paint color in a retail store under lighting that differs from the actual lighting in their space.

Most homes have some combination of natural, incandescent, and fluorescent lighting. However, some homes now are using the newer and more energy efficient lighting such as compact fluorescent lighting (CFL), light-emitting diodes (LED), and fiber optic lighting. Incandescent lighting can bring dullness to some colors and fluorescent lighting can completely distort color. Incandescent lighting generally makes colors appear warmer. Fluorescent lighting makes colors appear warmer or cooler depending on the color of the lightbulb or tube. In general, most fluorescent lighting will make colors appear cooler compared to incandescent lighting. Halogen lighting renders the truest presentation of colors. Compact florescent lighting affects colors in various ways depending on the color rating of the bulb. The chart, 11-19, shows the impact of various lighting types on colors. You will learn more about types of lighting in Chapter 17.

Location of the Room

The direction the room faces—north, south, east, or west—must be taken into consideration when choosing the base color and color harmony. If a bedroom is located on the north side of a house, the subdued light of the northern exposure may make colors appear cooler. To make the room appear warmer, choose

11-19
Colors change when viewed under different types of artificial light.

Color and Artificial Lighting					
Type of Artificial Lighting	**Yellow**	**Orange**	**Red**	**Blue**	**Green**
Standard Incandescent	Warms	Strengthens	Enriches	Dulls	Darkens
Tungsten-Halogen Incandescent	Warms	Strengthens	Enriches	Dulls slightly	Darkens slightly
Deluxe Cool-White Fluorescent	Enriches and intensifies	Close to true hue	Warms	Enriches	Brightens
Deluxe Warm-White Fluorescent	Brightens	Strengthens	Enriches	Darkens and enriches	Enriches
Cool-White, Bright-White CFL	Enriches and intensifies	Close to true hue	Warms	Enriches	Brightens
Warm-White, Soft-White CFL	Warms	Strengthens	Enriches	Dulls	Darkens

a color harmony that uses warm colors. A southern exposure receives the most sunlight and generally makes colors appear bright and warm. Sometimes cool colors are preferred for rooms with southern exposures, 11-20.

You cannot assume, however, the quality of light entering a room from a specific direction is always the same. The light entering a bedroom with a northern exposure will change significantly, for example, if it reflects off a bright white house next door. Also, a room with a southern exposure will not be sunny if a covered porch overhangs the windows and doors. Even the light that filters through trees outside a window can change the quality of sunlight entering the room. Consequently, the best rule of thumb is to view a color sample in the actual room at different times of day and night to examine all lighting factors.

When considering location, you also need to think about the colors used in adjoining rooms. The new colors you choose should blend with those used in adjoining rooms. In general, color should not change abruptly from room to room. Instead it should make a gradual transition from one space to another.

If the location of a dining room is next to the living room, you can use the same base color in both rooms. You might use an analogous color harmony with yellow as the base color of the color scheme in both rooms. In the living room, consider selecting yellow as the dominant color with the other analogous hues playing secondary roles. Then use the same analogous color harmony in the dining room but expand the harmony from three to five hues and add interest by changing the tints or shades of the hues selected. You might also choose to have yellow play a less-dominant role in the dining room than it did in the living room. Introducing a color in the split-complementary color harmony with yellow as an accent will add excitement

to the room. Since yellow is the base color of all the harmonies in both rooms, it provides a smooth transition.

There is an exception to the rule of blending colors in adjoining rooms. In homes using contemporary design, the walls of adjoining rooms may intentionally have different, bold colors. Devote special care, however, to applying the basic rules of color harmonies so the abrupt transitions result in good design.

Using Color Correctly

As you work with color, the following guidelines will help you use color well:

- Applying colors to large areas makes them appear to gain intensity. Because of this, a color you select from a paint chip may appear too intense or dark when painted on all four walls of a room. At other times, a paint chip that appears soft and easy on the eye will fade to nothing when you apply it to the four walls of a room. It is advisable to paint a large swatch of the color on the wall or piece of foam board to help visualize how a paint color will appear on a wall.

- Using contrasting colors draws attention. For example, a white sofa against a dark wall will draw more attention than a white sofa against a white wall,

11-20
Because this bedroom has a southern exposure, the designer chose cool colors to decorate the room. These colors keep this room looking serene, light, and airy.

11-21. While you may want to avoid a totally neutral room, remember too many strong contrasts in a room can be confusing and tiring.

- Color harmonies are easier on the eye when one color, the base color, dominates. The dominant color should cover about two-thirds of the room area. When you use equal amounts of two or more colors in a room, your color selections can become a distraction and appear cluttered as each color competes for attention.

- When choosing colors for large areas, such as walls and floors, select low-intensity colors. If you use high-intensity colors in large amounts, they can become overpowering. Instead, use high-intensity colors in small amounts as accent colors in accessories or small pieces of furniture.

- Heavily textured surfaces make colors appear dark. This is because the light strikes the surface at different angles, making the item appear to have greater depth, 11-22. When trying to match

11-21
Color harmonies look best when your base color dominates the room.

fabrics, it is important to have samples of the fabrics you are matching. For example, if you are matching drapery fabric to carpet, make sure you have samples of the carpet with you.

- If a room is very large, consider choosing colors that will make it look smaller. Shades, high-intensity colors,

11-22
The cabinetry and wicker seating use the same green color, but the chair texture makes the room look darker.

Lexington Furniture Industries

and warm hues that have advancing qualities make a room appear smaller.

- If a room is small, color can make the room appear larger. Tints, low-intensity colors, a monochromatic or analogous color scheme, or cool hues that have receding qualities make a room look larger.

Choosing the right colors, creating color harmonies, and following the color guidelines is important, 11-23. This will help you make color work well for you, your home, or your customer.

11-23
Using the color guidelines to choose the right colors and create pleasing color harmonies is important for you or a client.

Photography Courtesy of Calico Corners—Calico Home Stores

CAREER FOCUS

Photography Courtesy of the
Color Marketing Group

Color Designer

If you share some of the following interests, you may want to consider a career as a color designer.

Talents and Skills: Do you like to experiment with the colors of your clothing and accessories? Do you realize that color plays an important role by having a positive or negative impact on emotions? Do you enjoy being in spaces where the colors give you a sense of peace? Have you found enjoyment working with colors and paint throughout your education? Skill requirements for a color specialist include: an excellent eye for color; thorough understanding of color psychology, the color wheel, and how to use different color harmonies; and the ability to organize details and research information. In addition, excellent speaking, writing, and listening skills are needed to communicate with a client.

Career Snapshot: Color designers work with manufacturers and interior designers. They provide many different design services as well as marketing. A color designer must have a strong combination of the two. They consult manufacturers about colors that will work best for trends in new furniture, paint, wall coverings, fabrics, rugs, and other accessories. For example, a color designer may work for a textile firm and may recommend yarn colors that will be the most popular and marketable. Color designers must be able to recognize very subtle differences in colors. They must stay current in their research to predicting color trends.

Education/Training: A bachelor's or a master's degree is preferred. Courses include color theory, psychology of color, art, art history, interior design, and computer programs.

Licensing/Examinations: No license required.

Professional Associations: The Color Marketing Group (CMG) (www.colormarketing.org/), The American Society of Interior Designers (ASID) (www.asid.org), the International Interior Design Association (IIDA) (www.iida.org), the Inter-Society Color Council (ISCC) (www.iscc.org)

Job Outlook: The many career possibilities for a color designer in interior design will grow faster than average through 2018. Color designers may work for a large firm that specializes in color design, an interior designer specializing in color design, or an individual company as a consultant. Some choose freelance work for projects of interest.

Summary

Color is one of the most important elements of design. It can create and communicate different moods. Color has it own physiological and psychological effects on people.

The basis of all color relationships is the color wheel. Colors in the middle ring of the color wheel are primary, secondary, or intermediate colors. Color has three characteristics—hue, value and intensity. The cool colors are located on one side of the wheel, and the warm colors are on the other.

When colors are used together in a pleasing manner, color harmonies are created. They may be monochromatic, complementary, split-complementary, double-complementary, analogous, triadic, or neutral. Neutral colors are black, white, gray, tan, beige, and brown.

When choosing a color harmony for a personal color scheme, first choose the right colors for a home and the lifestyle of the occupants. Then following certain guidelines will coordinate the colors you select into good design.

Review the Facts

1. What factors influence the psychological impact color has on people?

2. Summarize the feelings each of the following colors evokes in people: red, green, and violet.

3. Name the secondary colors. What primary colors, in what proportions, are used to make each?

4. Which color name is listed first in the name of a tertiary color?

5. Contrast value and intensity of color.

6. What are the differences between a tint, shade, and tone?

7. Summarize how to neutralize a hue.

8. Name two warm colors and two cool colors.

9. Identify an example of each of the seven color harmonies.

10. What factors influence the way color harmonies are used in planning an interior design?

11. Summarize the guidelines for using color correctly in a room design.

Think Critically

12. **Draw conclusions.** No two people perceive color in exactly the same way and indeed some people are unable to distinguish between certain colors at all. How could these behaviors pose an obstacle to an interior designer's presentation to a committee in charge of finalizing selections for new corporate offices? Draw conclusions about what techniques the designer could use to overcome objections.

13. **Identify alternatives.** Assume you are working with two clients who want to redesign the master bedroom in their home. The room has a northern exposure with little natural lighting. One client prefers warm, intense hues while the other prefers cool hues. In addition to sleeping, your clients also use the room for reading. What color alternatives would you suggest that both clients will find pleasing? How can lighting impact your color choices?

Community Links

14. **Model home tour.** Visit a model home and observe the use of color. Record your observations. Did the colors match your preferences? Did the colors reflect current trends? How were colors used to create mood in various rooms? Identify several psychological impacts the colors may have on some people. Summarize your findings in a brief report to the class.

15. **Analyze color.** Analyze the color scheme of your bedroom or other room in your home, or in the home of someone you know. Which of the colors used is your favorite? How long has this room had this appearance? What color scheme was used before? If you could redecorate next week, what colors would you select? What do you think your color preferences reveal about your personality? Take one or more pictures of this room with a digital camera to place in an electronic presentation. Include examples and colors you might want to use in the future. Share your electronic presentation with the class.

16. **Color comparison.** Locate a home or business in the community whose exterior has a pleasing combination of colors. Identify the colors used and how they were used. Also, identify a building's exterior that represents the opposite of pleasing to you. What colors are used? Which colors would you change if you had the job of updating the look of the building on a budget?

Academic Connections

17. **Social studies.** Search the Internet for current color trends in residential design. What cultural influences, elements of nature, or other factors inspire the new color trends? How strongly does culture influence color? Which of the new color trends do you find most appealing? Share your findings during a small group discussion.

18. **Science.** Use Internet or print resources to investigate how light reflectance value (LRV) can influence an interior designer's choice of colors for a room design. How might LRV influence the aesthetics and function of a room design? Write a summary of your findings to share with the class.

Technology Applications

19. **Analyze color harmonies.** Use a digital camera to take pictures of 10 rooms that display good interior design. (Perhaps some are in your home or in historical homes that you have visited.) For each room, identify the type of color harmony that predominates. Also, analyze possible reasons for the color harmonies selected, given the purpose of each room. Using presentation software, combine your photographs and explanations to share with the class.

20. **Computer design project.** Using CADD or another popular interior-design software program, create two small rooms of the same dimensions. Cover the walls of one room with light, dull, cool colors. Cover the walls of the other room with dark, bright, warm colors. Analyze which room looks larger and which looks smaller. Why? Print a copy of the room colors for each room. Write a brief report summarizing your analysis.

Design Practice

21. **Color consulting.** Imagine you are a professional color consultant who has been hired to help select the room colors for a new community center in your neighborhood. Based on your knowledge of the psychological effect color has on people, what colors would you use in each of the following spaces? Why?

    - children's recreation room
    - reading room for older adults
    - hospitality room with a snack bar
    - small nature museum room
    - drama room for theatrical rehearsals

22. **Portfolio.** Continue the storyboard for the elements of design you started in Chapter 10. Add color as a design element and provide samples of all color harmonies, labeling the colors used. Keep a copy of your storyboard in your portfolio.

Leading the Way with Color

Do you find the psychology of color fascinating? Are your interested in the impact of color on overall room design? If you are, consider joining forces with a community organization, such as Rebuilding Together®. Such groups repair and modify homes for people with limited incomes, including older adults, people with disabilities, and veterans. For an FCCLA *Community Service* project, consult a leader in the organization about working with one or more clients to create a functional and aesthetically pleasing color palette for a room or entire home.

Use the FCCLA *Planning Process* and the *Community Service Project Sheet* to plan, carry out, and evaluate your project. See your adviser for information as needed.

CHAPTER 12

Using the Principles of Design

Terms to Learn

proportion
golden mean
golden section
golden rectangle
scale
visual weight
balance
formal balance (symmetry)
informal balance (asymmetrical)
emphasis
rhythm
repetition
gradation
radiation
opposition
transition
harmony
unity
sensory design

Chapter Objectives

After studying this chapter, you will be able to

- evaluate the use of the principles of design in residential and commercial interiors.
- summarize the goals of design.
- analyze the effects of sensory design.

Reading with Purpose

After reading each passage of this chapter, answer the following question: If you were explaining the information in this chapter to a friend who is not taking this class, what would you tell him or her?

In the previous two chapters, you learned about the elements of design. When the elements of design are applied using the principles of design, you can achieve the goals of design. In this chapter, you will learn how to use this process to create well-designed rooms.

The Principles of Design

The principles of design are guidelines for working with the elements of design. When you understand the principles of design, you can use the elements of design successfully. The principles of design are proportion and scale, balance, emphasis, and rhythm.

Proportion and Scale

Proportion and scale are closely related but different. They both describe size, shape, and amount. They are both concerned with the relationships of objects and parts of objects.

Proportion

Proportion is the ratio of one part to another part or of one part to the whole. It is an important factor when selecting and positioning furniture and accessories in a room. For example, proportion is a consideration when choosing a shade for a lamp. The lamp base and the lampshade need to be in proportion to each other (parts of the same object). Proportion is also a factor to consider when choosing the surface on which to place the lamp. The lamp and table need to be in proportion to each other (different objects in the same group). The accessories that surround the lamp are also considered. The accessories must be in proper proportion to both the lamp and the table (different objects in the same group).

When developing a design scheme, ratios such as 3:5, 5:8, and 8:13 are more effective than ratios of 1:1 or 1:2. For instance, a rectangle has more pleasing proportions than a square. These ratios also apply to rooms, furniture, and accessories, 12-1.

The Greeks were masters of the use of proportion. They developed guidelines that have been used for centuries. Study 12-2 as you read about the Greek guidelines for developing pleasing proportions:

- The **golden mean** is the division of a line midway between one-half and one-third of its length. This unequal division is more pleasing visually than an equal division or a division at a point that is less than one-third of the line's length. Interior designers often apply the golden mean when planning wall arrangements, tying draperies, and hanging pictures.

- The **golden section** is the division of a line or form in such a way that the ratio of the smaller section to the

12-1
Good proportion is important in furnishing a room.

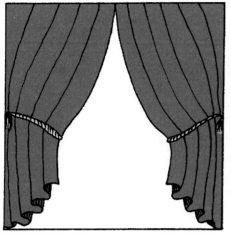

Golden mean

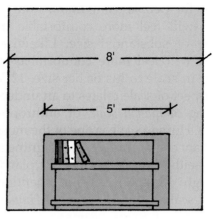

Golden section
Ratio 5:8

Golden rectangle
Ratio 1:1.618

larger section is equal to the ratio of the larger section to the whole. This relationship is based on the progression of the numbers 1, 1, 2, 3, 5, 8, 13, 21, 34, 55 and so forth. Notice that the number 2 and each number following is the sum of the two previous numbers.

When using the golden section to plan a design, you will find that the ratio of 3:5 is about the same as the ratio 8:13 and other similar ratios. Using the concept of the golden section can help you develop more pleasing proportions in your designs.

- The **golden rectangle** has sides in a ratio of 1 to 1.618. It is based on the ratio of the golden section. To form a golden rectangle, divide two equal lines following the golden section. Then combine the short segments and long segments to form the rectangle. One example of the golden rectangle is the Parthenon in Athens. The golden rectangle is frequently an aspect of good design. You can find many examples of the golden rectangle in houses and their furnishings.

Most people do not actually measure proportions. They can tell by looking at a rug on a floor if it is in the proper proportion. Likewise, they can tell if a bed or sofa visually "fits" its room. People tend to develop an awareness or sense of proportion based on their own visual perceptions.

Scale

Scale refers to the relative size of an object in relation to other objects. For example, a chair is a small piece of furniture in comparison to a bed. A twin bed is small in comparison to a king-size bed. However, the twin bed is still larger than the chair.

When the scale of furnishings relate to the space they occupy, they are visually pleasing. For example, large rooms require large-scale furnishings. A king-size bed is appropriate in a large bedroom. However, it might seem too large for a small room. Small rooms require small-scale furniture.

The furnishings within a room should be in scale with one another. For example, a large sofa requires a large coffee table. A small sofa would not go well with a large coffee table.

12-2
The golden mean, golden section, and golden rectangle are all guidelines to help you achieve good proportion.

Rea-Lynne Gilder

Furnishings also need to be in scale to the people using them. A large person will feel more comfortable in a chair of substantial size. Likewise, a child will feel more comfortable in a chair in scale to his or her size, 12-3. This aspect of scale relates to an understanding of *human scale*, or anthropometrics. Human scale is one of the most important considerations in designing a space—either interior or exterior plans. Although Maslow did not mention human scale in his *Hierarchy of Human Needs*, several terms he mentions can strongly relate to human scale. These terms include fulfillment, dignity, relationships, security, protection, and shelter. Peoples' personal size, capabilities, and limits influence how they interact with their environments.

Human scale influences such common everyday objects as the standard door that is 6-feet 8-inches tall by 3-feet wide, steps and ramps that are easy to ascend, or residential elevators that are wide enough to accommodate a wheelchair. Human scale also influences how you feel in a space. For example, think about how differently you feel when you compare the ceiling of a concert hall to the ceiling in your home. Understanding of the subtle aspects of human scale is one of the most important skills to develop in any of the environmental design professions.

Another aspect of scale is **visual weight**. Visual weight is the perception that an object weighs more or less than it really does. For example, a wooden chair and an upholstered chair may have the same dimensions. However, the upholstered chair will look larger and heavier than the wooden chair. Thick lines, bold colors, coarse textures, and large patterns add to visual weight.

When creating a design plan for a small room, choose furniture that has light visual weight. This will prevent the furniture from making the room look crowded. Likewise, choose accessories that are in scale to the furniture. In a small room, it is wise to "think small" in regard to furniture and accessories.

Balance

Balance implies equilibrium among parts of a design. It is a perception of the way arrangements are seen. When there is balance, there is a sense of equal weight on both sides of a center point, 12-4. There is not a visual pull in one direction more than the other. Balance can be either formal or informal. Both types of balance can be used in the same room or space.

In **formal balance**, or symmetry, there is identical proportion and arrangement of objects on both sides of a center point. *Symmetry* is another name for formal balance. Elegant and formal rooms often use this type of balance, 12-5. It is especially appropriate for traditional design styles. It is also useful in exterior design. Formal balance is easy to achieve and

12-3
The appropriate scale of these furnishings and chair provide greater comfort and accessibility for the children.

Calico Corners—Calico Home Stores

MATH MATTERS

How to Read a Scale Ruler

Architectural drawings are drawn in proportion to actual size. A floor plan of a room, for example, represents the actual dimensions of the room. This is done by using a scale; one measurement represents another.

A scale ruler is used to create and read these drawings. A six-edged triangular ruler is one of the most common scale rulers. One edge has a 12-in. ruler with each inch divided into 16 units. The other edges have two scales each—one is read from right to left and the other is read from left to right. The scale that reads from left to right is half as large as the scale that reads from right to left.

To use the ruler, find the scale you need and make sure you read it from the correct direction (left to right or right to left). House plans are usually drawn at a standard scale of *¼ in. equals 1 ft.* Each ¼ in. on the drawing represents 1 ft. on the actual house. Always use zero—not the ruler's edge—as the start point of the measurement.

Example 1: A house plan shows the length of a room as 3 in. How long is the actual room if you use the scale ¼ in. = 1 ft.?

Answer: If ¼ = 1, then 1 = 4; 3 × 4 = 12 ft.

Example 2: A room is 12 ft. wide by 15 ft. long. How would a) width and b) length be expressed in a drawing using the scale ¼ in. = 1 ft.?

Answer:

a. Width. 12 ÷ 4 = 3 in.
b. Length. 15 ÷ 4 = 3.75 in.

makes people feel comfortable because of its orderliness.

With **informal balance**, there is an arrangement of different but equivalent objects on each side of a center point. *Asymmetrical balance* is another name for informal balance. Although the sides are not alike, neither side overpowers the other. This creates a feeling of equilibrium.

You can achieve informal balance in various ways. In order to balance a heavy object and a light object, place the heavier object closer to the center line than the light object. Several smaller objects can balance a single, large one. If objects are the same size but of unequal distance from you, the object closest to you will appear larger.

An object that has visual weight can also balance a single, large object. Color, texture, and form all create visual weight, 12-6. Bold, warm colors will appear

12-4
The same accessories can be arranged in many different ways to create balance.

Rea-Lynne Gilder

12-6
The arrangement of accessories on this table is an example of informal balance.

12-5
The symmetry created in the entrance to this dining room is an excellent example of formal balance.

Group 3, Architectural and Interior Design. Hilton Head Island, South Carolina. Photography provided as a courtesy of John McManus, Savannah, Georgia.

heavier than subdued, cool colors. Decorations added to an object give it visual weight. Typically, large objects appear heavier than small objects.

Balance is a very important principle to follow when arranging accessories and furnishings. The furnishings on each half of a wall or opposite walls should balance with each other. Likewise, the accessories chosen for display on a table or in a bookcase should also balance with each other. The type of balance used helps determine the mood of a room. Formal balance creates an air of formality. Informal balance creates a casual atmosphere. In 12-7, the double doors in the entry create formal balance. Also in this image, the arrangement of furniture and accessories illustrate informal balance.

Emphasis

Emphasis creates a center of interest or focal point in a room. It is the feature that is seen first and repeatedly draws attention. Every well-designed room has a focal point. With one area of emphasis, the eyes are immediately drawn to that point when you enter a room. This gives a feeling of stability and unity to the room. When planning a focal point, keep the following guidelines in mind. The focal point should

- be worthy of the attention it will receive

- dominate the room, but not overpower it or the design

- not compete with other features, which results in confusion

Architectural features, such as picture windows and fireplaces, can provide a focal point for a room. Likewise, you can create a focal point through the use or special placement of various items. These include furniture groupings, colorful rugs, striking works of art, mirrors, shelves of books, or other collections, 12-8. Unusual accessories and objects, or their placement in a room, can also serve as focal points. For example, a beautiful piece of antique furniture in a contemporary setting is eye-catching. Similarly, the inclusion of contemporary sculpture as an accessory in a very traditional setting could create a prominent focal point. Special lighting cast upon a significant object can also create a focal point.

The focal point gives order and direction to a room. Everything else in the setting should relate to it through color, texture, proportion, scale, and theme.

Color is usually the first aspect of a focal point to catch one's attention. Carrying it throughout the room in accessories, window treatments, and upholstery fabric can further emphasize the color. You can emphasize the texture of the focal point throughout the room in similar ways.

The size of the point of interest should be in proportion and scale to the room and its furnishings. A massive focal point will

12-7
The structure of the doorway and placement of furnishings and accessories in this space represent both formal and informal balance.

be too large for a small room. However, a large room or a room with a cathedral ceiling demands a focal point that will not be dwarfed by the room size.

The usage of a room determines the theme of the room. The focal point should set the stage for the furnishings. For

12-8
The focal point of this room was created by the placement of striking artwork over the fireplace. Notice how the use of lighting enhances the focal point.

Group 3, Architectural and Interior Design. Hilton Head Island, South Carolina. Photography provided as a courtesy of John McManus, Savannah, Georgia.

example, the common use of a living room is for socializing. If the fireplace is the focal point, group comfortable seating that permits socializing around the fireplace.

Rhythm

Rhythm smoothly leads the eyes from one area to another in a design. Rhythm results when an element of design forms an organized pattern. For example, a continuous line found in window and door frames produces rhythm. You can achieve rhythm in a room design through repetition, gradation, radiation, opposition, and transition.

Repetition is the basis for all types of rhythm. Repeating an element of design—such as color, line, form, or texture—creates rhythm by **repetition.** Repetition is one of the easiest ways to achieve rhythm in a design. For instance, you can create rhythm by repeating a dominant color throughout a room. The repeating lines in bookcase shelves create rhythm, 12-9. Repetition

of form occurs when you use rectangular end tables and a rectangular coffee table in the same setting. Texture may be repeated in fabrics used in draperies and upholstery.

Gradation is the type of rhythm created by a gradual increase or decrease of similar elements of design. The eyes travel through the levels of progression. For example, color value can change from dark to light or from light to dark. Lines can vary from thick to thin in a design. Objects that have the same form can increase or decrease in size, 12-10. Textures can range from smooth to rough.

In rhythm by **radiation**, lines flow outward from a central point as in a wagon wheel, 12-11. Sunburst designs are examples of rhythm by radiation. Accessories usually show radiation in home furnishings. For example, a flower arrangement or a cushion may have

12-9
The beams in this bedroom create rhythm by repetition.

Group 3, Architectural and Interior Design. Hilton Head Island, South Carolina. Photography provided as a courtesy of John McManus, Savannah, Georgia.

12-10
These nesting tables are a good example of rhythm by gradation. The eyes move from the largest table to the smallest.

radiating lines. A window that forms a half-circle with a sunburst design is a good example of rhythm by radiation.

In rhythm by **opposition**, lines meet to form right angles. You will often find rhythm by opposition in the construction of a room as well as in the furnishings. For example, you can find it at the corners of windowpanes, picture frames, fireplaces, tables, and other furniture. Rhythm by opposition also exists in floor treatments, 12-12. The simple ways you accessorize and decorate can also create rhythm by opposition. For instance, three books lying on their sides may hold a row of books in place. The three books form a right angle to the other books on the shelf.

Curved lines that carry the eyes from one part of an object or room to another part create rhythm by **transition**. See 12-13. Transition leads the eyes in, through,

and over an object until they have seen the whole object. You can find curved lines in architectural features and in furnishings. An arched window will lead your eyes from one side to the other. A drapery swag will draw your attention from one part of the drapery to another.

12-13
These circles in this custom fixed window design and the arched top are an example of rhythm by transition. They lead the eyes up to the entire window.

Photo Courtesy of Andersen Windows, Inc.

Goals of Design

As you work with the elements and principles of design, you need to keep in mind the goals of design. The goals of design are function and appropriateness, harmony with unity and variety, and beauty. These goals help make sure that your design works together as a whole. Also consider the use, convenience, and satisfaction of the household as you work to achieve the goals of design.

Function and Appropriateness

Function and appropriateness are closely related. If furnishings serve their various functions (or purposes), they are appropriate and suitable. The people who live in a dwelling determine the functions of rooms and furnishings within the rooms. When furnishings provide service, comfort, and pleasure with minimum care, they are functional and appropriate. There are three guidelines to follow when thinking about function and appropriateness in the home.

- Furnishings should be appropriate for the function of the dwelling. For example, formal dining room furniture is not appropriate for a vacation cabin.

- Furnishings should be appropriate for each room. For instance, a living room is not an appropriate place for a refrigerator.

- The form of furnishings should be appropriate for their function. Their designs should adapt to the structure of the human body. Their arrangements should meet the needs to reach, stand, sit, and move within a room.

Above all, a home should be appropriate and functional for all members of the household. It should fit the personalities, lifestyles, needs, and wants of those who live there.

Harmony with Unity and Variety

Harmony is an agreement among the parts. Using the elements of design effectively according to the principles of design creates harmony. A designer uses one idea and carries it throughout the design.

Think about harmony in design as it compares to the beautiful sounds of an orchestra in concert. The instruments or "elements" are in tune, so the resulting sound is harmonious. The total effect is more important than any of the parts.

Harmony results when there is unity among the elements. **Unity** occurs when all parts of a design relate to one design idea. When unity is present in a design, you see the room as a whole—not as separate pieces, 12-14. By repeating similar elements of design, you can achieve unity. For example, the furnishings and accessories in a room may all be square or rectangular. This ties the room together.

It would be monotonous, however, for the room to have only square and rectangular furnishings and accessories. Adding a few circular or triangular accessories creates variety. Unity with some variety makes a design more interesting. Without variety, the limitations on the elements and principles of design can result in an uninteresting, lifeless room.

While an area or room needs some variety, too much variety can cause confusion. Variation is like seasoning in food. The right amount of seasoning makes food tasty. Too little or too much may make it unacceptable. Consequently, the goal of good design is unity with some variation.

When working to achieve harmony, let only one type of each element of design dominate. For example, one color should dominate. This color can be the base color of your color harmony. Smaller amounts of a coordinating color can be used as an accent. This will assure harmony and unity with variety in the design. The overall appearance of a room will be pleasing. If you use several colors in equal amounts in a room, the room may be a confusing combination of parts.

12-14
When the elements and principles of design are used effectively, a harmonious room such as this is created.

Interiors by J. Banks Design

Planning a Harmonious Color Scheme

When planning a color scheme, there are several steps to create an integrated and coordinated look among the rooms. These steps include the following:

Step 1: Select two or three colors that will convey the mood or "feel" you want in the space. Each of these colors will serve different purposes in different rooms; however, just one color at a time is usually dominant in a particular space. The other colors you choose may have vivid impact and strong contrast, or they may blend softly with slight contrast.

Step 2: Add a neutral tone. The neutral tone allows for separation of the major colors, making them more powerful and noticeable. This enhances the visual depth and dimension of the space. The neutral color should relate to the major colors and therefore add to their harmony. Neutrals add unity when appearing consistently on similar surfaces, such as wood moldings, doors, and ceilings. As you learned in Chapter 11, neutral tones are combinations of black, gray, and white. You can also use brown, tan, and beige.

Step 3: Add an additional color in a very controlled way. This additional color will give a "punch" to specific areas and adds variety. Successful punches of contrasting color help to make a space memorable. The word "punch" describes an eye-catching color. It gets your attention right away—and it may be the first thing you notice in a room. A strong contrast catches your eyes. Punch occurs by color, through shape, and by using other design elements.

In order to use a coordinated color scheme effectively, it is important to plan the application of color for each room or space. As the colors trade places and emphasis in each room, they create different personalities for each space.

The following two photograph examples involve a living room with the adjacent dining room and den. The color scheme consists of three colors with strong contrast. The designer chose them to convey a "spring garden" effect: yellow, red, and green. Neutral ivory is the neutral tone. A strong, clear blue gives the punch. This is how the color scheme works in these rooms.

In the dressy living room, 12-15A, you can easily identify yellow as the dominant color covering the sofa and tall walls. This provides a soft, sunny backdrop for the stronger garden colors. Neutral ivory predominates in the rug, and its lightness relates the floor to the walls. The rich supporting reds and greens of the chairs rest comfortably against the light, sunny background. The play of the same colors in the sofa pillows, candles, and floral arrangement on the coffee table strengthens the harmony. Note that the reddish-brown finish of the wood furniture is a purposeful choice, adding to the overall coordination of the room. Finally, the designer adds the "punch" with limited dashes of a strong, clear blue.

A

B

In the den, 12-15B, the yellow walls and neutral floor again combine to create a unified backdrop of dominant color. A collage of pictures and plates in light and dark neutrals offers interesting contrast and a definable pattern to the tall walls. The softer reds and greens and plentiful neutrals of the large, sectional sofa allow the busy upholstery pattern to exist with the wall collage. The energetic color and pattern of this side of the room is in balance with the simplified blocks of color on the opposing wall. Note the large, neutral club chairs stand out against a solid cherry wall and mantle with a deep-green marble fireplace surround. Airy greenery, strategically placed throughout the room, accents and lightens the look of the heavy walls and furniture, contributing to an inviting, relaxing look.

Beauty

In addition to being a characteristic of design, beauty is also a goal of design. Each person has a unique concept of beauty. However, the word beauty generally describes well-designed and aesthetically pleasing objects.

The development of elements and principles of design is the result of studying objects that most people consider beautiful. If the arrangement of the elements of design follows the principles of design, the result will appear beautiful to most people. The separate elements enhance one another and heighten the overall effect of beauty. Beauty gives a house, its furnishings, and its surroundings a distinction. Although beauty is not the only goal in planning and furnishing a home, it is what makes the visual appearance memorable.

Sensory Design

Good design responds to all sensory needs and serves people of all ages, sizes, and physical capabilities. Design that considers the senses enriches the total environment. **Sensory design** is the application of design that affects the senses of sight, hearing, smell, and touch. It helps make housing more accessible and functional for people with limitations as well as those without limitations.

Most types of design affect the sense of sight. People can tell if they like a design by how it looks. With housing design, however, the other senses need consideration, too. Using specific materials in construction and design can control the noise levels in a room. For instance, hard and smooth surfaces make sounds louder by reverberating or bouncing them around a space. Rough and soft surfaces absorb sound, which creates a quiet atmosphere, 12-16. As you design a room, think about what kinds of sounds you want to hear in the room. Then think about the kinds of materials

12-16
This dining room uses an area rug and upholstered chair cushions to absorb sound.

Interiors by J. Banks Design

12-17
Placing fresh flowers and fruit in these accessories enhances the sensory design of the room.

you need to include in your design to create this atmosphere.

The smell of a room can evoke feelings and emotions. Fresh flowers placed in a room may provide a fragrance that many associate with elegance, 12-17. A lemon scent used in cleaners can create the impression of freshness. Pine reminds people of the outdoors. Candles, herbs, and spices used as accessories in design can create certain atmospheres in a room.

The sense of touch also affects your response to design. The texture of various materials used in design can communicate specific feelings. Marble is cold and hard, silk can be soft, and wood can be rough or smooth. People who are visually impaired rely on their sense of touch to direct them. For example, braille used in elevators helps them identify specific floors.

The temperature of a room also affects design. As you know, the choice of colors for a room can convey either warmth or coolness. In addition, people are sensitive to actual temperature changes, which can affect their comfort level. Heating and cooling systems help keep a room comfortable.

CAREER FOCUS

Interior Designer—Restaurants

Do you enjoy eating out in a comfortable, pleasing, relaxed atmosphere? If you do, creating designs for restaurant and other commercial hospitality interiors may be for you!

Interests/Skills: Do your interests include enjoying working on artistic and creative projects? Are you interested in food preparation, cooking, and food presentation? When you enter a restaurant for the first time, do you study the décor? Along with effective communication and presentation skills, interior designers for restaurants and other hospitality facilities need a strong understanding of how restaurants operate to make logical design decisions. For example, understanding the flow of food from kitchen to a customer's table helps in circulation design. As a designer, you have to work well with your client and their ideas. Effective marketing and research skills are especially important for designers of these facilities.

Career Snapshot: To offer relaxing vacation opportunities for families and individuals, hospitality interior designers create pleasing spaces for restaurants, resorts, hotels, cruise ships, and airplanes. Their designs enhance local community and urban plans. More and more people depend on having good meals away from home. Restaurant dining has become a way to relax and unwind. Because the food industry has a lot of interest and money, it is important for industry to develop trends that impact customers. This includes interior designs that appeal to potential and current clients. A unique design can help set the tone for a restaurant or other hospitality facility. It can achieve a certain mood. Well planned interiors contribute to the success and the profits of any establishment.

Education/Training: Completion of a bachelor's or master's degree is preferred. Classes include business management, lighting, computer technology, color theory, textiles, and CADD. Additional courses in culinary arts and psychology would make the designer more competitive in the job market.

Interiors by J. Banks Design

Licensing/Examinations: Approximately one half of the states require interior designers to be licensed. The National Council for Interior Design Qualification (NCIDQ) administers an examination that interior designers must pass in order to obtain a license and to be competitive in their career.

Professional Associations: The American Society of Interior Designers (ASID) (www.asid.org), The International Interior Design Association (IIDA) (www.iida.org)

Job Outlook: Jobs are expected to grow at a faster than average rate through 2018. Outlook will be especially good for designers who specialize in ergonomic design or environmental (green and sustainable) design.

Source: Information from the Occupational Outlook Handbook (www.bls.gov/OCO) and the Occupational Information Network (O*NET) (www.online.onetcenter.org)

Summary

The design principles guide the application of the elements of design. The principles of design are proportion and scale, balance, emphasis, and rhythm.

Proportion and scale both describe size, shape, and amount. They are also concerned with the relationships of objects and parts of objects. Guidelines for using proportion are the golden rectangle, the golden mean, and the golden section. Visual weight, an aspect of scale, is a perception that an object weighs more or less than it really does.

Balance can be formal or informal. It is a perception that both sides of an imaginary centerline are equal. Balance can be attained through the arrangement of objects and the use of color, texture, and form.

Emphasis creates a focal point in a design. The focal point gives order and direction to a setting.

Rhythm leads the eyes from one area to another in several ways. The design may be repeated. Gradation may be used to gradually increase or decrease similar elements. Lines may flow outward from a central point or meet to form right angles. Curved lines may carry the eyes from one part of an object to another.

The goals of design can be achieved when the elements and principles of design are used together well. The goals of design are function and appropriateness, harmony with unity and variety, and beauty. Using harmony with unity and variety helps create a color-scheme plan that coordinates the look between rooms. Sensory design responds to the needs of people of all ages and incorporates the senses into design.

Review the Facts

1. Contrast proportion and scale.

2. Which is more pleasing, a sofa with an adjacent coffee table in a 1:2 ratio or in a 2:3 ratio? Why?

3. Large-scale furnishings need _____-scale accessories.

4. How does human scale influence design?

5. Contrast formal balance and informal balance. Sketch an example of each.

6. How can a designer use emphasis to create a focal point? Give an example.

7. What are the five kinds of rhythm?

8. How are the design goals of function and appropriateness related?

9. What are three guidelines to follow to make sure that a design is functional and appropriate?

10. How do unity and variety impact harmony?

11. Identify three steps to use when planning a color scheme for a room.

12. What is the relationship between beauty and the elements and principles of design?

13. Give an example of how sensory design can benefit you.

Think Critically

14. **Analyze design priorities.** Imagine that you rent an apartment and need to design your living room, which currently is empty. Analyze your lifestyle and personal preferences in relation to your design priorities. What would you select for the focal point of this room? What other accessories would you include in the room to complement the focal point?

15. **Recognize alternatives.** Suppose a client hired you to create a room design which involved purchasing several new pieces of furniture and some accessories. Within days of completing the project and a positive client walk-through, you receive a complaint call from the client regarding a new mantel clock that ticks too loud and a new chair that has scratchy upholstery and an uncomfortable fit—both of which were special order items. Your client wants you to replace the items, claiming poor design. (Note your client signed a letter of agreement which indicates there are no returns on special orders.) What alternatives can you recognize for solving your client's problem? Your client is an influential community member whose business you greatly value.

16. **Analyze effects.** Think about a room in your home or other location that you find particularly pleasing. Analyze the use of the principles of design in the room. What effect do the principles of design have on the aesthetics (beauty) and function of the room? Discuss your analysis with a classmate.

Community Links

17. **Evaluate design.** Tour a model home (or furniture store with designer room displays). Pay special attention to the interior design of the living room, dining room, and master bedroom. Evaluate how the principles of design are represented in the home (or room displays). List the principles and explain how they are represented. Does the home (or room displays) meet the goals of design? Give examples of how each goal is or is not met. Share your findings with the class.

18. **Golden guidelines.** Look around your school or place of employment and identify where the golden mean, golden section, and golden rectangle are used. If they are not used, make suggestions where they could be applied. Write a one-page report on your observations.

19. **Sensory design.** Interview a community member who has a special need or physical limitation. Determine ways that good housing design can make his or her housing more accessible, functional, and appropriate—enhancing the quality of his or her life. What aspects of sensory design could make the home more accessible and increase the enjoyment of the space?

Academic Connections

20. **Math.** Investigate the relationship between the golden section, golden rectangle, and the *Fibonacci sequence* of numbers. What is the application to interior design? Write a summary of your findings.

21. **Social studies.** Research the use of golden section and golden rectangle in music and art by such noteworthy historical figures as Chopin and Leonardo Da Vinci. Locate one or more examples to share with the class.

22. **Math.** To practice using a scale ruler, create two floor plans for a room in your home or the home of someone you know. Create one floor plan using a standard ¼ in. scale and choose a second scale on the ruler for your second plan. Which scale would you prefer to use when working with an interior design client? Why? Share your floor plans and explanation with the class.

Technology Applications

23. **Photo essay.** Working with a team of classmates, assemble a variety of room accessories such as books, bookends, plants, clocks, pictures, photographs, baskets, sculptures, and vases. Create an area in your classroom for display, such as a long desk or bookshelf. Take turns arranging the accessories in different ways to give examples of both formal and informal balance. Use a digital camera to take photos of each design. Identify how the principles of proportion, scale, balance, emphasis, and rhythm are displayed in each photo. Combine your images in a photo-essay format using presentation software. As your team presents its photo essay to the class, discuss what you notice about the visual weight of the accessories as you change their position in each arrangement.

24. **Design examples.** Search the Internet for two room examples that effectively use the goals of design. Then locate two contrasting examples—those that show poor use of the goals of design. Present your examples to the class and give supporting reasons as to why the room designs effectively or ineffectively utilize the goals of design.

25. **Wall design.** Use a CADD software program to design a wall against which you need to place a large piece of storage furniture (as is used in a dining room or bedroom). Create five different designs, making sure to utilize each of the design principles. Print a copy of each design. Mount your designs on poster board to share with the class. Explain how each design arrangement effectively uses the principles of design.

Design Practice

26. **Design for human scale.** Suppose a client has hired you to create a design for a very small living room that measures 10 ft. by 12 ft. Expanding the space is not an option because the dwelling is part of a condominium complex. Because previous furnishings have been uncomfortable, your client's greatest concern is that the furnishings "fit" his or her 5 ft. 3 in. stature. Create a floor plan for the room layout. Select photos of furnishings that meet your client's requirements. Summarize how the proportion and scale of the furnishings fit both your client and the room.

27. **Design for harmony.** Use Internet or magazine resources to locate three living room designs that effectively use harmony with unity and variety. Analyze the photos. Summarize the items in each photo that help bring harmony with unity and variety to each design.

28. **Portfolio.** Because good organizational skills are important for an interior designer, use word-processing software to create a checklist that includes the elements and principles of design and a brief explanation of each. Use your checklist as an organizational tool for further design projects.

Using the Principles and Elements of Design

Prepare an FCCLA STAR Event *Illustrated Talk* on a topic related to using the principles and elements of design. For example, you might use the principles and elements of design to organize a presentation about a low-cost design for a child's bedroom, a teen's room, or a room for an older adult.

Use the *Illustrated Talk* guidelines found in the FCCLA *STAR Events Manual* on the Internet (www.fcclainc.org). See your adviser for information as needed.

CHAPTER 13

Textiles for Environments

Terms to Learn

textiles
fiber
cellulosic natural fiber
protein natural fiber
resiliency
manufactured fiber
polymer
generic name
trade name
extrusion
spinneret
yarn
blend
combination yarn
weaving
warp yarn
grain
weft yarn
wale
float
nap
knitting
tanning
bonded fabrics
structural design
applied design
finishes
tufted
needlepunching
upholstery
comforter
flammable

Chapter Objectives

After studying this chapter, you will be able to

- analyze factors about fiber, yarn, and fabric manufacturing for use in textile products for residential and commercial environments.

- evaluate characteristics of textiles for use in residential and commercial environments.

- summarize features of textiles for floor treatments, including methods of care and maintenance.

- analyze appropriate textiles for upholstery and window treatments.

- summarize characteristics of textiles suitable for the kitchen, bathroom, and bedroom.

- summarize the key features of textile laws that protect consumers.

Reading with Purpose

Imagine that you own a textile supply business and have several employees working for you. As you read the chapter, think about what information you would like your employees to know about textiles. When you finish reading, write a memo to your employees and include key information from the chapter.

Textiles are any products consisting of fibers, including fabrics. You come in contact with a variety of textiles in your home and other environments every day. Your clothes are made from textiles and so are many other products. They include carpets, rugs, upholstery, curtains, table linens, towels, and sheets.

You need to choose textile products carefully when designing interiors and making furnishing decisions for yourself and potential clients. It is important to understand the characteristics of the many fibers and fabrics used in textiles. You also need to know how to maintain and care for them.

Understanding Fibers, Yarns, and Fabrics

To understand how to use and care for textiles properly, it is important to know how they are made. Textiles begin as fibers. Manufacturers spin fibers into yarns, which they then make into fabrics and other textile products.

Fibers

Fibers are the raw materials of which yarns and fabric consist. They are long, thin, and hairlike. Fibers are obtained from either natural or manufactured sources.

Natural Fibers

Natural fibers come from plant or animal sources. There are two categories of natural fibers—cellulosic natural fibers or protein natural fibers.

Cellulosic natural fibers come from the cellulose in plants. In general, they are highly absorbent, launder well, and seldom experience insect damage. However, they burn easily and mildew can stain them. Also, prolonged exposure to sunlight can cause yellowing. The fibers are low in elasticity and may wrinkle easily. See 13-1 for specific traits and uses of some cellulosic natural fibers.

Protein natural fibers come from animal sources. They burn slowly and have good elasticity. They also have **resiliency**, an ability to return to the original size and shape. These fibers require careful cleaning, however, and they often need to be dry-cleaned. See 13-2 for characteristics and uses of some natural protein fibers.

Manufactured Fibers

Wood cellulose, oil products, and other chemicals make up **manufactured fibers**. There are two classifications of manufactured fibers—cellulosic and noncellulosic. Cellulosic fibers consist of cellulose, a naturally occurring polymer. A **polymer** is a chemical compound that forms from the union of small molecules that contain repeating structural units. Noncellulosic fibers consist of simple molecules or inorganic fibers. (*Note:* Inorganic fibers do not come from natural sources.) Each fiber has a **generic name**, which describes a group of fibers with similar chemical compositions. **Trade names** are names companies use to identify the specific fibers they develop.

Making most manufactured fibers requires using an **extrusion** process to form and shape the fibers. Raw materials for manufactured fibers consist of thick solutions. These solutions form by dissolving the raw materials in chemicals. The process and chemicals vary according to the type of fiber in production. Once the solution formation is complete, the solution is forced through an opening in a *spinneret* to form a fiber. The **spinneret** is a small nozzle with tiny holes that is much like a showerhead. Each hole in the spinneret extrudes one fiber. Once the fiber exits the spinneret, it solidifies.

Each manufactured fiber has its own characteristics. However, all manufactured fibers have some traits in common. For example, they generally launder well and are mothproof. They are hypoallergenic, which means you are not likely to develop an allergy to them. See 13-3 for some common manufactured fibers and their traits and uses.

Cellulosic Natural Fibers			
Fiber	**Source**	**Characteristics**	**Uses**
Cotton	Cotton plant	Absorbent Strong Dyes well Shrinks in hot water	Sheets Bedspreads/comforters Rugs Towels Upholstery Draperies
Flax (Linen is the fabric name)	Flax plant	Absorbent Strong Wears well	Table linens Upholstery Bedspreads/comforters Kitchen towels Draperies
Ramie	China grass	Dyes well High gloss or shine Shrinks	Table linens
Kapok	Ceiba tree	Light Soft Not washable	Pillows and pad filling
Bamboo	Bamboo plant	Soft Absorbent	Kitchen towels Bath towels
Sisal	Sisal plant	Strong Durable	Carpet Rugs

13-1
Cellulosic natural fibers come from a variety of plant sources.

Protein Natural Fibers			
Fiber	**Source**	**Characteristics**	**Uses**
Silk	Silkworm cocoon	Strong Absorbent Dyes well Lustrous Water spots easily Poor resistance to prolonged sunlight exposure	Draperies Lampshades Wall hangings Upholstery
Wool	Hair of sheep	Absorbent Wrinkle resistant Not moth resistant Shrinks	Rugs Carpets Curtains Blankets Draperies Upholstery

13-2
Protein natural fibers are strong and absorbent.

13-3
Each manufactured fiber has its own unique traits.

Manufactured Fibers			
Generic Name (Some Trade Names)	**Type**	**Characteristics**	**Uses**
Acetate Celanese Chromspun Estron	Cellulosic	Drapes well Dyes easily Weak Heat sensitive Poor abrasion resistance	Bedspreads Draperies Upholstery Sheers
Acrylic Acrilan Creslan Duraspun	Noncellulosic	Warm Lightweight Resists wrinkles Low absorbency Heat sensitive	Blankets Carpets Draperies Rugs Upholstery
Glass Fiberglas	Noncellulosic	Strong Resists sun fading Nonabsorbent	Curtains Draperies Insulation
Lyocell Tencel Lenzing Lyocell	Cellulosic	Stronger than other cellulosic fibers Absorbent Drapes well Soft Wrinkle resistant	Bedding Draperies Slipcovers Upholstery
Metallic Lurex Chromoflex	Noncellulosic	Resists shrinking Durable Nonabsorbent Increases fabric stiffness	Drapes Rugs Tablecloths Upholstery
Modacrylic SEF	Noncellulosic	Warm Dyes easily Resists flames and wrinkling Weak Nonabsorbent Heat sensitive	Blankets Carpets Curtains Draperies Rugs
Nylon Anso Supplex	Noncellulosic	Strong Resistant to chemical damage and abrasion Does not stretch, shrink, or absorb water Creates static electricity	Carpets Curtains Draperies Slipcovers Table linens Upholstery
Olefin Essera Herculon	Noncellulosic	Lightweight Strong Resistant to abrasion Heat sensitive Nonabsorbent	Carpet backs Carpets Slipcovers Upholstery
Polyester ColorGuard Dacron Fortrel	Noncellulosic	Strong Resistant to abrasion, creases, and shrinkage Holds its shape Low absorbency Heat sensitive	Bedding Carpet Curtains Draperies Rugs Table linens Upholstery Wall coverings
Rayon Lenzing Modal Zantrel	Cellulosic	Highly absorbent Soft Dyes easily Drapes well Weak	Bedding Bath towels Draperies Slipcovers Table linens Upholstery

Yarns

Fibers are spun or twisted into yarns, 13-4. A **yarn** is a continuous strand of fibers that may consist of *staple fibers* (short fibers) and/or *filaments* (long, continuous fibers). Many natural fibers are staple fibers, while many manufactured fibers are filaments. A yarn may consist of a single type of fiber like wool or nylon. Combining two or more different fibers in making yarn—such as cotton and polyester—forms a **blend**. Blends bring out the good qualities of the fibers and minimize the less-favorable characteristics. Combining two or more different yarns creates a **combination yarn**.

Fabric Construction

The type, amount, and size of fibers along with their usage help determine the fabric traits. How fabrics are constructed is also important. The methods include weaving, knitting, felting, or bonding.

Woven Fabrics

Many fabrics for home use are woven, 13-5. **Weaving** is the interlacing of two sets of yarns at right angles. The **warp yarns** run the lengthwise direction and form the lengthwise grain. **Grain** is the direction threads run in a woven fabric. Extra warp yarns form the selvage, which is the lengthwise woven edge of the fabric. The **weft yarns** are the filling yarns that run in the crosswise direction. They form the crosswise grain.

Manufacturers generally use one of three basic weaves to form woven fabrics. They are the plain weave, twill weave, and satin weave. Each weave varies according to how the yarns are crossed or interlaced. All other weaves are variations on these three basic weaves, 13-6.

- **Plain weave.** The plain weave is the simplest weave. The weft yarn goes over and under each warp yarn. A variation of the plain weave is the basket weave. Two or more weft yarns are interlaced with two or more warp yarns. The rib weave is

13-4
Cotton fibers are twisted and pulled into small strands to make fine yarns.

National Cotton Council of America

13-5
Many woven fabrics are used in this room. They are found in the sofa, chair, and ottoman upholstery, as well as in the window treatment and pillows.

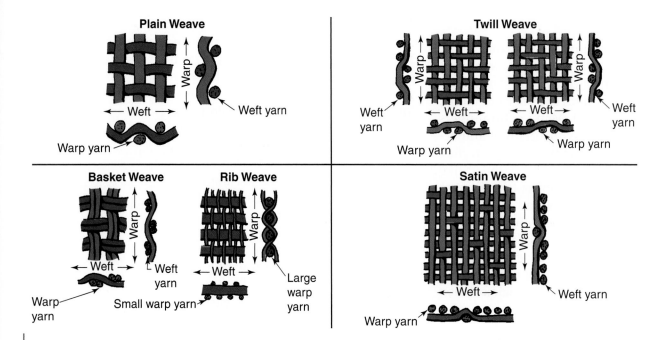

13-6
Each weave is constructed differently. This gives each type of fabric a different look and feel.

another variation of the plain weave. Coarser weft yarns are combined with regular warp yarns to give a corded effect.

- **Twill weave.** In the twill weave, the warp or weft yarn passes over two or more yarns. Each succeeding pass begins one yarn above or below the last one. The result is a **wale**, which is a diagonal rib or cord pattern. A twill weave can be even or uneven. Weaving the weft yarns over and under the same number of warp yarns, creates an even twill weave. When the number of the weft yarns and the warp yarns are not the same, an uneven twill weave forms. Twill weave fabrics are stronger than plain weave fabrics and tend to show soil less quickly.

- **Satin weave.** The satin weave has long **floats**, or segments of yarn on the surface of the fabric. Either the warp yarns or weft yarns float over four or more opposite yarns, and then go under one. Each successive float begins two yarns away from the beginning of the last one. The

satin weave is smooth and slippery. It drapes well and is good for linings. However, satin weave fabrics are less durable than fabrics in other basic weaves because the long floats tend to snag easily.

The *pile weave* is a variation of the plain and twill weaves. Pile fabrics have yarn loops or cut yarns that stand away from the base of the fabric. In 13-7, you can compare a plain weave, loop-pile weave, and a cut-pile weave. Examples of pile weave fabrics are velvet, velveteen, corduroy, terry cloth, and frieze.

Pile fabrics have a **nap**, which is a layer of fiber ends that stand up from the surface of the fabric. The nap appears different when you view it from varying directions. It is important the nap runs in the same direction throughout a product. For example, if you make draperies that have two or more panels, the nap of the pile fabric needs to run in the same direction on all of the panels.

Usage of two other weaves—the jacquard and leno weaves—is common in home-furnishings fabrics. Damask, tapestry, and brocade fabrics are examples of the *jacquard weave* you will often

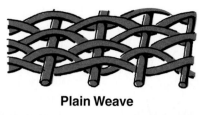

Plain Weave

Loop-Pile Weave

Cut-Pile Weave

13-7
A pile weave fabric has additional yarn covering the surface.

find in upholstery, draperies, and table linens, 13-8. Fabrics for curtains and thermal blankets often use the *leno weave*, 13-9. In addition, weaving small geometric shapes such as diamonds or squares into fabric is an example of the *dobby weave*. The primary use of the dobby weave is for upholstery fabrics and some drapery fabrics.

Knitted Fabrics

Knitting is the looping of yarns together. The size of the loops and how close together they are varies, as well as the way the loops are joined, 13-10. Depending on whether one or two needles are used, knits can be single or double knits.

Weft knits are either circular or flat. They produce single knits, double knits, jersey, rib knits, and jacquard. Warp knits are flat. They are generally tighter, flatter, and less elastic than weft knits.

The main use for knitted fabrics is as backing for other fabrics for the home.

13-8
The tapestry fabric used on the chairs is an example of a jacquard weave.

Leno Weave

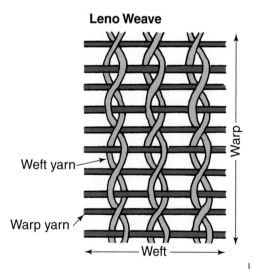

Weft yarn

Warp yarn

Warp

Weft

13-9
The leno weave is loosely woven and has open spaces.

13-10

Knitted fabrics vary according to yarn size, yarn texture, and loop construction. The weft stitch allows more stretch than the warp stitch.

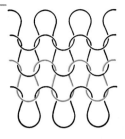 

Weft Stitch   **Warp Stitch**

This is because they lack the stability and body needed for many home textiles. However, there is increasing use of these fabrics for upholstery.

Other Types of Fabrics

There are other fabrics used in residential and commercial interiors that are not woven or knitted. They vary in method of construction.

Manufacturers make nonwoven fabrics by joining fibers together with adhesives or by entangling fibers with heat fusion. During these processes, the masses of fibers interlock and hold together. Felt and fusible interfacing are examples of nonwoven fabrics. Nonwoven fabrics are generally not as strong as woven or knitted fabrics, and they do not have as much stretch.

Vinyl and other plastic materials are not made from fibers. Instead, they are thin, nonwoven sheets. The finishing processes for these sheets can make them look like woven fabrics or leather. Vinyl usually has a knit-fabric backing to give it stability and strength.

Leather is sometimes classified as a nonwoven fabric. The process of **tanning** leather requires use of a complex acid compound, or tannin, which causes the leather to become soft and resistant to stains, fading, and cracking. Its strength and durability makes it ideal for some home and commercial uses.

Bonded fabrics consist of two layers of fabric that are permanently joined together with an adhesive. Heat sets the bond. Sometimes a face fabric is bonded to a lining. At other times, a face fabric is bonded to synthetic foam. When bonded to another fabric, the face fabric typically has a better appearance and will form the outside of a textile product such as upholstery.

Fabric Modifications

Manufacturers can modify fabrics to improve their appearance, feel, performance, and durability. They can make these changes through design, dye, and finishes.

Design

Designs in fabrics may be structural or applied. Fabric producers make **structural designs** by varying the yarns while weaving or knitting the fabric. The size, texture, and placement of the yarns all affect the final pattern. **Applied designs** are printed onto the surface of the fabric. You can see them distinctly only on one side of the fabric.

Dye

Dyes give color to fabric. There are four main methods of dyeing fabric, depending on when color is added. Applying color to fibers, yarn, or fabric occurs through the following methods:

- **Stock dyeing.** Adding color to the fibers, or *stock dyeing*, is done before spinning the fibers into yarn. The method of dyeing is uniform and long lasting.

- **Solution dyeing.** Adding color to manufactured fiber solutions before forcing them through the spinneret creates a consistent color throughout the fiber.

- **Yarn dyeing.** Adding color to the yarn before making it into fabric— or *yarn dyeing*—is one of the oldest dyeing methods. This method is widely used and color absorption is good.

- **Piece dyeing.** The easiest and least expensive method of dyeing is adding color to the fabric, or *piece dyeing*. It usually requires using a single color.

Finishes

Finishes can improve the appearance, texture, and performance of fabrics. They are applied only to the fabric, not to the fiber or yarn. Manufacturers are able to produce many finishes for fabrics. See 13-11 for a description of common fabric finishes and the wide variety of benefits they provide.

Textiles for Residential and Commercial Use

Textiles are fabrics for use in residential and commercial buildings. The textiles you choose for yourself or for potential clients will depend on where and how you will use them. You need to consider the appearance, durability, maintenance, and comfort of the fabric. You should also think about the ease of working with the fabric and the cost. Your knowledge about fabric types and construction will help you make these decisions.

Basic Textile Finishes	
Type of Finish	**Benefits**
Antibacterial; antimicrobial	Prevents growth of bacteria, mold, and mildew; prevents odor
Antistatic	Prevents buildup of static electricity
Bleaching	Whitens natural fabric from the mill
Crease-resistant	Prevents fabric from wrinkling
Durable press	Prevents fabric from wrinkling
Flame-resistant; flame-retardant	Reduces fabric burning and flaming from exposure to flames or high heat
Moth resistance	Discourages moths and carpet beetles from attacking wool fibers
Napping	Produces a raised surface by lifting fiber ends
Preshrinking	Prevents fabric from shrinking more than a small amount
Sizing	Provides extra body and weight to fabric through a solution of starch
Soil release	Makes stain removal easy
Stain resistance (soil resistance)	Makes fibers less absorbent so stain removal is easier
Waterproof	Prevents water from soaking into the fabric
Water repellent	Resists water but does not make fabric waterproof

13-11
The application of finishes to fabrics can improve their appearance, durability, maintenance, and comfort.

A

B

13-12
Fabrics can convey different moods, as demonstrated by different collections of pillows. The atmosphere can range from cheerful and formal (A) to relaxed (B).

(A) Calico Corners—Calico Home Stores

Appearance

Appearance is the overall visual effect. For instance, a fabric may appear soft or stiff. It may also appear bulky or sheer, light or dark, rough or smooth, bright or dull. Fabrics can make a room appear elegant or invite relaxation. See the two examples in 13-12.

Durability

Durability is the capacity to be long lasting under normal conditions. You want fabrics to last as long as possible to limit replacement costs. Fabrics that receive heavy use, especially those for commercial environments, need to withstand wear. Tightly woven fabrics or fabrics with bulky yarns have the most durability.

Maintenance

Maintenance is the care fabrics require to keep them clean and looking their best. Following instructions and using proper cleaning techniques—either laundering or dry cleaning—ensure good results with fabric care. You also need to consider the cost of maintaining fabrics. Choosing textiles to launder at home can help avoid the high costs of dry cleaning—both financial and environmental. Most textiles have suggested care instructions. Those for commercial use must also withstand frequent cleaning with disinfectant solutions.

Comfort

Most people want fabrics that make them feel comfortable. Comfort is a psychological consideration and is different for each person. A fabric can give visual comfort if you like its appearance. It can give physical comfort if it is soft or pleasant to the touch.

Ease of Construction

If you are going to sew some textiles yourself, you need to consider the ease with which you can manage the fabric. Heavy, closely-woven fabrics are harder to handle than lightweight, loosely woven fabrics. However, loosely woven fabrics tend to catch on objects and snag easily. Also, stitching is more difficult to see on dark fabric than light fabric.

Cost

Cost is always an important consideration, but do not base your decision on cost alone. Buy the best fabric for its use. A good-quality fabric at a high price may be more economical in the long run than buying a low-quality fabric at a low price. Also, keep in mind the costs of installation, maintenance, and replacement in addition to the initial price. Evaluate fabrics based on these important factors before you make a purchase.

Textiles for Floor Treatments

Buying carpets and rugs for residential and commercial use is a major purchase. There are many different construction methods, textures, fibers,

GREEN CHOICES

Consider Environmentally Friendly Carpet

New carpeting often releases volatile organic compounds (VOCs) (compounds with high vapor pressure and low water solubility) into the air as gases. If people inhale them, these gases can have a negative impact on health. These gases are often associated with the smell of new carpeting and can last for weeks to months in an interior environment.

Use the following tips for selecting carpeting that is kind to the environment and to the occupants:

- Check the label to ensure carpeting components have undergone testing by the *Carpet and Rug Institute (CRI)* in its indoor air quality testing program. The Green Label and the Green Label Plus (icons within a small green house) indicate that the product has been tested and that it meets the CRI's standard for low emissions.
- Air out the carpet before installing. Often the installer can do this for you before it is delivered to your home.
- Use felt padding versus rubber padding.
- Use low-emitting, non-solvent adhesives if carpet installation requires gluing it down.
- Follow proper carpet cleaning guidelines. Improper cleaning can trap VOCs, dust mites, and allergens.

finishes, and green options from which to choose. In order to make a good decision, it is important to know what choices are available.

Construction Methods

There are several methods manufacturers use to construct carpets and rugs, including weaving, tufting, and needlepunching, 13-13. Each of these methods combines the pile yarn, which is the part you walk on with the backing material, which is the part that holds the yarn together.

- **Weaving.** Much like fabrics, manufacturers use looms to weave carpets and rugs. The pile yarns and the backing are interwoven. Velvet, Axminster, and Wilton are the three main types of weaves carpet producers use to make woven carpets and rugs. Usage of wool yarns or wool-blend yarns is common with these carpet weaves. Less than two percent of today's carpeting is woven.

- **Tufting.** Looping the yarns into a backing material and securing them to the backing with an adhesive (often a rubberized latex compound)

is a process carpet producers use to make **tufted** carpets and rugs. Tufting is easy to do and is less expensive than weaving and is the most common method of producing carpet and rugs today.

- **Needlepunching.** The process of interlocking fibers by using felting needles is **needlepunching**. This process produces a flat carpet that resembles felt. Its main use is for indoor/outdoor carpets and rugs.

Textures

Pile is another name for carpet texture. Carpet producers create different textures in carpets and rugs when the yarns are cut, left uncut, twisted, untwisted, or cut in different lengths. The five types of pile that result from these processes are *cut, level loop, multilevel loop, cut and loop,* and *shag.* Level loop pile wears the best. Multilevel loop pile results from a combination of cut and looped yarns.

Twisting the pile yarns can also achieve texture. At other times, the addition of flecks of color results in the appearance of texture.

The thickness of the yarns affects texture, too. Thicker yarns create more plush carpeting and rugs. Density refers to the number of *tufts* or yarns per square inch. Carpets with a high density look better and are more durable.

Fiber Content

Fiber content greatly affects the quality of carpets and rugs. Wool, nylon, acrylic, rayon, olefin, and cotton are the major fibers manufacturers use for carpets and rugs. Each has unique traits that affect carpeting and rug products.

Wool is an ideal fiber for carpets and rugs because it is very resilient. It is also durable and resistant to soil and stains. Wool, however, is expensive. Therefore,

13-13

The carpeting construction method affects the appearance and durability of the carpeting.

Woven Carpet or Rug

Tufted Carpet or Rug

Needlepunched Carpet or Rug

LINK TO SCIENCE & TECHNOLOGY

Nanotechnology and Household Products

A technological revolution is taking place involving objects so small they can't be seen through most microscopes. Researchers have been exploring the properties and behaviors of objects at the *nanoscale*, which ranges from 1 to 100 nanometers. There are 25.4 million nanometers in 1 inch. Using what they learned, scientists and engineers are creating new materials and endowing already existing ones with amazing new properties.

Some of the products you use every day were probably created using nanotechnologies. These include UV-ray-blocking sunscreens; wrinkle- and stain-resistant clothing, bedding, and towels; and even certain foods and beverages. In addition to producing consumer products, cutting-edge nanotechnologies in health care helps doctors treat some diseases more effectively.

One of the most popular nanotechnology applications so far is the creation of household products with built-in disinfectants. Many of these products—from refrigerators and cutting boards to bathroom fixtures and bath towels—contain nanoparticles of silver metal, which has germ-killing properties. In addition to textiles with stain and germ-fighting properties, fiber scientists are creating fabrics that

- repel mosquitoes without pesticides
- absorb and neutralize harmful airborne chemicals, such as indoor air pollutants
- hold color without the use of dyes

Many governments and industries are pumping billions of dollars into nanotechnology research and development. Some believe that the world's most pressing problems—including pollution, disease, and energy—can eventually be solved using nanotechnologies.

However, other experts believe more research must be directed toward analyzing safety and environmental issues related to nanoparticles. The long-term affects of using some products made with nanotechnologies is unknown. For example, do germ-killing products possibly kill off beneficial microorganisms that live in and on the body, in addition to harmful ones?

It is hard to know which products contain nanoparticles and which do not. There is currently no requirement for manufacturers to print this information on consumer product labels. The Project on Emerging Nanotechnologies maintains a list of nanotechnology-based consumer products at www.nanotechproject.org/inventories/consumer.

For more information, read "Nanotechnology: Big Things from a Tiny World" and other informative articles from the government's U.S. National Nanotechnology Initiative at www.nano.gov.

manufacturers generally use wool only for luxury carpets and rugs.

Nylon is the most commonly used fiber for carpets and rugs today. It is very durable, resilient, and soil resistant, but oily stains are difficult to remove. Nylon is less costly than wool. See 13-14.

Kitchen, bathroom, and outdoor carpets often consist of olefin fiber. It is very durable and resistant to soil and stains. Olefin is also fairly resilient and resists mold and mildew. Prices for olefin carpets range from medium to low.

Polyester fibers offer a soft, luxurious texture to cut-pile carpets and rugs. These fibers have good color clarity and resist fading. They are easy to clean and stain resistant.

Acrylic looks like wool. It also has good resilience, durability, and soil-resistance like wool. However, oily stains are difficult to remove. Acrylic costs less than wool but more than nylon.

Rayon carpets and rugs are attractive, but not very practical. They are low in resilience, durability, and soil resistance.

Rayon rugs are, however, low in price and used when quality is not an important factor. Scatter rugs and inexpensive room-size rugs are sometimes made of rayon.

Cotton rugs are attractive and durable, but low in resilience and soil resistance. Prices vary according to the type of cotton, but are generally low. The most common use of cotton is for washable scatter rugs for bathrooms and kitchens.

Finishes

The application of finishes to carpets and rugs is mainly for functional reasons. For example, an antistatic finish reduces static buildup. A flame-resistant finish prevents the fabric from burning easily. Stain-resistant and soil-release finishes make carpet care easier.

Textiles for Upholstered Furniture

Upholstered furniture has full or partial coverings of fabric, 13-15. **Upholstery** is the fabric, padding, or other material manufacturers use to make a soft covering for furniture. When you choose upholstery fabric, consider where and how you will use the furniture.

For furniture that will receive constant wear, choose fabrics that are durable, stain-resistant, and easy to clean. Wool, mohair, and such manufactured fibers as nylon and acrylic are very durable. They are often available in blends. Upholstery for commercial use may require a higher level of durability than that for residential use.

By knowing the fabric content, you will know how well the fabric will clean and withstand wear. The fibers and finishes manufacturers use to produce

13-14
This wool carpet is both durable and resistant to stains and is a good selection for a dining room.

Photography Courtesy of Karastan

these fabrics influence cleaning and durability.

Choose upholstery fabrics according to their use in formal and informal settings. Formal rooms have an elegant appearance. Designers and manufacturers most often use such fabrics as plain or textured satins, damask, velvet, velveteen, brocade, faille, mohair, or matelassé in formal settings. These fabrics often consist of silk or a blend of natural and manufactured fibers, 13-16.

For informal or casual settings, patterns can range from a very small print to a large scenic design. You can use a wide variety of fabrics, including chintz, polished cotton, gingham, sailcloth, burlap, denim, poplin, or corduroy.

Textiles for Window Treatments

Window treatments—such as draperies and curtains—require the use of fabric. When making your selections, you need to consider the purpose and style of the room in either residential or commercial settings. You also need to consider the colors and patterns in use throughout the room. Finally, the cost of the fabric and its care are other factors to consider.

Purpose and Style of Rooms

A window covering can regulate the natural light that enters a room. Sheer fabrics will filter the light. They offer a feeling of privacy in the daytime. You will be able to see out, but others will not be able to see into the room. However, sheers do not provide privacy at night, 13-17.

When closed, opaque window treatments will not allow you to see out. They can shut out light and provide

13-15
The chairs in this room are partially upholstered, while the sofa is completely upholstered.

13-16
You can add an accent to a simple piece of upholstered furniture by adding a contrasting pillow.

13-17
The sheer fabric selected for this window treatment softly filters the light entering the room.

privacy both day and night. This is an important consideration when choosing fabrics for some rooms, such as bedrooms. Opaque fabrics are usually heavy and thick. Lighter-weight fabrics may not give the privacy you desire.

As you choose window treatments, consider the styles of the rooms in which they are used. In work or informal areas, denim, poplin, and other casual fabrics are good choices. In more formal settings, you may use damask, antique satin, or similar fabrics.

Colors and Patterns

The fabric colors and patterns in window treatments should match or complement the room furnishings, as in 13-18. You may choose a dominant color for window treatments. It could be a color that is in the upholstery or carpet. When choosing patterns, select large patterns for large rooms and small prints for small rooms.

Cost and Care

You can buy ready-made or made-to-order window treatments. Also, you can purchase fabric and make them

yourself. However, it is important to remember that the more fabric and detail a window treatment requires, the more it will cost.

You should also consider the cost of caring for window treatments. Most draperies and some curtains require dry cleaning, which can be expensive. Other window treatments consist of washable fabrics that you can launder at home. However, very large window treatments will require professional laundering because of their size.

Textiles for Kitchen, Bath, and Bed

Textiles for use in the kitchen, bathroom, and bedroom are called linens, although few actually consist of linen fiber today. You need to consider their appearance, durability, and care requirements.

Kitchen

The main linens used in the kitchen or dining room are table coverings and towels. Easy care and durability are key characteristics for these linens.

Table Coverings

Table coverings include tablecloths, place mats, and napkins, 13-19. Silence cloths that go under the tablecloths to reduce noise are also a form of table covering.

Thinking about how you will use table coverings will help you choose the best type. Is the table covering intended for use everyday or only for special occasions? Will you use the table linens for a formal dining room or a breakfast nook? Will the table linens be used in a commercial setting such as a restaurant? Knowing answers to these basic questions will help you select an appropriate fabric.

Linen was the preferred fabric for table coverings, but it requires ironing. Easy-care fabrics are most popular with people today. Many table coverings are available in fabrics that require little or no ironing and have soil-release finishes.

Towels

Kitchen towels are usually made of either cotton, a blend of polyester and cotton, or linen. Linen is good for lint-free towels because it does not have a nap and dries more quickly than cotton; however, linen is not used as much now as in the past. All towels you choose should have the following qualities in this order. They should

- absorb water quickly and easily
- provide durability
- look attractive
- be easy to launder

Towels are available in a variety of colors and patterns. Some have borders and woven designs. Any additional decoration—such as special borders or monograms—will increase the cost of towels. This, however, does not make them better-quality towels.

Bathroom

Linens for use in a residential or commercial bathroom include towels, bath mats, and shower curtains.

Towels

Bathroom towels come in several sizes. These include a bath sheet (extra large), a bath towel (large), a hand towel (medium), and a washcloth (small). Sometimes even smaller towels—guest towels or fingertip towels—are also available. Bath towels often come in sets. You may use a variety of towel colors to coordinate with other colors in a room design, 13-20.

Manufacturers make many towels from cotton terry cloth because it is absorbent. Also, the loops absorb moisture well. Some towels are a cotton and polyester blend. The polyester decreases drying time, adds strength, and reduces shrinkage. The tighter the fabric's weave,

13-18
The colors and patterns in this window treatment complement the other fabrics and furnishings in the room.

Calico Corners—Calico Home Stores

the more durable and absorbent are the towels. Velour terry cloth towels have a cut pile on one side, which gives the towels a velvetlike appearance.

Bath Mats

Some bath mats consist of a fabric resembling towels but heavier. Others are tufted and have latex backing to keep

13-19
Table linens and napkins often coordinate with the tableware.

13-20
The blue and white towels coordinate with the color of the sliding pocket door and the wall covering in the room.

Photograph Courtesy of JELD-WEN Windows and Doors

them from slipping. Still others are made of yarn sewn onto a backing. You may see bath mats made from braided fabrics. Fibers used to make bath rugs include cotton, rayon, and various blends. They often have colors that match or coordinate with the bath towels.

Shower Curtains

Shower curtains prevent water from spraying outside the shower area. They are made from plastic or fabric that has a waterproof finish. Shower curtains have a wide variety of colors and patterns. Often they coordinate with bath towels, bath mats, wall coverings, and window treatments.

Bedroom

Bedding—or linens for bedroom use—includes sheets, pillowcases, blankets, bedspreads, comforters, as well as accessories such as shams, pillows, and dust ruffles.

Bed Linens

Sheets and pillowcases are usually available in matching sets. The sheets may be flat or fitted. A flat sheet can serve as the top or bottom sheet. A fitted sheet, however, snugly fits the shape of the mattress and functions only as a bottom sheet. Sheets and pillowcases are available in various sizes to fit the different bed sizes. These range in size from standard (for twin and full-size beds) to queen and king sizes. Also, sheets designed to fit waterbeds are available.

Sheets and pillowcases are usually made of cotton or a cotton/polyester blend. Cotton sheets are more absorbent, but polyester reduces wrinkling. Sometimes sheets are made from acetate or nylon. Classifications for cotton sheets are usually percale, muslin, or flannel.

- *Percale* is a high-quality, lightweight, tightly woven plain-weave cotton or cotton/polyester fabric. It has a smooth, silklike feel and launders easily.

- *Muslin* is also a plain-weave cotton fabric that ranges from lightweight to heavyweight. Although muslin sheets can have a soft feel, they are not as smooth as percale.

- *Flannel* has a napped surface that provides extra warmth.

When purchasing sheets and pillowcases, look at the thread count. The higher the thread count is, the more closely woven is the fabric. Closely woven fabrics have a softer and smoother feel. Fine percale sheets cost more and may have a thread count of 200 to 300. Lower thread-count sheets are lower in price.

You also need to be concerned about the washability of sheets and pillowcases for both residential and commercial uses. Since they require frequent laundering, sheets and pillowcases need to be colorfast and durable. For use in such commercial institutions as hotels and hospitals, sheets and pillowcases must also be durable enough to withstand disinfectants.

Blankets, Bedspreads, and Comforters

Blanket items come in weights suitable for different seasons of the year. In certain climates and air-conditioned homes or commercial buildings, using blankets all year is a requirement. Light cotton or rayon blankets are ideal for summer. They are easy to launder and less expensive than heavy blankets. Thermal blankets made by using the leno weave are often a good choice. The open spaces in the weave form pockets that trap air and serve as insulation. Wool, acrylic, or a wool and acrylic blend are good for cold winter nights. Again, comfort, attractiveness, and durability are considerations in choosing blankets. For commercial uses, blankets must utilize washable fabrics and be able to withstand the use of disinfectants.

Most people purchase bedspreads for their attractiveness. They come in a variety of fabrics. You can make a satisfying choice if you know your fabrics. While some bedspreads are washable, many require dry cleaning.

In addition to a bedspread being attractive, it should be the correct size for the bed. It should also harmonize with the other furnishings in the room. Matching bedspread, window treatments, and sheet sets are available for residential and commercial settings.

Comforters are thick bed coverings that consist of two layers of fabric with filling sandwiched between them. People choose them for their attractiveness and warmth. The fabric layers make a comforter covering attractive, 13-21. Rayon, acetate, and silk comforter coverings look and feel luxurious. Comforter coverings made from sateen, polished cotton, and challis do not have the same luxurious appearance and feel. However, they are more durable, yet very attractive.

The filling makes the comforter warm. The warmest comforters have

13-21
The comforter and its coordinating pillows, and upholstered head- and footboard make this bed very attractive and comfortable.

Calico Corners—Calico Home Stores

wool or down filling. Down is the soft, fine feathers from ducks or geese. Down is light and resilient, but quite expensive. As a result, manufacturers sometimes use lower-quality feathers instead. Other comforter fillings include polyester or cotton and kapok, which tend to mat or clump.

Textile Laws

There are many laws in the United States that regulate textiles. The intention of these laws is to inform and protect consumers from false labeling and advertising, 13-22. The following summary addresses three major textile acts that apply to household textiles.

Textile Fiber Products Identification Act

According to this law, textile labels must list fibers in a textile product in order of predominance by weight. If the fibers make up less than five percent of a fabric,

13-22
As you shop, read labels to learn what fibers and finishes are used in the various fabrics.

A

B

the manufacturer can list them as "other fiber or fibers." Fabric producers must list natural and manufactured fibers by their generic names, but may also include the trade names. The product information labels must be attached to the product. However, certain items, such as already installed upholstery fabrics, mattress materials, and carpet backings are exempt. In addition, the content label must identify the manufacturer and where a product is processed or manufactured.

Wool Products Labeling Act

This law requires all products containing any quantity of wool to include a label identifying the kind and amount of wool used. Wool products must be labeled as one of the following types:

- New or virgin wool—wool fiber that has never been used or reclaimed from a product or used by a consumer.

- Recycled wool—wool fiber recovered from woven or felted-wool products that may have had consumer use. (Felted wool consists of wool fibers held together by moisture, heat, pressure, and chemicals.)

Products made from wool must have labels identifying the percentage of each type of wool used. The product labels also require the name of the manufacturer and must list the name of the country where the wool or wool product was processed and manufactured.

Flammable Fabrics Act

This law prohibits the sale of fabrics that burn quickly, or **flammable** fabrics. The *Flammable Fabrics Act* covers fabrics in textile products home use, such as carpets, rugs, mattresses, mattress pads, blankets, draperies, and upholstery. As the result of this law, came the development of many new flame-resistant finishes to protect consumers.

CAREER FOCUS

Materials Scientist

Have you wondered about why and how natural or manmade fabrics have certain characteristics such as flame resistance and durability? Then you may be interested in a career as a materials scientist who develops new or improved textiles for use in the interior environment.

Interests/Skills: Do you like to ask questions and solve problems, particularly using math? Do you like to look at different ways of solving problems and often ask why something is done in a certain way? Do you like to create new things? When something goes wrong in an experiment, do you like to try to find out what happened and fix it? Material scientists need critical-thinking skills as they use logic and reasoning to identify the strengths and weaknesses of alternative solutions, conclusions, and approaches to problems. They need good reading and listening skills. A scientist developing materials in a laboratory needs to manage his/her own time and the time of others.

Career Snapshot: Materials scientists research and study the structures and chemical properties of various natural and manmade materials. They work in laboratories to develop projects and procedures to solve problems, develop new procedures, strengthen/combine materials, or make new products in textiles or other materials. These natural and manmade textiles are used in a wide range of products and structures from airplanes to clothing and household goods. Materials scientists observe, receive, and obtain information for all pertinent sources. They analyze information and evaluate results to choose the best solution to problems. They communicate with supervisors, peers or persons working for them, often working in teams to solve problems. They must be very exact or highly accurate in performing the job. There is usually freedom to make decisions and to structure work. The scientist publishes research and writes reports of their experiments, findings, and conclusions.

Education/Training: A bachelor's degree is required in chemistry or a related field such as engineering that requires extensive background and knowledge in chemistry. Most jobs as a materials scientist require a master's degree or a Ph.D. There may be some on-the-job training but most jobs assume the person will already have the required skills, knowledge, work-related experience and/or training. Persons interested in materials science should seek experience in academic laboratories or through internships, fellowships, or work-study programs in industry. Most employers prefer to hire individuals with several years of postdoctoral experience.

Professional Association: American Chemical Society (ACS); Materials Research Society (MRS).

Job Outlook: Employment of materials scientists is expected to be slower than the average of all occupations. Job opportunities are more favorable for individuals with a master's degree or Ph.D.

Source: Information from the Occupational Outlook Handbook (www.bls.gov/OCO) and the Occupational Information Network (O*NET) (www.online.onetcenter.org)

Summary

Fibers come from plant and animal sources, wood cellulose, oil products, and other chemicals. Each fiber has its own traits. You can make wise fabric choices by understanding fiber traits and the ways used to construct fabrics. Fabrics can be woven, knitted, felted, tanned, or bonded. Other factors to consider when choosing fabrics are the design, color, and finishes.

Uses for some textiles include floor treatments, upholstery, and window treatments. Other textiles are used as various types of linens in the kitchen, bathroom, and bedroom. The function and placement of the textiles are important. You need to consider how the fabrics will look with other furnishings in the room. Durability, maintenance, comfort, ease of use, and cost are other factors to consider.

Various textile laws inform and protect consumers. Some laws require specific labeling information on textiles. Labels can help you wisely choose household textiles.

Review the Facts

1. What is the difference between cellulosic natural and protein natural fibers? Name two examples of each type of fiber.

2. Distinguish between natural and manufactured fibers.

3. List five manufactured fibers and two characteristics of each.

4. How do fibers and yarns differ?

5. Contrast weaving and knitting.

6. How are bonded fabrics made?

7. What is the benefit of fabric modifications?

8. Why are the factors of appearance, durability, maintenance, and comfort important when choosing textiles for home or commercial use?

9. In addition to the initial price, what three costs are important to consider before buying textiles? Why?

10. Describe the weaving and tufting processes used in carpet construction.

11. Name three fibers and the type of carpet or rug made from each.

12. List three factors to consider when choosing upholstery fabrics.

13. What purposes influence the selection of window treatments?

14. Why are opaque window treatments a better choice for a bedroom than sheer window treatments?

15. What fabrics and their characteristics are suitable for kitchen table coverings and towels?

16. What fabrics are suitable for bath towels? Why?

17. Which fibers and fabrics would you choose for sheets, blankets, and bed coverings for a cold climate? a warm climate? for commercial use?

18. Choose a textile law, summarize its key features, and explain how it protects consumers.

Think Critically

19. **Analyze characteristics.** Imagine you and your college roommate want a new area rug for your dormitory room. Your budget is limited and you want to buy a rug that will be durable, affordable, resilient, and soil resistant. To accomplish these goals, analyze the following characteristics: construction method—weaving, tufting, or needlepunching; type of pile and density; and fiber content and finish. Write a summary indicating your choice of characteristics and reasons supporting your choices.

20. **Draw conclusions.** The U.S. Government has created many laws to inform consumers and protect them from such dangers as fabrics that burn too quickly. Suppose you were shopping one weekend at a neighbor's yard sale. Draw conclusions about whether you would feel comfortable buying blankets or draperies that no longer had labels showing fiber content and flammability ratings. Would the money you could save by purchasing these items represent a good bargain to you? Explain your reasons for either making or not making such a purchase.

21. **Evaluate labels.** Choose five textile products from one room of your house. Read any labels you find on them. Record the information required by law that appears on each. Evaluate how the label information benefits consumers. Share your findings with the class.

Community Links

22. **Textile descriptions.** Visit a store or showroom for a local supplier of residential and commercial textiles. If this is not possible, use Internet or print resources for suppliers of home textiles to research and list descriptions of the fiber content, cost, and care requirements for fabrics suitable for each of the following:

    A. upholstery

    B. window treatment

    C. bedroom linens

23. **Carpeting choices.** Presume you are choosing new carpeting for the family room of a home. Because the family actively uses the room as a media room and game room, durability is very important. Determine what fiber type, construction method, texture, and finish you want for the carpeting. Then review the Web sites of carpet suppliers in your community. What choices are available to meet your needs? Print a copy of your choice to share with the class. Summarize the carpet features that meet the family's needs.

Academic Connections

24. **Writing.** As a consumer reporter for a local TV station, you have been assigned to write a consumer bulletin that explains the important factors consumers should know before buying carpeting. If possible, use digital photographs identifying carpeting features to enhance your bulletin. Have the class critique the usefulness of the information in the bulletin.

25. **Science.** Use Internet or print resources—such as the Web site for the *American Chemical Society* (ACS)—to research the role of *polymer chemists* in developing new textiles and modifying performance features of existing textiles. How do demands for recyclable and degradable fibers impact the work of polymer chemists? Write a report or present your findings to the class using presentation software.

Technology Applications

26. **Fiber production facts.** Use the Internet to research which countries are the largest suppliers of various natural and manufactured fibers. How many metric tons were produced globally of the 10 most commonly used fibers in today's homes? For what percentage of fiber production is the United States responsible? Use presentation software to create a chart or graph showing your findings. Share your findings with the class.

27. **Nanotextiles at home.** Further investigate the use of nanotechnology in the manufacture of textiles for residential and commercial use. What are the key features? What are the benefits to consumers? What new textile products are on the horizon for residential and commercial consumers? What are some of the drawbacks consumers should consider? Use reliable Internet (such as www.nano.gov) and print resources. Summarize your findings in an oral report for the class.

Design Practice

28. **Renovation project.** Presume a client has hired you to select the textiles for room renovations occurring in three rooms of his or her house—kitchen, bathroom, and master bedroom. List the textile items needed for each room. Use Internet or print resources (such as supplier catalogs) to locate photos of each textile item on your list. Mount the photos by room on poster board. Label each textile photo with a brief description of the textile features. Then have a classmate serve as your client. Role play the presentation of your textile choices to your client during class. What evidence did you give to support your choices?

29. **Office textiles.** A client in your community wants you to select upholstery and carpeting for an office renovation. The office areas include a meeting room that holds 12 people around the conference table, the owner's office which adjoins the meeting room, and a reception area. All three areas will require upholstered seating and carpeting. Locate samples for three possible design options. Mount them on poster board to share with your client.

30. **Portfolio.** Create a vignette of fabrics you would choose for a bedroom design for a future apartment. Label each fabric, identifying its fiber content, finishes, care method, and proposed use.

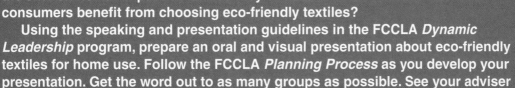

Informing Citizens About Eco-Friendly Textiles

Are you concerned about the environmental impact of textiles in your home and surroundings? What sustainable methods do manufacturers use for producing textiles for the home? What should consumers know about the environmental impact of textiles they choose for their homes? How can consumers benefit from choosing eco-friendly textiles?

Using the speaking and presentation guidelines in the FCCLA *Dynamic Leadership* program, prepare an oral and visual presentation about eco-friendly textiles for home use. Follow the FCCLA *Planning Process* as you develop your presentation. Get the word out to as many groups as possible. See your adviser for information as needed.

CHAPTER 14

Creating Interior Backgrounds

Terms to Learn

floor treatment
flooring materials
tile
ceramic tile
porcelain tile
floor coverings
soft floor covering
resilient floor covering
laminate
cork
gypsum wallboard
plastic wallboard
paneling
synthetic
plaster
wall treatment
paint
faux finish
stenciling
wall covering
ceiling treatment
acoustical
countertop
solid surface
engineered quartz
butcher block

Chapter Objectives

After studying this chapter, you will be able to

* compare and contrast floor treatments.

* analyze materials for wall construction and wall treatments.

* summarize various ceiling treatments and how they serve as interior backgrounds.

* evaluate countertop materials for kitchens and bathrooms.

* demonstrate how to plan satisfying interior backgrounds.

Reading with Purpose

Write all of the chapter terms on a sheet of paper. Highlight the words that you do not know. Before you begin reading the chapter, look up the highlighted words in the glossary and write the definitions.

Floors, walls, and ceilings create interior backgrounds for furnishings and accessories in rooms. They also hide construction details and provide insulation. How they are treated helps to determine the total look of the room and create a desired mood. Preferably, the materials you select will reflect careful consideration of both *sustainable* and *green* design.

Floor Treatments

The floor treatment is usually the first background interior designers will plan for a room. **Floor treatments** consist of flooring materials and floor coverings. There are many types of flooring materials and floor coverings from which to choose. However, before you choose a floor treatment, you should consider its appearance, comfort, durability, cost, sustainability, and maintenance.

Flooring Materials

Flooring materials are materials that form the top surface of a floor. They do not include the subflooring; however, part of the installation process is to secure the flooring materials to the subfloor, making it fairly permanent.

Common flooring materials include wood, tile, concrete, and brick.

Wood

Wood has always been a popular flooring material. With an appropriate finish, it can coordinate with all styles of furniture. It offers beauty and warmth to a room, 14-1. Wood has some resilience and is durable, but can be scratched and dented. The cost of wood flooring is moderate to high, depending on the type and quality of wood chosen. Hardwoods are typically more expensive than softwoods. Oak, hard maple, beech, birch, hickory, mahogany, cherry, and teak are common hardwoods used for floors. Oak is the most common because of its beauty, warmth, and durability. Hard maple is also common because it is smooth, strong, and hard.

Southern yellow pine, Douglas fir, hemlock, and larch are common softwoods used for floors. Use of redwood, cedar, cypress, and eastern white pine occurs where they are readily available. Bamboo, which is actually a form of grass, is a sustainable alternative to many wood products. There are two different kinds of wood floor installations. They include unfinished solid wood and prefinished engineered wood flooring.

When installing solid wood floors that require finishing, the floors must have enough time to adjust to the house environment. Wood that needs finishing will expand and contract during fluctuations in humidity and temperature. The floor finishing process requires multiple steps of repeated sanding and staining. The last step involves sealing the floor surface with a protective coating.

An alternative to a solid wood floor is a floor made of engineered wood, available in many styles and finishes. These floors are prefinished at the factory and, therefore, already sanded and stained. You can install engineered wood floors

14-1
This hardwood floor adds warmth and beauty to the room.

over concrete and wooden subfloors. Solid wood floors, however, require a plywood underlayment when installing them over concrete. The construction method for making engineered wood floors helps them to withstand moisture. They have more stability than solid wood and will expand and contract less with seasonal changes in the environment.

Construction of certain types of engineered wood flooring may involve layering, or laminating, woods of different quality. This process can lower the cost of the product and increase its structural integrity. It also offers a more earth-friendly solution to the use of other flooring materials. Infusion of a substance such as acrylic into this laminate flooring gives it greater durability.

Strip flooring is the most common method of installing engineered wood floors which involves nailing down thin strips of wood that are tongue-and-grooved to keep them close together. *Plank flooring* is a similar installation method that utilizes wider widths of wood. Another style of wood flooring is *parquet flooring*. Creating decorative patterns—such as alternate plank and parquetry, 14-2—adds interest to a wood floor.

Wood finishes of polyurethane, plastic, wax, and oil make the task of maintaining wood floors easy. They protect the wood from moisture, stains, and wear. If properly maintained, a quality wood floor can last the lifetime of the house.

Tile

Tile is a flat piece of kiln-fired clay or natural stone that is available in a wide range of sizes, colors, finishes, and patterns. Tile feels cool to the touch and is therefore more popular in Sunbelt areas than in colder climates. The primary tile choices for residential use are ceramic, porcelain, natural stone, and quarry. Because of the amount of

14-2
The use of parquet flooring adds interest to any room.

labor installation requires, tile can be expensive to install. As with most hard surfaces, consider safety when selecting such products in regard to slip resistance for your interior design projects.

Ceramic Tile

Ceramic tile is a flat piece of kiln-fired clay coated with a protective glaze. High-quality ceramic tile is harder, more durable, and more expensive than ceramic tile of lesser quality. Ceramic tile is a durable choice for a floor treatment, but quality and cost can vary considerably. Keep this factor in mind when choosing ceramic tile for yourself or a client.

Glazed ceramic tile is water- and stain-resistant, which makes it easy to maintain. To further protect the floor, you can seal the grout to make it resistant to stains, too. Grout is the cement-like mortar substance that fills the spaces between the tiles. Maintaining ceramic floor tile clean requires mopping with soapy water.

In the past, the common use of ceramic tile was in bathrooms and entryways. However, current interior design trends often promote using ceramic tile for flooring throughout a house or

MATH MATTERS

Estimating Wood Flooring Cost

This exercise will show you how to estimate the cost of wood planks for a new floor. Suppose a rectangular-shaped room has a length of 14 ft. 0 in. and a width of 11 ft. 7 in. It also has a closet that is 4 ft. by 3 ft. In this example, the hardwood planks are sold in boxes of 24 sq. ft. per box. Each box costs $82.00, not including taxes and the cost of installation supplies.

1. When measurements contain inches, round up to the nearest foot. Round up 11 ft. 7 in. to 12 ft.

2. Figure the square footage of the floor space you will cover. Identify the rectangles in your space, figure the area of each, and total the square footage. The formula for calculating the area of a rectangle is length multiplied by width, or l × w. The area of the room is 14 ft. x 12 ft. = 168 sq. ft. The area of the closet is 4 ft. × 3 ft. or 12 sq. ft. Add 168 and 12 to get 180 sq. ft.

3. Experts recommend adding about 10 percent to total square footage because of variations in the grain and coloring of wood flooring. Installers want to avoid dramatic changes in coloring from one plank to the next. They achieve a natural look by matching each plank for color with surrounding planks. Also, some leftover planks should be stored in case one or more planks need replacing in the future. If you purchase an extra 10 percent of wood flooring (10 percent of 180 = 18), you'll need 180 + 18, or 198 sq. ft.

4. Calculate how many boxes you'll need. Divide the square footage of the floor by square feet per box, for example, 198 ÷ 24 = 8.25 boxes. You will not buy a fraction of a box, so round up to 9.

5. Calculate the total cost for the wood planks. If each box costs $82.00, 9 boxes will cost $738.00.

structure, 14-3. Manufacturers can produce ceramic tile in almost any color, pattern, or finish. Recent advances in computer imaging and glazing techniques enable the creation of ceramic tile to resemble natural stone and marble.

Porcelain Tile

Porcelain tile is the highest quality ceramic tile made. The tile has a white or light clay-colored body that is kiln-fired at a very high temperature. The result is a very strong and durable product. Because of its strength, porcelain tile withstands freezing temperatures which makes it suitable for indoor and outdoor use. However, avoid using tiles with a smooth, high-gloss surface for outdoor living spaces because they become very slippery when wet.

The color of a porcelain tile often penetrates the tile's entire thickness. In contrast, the color of a ceramic tile is only on the surface. Porcelain tile is more expensive than ceramic tile.

Quarry Tile

Quarry tile is available in black and a range of gold hues, beiges, reds, browns, and grays. Manufacturers make quarry tile from clay mixture (the consistency of dough) that goes through an extrusion process and is kiln-fired at a high temperature. For example, manufacturers use a terra cotta clay mixture to form red tile. Quarry tile is very strong and durable. It resists grease, chemicals, moisture, and changes in temperature. The shapes and textures of quarry tile vary, and it can be glazed or unglazed. Glazed quarry tile is easy to maintain with soapy water. Applying a protective sealer to unglazed tile will make it as easy to clean as glazed tile.

Natural Stone

Natural stone floors are beautiful and durable, but are usually costly to purchase and install. Stone comes in a variety of types, sizes, and qualities. Five types of stone, commonly available in the following colors, are very popular for home use:

- limestone—taupe, white, light and dark brown, and gray; with gold or light green veins
- travertine—usually cream or beige
- granite—almost any color
- marble—almost any color
- slate—usually gray, gold, or green

For your interior design backgrounds, you may choose to use stones in their natural shapes or those cut into geometric shapes. You can achieve attractive designs by mixing different types and shapes of stone together. The texture of stone tile may be rough or polished. Polished stone creates a formal appearance, while rough stone has a more rustic and informal look.

Stone floors are fairly easy to maintain by mopping with a solution of white vinegar and water. A sealer protects them from grease, oil, and household stains. You can use stone floors throughout the house including entryways, kitchens, living and dining rooms, and bathrooms.

Concrete

Concrete can have a smooth or textured surface. You can use a smooth surface as a finished floor. Adding color in powder form when mixing concrete

14-3

The tile used throughout the entire house helps bring continuity to a design scheme.

Florida Tile Industries, Inc.

blends the color throughout the floor. Installers can also add color by painting concrete with a special paint.

Concrete is extremely sturdy and durable, but uncomfortable to stand on for long periods. Entryways, basements, patios, and garages are common uses for concrete floors. For easy maintenance, apply a coat of nonslip wax on indoor concrete floors. Concrete floors are relatively inexpensive because they do not require subflooring.

Brick

Brick floors are beautiful, durable, and costly. They look best in informal design settings, 14-4. Because bricks come in many sizes, colors, and textures, you can use them in a wide variety of patterns. The care of brick floors is similar to that of stone floors.

Floor Coverings

Floor coverings are surfaces placed over the structural floor. Although they may adhere to the floor, they are not part of the structure. Floor coverings last several years and are expensive. However, they are not as expensive

14-4
These brick floors look beautiful in this comfortable setting. The use of black in the wicker furnishings helps create a wonderful blend of both formal and informal design.

Calico Corners—Calico Home Stores

as other flooring materials and many people change them more often. Floor coverings include soft floor coverings and resilient floor coverings.

Soft Floor Coverings

Carpets and rugs are types of **soft floor coverings**. As you may recall from Chapter 13, these are floor treatments that consist of manufactured or natural fibers. Manufactured fibers include nylon and olefin, while natural fibers include wool, cotton, bamboo, and sisal. Carpets and rugs insulate cold floors, provide sound control and walking comfort, and add color and texture to a room, 14-5. They vary in their methods of construction as well as their textures and finishes.

Soft floor coverings can cover the entire floor or portions of it. Classified by how much floor they cover, common soft floor coverings are wall-to-wall carpeting (broadloom and modular), room-size rugs, and area rugs.

- *Wall-to-wall carpeting* covers an entire floor, making rooms appear large and luxurious. You can typically purchase it on a roll (broadloom). It can hide any damage or faults in the floor surface. Maintain wall-to-wall carpeting with routine vacuuming. Remove stains by applying an appropriate cleaning product as suggested by the manufacturer.

- *Modular carpeting*, or carpet tiles, has similar characteristics to broadloom

14-5
Wall-to-wall carpeting is an example of a soft floor covering.

Photography Courtesy of Karastan

but is in the form of smaller square or rectilinear pieces. It typically has a built-in cushion and is easy to install. It gives owners the opportunity to replace small areas (due to stain or wear) without replacing the flooring in an entire space.

- *Room-size rugs* expose a small border of floor. They can show off a beautiful wood floor while keeping the warmth and comfort of the soft floor covering, 14-6. Maintain room-size rugs in the same manner for maintaining wall-to-wall carpeting. A disadvantage using a room size rug is that the rug and the adjacent floor require separate cleaning procedures.

- *Area rugs* vary in size, but are not as large as a room-size rug. Interior designers often use area rugs to define areas of a room, add interest, and even serve as a focal point. You can move them from

14-6
A room-size rug provides comfort without covering the beauty of the floor beneath.

Photography Courtesy of Karastan

A

B

C

14-7
These area rugs and carpeting are examples of three different design styles: Traditional (A), Country (B), and Modern or Contemporary style (C).

(B) Photography Courtesy of Karastan;
(C) Photography Courtesy of Karastan

one furniture grouping to another to create a new look, 14-7. Maintain area rugs with routine vacuuming and spot-stain removal. One big advantage of area rugs is they are portable—you or a client can move them with the household. Sending them out for professional cleaning is also an option.

Manufacturers generally recommend the use of padding under carpeting and rugs to reduce wear and increase resilience. It also adds luxury and warmth. Padding is made of hair, jute, sponge, or foam rubber. Different types of carpeting and rugs require the use of specific products for padding. Always check the carpet or rug manufacturer's recommendations when buying padding.

As time passes, carpeting and rugs will show wear and dirt in areas of highest traffic. Scheduling a professional cleaning service to do a thorough cleaning or renting the proper equipment and following the manufacturer's care directions are two options of carpeting and rug maintenance.

The carpet industry was one of the first to understand sustainable practices and their part in ecological issues and landfills. Many carpet companies are implementing reclamation programs, reprinting carpet systems, and recycling backing and fibers. They are also encouraging the use of carpet tiles over broadloom to reduce the impact of carpet in landfills.

Resilient Floor Coverings

Resilient floor coverings are floor treatments that are generally nonabsorbent, durable, easy to maintain, and fairly inexpensive. They provide some cushioning for walking comfort and noise control. Vinyl floor coverings, laminate floor coverings, and cork tile are types of resilient floor coverings. They are available in a wide range of colors and patterns to enhance any interior design scheme.

Vinyl floor coverings, 14-8, are available in many colors, patterns, and textures. The quality of the flooring varies with the cost. Vinyl floor coverings resist wear and stains, but abrasion can damage the surfaces of the flooring. They are available in either tile or sheet form. These floor coverings need little or no waxing. Some sheet vinyl has a layer of vinyl foam on the bottom, resulting in a floor with good walking comfort and sound absorption.

Solid vinyl floor coverings are growing in popularity. They are a higher quality than sheet vinyl because of their all-vinyl composition. In contrast, sheet vinyl only has a vinyl top layer. Solid vinyl flooring products are available in many striking colors, styles, and patterns. These floors may have the appearance of fine hardwood, elegant stone, marble, slate, granite, or a geometric pattern. They are available in planks, tiles, blocks, or squares. Interior designers often combine these different shapes and patterns in the same floor

14-8
This vinyl floor covering is attractive and easy to keep clean.

©Armstrong World Industries

to provide an endless opportunity for creative custom designs.

Because of its environmentally friendly manufacturing process, linoleum is regaining popularity. It is also available in a wide variety of colors and patterns. Manufacturers use a combination of natural linseed oil and jute backing to form linoleum. This product is durable and provides a cushion for tired feet. It also does not introduce toxic chemicals into interior environments as do many man-made materials.

Laminate floors vary in quality depending on their construction. Manufacturers make **laminate** products by uniting one or more different layers, usually a decorative surface to a sturdy core. In order to make the best laminate floors, manufacturers fuse four layers of materials under intense heat and pressure. This process creates a single unit with a decorative surface and a sturdy core. The layers consist of a moisture-guard backing, a core of high-density material for structure, the pattern design, and a wear- and stain-resistant finish. The final product resists traffic wear, stains, and fading, 14-9. Laminate floors are easy to clean, comfortable for walking, and good at sound absorption. They are not, however, as resilient and durable as quality solid vinyl flooring.

Cork is the woody bark tissue of a sustainable plant. Manufacturers use this bark to create *cork tiles* that are rich in appearance and good for walking comfort and sound control. An application of a protective coating helps keep cork tile water resistant, durable, and easy to maintain. Without a protective coating, cork wears rapidly, dents easily, is difficult to maintain, and is susceptible to grease stains. Cork is not a resilient floor covering without the protective coating.

Walls

Walls make up the largest surface area of a room. They provide protection from the outdoors and reduce the amount of noise

14-9
Laminate flooring is durable and easy to clean.

entering a room. They hide pipes, wiring, and insulation. They also divide space within a dwelling and provide privacy.

Wall Construction

When designing interior backgrounds, considering the type of wall construction is an important factor. Builders use a variety of materials to construct interior walls. These materials include gypsum wallboard, plastic wallboard, paneling, plaster, and masonry. The materials used in wall construction will help determine what type of treatment to use. (You will learn more about wall treatments later in this chapter.)

Gypsum Wallboard

Gypsum wallboard is the most common building material used for interior walls and ceilings. Other names for this product include *drywall* and *sheet rock*. It comes in panels that are 4-feet by 8-feet and 4-feet by 12-feet. The use of larger panels minimizes the number of joints or seams. To achieve a seamless wall surface, installers use joint tape and a fast-drying joint compound to cover the drywall seams. A smooth wall surface often requires sanding and applying several coats of joint compound. Then the walls are ready for such surface finish treatments as paint, wall coverings, or fabric.

HEALTH/SAFETY

Reducing Mold with Paperless Drywall

Mold growing in drywall can be a major concern to the health of a family and the indoor air quality of a home or building. There are many forms of mold, and some are toxic—especially to people with mold allergies. Exposure to water and moisture causes mold spores to multiply. Mold in drywall also impacts the maintenance and value of a home.

Mold thrives on the paper component of traditional drywall. That is why researchers have developed a new paperless drywall. Instead of paper facings, this new product uses fiberglass mats for the facing. The design community considers paperless drywall more sustainable for several reasons. Paperless drywall is more sustainable because it

- lasts longer than other wallboards with exposure to moisture
- is mold and moisture resistant
- has the *Greenguard Environmental Institute* certification as a product with low emissions of volatile organic compounds (VOCs)

The U.S. Green Building Council—developers of the Leadership in Energy and Environmental Design (LEED) Green Building rating system—values products with a longer sustaining life. Such products have low VOC emissions and provide good air quality. Builders used this product in reconstructing homes in New Orleans after Hurricane Katrina.

The architects who designed this basement made a sustainable design choice by specifying a mold and moisture resistant drywall in the construction.

Used with permission of Georgia-Pacific, Gypsum LLC.

Plastic Wallboard

Plastic wallboard is a building material with a durable decorative finish that contractors commonly use for interior walls. It comes in both enamel and plastic laminate finishes, which make it easy to maintain. Its primary use is in bathrooms and kitchens.

Paneling

Paneling is a building material that is usually made of plywood but can be produced from a synthetic material. A **synthetic** is a manufactured material that imitates or replaces another. Paneling comes in many different colors and textures, and is commonly available in 4-foot by 8-foot panels. Builders can apply it directly to the wall frame. However, it is possible to achieve a more substantial wall installation by applying it over gypsum wallboard. Paneling is appropriate for almost any room, 14-10.

Plaster

Plaster is a paste used for coating walls and ceilings that hardens as it dries. Plastered surfaces can be either smooth or rough, and usually have a finish coat of paint. Applying plaster requires special skills and equipment, so it costs more than most other types of walls. Usage of this product is rare except in older homes and some commercial buildings.

Masonry

Masonry walls can serve as both exterior and interior walls. Cement blocks are a commonly used form of masonry. Sometimes they are painted. Since cement blocks are large, they belong in large rooms decorated with large pieces of furniture, rough textures, and bold colors.

Brick or *stone* may form entire walls—primarily decorative walls and fireplace walls, 14-11. They are beautiful and durable, and they require little or

14-10
The paneling in this traditional room provides a feeling of warmth.

no upkeep. However, they are costly to install. Interior designers often use both brick and stone for informal settings.

Some of the materials used in wall construction can also serve as the wall treatment. Because they are decorative in their original state, paneling, bricks, and stones do not need additional wall treatment.

Wall Treatments

A **wall treatment** is a covering that is applied to an interior wall. Common wall treatments are paint, wall covering, fabric, cork, ceramic tile, mirrors, glass, and reflective metals. Applying these wall treatments varies from easy to difficult. Some treatments are inexpensive while others are high in cost.

As you choose a wall treatment for an interior design project, keep in mind that it should harmonize with the floor and ceiling. It should add to the general mood of the room. Most of all, it should reflect the personalities of the people who use the room.

Paint

Paint is a mixture of pigment and liquid that thinly coats and covers a

14-11
A brick wall is an attractive background for an informal room.

Masco Corporation/
Scholz Design Architects

paint—either vinyl or acrylic latex—for interior wall surfaces because it is easy to apply and dries quickly. Equipment cleanup is also easy. Solvent-based paint—or oil-based or alkyd paint—is thinner and takes longer to dry. Also, it is much harder to clean the paint equipment when using a solvent-based paint.

Paints vary in how glossy or shiny their surfaces look. Paint surface finishes include

- *Enamel paints* that have the most gloss. They give a protective and decorative finish to kitchen and bathroom walls, wood trim, windowsills, radiators, masonry, and heating pipes.

- *Semigloss paints* that have less gloss and are slightly less durable than enamel paints. You can use them in most of the same places as enamel paints.

- *Satin* or *eggshell* paint finishes that have a slight sheen. Paint professionals usually use them on walls. They are slightly less durable than semigloss paints.

surface. It is the fastest and least costly way to cover wall surfaces and change the look of a room, 14-12. There are two categories of paint: water-based and solvent-based. Most designers and paint professionals choose water-based

GREEN CHOICES

Be Kind to the Environment—Select Nontoxic Paint

Indoor air is more polluted than outside air, according to the US Environmental Protection Agency (EPA). Indoor air quality is one of the top five hazards to human health. Paints and finishes are among the major causes of this hazard.

Low-level toxic fumes and chemicals move into the air for years after painting with certain paints. Most of these toxins come from the volatile organic compounds (VOCs)—in the form of solvents in the paint. In the past, the VOCs were necessary for the paint to do well over time.

Through new environmental regulations and consumer demand, low-VOC and zero-VOC paints and finishes are now available. Most paint manufacturers now produce one or more of these nontoxic paints. In addition, following the environmental disaster of *Hurricane Katrina,* new paint products are now available that have nontoxic, antimicrobial ingredients to inhibit the growth of mold on paint surface. This provides for a healthier air quality and interior environment. These new paints are durable, are reasonable in cost, and are less harmful to human and environmental health.

- *Flat wall paints* that have no gloss. They give a soft finish to walls and ceilings. Do not use them for windowsills or kitchen or bathroom walls and woodwork which are susceptible to moisture, mold, and mildew. Flat paints are usually the least expensive and the most difficult to clean.

When you choose paint, choose a color that is slightly lighter than the color you want. When applying the paint color to walls, it appears stronger and darker than the color on the paint chip. This is because you see so much more of the color on the wall than on the sample. Textured paints give walls a rough surface. You can use them to cover cracks or irregularities in walls and ceilings. Refer to the label directions before applying texturizing paints. Application of these paints can also minimize the appearance of other designs.

Keeping a record of paint type and color is important. Retaining a chip from the paint company is one way to accomplish this. However, sometimes paint chips are not available particularly if the paint is custom mixed. One way to secure this information for your records is to paint one side of an index card once a room is painted. On the reverse side, write the brand name and color name and formula of the paint. This information can make color matching more efficient in the future. In addition, it will make it easier when coordinating window treatments, floor treatments, or furniture.

Faux Finishes. Paint is usually associated with walls finished in solid colors. However, a number of different textures and patterns create decorative wall finishes through special applications, or **faux finishes**, from the French word meaning "false or fictitious." Paint professionals can achieve faux finishes by applying paint to the wall with tools other than a

14-12
Paint gives this room a cheerful, light, and airy appearance.

Photography Courtesy of Karastan

common paintbrush. For example, *sponging* is a faux finish that requires dipping a sponge in paint and dabbing it on the wall to add pattern. *Ragging* is another faux finish by which you apply paint with pieces of cloth. *Combing* involves using a rubber comb or other combing device to create a faux finish that results in stripes, swirls, or other unique patterns. A finishing technique called *marbleizing* creates a wall treatment that looks like marble stone. Many other faux finishes are available to create a unique look. See 14-13 and 14-14.

The application of paint in an artistic manner can also create a wall scene or mural so lifelike that it "fools the eye." The name of this technique is *trompe l'oeil*, which means "illusion" in French. Designers and painters can

14-13
To achieve this look, the room was painted with the same base color to seal the tape and avoid bleeding. A glazing liquid was then painted in a thick layer into the taped-off areas. Once dried, the tape was peeled off, giving a rich wall covering effect.

©2009 Sherwin-Williams Company

14-14
The walls appear to have a wall covering, but the stripes are actually examples of a faux-finish technique called *combing*.

©2009 Sherwin-Williams Company

use this technique to turn a plain wall into a grand three-dimensional garden, complete with stone walls, fountains, and beautiful plants, 14-15. The same technique can be used to paint the four walls of a child's playroom with beach scenes showing blue sky, sand, water, swimming fish, and dancing dolphins. Faux finishes and trompe l'oeil can create endless possibilities, but good results require patience and talent.

Stenciling Finish. In addition to faux finishes, paint professionals can apply paint with a stenciling technique to add interest to a wall. **Stenciling** is applying paint by using a cutout form to outline a design or lettering. You can either create these stencil patterns or purchase them ready-made. For a professional finish, apply paint to the open area of the stencil to transfer the design to the wall. The designs may vary from simple to complex and may entail one coat of paint or many to achieve the proper detail.

Wall Covering

A **wall covering** is decorative paper or vinyl applied to a wall with a special paste. It can copy the look of almost any surface, such as brick, stone, wood, and leather. Wall coverings can bring the look of the outdoors in through the creation of murals showing outdoor scenes. Because of the variety of patterns available, the use of wall coverings can enhance any room and create any style, 14-16.

Wall coverings are practical as well as beautiful. Some wall coverings have a thick vinyl coating, which makes them durable and easy to clean. Others consist of solid vinyl. Vinyl-coated or solid vinyl wall coverings are often desirable for kitchens and bathrooms because they resist stains and water.

Fabric

Fabric is another product you can use to cover walls. You can use special glue, tape, or staples to attach it to walls. Other applications include stretching it over a frame and hanging it on the wall, or stretching it between curtain rods at the ceiling and floor. Fabric can add color, warmth, texture, and interest to a room.

Closely woven, medium-weight fabrics are the best choices for wall treatments. Look for fabric that will not fade,

HEALTH/SAFETY

Avoiding Lead Paint Dangers

At the time of the lead-based paint ban in 1978, lead-based paint was present in more than 38 million homes in the U.S. Even small amounts of lead in dust, dirt, or water, can be dangerous. This toxic metal can cause nerve damage, behavioral problems, learning disabilities, reduced IQ, and other serious health problems, particularly in infants, young children, and people with high blood pressure. Lead can cause seizures and death. Pets are also subject to lead poisoning.

Although today's household paints are lead-free, it is possible to release lead trapped in old layers of paint—especially when renovating pre-1978 homes. For example, such projects as sanding surfaces, puncturing walls, and replacing old windows can cause lead contamination of homes and yards. Children can swallow paint chips. Invisible lead dust from paint and lead-contaminated soil is easy to inhale or ingest. Before starting any renovations, interior designers and owners of older homes may want to have these homes tested for lead.

After April 2010, contractors who disturb painted surfaces in pre-1978 homes must be lead-certified by the U.S. Environmental Protection Agency. Consumers should ask to see the contractor's license. Contractors must also follow specific work practices to prevent lead contamination.

For more information, go to the EPA's Web site and the National Lead Information Center at www.epa.gov/.

14-15
A faux finish was applied to this wall to create a trompe l'oeil illusion of a stone wall.

©2009 The Sherwin Williams Company

14-16
Consumers and interior designers can coordinate wall covering selections with paint colors by using a CADD system.

Courtesy of Software by Chief Architect

stain, shrink, or mildew. Because fabric applied to walls can be difficult to clean and maintain, it can trigger allergic reactions.

Cork

Cork makes a good wall treatment for rooms that require sound insulation. Cork also adds warmth and textural interest to a room.

Ceramic Tile

Ceramic tile comes in a wide variety of sizes, shapes, and patterns, 14-17. You can use it to create many different styles and designs. The tiles are durable and easy to maintain. Decorative ceramic tiles on a wall can be the point of emphasis in a room.

Mirrors, Glass, and Reflective Metals

Using large mirrors, glass, and reflective metal tiles or strips on all or part of a wall can add interesting design

details to a room. Because of repeating reflections in a room, mirrors can make rooms look larger. Covering an entire wall with mirrors will make a room look twice its actual size.

Large expanses of glass in windows and glass doors also serve as a type of wall treatment. This is because they occupy wall space. Using glass extends the indoor space and brings the outdoors in, creating the illusion of a larger space. For example, the use of glass blocks allows light to enter a space while preventing a clear view into the room. An application such as this is suitable for a bathroom window area where light and privacy are requirements.

The application of reflective metal tiles or strips to a wall also allows the reflection of light into a space. The effect of mirrors, reflective metal, and glass wall treatments can be dramatic, 14-18. These wall treatments are especially popular in spaces with a more modern or contemporary design. By comparison, however, these treatments are more expensive than other wall treatments such as paint and wall coverings. Take care to assure that the reflected image enhances the design of the room.

As you have learned, the various walls and wall treatments provide many different looks. Each one has its advantages and disadvantages. Choose the one that fits the mood of the room and best meets the needs and wants of you or a client.

Ceiling Treatments

A **ceiling treatment** is a coating, covering, or building material applied to the ceiling area. The ceiling of a room is often the background people notice least, but it performs many tasks. It holds and conceals insulating materials that help control the house temperature. It hides electrical wiring. Some ceilings also hide water lines and gas lines.

14-17
The installation of the ceramic tile backsplash and floor creates this sophisticated design.

14-18
The reflective metal backsplash on the wall brings a sense of drama to this kitchen.

14-19
The high ceiling and use of skylights give this hallway a spacious, airy appearance.

The height of the ceiling can help create certain moods. Minimum and most typical ceilings are 8 feet from the floor. Higher ceilings give a feeling of spaciousness and usually create a formal atmosphere, 14-19. You can create the feeling of a higher ceiling by painting it a light color. You can also create the illusion of height by using vertical lines on the walls. (*Note:* Painting a ceiling requires an extension handle for the paint roller. It allows an individual to paint a ceiling without using a ladder, which is safer.)

Lower ceilings make rooms seem smaller and usually create an informal mood. Painting a ceiling a dark color or adding patterned materials will make it appear lower. Another way to make ceilings look lower is to use horizontal lines on the walls.

The four most common materials used for ceilings are plaster, acoustical plaster, acoustical tile, and gypsum wallboard. **Acoustical** means that the material will reduce or absorb sound.

- *Plaster* is one of the earliest forms of ceiling treatments. People seldom use it today except in restorations of older houses. Its surface can be either smooth or rough. Flat paint is the usual surface covering for plaster ceilings.

- *Acoustical plaster* has a rough texture. It helps absorb sound and thus reduces the noise in a room. Application of this plaster requires spraying it onto the ceiling's surface. Acoustical plaster is difficult to paint, clean, and repair.

- *Acoustical tile*, 14-20, is decorative and functional. It comes in many patterns and colors. It absorbs sound and is easy to clean. Application of these tiles generally involves hanging them from a grid to hide mechanical, plumbing, and electrical components above the ceiling.

- *Gypsum wallboard* is a common ceiling treatment. It can be finished with a smooth surface or with a rough texture that resembles plaster. Manufacturers produce ceiling wallboard differently than that used for wall applications to resist sagging. As with other wallboard applications, paint is usually the final finish.

14-20
Acoustical tile absorbs sound and is easy to maintain.

©Armstrong World Industries

When planning backgrounds for interior design projects, keep the goals of design in mind. This will help you achieve pleasing results in any room throughout a dwelling.

Countertops

A **countertop** is a durable work surface installed on a base cabinet. Cabinets with countertops are found in kitchens, bathrooms, and play and work areas. Counter tops should be functional and attractive. Because they involve a substantial financial investment, you cannot replace them as easily as the paint on a wall. Therefore, use special care when making countertop selections.

Countertop Materials and Treatments

For the kitchen area, countertops should be stain-, scratch-, and heat-resistant. Perhaps no surfaces in a home will receive as much wear and tear as those in the kitchen. Common countertop materials include laminates, ceramic and porcelain tiles, and wood (such as butcher block). Popular countertop choices on the market today include solid surfaces, engineered quartz, stone such as granite, and metal.

Laminate

One of the more affordable countertop choices is a laminate, 14-21. Manufacturers achieve the colors, textures, and designs by combining decorative surface papers with resins that they bond under heat and pressure with other materials. This process forms a single unit with a decorative surface on a rigid base. Laminate countertops come in a wide range of colors and textures. Designs include solid colors, various patterns, and finishes that resemble metal, stone, or wood. Edge finishes include beveling or rounding. As with other products, there are different quality grades on the market. Less expensive laminates will not offer the durability of more expensive, name brand laminates.

Laminates are relatively easy to maintain by wiping with a damp cloth or sponge. The product will show seams in the installation where sections are joined. It is best to select a product that comes in significant sheet size to minimize the need for seams. Some textured-laminate surfaces may be scratch-resistant. New products are available that are more resistant to stains than earlier laminate surfaces. If stains occur, application of a mild household cleaner to the area and gentle rubbing

14-21
Quality laminate countertops are very attractive and affordable. There are hundreds of different colors and patterns from which to choose.

Photo Courtesy of Wilsonart International, Inc.

with a soft brush generally removes the stains. However, it is difficult or impossible to repair such damage to laminate countertops as chipping and burns.

Solid Surface Material

A **solid surface** is a durable countertop material that contains the color and pattern of the surface throughout. Manufacturers construct this product with an advanced blend of materials and minerals in an acrylic or polyester compound. Solid-surface countertops are easy to clean and available in many colors, but much more expensive than laminates. When installed, the surface appears continuous, showing no seams. Also, solid surfaces can blend seamlessly into sinks of the same material. Because the product can be shaped and molded, various custom edges are available.

Solid surfaces are scratch-, stain-, and heat-resistant. If damage does occur, these surfaces are repairable and renew-able. They do not require sealing and are bacteria-resistant. Solid surfaces are available in many colors, and new additions to the market look like natural stone.

Ceramic and Porcelain Tile

Tile can be expensive due to the labor costs for installation. Ceramic tiles come in many colors and patterns. They are easy to maintain and are heat- and scratch-resistant. To prevent staining, sealing the surface of the grout is essential. Ceramic tile is subject to chipping if struck by a heavy object.

Likewise, porcelain tiles are expensive to install and require sealing. However, since the surface color usually penetrates porcelain tile, it can keep a like-new appearance in spite of scratches.

Natural Stone

Natural stone, such as granite, is elegant and expensive. Since stone is porous, it requires sealing to make it stain-resistant. In addition, stone countertops are prone to scratching and can break if struck with a heavy object. Due to the weight of stone, install it on very sturdy cabinet bases.

Engineered Quartz

A popular type of countertop that looks like natural granite or marble is **engineered quartz**. It is a stonelike countertop material that is a combination of quartz particles with a mixture of binders. Manufacturers subject the mixture to a high-tech compression and heating process. The surface has a polished granite or marble appearance and does not require a sealant as is needed with granite or marble.

Engineered quartz surfaces are popular for several reasons. They are less costly than granite and marble; easy to maintain; and much more heat-, stain-, and scratch-resistant. Manufacturers usually guarantee these surfaces against defects by a limited warranty, which is not available with natural stone, 14-22.

Metal Surfaces

Use of metal surfaces for countertops is more common in commercial kitchens than in residential kitchens. The most common metal surface is stainless steel, but use of zinc and copper are also common for countertops. Metal countertop surfaces are expensive. Stainless is easy to clean, but can scratch. It is a good idea to use a cutting board with stainless steel counters.

Butcher Block

Butcher block is a work surface made by fusing a stack of long, thin hardwood strips. The exposed sides form the countertop surface. Butcher block is not heat- and stain-resistant and is less durable than most other countertops. Also, it can harbor any food bacteria that come in contact with it.

14-22

An engineered quartz countertop provides the home owner with both a beautiful design and a warranty.

Silestone® Photo Courtesy of Consentino USA

Fiberglass

Bathroom countertops use many of the materials used in kitchens, but there is an additional product to consider for that room. Manufacturers mold *cultured marble* countertops from fiberglass compounds. They are more expensive than laminates but less expensive than solid surface, tile, and stone countertops. As in the case of solid surface materials, you can obtain a bathroom sink and countertop all in one unit. Cultured marble countertops are scratch- and stain-resistant, easy to maintain, and durable if cared for properly. They come in solid colors, marblelike patterns, and polished or matte finishes.

Planning Background Treatments

The backgrounds for interior design schemes set the stage for the furnishings you choose. Although they do not need to be costly, they do require careful planning. This is especially important for floor and wall treatments.

Planning Floors

Floor treatments receive more wear than other background treatments. They are usually more expensive, too. Unless design plans require replacing a floor covering within a couple years, choose one that is durable. Try to choose a color and style that is neutral enough to allow changes to an interior design scheme.

The floor treatment accents the entire room and helps tie the many parts of the room together. Choosing different floor treatments for each separate area of the house, causes a lack of design continuity and the spaces will not flow well. Using a single treatment such as carpeting or hardwood throughout some houses may be preferable. Doing so can make the house seem larger and more unified.

This can be especially important if your house is small. In contrast, for larger, open-plan spaces, varied flooring can help define areas that serve different functions.

Planning Walls

Classic wall treatments are those that continue to be in style year after year. Choosing a classic wall treatment will save the cost of changing the wall treatment as styles change. Off-white is a classic wall-treatment color. As a background, it lets you use a great variety of colors and designs in a room. It also helps make rooms appear more spacious, 14-23.

Bold, bright wall treatments can give a room a dramatic look. Painted graphic designs, murals, and wall coverings with bold patterns make colorful focal points. Bold treatments tend to make rooms look smaller, so use them carefully. Be sure to choose wall treatments and furnishings that do not compete for attention.

The most common wall treatment is paint. It is important to choose the right paint for the room. Use washable paints in rooms that receive much use, such as kitchens and children's bedrooms. Keep painted surfaces clean to avoid repainting as often. Enamel and semi-gloss paints are easier to clean than flat paints.

Wall coverings are available in a wide variety of types and designs. Professional paperhangers generally hang wall coverings. However, if you or a client chooses to hang the wall coverings, there will be savings on installation costs.

Planning Countertops

Apply the same careful attention to countertops as you give to floors, walls, and ceilings. Countertops impact the visual effect of your interior design scheme as much as decisions on any

14-23
Off-white paint is a classic wall treatment. It allows greater variety of design and makes rooms look more spacious.
Photography Courtesy of Pottery Barn

other background treatments. Countertops also have an important impact on how a space functions and how easy it is to maintain.

As with all design decisions, make countertop choices after considering the total appearance of the room. Walls, countertops, floors, and ceilings must all work well together to create a pleasing design scheme that functions successfully.

CAREER FOCUS

Interior Designer—Schools

Can you imagine yourself as the interior designer for a school in your community? If you can, you may want to consider a career as civic contract designer who designs schools.

Interests/Skills Are you interested in developing the youth of the next generation? Do you believe design can affect relationships between teachers and their students? Have you thought about better ways to navigate the crowded hallways between classes or how to make the cafeteria more functional for students and staff? Project organization and time management skills are essential for civic designers. Designers must be able to convey their thoughts and ideas so others understand them. For example, effective communication about design plans between designers, architects, and school board members helps improve the quality of education.

Career Snapshot: Designers must educate themselves about any special requirements. They need to know the age group for whom they are designing. Educational buildings age rapidly and constantly need to be brought up to current codes and standards. For these types of projects, designers need experience with designing existing spaces. Current trends point the way to eco-friendly design and using sustainable products that promote a healthy environment. As a result, designers must constantly update their education.

©2005 Image by Greg Loflin--The Loflin Group/ LS3P ASSOCIATED, LTD. Knightdale High School, Knightdale, North Carolina.

Education/Training: Completion of a bachelor's or master's degree is preferred. Classes include business management, lighting, textiles, and CADD. To specialize in designing spaces for schools additional courses in psychology of learning, education, and ergonomics are essential. Continuing education is a career-long requirement.

Licensing/Examinations: Approximately one half of the states require interior designers to be licensed. The National Council for Interior Design Accreditation administers an examination that interior designers must pass in order to obtain a license and to be competitive.

Professional Association: The American Society of Interior Designers (ASID) (www.asid.org), The International Interior Design Association (IIDA) (www.iida.org)

Job Outlook: Jobs are expected to be in demand through 2018. Outlook will be especially good for designers who specialize in ergonomic design or sustainable design. Also, because of the large number of aging schools, the job market will be strong for designers with knowledge of the special needs of this sector.

Source: Information from the Occupational Outlook Handbook (www.bls.gov/OCO) and the Occupational Information Network (O*NET) (www.online.onetcenter.org)

Summary

Floors, walls, and ceilings serve as backgrounds for the furnishings and accessories in a room. Floor treatments include flooring materials or floor coverings. Flooring materials include hardwoods, softwoods, tile, natural stone, concrete, and brick. Floor coverings consist of soft floor coverings and resilient floor coverings.

Wall construction provides the basis for wall treatments. Builders can construct walls from gypsum wallboard, plastic wallboard, paneling, plaster, and masonry. Finish applications for wall treatments include paint, wall covering, fabric, cork, ceramic tile, mirrors, glass, and reflective metals.

The height and the treatment of ceilings are important factors. High ceilings give the feeling of formality and openness. Low ceilings create an informal, close feeling. Different ceiling treatments can create the illusion of higher or lower ceilings. Common ceiling materials are plaster, acoustical plaster, acoustical tile, and gypsum wallboard.

Countertops are another consideration when designing background treatments. They should be functional, yet attractive and durable.

Interior backgrounds last for several years and involve considerable cost. Select treatments for countertops, walls, floors, and ceilings so they set the stage for the furnishings and accessories.

Review the Facts

1. Why are interior backgrounds important to a design scheme?
2. Contrast flooring materials and floor coverings. Give an example of each.
3. Give an example of when you would use each of the following flooring materials: wood, tile, natural stone, concrete, and brick.
4. What is the difference between soft floor coverings and resilient floor coverings?
5. What products are generally used to construct interior walls?
6. Summarize four wall treatments.
7. How can you make a ceiling appear higher than it actually is? lower?
8. What is the benefit of using acoustical plaster or tile as a ceiling treatment in a room?
9. Give an example showing when you would use each of the following countertop materials and treatments: laminate, solid surface, ceramic and porcelain tile, natural stone, engineered quartz, metal, butcher block, and fiberglass.
10. Why is it a good idea to use neutral backgrounds in a home?
11. What is the result of bold wall treatments in a room?
12. Why should you pay just as much attention to countertop treatments as you do to other interior background treatments?

Think Critically

13. **Analyze interior treatments.** Economics often influences the choices people make for interior backgrounds. Presume you have the job of designing an affordable and durable interior for a new home built by Habitat for Humanity. A nuclear family with two daughters under age 10 will occupy the home. What treatments would you select for the flooring, walls, ceilings, and countertops? Analyze and determine the interior selections. Explain your choices to the class.

14. **Draw conclusions.** Assume you are selecting wall construction materials for a basement family room. Draw conclusions about which material(s) you would use. Write a short summary of your conclusions.

Community Links

15. **Flooring collage.** Research Internet sites for local stores or manufacturers that sell flooring materials and floor coverings. Print photographs showing examples of products with information about their cost, warranties, and durability. Make two collages: one showing various flooring materials, and one showing several floor coverings. Display your collages to the class as you summarize your findings.

16. **Wall covering display.** Visit a store that sells wall treatments. Obtain samples of six or more different wall coverings—three for residential use and three for commercial use. Display your samples to the class, and explain the effect of each if it were installed in your classroom.

17. **Scale model.** Obtain samples of wall coverings, paint, tile, flooring, and countertops from your local home improvement store. Use a small box to make a scale model of a kitchen or bathroom. Then use the samples to create the interior backgrounds for the room. Show your model room to the class and explain the principles of design you used to make these selections.

Academic Connections

18. **Social studies.** The use of wall, floor, and ceiling treatments changed continually throughout history. Select a specific country and historical period, and research the types of interior backgrounds that were used. Write a report describing the social, environmental, historical, and geographical influences that shaped the creation of these background treatments. Share your findings with the class.

19. **Science.** Investigate the process paint manufacturers use to create paint products that have low emissions of volatile organic compounds (VOCs). Why should interior designers promote the use of such products with their clients? Write a summary of your findings.

Technology Applications

20. **Wall covering technology.** Use Internet resources to investigate technological advances in manufacturing eco-friendly wall coverings. Evaluate the features of these products including care and maintenance. Write a summary of your findings to share with the class.

21. **Acoustical tile research.** Search the Internet for information on the technological trends for acoustical ceiling materials and the design options available to designers and consumers. Check at least three manufacturers to find the recommended uses of their ceiling materials and the effect of their products on controlling noise. Document the Web sites you explore, and write a brief report on the information you find.

Design Practice

22. **Residential backgrounds.** As part of a renovation project, your client has asked you to identify several wall, ceiling, and floor treatments to use in the kitchen, family room, and master bathroom. For each treatment, your client wants information about special features, durability, and care requirements. Use presentation software to assemble photos and descriptions of each of your background choices. Share your potential plans with your client (the class).

23. **Commercial backgrounds.** Presume you have been contracted to design the background materials for use in the cafeteria and library of a new high school. School officials desire a classic design scheme with a contemporary edge. What wall, ceiling, and flooring choices would you make for each area? Why?

24. **Portfolio.** Select examples of each type of background material described in this chapter. Collect and mount samples of flooring materials, floor coverings, wall treatments, ceiling treatments, and countertop treatments. Label each treatment type and note the appropriate features, use, and care of each. Save your background collection in your portfolio for use with future design projects.

Working Toward Owning a Business

Are you artistic? Do you like creating attractive wall treatments with faux finishes? Perhaps you are interested in owning your own painting business and specializing in faux finishing.

Use the FCCLA *Planning Process* and the *Power of One—Working on Working* guidelines to develop a business plan for your enterprise. See your adviser for information as needed.

CHAPTER 15

Furniture Styles and Construction

Terms to Learn

Casual style
Country style
Eclectic style
antique
collectible
reproduction
case good
wood grain
deciduous
coniferous
solid wood
bonded wood
veneered wood
pressed wood
mortise-and-tenon joint
double-dowel joint
dovetail joint
tongue-and-groove joint
butt joint
corner block
coil springs
flat springs
innerspring mattress
foam mattress
memory foam mattress
waterbed
box springs

Chapter Objectives

After studying this chapter, you will be able to

- analyze various furniture styles.
- evaluate quality furniture construction.
- summarize consumer protections for buying furniture.

Reading with Purpose

As you read the chapter, record any questions that come to mind. Indicate where the answer to your question can be found: within the text, from your teacher, in another book, on the Internet, or by thinking about your personal experiences. Pursue the answers to your questions.

Once you create the interior backgrounds for a design scheme, continue the process by deciding how to furnish it. The first two steps in furnishing an interior space are choosing furniture styles and evaluating furniture construction. You will learn about selecting furniture for a design scheme in Chapter 16.

As you recall, design has three characteristics: function, construction, and aesthetics. This chapter focuses on two of those characteristics as they relate to furniture—aesthetics and construction. By focusing on the aesthetics of furniture, you will learn to recognize the physical characteristics that make individual styles unique and appealing. In addition, you will learn about the history and evolution of different furniture styles. Then you will learn to evaluate the quality of the construction.

Choosing Furniture Styles

Choosing furniture styles is a matter of taste, or personal preference. There is no right or wrong furniture—just furniture that is best for you or an interior design client. Studying the various styles can give you a good idea of which styles are pleasing and fit a design plan. Learning furniture styles will also help you use each piece of furniture to its best design advantage.

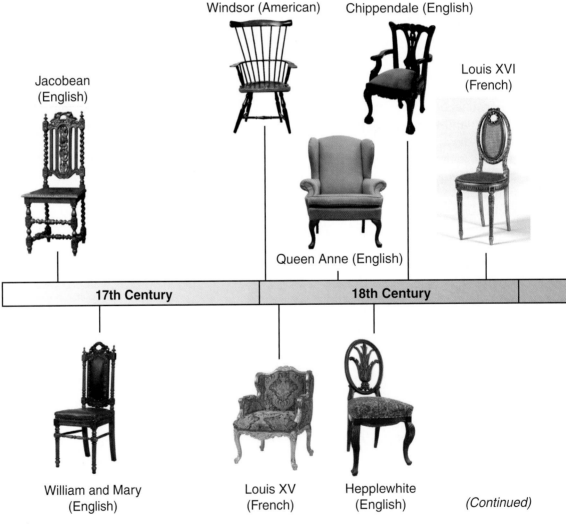

Windsor (American)

Chippendale (English)

Louis XVI (French)

Jacobean (English)

Queen Anne (English)

William and Mary (English)

Louis XV (French)

Hepplewhite (English)

17th Century

18th Century

(Continued)

15-1

Furniture design styles have changed throughout history. Available resources, lifestyle, and the styles and tastes of an era all influence furnishings.

Furniture style refers to design only. It does not refer to the cost or the quality of construction. Any style, from Queen Anne to contemporary, can be made of good or poor materials using good or poor construction methods.

Furniture Styles

The first documented fine furniture styles were those of the Ancient Egyptians in 3000 B.C. Fine quality Oriental furniture dates back to 300 B.C. Styles from Ancient Rome can be documented from 700 B.C., while styles from Ancient Greece date back to 1100 B.C.

For about 800 years (400 to 1200 A.D.), fine furniture making almost became a lost skill. It began its recovery in the 1200s with the emergence of Gothic art in Western Europe. Gothic art influenced both architecture and furniture design with the use of arches and columns. Many furniture styles used today date back to the traditional designs from the early 1600s.

Traditional Furniture Styles

Traditional, or period, furniture styles were developed during different periods of history. Traditional furniture styles are designs created in the past that have survived the test of time and are still in use today. This chapter discusses traditional styles from France, England, and the United States. Figure 15-1 shows a

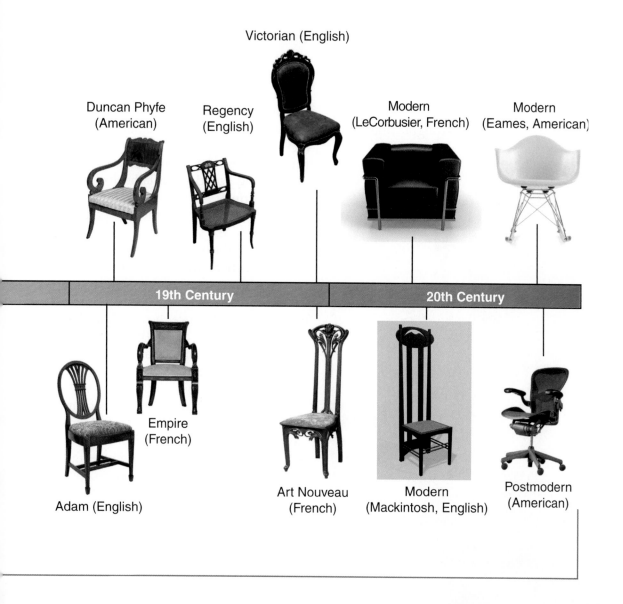

general time reference for some traditional and nontraditional furniture styles. Most furniture styles are named after the rulers of the era or the craftsmen who actually created them.

Traditional Styles from France

While Louis XIII was King of France, 1610-1643, furniture styles were grand and formal. Rich inlays, carvings, and classical motifs were typical.

At the end of the Renaissance period, Louis XIV, the Sun King, ruled France from 1643–1715. He built the Palace of Versailles and filled it with extravagant furnishings. The furnishings had heavy ornamentation and gold overlays. These characteristics mark the influential *French Baroque* period.

During the reign of Louis XV, 1715–1774, furniture styles had smaller proportions and became more delicate. Curved lines and soft colors were dominant.

Before the French Revolution, Louis XVI and Marie Antoinette ruled France, 1774–1792. Simple, straight lines and classic motifs, such as fluted columns, were popular in furniture.

When Napoleon ruled France, 1804–1815, he dominated everything—even furniture styles. The dignified style called *Empire* became popular. The furniture was large and heavy. Ornamentation included Napoleon's initial and military symbols. Usage of Egyptian, Greek, and Roman motifs was also common.

During the seventeenth and eighteenth centuries, artisans began copying styles that were popular in the court at Paris. The *French Provincial* style was practical, functional, and comfortable. Usage of local woods and simplified decorations was characteristic of these furniture copies, 15-2.

Traditional Styles from England

During the reigns of James I and Charles I, 1603–1649, *Jacobean* furniture became popular. The decorative features of this heavy oak furniture utilized the techniques of turning and fluting. *Turning* is an ornamental detail used on furniture legs and other pieces made by rotating wood on a lathe to create a spiral effect. *Fluting* is another ornamental detail made by carving parallel grooves into the wood.

During the reign of Queen Anne, 1702–1714, there was an Oriental influence in furniture. The use of cabriole legs in the *Queen Anne* style represents the Chinese influence. A *cabriole leg* has a gentle S-shaped curve that ends in a decorative foot. Carved fans and shells are also characteristic of this graceful and comfortable style.

Several furniture styles became popular during the reigns of Kings George I, II, and III, 1714–1820. *Georgian* is the style name people sometimes use for furnishings of this era. However, they are often labeled to reflect the names of their designers—Thomas *Chippendale*,

15-2
Country French style of furniture is used frequently today. It is an interpretation of the French Provincial style.

Calico Corners—Calico Home Stores

the *Adam* Brothers, George *Hepplewhite*, and Thomas *Sheraton*.

Thomas Chippendale was the first person to publish a book entirely about furniture designs, and his designs became popular worldwide. Gothic and Chinese influences were part of the Chippendale design. Details such as the use of splat-back chairs and curved top edges on the backs of chairs and sofas were typical. Early Chippendale furniture has S-shaped legs with claw and ball feet, 15-3. Later, due to Chinese influence, his furniture had straight legs.

Furniture from the Adam Brothers, Robert and James, was designed to complement their architectural designs. The furniture was classic and symmetrical. The pieces had simple outlines, rectangular shapes, and tapered, straight legs.

George Hepplewhite is most famous for his graceful chair designs. The backs of the chairs had shield, oval, and heart shapes, 15-4.

The furniture designs by Thomas Sheraton had characteristic straight lines. He included motifs of urns, swags, and leaves. Mechanical devices—such as disappearing drawers, folding tables, and secret compartments—were key features of his furniture.

The *Regency* furniture style, 1810-1837, is named after the Prince of Wales whose reign as regent was nine years. The style

15-4
This chair has a shield back, which is characteristic of Hepplewhite.

Hickory Chair Co.

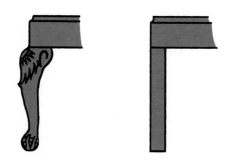

15-3
Curved legs with claw and ball feet were early Chippendale designs. His later designs had straight legs.

reflects an interest in the ancient cultures of Greece, Rome, and Egypt. Bold, curved lines were dominant.

During the reign of Queen Victoria, 1837-1901, the *Victorian* furniture style became popular. Machines could make detailed pieces of furniture quickly and easily. This led to the excessive use of ornamentation that was typical of the style, 15-5. Massive proportions and dark colors were also features of this style.

Traditional American Styles

The first European settlers in North America built sturdy, practical furniture. These *Early American* furnishings were simplified versions of the Jacobean style, which was popular at that time in England. The colonists used native woods, such as maple, pine, and oak. They began making furniture with less massive proportions. Ladder-back chairs and canopy beds were common. Windsor chairs were also popular, 15-6.

Later the Colonial style became popular. England's Queen Anne and Georgian styles were the basis for this furniture.

15-5
This vintage example of Victorian furniture is still found in many American homes today.

15-6
The Windsor chair is typical of Early American furnishings.

The fully upholstered wingback chair became popular in the colonies during this period. The chair design featured a high back with winglike sides that provided protection from drafts, 15-7. Graceful lines, S-shaped legs, and comfortable forms were characteristics of this period.

After the American Revolution, England's influence declined in all areas, including furniture styles. The *Federal* style became popular in the United States. It combined classic influences with patriotic symbols, such as eagles, stars, and stripes.

Duncan Phyfe was a major furniture designer of this period. His most notable design utilized the lyre motif in chair backs. Other features of his designs include brass-tipped dog feet, curved legs, and rolled-top rails on chair and sofa backs.

In the early 1800s, the Shakers—a religious group—gained recognition for their use of the circular saw in making furniture. *Shaker* furniture was very plain in design, but often painted in bright colors. Best known for their side chairs and rockers, Shakers did make other furniture, too, 15-8.

Twentieth-Century Furniture Styles

At the beginning of the twentieth century, designers reacted against the cluttered look of the Victorian era. Instead, they wished to create furniture designs that represented a more modern lifestyle. They designed furniture with simpler lines and forms. The primary characteristic of Modern furniture was the use of abstract form. A strong influence on these furniture styles was the ability of manufacturing companies to mass-produce pieces of furniture with automated machinery.

Also significant to the styles of this period was the influx of many architects into the field of furniture design. The leading architects included Gerrit Rietveld, Walter Gropius, and Frank Lloyd Wright. Twentieth century design also benefited from a vast international influence. Significant styles of the Modern period include Art Nouveau, De Stijl, Bauhaus, Organic, Art Deco, and Modern Scandinavian.

Art Nouveau

The *Art Nouveau* style began as a revolt against historical revival styles. The term is French for *New Art*. The movement actually began in the 1800s and lasted until the early 1900s. The rejection of traditional styles by the Art Nouveau movement greatly influenced furniture design in the 1900s. Reflecting a revival of interest in the decorative arts, the use of Japanese motifs was characteristic of this style. Other characteristics include long, slightly curved lines that reflect natural growing forms of plants, such as blossoms, vines, and stalks. These lines typically end abruptly in sharp whiplike curves. The use of curved lines was common in chair legs and backs. Pieces with this design are still popular today. You will typically find them in modern homes and restaurants.

De Stijl

De Stijl, which means *The Style*, began as an art movement around 1917 in the Netherlands. Gerrit Rietveld—a Dutch architect and furniture designer—led the movement. With abstract art as an influencing factor, the furniture style utilized geometric forms such as rectangles. The only colors Rietveld used were the three primary colors of yellow, blue, and red. His work influenced many later furniture styles in the 1900s.

Bauhaus

In the early 1900s, the German *Bauhaus* movement strongly influenced the direction of furniture design. Architect Walter

Gropius established the Bauhaus school of design in Weimar, Germany in 1919. The Bauhaus philosophy was simple— *form follows function*. In other words, if the intention for a furniture piece was sitting (as in the example of a chair), it was given a form that made that function possible.

Typical Bauhaus furniture designs were very simple. For chairs, use of chrome-plated steel tubing for support with seats and backs of canvas, wood, cane, or leather was common. Famous

15-7
The upholstered wingback chair was popular in the American colonies.

15-8
These Shaker rocking chairs face a Shaker sewing stand that has a drawer on each side.

Photo by Paul Rocheleau, Hancock Shaker Village

examples of this movement are the chair designs by Marcel Breuer and Mies van der Rohe. Their designs became popular worldwide. Production and use of these designs in this Classic Modern style continues today, 15-9.

Arts and Crafts

As you recall from Chapter 6, John Ruskin (1819–1900) and William Morris (1834–1896) began the *Arts and Crafts* movement in protest to the shoddy industrial production of goods in Victorian design. Ruskin and Morris urged a return to creative, quality handwork by craftsman who use materials honestly and with less-elaborate detail, 15-10. In post-Civil War America, the name of the Arts and Crafts movement was shortened to the *Craftsman* movement. The name "Craftsman" came from the title of a popular magazine publication by a famous furniture designer, Gustav Stickley (1858–1942). The first issue of his magazine in 1901 was dedicated to William Morris. The second edition was devoted to John Ruskin.

Other names for Stickley's furniture are *Mission* or *Golden Oak* style. His furniture expressed his unique design sense and mastery of form, proportion, and color. The furniture designs were simple, functional, and sturdy. He placed emphasis on the details of *joinery*—the art of joining pieces of wood. Tenon and key joints, exposed tenons, and visible dowels gave Stickley furniture a handmade appearance. Through furniture design reform and with his well-made, well-designed furniture, Stickley created an authentic body of work with enduring qualities.

Organic Design

Organic style denotes the furniture designs by American architect Frank Lloyd Wright (1869–1959) and his followers. Wright was known for his Prairie style architecture. His home and structure designs complement their natural surroundings. Wright positioned his houses to work within the natural terrain of the land and take advantage of sunlight and prevailing breezes.

15-9
This photo shows two *Barcelona* chairs, by designer Mies van de Rohe, in a contemporary setting.

15-10
As a classic example of Arts and Crafts era furniture, this Morris-style chair displays quality craftsmanship and simplicity.

These structures utilize basic materials such as wood, masonry, and glass.

Wright believed that furniture should fit easily and naturally into its surroundings. He created furniture designs specifically to fit the design of each house. While the furniture designs varied according to each specific house, Wright's use of geometric shapes, flat surfaces, and slats were common elements in his furniture, 15-11.

Art Deco

The most popular international decorative style in the 1920s and 1930s was *Art Deco*. Images suggesting the public's interest in speed, such as fast-moving trains, ocean liners, and cars were characteristic of this style. Unusual combinations of industrial materials and traditional luxury materials in the construction of Art Deco pieces supported this interest. For example, manufacturers often paired brushed steel with exotic wood, ivory, or gilt bronzes. (*Gilt* refers to the application of gold or a material that looks like gold onto a surface.) Other diverse styles—such as mechanical design and Native American, Ancient Egyptian, and African art—were influential on these furniture designs.

Modern Scandinavian

Modern Scandinavian design began in Denmark, Norway, and Sweden in the late 1920s. During the twentieth century, its influence on furniture design is evident in chairs consisting of molded wood seats or arms. The perfection and first application of this technique—shaping many veneers of wood by applying steam or heat—was in the construction of molded snow skis. White birch was a typical wood choice because of its hard surface and firmness, but unusual pliability. Clean, simple lines and natural wood were key features of this style, as were simple upholstery fabrics of wool, cotton, or linen.

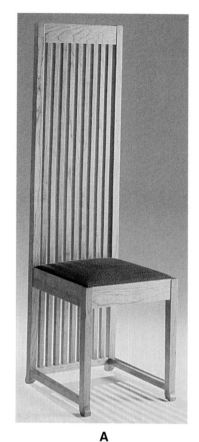

A

B

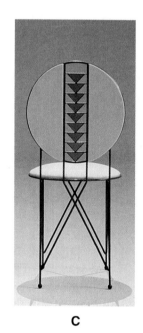

C

D

15-11
Frank Lloyd Wright designed his modern furniture to correspond to his Prairie style house designs.

Courtesy of the Frank Lloyd Wright Foundation

15-12
This is the basic Eames molded plywood chair design. It is functional and beautifully simple.

Photography Courtesy of Herman Miller, Inc.

The furniture style was very popular because it was warm, natural, and easy to maintain. It was considered functional and elegant. The smaller scale of the pieces worked well in apartments and smaller homes, 15-12.

Late Twentieth-Century Styles

Later styles of furniture in the twentieth century include the *Retro, Radical Modern,* and *Postmodern* styles. The Retro style of the 1950s and 1960s utilized many of the same elements that were popular in the early 1900s. The use of triangular, boomerang, and rhomboid shapes is characteristic of this style. (Recall from math that a rhombus is a slanted parallelogram.)

The single most important furniture design of this period was a simple chrome and molded-plywood chair designed by the American designer Charles Eames. Because of the importance of this design, some consider Eames as part of the Classic Modern group. His work, however, came many years after the Bauhaus and International style.

Some retro armchairs feature forms that hug the body. One such design was the *butterfly chair* by Harry Bertoi, an American sculptor and designer.

Modular furniture units also evolved during this period. These units were composed of separate seating pieces in standardized sizes. Because of great flexibility in space planning, designers could group these pieces together or separately in a variety of seating arrangements. Polyfoam was used in these pieces instead of the typical coil springs and webbing. By using the polyfoam, the modular units weighed less and were easier to move. Also, the polyfoam was less costly than the typical coils and webbing.

Radical Modern design was popular in the late 1960s. Furniture of this style was inexpensive and serviceable, but not long-lasting. One such style was the *beanbag chair*. It was constructed of vinyl, leather, or cloth, and was filled with plastic beads. This chair design conforms to the body of the seated person.

The Postmodern design style of the late 1900s (1970 and beyond) used traditional shapes from other styles of furniture, but constructed them in different materials and finishes. Examples of this are the chairs created by American architect Robert Venturi. He designed a Queen Anne chair of bent plywood. He also created bent plywood versions of a Sheraton chair and an Art Deco chair. The results were artistic and lighthearted reinterpretations of historical design.

Other furniture designers of this period purposely designed furniture that machines could not produce. The goal of this movement was to remove furniture design from a factory manufacturing process and return it to the realm of art.

Twenty-First Century Furniture Styles

Currently there are five dominant furniture styles popular in the United States. According to the American Furniture Manufacturers Association, the current styles are Contemporary, Traditional, Casual, Country, and Eclectic, 15-13. Furniture in the five styles is available in many different price ranges and levels of construction quality.

Contemporary

Contemporary furniture style is composed of designs that are the very latest introductions to the market. They take advantage of the newest materials and manufacturing methods. Many contemporary designs trace their origin to the Modern or International style designs created during the twentieth century, when function was such an important influence.

A

B

C

D

15-13
These rooms show examples of furniture styles that are currently popular in the United States. The furniture designs include Contemporary (A), Traditional (B), Casual (C), and Country styles (D).

Usage of plastics, metals, wood, and glass create an endless range of visual effects. Pieces of contemporary furniture have simple lines and forms. The feeling is streamlined and sleek. Geometric shapes such as circles, rectangles, triangles, cylinders, and cubes are often part of these designs. Colorful fabrics and accessories add beauty and variety to contemporary rooms by enhancing the furniture's simple lines.

In other room designs, contemporary furniture may appear very stark. In such a case, the use of color and accessories may be minimal.

Traditional

The Traditional furniture made today continues to be inspired by the early designs of French, English, and American periods. Symmetry and graceful, carved curves are key characteristics of this furniture style. The fabric colors are rich, and the wood finish tends to be dark with a polished sheen. Use of this style of furniture conveys a sense of elegance.

Casual

Casual style furniture is a style that emphasizes comfort and informality. The feeling this type of furniture creates is opposite the elegant mood created by traditional furniture. The emphasis is on comfort, and often the sofas and chairs have an overstuffed look. Fabric designs are carefree in both look and function. Pine, ash, oak, and maple are the common types of wood used. This furniture style is an evolution of the American lifestyle. Its beginnings do not date back to any single historical period of design.

Country

Country style furniture traces its origins to the lifestyles of rural areas. There are many subcategories of Country style furniture depending on the country that influenced the particular design. These styles include American, English, Italian, French, and Irish Country. Characteristics of the style may vary somewhat between countries.

In general, Country style furniture uses painted or distressed wood finishes that convey a feeling of age. Natural pine, cherry, and oak are also used. The chairs and sofas are plump and comfortable. Fabric designs also convey a timeworn appearance.

Eclectic

In the **Eclectic style**, furniture and fabrics cross over styles and periods. The style can be a mix of different ethnic, historical, and international influences as well as works by different artisans or manufacturers. Since an eclectic room may use a variety of furnishing styles, effective use of the principles of design helps create a unified look. For example, the furnishings in an eclectic room should be in proportion to one another and somewhat related in mood. Carefully considering the combinations of textures and colors also helps unify the design scheme.

Antiques, Collectibles, and Reproductions

While Contemporary, Casual, Country, Traditional, and Eclectic are the dominant styles in furniture, antiques, collectibles, and reproductions continue to be popular choices. Such purchases can mix well with many styles of furniture.

Antiques

Antiques are pieces of furniture made over 100 years ago in the style of the period. As furniture styles become outdated, good-quality pieces have become hard to locate. Some antiques are reasonable in cost. However, furniture that is very old and reflects good construction can be quite costly. Fine antiques are those of good quality. The very finest antiques are museum quality, as in 15-14. Such pieces are very rare and expensive.

Collectibles

Collectibles are highly valued furnishings less than 100 years old, but no longer made. If kept long enough, they will become antiques.

Reproductions

Reproductions are copies of antique originals. Manufacturers sometimes make them to look worn or used. For example, they may add false wormholes to the finish for an older appearance. Reproductions may or may not be accurate imitations. Determining whether a furniture piece is authentic or a reproduction requires careful inspection and research. See 15-15 for an example of an accurate and authentic reproduction.

Evaluating Furniture Construction

Many furniture styles are made with wood, plastic, metal, wicker, or glass. The materials can be used alone or in combination with other materials. The furniture you select for a design scheme depends on the desires of the household, the mood of the room, and money available to carry out the design. Evaluating the functional quality of furniture for usefulness, convenience, and organization is vital for a successful design. You will also need to evaluate furniture's aesthetic value, such as its pleasing appearance or effect. (The elements of design also apply to furniture.)

Knowing how to evaluate the quality of furniture construction is very important. The materials used in the construction of the furniture should meet

15-14
The antique furniture in this room is museum quality.

Rhonda Hull Interiors, Rhonda Hull, Allied ASID, ASID Historical Renovation Merit Award 2007, Harper House Hickory Center. Photography by Bob Huffman, Hickory, North Carolina.

15-15
This lowboy is a fine reproduction of an original antique. The original is found on the historic Tuckahoe Plantation along the James River in Virginia.

Hickory Chair Co.

industry standards and be the highest quality a person can afford. Furniture should also be safe and durable. Understanding furniture construction can help you choose the highest-quality furniture for the money available, 15-16.

Wood in Furniture

Wood is the most common material used in furniture construction. A **case good** is a furniture piece in which wood is the primary construction material. Such furniture includes tables, desks, dressers, headboards, and chests. Fine wood may also be part of the structural framework of furniture that has a covering of another material, such as upholstery.

Wood used in furniture construction can be classified according to the following factors:

- type and quality of wood grain
- hardwood versus softwood
- solid versus bonded wood
- type of wood joints
- finished versus unfinished wood

These factors affect the quality of the piece. When looking at furniture, be sure to consider each factor to determine if the price reflects the quality.

Grain

A **wood grain**, or pattern, forms as a tree grows, 15-17. The stump or base of a tree has a beautiful, irregular grain

caused by the twisted and irregular growth of the tree's roots. Crotch wood has a special grain caused by branches growing out from the trunk of a tree. Burls, which are woody, flattened outgrowths on trees, have a unique and highly prized grain. It is very important to evaluate the appearance of the grain when you are selecting a case good.

Lumber is cut to show off the grain. The way it is cut can affect the appearance of wood grain in furniture. Quarter slicing, rotary cutting, and flat cutting are methods that create different looks with the same kind of wood.

Hardwood and Softwood

Furniture makers can construct furniture entirely from hardwood, softwood, or a combination. Hardwood comes from **deciduous** trees, or trees that lose their leaves. The most popular hardwoods used for quality furniture include walnut, mahogany, pecan, cherry, maple, and oak. Hardwood does not dent easily. It is usually stronger than softwood and is more costly.

Softwood comes from **coniferous** trees, or evergreen trees that do not shed their leaves. Softwood does not have as beautiful a grain as hardwood, and it dents easily. Cedar, redwood, pine, fir, and spruce are the most common softwoods used for furniture. Some softwood is harder than some hardwood, so the names may be somewhat deceiving. Figure 15-18 shows examples of various wood species.

Solid Wood and Bonded Wood

Solid wood means that all exposed parts of a piece of furniture are made of whole pieces of wood. Such furniture is usually expensive, especially if it is made of hardwood. The disadvantage of solid wood is that it has a tendency to warp, swell, and crack.

15-16
If you buy furniture made by a well-known company, you can be assured that high quality wood was used.

15-17
Wood grain varies according to the part of the tree from which the lumber comes (crotch, burl, or stump wood) or the way it is cut (flat, rotary, or quartered).

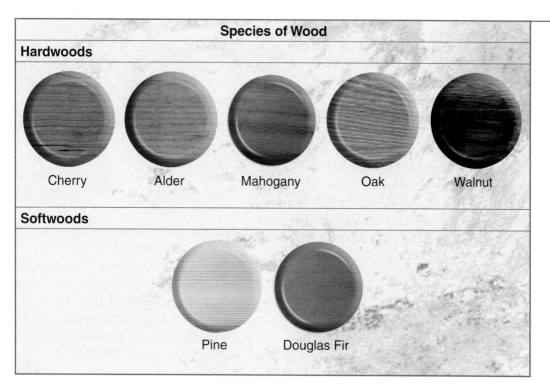

15-18
Notice the differences in the wood grain and the colors of these woods. In furniture, each of these woods provides a different look.

Photography Courtesy of JELD-WEN Windows and Doors

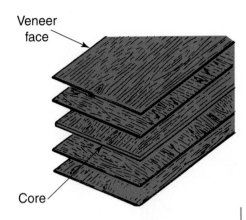

Veneer face

Core

15-19
In plywood, the grains of alternate veneers run at right angles to one another. This adds strength to the plywood.

The application of glue and pressure to several layers of wood forms **bonded wood**. Bonded woods include veneered wood and pressed wood.

Bonding three, five, or seven thin layers of wood to one another, to a solid wood core, or to a pressed wood core creates **veneered wood**, or plywood. See 15-19. Fine woods make up the outside layers. Less expensive woods make up the inside layers or core.

Since the outside layer of veneered wood utilizes more expensive woods, veneering makes fine woods available at a moderate cost. Rare woods and beautiful grains are also available. Veneering permits the use of fragile woods, since the inside layers add strength. A disadvantage of veneered wood is the adhesive may not stick permanently, causing the veneer to loosen and chip.

Most of the furniture made since 1900 is partly veneered. Today, veneered furniture is more common than solid wood furniture.

Pressed wood is made of shavings, veneer scraps, chips, and other small pieces of wood. Other names for pressed wood include *particleboard, wafer board*, or *composite board*. These wood types are less expensive than solid or veneered wood. Furniture makers often use pressed woods on parts of furniture that do not show. Furnishings that need a tough, durable surface may have a top layer of more expensive wood or plastic laminate.

Wood Joints

When selecting furniture, especially case goods, pay close attention to the method used for fastening, or joining, the wood pieces. Furniture makers can use many different ways to fasten wood pieces, including the use of wood joints. Figure 15-20 shows common wood joints. Usage of glue on all wood joints adds strength and durability. Common wood joints include the following:

- **Mortise-and-tenon joints** are some of the strongest joints used for furniture. The glued tenon fits tightly into the mortise, or hole. This method of joinery uses no nails or screws. Common uses for mortise-and-tenon joints include joining legs or rails to tables, chairs, and headboards.

- **Double-dowel joints** are very common and very strong. Glued wooden dowels fit into drilled holes in both pieces of wood.

- **Dovetail joints** fasten wood pieces at corner joints. These joints utilize flaring tenons and mortises which fit tightly, interlocking two pieces of wood. You can find them in drawers of good-quality furniture.

- **Tongue-and-groove joints** form by fitting a tongue cut on one edge of a board into a matching groove cut on the edge of another board. These joints are invisible if they are made skillfully. They are used where several boards are joined lengthwise, such as in making tabletops.

- **Butt joints** involve gluing or nailing one board flush to another board. They are the weakest of the wood joints.

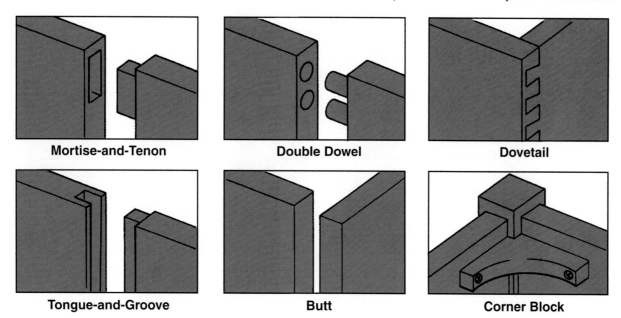

Mortise-and-Tenon   **Double Dowel**   **Dovetail**

Tongue-and-Groove   **Butt**   **Corner Block**

15-20
Joints are an important factor in determining the quality of furniture pieces.

- **Corner blocks** are small pieces of wood attached between corner boards. They support and reinforce the joint. Furniture makers use them in the construction of chairs and tables. They keep one side from pulling away from the other.

Finished and Unfinished Wood

You can purchase wood furniture finished or unfinished. Most furniture pieces are already finished. Manufacturers may use one or more ways to treat finished furniture to protect and improve the appearance of the wood surface. Some finishes include stains, sealers, waxes, and paints. Water-based stains and oil-based stains bring out the natural beauty of hardwoods and softwoods respectively. Sealers can be penetrating sealers or surface sealers. Plastic sealers resist moisture and are frequently used. Use of wax preserves the wood and gives it an attractive finish. Paint finishes can hide surfaces that are unattractive. Paint can also enhance an existing furniture piece by applying decorative finishes.

The wood in unfinished furniture is in its natural state following construction. Untreated wood surfaces appeal to those who want to finish the furniture themselves, often to achieve a unique look. The initial cost of unfinished furniture is low. Before buying such furniture, it is important to factor in the finishing costs in money, time, and effort.

You or a client may choose to finish furniture by applying a wood stain and a sealer or wax. Paint is another finish choice. Consider applying the paint in a solid color application or in a custom and novel application of a faux finish, such as sponging or ragging. Marbleizing a plain wooden table surface creates the impression of a marble stone top. Applying trompe l'oeil painting techniques to unfinished furniture can add an interesting effect. For example, creative painting can transform a plain wooden chest into a seaside scene with a sailing ship. These paint treatments can turn a bargain piece of unfinished furniture into a custom work of art. Review the descriptions of these finishes in Chapter 14.

15-21
A checklist is a useful tool when evaluating wood furniture.

Wood Furniture Checklist
• Do doors shut tightly without sticking?
• Are corner blocks used for reinforcement?
• Are dust panels provided between drawers?
• Do drawers slide easily?
• Are legs attached with mortise-and-tenon or dowel joints?
• Do legs stand squarely on the floor?
• Have insides of drawers, backs of chests, and undersides of tables and chairs been sanded and finished?
• Are surfaces smooth?
• Are surfaces solid, veneered, or laminated?
• Has a protective plastic coating been used on surfaces that will receive hard wear?
• Will the furniture piece fulfill your use, style, color, and size requirements?
• Is the furniture affordable?

When buying wood furniture, check the quality characteristics in 15-21. You should also read the labels carefully. They offer information about the finishes, the purpose of the finishes, and the care they should receive. It is important to understand all the terms on the labels. For instance, solid walnut means the exposed wood (in this case, walnut) is the same wood used throughout the entire piece.

GREEN CHOICES

Determining "Sustainability" in Furniture and Furnishings

Consumers, interior designers, and retailers now have a way to select furniture and furnishings constructed using environmentally friendly practices and materials. The *Sustainable Furnishings Council* has established standards for "Best Practices for Sustainability" in the furniture and home furnishings industry. Over 400 companies are members of the council and display a seal on their labels and advertisements in catalogs, marketing materials, and advertisements. In addition, those members with significant achievement in sustainability receive authorization to use the Council's hangtag on their products.

The seal assures the furniture manufacturer has steps taken to reduce carbon emissions, reduce waste, and reduce nonrecyclable materials. Further, the hangtag designates exemplary principles used in producing the product from the forest to the showroom floor.

Learn more about the Sustainable Furnishings Council and their members at the following Web site: www.sustainablefurniturecouncil.org/

Genuine walnut means that walnut is the face veneer, but other woods form the core. Walnut finish means the piece of furniture has been finished to look like walnut.

Plastic, Metal, Rattan, Wicker, Bamboo, and Glass Furniture

Plastic, metal, rattan, wicker, bamboo, and glass are other materials used in furniture construction. Evaluate all materials for quality when buying furniture.

Plastic

Plastic furniture is usually less costly than wood. It is lightweight, sturdy, and easy to clean. Generally, it looks best in modern and contemporary settings.

Plastic used for furniture should not imitate other materials, such as wood. Instead, the furniture design should take advantage of the special properties of plastic. When evaluating for plastic furniture, ask yourself the following questions:

- Is the piece strong and durable?
- Are the edges smooth and the surfaces flawless?
- Are color and gloss uniform?
- Are the reinforcement parts (that are not part of the design) hidden?

Metal

Metal is popular for both indoor and outdoor furniture. Wrought iron, steel, cast aluminum, and chrome are all used for different furnishings. Manufacturers often combine metals with other materials, such as wood, fabric, glass, or marble, 15-22. When evaluating metal furniture, ask yourself the following questions:

- Is the metal or metallic finish rustproof?
- Is the surface smooth?
- Are sharp edges coated or covered?

15-22
The free-standing storage piece in this bathroom is made of polished-nickel-plated steel with marble shelves. Notice the side rails that help secure the accessories, and you can also use them for hanging towels.

Photo Courtesy of Pottery Barn

Rattan, Wicker, and Bamboo

Rattan, wicker, and bamboo furniture combine natural wood frames with woven stems or branches. Rattan furniture utilizes the stringy, tough stems of different kinds of palm trees. These stems bend easily and are strong. Rattan furniture works well in casual or informal room settings.

Popular since the 1800s, the original use of wicker furniture was for outdoor furniture. Construction of wicker furniture requires loosely weaving thin, flexible branches (often from willow trees) around a frame. After the weaving is complete, paint, lacquer, or varnish are common finishes for wicker furniture. Wicker is lightweight and durable. It is also water resistant and has a natural gloss. Use of wicker furniture is now common in both indoor and outdoor settings, 15-23.

Construction of bamboo furniture uses various woody, mostly tall tropical grasses including some with

15-23
Wicker furniture is popular for informal indoor settings.

Photo Courtesy of Karastan

15-24
Upholstered furniture may be completely covered in fabric or some wood may be exposed.

Calico Corners—Calico Home Stores

strong hollow stems. These stems, or canes, form the frame of the furniture. Some manufacturers combine bamboo and rattan in one piece of furniture. For example, bamboo can form a chair frame and woven rattan can form the seat. Use of bamboo is most common in casual room settings. When evaluating rattan, wicker, or bamboo furniture, ask yourself the following questions:

- Are the strands smooth and unbroken?
- Are the joints well wrapped and secure?
- Is the finish a high quality?

Glass

Glass is usually combined with metal or wood. It is popular for table-tops and cabinet doors. When glass is a part of the furniture you are choosing, ask yourself the following questions:

- Does the furniture use tempered glass for safety and durability?
- Does the furniture design hold the glass firmly in place?
- Are glass surfaces free from bubbles, scratches, and other defects?

Upholstered Furniture

Another name for chairs, sofas, and other pieces of padded furniture is upholstered furniture. Most or all exposed surfaces of a furniture piece have a covering of fabric, 15-24. This outer covering hides the inner construction details. Because you cannot see these details, choosing good-quality upholstered furniture can be difficult. The information that follows will help you evaluate upholstered furniture.

Upholstery Fabrics

Fabric is an important part of upholstered furniture. It is also a clue to the overall quality of a piece. Good-quality furniture has durable, well-tailored upholstery fabric.

HEALTH/SAFETY

Furniture Design and Ergonomics

Furniture, particularly workplace and home office furniture, is sometimes described as "ergonomic." The manufacturer or retailer claims certain furniture designs use principles from the science of ergonomics. The goals of ergonomics are to minimize injury and maximize comfort and efficiency of use. However, interior designers and consumers should beware because any product can be labeled as ergonomic in the U.S. Ergonomics guidelines have been developed by the Business and Institutional Furniture Manufacturer's Association (BIFMA).

True ergonomic products require that designers understand both the physical and psychological characteristics of their users. They consult anthropometric data, or human body measurements, and study how people interact with furniture and other elements of their environments.

As a result, ergonomic furniture is often adjustable and can be comfortably and safely used by people of different sizes. Controls are simple to use and easy to reach and manipulate without straining. Seats and chair arms are usually padded and covered with nonslip breathable coverings. Many include lower-back supports that maintain the lumbar curve in the lower spine. Ergonomic tables are designed with adjustable-height legs.

Ergonomics is a broad and varied field that covers much more than furniture design. For more information, about ergonomics and ergonomic products, visit the Web sites of the following organizations:

- Business and Institutional Furniture Manufacturer's Association (bifma.org)

- Human Factors and Ergonomics Society (hfes.org)

- U.S. Department of Labor's Occupational Safety & Health Administration (osha.gov)

Upholstery fabrics are made primarily of blends or combination yarns. Manufacturers weave yarns to create fabrics with different patterns and designs. Upholstery fabrics come in many attractive colors and interesting textures. They can be heavy-, medium-, or lightweight, although lightweight fabrics do not wear as well as the others. When choosing upholstery fabrics, consider the following points:

- Woven fabrics with close, tight weaves are better quality than fabrics with open, loose weaves.

- Long floats, such as in the satin weave, tend to snag.

- Fabrics with equal number and size of warp and weft yarns are more durable.

- Flame-resistant fabrics are safer than untreated fabrics.

- Stain-resistant finishes make woven fabrics easier to clean.

- Colorfast materials are preferred.

- Medium to dark colors, patterned materials, tweeds, and textured fabrics do not show soil easily.

- Labels on fabric samples give content and care information.

- Fabrics use earth-friendly products, 15-25.

Earth-Friendly Upholstery

15-25
This earth-friendly sofa has very soft back cushions that are made from recycled plastic drink bottles.

Photography Courtesy of Lee Industries

Upholstery Tailoring

When evaluating upholstered furniture, you need to look at the tailoring details. A quick way to check is to evaluate a cushion cover. If the cover can be removed, check the seams and filling material, and see if it has an inside casing.

For a more thorough evaluation, check the entire piece of furniture. The more yes answers you have to the questions in the following checklist, the better tailored the upholstery:

- Is expert sewing evident?
- Are threads secure and trimmed?
- Is the fabric smooth, tight, and free from puckers?
- Does the fabric pattern, such as stripes and plaids, match?
- Are curved shapes and corners smooth?
- Are skirts lined and do they hang straight?
- Are buttons and trims securely fastened?
- Are staples and tacks concealed?

Frames, Springs, and Cushions

Upholstered furniture frames are made of wood or metal. As you evaluate the frames, keep in mind the points for choosing wood or metal furniture. You should choose a solid hardwood frame that is heavy and substantial. The joints should be secure, utilizing screws and corner blocks.

Springs are a part of the inner construction. The type and number of springs in a seat base help determine the quality. There are two types of springs: coil and flat, 15-26. **Coil springs** have a spiral shape without padding and covering. Heavier furniture utilizes coil springs. An average-size chair generally has nine to twelve springs per seat. Up to

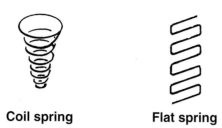

Coil spring   **Flat spring**

15-26
Coil springs are used in heavy furniture. Flat or zigzag springs are used when a minimum of bulk is desired.

eight ties per spring securely attach the springs to steel bands or webbing. This construction method provides support and enhances durability in a high-quality upholstered piece.

Lightweight pieces of furniture with sleek lines usually have flat or zigzag springs. **Flat springs** are flat, S-shaped springs that may have metal support strips banded across them. They offer firm comfort at lower cost.

Cushions need to be the proper size. They should fit snugly into the furniture. They need to give body support. Cushions often consist of urethane foam or foam rubber, but some manufacturers are now making seat cushions from a 20 to 30 percent soy-based material that is biodegradable (an alternative to petroleum-based materials that are not). These materials are durable, lightweight, and resilient. Manufacturers can mold these materials into many shapes, sizes, and degrees of firmness.

Covered or pocketed coils are sometimes used in cushions. They usually have a covering of a thin layer of foam rubber and a layer of fabric. Other cushions may have a filling of down and feathers. These are very comfortable, but less durable than foam. They are also more costly.

Cushion filling can also be in the form of loose fill. Shredded foam, kapok, and polyester fiberfill are all types of

loose fill. They are less expensive than the shaped fillers. However, because loose fill takes the shape of the casing, it may not retain its original shape. Furniture styles that have soft pillow cushions use loose fill. In addition, back cushions often use an ultrasoft fiber filling derived from recycled plastic drink bottles.

The cutaway illustration in 15-27 shows the inner construction of an upholstered chair. You can see how the combination of different materials provides seating comfort.

When choosing upholstered furniture, comfort is a very important factor to consider. For example, a sofa that does not feel comfortable is a poor buy. In making furniture selections, sit on a sofa or chair as you would at home. Check the height and depth of the seat. Check the height of the back and arms. Be sure it fits your body's proportions. If you are working with an interior design client, be sure your client has an opportunity to check out the comfort of potential furnishings, too. See the list in 15-28 for other points to consider when selecting upholstered furniture.

Beds

People spend about one-third of their lives sleeping. Therefore, choosing the best bed you or a client can afford

15-27
Making a chair durable, yet comfortable and attractive requires several work steps.

Monsanto Textiles Company

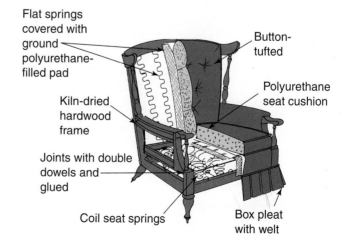

Flat springs covered with ground polyurethane-filled pad

Button-tufted

Kiln-dried hardwood frame

Joints with double dowels and glued

Polyurethane seat cushion

Coil seat springs

Box pleat with welt

15-28

Check these points before you buy pieces of upholstered furniture.

Upholstered Furniture Checklist
• Are the legs and joints securely attached?
• What kinds of springs have been used?
• What are the cushion materials and how are they constructed?
• Are the cushions reversible?
• Does the outer covering have a well-tailored appearance?
• Will the outer covering give good wearability for the intended purpose?
• Does the outer covering have a stain-resistant finish?
• Is it appropriate in style, design, and color for the room design?
• Is the furniture affordable for you or a client?

15-29

The use of a headboard adds interest to the design of this bedroom.

Calico Corners—Calico Home Stores

is important. A bed includes a mattress, frame, and springs. Addition of a head-board and footboard can help increase the charm of a design scheme, 15-29. Comfort is important when choosing a bed. Before buying a bed, a person should lie on it. That is the only way to determine if it is comfortable.

Since the inside construction of a mattress or box spring is not visible, choose a reliable brand. Many manufacturers have illustrations or miniature mattresses and box springs available for inspection when visiting a dealer. Check samples for support and durability.

Mattresses

There are many types of mattresses available. One of the most popular types is the innerspring mattress. An **innerspring mattress** contains a series of springs covered with padding, 15-30A.

The springs vary in number, size, placement, wire thickness (gauge), and whether they are individually pocketed. These factors determine the firmness and comfort of the mattress. Manufacturers say a good-quality full-size innerspring mattress should have the following features:

• at least 300 firmly-anchored, heavy coils

• good padding and insulation placed over and between coils

• a tightly woven cover with a border that does not sag

Foam mattresses are made of latex or polyurethane foam. The foam is cut or molded to shape and usually has a tightly woven covering of cotton cloth. The mattress may be solid foam or

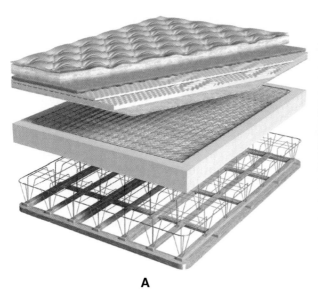

A

B

the more-pliable molded foam. Foam mattresses are lightweight, less durable, and less costly than innerspring mattresses. They vary in thickness, firmness, and quality. A good-quality mattress will be about 9 inches thick. It will have some holes or cores in it. The greater the number of cores, the softer the mattress will be. People with allergies often prefer foam mattresses or mattresses with hypoallergenic padding.

The newest foam mattress is the memory foam mattress. A **memory foam mattress** molds to the body during sleep, but quickly returns to its original shape once a person gets out of bed, 15-30B. In the 1970s, the National Aeronautics and Space Administration (NASA) developed this foam for use by astronauts in space. However, NASA never used this foam in space, but instead sold the technology to a company that has since developed the foam for consumer use.

A **waterbed** is a bed with a mattress consisting of a plastic bag or tubes filled with water. It conforms exactly to body curves and provides good, firm support. There are two types of waterbeds: hard-sided and soft-sided.

- *Hard-sided waterbeds* consist of a heavy-duty plastic water bag, a wood frame, a watertight liner between the mattress and frame to contain any leaks, and a water-heating device. Waterbeds range from full-motion to waveless types and require special bed linens. When a queen-size waterbed is full of water, it weighs about 1,600 pounds.

- *Soft-sided waterbeds* consist of a firm foam frame that surrounds the water-filled mattress. The mattress sits on a platform and looks much like a traditional innerspring mattress. One advantage of a soft-sided waterbed is that the owners can use traditional bed linens.

Buildings must have strong foundations to support them. Some rental properties prohibit waterbeds.

Air mattresses are easy to fill and empty. When empty, they require very little storage space. For these reasons, they make good portable beds. Camping is the primary use for air mattresses, but they are also handy for overnight guests.

15-30
When buying a mattress, it is important to check the quality of its construction, as shown in the layering of this high-quality mattress (A). Memory foam mattresses offer good support during sleep (B).

(A) Serta® 2009
(B) Serta® 2009

Springs

Most conventional beds have springs to support the mattress. Bedsprings have three basic forms: box, coil, and flat. Most people prefer box springs even though they are the most expensive. **Box springs** consist of a series of coils attached to a base and covered with padding. The coils may vary in number, size, placement, and gauge. Coil springs are between box springs and flat springs in terms of quality and cost. Flat springs are the least expensive.

When buying an innerspring mattress and springs, buy them in a matching set. When purchasing them as a set, the coils in the mattress line up with the coils in the springs. This makes the bed more comfortable.

Frames

There are many types of bed frames. The most common type is a metal frame on top of which you place a box spring and mattress. Sometimes springs, usually flat springs, are already built into the frame, 15-31. An electric adjustable bed is like a metal frame bed, except a person can adjust the frame up and down according to his or her needs. It is more expensive than a conventional metal frame.

Some bed frames, such as futons and sofa beds, have a dual purpose. You can also use them for seating. A futon frame is a wooden bed frame that is low to the ground. A cotton mattress is placed on top of it to make a bed. Futons can be folded up to make a chair or sofa. In the case of a sofa bed, pulling out a concealed mattress converts a sofa into a bed.

Consumer Protection

Buying furniture is a big investment. To help protect the investment, the government has agencies that protect consumers. The Federal Trade Commission (FTC) monitors advertising for truthfulness, while the Consumer Product Safety Commission (CPSC) oversees product safety.

In addition, federal laws also provide consumer protection. The Flammable Fabrics Act prohibits the sale of highly flammable fabrics for apparel and home furnishings. The Textile Fiber Products Identification Act requires a listing of fibers in their order of predominance by weight. It also requires generic names of fibers to appear on labels of all textile products, such as upholstery, carpets, and draperies.

Some fiber producers, fabric manufacturers, and furniture companies set their own high standards to surpass government requirements and industry standards. These companies guarantee the durability and performance of their products after consumers buy them. Information about guarantees and superior-quality materials appear on furniture labels. It is the consumer's responsibility to read the labels before buying any furnishings to know what to expect from the product.

15-31
Many people find traditional metal bed frames appealing and comfortable. When would you make a different choice?

Group 3, Architecture and Interior Design, Hilton Head, South Carolina. Photography provided as a courtesy of John McManus, Savannah, Georgia.

CAREER FOCUS

Upholsterer

Have you noticed upholstered furniture and often thought about replacing the fabrics? Maybe you would like to create final products in household furniture pieces by becoming an upholsterer.

Interests/Skills: Do you like to make things with your hands? Are you interested in creating or repairing the fabrics and cushioning on furniture? Do you like using math to solve problems? Do you like to create new things? Using math to estimate yardage needed in repairing or re-doing the fabric on a piece of furniture is necessary. Skill in using tools, equipment, and machines is required.

Calico Corners—Calico
Home Stores

Career Snapshot: An upholsterer makes repairs or replaces upholstery or coverings of household or institutional furniture. This involves estimating amount of material needed and accurately quoting a bid based on labor and materials. It involves knowing the characteristics of fabrics including their ease of using in upholstery but also the durability over time. A good upholsterer pays close attention to detail and design to create a high quality product.

Education/Training: Although a college degree is not required, serving as an apprentice is essential to develop the knowledge and skills needed on the job. This training may take up to ten years to learn all the essentials to be a skilled and accomplished upholsterer.

Job Outlook: Employment of upholsterers will be as fast as the average of all occupations through 2018. The largest source of positions is in household and institutional furniture manufacturing.

Source: Information from the Occupational Outlook Handbook (www.bls.gov/OCO).

Summary

Furniture styles are always changing. Many styles link to a certain country or historical period. Traditional designs are styles with enduring qualities that make them popular yet today. Characteristics of twentieth century furniture styles, or Modern styles, are in opposition to Traditional styles. Current furniture styles include Contemporary, Traditional, Casual, Country, and Eclectic.

Understanding furniture construction and materials can help you evaluate furniture and recognize good quality. Special joints hold together furniture consisting of wood and wood veneers. Plastic, metal, rattan, wicker, and glass are other materials used to make furniture. Some furniture is upholstered. Knowledge of upholstery fabrics and construction details will help you make good choices.

Government agencies and federal laws concerning consumer goods and textiles protect the consumer's furniture investment. Some manufacturers set higher standards for their products.

Review the Facts

1. Summarize three traditional styles of furniture.
2. Which following furniture style is not a Traditional style: (A) Louis XV; (B) Chippendale; (C) Colonial; (D) Organic?
3. What factors influence the unity of an eclectic design style?
4. Summarize the difference between an antique and a collectible.
5. Contrast a case good with an upholstered piece of furniture.
6. Summarize the differences between hardwood and softwood.
7. What are the benefits of using veneered wood for furniture?
8. List six joints used to fasten the structural pieces of wood furniture. Which is the weakest and which is the strongest?
9. What is the difference between solid wood and genuine wood?
10. Which furniture material is popular for indoor and outdoor use?
11. What questions should you ask when evaluating the quality of the following types of furniture: (A) plastic; (B) metal; (C) rattan, wicker, and bamboo; and (D) glass?
12. What characteristics indicate quality in an upholstered piece of furniture?
13. Contrast coil springs and flat springs in terms of bed comfort and cost.
14. Identify two government agencies that protect consumer interests when buying furniture, and briefly explain what each does.

Think Critically

15. **Draw conclusions.** Select and research a historical period of furniture design. Draw conclusions about how social, economical, political, and artistic trends of the era influenced the furniture design. Include illustrations of important furniture design characteristics. Share your findings with the class.

16. **Analyze upholstery.** Different pieces of furniture require different considerations when selecting upholstery fabric. Analyze the guidelines to follow in selecting fabric for a family room sofa for an active family with small children. How might the guidelines change for a retired couple who is selecting new sofa fabric for a formal living room? If possible, obtain samples of fabrics that you would recommend for each setting. Defend your analysis with the class.

Community Links

17. **Field trip.** Take a field trip to a store that sells antique furniture or reproductions of antique furniture. With the help of a salesperson, identify as many different historical styles as you can. Note the types of furniture, the countries of origin or association, and the characteristics the furniture possesses of a specific historical period. Which antique and reproduction styles are most popular with customers? After your field trip, answer the following question: How can understanding the availability, characteristics, and popularity of certain antiques and reproductions benefit you in an interior design career?

18. **Interview.** With a classmate, interview a furniture salesperson about the details of furniture construction in the products he or she sells. Check the labels attached to three types of furniture. What consumer information do the labels provide?

19. **Finish comparison.** Visit a building supply store or local hardware store and examine the selection of wood stain available. Look for a store display that shows the application of the same color stain to different types of wood. How do additional finishes, such as a polyurethane sealer or wax, cause differences in appearance? Note all variations in appearance. What factors influence the differences in appearance? Share your findings with the class. If possible, show examples of finishes.

Academic Connections

20. **Writing.** Suppose you have an interior design client who wants you to design his or her family room based on a photo of an *Arts and Crafts* period bookcase. Your client likes the bookcase, but knows little about the *Arts and Crafts* period. As an interior designer, you feel it is your responsibility to give your client as much information about this style as possible before committing to a design plan. Use Internet and print resources to research information about the *Arts and Crafts* movement to share with your client. Locate photos to help illustrate the information you find. Then use desktop publishing software to create an illustrated report for your client.

21. **Science.** Arrange a trip to a lumberyard. With the help of a salesperson, examine the various types of wood. Analyze the grain patterns in several pieces of wood and determine the part of the tree from which each was cut. Determine the characteristics of the wood: hardwood or softwood, solid or veneered, and finished or unfinished. Write a report summarizing your findings.

22. **Social studies.** Research the Federal Trade Commission Web site to identify laws and label requirements that protect consumers when buying a mattress. For instance, what does a white label represent? What does a red or yellow label mean? Use presentation software to give an illustrated report of your findings to the class.

Technology Applications

23. **Furniture style quiz.** Learn about furniture styles and/or your preferences by taking an online quiz. Search the Internet by using the keyword *furniture quiz*. Look for a quiz from a reputable furniture dealer or design source. After taking a quiz, how would you describe various furniture styles to client or salesperson? How can you use this information when you shop for furniture for yourself or a client?

24. **CADD furniture design.** Use a CADD furniture-design software program to design a unique chair. Your chair design should focus on aspects that display good function, aesthetics, and construction. Determine the material you will use for this chair—wood, rattan, wicker, bamboo, plastic, or metal. If you choose to use wood, identify whether you will use a hardwood or softwood, solid versus bonded wood, and the type of wood finish. Also show details about the type of wood joints you will use in the chair construction. Share your design plan with the class.

Design Practice

25. **Future furniture design.** Imagine it is the year 2050, and you are designing furniture for use in a home. Predict whether the furniture will be completely different from anything ever designed before, or whether it will have design components from earlier eras. Then use a CADD software program to sketch different pieces of furniture that might be used in this future period. Share your designs with the class, explaining why and how they are relevant for future lifestyles.

26. **Portfolio.** Use Internet or magazine resources to locate pictures of different furniture styles. Then create a storyboard showing a chronological timetable of the furniture styles. Organize them by date and country of origin. Save your storyboard in your portfolio for future reference.

Taking the Lead—Providing Furniture to People in Need

Many communities have nonprofit agencies that collect gently used furniture and redistribute it to people in need at low or no cost. Local social service agencies generally provide lists of people in need of furniture to such organizations.

As an FCCLA *Community Service* project, use your leadership skills and the FCCLA *Planning Process* to develop a project related to providing furniture to people in need. Perhaps you can work with a local group or start a service of your own. If you decide to start a service of your own, consider stepping up to an FCCLA STAR Event project on *Entrepreneurship*. See your adviser for information as needed.

CHAPTER 16

Arranging and Selecting Furniture

Terms to Learn

space planning
scale floor plan
template
clearance space
prioritize
ergonomics
comparison shopping
loss leader
seasonal sale
closeout sale
multipurpose furniture
unassembled furniture
recycle
restore
renew

Chapter Objectives

After studying this chapter, you will be able to

- analyze ways to arrange furniture effectively.

- evaluate how to select appropriate furnishings.

- determine ways to stretch available furniture dollars.

Reading with Purpose

After reading each passage (separated by main headings), stop and write a four-sentence summary of what you just read. Be sure to paraphrase—using your own words.

In the previous chapter, you learned about furniture styles and ways to identify quality in construction and materials. This chapter explores the next steps in furnishing a home—selecting furniture. If you select furniture before considering its placement in a home, you may choose items that will not fit or result in good room design. Knowing how to properly arrange furniture will help you choose only the furniture necessary. It will also help you or a client get the most from the furniture budget.

Arranging Furniture

Before selecting furniture for a room, you need to plan how to arrange it. The first step in this process is space planning. **Space planning** is the process of placing furnishings for a well-functioning and visually pleasing area. To plan a space, first measure the dimensions of the room. Room measurements let you know how much space is available in the room and how much furniture will fit in it. After taking measurements, several design tools can help you develop a space plan for a functional and attractive furniture arrangement.

Developing a Scale Floor Plan

To begin space planning, measure the length and width of each room. Then measure and determine the location of all the existing room features, such as doors, windows, electrical outlets, heating and cooling vents, and air intakes. In addition, measure the dimensions of any alcoves or other permanent features, such as fireplaces, cabinets, or built-in furniture pieces, too. All measurements should include the floor placement of the features as well as their wall height.

Before arranging furniture, you need to develop a scale floor plan. A **scale floor plan** is a reduced-size drawing that is directly proportional to the actual size and shape of a space or room. A common floor plan scale is ¼ inch equals 1 foot.

This means that ¼ inch on the drawing is equal to 1 foot in real life. You can create a scale floor plan from house plans used to build a home, as described in Chapter 7.

If the house plans are not available, there are two ways to create a scale floor plan. One way involves a manual process of using graph paper and templates. The second involves using a computer aided drafting and design (CADD) program to assist you. You will learn more about how interior designers use the CADD method in Chapter 19. Whichever method you choose, use the common scale of *¼ inch equals 1 foot*.

Graph Paper and Templates

To begin, draw the room on graph paper and include the features and dimension measurements. Use the symbols from Figure 7-3 to indicate the doors, windows, electrical outlets, and other features.

After creating a scale floor plan, you can use furniture templates to represent the furniture in the room. A **template** is a small piece of paper or plastic scaled to the actual dimensions of the furniture piece it represents. Manufactured plastic templates allow you to simply trace the shape of the furniture onto your plan. If you do not have access to manufactured templates, you can create your own by cutting small pieces of paper scaled to the actual dimensions of the furniture it represents. All templates must be the same scale as the floor plan, which usually is *¼-inch equals 1 foot*.

To create furniture templates, measure the length and width of the furniture you want to use. You may choose different colors of paper for different pieces of furniture. Cut them out and arrange the templates on the scale floor plan until you find the best arrangement, 16-1. Sometimes all the planned furniture pieces fit well. At other times, they may not. This is a much easier way to determine good furniture placement than

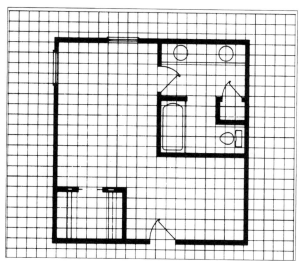

Step 1. Draw the dimensions of the bedroom on graph paper showing windows and doors in their correct positions.

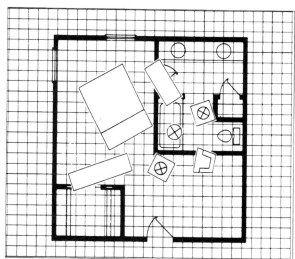

Step 2. Make furniture templates to be placed in the room, and cut them out.

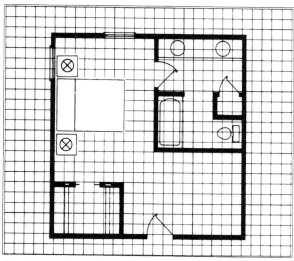

Step 3. Place the bed first.

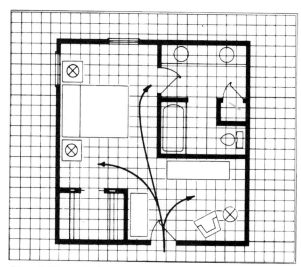

Step 4. Place the remaining furniture, keeping circulation paths clear.

16-1

Using a scale floor plan makes planning furniture arrangements easy.

actually moving heavy pieces of furniture back and forth.

Factors to Consider When Arranging Furniture

Several questions will help you develop the best space plan for a furniture arrangement. How will you or a client use the furniture? What space does it

need? How will room features and traffic flow affect furniture placement? Also consider the principles of design.

Furniture and Room Use

How furniture is arranged depends on how it is used. Each piece of furniture has one or more specific uses and requires a certain amount of space as a result. For instance, a chest of drawers takes up floor space and wall space. Clearance space is also needed in front to open the drawers. **Clearance space** is a measurement term for the amount of space to leave unobstructed around furniture to allow for ease of use and a good traffic pattern. See 16-2 for a list of clearance space requirements for furniture.

A furniture arrangement also depends on the room use. Before arranging furniture in a room, think about the activities that will take place there and the amount

16-2
In the process of space planning you must maintain adequate clearance space for proper traffic circulation.

Standard Clearance Spaces	
Room	**Clearance Space in Inches**
Living Room	
Around seating, such as chairs and sofas	18-30
Between sofa and coffee table	15-30
For minor traffic pattern area	18-48
For major traffic pattern area	48-72
Dining Room	
Between chair backs and wall or buffet (for diners remaining seated)	18-24
Between chair backs and wall or buffet (for self-service or host/hostess service)	30-36
Between table edge and wall or buffet (for self-service or host/hostess service)	18-30
For leg room in front of chair	48
Kitchen	
Between oven and opposite work space (opening door)	40 minimum
Between refrigerator and opposite work space (opening door)	36 minimum
Between dishwasher and opposite work space (opening door)	40 minimum
For circulation space	24
For work zone space between counter and nearby obstacle	48
Bath	
For activity zone in front of sink	18
For circulation space	24
Between front of sink and opposite wall or obstacle	40 minimum
Bedroom	
For activity zone in front of dresser to allow for work space and opening	42-48
For work zone space for making beds	26-40
For circulation space	24
Between twin beds	24

of space available. Then consider where within the room each activity will focus.

List the basic furnishings needed for each activity area, and determine the amount of space the furniture will occupy. For instance, you might want to create a conversation area in the living room, 16-3. A furniture grouping of chairs, sofas, tables, and lamps should be no more than 8 to 10 feet across. To encourage conversation, the area should form part or all of a circle. In the grouping, conveniently arrange lamps and other accessories in relation to their use. Give attention to the availability of electric outlets in planning the placement of lamps.

Room Features

When developing a space plan, arrange furniture so it does not interfere with the features of the room such as windows, doors, outlets, and air vents.

Do not place furniture where a door will hit it, and try not to block electrical outlets or air vents. Also, avoid placing furniture in front of a window, which makes opening and closing the window difficult. In addition, plan furniture arrangements around special architectural features. For example, furniture should not block a fireplace or built-in bookshelves.

By using a scale floor plan, you can see the placement of the features. If you have trouble visualizing furniture placement in relation to the features, add walls to your plan and indicate the features, 16-4.

Traffic Patterns

As you recall from Chapter 7, traffic patterns need to provide enough space for people to move about freely. Place each piece of furniture so people can

16-3
The furniture in this grouping is arranged to encourage conversation.

Photo Courtesy of Lindal Cedar Homes, Seattle, Washington

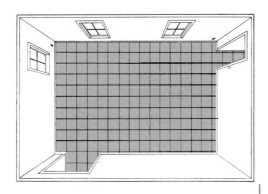

16-4

A three-dimensional scale floor plan can be created by sketching doors and windows on walls drawn to scale. The walls can then be folded up, fastened at the corners, and placed on top of a scale floor plan.

Drexel Heritage Furnishings Inc.

circulate easily throughout the room. To accomplish this, you must maintain proper clearance space around each piece of furniture. When placing furniture in a high-traffic area, consider increasing the clearance space. A furniture placement should not create an obstacle course or block traffic patterns between rooms.

Selecting Furniture

Once you know how much space is available and the plans for using it, you can begin selecting furniture. This process involves several steps. These steps include

- prioritizing furniture needs
- determining how much to spend
- identifying lifestyle needs
- identifying personal furniture style
- determining design preferences

LINK TO SOCIAL STUDIES & CULTURE

What Is Feng Shui?

Feng shui [fuhng SHWAY] is a Chinese art and philosophy that began over 8,000 years ago and spread throughout Asia. The words literally mean *wind* and *water*. Millions of Asian people use feng shui in their everyday lives with the belief that it helps bring harmony, happiness, and balance to their surroundings. Practitioners also believe it involves qi [CHEE], a kind of energy that can affect the quality of life. As part of the philosophy, certain colors, materials, and designs encourage greater harmony and balance to those who enter a building and the people within.

Some aspects of feng shui, particularly the feng shui of furniture arrangement, have caught on in the West. Here are a few examples that show how this art may be used in the home:

- Place the bed so the door is visible without directly facing the door. If the bed directly aligns with the door, it is thought that the flow of qi may disturb sleep.

- Place an even number of chairs around a dining table to promote good luck.

- Make the front entry door inviting and accessible to visitors.

- Arrange the kitchen so that the cook can see everyone who enters.

Hundreds of Web sites sell feng shui books and decorative items. Some colleges offer feng shui classes. A few U.S. corporations hire feng shui consultants to plan the construction and interior decor of buildings and resorts. Many people market themselves as experts, but consumers should be skeptical.

- deciding where and how to shop
- choosing when to shop

By following these steps, you can approach the furniture selection process in an organized manner. Such organization will help make the experience both time-efficient and enjoyable.

Prioritizing Furniture Needs

Few people can afford to buy all the furniture they need at once. Consequently, the first step in selecting furniture is prioritizing furniture needs. To **prioritize** means to rank goals in order of importance. This means deciding which pieces are first on the priority list, such as furniture for sleeping, eating, seating, working, and storage, 16-5. It is important to make these purchases first. When the budget allows, buy the furniture used less often and accessories that accent the large furniture pieces.

When selecting home office furniture, allow enough space for a continuous counter plus adequate cabinet and file storage. Most importantly, select a desk chair with *ergonomic* design. **Ergonomics** involves the design of consumer products and environments to promote user comfort, efficiency, and safety. For example, an ergonomically designed chair has a tilting chair back and adjustable seat height and arm rests. All these features take the strain off your muscles when you work at a desk or computer.

Discuss furniture priorities with all household members and ask for their input. This will allow you to make decisions that satisfy everyone. Listing all the ideas on paper will help prevent misunderstandings and make the priorities clear.

Determining How Much to Spend

After prioritizing furniture needs, the next step is deciding how much money to spend. Identifying a specific

16-5
The need for home office space is growing, and so are the available choices of functional and stylish furniture.

Photography Courtesy of Pottery Barn

dollar amount will clarify how many items on your list you can afford. All members of the household should express their views on this decision. Make a budget and be sure to follow it. Overspending is not likely to give the same satisfaction as spending only what you can afford, 16-6.

16-6
Begin your selections by first prioritizing your needs. Begin with what you can afford and gradually add more furnishings and accessories as time passes and as your budget allows.

MATH MATTERS

Buying Furniture on Credit

The purchase of new furniture can be costly. People who don't have cash often buy on credit and many furniture stores offer financing plans. Customers take furniture home after signing a contract agreeing to make regular payments for a specific period of time or before a certain date. Some stores require that people make a down payment, which is a portion of the purchase price. The down payment amount is subtracted from the total owed.

Buying on credit is more expensive than buying with cash because a finance charge is added. The charge is calculated by the creditor or the lender and consists of interest plus fees. There are several different formulas for calculating a finance charge. It is expressed as a percentage; the higher the percentage, the more costly the credit.

For example, suppose a $500 coffee table is purchased on credit and must be paid in 12 months. The finance charge will vary depending on the percentage. Suppose that interest paid in a year is

$50.08 at 18%

$58.72 at 21%

$67.36 at 24%

At 24 percent, a customer using credit would pay about $67 more for the coffee table than a cash-paying customer. Before you use credit, take time to read the contract carefully and make sure you understand the terms before you sign. A number of groups, including American Consumer Credit Counseling, provide online calculators to help consumers figure the cost of financing.

Smart shoppers buy the best merchandise for the best price. Sometimes, however, trade-offs are made. For example, spending more money for a kitchen table than budgeted will require adjusting the spending plan. This may require cuts in other areas, waiting longer than planned before the next purchase, or eliminating one or more items from the list.

Identifying Lifestyle Needs

Choose furniture that fits the household lifestyle. Consider the following when making furniture selections to fit lifestyle needs:

- **Family.** If a person is single, are there plans to marry in the near future? Do young married couples plan to have children? If so, furniture selections must be durable and withstand wear.

- **Health.** Does a family member have special health considerations or challenges that impact family lifestyle? Such conditions may require purchasing certain materials, fabrics, or finishes.

- **Pets.** Are pets a part of the household? The same emphasis on durability is also a requirement.

- **Entertainment.** What type of entertaining do household members usually do: formal, informal, or both? If a household does not entertain with formal meals very often, having a formal dining room set is a waste of money and space. Furniture has little value if it is not used.

- **Relocation.** Do one or more household members have careers that may subject them to transfers and moves? If so, it is necessary to make furniture selections that are adaptable to many spaces.

Identifying Furniture-Style Preferences

To begin, review the twenty-first century furniture styles discussed in Chapter 15. Design magazines, store advertisements, and furniture brochures are other sources of style information. In addition, you can look at product catalogs of name brand furniture on the Internet. It is often helpful to compile a notebook of pictures showing examples of furniture that you consider attractive. Are you most comfortable with *Casual, Contemporary, Country, Traditional,* or *Eclectic* styles? Keep in mind that good design is timeless. However, the newest styles do not necessarily convey good design.

Determining Design Preferences

When identifying design preferences, apply the design information studied in Chapters 10 through 15. Browse through interior design magazines and assemble picture files of fabrics, wall coverings, accessories, and other items of interest. Make a list of favorite colors, go to a paint store and select sample color chips, or obtain a paint fan deck from a favorite paint supplier. What materials, patterns, and textures do you and others find appealing? Examining and gathering samples of fabrics and wall coverings can give you a sense of your own personal design preferences, 16-7. Understanding your own preferences will also help you understand the preferences of others.

Become familiar with interior design and decorating trends. This will help you spot fads. Certain trends have a lasting appeal, but fads do not. Think about how long certain selections will remain enjoyable. Furniture and design selections can be costly. Most people are not able to replace these selections with the

16-7
Gathering a collection of fabrics and finishes can help you get a sense of your design preferences.

Calico Corners—Calico Home Stores

same frequency as they would buy new clothes. Gathering input from all household members is important to ensure the design will be one that everyone enjoys.

After researching your style preferences, you may desire additional guidance from available resources and services. Interior designers, both in private design firms and as in-store consultants, are professionally trained to listen and direct customer design plans. They can draw the customer's floor plan and pull together samples of wall, floor, and ceiling treatments for a space. These samples may include paint colors, fabric samples, and pictures of possible furnishings and accessories. Such a display shows a customer how the colors, patterns, and textures will combine in a completed room. Some interior designers will also draw a picture or rendering of how the finished room will appear. Designers who are members of professional groups, such as the *American Society of Interior Designers* (ASID), are the most qualified sources for professional advice.

Deciding Where and How to Shop

Many different types of stores sell furniture and accessories. Generally, the more services a store provides, the higher are the prices. Before buying, doing some comparison shopping can save money. **Comparison shopping** involves comparing the qualities, prices, and services linked to similar items in different stores. You can save time and energy by checking prices using the Internet or your telephone.

Retail Stores

Retail stores, such as department or furniture stores, offer the most services to customers. For example, retail stores typically will deliver, unpack, and set up the merchandise in a customer's home. However, the prices are usually higher to pay for these services. Some stores provide interior design and decorating services. Design professionals do scale floor plans, evaluate a customer's home, show a wide selection of furniture, and take custom orders. Most furniture retailers require placement of custom-furniture orders one to three months in advance.

Shop at retail stores with reliable service and buy furniture from manufacturers with good reputations. A good store will back up the merchandise it sells, and the manufacturer will replace defective products, 16-8.

Furniture stores usually have a larger selection of furniture than do department stores. Both types of stores can order furniture they do not have in stock. Allow extra delivery time for custom furniture.

Some retail stores offer their products at *discounted* prices. In order to give discounts, these stores may offer less service. You may need to wait for assistance in the store or for delivery of your purchase. Delivery services for larger items may be unavailable, or available only for an extra charge. If you later find a problem with the product, service may be limited. If you are willing to forego convenience for lower prices, you may be able to find bargains at these stores.

Warehouse Showrooms

Generally, showrooms handle only a few brands of merchandise. In addition to brand names, they may also sell off-brands. With ready-made furniture, you will have fewer fabric choices. The advantages of shopping in warehouse showrooms are savings and quick service. You can take the item with you or have it delivered in a few days.

Internet and Catalog Shopping

Catalogs let you shop by mail from any location. By shopping from catalogs or online, you can shop, purchase, and order furniture without ever leaving home. You can find store brand merchandise as well as name brand merchandise. Some online shopping and catalog sources may give you access to closeout items that have lower prices.

The main disadvantage of Internet and catalog shopping is inability to inspect the furniture for quality or comfort. In addition, the actual color of the wood and upholstery may look quite different from its picture. Before ordering, request actual fabric samples and finishes for inspection.

Additionally, it is important to research the supplier reputation. What is the return policy and how helpful is the customer service department? Since the items require shipping, damage could occur in transit. If damage occurs, what is the company's responsibility and what is the customer's responsibility? Also, keep in mind that shipping fees will add to the cost of the product. 16-9.

Other Furniture Sources

Salvage stores, garage sales, auctions, and flea markets can provide great bargains if you have time to shop carefully. Some items may need repairs or refinishing. You can decide whether a price is low enough to make fix-up and freshen-up efforts worthwhile.

16-8
When selecting furniture from a manufacturer with a good reputation, you make a wise investment.

16-9
Make sure you check the company's merchandise-return policy before ordering furniture from an Internet site or catalog.

Deciding When to Shop

When to shop is as important as *where* and *how* to shop. If people are hurried, tired, or shopping in crowded conditions, they may not make the best decisions—ending up with purchases they do not really want. The choice of a time to shop depends on personal circumstances and desires. Wise consumers budget their time with the same care they budget their money. Some shoppers enjoy doing lots of research and browsing before they buy, others recognize what they like and buy it.

Shopping at certain times can save money. Stores sometimes have high-quality furniture on sale. Some sales can significantly lower prices. There are many different types of sales, and understanding each can help consumers spend money more wisely.

Loss-Leader Sales

Loss leaders are items priced well below normal cost to entice people into a store to buy them plus items not on sale. The store management hopes people who come for the sales will also buy several other items that are not on sale. When shopping this kind of sale, buy only those items offered at a good price. For instance, you may find a chair is on sale, but the matching sofa is not. If you want to buy only the chair, it may be a good bargain. However, if you want to buy the chair and matching sofa, you may be able to get a better deal somewhere else.

Seasonal Sales

Stores hold **seasonal sales** at the end of a selling season to eliminate old stock and to make room for new items. For instance, patio furniture is often on sale in August to make room for furniture for college dorm rooms. During seasonal sales, consumers will find many discounts on high-quality products, 16-10.

16-10
Good bargains are often available when people wait for seasonal sales.

Bargain Months for Furnishings		
January	**February**	**March**
Appliances, blankets, carpets and rugs, furniture, home furnishings, housewares, and white goods	Air conditioners, carpets and rugs, curtains and draperies, furniture, home furnishings, housewares, and storm windows	Laundry appliances and storm windows
April	**May**	**June**
Gardening specials	Blankets, carpets and rugs, linens, and TV sets	Building materials, furniture, lumber, and TV sets
July	**August**	**September**
Air conditioners, appliances, carpets and rugs, fabrics, freezers and refrigerators, stereos, white goods	Air conditioners, bedding, carpets and rugs, curtains and draperies, fans, gardening equipment, home furnishings, housewares, summer furniture, and white goods	Appliances, paint, and TV sets
October	**November**	**December**
China and silverware	Blankets, housewares, and home improvement supplies	Blankets and housewares

Closeout Sales

If a store is moving to another location or going out of business, management often holds a **closeout sale**. It is better for the store to sell the merchandise at a low price or even at a loss than to move many heavy goods. It is even more important to sell all the merchandise if the store is closing.

When buying furniture from a company that is going out of business, do not expect any after-sale customer service. Customers generally must deal directly with the product manufacturer if a problem arises.

Sales of Damaged and Discontinued Items

Many stores mark down prices on items with slight damage. Make sure you know where and how bad the damage is. A desk with a surface scratch may be a good bargain if the price is low. If the drawers do not open easily, the desk may not be a bargain.

Discontinued-item sales offer high-quality goods at low prices because the seller wants to eliminate items no longer in production. However, once the sale items are gone, you will not be able to purchase matching items. For example, you may find discontinued wall covering on sale. If there is enough for you to cover a complete area, it is a bargain.

When shopping at sales, keep in mind the saying, "Let the buyer beware." When prices are below the normal cost of items, there is always a reason. It is up to the buyer to learn why and decide whether the lower price really represents a good value, 16-11.

Information Sources

Before making a final furniture selection, consult various sources for information on furniture of interest. These sources will provide information on the quality and reliability of

16-11
Sometimes an advertised sale applies only to selected items. Always check whether the "sale" price is lower than the everyday price.

the furniture. They will also help you become familiar with other furniture that is available. Begin by checking for important information on the Internet or at your local library. The Internet offers a tremendous opportunity to research and compare products.

Books and Magazines

You can find home furnishing books and magazines at the public library or you can purchase them. Some books and articles tell how to refinish furniture. Some provide ideas on furniture selection and arrangement. Others give sources and costs for the merchandise featured. Many often include money-saving ideas.

Product-Rating Organizations

Consumer Reports and *Consumer Guide*® are publications from organizations that test and rate products. They provide information about quality, price, and other factors, such as warranty information. The reports are available as monthly magazines and annual buying guides. You can find these and other product-rating reports on the Internet, in a library, or at a bookstore.

Advertisements

Advertisements in newspapers, magazines, radio, TV, and on the Internet often contain useful information. Use advertisements to compare brand names, features, and prices.

Labels and Seals

Labels on furniture may contain information about the materials used, coverings, fillings, country of manufacture, and origin of style. For example, if the product is made in the United States, the label will state "Danish Style" rather than "Danish." The label may indicate that the materials used are *all new or partly made from used materials*. Labels also include care information. Other labels and seals indicate whether furniture is rated green or sustainable.

Better Business Bureau

The Better Business Bureau (BBB) is a nonprofit organization sponsored by private businesses. It publishes information on how to shop wisely for products and services. Your local BBB can give you information about stores and business people in the area. The BBB also maintains a record of consumer complaints against local businesses and tries to settle disputes.

Stretching Your Furniture Dollars

Stretching your furniture dollars can help you acquire more furniture for your money. There are many reasons you may need to do this. For example, when you move into your first home, your take-home pay may not cover many furniture needs. You may find it necessary to furnish your home with rented or used pieces until you can afford new furniture.

Another reason is the likelihood of increasing housing costs as the size of your household increases. Consequently, finding ways to save money on furniture may become more important as you move through the life cycle.

You can stretch your furniture dollars by doing the following:
- shopping for bargains
- using multipurpose furniture

GREEN CHOICES

Furniture Going Green

Although many green products are in the marketplace, shoppers and professionals now have the opportunity to buy "green" furniture. This does not of course refer to the furniture's color but to its materials and construction practices. Look for furniture on the market that has a label or seal that includes the following green items:

- certified sustainable wood frames (produced from wood secured from forests in environmentally sound methods)
- water-based finishes (versus the finishes that do harm in the atmosphere)
- soybean cushions (versus foam)
- organic and natural fibers
- planting a tree for each purchased furniture piece

- buying unassembled furniture
- reusing old furniture
- creating an eclectic look

Shopping for Bargains

A good way to find furniture bargains is to buy furniture on sale. However, no matter how much the item costs on sale, it is not a bargain unless you need and can afford it. Also, the item is not a bargain if you would really rather have something else. A true bargain improves the quality of your life.

Sometimes what seems like a bargain may not be a bargain at all. One item may cost less than a similar item, but it may require more time or effort to acquire. For instance, carpeting at a store 50 miles away may cost 20 percent less than carpeting at a nearby store. This savings may be worth the long drive to some people, but not to others.

Although durable, simple furniture may not seem like a bargain, it really is. Complex furniture is often more expensive than simple furniture. Carving, latticework, turnings, and other extras add to the cost of furniture, 16-12. You can easily update the appearance of furniture with simple lines and colors by changing accessories.

Using Multipurpose Furniture

Multipurpose furniture is furniture that serves more than one purpose. For example, you can use a sofa bed for sitting or sleeping. Flat-topped trunks and chests make usable end tables and coffee tables while functioning as storage pieces.

Unassembled Furniture

Unassembled furniture, which is furniture sold in parts that require assembly, may or may not be finished. It is

16-12
The detailed turning found in the legs of this table and chair set makes it more expensive than a set with simple, straight legs.

Calico Corners—Calico Home Stores

often a lower quality than most assembled furniture. By assembling furniture yourself, you save money. Since packaging for unassembled furniture is usually very compact, you can save delivery costs by hauling it home yourself.

You can creatively assemble pieces from items not normally considered furniture. For example, bricks and boards easily combine to make bookshelves.

16-13

A round board mounted on any kind of base and covered with an interesting fabric can become an attractive table.

Group 3, Architectural and Interior Design, Hilton Head Island, South Carolina. Photography provided as a courtesy of John McManus, Savannah, Georgia.

Covering a round piece of board with a large circular cloth makes an attractive table, 16-13. You can also assemble plastic or wooden cubes in a wide variety of ways to create furniture. Combine

16-14

These cubes can be arranged in many different ways to create shelves and storage space.

Hold Everything

them to create shelves, tables, desks, and seats. Divide some cubes for shelf space or to accommodate drawers, 16-14. Although plastic cubes come in many colors, you can paint wooden cubes to coordinate your interior design scheme.

Reusing Furniture

After acquiring new furniture, you can still reuse your old furniture. This will help you stretch your home furniture dollars even more. To reuse your furniture, you can recycle, restore, or renew it.

Recycling Furniture

To **recycle** means to adapt to a new use. Recycling furniture means using furniture for a new use after it no longer serves its original purpose. For instance, some people may use outdoor furniture first in a living room, dining room, or family room. As their budget allows, they replace the outdoor furniture with indoor furniture and then use the outdoor furniture to decorate a patio. Other outdoor furniture may also be used indoors. For instance, some people use patio benches as coffee tables, end tables, or additional seating.

Consider recycling furniture pieces in your own home or passing them on to others to use. You can also buy used furniture from other sources to recycle in your home. Garage sales, secondhand stores, and relatives are good sources of used furniture.

Renovating Furniture

People often renovate furniture by either restoring or renewing it. It usually costs less to renovate an old piece of quality furniture than to buy low-quality, new furniture. You can choose to renovate furniture yourself, or hire a professional, 16-15. If you choose to do it yourself, keep in mind that it takes time, patience, and work. It also takes money for supplies and equipment.

When considering whether to renovate a piece of used furniture, answer the following questions:

- Is it well designed?

- Will it blend well with the other furnishings?

- Is it well constructed and worth repairing?

- Can it be used *as is*?

- Do you have the time, patience, and energy to do a good job?

- Do you have the necessary equipment and supplies to do the job, or the money to buy them?

- Do you have a suitable place to work?

When you **restore** a piece of furniture, you return it to its original state as much as possible. There are several steps to restoring a piece of furniture, including repairing, refinishing, and possibly

16-15
Some furniture renovations require the help of a professional.

reupholstering. For example, suppose you want to restore an antique chair. Using the following steps will help you effectively complete this task:

1. Remove the paint and sand all the finish off the wood.

2. Make any necessary repairs, such as redoing the joints.

3. Apply a wood finish as close to the original as possible.

4. Do any needed reupholstering. Carefully remove the original upholstery fabric and use it as a pattern for the new upholstery. For a proper restoration, select an upholstery fabric pattern that is similar in design to the type of fabric original to the piece.

This process takes much time and skill. You must have a strong interest in restoring furniture to make it worthwhile.

If a furniture piece is in good condition, but the upholstery is worn or out of date, you can **renew** it. To renew furniture means to give it a new look. The steps in this process are similar to those followed in restoration, with one important difference. When you renew furniture, you update it and do not attempt to restore it to its original condition. Based on the fabric and/or paint finish you select, an old piece of furniture can take on a totally different appearance.

Creating an Eclectic Look

Another way to stretch available furniture dollars is to create an eclectic look in your home. Eclectic is a design style based on a mixture of furnishings from different periods, styles, and countries. (Refer to Eclectic style in Chapter 15.) You can use this look while you are acquiring furniture piece by piece, or you can use it on a permanent basis, 16-16.

16-16
This mixture of contemporary and traditional furnishings works well together to create an eclectic look.

Calico Corners—Calico Home Stores

CAREER FOCUS

Interior Designer—Community Medical Complex

Can you imagine yourself as the interior designer of a medical complex for your community?

Interest/Skills: Perhaps you feel that a doctor's office should be comfortable and inviting. Interior designers who specialize in health care facilities have a passion to help others and provide comfort during challenging times. With ability to creatively see in your mind's eye how spaces could look, as a designer, you would organize a plan space for arrangements. Attention of detail is an important skill. Strong computer skills, especially in using CADD software, are especially important for complicated projects. Because many people are involved in developing a medical complex, exemplary communication and teamwork skills are essential in working with clients and contractors to finish the job on time. Medical interior designers need to be able to work with a budget and calculate all job costs.

Career Snapshot: Medical interior design involves working with the client and the architects. The designer develops a plan that keeps the client happy. Along with following a budget and local building codes, an interior designer is responsible for the flooring, all the fittings, decorating, and the accessories. Work hours are irregular due to the nature of the work.

Education/Training: A bachelor's or master's degree is preferred. Computer courses in CADD are essential. To specialize in medical interior design, classes in psychology, biology, physiology, and medical facility management are also necessary.

Licensing/Examinations: Approximately one half of the states require interior designers to be licensed. The National Council for Interior Design Qualification (NCIDQ) administers an examination that you must pass in order to obtain a license.

Professional Associations: The American Academy of Healthcare Interior Designers (AAHID), the International Interior Design Association (IIDA), the American Society of Interior Designers (ASID)

Job Outlook: Interior designers can expect job growth to be as fast as average through 2018. Designers with a broad range of skills and experiences will be in demand. When you first start your career, work as an assistant with experienced designers to gain more knowledge and skill. As your career progresses, build a portfolio. Large numbers of aging Americans make the job market strong for designers with knowledge of their special needs.

©2002 Image by Rick Alexander/LS3P ASSOCIATED, LTD.

Source: Information from the Occupational Outlook Handbook (www.bls.gov/OCO) and the Occupational Information Network (O*NET) (www.online.onetcenter.org)

Summary

Using a scale floor plan aids in arranging furniture. It shows the dimensions and features of a room and allows the movement of furniture templates to create the best space plan. Good furniture arrangement is dependent on how the furniture and the room are used. Arrangements should provide for adequate clearance space to avoid interfering with room features and traffic patterns.

Selecting furniture involves several steps and begins with prioritizing furniture needs. Then you decide how much you can afford, what is your lifestyle, what are your furniture styles and design preferences, where and how to shop, and when to shop. Finally, you should consult information sources.

To acquire more furniture for your money, you can stretch your furniture dollars in a number of ways. Shopping for bargains, choosing multipurpose furniture, or buying furniture that needs finishing or assembly can save money. Reusing furniture also saves money. Using an eclectic look in your rooms can be a design solution while you acquire furniture over a period of time or it may be a permanent style choice.

Review the Facts

1. Why is using a scale floor plan an effective method for deciding furniture arrangements?

2. Identify three factors to consider when planning a furniture arrangement.

3. Why are traffic patterns and clearance space important to creating effective furniture arrangements?

4. Explain the importance of prioritizing furniture needs.

5. Why should consumers decide on the amount of money to spend for furniture before shopping begins?

6. Summarize a lifestyle need that may impact how to select appropriate furniture.

7. List three places to shop for furniture and give one advantage of each.

8. Identify possible shopping drawbacks with each of the following types of sales: (A) loss leader; (B) seasonal; (C) closeout: (D) damaged and discontinued items.

9. What are five sources of information useful for selecting furniture? Choose one and summarize why it will be useful to you.

10. Name five ways to stretch furniture dollars.

11. When is renovating a piece of furniture most cost-effective?

12. Contrast restoring furniture with renewing it. When might you do each?

13. Summarize the steps in restoring furniture.

14. Why does the eclectic design style help people stretch their furniture dollars?

Think Critically

15. **Analyze priorities.** A client of yours needs assistance in furnishing a small two-bedroom apartment. The kitchen, dining, and living areas are open to one another. The family has one school-age child who plays soccer for a community team. Your client has beds and dressers, and a limited budget for making furniture purchases. Analyze what furniture items are priorities for your client. What items are lower on the priority list? What cost-saving options would you suggest?

16. **Recognize value.** What ways can you determine if a piece of furniture is a valuable bargain? Write your response in a one-page paper. Support your response with appropriate examples.

17. **Assess preferences.** Suppose you have a new interior design client. This is the first time your client has worked with a designer in regard to a design scheme for the home. You do not have any information about your client's furniture-style preferences. What approach would you take in assessing your client's preferences? What questions might you ask? Write a short paper summarizing your approach to assessing your client's preferences.

Community Links

18. **Scale floor plan.** Select and measure one room in your home or in a home of someone you know. Following the chapter guidelines, draw a scale floor plan of the space on graph paper. Make templates of either existing furniture or new furniture, and create two different plans for arranging the furniture. Carefully consider clearance space and allow for traffic patterns.

19. **Price comparison.** Compare prices on identical pieces of furniture of the same brand name and manufacturer—such as a sofa or dining room table—by visiting two different local stores. Then use the Internet to locate one or more sources for the same pieces of furniture, and identify the prices and the shipping costs. Are the prices similar or different? What factors do you think might impact price differences or similarities? Which location had the best price? Share your findings with the class.

20. **Going green.** Because many consumers today desire products that are *green* or *sustainable*, some furniture stores are offering options to meet consumer preferences. Visit one or more furniture stores in your community to investigate the availability of green furniture products. What options are available? Interview a sales associate regarding green purchasing trends at the store or in the community.

Academic Connections

21. **Writing.** Presume you are a consumer reporter for a local news publication. Your assignment is to evaluate sofas and chairs from a manufacturer of your choice. You are to evaluate the product construction and materials used in manufacturing. In addition, identify care and maintenance methods recommended by the manufacturer. What are the manufacturer's customer service policies? How can this information benefit consumers and interior designers alike? Write a report summarizing your findings.

22. **Science.** Use Internet or print resources to investigate how eco-friendly fibers and fabrics go through the manufacturing process from the farm to a consumer's home. What factors about the growing process make these fabrics *organic* or eco-friendly? What processes do fiber and fabric manufacturers use to create these eco-friendly materials for home use? How do these materials benefit consumers? society? Prepare a summary of your findings to share with the class.

23. **Math.** Suppose the sectional sofa you have identified for your new family room design is on sale at a local furniture store. The sofa cost is $1295.00—a 30 percent savings off the original price. Because you have not had time to save the funds for your sofa, you decide to use a credit card to make the purchase. The credit card interest rate is 13.9%. The credit card company requires a minimum payment of 2% of the total purchase; however, you are able to pay $100.00 per month toward the bill. Use the *Credit Card Interest Calculator* on the American Consumer Credit Counseling Web site to calculate the cost of financing the sofa. How many months will it take you to pay for the sofa? How much will the total interest cost? What are the pros and cons of buying the sofa with credit?

Technology Applications

24. **CADD floor plan.** Use a CADD design program to create a scale floor plan and furniture arrangement for a living room that measures 20 feet by 18 feet. Show the placement of one door and three windows. Place furniture pieces—such as a sofa, two chairs, two side tables, and a coffee table—in the room in three different arrangements. You may decide to delete or add more furniture keeping in mind the best quality available within your client's budget constraints. Use the chart in Fig. 16-2 to check the clearance-space measurements between furniture pieces in your designs. Do your designs meet recommendations? If not, redesign the arrangements as necessary to meet the recommended clearances.

25. **Customer service policies.** Search the Internet for several furniture manufacturers that sell furniture online. Locate the customer service policies of the companies on the Web site. Identify whether the following questions are answered:

    A. How does the company handle returned items?

    B. How does the company handle items damaged in shipping?

    C. What are the shipping costs?

    Print off copies of the answers to these questions from each manufacturer. Based on what you find, how would you advise a client who is considering shopping for furniture online? If the policies are not explained online, how could a consumer get the information? Summarize your advice and recommendations in writing.

26. **Shopping online.** Use the Internet to investigate resources for buying furniture. What options to consumers have? How do costs differ for online buying? What alternatives do consumers have for finding furniture bargains for little or no cost? How might a consumer determine which online shopping sites are reliable?

Design Practice

27. **Combination design.** Suppose a client asked you to design a living and dining room combination in a space measuring 20 by 26 feet. Since the space has windows overlooking spectacular views on two walls, your challenge is to avoid obstructing the view. The windows extend from the ceiling to three feet off the floor, and the room has one windowless wall. The fourth side of the space is open to the kitchen and a hallway leading to other rooms. Select and place furniture appropriate for a young couple that enjoys informally entertaining up to a dozen friends at a time. Identify the furniture pieces you would choose for the room. Also, create a floor plan showing the placement of the pieces. You may add electrical floor plugs for lamps and other electrical needs.

28. **Portfolio.** Review the floor plans you have created for this chapter. Refine the plans. Then use presentation software to create a design presentation suitable for client review. Save your presentation as an example of your work.

Chapter Service Project

With your team, use the FCCLA *Planning Process* to plan, carry out, and evaluate a project for the FCCLA *Chapter Service Project* STAR Event. Develop a project that involves collecting and recycling home furnishings. Consider partnering with such organizations as *Habitat for Humanity* and the *Habitat Restore* or *Goodwill Industries International, Inc.*

Use the *STAR Events Manual* on the FCCLA Web site (www.fcclainc.org) to identify specific competition requirements for your project. See your adviser for information as needed.

CHAPTER 17

Window Treatments, Lighting, and Accessories

Terms to Learn

window treatment
draperies
curtains
shades
shutters
blinds
incandescent light
lumen
tungsten-halogen (quartz) light
fluorescent light
compact fluorescent lamp (CFL)
fiber optics
light-emitting diode (LED)
reflected light
absorbed light
diffused light
color temperature
color rendering index (CRI)
general lighting
direct lighting
indirect lighting
task lighting
wattage
foot-candle
accent lighting
structural light fixture
nonstructural lighting
accessories

Chapter Objectives

After studying this chapter, you will be able to

- summarize different types of window treatments.

- contrast types of lighting available for residential and commercial uses.

- summarize the properties of light.

- plan residential lighting for visual comfort, safety, and beauty.

- distinguish between structural and nonstructural lighting.

- summarize guidelines for the use, placement, and care of accessories.

Reading with Purpose

Write the main headings in the chapter on a sheet of paper, leaving space under each heading. As you read the chapter, write three or more main points that you learned as you read each passage.

Some of the final steps for furnishing a room are selecting window treatments, providing good lighting, and choosing accessories that reflect the personality of those who inhabit the space. You will continue to use the elements and principles of design that you learned in Chapters 10 through 12 as you learn to add the finishing touches to a design scheme.

Window Treatments

Window treatments are applications added to window units either for helping control the home environment or for purely decorative purposes. Be sure to consider the style, size, and location of windows when choosing window treatments. Other very important considerations for selecting window treatments include the need to control sunlight and noise, and to provide the ventilation, privacy, and insulation for each room.

Some window treatments can help control the amount of natural light that enters a room by blocking all or part of the light from entering. For example, a treatment should provide both sun control and privacy in a sleeping area for adults or children. However, privacy and sun control may be less important for a child's playroom. For a sunroom, window treatments should allow as much light and air ventilation as possible. In contrast, a media room or home theater requires window treatments to regulate or block the amount of sunlight entering the room.

Window treatments include draperies, curtains, shades, shutters, blinds, and decorative top treatments. The right window treatments can enhance the appearance of a room. Certain treatments can also camouflage windows that are not in proportion to the rest of the room.

Sometimes windows require no treatments, especially when privacy is not a concern. If the shape of the window is too difficult to treat or if the window itself is an important architectural focal point of the room, you may choose to leave it untreated. In 17-l, the uniquely shaped windows are left uncovered to give the room a dramatic look and let light enter freely. Furthermore, if windows provide a beautiful view of the outdoors, you may prefer having no window treatments.

Another consideration in the selection of the type of window treatment is the feeling you wish to create in the room. Is the mood of the room to be formal or informal? Is the style of the space to be traditional or contemporary? Depending on the design of the window treatment, an interior designer can create many different moods and effects.

Other important considerations for the selection of window treatments deal with the initial cost of purchasing the treatments and the subsequent cost of

17-1
These striking windows need no treatment.

Image Courtesy of Andersen Corporation

GREEN CHOICES

Promoting Indoor Air Quality

Rising energy costs for home heating and cooling can lead to more ways to tighten the home. Often the ventilation is reduced to the point that indoor air quality (IAQ) issues can become a problem. Because interior designers promote the health and safety of the public, they should take care to specify interior building components to promote good indoor air quality.

Interior designers responsibilities to green and sustainable design include but are not limited to

- Selecting wood products for cabinets, floors, wall panels and furniture that reduce the amount of formaldehyde and other volatile organic compound (VOC) emissions.
- Specifying paint products that are water-based latex instead of oil-based paints with VOC emission rating documented at less than 100 grams per liter. It is good practice to ventilate the space for five days after painting prior to occupancy.
- Since carpet floor coverings can also emit harmful gases, selecting carpeting that the Carpet and Rug Institute (CRI) certifies to have passed their indoor air quality testing program.
- Specifying renewable flooring products such as bamboo or linoleum that help reduce the amount of land and natural resources that went into their production.
- Designing around standard product sizes to reduce material waste.
- Selecting materials that can be recycled in their next life or that are sustainable to reduce adding to landfills.

maintaining them. Keep in mind that custom or made-to-measure window treatments are more costly than ready-made treatments that are mass-produced. In today's market, more and more attractive ready-made styles and options are available. Also, pattern companies offer many designs for creating your own window treatments or for hiring a drapery workroom to do so.

Whether you purchase or create your own window treatments, give careful consideration to the fabrics you select. Are they colorfast? Do they require dry cleaning or laundering? Can simple dusting or vacuuming maintain the appearance of the treatments? Do not invest in a window treatment that you or a client have neither the time nor money to maintain.

Draperies and Curtains

Draperies and curtains are the most common window treatments. They are extremely versatile and can fit into any decor. The type of draperies or curtains you choose depends on the room's decor and the function of the windows.

Draperies

Draperies are fabric panels with pleats that cover windows completely or are pulled to the side. Depending on the design and type of fabric, draperies can fit in any style decor. Draperies can be opaque or translucent. *Opaque* draperies block light, while *translucent* draperies permit the passage of light. They can be lined or unlined. Lining draperies blocks some sunlight from entering the room and protects the draperies from sun fading. The lining also adds body, makes draperies hang or drape better, and increases their ability to insulate.

You can use draperies alone or with other window treatments, such as curtains, shades, blinds, and decorative top treatments. In 17-2, center draw-drapery panels were the designer selection for this window. Opening them during the day allows light to enter the room. Closing them at night provides complete privacy and helps insulate the room. A decorative top treatment hides the drapery hardware.

The names of different types of draperies represent how they operate. *Draw draperies* open and close from the center or side with a pull stick or cord on one end of the curtain rod. You cannot open or close *stationary draperies*. Permanent placement of stationary draperies is usually at one or both sides of a window.

Curtains

Curtains are flat fabric panels that hang to the left and right of a window or may completely cover it. Like draperies, the design and fabric selected for the curtains impacts the style and mood of the room. Curtains usually have a rod-pocket hem at the top. You slip the curtain onto the curtain rod through the rod pocket and gather it to the desired fullness. Some curtains may hang from the curtain rod with decorative drapery hardware or tabs of sewn fabric. The rod itself may be plain or decorative, such as a grooved wooden pole or a pole of brushed nickel or wrought iron, as in 17-3. Ruffles, bands of fabric, and trim can add interest to the panels. The use of tiebacks to pull the curtain panel away from the window gives a curvy shape to the panel instead of simply a straight line.

17-3
These bedroom curtains are mounted on a metal rod and are attached with metal rings. The designer used two fabrics, a floral pattern and a solid, to create this beautiful installation.

Calico Corners—Calico Home Stores

17-2
These drapery panels provide sunlight during the day and privacy at night. The valance top treatment is both decorative and functional since it hides hardware.

Calico Corners—Calico Home Stores

The amount of light, insulation, or privacy curtains provide depends on the fabric. Curtains from sheer fabric give a room a light, airy feeling. For more privacy, use heavier fabrics. Using heavier fabrics, however, may make the room appear darker.

Cafe curtains are horizontal panels hung in tiers to cover part of a window. The top of each panel is joined to rings that slip over a curtain rod. Cafe curtains do not have a draw cord as do draw draperies. Instead, you open cafe curtains by pushing them to the window sides to control air, light, and privacy. With cafe curtains, one tier generally covers only the bottom half of the window. More than one tier can completely cover a window. By changing the width or the number of tiers, you can achieve a variety of looks with cafe curtains. Use cafe curtains in an informal setting.

The length of draperies and curtains should fall to *stool length*, *apron length*, or *floor length*. If the bottom edge of a window treatment falls at any other place, it will look either too short or too long. To correctly measure the length of draperies and curtains, use the methods in 17-4.

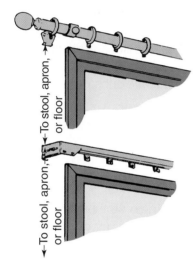

Draperies
Hang traverse rod 1 inch above the frame for decorative rods and 2 inches above the frame for conventional rods. In either case, the rod should be at least 4 inches above the glass.

Measure from either the bottom of the decorative rings or the top of the conventional rods. Measure to the stool, apron, or floor. If measuring to the floor, subtract 1 inch for clearance.

Curtains
Measure from the top of the frame to the stool, apron, or floor. If measuring to the floor, subtract 1 inch for clearance.

Cafe curtains
Top tier: Measure from the top rod to the desired hem. This tier usually covers the lower rod.

Lower tier: Measure from the lower rod to the stool, apron, or floor. If measuring to the floor, subtract 1 inch for clearance.

A   B   C

17-4
Different methods are used to measure draperies, curtains, and cafe curtains.

HEALTH/SAFETY

Window Treatment Dangers

Each month a child between 7 months and 10 years old dies from strangulation in cords attached to window treatments. Infants who are sleeping or playing can accidentally become entangled in the cords. Young children peering through windows can fall and become caught in the cords.

In 2009, after 15 years of issuing consumer warnings and recalling more than five million window coverings, the U.S. Consumer Product Safety Commission (CPSC) acted again. The CPSC was joined by the Window Covering Safety Council (WCSC), an organization of manufacturers, importers, and retailers. They announced a voluntary recall affecting millions more blinds and shades. Recalls affect Roman shades, roller and roll-up blinds, and vertical and horizontal blinds.

In homes where infants and children live or visit, the CPSC recommends that consumers examine their window treatments and replace products with exposed cords. Exposed cords may be found on the front, back, or sides of a product. It is best to use only cordless window coverings on all windows. Check the CPSC's window coverings recall list and avoid those products. Also, never leave cribs or items children can climb, such as toys and furniture, near windows.

For information about recalls and the latest recommendations, check CPSC's Web site at www.CPSC.gov.

Shades, Shutters, and Blinds

Shades block unwanted light, such as intense sunlight in the afternoon or streetlight at night. They are simple to operate and can cover all or part of a window. Shades vary in appearance to go with almost any decor. The fabric and other materials used in their construction affect the amount of light control, insulation, and privacy they provide.

- *Roller shades* come in various colors. They also come in various degrees of opaqueness. Many people commonly use these shades in informal rooms.

- *Roman shades* are fabric window treatments that stack into horizontal pleats when they are raised, but hang flat when closed. Installation of most Roman shades is generally within the window molding.

Depending on the fabric choice, they can adapt to many design styles.

- *Balloon shades* are also of fabric construction and form soft poufs along the bottom, 17-5. These shades are similar in operation to Roman shades. They received their name from the balloon shape they take when they are raised. Balloon shades are also very adaptable to different design styles depending on the choice of fabric and pattern.

- *Pleated shades* are very popular in today's market. Manufacturers use synthetic materials to construct them, and they are available in accordion or honeycomb styles, 17-6. Like Roman and balloon shades, pleated shades are raised and lowered with a cord. They are available in many solid colors, patterns, and textures.

They may be opaque or translucent. The honeycomb style shades offer excellent insulation qualities due to an insulating channel of air between the shade layers. They work extremely well in contemporary settings.

Because some window treatments block air movement, you cannot use them on windows that provide ventilation. Shutters are appropriate choices for these windows. **Shutters** are vertical panels that are hinged together to open and close much like a folding door. They are constructed of wood or synthetic materials. Within the frames of the vertical panels are movable horizontal slats or louvers. The louvers are

17-5
The weight of fabric selected for balloon shades determines the amount of sun control, insulation, and privacy.

Calico Corners—Calico Home Stores

A

B

17-6
The pleated shades selected for this large window area are both beautiful and functional (A). To add interest to the pleated shade in this child's room, a shirred fabric valance was added (B).

(A) Permission granted by Hunter Douglas, Inc. to use copyrighted designs. Designs © Hunter Douglas, Inc.
(B) Kirsch

adjustable to allow sunlight control, ventilation, and privacy. The width of wooden louvers in shutters may vary from 1½ to 4½ inches. They adapt well to both formal and informal room settings.

Blinds are window treatments with slats that can be tilted, raised and lowered, or moved to the side. They are often made of wood, metal, plastic, or fabric. Blinds can be custom-made to fit windows with unusual shapes or placements, 17-7. There are three basic styles of blinds.

- *Horizontal blinds*, or venetian blinds, can be raised completely to uncover a window. Adjustments to the angle of the slats help control the amount of air and light entering the room. The slat widths vary from 2 inches to 3 inches. Horizontal blinds appear most often in informal settings.

- *Miniblinds* are horizontal blinds with narrow 1-inch slats. They operate exactly like other horizontal blinds in regard to raising and lowering and adjusting the slats. They also are most often used in informal rooms.

- *Vertical blinds* have slats that move to one side to uncover a window. The slats are generally 4 inches wide and vary in length. In order to control the amounts of air and light that enter a room, the angle of the slats can be adjusted. Usage of vertical blinds is more common in contemporary designs.

Decorative Window-Top Treatments

Decorative window-top treatments easily combine with draperies, curtains, shades, shutters, or blinds to add interest to the window installation. Such decorative top treatments include the following:

- **Swag.** A *swag* treatment has softly pleated fabric hanging in a curve across the top of the window. (Refer again to 17-2.)

- **Valance.** A *valance* is a horizontal treatment across the top of the window. It can hide the drapery or curtain hardware. The many styles of valances depend on the cut and construction of the fabric, the degree of gathering, and the installation hardware used. (Refer again to 17-5.)

- **Cornice.** A *cornice* is also a horizontal treatment that is usually constructed of wood. The wood is then padded and covered with fabric. Some formal cornices may actually be wood that has been carved in an attractive design. Other more informal cornices may have been painted or stenciled with a design.

- **Lambrequin.** The construction of a *lambrequin* follows the same manner as a cornice, but also extends down the left and right sides of the window.

Decorative window-top treatments may use matching or complementary fabrics and designs to add interest to the treatment. Also, using such trims as decorative braid, tassels, and cording can add a custom touch. Depending on the fabric choices, you can use these top treatments in many different room styles.

Types of Artificial Light

Natural light is not always available so artificial light is also needed. Previously, the two main kinds of artificial light used in homes were incandescent and fluorescent light. However, other types of light sources are replacing old technologies and are becoming more available to consumers.

A—Miniblinds Between Glass Panels

B—Wooden Blinds

C—Miniblinds

D—Vertical Blinds

17-7
Special miniblinds were installed between the panels of glass in these windows to control light (A). The wooden blinds installed in these windows are a complement to the masculine feeling of the room. The arches are left untreated to create a focal point (B). By adjusting these miniblinds, a person enjoying this space can have privacy or a wonderful view of the neighborhood (C). These custom vertical blinds provide an excellent solution to the treatment of this arched window (D).

Incandescent Light

Incandescent light is produced when electric current passes through a fine tungsten filament inside a bulb. The electricity heats the filament until it glows and gives off light, 17-8. Over time, the filament deteriorates, leaving a dark coating on the bulb. This coating lowers the light level coming from the bulb, making it very inefficient. Incandescent bulbs vary in shape and size, but they all work the same way.

Incandescent lightbulbs used in homes range from 15 to 250 watts. (See Chapter 9 for an explanation of watts.) When comparing two incandescent bulbs, the one with the higher wattage will give more light. For two incandescent bulbs with the same wattage, compare the lumen output of the bulbs. A **lumen** is a measurement of the amount of light a bulb produces. A higher lumen number means the bulb emits more light, therefore, making it a more efficient choice. Incandescent bulbs, in general, are not very efficient sources of light. They produce very little light for the energy used, and use most of their energy for the production of heat.

Most incandescent bulbs for home use have a *frost finish* that covers the entire inside surface of the bulb. The main purpose of the frost finish is to reduce glare and make shadows appear softer. Some people prefer to use clear bulbs that do not have the frost coating in some light fixtures. Bulbs without a frost finish produce a great deal of glare. To eliminate the glare, use them only in fixtures that hide the bulbs completely from view.

Many kinds of special incandescent bulbs are available. One is the *three-way bulb*. Sets of filaments operate separately or together to produce different amounts of light. For example, a three-way bulb may have the light level options of 50, 100, and 150 watts. Some bulbs have silver or aluminum coatings on the sides of the bulb which focuses the light in one direction. Other bulbs have a silicone coating. This coating prevents the glass from shattering if the bulb breaks.

In the coming years, incandescent bulbs will become a thing of the past. In 2007, The Energy Independence and Security Act passed in the United States established energy efficiency standards for many types of lightbulbs. These include incandescent bulbs and the proposed phase-out of incandescent and other inefficient bulbs over time. The law states that all lightbulbs must use 25 to 30 percent less energy by 2014.

Tungsten-Halogen (Quartz) Light

Tungsten-halogen (quartz) lights are another form of incandescent lighting. In this type of bulb, halogen gas combines with tungsten molecules to activate a filament inside a quartz enclosure. Halogen bulbs burn more intensely than standard incandescent bulbs.

Tungsten-halogen bulbs have many advantages over regular incandescent bulbs. They produce a whiter type of light. The amount of light in an

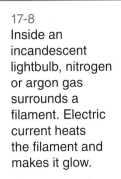

17-8
Inside an incandescent lightbulb, nitrogen or argon gas surrounds a filament. Electric current heats the filament and makes it glow.

U.S. Department of Energy

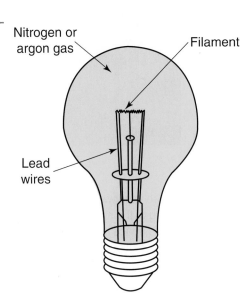

Nitrogen or argon gas

Filament

Lead wires

aging tungsten-halogen bulb does not decrease as much as in regular bulbs. Also, tungsten-halogen bulbs last up to three times longer than regular incandescent bulbs. Tungsten-halogen bulbs are less energy efficient than fluorescent lights, but more energy efficient than other types of incandescent lights. These lights, however, become extremely hot. Care should be taken when handling them or placing them near combustible materials.

Fluorescent Light

Fluorescent light is produced in a glass tube by releasing electricity through a mercury vapor to make invisible ultraviolet rays. A coating of fluorescent material on the inside of the glass tube converts these rays into visible light rays. There is a delay between the release of electric current and the production of light.

Fluorescent light is more energy efficient than incandescent light. A fluorescent tube produces about four times as much light as an incandescent bulb of the same wattage.

Fluorescent tubes are more expensive than incandescent bulbs, but they last longer and are less expensive to use. Fluorescent tubes can last up to 20,000 hours and use about 40 watts of electricity. Fluorescent tubes are straight or circular, and available in various sizes.

The color of light from a fluorescent tube varies by changing the coating of fluorescent material in the tube. The two types of tubes are cool-white light which intensifies cool colors like blues and greens and warm-white light which intensifies yellows, reds, and oranges. Common uses for both types of lights are often in kitchens, bathrooms, and workshops. Deluxe cool-white light closely imitates natural daylight. Full-spectrum fluorescent tubes are designed to replicate natural daylight.

Compact Fluorescent Lamps (CFL)

The **compact fluorescent lamp (CFL)** is a type of fluorescent lamp that is replacing old incandescent bulbs. Compact fluorescent bulbs screw into regular lightbulb sockets and come in many sizes and shapes, 17-9. Some CFLs have a cork-screw shape and newer models look like standard incandescent bulbs. CFLs produce light differently than incandescent bulbs. With an incandescent bulb, electric current runs through a wire filament and heats the filament until it starts to glow. In a CFL, electric current runs through a tube containing argon gas and a small amount of mercury vapor. This generates *invisible* ultraviolet light that excites a fluorescent (or phosphor) coating on the inside of the tube. When this coating

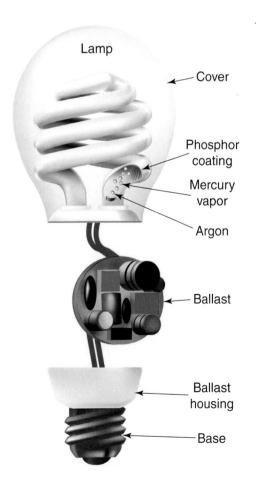

17-9
Although compact fluorescent bulbs look and function differently from regular incandescent lightbulbs, you can use them in the same fixtures.

Provided by ENERGY STAR at www.energystar.gov

is excited, it emits *visible* light. CFLs use about 75 percent less energy and operate for nearly 9,000 hours while using fewer watts of electricity, 17-10.

Compact fluorescent lamps help the environment. Overall, CFLs create less energy during manufacturing. For example, it takes just as much time to produce six to 10 incandescent bulbs as it takes to make one CFL. During the life of a CFL, it will use four times less energy than six to 10 incandescent bulbs in the same time period. The electricity you save by replacing an incandescent bulb with a CFL equals the energy produced by burning about 450 pounds of coal.

Handle CFLs carefully when taking them home after purchase. Broken CFLs can emit a small amount of dangerous mercury, a risk to human health. Do not throw CFLs into the regular trash to avoid contaminating landfills with mercury. You must recycle or properly dispose of CFLs according to your community's waste removal guidelines. Many home-improvement stores and community agencies also offer free recycling for CFLs.

Lighting from Fiber Optics

Fiber optics is a type of heatless light produced by passing an electric current through a cable containing very fine strands of glass. These cables are primarily used in communications (such as Internet and TV), but are also useful for lighting. Optical fibers permit such transmissions over longer distances and at higher bandwidths than other forms of communication. *Bandwidth* refers to how much data you can send through a network connection. Fiber optic lighting gives off no heat or ultraviolet rays that can distort colors.

Fiber optic lighting lends a dramatic effect in interior spaces. In museums, it can recreate star constellations on ceilings as well as give finishing effects to exhibits. Using fiber optic lights can also provide energy-efficient and somewhat unique decorative lighting at home.

Light-Emitting Diodes (LED)

Extremely long-lasting bulbs are made from **light-emitting diodes (LED)**. LEDs are composed of crystals on silicon chips about the size of a grain of salt. These crystals produce light when a low electric current passes through them. An LED bulb can last 100,000 hours or more. In comparison with other bulbs, it will last about 10 times longer than CFLs and over 100 times longer than incandescent bulbs. The initial cost of LED lighting is currently much more expensive than incandescent lighting. However, LED lighting lasts longer,

17-10
This chart compares incandescent and CFL lamps. Notice that the CFLs use less energy but provide the same lumen output.

Comparing Incandescent and CFL Lamps		
Incandescent Bulbs (Watts)	**Minimum Light Output** (Lumens)	**ENERGY STAR Qualified Equivalent CFLs** (Watts)
40	450	9 to 13
60	800	13 to 15
75	1,100	18 to 25
100	1,600	23 to 30
150	2,600	30 to 52

U.S. Department of Energy, ENERGY STAR at www.energystar.gov

consumes less energy, is more durable, and gives off less heat than other traditional lighting methods. LED lighting will most likely replace many other types of lighting sources in the future.

The small size and flexibility of LEDs make them a promising option for a number of general lighting purposes. For example, with interior spaces you may use LEDs for recessed down lights, under-cabinet lighting in the kitchen, and as portable desk/task lighting. LED lights are also useful in outdoor lighting especially for landscaping. They can provide necessary surface brightness while using less energy and requiring less maintenance.

The Properties of Light

You can use light to achieve several different effects in your home. To do this, you first need to understand the various properties of light. Objects and surfaces can absorb or reflect light. It can shine directly on a certain spot or lighten a whole room. By knowing the properties of light, you can make light work for you.

Reflected Light

Light, color, and texture are closely related. Without light, there is no color. In turn, colors reflect and absorb various amounts of light. Surfaces with rough textures look dark because tiny shadows form where the light does not reach. Together, light, color, and texture greatly affect the appearance of rooms.

Reflected light is light that bounces off surfaces. It seems to come from these surfaces as well as from its source. Light colors and smooth, shiny surfaces on objects and backgrounds all reflect light. Background treatments in the home also reflect light. Some surfaces reflect so much light that they produce glare or

bright light shining in a person's eyes. It is best to avoid lighting placement that would create glare. See 17-11 to learn how much light various backgrounds can reflect.

Absorbed Light

Absorbed light is light that is drawn in by a surface. Rough textures and dark colors absorb most of the available light rays. If light is absorbed, it cannot be reflected. For example, suppose you use rough textures and dark colors in large areas of your home. Because these rough textures and dark colors absorb light, the areas appear smaller. A room with many dark surfaces may need additional light for certain activities.

Diffused Light

Diffused light is light that scatters over a large area. It has no glare, which is the most troublesome aspect of lighting. Instead, it creates a soft appearance. Devices that diffuse light—or *diffusers*—spread the light evenly. An example of a diffuser is the frosted or white finish on incandescent and fluorescent bulbs. Other diffusers are more apparent, such

Reflected Light		
Background	**Minimum**	**Maximum**
Ceilings		
Pale color tints	60%	90%
Walls		
Natural wood	5%	50%
Light colors	70%	80%
Medium colors	35%	60%
Dark colors	5%	25%
Floors		
Carpeting, tiles, woods	15%	35%
Countertops	30%	50%

17-11
This chart gives minimum and maximum amounts of reflected light.

as the covers for light fixtures. These diffusers are usually made of frosted or translucent glass. Lamp shades also serve as diffusers.

Light Temperature

The light given off by various light sources differs in **color temperature**. The color of a light is rated in *kelvin* (K)—a temperature scale. Light from these sources is divided into the following three general tones:

- Orange (incandescent), which is 2700–3000°K

- White (halogen), which is 3000–3600°K

- Blue (fluorescent), which is 3000°K for warm, and 4000°K for cool

The color of the light affects how things will appear in that light. When selecting lights for a certain purpose or space, keep in mind how the light will affect the surfaces around it. For example, skin tones are best viewed by light with a color temperature in the warm range of about 2800–3500°K. Color temperatures are listed with most light sources.

Color Rendering Index (CRI)

The **color rendering index (CRI)** of light indicates how well light from a source will bring out the true color. The CRI scale is from 1–100, with 100 equaling the color rendering of daylight. A CRI of 80 or above is good. The closer the CRI of a light source is to 100, the more accurately the light will reproduce color. Information for many light sources will list it as a CRI rating.

Functions of Lighting

Lighting serves several purposes. It illuminates areas that may pose a safety hazard. Lighting also focuses attention on beautiful objects or attractive architectural features. The most common use of lighting, however, is illuminating the environment so people can comfortably see, especially when performing certain tasks.

Lighting for Visual Comfort

To create visual comfort in your home, you need two basic types of lighting: general (ambient) and task. The type and amount needed vary from room to room.

General Lighting (Ambient)

General lighting, or ambient lighting, provides a uniform level of light throughout a room. Achievement of general lighting occurs through either of two ways: direct or indirect lighting.

- **Direct lighting.** Lighting that shines directly toward an object is **direct lighting**. It provides the most light possible to a specific area, such as when using a lamp in a room, 17-12. If used alone, direct lighting creates a

17-12
The use of direct lighting in this kitchen helps make food preparation and cooking easier and safer.

sharp contrast between light and dark areas, which can cause eye fatigue. Therefore, if you need direct lighting for a task, use other lights in the room, too.

- **Indirect lighting.** You can also achieve general lighting through indirect lighting. **Indirect lighting** is directed toward a surface, such as a ceiling or wall that reflects the light into the room, 17-13. Indirect lighting may provide soft light for a large area. However, it does not provide enough light for detailed work.

General lighting should light a room well enough for occupants to see objects clearly and move about safely. The amount of general lighting needed depends on the shape, size, and use of the room.

Task Lighting

General lighting does not always supply enough light for visual comfort. In such cases, you can supplement with task lighting. **Task lighting** is lighting used in areas where specific activities require more light. Using the right amount of task lighting helps prevent eyestrain.

The amount of task lighting you need depends on the activity. The finer the detail or the faster the action taking place, the more light you need. For instance, playing table tennis requires more light than shooting pool. Tasks such as writing letters, carving wood, or sewing require higher levels of task lighting to assure that you can see well enough to perform the task.

Task lighting in one part of a room can serve as general lighting for another part. For instance, if you are reading in one corner of a family room, the lamp that you use for task lighting adds to the general lighting of the entire room.

To get the right amount of good quality light, combine general and task lighting. Together, they give adequate light without sharp contrast.

17-13
Indirect lighting is reflected on the wall and plant on the left side of this room. Direct lighting accents the floral arrangement on the center table.

Randall Whitehead/ Lighting Designer: Randall Whitehead, Light Source

Measuring Light

The following terms are important to the measurement of light. **Wattage** is the amount of electricity a bulb uses. As you recall, a *lumen* is a measurement of the amount of light a bulb produces. One lumen is the amount of light produced by a source equaling the intensity of one standard candle. **Foot-candle** is a measurement of how much light reaches an object or a surface. One foot-candle is the amount of light a standard candle gives to an object one foot away. One foot-candle equals one lumen per square foot. You can measure the amount of light reaching a surface (foot-candle) with a light meter. See 17-14 for amounts of light needed for various activities.

Lighting for Safety

Lighting for safety is very important. It can help prevent accidents and fires. Accidents can occur in dim and dark areas. To guard against accidents, plan lighting where it will work best for you. If you can answer "yes" to the following questions, you will know your lighting promotes safety. Can you

17-14
Use this chart to determine the approximate amount of light needed for certain activities.

Lighting for the Home	
Task	**Base Foot-Candle Levels**
Dining	15
Grooming	50
Ironing	50
Kitchen Tasks	
• Food preparation and cleaning that involves difficult seeing tasks	100
• Serving and other noncritical tasks	30
Laundry Tasks	
• Preparation, sorting, and hand washing	50
• Washer and dryer areas	30
Reading, Writing, and Games	
• Reading reproductions and poor copies, writing, and intense studying	75
• Reading books, magazines, and newspapers,	30
• Playing games	30
Sewing	
• Dark fabrics	150
• Medium fabrics	100
• Light fabrics	75
• Occasional sewing or high contrast fabrics	30

- light your way as you go from room to room?
- switch lights on or off from each doorway?
- turn on stairway lighting as you go up or down stairs?
- light entrances as you enter?
- control garage or carport lighting from inside or outside the house?
- control outside lighting from inside the house?

Another aspect of lighting for safety concerns safe wiring. If wiring is unsafe, it can start fires in the home. To assure safety, the wiring used for lighting should meet standards set by various groups. For example, the National Electrical Code® is a standard with which all wiring should comply. Often there are local requirements, too.

When you purchase electrical lighting fixtures, buy only those with a safety seal from a safety-testing organization such as Underwriters Laboratories (UL), 17-15. The seal tells you that the light was manufactured according to safety standards. However, a safety seal does not guarantee that the parts will remain safe. You need to use lights safely and watch for possible dangers. Always read and follow the instructions for the use and care of the lights. This includes using bulbs of the correct wattage for the fixture as the manufacturer specifies. Using a larger wattage bulb than specified could possibly lead to

17-15
A seal on a lamp showing UL or CSA assures you the lamp was made according to safety guidelines.

Underwriters Laboratories

17-16
Exterior lighting gives this stylish home a dramatic appearance.

California Redwood Association

overheating and a fire or damage to the light fixture.

Lighting for Beauty

While all light can be decorative, the purpose of some lighting is for beauty alone. Soft light can create a quiet, restful mood. Sharp light can highlight the focal point in a room. When lighting serves as a highlight, it is called **accent lighting**. Some lighting is decorative, merely because of the lighting fixture's design which adds beauty to a space.

You can also use decorative lighting outside the home, 17-16. Homes may have yard lights next to the street. Lights near entrances are also common. Lighting patios for night use adds to the outdoor living space which makes the lighting functional as well as decorative. In such areas, the light should be attractive. Avoid harsh and glaring light that you and your neighbors may find annoying. With the right choices, you can have pleasant, glowing light.

Structural and Nonstructural Lighting

Lighting affects the appearance of a room. So does the delivery of light to a room. The two ways of delivering light are through structural and nonstructural lighting.

Structural Lighting

A **structural light fixture** is one that is permanently built into a home. It is either included in the original plans or added during a remodeling project.

When you choose structural light fixtures, keep them in harmony with other aspects of the room's design. When choosing fixtures, consider the following points:

- Diffused light gives more visual comfort than exposed bulbs, which can produce glare.

- Fixtures that can change position allow for usage in more than one way. Some fixtures you can raise or lower. Others swing or swivel for a variety of effects.

- Fixtures that provide different light levels—such as three-way bulbs or dimmer switches—allow for more flexibility with light levels in the home.

There are many types of structural lighting fixtures, as you can see in 17-17. *Valance lighting fixtures* are mounted over windows and hidden by the window

A—Recessed Downlights

B—Track Lighting

C—Task Lighting

D—Combination Lighting
(surface-mounted decorative, recessed, and natural light)

17-17
Structural lighting can create special effects in a room. It must be planned while the dwelling is being built or remodeled.

valance. Since the window valance is open at the top and bottom, fluorescent light is directed upward and downward, giving both direct and indirect lighting.

Bracket lighting fixtures are just like valance lighting fixtures, except they are used on walls or over work areas. The fluorescent light shines upward and downward. Bracket lighting can serve as general or accent lighting.

Cornice lighting fixtures are concealed sources of light that are mounted to the wall near the ceiling. Fluorescent light shines downward, giving direct light only. You can use cornice lighting on almost any wall for a variety of effects.

Cove lighting fixtures are also mounted near the ceiling. Fluorescent light is directed upward, giving indirect light only. Cove lighting provides good general lighting; however, you must supplement it with local lighting. It also gives a room a feeling of height.

Recessed downlights are small, circular lights installed in the ceiling. Using several of these lights spaced throughout the ceiling offers good general lighting. Too many recessed lights, however, can give a "Swiss cheese" effect to the ceiling. Using just a few creates effective accent lighting. The typical scalloped pattern of light and shadow produced by recessed downlights gives a dramatic look to a wall.

Wall washers are also installed in the ceiling. They have a contoured inner reflector that directs nearly uniform light on walls from ceiling to floor. This gives walls a smooth look. If the wall-washer fixtures are located closer to the wall, they can emphasize a textured wall surface.

Soffit lighting fixtures consist of an enclosed box attached to the ceiling. Often, a plastic panel at the bottom of the soffit box diffuses the light as it shines downward. Soffit lighting is used where a large amount of local light is needed, such as over a kitchen or bathroom sink.

Strip lighting is a structure consisting of a strip of receptacles that hold a series of incandescent lightbulbs. It is often used around mirrors in a bathroom or dressing room to provide good task lighting.

Track lighting consists of several light fixtures mounted on a metal strip. You can arrange the fixtures in varying positions to shine in different directions and create different effects.

Nonstructural Lighting

Nonstructural lighting is lighting that is not a structural part of the house. You can move, change, and replace these lights more easily than any other form of lighting.

Lamps are the most common type of nonstructural lighting. They can serve decorative purposes as well as provide good general and task lighting. When choosing lamps, keep the following points in mind:

- A sturdy or heavy base prevents tipping.
- Some have a diffusing bowl that prevents glare.
- A harp makes it possible to change the height of the lampshade. A harp is a metal hoop or arch that supports a lampshade.
- The colors and textures of lamps and lampshades should harmonize.
- Light-colored, translucent lampshades give the most light.
- Adjustable lamps are the most practical. You can raise or lower some, such as swag lamps. Some have swinging arms and some use three-way bulbs.

You can combine structural and nonstructural lighting in many different ways, 17-18. The goal is always to achieve good lighting throughout the dwelling.

17-18
Lamps, recessed downlights, and accent lighting provide artificial light for this room. A large window area provides natural light during the day.

American Lighting Association

Choosing Accessories

Accessories are items smaller than furnishings that accent the design of a room or area. An accessory should have a purpose in the room. It should not just fill a space. Accessories can be decorative or functional. Some accessories serve both purposes.

- *Decorative accessories* add beauty to a room. Some examples of decorative accessories are plants, floral arrangements, pictures, paintings, sculptures, wall hangings, and figurines.

- *Functional accessories* accent the room while serving another purpose. They may include such items as pillows, quilts, lamps, mirrors, books, bookends, candles, candlesticks, and clocks.

Whether for a residential or commercial design, it is a common practice to use functional and decorative accessories together. An example of an accessory that is both decorative and functional is a lampshade of a special design.

Accessories often reflect the personalities of those who use the space. They can show a preference for such items as pictures, clocks, antiques, or treasured objects from other countries or cultures. Some items may have sentimental value such as photographs, souvenirs, or trophies. Others may be parts of collections such as rare coins or antique porcelain plates.

Whether an accessory is functional or decorative, it should blend with the style and period of the room, 17-19. Sometimes an accessory may be useful, beautiful, or meaningful to a person, but does not fit the purpose or scheme of the room. At that point, you should ask yourself if it really "belongs." If the item adds a special statement of about individuality to the room, you may choose to include it.

If an accessory detracts from the overall room design, consider placing it somewhere else in the home or structure. For example, some people have a personal collection of plaques, awarded for excellence in sports. This collection is obviously very important, but it does not fit the design of a formal living room. The plaques are more suitable for display in a family or recreation room.

Accessories that are near one another should have something in common. The common factor may be color, texture, style, or purpose. This shared element will help tie the furnishings in a room together, 17-20. Determine other decisions on the placement and arrangement of accessories by applying the elements and principles of design that you learned in previous chapters.

When acquiring and purchasing accessories, give some thought to the price of the initial investment. Setting priorities about what you (or a client) want and can afford is essential. Select

A   B   C

17-19
These lamps are good examples of accessories that are both functional and decorative. The styles shown are Modern (A), Contemporary (B), and Casual (C).

accessories that are both functional and decorative first. Then consider accessories that are versatile and could be used in different rooms and spaces. Later, you may wish to start a collection of accessories based more on their decorative value for a specific space, such as a collection of landscape photographs for use in a study or office.

In addition to cost, function, and versatility, think about the maintenance accessories require. For example, a display of silver serving pieces may look lovely on a dining room table. However, you must be certain that you want to dedicate the time it takes to dust, polish, and maintain the silver before purchasing such items.

Also give consideration to the replacement cost of the accessories. A collection of expensive, fragile, hand-painted figurines is not practical to display within reach of small children. Store such purchases safely out of reach, or postpone the investment until the children are older.

17-20
You can create different moods in a room by the accessories you choose.

CAREER FOCUS

Civil Engineer

Can you imagine yourself working as a civil engineer? Read more about this challenging and exciting career.

Interests/Skills: If you share any of the following interests you may choose to explore a course of study that would lead to a career as a civil engineer. Do you like practical projects that involve hands-on activity? Do you enjoy fact-finding and problem solving? Civil engineers use these skills: mathematics, science, critical thinking, active listening, active learning, complex problem solving, monitoring, judgment and decision-making, and negotiation.

Career Snapshot: Civil engineers design such things as roads, buildings, airports, tunnels, dams, bridges, or water supply and sewage systems. They must consider many factors in their designs, from the costs to making sure the structure will stay intact during bad weather. This is one of the oldest types of engineering. Many civil engineers manage people and projects. A civil engineer may oversee a construction site or be a city engineer. Others may work in design, construction, research, and teaching. There are many specialties within civil engineering, such as structural, construction, environment, and transportation.

Education/Training: Civil engineers typically enter the occupation with a bachelor's degree.

Licensing/Examinations: State licensing is required for civil engineers. A license requires 4 years of relevant work experience and passing an exam. Beginning engineers often work under an experienced engineer to get their required work experience.

Professional Association: American Society of Civil Engineers, (ASCE) (www.asce.org)

Job Outlook: Jobs for civil engineers are expected to grow about as fast as the average for the next decade.

Source: Occupational Information Network (O*NET) (www.online.onetcenter.org) and the Occupational Outlook Handbook, Bureau of Labor Statistics (www.bls.gov)

Summary

The finishing touches of furnishing a room are window treatments, lighting, and accessories. Window style, size, and location influence their treatment. The amount of natural light you want to let in is also a factor. There is a variety of window treatments available. They include draperies, curtains, shades, shutters, and blinds. Decorative window-top treatments may be used in conjunction with most of these treatments. Window treatments can be made from a variety of fabrics and materials.

Artificial lighting supplements natural light. Types of artificial lighting- include incandescent, fluorescent lighting, compact fluorescent, and light-emitting diodes (LED). Each type has its advantages and disadvantages. Light can be used to achieve different effects. It can create visual comfort through general and task lighting. As you work with light, you need to consider using it for safety and beauty.

Some lighting comes from structural fixtures, which are a part of the house. Other lighting comes from nonstructural items, which are separate from the house's structure. What you choose will depend on the type of lighting you need or desire.

Accessories are part of the design scheme. They can be decorative, functional, or a combination. They reflect the personality and lifestyle of the household. Successful placement and arrangement of accessories requires an understanding of the elements and principles of design.

Review the Facts

1. Contrast draperies and curtains.
2. Why are shutters and blinds appropriate for windows that are used for ventilation?
3. How do incandescent lights differ from fluorescent lights in terms of purchasing cost and operating cost?
4. List two energy-efficient types of lightbulbs.
5. List three properties of light, and give an example of each.
6. Why do homes need both general and local lighting?
7. List five structural light fixtures.
8. Explain the difference between functional and decorative accessories.
9. Why should accessories placed near one another have something in common?

Think Critically

10. **Analyze window treatments.** Imagine you have just signed a lease for an apartment on the third floor of a five-story building, across a noisy street from a same-size apartment building. Suppose that all your windows face the street. Analyze the types of window treatments you would select and prioritize a buying plan. Your new apartment has the following windows:
    - bedroom—large double-hung window
    - bathroom—small awning window
    - kitchen—jalousie window over the sink
    - living room—sliding patio doors leading to a balcony

11. **Analyze room light.** Analyze one of the rooms in your home, and identify which surfaces reflect light and which absorb it. Under what circumstances is the reflected light helpful? When does it create problems? How does the light that is absorbed affect the look of the room?

Community Links

12. **Observe window treatments.** Identify the various types of window treatments used in your home and/or school. What function does each serve? Do the window treatments control light? provide privacy? provide insulation? Are they purely decorative, or both functional and decorative? Are there any safety considerations for the types of window treatments? Discuss your observations in class.

13. **Lighting safety.** Take a tour of your school building and grounds. Determine which areas have lighting that is adequate for safety. Identify specific areas that you feel have inadequate lighting. What solutions would you recommend to improve the lighting for safety? Share your recommendations with the class.

14. **Research electrical codes.** Research your local electrical wiring code requirements. Find out who is responsible for inspection. What problems would you anticipate if there were no requirements or inspections?

15. **Accessory options.** Visit a local store that sells an assortment of home accessories. Make a list of the accessories you would buy if you had a budget of $300.00. Consider your lifestyle and interests as you make your selections. Would all of these accessories work together in the same room? If not, which rooms would you use them in? Now, assume that your budget has been cut in half and you have only $150.00 to spend. Which accessories would you eliminate and which would you keep?

Academic Connections

16. **Science.** Use Internet or print resources to investigate *light temperature*—both warm and cool—and *color rendition* as it relates to light. What system is used for measuring light temperature? color rendition? How is this information used on lighting packaging? How can light temperature and color rendition impact your lighting choices as an interior designer? Write a summary of your findings to share with the class.

17. **Social studies.** Use Internet or print resources to read about *The Energy Independence and Security Act of 2007.* What principles are outlined in this legislation? How will mandated energy requirements help consumers? How will it impact the availability of different types of energy-saving lighting? Give an oral report of your findings.

Technology Applications

18. **Window treatment options.** Search the Internet for companies that sell window treatments and observe their latest products. Find three types of window coverings or treatments that offer new designs, materials, or features—especially those with consumer safety in mind. What technology makes these window treatments unique? Print examples of the products you find and bring them to class. Give a brief presentation, explaining each new product and reporting their price ranges.

19. **Lamp comparison.** Visit a local do-it-yourself store and find an example of the following types of light sources: frosted incandescent bulb, clear incandescent bulb, CFL, fluorescent tube, halogen bulb, and LED lamp. On a sheet of paper, make a chart to compare their wattage, lumens, cost, and hours of life. Also add CRI and color temperature if listed on the packaging. How do the different types of light compare? Share your findings with the class.

Design Practice

20. **Window treatment design.** Presume a client has hired you to create a new custom window treatment for a living room picture window. Your client prefers a contemporary design style. The window measures 72 inches wide and 64 inches high. The bottom of the window is 18 inches from the floor and is centered on a wall that is 18 feet long. The room has ceilings that are nine feet high. Use a CADD program to create an elevation view and rendering of your custom window treatment design. Print a copy to show your client. Write a summary indicating the types of textiles or other materials that make this design plan unique. Save a copy of your plan for your portfolio.

21. **Accessory and lighting design.** Suppose a friend asked you to plan the accessories and lighting for her bedroom scheme. She has a 16- by 20-inch piece of custom art and a few family photos she wants to include, but the rest is up to you. There are only two available walls in the bedroom: one is 11 feet by 8 feet and the other is 14 feet by 8 feet. Develop a design plan. Create wall elevations to show your accessory arrangements and lighting plans. Write a summary to accompany your design.

22. **Portfolio.** Create a floor plan for a kitchen or bathroom that includes recommendations for structural and nonstructural lighting. Explain the reasons for your selections.

Team Interaction with Older Adults

Older adults need interaction with other people, especially those who live in group settings or spend their days in an adult day services center. Activity-space arrangements can stimulate interaction or hinder it.

As part of an FCCLA *Community Service* project, contact the director of a long-term care facility or adult day services center in your community. Discuss ways that you and your team can encourage interaction with the older adults or meet some other needs. Ideas may be as simple as rearranging an activity room or adding decorative accessories that invite interaction. In addition, identify ways that you and your team might have regular interaction with these adults.

Use the FCCLA *Planning Process* and *Community Service Project Sheet* to plan, carry out, and evaluate your project. See your adviser for information as needed.

CHAPTER 18

Selecting Appliances and Electronics

Terms to Learn

appliance
EnergyGuide label
ENERGY STAR label
warranty
full warranty
limited warranty
induction cooktop
self-cleaning oven
convection oven
microwave oven
dehumidifier
humidifier
software programs
hardware

Chapter Objectives

After studying this chapter, you will be able to

- analyze information for selecting appliances and consumer electronics.

- evaluate choices in styles and features of various kitchen, laundry, and climate control appliances, including manufacturers, materials, care, and maintenance.

- appraise other appliances and consumer electronics for safety, cost, and quality.

- select appliances and consumer electronics to meet specific needs.

Reading with Purpose

Before reading this chapter, skim the chapter and examine its organization. Look at the bold or italic words, headings of different colors and sizes, bulleted lists or numbered lists, table, charts, captions, and features.

Photography Courtesy of Bosch Home Appliances

Creating an attractive interior design is only part of the inside story. To meet personal needs and values, a home or commercial space must also be functional. Appliances greatly increase the usefulness of various areas in the home or workplace.

Appliances are devices powered by gas or electricity. Large appliances, such as refrigerators and ranges, are major appliances. Smaller appliances, such as toasters and hair dryers, are small or portable appliances. Appliances play a significant role in the kitchen and laundry area. They are also used in other areas throughout a home or space. Appliances help people meet their basic needs. Choosing appliances carefully can help create a home or workplace environment that is safe, comfortable, and efficient.

Consumer Satisfaction

Satisfaction with appliances depends largely on consumer choices. However, appliance manufacturers and retailers will also affect consumer satisfaction.

As a consumer or interior designer, you have a responsibility to obtain information about the appliances you buy. See 18-1. You need to know the various options that are available. Appliance options should match the needs and desires of the people in a household. Determining the amount of money you or a client can afford to spend on an appliance is an early priority. In addition, you should understand the warranties and service available for appliances. Reading and understanding use and care information before operating an appliance is essential. Fulfilling these responsibilities helps improve consumer satisfaction with appliances.

Manufacturers have a goal of preserving their reputations and keeping customers happy. When appliance buyers are content with their purchases, they become repeat buyers. Unsatisfied customers and returned merchandise can put a manufacturer out of business.

To assure your satisfaction, manufacturers strive to make appliances safe, dependable, and affordable. They provide a variety of models that meet varying consumer needs and preferences. Appliances generally conform to performance standards set by the American National Standards Institute (ANSI). Manufacturers give warranties and detailed instructions about the use of their appliances—either in print or on DVDs. Most manufacturers also offer free cookbooks, toll-free phone numbers, and helpful Web sites for more information about their products and how to use them.

The success of retail appliance businesses also relies on customer satisfaction. To meet the various needs of different consumers, retailers provide a selection of models. Responsible retailers train their salespeople to clearly explain the features of all models. Most retailers deliver and install appliances, and offer maintenance services, too. Some retailers offer free classes and demonstrations. Reputable retailers serve as a go-between for the customer with the manufacturer to make sure the conditions of the warranty are met.

18-1
When consumers shop for appliances, they should be prepared to ask many questions.

Photography Courtesy of Bosch Home Appliances

Appliance Considerations

Consumers can expect most major appliances to last 10 years or more. When buying appliances, they must consider both present and future needs. Here are some questions about which to think:

- Will the household be expanding or compacting in the next decade?

- Is a household move in the near future?

- If a move is in the future, will the appliances be taken to the new home?

Major appliances account for a large part of a housing budget. This is especially true when completely equipping a home, 18-2. If you rent a home that has appliances in it, part of your rent goes toward the cost of appliance maintenance. Because appliances are so costly, their purchase requires careful consideration. Purchase and operating costs, features, size, safety, and quality are among the factors consumers should consider.

Purchase Price

When considering a major appliance purchase, consumers must think about whether the appliance cost fits the household budget. The cost of appliances varies greatly from brand to brand and from model to model. Larger appliances with many features will cost more than smaller, more basic models. The materials from which appliances are made can also impact the price. For example, stainless steel is typically more costly than more traditional appliance materials. Prices also vary from one retailer to another. Consequently, smart consumers shop around and compare prices.

The purchase price of an appliance is only part of its true cost. When

18-2
A fully equipped kitchen is a convenient, but costly, part of housing.

Laura B. Trujillo, ASID, Illinois Chapter

shopping, inquire about delivery and installation charges and extra fees for hauling the old appliance away. If a consumer pays for an appliance on an installment plan, there will also be a finance charge.

Energy Cost

Energy costs are another part of the expense of major appliances. In the past, purchase price was the only cost consideration when buying appliances. Today, the wise consumer also considers long-term operating costs. Purchase price plus operating cost reveals the true lifetime cost of an appliance. When examining appliance energy usage, two labels are helpful to consumers. The EnergyGuide label and the ENERGY STAR label offer different information.

The bright yellow and black **EnergyGuide label** states the average yearly energy use and operating cost of an appliance. The U.S. government requires these labels on new refrigerators, refrigerator-freezers, freezers, dishwashers, clothes washers, and water heaters. Room air conditioners and furnaces

GREEN CHOICES

Environmentally Friendly Appliance Decisions

Many companies now offer environmentally friendly products and buildings. As a consumer or interior design professional, how can you be sure that products or buildings will perform as advertised? In other words: will a certain washing machine use less water? or will a house require less energy to operate?

You can rely on testing labels and certification programs to help answer these questions. An example of using a verified label is the ENERGY STAR label for appliances. Choosing household appliances with the ENERGY STAR label makes saving energy easier. The energy efficiency percentage is different for various products, but ENERGY STAR qualified appliances use at least 10 percent less energy than the average appliance without the label.

have an energy efficiency rating versus a label.

EnergyGuide labels enable you to compare average cost estimates for similar appliances, 18-3. This helps you determine which appliances are the most *energy efficient*, or use the least amount of energy. Of course, those that use the least energy are the least costly to operate.

To roughly estimate the cost of 10 years of operation, for example, multiply the operating cost figure on the Energy-Guide label by 10. You will notice that many inexpensive, "no-frills" appliances usually cost the most to operate. In contrast, more expensive appliances, with all the features customers might want, will cost less to operate over time. This means the money you save when purchasing some less-expensive models you may eventually use to pay the extra energy costs needed over their lifetime. Of course, buying an energy-efficient appliance on sale represents even more savings. When buying appliances for the long-term, therefore, consider both purchase price and operating costs.

The **ENERGY STAR label** is not a requirement, but it serves as an easy-to-use energy guide for consumers. ENERGY STAR qualified appliances are the most energy efficient in their group. Typically these products are at least 10 percent more energy efficient than similar products that meet minimum government energy standards. For example, ENERGY STAR qualified clothes washers use about 30 percent less energy and use over 50 percent less water than regular clothes washers. An

18-3
EnergyGuide labels allow consumers to compare the average yearly energy costs of similar major appliances.

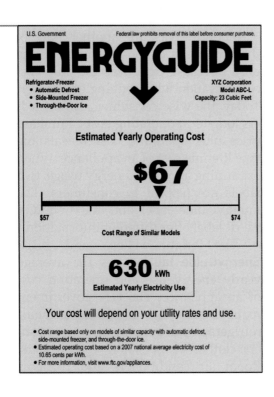

ENERGY STAR qualified refrigerator uses 20 percent less energy than a new non-ENERGY STAR qualified model. The requirements for meeting ENERGY STAR designation change over time for many reasons. One good reason is that more appliance companies are improving the energy efficiency of their products. As a result, the government modifies the ENERGY STAR requirements to remain a meaningful energy-efficiency guide to consumers. The U.S. Environmental Protection Agency (EPA) and the U.S. Department of Energy (DOE) sponsor the ENERGY STAR program.

The ENERGY STAR label makes it easy to locate energy-efficient products without giving up features, quality, or personal comfort. You can find the label on products in 30 different categories, including appliances, electronics, office equipment, lighting, heating and cooling equipment, windows, and even new homes, 18-4. Consumers can save money monthly on their utility bills by choosing ENERGY STAR products.

Using products with an ENERGY STAR label not only saves money in operating costs, but also helps save the environment. Effective environmental use focuses on reducing water use, promoting cleaner air, and using construction materials wisely.

18-4
The ENERGY STAR label assures the consumer that the appliance is one of the most energy efficient models on the market.

Image Courtesy of ENERGY STAR

Finishes and Features

Appliances are available with a wide range of finishes and features. Careful planning will help you choose the look and features that best meet your needs. When shopping, ask yourself some of the following questions: Is it available in the color you want? Will it coordinate with the other furnishings and appliances in the room? A particular design trend for consumer kitchens in recent years is the look of a "commercial kitchen." Designers label this the "Professional Look." For appliances, this means selecting models with a stainless steel finish, 18-5.

When deciding what appliance features you need, consider the people

18-5
The sleek look of stainless steel is apparent in the background refrigerator and the two refrigerator drawers built into the island in the foreground.

Photo Courtesy of Sub-Zero

MATH MATTERS

Estimating Appliance Energy Consumption

You can estimate the amount and cost of electricity used by appliances and consumer electronic products. As you recall, energy use is measured in *watts*. Energy use is expressed in kilowatt-hours (kWh). On its Web site, the U.S. Department of Energy gives the following formula to calculate energy used by a product each year:

Wattage × (Hours Used per Day) × (Days Used per Year) ÷ 1000 = Daily kilowatt-hour (kWh) consumption

Suppose you want to know how much it costs to operate a refrigerator during a year's time. Products are marked with the maximum wattage they draw. Suppose the refrigerator is marked 725, meaning it draws a maximum of 725 watts. Since refrigerators cycle on and off and don't operate continuously at maximum wattage, divide the hours used per day by 3. If you plug the information you have into the equation, you get:

(725 × 8 × 365) ÷ 1000 = 2117 kilowatt-hour (kWh)

To figure out what this would cost, look up the current rate—given in cents per kWh—charged by your electricity provider. If the utility charges 9.17 cents/kWh, you would calculate the following:

(2117 kWh used per year) × ($.0917 cents per kWh) = $194.13

It would cost approximately $194.13 to operate the refrigerator for a year. For more information, visit The U.S. Department of Energy's *Energy Savers* Web site (www.energysavers.gov/) and click on Appliances and Electronics, Estimating Energy Use.

who will use it. Is the appliance easy to use? Does it perform all the tasks the household requires? Does it have extra features that household members will not use? Extras add to the price.

Does anyone in the household have special needs? For instance, people in wheelchairs cannot reach as high or as far as others. Front-mounted controls are ideal for these appliance buyers. People with difficulty grasping or turning knobs, for example, may find electronic touch pads easier to use.

After deciding which appliance features meet needs, not just wants, consider items that have these features to find the best purchase. Although consumers can add some features later—such as icemakers—factory installed components are preferable.

Size

Size is another consideration when purchasing a major appliance. How large should the appliance be to meet the needs of the household? How many people will be using the appliance now and in the future? Does the household need a large or extra-large model, or something more compact? Will the appliance fit the space planned for it? Does it fit through doorways and hallways?

Safety

When purchasing a new appliance from a reputable dealer, you can be sure that it meets current safety standards. In contrast, appliances (usually portable appliances) purchased at flea markets or garage sales often do not meet current safety standards. In addition, a bargain appliance with an unfamiliar brand name may mean that the appliance does not meet safety standards.

Usually the first page of any owner's guide addresses appliance safety. Look for a seal certifying that the appliance conforms to safety standards. Consumers can find these seals on the back of major appliances, on the name plate, and in the use and care material. On small electric appliances, the seal is usually on the name plate or attached to the electrical cord. Common safety seals found on electric or gas appliances include

- *UL* from Underwriters Laboratory

- *ETL* from ETL SEMCO, a division of Intertek Testing Services Ltd.

- *CSA* from the Canadian Standards Association

With safety as the common goal, many groups join forces to develop safety standards. Appliance manufacturers, safety-testing organizations, and the U.S. Consumer Product Safety Commission lead the way in such efforts. Safety standards exist for each appliance category and undergo periodic review.

In addition, manufacturers often include ground fault circuit interrupters (GFCI) on the cords of some small appliances for safety. As you recall GFCIs are safety devices in outlets or on electrical cords that prevent electrical shock. It interrupts the unintentional flow of electricity to avoid shock, burns, and possible fatalities in the home. See Chapters 9 and 21 for more information about GFCIs.

In the home, appliance safety depends primarily on proper installation and use, 18-6. The literature that accompanies the appliance identifies these requirements. Make sure the house has

18-6
An important safety issue with microwave ovens is using the right model for over-the-range installation. This model is designed specifically for that purpose.

the correct electrical or gas connections. A 120-volt, major electrical appliance should have a three-prong plug. The third (round) prong grounds the appliance. If a grounded appliance has damaged wiring, electric current will flow to the ground rather than through your body. Because the grounding prong prevents electrical shock, appliance owners should not remove it. Also, avoid circuit overload by making sure the home has adequate electrical service for the appliance before installation.

Some appliances provide additional safety in the form of extra features. For example, some ranges provide child-proof control locks, which prevent children from turning on the oven or burners. Some consumers regard such extra safety features as a need.

HEALTH/SAFETY

Eliminate Hazards for Appliance Safety

Almost any household item can pose a hazard to unsupervised infants and children. Appliance entrapment and tip-over hazards are high on the list. Sadly, some children suffocate or are crushed by heavy appliances when playing with items in ways that are contrary to the manufacturer's instructions. Here are some safety concerns that deserve special attention.

- **Eliminate entrapment hazards.** Current law and voluntary safety standards require that the doors of refrigerators and chest freezers easily push open from the inside to keep from trapping children. Yet people often keep chest freezers made before 1970 with the old hook-and-latch lock as spare storage containers long after they stop operating. Tragically, when children use such an appliance as a hiding place they cannot escape. As a safety precaution, owners should remove one part of the locking mechanism to disable chest-type freezers. Your state may also require removal of the freezer cover before you can discard it.

- **Eliminate appliance tip-overs.** When buying new appliances, make sure installers use anti-tip hardware and follow the safety instructions manufacturers provide. For example, installers should secure a free-standing range to a wall to keep it from tipping forward if a child leans, sits, or stands on an open oven door.

To prevent appliance related accidents in the home, supervising young children and using items safely are key.

Quality

The quality of an appliance is a key purchase consideration. Appliances that require frequent repairs are costly and troublesome to operate. You want appliances that will work dependably for many years.

Asking a few questions may help evaluate quality. Is the appliance well constructed? Is the manufacturer reputable? Is the use and care manual thorough and easy to understand? Does the retailer or manufacturer offer after-sale service?

Assessing quality also involves reading the warranty. A **warranty** is a manufacturer's written promise that a product will meet certain performance and quality standards as outlined in the warranty. When reading a warranty, be sure to find out how long the warranty lasts and what it covers—the entire product or only certain parts. Does the warranty include labor fees?

A warranty may be full or limited. A **full warranty** provides the consumer with free repair or replacement of a warranted product or part if any defect occurs during the warranty period. Under a **limited warranty**, a warrantor provides service, repairs, and replacements only under certain conditions. For example, the warrantors can charge for repairs. Consumers may also be responsible for shipping the item back to the warrantor or taking other steps to get repairs.

In addition to the full and limited warranties, one option to consider is the extended warranty. For an extra fee, the consumer can add several years to the manufacturer's warranty. Read an extended warranty document very carefully to decide if it is necessary. Many times, extended warranties are not a wise purchase.

Choosing Kitchen Appliances

All aspects of food storage, preparation, and cleanup, require the use of kitchen appliances, 18-7. The purchase considerations already discussed pertain to all these appliances. Use the following information to help select appliances wisely.

Refrigerators

Refrigerators are a necessity for storing fresh foods. Perhaps that is why nearly every home in the United States has at least one refrigerator.

Styles

Refrigerators are available in a few basic styles. A *one-door refrigerator* does not have a freezer. Instead, it has a frozen-food storage compartment. This compartment is colder than the rest of the refrigerator, but its use is limited. It is not designed to freeze foods. It provides only short-term storage for commercially frozen foods and keeps ice cubes.

A variation of the one-door refrigerator is the *compact refrigerator*. It is suitable for rooms in college dorm rooms, hotel rooms, and small apartments. Consumers can purchase or rent them at a low price. Compact models may be capable of freezing ice cubes, but are usually not suitable for storing frozen foods.

Most refrigerators available today are *two-door refrigerator-freezers*. These models have separate freezer sections that freeze food. The freezer section

18-7
The tasks of storing food, cooking meals, and washing dishes are all made easier with the help of appliances.

Photography Courtesy of Bosch Home Appliances

temperature remains about 0°F. The freezer section may be above, below, or at the side of the refrigerator, 18-8.

The consumer can choose a built-in refrigerator, which is the same depth as the kitchen counter and is actually bolted to the cabinets. These refrigerators allow you to add panels to match the cabinets, making the refrigerator appear to be part of the cabinetry. A less-expensive option is to buy a freestanding refrigerator that allows you to add partial panels to the front to give a built-in look.

The refrigerator drawer is a new option that saves floor space. The drawer unit—which can be a refrigerator or freezer or a combination of the two—is installed in place of a base cabinet. These innovative refrigerators are convenient for small kitchens, efficiency apartments, recreation rooms, or even master bedrooms.

18-8
Some refrigerator-freezer owners prefer having the refrigerator section on top and the less-used freezer at the bottom.

Photography Courtesy of Bosch Home Appliances

Features to Consider

Refrigerators and refrigerator-freezers are generally available in several basic colors to fit the wide range of design schemes. Special features include individual compartments and temperature controls for meat, produce, and dairy products, 18-9A. Adjustable shelves allow easy storage of large items. Another option on some models is a reversible door that hinges on either side of the refrigerator. The ability to change hinge location can allow better access to adjacent counter space. A reversible door is particularly helpful when moving a refrigerator to a new residence that may present different traffic patterns. Ice and water dispensers also are features that many people want.

A

B

18-9
The temperature control is located on the outside of the refrigerator and is convenient to adjust (A). Storage should not be a problem with many compartments of this refrigerator (B).

Photography Courtesy of Bosch Home Appliances

The refrigerator's defrost system is a feature to consider. In general, one-door models often require *manual defrosting*. This means that frost accumulates inside the refrigerator, reducing the efficiency of the appliance. When the frost becomes ¼-inch thick, the appliance must be turned off so the frost can melt. This usually requires emptying the appliance and drying the compartments before turning it on again.

Refrigerator-freezers may have either partial or full automatic defrosting. *Partial automatic defrosting* models do not accumulate frost in the refrigerator compartment. However, the freezer compartment must be defrosted manually. In *full automatic defrosting* models, no frost accumulates. These frost-free models are convenient, but are more costly. They also use more electricity, but the convenience may be worth the cost.

Storage space is another important consideration. The measurement of space inside a refrigerator is in cubic feet. An 18-cubic-foot refrigerator-freezer may be the ideal size for a family that shops frequently or eats out often. In contrast, the same appliance may be too small for a family that shops less frequently or buys food in bulk.

The amount of refrigerator versus freezer space is another important consideration. All 18-cubic-foot models, for example, do not have same-size refrigerator and freezer sections. Make sure both compartments provide the necessary storage space. Check the interior dimensions and the shelf sizes, 18-9B. Will the storage accommodate all needed items? A range of sizes is available to meet the needs of various households.

Another consideration is the amount of kitchen space available for a refrigerator. Measure the height, width, and depth of the space you have. Take the measurements with you when you shop. A checklist for buying refrigerators is shown in 18-10.

Freezers

When more freezer space is a requirement, consumers may want to buy a separate freezer. The size needed depends on how consumers will use it. Will it simply provide backup storage

Checklist for Refrigerators
• Does the refrigerator require defrosting?
• Are interior and door shelves adjustable for more flexible use of space?
• Is space available for heavy and tall bottles?
• Is the interior well lighted?
• Is the refrigerator interior easy to clean?
• Are shelves made of strong, noncorroding, rust-resistant materials such as glass?
• Are all interior parts easy to remove and/or accessible for cleaning?
• Is the fresh-food section easy to reach, use, clean, and organize?
• Are door shelf retaining bars strong and securely attached?
• Is crisper space adequate? Is it designed to keep moisture inside?
• Is the freezer section easy to reach, use, clean, and organize?
• Is the refrigerator easy to move for cleaning?
• Is the refrigerator's energy consumption, as shown on the EnergyGuide label, reasonable for its size and features?

18-10
Consider these points before choosing a refrigerator.

or will extra freezer space be a regular need? People who preserve homegrown fruits and vegetables, buy food in bulk quantities, or freeze make-ahead meals usually need more freezer space.

Styles

The two styles of freezers are chest and upright. Large, bulky packages are easier to store in a chest model. Chest freezers use less electricity because less cold air escapes when opening the door. One disadvantage of chest freezers is that they require more floor space. Another is that users must lift the food when removing it from the freezer. Chest freezers require manual defrosting.

Food is easier to see and remove in an upright freezer. These freezers only require a small amount of floor space, but they cost more to operate.

You can choose an upright freezer with either a *manual defrost* or a *full automatic defrost* system. Full automatic defrost models are convenient, but the purchase price and operating costs are higher. Figure 18-11 shows a checklist for freezers.

Ranges

Recent years have seen many changes in ranges. These changes have been due to advances in technology and consumer interest in the speed of cooking and cleanability. You will have several factors to consider when choosing a range.

A consumer's first decision concerns the energy source. The choice of either electricity or gas depends on the availability and cost of each as well as personal preference.

Electric Ranges

Electric ranges offer several styles of cooking surfaces. The *conventional coil* cooktop has wires encased in coils. The electric current flows through the coils to produce heat, and the heat transfers to cookware by conduction and radiation.

Some electric ranges feature a smooth *glass-ceramic* cooktop, which makes the range easy to clean. This surface usually hides radiant heating elements that radiate heat through the glass to the cookware. Because the glass is also heated, it is important that the cookware be very flat in order to conduct heat and cook efficiently. The induction cooktops also use a glass-ceramic surface.

Induction cooktops use a magnetic field below a glass-ceramic surface to generate heat in the bottom of cookware. The cookware *must* be magnetic. Cast iron and some stainless steel work

18-11 Consider these points before choosing a food freezer.	Checklist for Freezers
	• Will model fit your floor space and weight limitations?
	• Will the type of door opening be convenient in its location?
	• Are shelves and/or baskets adjustable?
	• Are all sections readily accessible?
	• Is the interior well lighted?
	• Does it have a safety signal light to let you know that power is on?
	• Is the freezer frost-free? If not, does it have a fast-defrost system?
	• Does it have easy-to-read and accessible controls?
	• Does it have magnetic gaskets to seal cold air in more completely?

well because they offer resistance to the passage of the magnetic waves, which generates heat. Heat from the cookware then transfers to food. The range surface does not heat up. Cleanup is easy because spills do not burn.

Gas Ranges

The combustion process between gas and oxygen in the air produces the heat in gas ranges. Regulating the flow of gas through a valve controls the heat. More gas causes a higher flame and hotter temperatures. In the past, users had to light a pilot light to use the burner. Current standards require electronic ignitions on all new ranges powered by natural gas or propane gas.

Gas ranges are available with two types of burners—conventional and sealed. *Conventional burners* do not fit snugly into the cooktop, so spills can leak under the burners to cause a mess. No opening exists between *sealed burners* and the cooktop surface, which makes cleanup easier. The energy usage of gas burners is measured in British thermal units (Btu), with larger burners consuming more Btus.

Styles

Ranges come in several styles and sizes. A consumer's choice depends on the capacity requirement and the available space. All ranges have a cooking surface with one or two ovens. *Freestanding* models are the most common, with many size, color, and feature options. The controls are usually located on the range backsplash at the back of the range. These ranges may stand alone or you can place them between cabinets for a built-in look, 18-12.

Slide-in and *drop-in* range models either slide into a space or rest on a base cabinet. They fit snugly between kitchen cabinets and counters. Chrome strips often cover the side edges and provide a built-in look. The controls for these

18-12
This quality freestanding range becomes a focal point in the kitchen. Note that the refrigerator in the background has panels on the front to match the cabinets.

Photo Courtesy of Sub-Zero/Wolf

models are on the cooktop surface and do not include a backsplash.

Built-in models provide cooking surfaces separate from the oven. This allows flexible kitchen arrangements. Installation of surface units is in a countertop, often a kitchen island. Oven installation is in a wall or custom-made cabinet. Some built-in ovens are double ovens. Many built-ins are single ovens installed above or below a microwave oven and/or a warming drawer. A *warming drawer* keeps hot food warm until serving time. Also, it warms-up dinner plates and serving pieces. Some warming drawers have humidity controls to keep selected foods moist, 18-13.

Features to Consider

Many consumers want a self-cleaning feature for the oven. **Self-cleaning ovens**

18-13
A warming drawer is an ideal appliance for someone who does a lot of baking or cooking.

Photo Courtesy of Wolf Appliance

operate at extremely high temperatures to burn away spatters and spills. The user simply wipes away the small amount of remaining ash. Because these ovens reach very high temperatures during cleaning, they have extra insulation. This also helps save energy during normal baking periods. The self-cleaning feature adds to the price of the range, but the cost of operating the cleaning cycle is less than the cost of chemical oven cleaners. Such ovens generally use three to four kilowatt-hours of electricity during the self-cleaning cycle.

A surface-cooking option to consider is the ceramic cooktop. These cooktops may have a variety of different element sizes including dual elements that give multiple size options. In addition, warm and serve elements that operate at very low temperatures to keep food warm without overcooking are also optional. Some have modular surface units the user can interchange with a grill, griddle, or wok, 18-14. Newer glass-ceramic cooktops do not use knobs, but instead have electronic touch controls that are part of the glass surface. With no knobs to clean, the surface is very easy to clean.

Other range features to consider include clocks, timers, and programmable cooking cycles. Delay and time-bake cycles allow you to start and stop the cooking process while away. Study the checklist for ranges in 18-15.

Convection Ovens

Convection ovens bake foods in a stream of heated air. Because these ovens continually force heated air directly onto the food, it browns the food and seals in juices. Convection ovens cook in about two-thirds the time and with less energy than conventional cooking. The user may need to adjust the cooking times for favorite recipes for convection cooking.

A convection oven can be part of a range, but can also be a separate built-in oven, or countertop model. You can use

18-14
The modular surface units in this cooktop have been replaced with a grill.

Jenn-Air

Checklist for Ranges
• Is the range suitable for cooking needs and kitchen space?
• Are cooktop burners or units an adequate size for the pans you will use?
• Is oven capacity adequate to meet regular cooking needs?
• Are controls placed for convenient and safe use?
• Are control settings and numbers easy to read?
• Is the range designed to simplify cleaning? Does it have a smooth backsplash, an absence of grooves and crevices, removable burners or units, and a self-cleaning oven?
• Does the range offer features that are important to family needs and use?

18-15
Consider these points before choosing a range.

most convection ovens in the convection mode, as well as the conventional mode without the fan. These ovens typically come with a "convection bake" option for baked items and a "convection roast" option for meats.

Microwave Ovens

Microwave ovens cook food with high-frequency energy waves called *microwaves*. These appliances can cook, defrost, and reheat foods in a fraction of the time required for conventional ovens. Microwave cooking can also save up to 75 percent of the energy used by conventional ovens, depending on the type and amount of food cooked.

As food absorbs microwaves, the molecules within the food vibrate against one another. The friction produced creates the heat that cooks the food.

The time requirement to cook foods depends on the type of food and the power level used for cooking. Most microwave ovens have 10 power levels. Protein foods—such as eggs, cheese, and meats—and thickening sauces require low power levels, as does defrosting. For most other foods, you can use medium and high power levels.

For even and efficient cooking, it is important to use cookware items that allow microwaves to pass through them. Generally, glass, ceramic, and some plastics allow microwaves to pass through them better than other types of cooking materials.

Users should carefully select cookware and containers to use in the microwave oven. The owner's manual generally recommends cookware and containers that are appropriate to use. For safety, use only cookware manufactured for use in the microwave oven. Glass, ceramic, and plastic containers that are safe are usually labeled as safe for microwave use. A general recommendation is to avoid placing metal in the microwave because of potential fire or damage to the microwave oven.

Styles

Several styles of microwave ovens are available. Countertop models are the most popular and offer a large number of features. Users can place them on a countertop, table, or cart, 18-16. Microwave ovens are available in a variety of sizes and oven wattages.

Microwave ovens with ventilation hoods are attached to the wall and cabinet above a range. These models are similar to countertop models; however, they may have less capacity, 18-17.

A microwave feature is sometimes built into "speed cook" ovens. The microwave mode can be used alone or together with convection air or light energy in a cooking cycle. In these ovens, the *microwave mode* cooks the

18-16
Countertop models of microwave ovens can be placed on carts, countertops, and tables.

food quickly and the *heat mode* browns and crisps it.

Features to Consider

Features available on microwave ovens include automatic programming, automatic settings, sensor cooking, browning elements, temperature probes, and turntables, 18-18. These features do the following:

- **Automatic programming.** This feature automatically shifts the microwave oven power levels at preset times. It allows you to program the oven to do several operations in sequence. For instance, you can set this oven to defrost a food product, cook it, and then keep it warm. Pretimed settings, as for popping

popcorn, are available on many microwave oven models.

- **Automatic settings.** These settings, available on some models, determine cooking times and correct power levels for you. You just set the controls for the type and amount of food, and the oven does the rest.

- **Sensor cooking.** This feature determines food doneness by either sensing the temperature or moisture levels in the oven. The oven will stop when it determines the food is cooked.

- **Browning elements.** Electric heating coils on the top of some ovens are an option. They add browning and crispness to food following microwave cooking.

- **Temperature probes.** This probe is a type of food sensor that helps you control cooking. It automatically turns off the oven or switches to a warm setting when food reaches a preset temperature.

Range Hoods

Hoods over cooking appliances help vent heat, moisture, toxins, smoke, grease, and odors from the kitchen, 18-19. Installers can vent hoods to the outside, and if using gas cooking appliances, this is the best type of hood to install. Unvented models use a special screen to collect grease, and sometimes a charcoal filter to remove smoke and odors. The unvented design does not remove moisture, heat, or toxins. Systems that vent to the outdoors do a more complete job of removing all pollutants produced in the home kitchen.

An alternative to a hood is a *downdraft ventilation system*. A fan below the cooktop pulls fumes down into a vent. The downdraft units are vented to outdoors.

18-17
Microwave ovens built for over-the-range installation have vent systems, too.

Checklist for Microwaves
• Is the oven cavity the right size and shape for your needs?
• Does it have the power settings and pretimed buttons you need?
• Is there a signal when the microwave oven finishes cooking and shuts off?
• Does it have a timer? If so, does the timer have enough minutes to allow you the flexibility you need?
• Are the controls mechanical (knobs and push buttons) or electronic (touchpads)?
• Are the controls easy to understand?
• Does a cookbook come with the microwave oven?

18-18
Consider these points before choosing a microwave oven.

Quieter operation of the exhaust fans comes with modern range hoods. You can also find remote fans in which the fan is not part of the hood itself, but outside the house. Many new styles and sizes of hoods are available. Some are focal points in the kitchen and make a strong design statement.

Dishwashers

A dishwasher can save the homeowner time, energy, and water. It also has the ability to clean dishes better than hand washing because it uses hotter water and stronger detergents. Dishwashers also dry dishes which avoids wiping them with towels that may carry pathogens.

Most dishwashers are built into the cabinetry, but some are portable/convertible models. Portable/convertible models are on casters, so users can move them easily to the sink from a storage area in the kitchen. Hoses in the back of the dishwasher connect to the sink for operation. With removal of the casters, users can convert this model into a built-in model. Newer types of dishwashing appliances include the dishwasher drawer, 18-20, and compact countertop models.

Features to Consider

Dishwashers often feature a variety of design options and cycles to meet various cleaning needs. Many door

designs and finishes are available. The consumer can choose between molded plastic and stainless steel for the interior liner. In addition to quiet operation, here are some other features consumers may find of value:

• special cycles for scrubbing pans, sterilizing baby bottles, or washing fine china

• adjustable upper rack to wash large or odd-sized items along with baskets for small items

18-19
This slim range hood is interesting and effective in removing odors and heat out of the kitchen.

Photography Courtesy of Bosch Home Appliances

18-20
This two-drawer design for a dishwasher allows faster cleaning of small loads of dishes.

Photo Courtesy of Fisher & Paykel

- continuous bottom racks for more capacity and adjustable rack tines for convenience
- top-rack only wash, hidden controls and heating elements, and a preheater to heat water to the ideal temperature
- a third rack for flatware or flat items, automatic detergent dispenser, or a food disposer to eliminate food particles

Many models offer energy-saving features, such as a non-heat drying cycle.

This can save up to one-third the electricity usage in a normal drying cycle, but dishes may not dry completely. See the checklist in 18-21 before choosing a dishwasher.

Trash Compactors

Trash compactors compress household trash to a fraction of its original volume. Compactors use heavy-duty plastic bags or special plastic-lined paper bags to collect trash. They are typically built into base cabinets. Trash compactors handle almost any kind of nonfood trash, including bottles, cans, and plastic containers.

Compactors are not intended for food scraps, due to the growth of bacteria and odor development. Also, they should not be used to dispose of highly flammable materials and aerosol cans. These items present safety concerns and should be discarded separately. With an increasing emphasis on recycling, trash compactors are less popular than in the past.

Food Waste Disposers

A food waste disposer easily eliminates the smell and mess of food scraps. With installation below the kitchen sink, this appliance catches and grinds most types of food scraps. It connects to a sewer line or drains into a septic tank.

18-21
Consider these points before selecting a new dishwasher.

Checklist for Dishwasher
• Are the tub and door linings durable and stain resistant?
• Does the wash system have two or more levels? (A single system takes considerable loading care to get all the dishes clean.)
• Will it hold at least 10 place settings? Do your favorite pots and pans fit?
• Does it offer more than one cycle, such as rinse/hold or prerinse cycles?
• Is an automatic wetting agent dispenser provided?
• Is the dishwasher insulated to eliminate excessive noise and heat?
• Does it have an energy saver switch to turn the heating element partially or completely off during some cycles?

Both batch-feed and continuous-feed models are available, with continuous feed the most popular. In *batch-feed* models, scrape the food down the drain opening into the grinding chamber. Then put the drain cover in place, turn on the cold water, and start the disposer. When the scraps flush away, turn off the water and remove the cover. In *continuous-feed* models, add food scraps to the disposer while it runs. This disposer also utilizes a stream of cold water to help grind the scraps and flush them through the drain.

Choosing Laundry Appliances

Doing laundry is a routine household task. Having a washer and dryer in a home is highly convenient. Users can do laundry whenever time allows without the trouble and expense of taking it to self-service laundry. Placement of laundry appliances can vary from the kitchen, a utility area, or in a second-floor laundry closet, 18-22.

Washers

Size is one of the most important variables in washers. Does the household do small loads of laundry on a frequent basis, or fewer, bigger loads? Will a full-size or compact unit meet family needs? Is a side-by-side washer/dryer pair or a stackable washer and dryer preferable? See 18-23. In small homes, stackable laundry appliances may be the best option because they take up less floor space or can be incorporated into a closet. A style reintroduced to the market is the combination washer/dryer. It is one appliance that serves as both a washer and dryer.

There are two basic types of washers for the home: top-loading and front-loading models. The top-loading models, or *vertical-axis machines*, have a

18-22
Placing the washer and dryer in a clothing closet adds convenience.

Photography Courtesy of Bosch Home Appliances

18-23
A stackable washer and dryer is a good choice where floor space is limited.

Photography Courtesy of Bosch Home Appliances

door on the top of the appliance. This style has been the one preferred by most American consumers. A standard top-loading model has an agitator in the center of the wash tub. Clothes wash in a tub partially full of water. The agitator moves the clothes around in the water to remove soil.

Several companies offer new water- and energy-efficient top-loading models. These models load from the top, but the wash action is very different from the standard models. Instead of having an agitator in the middle, they have another means for "tossing" clothes in the wash tub with only a small amount of water. Clothes rinse in a shower of water. These models use much less water than the typical top-loading models.

Front-loading models are also called *horizontal-axis washers*, 18-24. Because these models load from the front, they require more bending of the user than the top-loaders unless they are elevated with special pedestals available from manufacturers. While they cost more to purchase than traditional washers, front-loading models are highly efficient and use *much* less water and save energy, too. Horizontal-axis machines have a faster spin speed that wrings out more water. Less water means a shorter drying time. They also use less detergent, but require special low-sudsing, high-efficiency detergents. Look for "he" on the detergent label. Because there is no agitator, front-loading models are gentle on clothing.

To suit a variety of fabrics, washers have cycles, such as heavy-duty, normal, permanent press, and delicates. All cycles have the same basic steps: fill, wash, spin (drain), rinse, and spin again. Cycles vary in the length of time, amount of agitation or movement, water temperature, and number of rinses.

Features to Consider

Features on washers include dispensers that release detergent, bleach, and fabric softener into the wash water at the right times. Top-loaders also feature a control that lets the user match the water level to the load size. Front-loading machines weigh the load to determine the water use. Some washers have a water temperature control for the wash water.

Porcelain-coated and stainless steel tubs are rust-resistant and smooth enough to protect fine fabrics. If chipped, however, porcelain-enamel tubs can form rust spots. Plastic tubs are durable and rust-resistant, but may develop rough spots over time which may snag clothes. See the checklist in Figure 18-25 when buying a washer and dryer.

Dryers

Clothes dryers are often bought at the same time as washers. They are usually available in matching sets. Dryers should be large enough to dry a full load from the washer. An advantage of buying a matching pair is the dryer design handles the same load size as the washer. For easy loading, arrange the dryer so that the open door faces the clothes washer. This is especially important in the front-loading models.

18-24
This home owner chose to use the front-loading washer and dryer. Notice the convenient sink and clothing-hanging area.

Photography Courtesy of Bosch Home Appliances

Checklist for Washers and Dryers	
Washers	**Dryers**
• Will the washer fit your space limitations? • Does the washer have a self-cleaning lint filter? • Does the top-loading model have a water-level selector? • Is there a water temperature selector? • Does it have a minimum of regular, delicate, and permanent press cycles? • Is a presoak cycle available? a permanent-press cycle? a knit cycle? a delicate cycle? • Does the washer have a control to stop the machine and signal when the load is unbalanced? • Does the model have dispensers for bleach, fabric softener, and detergent? • Does the washer have an optional second rinse selector? • Is the tub and lid made of porcelain enamel or stainless steel?	• Is the lint trap in a convenient place for ease in removing, cleaning, or replacing? • Is the control panel lighted? the interior? • Is there a signal (buzzer or bell) at the end of the drying period? • Is there a safety button to start the dryer? • Does the dryer offer one heat setting or a choice? • Does the dryer have an automatic sensor to prevent overdrying? • Does it offer a wrinkle-guard feature? an air-only, no-heat setting? • Does it have a touch-up cycle to remove creases in dry clothes?

18-25
Before buying a washer and dryer, consider these points.

Dryers operate on gas or electricity. Compare installation and operating costs as well as purchase prices before you buy.

Features to Consider

Basic clothes dryer models have preset temperatures that are safe for most fabrics. Most dryers have both time and temperature settings. A permanent press feature prevents wrinkles from forming by tumbling clothes without heat at the end of the drying time. An *air-dry* option may be available to fluff items without using heat.

Most dryer models have a timer control, and some have either a temperature sensor or a *moisture-sensing system.* These sensors shut the dryer off when clothes reach a selected temperature or degree of dryness. Another feature of deluxe models guards against wrinkles. Some reverse the drum direction periodically to mix up the clothes. Others tumble dry clothes without heat for a few seconds every few minutes until they are unloaded.

Choosing Climate-Control Appliances

Appliances can help control the climate in your home. They can maintain humidity levels and temperatures that increase the comfort of the indoor environment.

Dehumidifiers and Humidifiers

The humidity level of the air in a home will determine the need for a dehumidifier or a humidifier. A **dehumidifier** is an appliance that removes moisture from the air. Excess humidity can cause discomfort as well as mildew, musty odors, rust, and other problems. If a home has an air conditioning unit, there may not be a need for a dehumidifier because the air conditioner removes moisture as well as heat.

A **humidifier** performs the opposite function of a dehumidifier. It adds moisture to the air. Dry air is a problem in some climates, especially during winter months when homes are heated. Static electricity and splintering wood floors and furniture are signs the air is dry.

Dehumidifiers and humidifiers can be portable or part of the heating-cooling system. When purchasing a new unit, follow the recommendations of a manufacturer that offers a wide variety to locate a type and size for a particular home.

Room Air Conditioners

A room air conditioner is an appliance for cooling a room or small area. There are three types of room air conditioners: window units, built-in wall units, and portable units. Regardless of the type, the air conditioner should have the cooling capacity appropriate for the needs of the room or area. Window units must fit the window opening for installation, 18-26. Built-in models fit an opening in an exterior wall. When it is not possible to use window units or built-in models, portable air conditioning units are the remaining option. These units are on castors and users can move them from room to room. They tend to be more costly than window or built-in models and may be less efficient.

When you shop for room air conditioners, you will need to know your cooling needs in detail. You can pick up a helpful form from a retailer that includes all the key questions to answer. For example, what direction does the room face? South and west exposures receive more sunlight and, therefore, require greater cooling capacity. What are the size and the shape of the area requiring cooling? How many people normally use the space at the same time? How much glass and insulation are in the area? Greater glass area builds up heat while greater insulation will control heat/cool air exchange.

The answers to these and other questions help in calculating the cooling needs of a home. A retailer or heating/cooling specialist can help with this step. Cooling needs and the cooling capacity of room air conditioners are expressed in British thermal units (Btu). Once the Btu range is known, check the EnergyGuide labels of similar models to compare energy efficiency ratings (EERs). Models with higher EERs use less energy and, therefore, cost less to operate. In addition, look for the ENERGY STAR label, too.

Also check the controls. Are they easy to reach and use? Can the user change the level of cooling to meet his or her needs? Can the user program it to change cooling levels automatically? Check the louvers for air direction. If possible, turn on the unit to check the noise level.

Many homes today have whole-house air conditioners as part of their HVAC system. For more information, refer to Chapter 9.

18-26
Room air conditioners come in different sizes both to fit the window space and also to handle the cooling requirements of different rooms or areas.

Whirlpool Home Appliances

Portable Space Heaters

A portable space heater is an appliance used for heating a room or small area. Numerous types of space heaters are available including those that rest on the floor or baseboard heating. There are also heaters than can be wall mounted and some heaters can rest on tables or other furniture.

A major energy source for space heaters is electricity, either in the form of electric space heaters, electric oil or water radiators, and electric baseboard heaters. Some space heaters also use kerosene for fuel, but some cities do not permit this use. For example, the District of Columbia Fire Code strictly prohibits the use of kerosene heaters in any location of Washington, D.C.

Features in portable space heaters are numerous, with safety and operational controls of top importance. These features may include

- an automatic cut-off when the heater is off balance or tips over
- an automatic cut-off when overheating of the unit occurs
- thermostatic controls with variable temperature settings and a remote control to adjust settings
- an oscillating fan to distribute warmth throughout the space

Choosing Other Appliances

Many other appliances, both essential and optional, are available for home use. Water heaters, vacuum cleaners, personal computers, and a variety of portable appliances are among those that people might consider buying.

Water Heaters

Many tasks in a home require hot water, including bathing, laundry, and a variety of cooking and cleaning tasks. Water heaters use either gas or electricity to heat water. The type of water heater you (or a client) choose will depend on the home heating system. For example, homes with gas heating will utilize a gas hot water heater. In contrast, homes with electric heating systems use electric hot water heaters.

When purchasing a water heater, considering size capacity is important. This will depend on the amount of hot water a household uses. The more people who live in a home increase the demand for hot water. Other appliances that require large amounts of hot water, namely a dishwasher and an automatic clothes washer, also influence water heater size.

Heating water adds to home energy costs. Therefore, it is wise to properly insulate the water heater. To do this, simply wrap an insulating jacket around the water heater to provide more insulation. Insulating hot water pipes to reduce heat loss is also important. Set the water heater thermostat at 120°F; however, if you have a dishwasher without a preheater, set the water heater thermostat at 140°F. Most new water heaters are preset at the factory to 120°F, and alterations to this temperature are not possible. In this case, make sure the dishwasher has a preheater. If possible, install the water heater near the kitchen and laundry areas. These steps will help save energy, too.

Vacuum Cleaners

A vacuum cleaner is a useful appliance for removing loose dirt from rugs and carpets. Uses also include cleaning hard-surface floors, draperies, and upholstery. Attachments allow vacuum cleaners to perform other cleaning tasks, too.

Some vacuum cleaners use a High-Efficiency Particulate Arresting filter, or HEPA filter. A HEPA filter removes additional allergens from the air before recirculating the air into the room.

A consumer's choice of a vacuum cleaner depends on what he or she wants it to do. There are many types available. These include canisters, uprights, mini-canisters, and hand-held and wet/dry vacuums. Some people choose to own more than one type to meet their various needs.

Canisters

Canister vacuums are easy to handle and do a good job of house cleaning, 18-27. They are effective on bare floors, stairs, and upholstery. Canister cleaners can be straight suction models, or they may feature a power nozzle attachment that increases the carpet cleaning capability with rotating beaters and brushes.

Uprights

Upright cleaners are the choice of many people purchasing vacuum cleaners. Their primary usage is to clean carpets. Most are adjustable for all types of carpet pile. Some adjust automatically, while others are set manually. Uprights are available in self-propelled models. Nearly all uprights have attachments for other cleaning tasks, such as removing dust from furniture.

Central Vacuum Systems

A central vacuum is a built-in system with a heavy motor and dirt collection container that stay in one place, usually a garage or basement. The user carries a flexible, lightweight hose from room to room and inserts it into wall outlets in convenient locations. The system can also have a power attachment and special cleaning attachments. The air is filtered to the outside of the home.

Portable Appliances

Portable appliances allow the user to move them easily from one area to another. They include everything from toasters to electric blankets to hair dryers.

In today's society, many consider major appliances to be basic necessities. Living without a refrigerator or water heater, for instance, would require a big adjustment in lifestyle. The same is not true for portable appliances. These small appliances provide many conveniences, but are not necessary in many situations.

Portable appliances tend to be less costly than major appliances. However, the procedure for choosing them is much like choosing major appliances. The first step is determining the specific needs of household members and household resources. Then shop and compare. Choose portable appliances to meet the specific needs of household members.

Check construction details, warranties, and prices. Decide which of the latest features you want and can afford. Determine whether a small appliance

18-27
The lightweight vacuum cleaner can easily be carried throughout the home.

Dirt Devil

LINK TO SCIENCE & TECHNOLOGY

Consumer Electronics Explosion

Between 1975 and 2008, the number of electronic devices in the average American home grew from 1.3 to 25. Examples of these devices are televisions, computers, book readers, gaming systems, digital cameras, personal media players, and phones.

Consumers must subscribe or buy services to use some consumer electronic products. Services include cell phone and Internet access, cable television, and satellite radio. Telecommunication industries, which provide these services, transmit voice, data, and images. For example, when you make a phone call, send an e-mail, text, or tweet, you are using telecommunications services. Many of these companies also sell their own products.

Electronic products are merging with each other and with various home appliances. Manufacturers are building flat-screen televisions into some refrigerator doors and Internet connectivity into many televisions sold today. This process, or *convergence*, involves the merging separate products into one. Other merged products include smart phones, personal digital assistants, and touch-screen devices that allow users to read books, visit Web sites, and download videos. New telecommunications technologies continue to change the way people communicate, work, learn, and have fun.

is necessary and whether it performs multiple functions. For example, can a mini-food processor chop nuts and grind coffee as well as grate vegetables? Look for recognizable brands, and be sure appliances have a seal indicating they meet safety standards. Read use and care information to help you select appliances that are easy to operate, clean, and maintain. As with other equipment, consider and plan for where and how to store portable appliances. Following these guidelines will help you make wise appliance choices, 18-28.

18-28
Portable appliances are available for a wide range of food preparation and cooking tasks.

(A) Zojirushi America Corporation; (B) T-Fal Corporation; (C) Hamilton Beach

A

B

C

Choosing Consumer Electronics

Consumer electronics differ from appliances in that they operate only on electricity or batteries. Appliances, as you recall, operate with gas or electricity. Consumer electronics serve many purposes in the home and workplace including education, communications, and entertainment. The electronic devices having the greatest impact on interior design schemes include computers, televisions, and their accompanying components or peripheral devices. Some computer electronics require additional furniture or mounting components.

Computers

A versatile electronic device typical in most homes and commercial environments is the computer. Desktop and portable laptop computers can meet an array of consumer space needs. Computers serve a number of purposes including tutoring students, entertaining children, and organizing entrepreneurs. Other common uses include sending and receiving communications and playing games. Developing household budgets, paying bills, managing household records, controlling household systems, and activating appliances are other computer-related activities.

When purchasing a computer for home or office, the first decision involves what the user wants it to do. **Software programs** are instructions that tell a computer what to do. For example, the operating system software controls the basic functions of a computer. Consumers can customize their computers by purchasing additional software. Software programs (or applications) can perform specific tasks to meet practically every need, whether creating a household budget or analyzing the nutritional value of meals. Review the software applications for the tasks you want to perform. Then find out what type of computer system and how much computer memory you need to operate these applications.

Hardware refers to the components in a computer system. The components include *input devices*, such as keyboards, touchpads, and digital cameras and video recorders. These devices are used to enter data into a computer. A *central processing unit (CPU)* is another hardware component. It follows built-in instructions as well as those on software programs. Computer speed depends on the power of the microprocessor and the amount of working memory, or *random access memory* (RAM). The higher the RAM, the faster the computer runs. The CPU generally includes a disk drive, which reads the information on software programs and stores it. An *output device*, such as a monitor, speakers, and a printer/scanner, allows a computer user to view and hear data. Another name for input and output devices is *peripherals*.

When buying a computer, consider everyone who might use it and all the ways they might use it, 18-29. Find out if the computer's memory capacity can expand to meet future needs. Ask whether telephone or online support service is available when questions arise. Investigating the purchase carefully will help you get the most use and value from this appliance.

Setting Up a Home Office

In addition to determining computer needs, also consider workspace setup and location. When setting up the home office, the purpose for the space will determine furnishings, equipment, and supportive wiring needs, 18-30. In

18-29
Telecommuters frequently use the computer to contact coworkers through e-mail.

18-30
Placing a personal computer in a kitchen work area helps keep household records organized.

addition to a powerful computer, perhaps many of the following items are required: a telephone, Internet connection, shredder, fax machine, copier, scanner, and printer. Often, one piece of peripheral equipment combines the functions of faxing, copying, scanning, and printing. Such multipurpose office equipment reduces surface-space needs. Most importantly, give attention to purchasing adequate surge protection, appropriate electrical wiring, cable connections, and electrical outlets.

Televisions

With the arrival of all-digital television broadcasts, many people are replacing their older boxlike TVs with sleeker *high-definition TV* (HDTV) sets. The impact of this transition for interior design varies. HDTV sets and the components that accompany them—cable and satellite TV boxes, gaming systems, and digital video recorders—require space. Some households choose to wall-mount their HDTV sets and use wall shelving for the components. Others choose either a built-in wall unit or a free-standing furniture unit. Because HDTV sets and their components use much electricity, appropriate electrical wiring, cable connections, and electrical outlets are essential.

CAREER FOCUS

Interior Designer—Kitchens and Baths

Can you imagine yourself as an interior designer who specializes in kitchen and bath design? If you can, read more about this challenging and appealing career.

Interests/Skills: Do you enjoy cooking and realize how important proper space planning is to creating an efficient food preparation area? Do you consider the kitchen a great space for family interaction? Skills include a vision for what a space could look like and balancing it with the rest of the home. When working with existing space, measurements and problem solving are very important.

Career Snapshot: Some residential interior designers specialize in designing kitchens and baths. The finished product needs to be a style that fits seamlessly with the rest of the home. Kitchens require a different approach to interior design than a living room or dining room. Designers must research products and select materials that provide for a safe environment. In kitchen design, they must be able to create a kitchen with properly placed work centers for storage, preparation, cooking, cleanup, and mixing. For bathrooms, the designer works with the client to determine what will work best to meet individual and family needs. In designing both kitchens and baths special attention must be given to the placement of electrical outlets, lighting, and ventilation. The designer must meet all local building codes.

Education/Training: A bachelor's degree is most often required. In addition, Certified Kitchen Designers (CKD) are certified through the National Kitchen & Bath Association (NKBA).

Photography Courtesy of Kohler

Licensing/Examinations: Approximately one-half of the states require interior designers to be licensed. The National Council for Interior Design Qualification (NCIDQ) administers an examination that interior designers must pass in order to obtain a license. In addition, designers specializing in kitchen and bath design would need to pass either the Certified Kitchen Designer (CKD) or the Certified Bath Designer (CBD) exam, both administered by the NKBA.

Professional Association: American Society of Interior Designers (ASID) (www.asid.org), International Interior Design Association (IIDA) (www.iida.org) and the National Kitchen & Bath Association (NKBA) (www.nkba.org)

Job Outlook: Customers often look to specialized positions for the best quality of service. Although not as qualified as an architect to do complex plans, a Certified Kitchen Designer can perform most similar services at a lower cost.

Source: Information from the Occupational Outlook Handbook (www.bls.gov/OCO) and the Occupational Information Network (O*NET)(www.online.onetcenter.org)

Summary

Choosing household equipment, including major and portable appliances, is part of housing decisions for you or your client. For satisfactory performance from appliances, choose products that meet your or your client's needs. Consider cost, features, size, safety, care, energy use, and quality when making appliance purchases.

Kitchen appliances include refrigerators, freezers, ranges, convection and microwave ovens, dishwashers, trash compactors, and food waste disposers. These appliances are available in a range of styles and features. Careful consideration will help in selecting those appliances that best meet your or your client's needs. Other appliances, including those used for laundry and climate control, must also be chosen with your needs in mind. Although they are a big investment, these appliances can improve the convenience, efficiency, comfort, and safety of your household.

Consumer electronics perform a variety of functions in the home and workplace. Computers and televisions can be a source of education, communication, and entertainment. They can impact the interior design of a space.

Review the Facts

1. Explain the difference between a full warranty and a limited warranty.
2. Which style of freezer is most energy efficient?
3. What type of material is used to make cookware for an induction cooktop? Why?
4. Explain why a convection oven cooks food faster and at a lower temperature than a conventional oven.
5. How is heat produced in a microwave oven?
6. Summarize the key features of a dishwasher.
7. Contrast the features of top-loading washers and front-loading washers. Which tends to be more energy efficient?
8. Explain the difference between a dehumidifier and a humidifier.
9. Why is insulation on a water heater important?
10. How does air filtering on a central vacuum system differ from that on most canister and upright vacuum cleaners?
11. What are three questions you might ask before purchasing a personal computer?
12. How can the transition from older boxlike TVs to high-definition TVs impact the interior design of a space?

Think Critically

13. **Analyze risks.** Suppose you found a small appliance (such as a toaster) for sale at a flea market or yard sale. It looked rather new, but it had no information about the use and care or warranty information. Analyze the potential risks of buying the small appliance.
14. **Draw conclusions.** Major appliances play a significant role in modern-day homes. For instance, most American homes have a clothes washer, range, and refrigerator. Use of these appliances is a part of everyday life. In contrast, many households tend to collect small appliances that are used infrequently. Draw conclusions about reasons for this fact.

Community Links

15. **Appliance comparison.** Review the Web site of a local store that sells major appliances. Compare the prices, energy costs, performance features, size, safety features, warranties, and quality of two brands of similar major appliances. Use the checklists given in this chapter to help you evaluate the two products. Share your findings with the class.

16. **Appliance use and care.** Locate a use and care manual for a major appliance. Summarize the kinds of information that it provides in a written report.

17. **Article review.** Locate and read two magazine or newspaper articles on new types of appliances or new appliance features coming in the future. Report your findings to the class. As an alternative, read two articles about consumer electronics and how they impact the interior design space in a home.

Academic Connections

18. **Reading.** Read two or more articles about tankless water heaters. Use reliable resources such as the Web sites for ENERGY STAR (www.energystar.gov/), the U.S. Department of Energy (www.energy.gov/), the U.S. Environmental Protection Agency (www.epa.gov/) or such magazines at *Consumer Reports.* What are the key features of tankless water heaters? How do materials and installation labor costs compare to the savings in energy? Give an oral report of your findings to the class.

19. **Math.** Suppose you are creating a design plan for a new kitchen for a client. Your client wants you to select two range models and two refrigerator models and compare the energy costs for each model for one year. Review the EnergyGuide labels for each range and refrigerator. Calculate the energy usage in kilowatt hours based on your local energy rates using the following formula:

Wattage × (Hours Used Per Day) × (Days Used Per Year) ÷ 1000 = Daily kilowatt-hour (kWh) consumption

Technology Applications

20. **Appliance technology.** Choose a kitchen or laundry appliance and investigate the technology used in the most current models. How does the appliance work? What are the pros and cons of the appliance? How do organizations such as ENERGY STAR and *Consumer Reports* rate the appliance? What conditions must the appliance meet to have an ENERGY STAR label? Put together your findings using presentation software and give your report to the class.

21. **Marketing analysis.** Analyze a TV infomercial for a household appliance or consumer electronics item. Summarize your observations by answering the following questions: What is the appliance or consumer electronics item and what does it do? According to the infomercial, why is it better than competing products on the market (if there are any)? How much does it cost? How persuasive is the infomercial? Give a report of your observations to the class. If possible, show a video clip of the infomercial.

22. **Appliance/electronics evaluation.** Locate a Web site that provides helpful comparisons of appliance features and prices for consumers. Review the information for two models of an appliance (large or small) or consumer electronics item of your choice. Use a computer to write a brief description of the appliance review in chart form. Based on the information presented, which model would you buy? Explain your decision.

Design Practice

23. **Home office design.** Presume you are designing a home office for a client's small business. The available space is 16 ft. by 20 ft. The painting and carpet installation are complete—both are warm neutral hues. A work surface and computer are essential. Your client also wants a small presentation area within the office space. The presentation area will require TV and component equipment. Use CADD software to design the floor plan showing the locations of the work and presentation areas. Then select photos of equipment and furnishings to best meet the client's needs. Write a summary of your recommendations to accompany the floor plan for your client.

24. **Portfolio.** A family you know is trying to decide what new refrigerator to buy. The household currently has an 18-cubic foot refrigerator-freezer that all members of this five-member household use. The family shops for groceries once per week, and refrigerated items usually fill all available space. They purchase few frozen foods. One of the family's three children uses a wheelchair. Everyone makes frequent trips to the refrigerator for ice and the pitcher of chilled water. Research the available options and make a recommendation. Keep a copy of your research and recommendation in your portfolio.

Investigating Appliance-Related Careers

Is a career linked to household appliances of interest to you? Do you find the challenge of appliance design and engineering interesting? Perhaps a career as a public relations specialist who promotes energy-efficient appliances may be another option.

In your career research, take the interactive *Career Scan* which is part of the FCCLA *Career Connection* program. This tool helps you rate your career development experiences and focus your attention on *Career Connection* units that meet your career goals. See your adviser for information as needed.

CHAPTER 19

Planning and Presenting Interior Designs

Terms to Learn

design process
letter of agreement
retainer
profile
ajacency matrix
criteria matrix
reupholster
interior wall elevation
bid
change order
outsource
liaison

Chapter Objectives

After studying this chapter, you will be able to

- summarize the phases of the interior design process.

- evaluate a client's needs, goals, and resources in creating design plans for residential housing and furnishings or for commercial interiors.

- apply design knowledge, skills, processes, and oral, written, and visual presentation skills to communicate design ideas.

- develop an interior design presentation.

- summarize the contract and financial elements for developing an interior design project.

Reading with Purpose

Read all parts of the chapter and write down three key points for each heading. Then write a summary describing how this chapter will help you apply concepts you learned in previous chapters.

The goal of an interior designer is to help solve a client's design problem by producing a usable, safe, and attractive space. The designer may begin with an empty new room or may redesign an existing space. The designer may also collaborate with builders, architects, and other tradespeople to create a new space. To create this new space, the interior designer follows an orderly process.

As you read this chapter, imagine yourself as an interior designer who is working with a client to develop a design concept for a room or area. Think about how each aspect of the design process and your prior learning will influence the decisions you make for your client's design plan.

What Is the Design Process?

In order to reach a client's goals, you will use the design process. The **design process** is a series of organized phases a designer uses to carry out a project in an orderly manner. Following the design process will help assure your clients that a design plan will help meet their desired results. The design process includes the following five phases:

1. **Programming**—gathering information from the client and other sources to guide the actual design

2. **Schematic design**—designer prepares preliminary sketches and compiles drawings, samples, and furniture photos to present as ideas to the client

3. **Design development**—the designer prepares the final design drawings and puts together a presentation board to show the client the complete design

4. **Contract documents**—designer makes purchases for the client, involves appropriate professionals for the project; and possibly initiates the bidding process for the final contract

5. **Contract administration**—involves actual construction and interior finishes, and ordering and installing furnishings and equipment

Not all design projects fit neatly into phases that have precise beginnings and endings. Indeed, the phases often overlap or occur at the same time. In addition, some designers argue that not all projects go through all steps in the phases. Regardless of the size or extent of a project, all projects involve some parts of all the phases in the design process. The rest of this chapter provides details on how to complete phases of the design process. These phases apply to both residential and commercial projects. *Residential* refers to where people live, such as homes and apartments. *Commercial* refers to business spaces where people go for services, such as hotels, restaurants, hospitals, day care centers, and banks.

Before beginning the design process, you will often have a consultation with the client about his or her needs, goals, and resources for the project. Careful listening is extremely important. You will need to understand the client's expectations for creating an attractive, functional environment for a home or business. It is also during this meeting that the designer will evaluate whether he or she has the experiences, skills, resources, time, and interest in completing the design with the potential client.

During an initial consultation, you and your client may sign a letter of agreement. The **letter of agreement** spells out the scope of project services responsibilities of each party. The designer's responsibilities include planning and carrying out a design plan and informing the client about fees. The client's responsibilities include providing the designer with necessary budget information, approving the design plan, and paying the designer's fees.

The letter of agreement generally requires the client to put down a **retainer**—an upfront fee the client pays to engage the services of a designer. Usually, the designer deducts the retainer from the balance due at the end of the project. The letter of agreement and the retainer protect both the designer and client in the event the project never develops. Once you create the design and the client approves it, you will draw up official contracts that include very specific details about the project. You will learn more about methods a designer uses to establish fees later in the chapter.

Phase 1: Programming

The main purpose of the Programming phase is to gather information from the client and other sources to guide the actual design. You will need to understand what the client wants in as much detail as possible. This usually requires meeting with the client to acquire this information; however, some designers have the client complete a questionnaire, 19-1. Either way, you need to ask very specific questions and discuss options that will help meet your client's unique needs. With commercial clients, it is important to do a little research about the business prior to the meeting. This will give you a better understanding of how the business space must function.

Gathering Client Information

During this part of the process, you will gather information about everyone who may use a space. In planning the

19-1
Meeting with your clients to acquire information about their design project is an essential part of the design process.

interior space of a house, this includes the number of family members, guests, and friends. Do any occupants have special needs the space must fulfill? For example, do older adults or anyone with a disability live in the home? How much privacy does each person require? You will generally create a profile for each occupant of the home along with profiles of guests and friends. A **profile** is a concise biographical sketch (or word picture) that portrays the key characteristics about the client. A residential client profile will include details about lifestyle, space functions, household activity needs, design style preferences, and future needs.

A commercial client profile will include details about business culture as well as space functions and design style preferences. Other business requirements a designer must consider include
- **Location of offices.** The designer will need to know the location of offices and how close they need to be to one another. For example, such as whether a manager's secretary is close to the manager or is located in a secretarial pool in a central location. Work flow and the needs of various departments also impact the arrangement of offices and their closeness.

LINK TO SOCIAL STUDIES & CULTURE

Americans with Disabilities Act

The Americans with Disabilities Act of 1990 prohibits discrimination against people with disabilities. According to this law, disability is "a physical or mental impairment that substantially limits one or more of the major life activities…" Life activities include working, learning, hearing, speaking, seeing, breathing, walking, executing manual tasks, and self-care activities such as eating, dressing, and bathing.

Architects and interior designers are familiar with ADA requirements that impact the design, construction, and alteration of public and commercial places. These places—hotels, restaurants, stores, medical offices, schools, local and government offices, for example—must be accessible to people with disabilities.

Following are a few examples of the many ADA requirements.

- Most buildings must have one or more entryways that are wheelchair accessible. For example, doorways must be wide enough to admit a wheelchair and ramps must be available if necessary.

- Signage, including signs at elevator entries, must include raised letters and braille characters for people who are blind or have low vision.

- Cafeteria food counters, drinking fountains, ATM machines, and public restrooms must be accessible.

The U.S. Department of Justice and the attorney general of each state can prosecute violations to the ADA. Individuals can also sue violators. Meeting ADA requirements can be costly. Requirements will sometimes be waived or altered if they impose an "undue burden." For more information about the ADA accessibility standards, go to www.ada.gov.

- **Accessibility of services.** For example, does the client prefer services such as printing and photocopying in a central location or in other strategic areas of the office?

- **Employee hierarchy.** Hierarchy within an office often determines the location of offices. For example, a top manager's office may be located the farthest from the entrance while the receptionist is within a few feet of the entry.

An adjacency matrix and a criteria matrix are tools to assist the designer in locating the rooms and space according to client needs. An **adjacency matrix** shows the desired relationship of room and space locations, 19-2. A **criteria matrix** looks at the impact of specific needs on various spaces. These specific needs include the need to control noise or provide visual privacy.

The details you require depend on the size and complexity of the project. Factors to consider when gathering client information also include codes that might affect the space design. These codes include construction, fire safety, general safety, mechanical, and accessibility codes.

Lifestyle and Function

The client's lifestyle includes all the various activities that occur in the home or space. As an interior designer, you must identify how the client thinks about *home*. Is home a place of rest and rejuvenation? Is it a place of constant activity? Is it a social place where many people gather for formal or informal meals, games, music, or media activities? How much space do household members need for privacy and interaction? For example, you will need to know if your clients use the bedrooms for more activities than sleeping, such as studying or watching television. What family history or cultural factors may influence the design? All this and more will help you create the best possible design concept for your client.

Space Requirements

When designing a functional pleasing space, you will need to know how much space to allow for each of the activities and functions that occur in the home. Traffic patterns and standard dimensions of furnishings are important parts to solving the design puzzle. Storage needs to be adequate for all of the client's belongings. Taking inventories of household equipment, sports equipment, furnishings, clothing, musical instruments, and other items for all occupants of the dwelling are important for allocating storage space. In addition, many homes today are sites of cottage industries and home offices that require more storage.

Design Preferences

Good communication is key to assessing your client's design preferences. Whether you are designing one room or a whole house, learning the likes and dislikes of each occupant will help in developing a design concept pleasing to all. In addition, visiting the client's home will give you great insight into the client's style needs and tastes. What might you learn by viewing a client's living space? The following factors provide clues for a successful design plan:

Adjacency Matrix						
Location of Space in Physician's Office						
Plan for Traffic Flow	Doctor's Office	Exam Rooms	Nurses' Station	Copy Services & Files	Registration	Lobby	Entrance
Entrance	3	3	3	3	1	1	–
Lobby	3	3	2	2	1	–	
Registration	3	2	2	2	–		
Copy Services/Files	3	3	1	–			
Nurses' Station	2	1	–				
Exam Rooms	1	–					
Doctor's Office	–						
1 = Near							
2 = Not so near							
3 = Far							

19-2
An adjacency matrix helps an interior designer show the desired relationships between room locations and space to meet client needs.

Madge Megliola, ASID

- What types of things surround a client's living space? Is the space uncluttered and have clean surfaces?

- How does the space make the client feel? Is it energizing or restful? close and cozy, or spacious and private?

- What color-scheme preferences does the client have? What backgrounds, lighting, and accessories bring comfort to the client?

- What new or existing furniture will the client want to use?

- What cultural artifacts and psychological elements seem to influence the client's taste?

- Is the client's style traditional or contemporary? Does your client prefer a vintage style?

Future Needs

Although clients generally have very specific ideas for their space today, the needs and goals for a home or office often change over the years. For example, when developing a design plan for a young family, a key goal may include accommodating play space for the whole family. How might this goal change as the family grows and children leave home?

Assessing the Environment

As you walk through a client's living space, you will assess a number of environmental factors about the space. Noting even the smallest details will help you effectively meet the design needs and goals for your client. The details to notice include the following:

- **Location of functional areas.** Where are the private, social, and work areas located? How do these areas relate to each other? How much space does the client allocate to each functional area? See 19-3.

- **Number and arrangement of rooms.** Whether your client wants to develop a new design plan for a single room or for the whole house, it is important to know the number of rooms and their arrangement in the space. For example, design plans for one room can impact another adjacent room.

- **Storage.** Does every bedroom have adequate closet space? Where are other storage areas located throughout the dwelling? Is there adequate space for bed and bath linens? Does kitchen storage adequately meet

client needs? Does your client require special storage, perhaps for sports equipment or musical instruments?

- **Backgrounds.** What ceiling, wall, and flooring backgrounds are in your client's current space? Does your client prefer paint or wall coverings, hardwood floors or carpeting, and drapery or nondrapery window treatments?

- **Furnishings.** What style does your client prefer in furnishings? Is the current style traditional or eclectic? Does your client prefer furniture designs from previous eras, such as the Victorian or Craftsman periods? Perhaps your client prefers contemporary furnishings with a futuristic edge. What items will help address functional and aesthetic needs?

- **Energy and environmental needs.** What energy needs and environmental factors does your client want to meet? Is replacement of windows with insulated windows and low-E glass on the agenda? Is an upgrade to a high-efficiency ENERGY STAR model for the heating and cooling system in order? Perhaps your client wants to install an active solar system or insulated window treatments.

- **Traffic patterns.** How do household members move through the house? Are there features that interfere with good traffic flow? What traffic flow needs does the client want to accomplish? How does traffic flow impact furniture arrangement?

- **Health and safety.** Creating a design that meets all codes and health and safety factors is essential.

Taking Measurements; Calculating Materials

An important part of successful design development is taking careful measurements. Accurate measurements will help you calculate or verify the

19-3
The well-defined relationships among the food preparation, dining, and living areas takes into consideration the client's needs for multiple activities in a space.

GREEN CHOICES

Considerations for Green or Sustainable Products

When developing a design plan for a client, interior designers should ask themselves the following questions when evaluating green or sustainable products:

- Does the manufacturer of the product strive to make improvements in the manufacturing process by reducing and reusing first, then recycling?
- Is the manufacturing process energy efficient?
- Does the manufacturer comply with their industry's voluntary testing programs?
- Does the manufacturing process release harmful substances?
- What are the raw materials used to create the product and where do they originate?
- Are the materials from renewable resources?
- Are the adhesives, coating and finishes used in the product healthy and safe?
- How is the product packaged and transported?
- Does the product do its job well?
- Is the product durable, biodegradable, or recyclable?
- Does the product nurture the health and well-being of its occupants?

Information Courtesy of REGREEN by ASID and USGBC

amounts of materials to order for a client's design concept. Creating a rough sketch of the floor plan for an area will help you accurately keep track of measurements.

Remember to use good measuring techniques, such as keeping the tape level when measuring horizontally. When measuring wall length, for example, run the tape measure along the floor next to the wall. When you cannot move furniture, track the tape along a straight floor seam or use a straight edge. For taking most measurements, use a retractable metal tape measure that is marked in feet, inch, and sixteenth-inch graduations for the most accuracy. As a designer, you will often need to calculate paint, wall coverings, flooring, window treatments, and upholstery materials.

Many variables can impact measurements. For example, a reupholstery job will require more fabric if the fabric

of choice has a pattern repeat than if the fabric is plain. Likewise, covering existing walls painted a deep red will require more paint. The information about taking measurements in this passage is just the starting point. Every design project will have its own unique set characteristics and variables that can impact the measurements you take.

Paint Calculations

When a design plan requires painting a room, most interior designers obtain an estimate from a quality painter. The designer determines the paint colors and the type of paint (such as flat or eggshell, semi-gloss or gloss) and gives this information to the painter. The painter determines how much paint a job requires. Because most painters purchase paint at a reduced cost from their suppliers, you will often get a better deal for the job if the painter supplies the paint. When developing an estimate, the painter

- evaluates how many coats a room will need for coverage (note that covering deep reds and yellows on existing walls often requires extra coats of paint)

- determines the amount of primer and whether to tint the primer the same color as the finish paint (note that tinting the primer may reduce the number of coats a room requires)

- calculates trim paint separately if the trim paint is different from the wall paint (trim includes crown and base moldings, door and window casings, and often doors)

To verify the accuracy of a painter's estimate, you may want to take your own room measurements. Keep in mind that one gallon of paint usually covers 350 square feet of wall space. Divide the total square footage of a room by 350 square feet to estimate the amount of paint. If the result is less than 0.5 gallon, generally two quarts will do. If the result is greater than 0.5 gallon, a gallon is usually more economical.

Ceiling Paint. When calculating the amount of ceiling paint, multiply the ceiling width by the ceiling length to determine the square footage of the area. Divide the square footage by 350 to identify how many gallons the job requires, rounding your answer up to the nearest gallon. Use the following formula for your estimate:

$$\text{Area} = \text{Width} \times \text{Length}$$

Wall Paint. To calculate the amount of wall paint to order, add together the lengths of the room walls (the perimeter) and multiply the total length by the room height to get the total area square footage using the following formula:

$$\text{Area} = \text{Perimeter} \times \text{Height}$$

Once you know the total area (square footage) of the walls, subtract the square footage of door and window openings (Area = Width × Length). Divide the total by 350 to obtain the total gallons of paint.

How much wall paint is required for a room measuring 13 ft. wide by 16 ft. long by 8 ft. high with one door (3 ft. wide by 7 ft. high) and two windows (3 ft. wide by 4 ft. long)?

Step 1: $P = 13 + 16 + 13 + 16$

Step 2: $P = 58$ ft.

Step 3: $A = 58$ ft. × 8 ft.

Step 4: $A = 464$ sq. ft. (total wall area)

Step 5: $A = 3$ ft. × 7 ft. (door area)

Step 6: $A = 21$ sq. ft. (total door area)

Step 7: $A = (3$ ft. × 4 ft.$) \times 2$ (window area)

Step 8: $A = 24$ sq. ft. (total window area)

Step 9: 45 sq. ft. = 21 sq. ft. + 24 sq. ft. (total window/door area)

Step 10: 464 sq. ft. - 45 = 419 sq. ft. (total wall area)

Step 11: 419 sq. ft. ÷ 350 = 1.19 gallons (round up to 1.5)

Because the answer includes 1 whole gallon and a fraction of a gallon less than 0.5, you will need 1 gallon plus 2 quarts of paint. (*Note:* Because of the minimal cost difference, it may be a good idea to round up to the next gallon to allow for touch-ups or to add another coat if necessary.)

Wall Covering Calculations

Similar to estimating materials and labor for room paint, interior designers often work with professional wall covering hangers to determine the material and labor requirements for hanging wall covering. Because these professionals work with wall coverings and their variables on a daily basis, they can efficiently estimate these costs. Once a client chooses a wall covering, the interior designer gives this information to the wall covering hanger. Factors that impact the amount of wall covering a job requires include

- type of wall covering (for example vinyl-coated paper or solid vinyl, prepasted or not)

- size of pattern and length of pattern repeat in the wall covering (pattern repeat impacts the usable yield of wall covering—a longer repeat reduces the usable square footage)

To confirm the wall covering estimate, calculate wall covering needs with the same formula for calculating wall area for paint. (Note: A single roll of wall covering covers about 30 square feet. Most suppliers sell wall covering in double rolls.)

Divide the total square footage of a room by 30 to determine the number of single rolls of wall covering. If your calculations reveal a fraction of a roll, round up to the next roll. Many experts do not subtract the square footage for door and window openings when estimating wall coverings.

Suppose your client decides to use a wall covering with no pattern repeat for the 13 ft. by 16 ft. room (464 sq. ft.) instead of paint on the walls. How many double rolls of wall covering would you need to order for this room?

> **Step 1:** 464 sq. ft. ÷ 30 = 15.5 rolls
>
> **Step 2:** 15.5 ÷ 2 = 7.75 double rolls (round up to 8 double rolls)

Resilient Flooring and Carpeting Calculations

Before taking measurements, create a rough sketch of the room or area in which your client wants resilient flooring or carpeting. There are several factors to remember about these flooring coverings.

The standard width of most resilient flooring and carpeting is 12 feet. Some resilient flooring has a pattern that influences the direction to lay the flooring. In addition, all carpeting has a grain or nap—the direction in which the fibers run. Installing carpeting so that the grain runs in the same direction as the entrance (or main entrance in case of multiple doors) to the room helps ensure the carpeting will wear better and last longer.

You will likely work with a floor covering supplier or installer to consider the best way to lay the resilient flooring or carpeting in the room so that the pattern or grain flows with the traffic pattern. This will also help determine where the seams (if any) will fall in the floor covering, 19-4. Planning the layout helps reduce the amount of waste and often saves the client money. A flooring seam should *never* run down the middle of a room. This is not pleasing to the eye and may cause the resilient flooring or carpeting to wear faster.

When taking floor-covering measurements, use the standard formula for calculating the room area (square footage). Then divide the square footage by 9—the number of square feet in a square yard. (*Note:* Resilient flooring and carpeting often sells by the square yard rather than square foot.)

When a wall measurement includes a fraction of a foot, always round the measurement up to the next whole foot. For example, if the width of a room measures 14.5 feet, round up to 15 feet before calculating square footage of the room. It is always better to have a little extra than not enough carpeting.

Suppose your client intends to carpet a great room that measures 16.5 by 24 feet. How many square yards of carpeting will you need to order?

> **Step 1:** 17 ft. × 24 ft. = 408 sq. ft.
>
> **Step 2:** 408 sq. ft. ÷ 9 = 45.33 sq. yd. (round up to 45.5 sq. yd.)

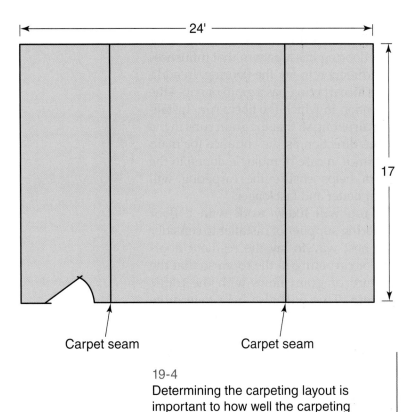

Carpet seam   Carpet seam

19-4
Determining the carpeting layout is important to how well the carpeting wears and its beauty.

Calculations for Shades and Blinds

Many styles of nondrapery shades and blinds are available to enhance the look of windows, block light, and provide privacy and insulating qualities. There are two ways to install shades and blinds: inside the window frame or positioning them over the window frame and trim.

If you are ordering shades or blinds for more than one window, number or letter the windows on a room or area sketch to make sure each gets the appropriate shade or blind. When writing measurements for shades and blinds, *always* note the width measurement first and the length measurement second to avoid confusion about how to install these window treatments, 19-5.

Inside Mount. Measurements for mount-ing shades and blinds inside the window frame require absolute precision. Use the following steps to take inside-mount measurements:

19-5
Taking precise measurements is essential for shades or blinds mounted inside the window frame. With shades or blinds mounted outside the window trim, measurements can be more flexible.

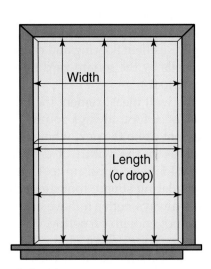

A. Inside mount measurements for shades or blinds.

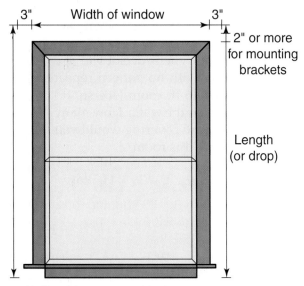

B. Outside mount measurements for shades and blinds.

Step 1: Measure the window width inside the window frame from left to right. Take three width measurements from the top, middle, and bottom of the window. Use the narrowest measurement for the width of inside-mount shades and blinds.

Step 2: Measure the length (or drop) of the window from the top of the frame to the stool on the left and right sides of the window and the middle. If the client does not want the shade or blind to touch the stool, subtract ¼ inch from your length measurement.

Outside Mount. Mounting shades and blinds outside the window trim offers greater privacy and light-blocking properties especially for bedrooms. Use the following steps for taking outside-mount measurements:

Step 1: Measure the window width from the outside edge of the trim on the left to the outside edge of the trim on the right along the top of the window. Add 3 or more inches to the width measurement on each side of the window for adequate coverage.

Step 2: Measure from a point at least 2 inches above the top of the window trim to the appropriate length (or drop) below the window apron. The 2-inch space above the window trim allows room for the mounting brackets.

Curtain and Drapery Calculations

Curtains and draperies are soft window treatments you can use to enhance the beauty of a room and help tie together the design details. Most curtain and drapery fabrics are 54 inches wide. Curtains or draperies may require 2 or 3 panels or widths of fabric per window depending on the fullness the client desires, pattern repeat, and whether the treatment needs lining. Some styles of window treatments—such as pleated draperies versus tab-top draperies—require more or less fabric than others. To obtain the basic yardage requirements for curtains and draperies, you will need to measure the area these treatments will cover. Take these measurements in inches using the following steps:

Step 1: Measure the width of the window and any wall space the treatments will cover. Then multiply this measurement by the number of fabric widths the client desires. For example, suppose your client wants full, sheer curtains on the living room picture window. The fabric type is sheer Georgette with no pattern repeat. The window measures 72 inches in width. Multiply this measurement by 3 for adequate fullness; then divide this number by 54 to determine the number of fabric widths.

> 72 in. × 3 = 216 in.
> 216 in. ÷ 54 in. = 4 fabric widths (panels)

Step 2: Measure the length of the window treatment from the top of the rod (usually 2 to 3 inches above the top window trim). Add 12 to 16 inches to this length to allow for top and bottom hems of the curtains or draperies. Assume your client wants the curtains to touch the floor and have deep hems. Your measurement is 92 inches finished length. Add together the total length and hem allowance. Then divide this total by 36 inches (the length of 1 yard of fabric).

> 92 in. + 16 in. = 108 in. (length)
> 108 in. ÷ 36 in. = 3 yd. (per panel)

Step 3: Multiply the number of yards-per-panel by the number of panels you need to obtain the total yardage for the curtains or draperies.

$$3 \text{ yd.} \times 4 = 12 \text{ yd. (fabric)}$$

Upholstery Fabric Estimations

If your client wants a new piece of upholstered furniture, you may need to determine how much fabric it will require. Factory-made upholstered furniture is usually less costly than custom pieces. For custom pieces, the fabric cost per-yard and the upholstery-workroom labor cost greatly influence the total price of a furniture piece. Most furniture and upholstery fabric companies have fabric estimation charts that can help guide your plans for the project budget. Figure 19-6 shows fabric estimations for a few key pieces of upholstery. For custom pieces, the fabric cost per-yard and the upholstery-workroom labor cost greatly influence the total price of a furniture piece.

Suppose your client decides to **reupholster**—or update fabric, padding, and springs for a piece of furniture he or she wants to keep. If your client agrees, involve a reputable upholsterer to determine the material and labor costs for the work. Generally, you can give the upholsterer the following information and he or she can determine the fabric yardage the project requires:

- height and width of the furniture piece
- number of cushions (seat and back)
- arms and legs, if any, and whether they are exposed
- skirting and piping requirements
- fabric width and pattern repeat

A common practice is to add 10 percent or more fabric to the estimate to account for seams, decorative trims, and stretchers (fabric pieces used for pulling upholstery taut to the frame). If the fabric of choice has a pattern, the upholsterer will likely increase the

---

19-6
Although standard upholstery yardages are available for most furniture pieces, precise measurements are necessary before ordering client fabrics.

Standard Upholstery Yardages (No Pattern Repeat)*	
Furniture Type	**Upholstery Yardage**
Traditional Sofa (6 ft. long)	10 to 12 yd.
Traditional Sofa (7 ft. long)	11 to 14 yd.
Traditional Sofa (9 ft. long)	13 to 18 yd.
Sectional Sofa (3 pieces)	30 to 34 yd.
Chaise Lounge	6 to 8 yd.
Club Chair	7 to 8 yd.
Slipper Chair (armless)	4 to 5 yd.
Wing Chair	5 to 7 yd.
Dining Chair (upholstered seat and back)	2 to 2.5 yd.
Small Ottoman	2 to 2.5 yd.
Medium Ottoman	2.5 to 3 yd.
Large Ottoman	5+ yd.
*Upholstery yardage is based on a standard 54 in. width of fabric. Estimates may vary with factors associated with such design or construction details as tufting, number and style of cushions, shirring, etc.	

yardage to account for the length of the pattern repeat. Note that pattern repeats can run anywhere from 3 to 50 inches, which will increase fabric yardage by 10 to 40 percent.

Estimating Costs

Estimating material and labor costs may be one of the most challenging factors in determining fees for your client. It is essential to provide clients with itemized details of all costs for materials and labor charges. Regardless of the method you use for setting fees, you will need to include overhead costs (such as business supplies and office rent and utilities) and build in profit to your budget estimation. Remember, your *budget* is a financial plan for coordinating available resources and expenditures.

Because labor costs vary greatly in different regions of the United States, you may need to check several sources for information about these costs. Obtaining price lists from quality contractors, product suppliers, tradespeople, and drapery and upholstery workrooms will help you create accurate estimates, 19-7. It is also important to determine who will pay for freight, shipping and handling. Some factors that influence labor costs include scheduling, location and equipment needs, economics, region or city, and clean-up costs. In addition, you may find prices of labor are higher when jobs are plentiful and lower when jobs are scarce, which follows the basic economic principles of supply and demand. Here are some points to remember when estimating labor costs for the following:

- **Paint.** Professional painters generally base labor charges on the amount of time it takes to paint 100 square feet. The amount of time is then multiplied by an hourly rate. Factors, such as the need for scaffolding or other special equipment also influence labor costs for painting.

19-7
Obtaining a price list from a quality upholstery workroom will help you calculate accurate price estimates. Upholstery workers, such as this woman, are able to calculate to the minute how long it will take to create an upholstered furniture piece.

Calico Corners—Calico Corners Home Stores

- **Wall coverings.** Labor charges for hanging wall coverings are generally on a per-roll basis. For example, hanging wall coverings may cost anywhere from $16.00 to $50.00 per single roll depending on the wall covering type and quality and the room layout.

- **Carpeting.** Professional carpet installers may base installation fees per-square-foot or per-square-yard. Note that installers will charge additional fees for removing old carpeting or moving furniture. Installation fees will also be greater in major markets, such as New York, Chicago, and Los Angeles. If the carpet requires padding, be sure to get the "installed" price.

- **Window treatments.** There are two labor costs for window treatments: workroom or fabrication costs and the installer's costs. In addition, there will be costs for fabrics (per yard), rods (per foot), and hardware for hanging window treatments. Because costs vary, it is best to obtain a price sheet from a reputable drapery workroom. Fabrication time (manufacturing time) can vary depending on how long it takes for the workroom to obtain the correct fabrics and the complexity of the drapery order. Four to six weeks or more is not uncommon for creating custom window treatments.

- **Upholstery.** Professional upholsterers have shop rates based on an hourly rate plus the amount of time required to remove and replace fabric. Repairing frames and springs or applying special accessory trims also add time to labor estimates. An experienced upholsterer will be able to calculate to the minute, how much time it will take to reupholster a furniture piece.

Establishing a Preliminary Project Budget

Once you take all of the measurements required for the design concept, you will need to make many financial decisions. These include establishing fees and developing a project budget. Many factors enter into establishing a preliminary project budget. The costs for products, furnishings, labor, and services vary for every project, 19-8. You will need to consider whether there is a need for other consultants such as those who, for example, specialize in planning licensed child care facilities. In addition, the costs involved for other professionals, such as architects, carpenters, and

electricians also affect the total project budget. The first step in planning a project budget is establishing designer fees and a payment schedule.

Designer Fees and Payment Schedule

Interior designers are unique in their talents, skills, knowledge, experience, personalities, specialty areas, and reputations. Likewise, fees and payment schedules also differ from one designer to the next. As a result, there is no usual fee for interior design services. The designer's experience and the project complexity usually influence fees and payment arrangements. Although some interior designers may negotiate their fees to suit a client's needs, most use one of the following methods, or combination of methods, to set their fees:

- **Fixed (or flat) fee.** With this fee method, you identify a specific sum to cover costs. One total fee applies to the complete range of services, from conceptual development through layouts, specifications, purchases, and final installation. This requires knowing in advance every cost, the time involvement for services, and the appropriate profit margin for the complete project.

- **Hourly fee.** For this form of compensation, you base the fee on the actual time you spend on a project or specific service. Hourly fees for interior designers can range from $60.00 to $350.00 per hour depending on the designer's experience and the project complexity.

- **Cost plus**. With this fee method, you purchase materials, furnishings, and services (such as carpentry, drapery workroom time, picture framing, and more) at cost. Then you sell these items to the client at cost plus a specific percentage agreed to with the client to compensate for your time and effort.

19-8
The fees for other consultants will need to be part of the total budget for a project.

- **Retail.** The retail method relates to the cost plus method because the client purchases products from the designer. In this method, the client pays the manufacturer's recommended price for the item as sold in stores or by the interior designer. You as the designer will keep the actual *markup profit* on the items, which can be 100 percent, while ordering items at the lower professional rate.

- **Per square foot.** For larger commercial projects, you may calculate costs on a per square foot basis, based on the area of the project.

The Preliminary Budget

Before beginning to develop a client's design concept, you must have a basic idea about what the client wants to spend and accomplish in the project. In addition to the designer's fees, there are other costs to consider when developing a preliminary project budget. The preliminary budget includes the amount of money the client allocates to spend on the design project. Developing a preliminary project budget that satisfies both the client and designer is a major factor in the designer/client relationship, 19-9.

When beginning a project with a client, it is important to understand the different ways clients approach setting a project budget. Clients may do the following:

- Ask you to make a budget estimate for completing the specific design concept. Such clients may react to your budget by accepting it fully or by asking you to adjust it to a lower or higher figure.

- Tell you the amount of money they are able to spend on the design project at the first meeting. The clients ask you to develop a concept within this budget.

- Work with you as funds become available. Clients may spread the work over a period of time or perhaps approach the design project one room or area at a time.

- Set no predetermined budget figure. The client simply wants you to work without any limitations. A designer may have this type of job once in a lifetime.

When setting a project budget, there are three key areas on which you and a client must agree. These areas include the following budget allocations:

- direct costs, such as furnishings, product manufacturing or fabrication, installation, construction, materials and finishes, and delivery services, as well as unusual travel costs the client or project may require of the designer

- indirect costs, such as sales taxes and contractor/delivery delays

- interior designer compensation

If you realize that the available budget will not accomplish the client's design project goals, you have several options. Revise the design to fit within the client's budget, if possible. You can also advise the client to increase the budget to accomplish what he or she wants. If you cannot reach a compromise on the budget and the quality that you must deliver, then you should tactfully remove yourself from the project. It is important that both the designer and client are clear on their expectations of each other.

Recording Project Needs

Once you have all necessary project details from your client, it is important to put this information in writing and create the client project file. Begin with a general statement about the design concept. Then you can put much of the program research you acquire into an

Preliminary Project Budget—Great Room

Presume your clients want you to redesign the great room off their kitchen. The room dimensions are: 18 ft. wide, 24 ft. long, and 8 ft. high. This room is a place where the family gathers to relax, watch movies, and play games. They plan to keep their traditional sectional sofa, but want it reupholstered. Your clients know they need additional seating, lighting, window treatments, and accessories. Here is the preliminary budget you have developed for this project.

Item	Quantity	Color/Style	Estimated Cost	Note
Bamboo flooring	432 sq. ft.	Natural bamboo with satin finish sealer	$13,000.00 installed	Existing subfloor in good condition
Painter, labor			$1,800.00	Two coats on walls and trim; one coat on ceiling; all surfaces in good condition, no prep work required
Wall paint	2 gal.	Taupe, flat latex	$72.00	Painter to supply paint
Ceiling paint	1 gal. + 2 qt.	Ceiling white, flat latex	$33.00	
Trim paint	1 gal. + 2 qt.	Ivory, semi-gloss oil-base	$65.00	
Sectional sofa				
Fabric	35 yd.	Chocolate brown, chenille	$3,000.00	No pattern repeat
Freight			$59.00	Freight is for custom order of fabric
Workroom	Recover only, no repairs		$2,500.00	
Installation			$35.00	Pick-up and delivery
Chairs	2	Fully upholstered matching club chairs, taupe multi-linen weave	$3,800.00	
End tables	2	Two-tier classic end table with center drawer, premium black walnut finish, with small gallery and castors in tarnish silver finish, 21w × 24d × 26h	$1,100.00	
Coffee table	1	42 in. square glass top with tarnished silver finish metal frame, tapered legs	$1,000.00	
Table lamps	2	30 in. round ceramic, ivory with brown wood base; ivory silk shades with brown linen trim	$700.00	
Freight			$40.00	Freight is for custom order of lamps

(Continued)

19-9
The project budget focuses around the total amount the client has allocated for the interior design project.

19-9 *(Continued)*

Item	Quantity	Color/Style	Estimated Cost	Note
Recessed ceiling lights	6	4 in. halogen bulb, white baffle	$450.00	Ceiling is prepared to receive housing, electrical conduit in place for connection
Installation			$450.00	
Lined draperies				
Fabric	27 yd.	Ivory linen with natural slub, soft weave	$2,300.00	Three windows, 35w × 66h outside measurement
Freight			$50.00	Freight is for custom ordered draperies
Workroom	6 panels	Soft pleat, full-length, 1 ½ width stationary panels	$1,080.00	
Drapery hardware				
Rods	3	4 in. decorative wood pole, premium black walnut finish	$225.00	Freight is for custom order on hardware
Brackets	3	Bracket pairs, finish to match	$60.00	
Finials	6	Decorative finials, finish to match with tarnished silver detail	$216.00	
Rings	42	Decorative wood rings, finish to match rod, 6 sets @ $7.00 per set	$144.00	
Freight	All window hardware		$100.00	
Installation			$450.00	

organized chart. For example, you will want to note how many people will use the space along with their names and ages. You will also want to note the functions of all areas. Identify room relationships along with needs relating to the environment, mechanical systems (heating, cooling, electrical), and the cultural and psychological factors that influence the comfort of the space.

Phase 2: Schematic Design

During this design phase, you will produce a number of schematic drawings—or quick, freehand sketches and drawings to show space arrangements for the project. Then produce various sketches and other documents for your client's review and approval, 19-10. Be sure to keep a file folder for each room or area that you will be designing. Compile drawings, samples, and photographs of

19-10
Many interior design projects begin with very basic sketches serving as design inspirations.

furniture and accessories in these separate folders for each area. Place an itemized list of all items for a room or area in each folder. Organizing the design details in this manner will be very helpful when it comes to developing the preliminary project budget.

Developing Space Arrangements

During this phase, you will create a visual idea of what the project will look like. Begin with brainstorming many ideas. The drawings can be in two or three dimensions. Two dimensions show only the width and length. Three dimensions show the width, length, and height or depth. Here are some types of drawings you are likely to produce during the schematic phase.

- **Bubble diagrams.** Bubble diagrams are simple, loosely connected circles or bubbles that show the relationships of the various zones (private, work, and social) in residential designs. In commercial designs, these diagrams may show the proximities of offices or services.

- **Rough sketches and floor plans.** After discussing possible ways to arrange the zones, you will create two-dimensional rough sketches and floor plans of how the space will look. These sketches will show wall locations with fixture and furniture arrangement possibilities.

- **Thumbnail perspectives.** These small, three-dimensional drawings will show exactly how the project will look.

Once you have the rough sketches and floor plans, you need to plan how to arrange furniture before you actually select it. As you recall from Chapter 16, *space planning* involves placing furnishings for a well-functioning and visually pleasing area. If working with new construction, you and your client may collaborate with an architect or contractor to determine dimensions. If working with an existing space, you will need to accurately measure it. Area measurements let you know how much space is available in the room, an important factor to consider in how much furniture can be added. After taking measurements, several design tools can help you develop a space plan for a functional and attractive furniture arrangement, 19-11.

Measurements for a Scale Floor Plan

Before developing your scale floor plan, measure the length and width of each room. Then measure and note the location of all the existing room features, such as doors, windows, electrical outlets, heating and cooling vents, and air intakes. In addition, measure any alcoves or other permanent features, such as fireplaces, closets, cabinets, or built-in furniture pieces, too. All measurements should include the floor placement of the features as well as their wall height. Note whether the room or area involves an open or closed floor plan because this can also impact furniture arrangement. Use the standard scale of *¼ inch equals 1 foot.*

Interior Designer's Tool Kit

Interior designers use the following tools to develop their designs:

- Computer
- Design software
- Printer
- Graphing paper (thin like tracing paper, marked off in squares, erases easily)
- Tracing paper
- Mechanical pencil and pencil lead
- Eraser
- Scale ruler
- Adjustable triangle
- Circle template
- T-square (or drafting board with a parallel bar)
- Retractable metal tape measure
- Flexible plastic tape measure
- Watercolor paint, colored pencils, or watercolor markers for renderings
- Designer color wheel/paint-fan decks
- Resource file with photos or samples of fabrics, wall treatments and coverings, floor coverings, cabinetry, hardware, furniture, wood finishes, fixtures, appliances and electronics, lighting, and accessories

19-11
These specialized tools help an interior designer create quality designs throughout the phases of the design process.

Computer-Aided Drafting and Design (CADD)

Although some interior designers may draw their scale floor plans by hand on graph paper, most interior designers typically use computer-aided drafting and design (CADD) software and a computer for creating a scale floor plan. A number of different CADD software products are available for interior designers. Some not only allow you to draw a floor plan to scale, but may also include features for estimating materials. Usually, it saves time to generate the floor plans with a computer. Not only can you develop the plans more quickly, but you can also use other options to view the plan in many different ways.

Many people have difficulty visualizing how a finished room will actually look from a floor plan. With the assistance of a computer, you can position furniture in a room and move it around to consider different arrangements. Also, most software allows you to produce interior wall elevations of the room. **Interior wall elevations** show how a finished wall will look. Such images or drawings may illustrate bookcases, cabinets, interior trim, mantels, stairs, and furnishings.

With some programs, or *virtual reality models,* you can view the room from a *walk-through* perspective. A walk-through provides a more realistic picture that allows you and your client to judge how well the furniture positions meet expectations. For instance, an area may seem more crowded in the walk-through view than it appears when only looking at the floor-scale drawing.

Learning how to use a computer software package may take some time, especially the more complicated programs. However, learning how to use such a program can be worthwhile if you are planning several room arrangements, working with a very challenging floor plan, or working with multiple clients.

Arranging Furniture

To help create furniture arrangements for residential or commercial projects, refer back to your client profile and all of the information about how the client uses the space. How will your client use the furniture? What space does it need? How will room features and traffic flow impact furniture placement? In addition, keep in mind the elements and principles of design discussed in Chapters 10, 11, and 12.

Furniture and Room Use

Furniture use greatly impacts its arrangement. Every furniture piece has specific uses and requires a certain amount of space. Furniture arrangement also depends on room use. Before arranging furniture in a room, consider the activities that will take place there and the amount of space available. Then determine where within the room each activity will focus.

Maintain a list of furniture needs for each activity area, and determine the amount of space the furniture will occupy. For instance, if a room requires a conversation area, group chairs, sofas, tables, and lamps in a full or partial circle. In the grouping, arrange lamps and other accessories conveniently in relation to their use. Give attention to the availability of electric outlets in planning the lamp placement. In some cases, electrical outlets may need to be added to accommodate good lighting design.

Room Features

Be sure to plan furniture arrangements around special architectural features. For example, furniture should not block a built-in entertainment center or a fireplace. A scale floor plan allows you to see the placement of the features.

If you have trouble visualizing furniture location in relation to the features, add wall elevations to your plan and indicate the features. When using CADD, you can view interior wall elevations. By using CADD, you can also create a three-dimensional view of the furniture placement, 19-12.

Traffic Patterns

When arranging furniture, plan traffic patterns to include space for people to move about freely. People should be able to easily circulate throughout an entire area. Maintaining proper clearance space around each piece of furniture is essential. When placing furniture in high-traffic areas, you may want to increase the amount of clearance space. Keep function and safety in mind to avoid creating obstacles within traffic patterns.

Choosing a Color Scheme

Once you know the dimensions of the space, furnishing requirements, and your client's preferences, it is time to choose a style and a color scheme for the project. As you learned in Chapter 11, using color effectively is an important part of any design plan. Begin with the preferences noted in your client profile. Does your client prefer warm or cool colors? Does your client want the space to be calm and relaxing or vibrant and exciting? Will the client's preferred design style (such as Victorian, Craftsman, or Contemporary) influence the color scheme? With the color wheel as your guide, consider selecting several color-scheme options from which your client can choose. Colors should coordinate with existing finishes elsewhere in the home or space.

A

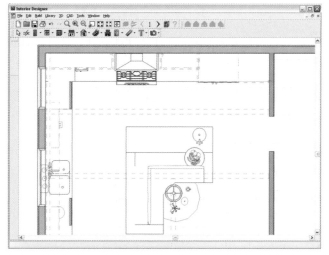

B

19-12
With CADD, you can also create three-dimensional views of a design. This illustration shows both the two-dimensional floor plan with the three-dimensional elevation.

Courtesy of Software by Chief Architect

Selecting Finishes, Furniture, Lighting, and Accessories

Once you and your client agree on a style and color scheme, you can begin selecting background finishes, furniture, lighting, and accessories. Consider the following factors when making your choices:

- **Background finishes.** Background treatments for floors, walls, and windows set the stage for all other details of your design. Depending on your design plan, you may be selecting paint or wall covering, carpeting or resilient flooring, and blinds or curtains and draperies. Your client may want to see a *memo sample* of wall covering—a sample that is large enough to show an entire pattern repeat. In addition, your client may want to see a small sample of the actual dye lot—a *cutting for approval (CFA)*—to confirm the actual color.

- **Furniture.** Design style, usage, color, and fabric types will influence furniture selections. Your client may choose to order all new furniture, or may keep one piece and have you select options that complement it.

- **Lighting.** Lighting provides visual comfort, safety, and beauty in a room. How will lighting options fulfill functional needs for reading, crafts, or watching movies? How will lighting enhance decorative pieces or fine art?

- **Accessories.** Remember to consider the functional and decorative aspects of accessories. How will the accessories reflect client personality and culture? How will the accessories help tie together the design plan?

Finalizing the Project Budget

After selecting all products, finishes, furnishings, lighting, and accessories, you will need to finalize the project budget, 19-13.

Final Budget—Great Room

Item/ Product	Description	Quantity	Style/Color	Est. Cost	Actual Cost	Notes
Bamboo flooring Materials Installation	Natural bamboo with satin finish sealer	432 sq. ft	Natural bamboo	$13,000.00	$13,867.20	$12,960.00 (slight price reduction) + Sales tax
Paint						
Walls	Latex flat	2 gal.	Medium Taupe	$72.00	$77.04	Sales tax
Ceiling	Latex flat	1 gal. + 2 qt.	Ceiling White	$33.00	$35.31	Sales tax
Trim	Oil-base semi-gloss	1 gal. + 2 qt.	Ivory	$65.00	$69.55	Sales tax
Labor	2 coats, walls and trim; 1 coat ceiling			$1,800.00	$1,926.00	Sales tax
Sectional sofa Fabric	Cotton/rayon chenille	35 yards	Chocolate brown, no pattern repeat	$3,000.00	$3,183.25	$2975 (slight price reduction) + Sales tax
Freight				$60.00	$58.23	Sales tax
Workroom				$2550.00	$2728.50	
Installation	Recover only; no repairs necessary Pick up and delivery			$35.00	$37.45	Sales tax
Chairs	Club style, fully upholstered, loose seat and back cushions	2	Taupe/multi, cotton/linen	$3,800.00	$4,066.00	Sales tax
End tables	Classic 2-tiered table, premium finish, with metal gallery and castors 21w×24d×26h	2	Premium black walnut finish with tarnish silver metal trim	$1,100.00	$1,177.00	Sales tax
Coffee table	42 in. square glass top with metal frame	1	Tarnish silver metal frame with tapered legs	$1,000.00	$1,070.00	Sales tax

(Continued)

19-13
Finalizing the preliminary budget may require adjustments to some costs because of changes in material costs or labor.

19-13 *(Continued)*

Item/ Product	Description	Quantity	Style/Color	Est. Cost	Actual Cost	Notes
Table lamps	30 in. high large round ceramic lamp	2	Ivory ceramic on brown wood base and ivory silk shade w/ brown linen trim	$700.00	$802.50	$750.00 (alternate supplier necessary for exact color) + Sales tax
Freight				$40.00	$42.18	
Recessed ceiling lights						
Lighting	4 in. halogen	6	White baffle and trim	$900.00 incl. installation	$963.00	Sales tax
Installation	Direct install; no new circuitry or switching required					
Lined Draperies	3 windows @36w × 66h (outside meas.)					
Fabric	Soft-weave linen with natural slub	27 yd.	Ivory; 100% "washed linen"	$2,310.00	$2,471.70	Sales tax
Freight				$50.00	$43.17	
Workroom	Full-length, 1½ width soft-pleat stationary panels, lined and inner-lined	6		$1080.00	$1155.60	Sales tax
Drapery Hardware						
Rods	4 ft. decorative wood pole, 1¾ in. diameter	3	Premium black walnut finish	$225.00	$240.75	Sales tax
Brackets	Decorative wood	3 pr.	Finish to match	$60.00	$64.20	Sales tax
Finials	Decorative wood	6	Finish to match with tarnish silver detail	$216.00	$231.12	Sales tax
Rings	Decorative wood		Finish to match	$144.00	$154.08	Sales tax
Installation		42		$450.00	$481.50	Sales tax
Freight	All window hardware			$100.00	$85.02	

Some parts of the preliminary budget may need adjustments due to changes in materials costs or labor.

Creating a Bid

After updating the preliminary budget, the designer then creates the final **bid**—or statement including products, work, and fees for the project. A bid includes the *actual costs* for the project. Fees and expenses that were initially "estimates" need to become final cost figures. The bid must be specific as to the furnishings, wall treatments, window treatments, floor treatments, lighting, and accessories you are selecting for the client and installing in the space. The bid must clearly list and explain the cost of your services and fees over the length of the project. Depending on the project length and complexity, you may want to develop the bid in such a way as to bill your design fee on a monthly basis. In addition, the bid must include the following:

- **Consultant fees and services.** If the design plan requires the services of outside consultants, such as architects and lighting specialists, the bid must include a list of their services and their fees for the job.

- **Subcontractor fees and services.** If the project requires construction, the final bid must spell out the work and actual fees for the subcontractors who will be doing the work. You may recommend that your client obtain several bids from subcontractors in a competitive bidding process. However, the subcontractor and your client should sign the final bid and contract for these services separately. You as a designer should never place yourself in a position in which you are legally responsible for the quality of work another person performs.

It is critical for the final bid to include all of the work necessary to complete the project to the designer's and client's expectations in a timely manner. Oversights in creating the bid—such as failing to build in time for late shipments—can lead to project delays and misunderstandings between the designer and client. Adequate planning and extremely good organization help avoid such problems.

As the project begins, it is unrealistic to think that clients never change their minds. Changes often occur especially in the case of new construction or remodeling projects. Unexpected situations may arise that require changes to the bid. In such cases, the designer or contractor prepares a **change order**—a document that outlines the details of

19-14
It is not unusual for clients to change their minds about part of a design as the project moves through the phases. This young couple is discussing a color change with their interior designer.

the plan changes. The change order will list the services, materials, or design changes to which the client and designer and/or contractor agree, 19-14. There is usually a fee for change orders. The contract should state in advance, how to handle changes once work on a design contract begins.

When you present the bid to a client, you must be able to anticipate and answer all of the client's questions. This is the time to discuss and make adjustments in the bid. Once the bid is final, you will present the client with a final contract. After the designer and client sign the contract (and the client signs any additional contracts with subcontractors and consultants), work on the design project begins.

Phase 3: Design Development

In this design phase, you will refine the design and produce the final drawings and details on color schemes and other selections, 19-15. Whether you create hand drawings or use CADD software, your final drawings will include

- floor plans

- elevations

- renderings

In addition, specifications for all the work is included and includes custom design work. The designer confirms that preliminary space plans and design concepts are safe, functional, and are aesthetically appropriate. They should also meet all public health and safety requirements. This includes code, accessibility, environmental, and sustainability guidelines.

Preparing a Professional Presentation Board

To prepare your professional presentation board (or sample board), you will

19-15
Because of the speed and accuracy of CADD software, many interior designers use such software to create their designs.

Photo Courtesy of Madge Megliola, ASID

need a large mat board or illustration board, typically 18 inches by 24 inches or 20 inches by 30 inches. You will identify the project by placing the name of your firm or business on the board and the name of your client. Then mount the floor plan and other items that follow to the board. It is important to note that the layout for the presentation board should utilize the same design elements and principles as the design plan, 19-16.

Floor Plans, Elevations, and Renderings. Mount the floor plan drawing and any elevations or renderings on the board to show the placement of all structural details, such as the locations of doors, windows, partitions columns, cabinetry, closets, and storage. These scale drawings will also show the placement and installation of all the furniture and lighting in the room.

Code and label each part of your floor plan with letters and/or numbers. For example, you may label the furniture with letters (A, B, C, and so forth) and the walls, window treatments, accessories, and light fixtures with numbers (1, 2, 3, and so forth).

	Tips for Preparing Presentation Boards
19-16 Creating a professional presentation board for your clients helps lead to project and career success.	• Attach some samples on your presentation board with hook-and-loop tape so that you can show your client alternative choices. • Consider proportion when preparing your board. Show furnishings in size proportion to each other. Show materials according to the proportion of their use in the space. For example, show a larger paint sample for a room next to a smaller one you will use for an accent wall. • Consider spatial relationships. Show lighting higher on the board than walls. Show floor patterns and coverings lower on the board. • Create the board showing samples in the chronological order of how a visitor will experience them in the space. • Avoid visual clutter. You do not have to mount everything on the board. Use supplemental booklets and back pockets on the board for presenting additional information on items of lesser importance. • Show consistency with labeling and print techniques. Your client should be able to read the board from 8 feet away. • Use technology as much as possible with your presentation. With advances in technology, more and more designers prepare their presentations with computers and design software. Become comfortable with photo-editing and design-presentation software early in your design career.

19-17
Selecting samples for your presentation board that convey the essence of your design plan takes careful evaluation, thought, and planning.

Photo Courtesy of Madge Megliola, ASID

Selection Samples. Mount on the board samples of each of the following items on which you and the client agree (19-17):

- paint and wall covering for the walls and trim
- wood finishes for furniture, cabinetry, and millwork (doors, windows, and trims)
- flooring finishes and materials
- photographs or drawings showing furniture styles, window treatments (shades, blinds, or curtains and draperies), light fixtures, bath fixtures, and accessories
- fabric swatches and trims for window treatments and each piece of upholstery
- carpeting samples and/or photographs of the rugs you propose for the space

Label each sample with the same letter or number code that you placed on the floor plan. If you labeled a sofa with the letter "A," you will also label its sample upholstery fabric and photo with "A." As you finish your presentation board, each sample on the board will have a code that shows its use and appearance in the space.

Schedules and Specifications. Prepare organized charts of detailed notes, or *schedules*, for all items that correspond to the code numbers and letters on the floor plan. Your schedules may include features for doors and windows, electrical and plumbing fixtures, door hardware, and finishes for ceilings, walls, and floors. These schedules will also include *specifications,* or plans for the types and quality of materials to use, such as manufacturer and color numbers and names along with application information for finish treatments.

To obtain or order fabrication of interior design products, the designer needs a way to communicate exact descriptions of these products to suppliers. He or she prepares written specifications to identify the name, quantity, dimensions, color, construction features, design details, and more for each item. The designer may record the specifications on standard hardcopy or online forms, or on custom spreadsheets he or she develops for individual projects. Subcontractors can use the specification document for bidding purposes and easily convert the information to order forms.

You will also need to prepare specifications for individual pieces of furniture, identifying manufacturers, finishes, dimensions, costs, and any other important details. The specifications also identify the manufacturers, materials, fibers, and fabric content of all the upholstery pieces, window treatments, and floor treatments. Organize your presentation board and write your schedules and specifications clearly to communicate well and anticipate any questions your client may have about the visual design concept.

Practicing Your Presentation

Before making a design presentation to your client, practice your oral presentation. You want your presentation to be as professional and flawless as possible. Also, prepare and practice your sales skills. Remember, as the designer you may need to encourage and coax your client to understand the details and importance of how and why you made your selections.

Presenting Your Design

When making your presentation, your goal is to give your client a good preview of what the final project will look like. The effective display of your presentation board will help convey this view to the client. In addition, you will need to give your client more details about your selections, such as the life cycles (how long items will last and when they might need to be replaced), functions, maintenance, performance, environmental features, and safety. See 19-18.

If your clients reject any part of your presentation, do not become defensive. Remember it is their home or business and they are the ones spending the money. Before the presentation, prepare yourself to rethink any areas that cause them concern. Once your client approves the final design, the next phase begins.

Phase 4: Contract Documents

Once your client approves all aspects of the design project, the Contract Documents phase begins. This phase involves making purchases and getting the appropriate professionals involved in the project. You will develop the contract documents using the construction drawings and the specifications you prepared during the design development phase. Whether your design plan is a residential or commercial project will influence how you prepare the contract document.

Residential Projects. You as the interior designer may act as a purchasing agent for your client and hire and supervise various contractors. For example, you may hire the drapery and upholstery workrooms that fabricate window treatments and upholstered furnishings. You may also hire painters, wall-covering hangers, and contractors who specialize in faux finishes for ceilings, walls, and floors. Usually, you will sell these services to your client using the *cost-plus method* or the *retail method* at a marked-up cost.

Commercial Project. With commercial interior design projects, you will often use a bidding process before developing the final contract. In the bidding process, all the various contractors (carpenters, plumbers, electricians, painters, etc.) have a chance to submit proposals on how they would complete the job. Each bidding contractor must submit construction drawings and specifications for each part of the project.

Several factors will influence which bidder gets the contract for the project. For some clients, the bidder offering the lowest cost is the one who obtains the contract and completes the work. This process reduces all qualifications to cost, which is not always in the best interest of the client and designer. For other clients, cost may not be the biggest factor. When competing contractors have reputations for quality work, it is often neither the lowest nor highest bidder who gets the contract. A contractor with a middle bid and a reputation for meeting all deadlines may win a contract over others who do quality work, but may

not always complete it on time. When all of the contractors submit bids for the client's response and the client makes a choice, this part of the design process is complete.

Phase 5: Contract Administration

The final stage of the design process, or Contract Administration, involves completing the project. During this phase, the interior designer will need to prepare a *punch list* for all tasks that need to be completed before the end of the project. This includes any construction as well as the ordering and installing of furniture, furnishings, and equipment. In addition, you will develop a time schedule that shows beginning and ending dates for each step of the project. Remember, some contractors will need to do their work before others. For example, electricians and plumbers must do their basic installations before a builder hangs drywall. Wall painting and trim finishes must be complete before installing window treatments and carpeting.

Sometimes the interior designer or design firm sells furniture, furnishings, equipment, and labor for the project. In these cases, the designer must be able to address some legal responsibilities that go along with such sales. For example, problems may arise that relate to faulty workmanship, equipment failure, warranties, product failure, customer service, repairs, returns, delivery and pickup, approval policies. The contract document should spell out what the designer is responsible for and for how long.

In order for designers to implement their design plans, they must have access to suppliers, artisans, and tradespeople who offer the types of goods and services they require. Many designers **outsource**, or hire out much of the implementation work to subcontractors who specialize in particular tasks. Painters, faux-finishers, wall-covering hangers, millworkers, upholsterers, and other craftspeople are excellent resources to trade professionals who design and specify only.

Similarly, designers use outsourcing to obtain fabrics and furnishings for their clients. Building and maintaining good relationships with quality manufacturers, their representatives, and other suppliers is highly important to the designer. Developing strong relationships with such sources is a good investment of the designer's time.

Usually the interior designer reviews and inspects work for quality, workmanship, and finishes. The interior designer serves as a **liaison**—or connecting agent—between the client and the other persons involved in the project. Supervision of construction and installation of built-ins often requires special certification and knowledge, 19-19. As a result, some states do not allow interior designers to supervise construction and installations.

In this phase, project completion occurs through the following activities:

- completion of paperwork to make purchases, finalizing bids, and preparing necessary drawings and specifications

19-19
Part of an interior designer's job is to inspect work on his or her projects for quality.

- completion of construction
- installation of furniture, furnishings, and equipment
- submission of bills to the interior designer, who in turn bills the client for payment
- completion of a walk-through to make sure all work is complete and satisfactory to the client (most commercial jobs require a formal walk-through)
- notation of missing items or damaged goods during walk-through
- obtain and replace missing or damaged goods
- initiation of final payments to the designer and to the contractors after all remaining items of the project are complete

Project and Time Management

As an interior designer, you will manage a project for overall performance in terms of the time schedule, costs, and quality. The ability or inability to develop the organizational skills for project and time management can either make or break the path to career success. The following notes some additional tasks that require project and time management skills of the designer:

- overseeing and coordinating the work of different tradespeople, such as the plumbers and painters
- scheduling the delivery and installation of all purchased items
- inspecting all purchases to ensure that they are of the quality expected when you placed the order
- reviewing and approving all invoices and bills upon receipt

In addition, the designer must be careful that this supervision does not take up more time than noted in the bid for her or his own design services. Successful designers work on multiple projects at one time while still marketing their businesses and contacting new clients.

CAREER FOCUS

Interior Designer

Do you consider yourself artistic and creative? Do you have a flair for design? If you do, a career in interior design may be for you!

Interests/Skills: Do you find yourself very aware of your surroundings when you are dining out in a restaurant, visiting an airport, shopping in a retail store, visiting a new school, or entering a bank? Can you imagine yourself as someone who designs the interiors of homes or businesses? Do you frequently like to think about designing or redesigning your own personal space? Future interior designers answer "yes" to these questions and must possess three important skills sets: artistic and technical skills, interpersonal skills, and management skills.

Career Snapshot: Although many interior designers follow a traditional career path focusing on the decorating aspects of design, more and more designers are involved in the architectural detailing as well as the aesthetics for interior spaces. Designers must be able to read construction documents (blueprints) and understand building codes. Many work with architects and builders to determine layouts and location of elements such as windows, doors, stairways, and hallways. For complex projects, interior designers may submit drawings to a building inspector for approval to make sure the design meets all codes.

Education/Training: Completion of a four- or five-year bachelor's degree through an accredited college or university is preferable and usually qualifies the graduate for a formal design apprenticeship program. Completion of a two-year associate's degree generally qualifies the graduate to be an assistant to an interior designer.

Skills for Interior Designers	
Artistic and Technical Skills	• Knows how to plan a space • Can present a plan visually so the client understands it • Has material and product knowledge for creating and furnishing a space • Knows how texture, color, lighting, and other factors combine and interact to give a space its "feel" or "look" • Understands the structural requirements of their plans • Understands health and safety issues in spaces • Is knowledgeable about building codes and many other technical aspects of buildings
Creative Ability	• Displays innovative and imaginative ability in creating design solutions • Adaptable to trying new design ideas within the parameters of good design • Displays good aesthetic judgment • Takes prudent risks to excel in solving design problems • Executes original/unique design plans to meet customer needs
Interpersonal Skills	• Feels comfortable in meeting and dealing with many kinds of people • Communicates clearly and listens closely • Maintains good client relationships • Works well with architects and other professionals on projects • Negotiates and mediates problems • Creates proposals and presentations that are clear, informative, and persuasive
Management Skills	• Handles more than one project at a time • Works under demanding timelines • Looks for new clients while working on other projects • Develops and implements a business plan in order to protect and grow the practice • Manages business budgets • Manages the budget for each client's project • Knows how to market oneself and interior design services to clients

Licensing/Examinations: After a one- to three-year apprenticeship to gain experience, interior design graduates can take a licensing examination through the National Council for Interior Design Qualification (NCIDQ). Although only 50 percent of states require licensing for interior designers, passing the exam is necessary to obtain a license and have a competitive career. You will want to identify your state's title and practice acts that impact interior designers. *Title acts* govern or control the use of a title, such as *certified interior designer*, but do not require licensing to practice interior design. States with *practice acts*, however, require licensing for those who practice interior design. These states also govern who can call him- or herself an interior designer. Practice acts generally do allow new professionals to practice interior design under the supervision of a licensed professional. Once new designers gain the necessary years of experience and professional skills, they are eligible to pursue licensing.

Professional Associations: The American Society of Interior Designers (ASID) (www.asid.org); the International Interior Design Association (IIDA) (www.iida.org)

Job Outlook: Although competition will be intense, the demand for interior designers is expected to grow faster than average. Because many consider interior design services to be a luxury, employment opportunities are subject to fluctuations in the economy.

Additional Information Sources: The Occupational Outlook Handbook (www.bls.gov/OCO); the Occupational Information Network (O*NET) (www.online.onetcenter.org)

Careers in Commercial Interior Design		
Specialty Area	**Facility Possibilities**	
Health Care Designers Specialize in designing interior space within the health care profession	Hospitals Cancer treatment centers Office reception areas (doctors and dentists) Orthopedic sports centers Assisted living homes Intensive care units (ICU) Birthing centers	Neonatal ICU Healing gardens Medical fitness centers Research laboratories Hospice care facilities Outpatient surgical clinics
Hospitality Designers Specialize in designing interior spaces within the hospitality industry	Restaurants Resorts Hotels and motels Cruise ships Airplanes	
Civic Contract Designers Specialize in designing interior places for public use	Museums Fire stations City halls Early childhood education centers Elementary, middle, and high schools	Libraries Universities Convention centers Performing arts centers Nonprofit agencies
Government Designers Specialize in designing buildings and offices for federal and state governments	Courthouses Police stations Detention centers Prisons Training centers	
Retail Contract Designers Specialize in designing interior involved in commercial sales	Large stores Small shops and boutiques Showrooms/galleries Shopping malls	
Office Contract Designers Specialize in designing interiors involved in businesses	Bank offices and lobbies Accounting firms Legal firms Corporate offices	

Summary

An interior designer uses the design process to carry out an orderly project. These phases are Programming, Schematic design, Design development, Contract documents, and Contract administration.

During programming, the designer gathers client information. Applying the principles and elements of design for all aspects of the project is crucial during the schematic phase.

After initial design approval, the designer makes a professional presentation board. During the formal presentation, the designer gives the client specific details about selections.

Handling contract documents includes making purchases, acquiring bids, and coordinating all professionals on the project. It also includes construction drawings and specifications. Project completion occurs during the contract administration phase. Some designers supervise and inspect all work done on a project.

Review the Facts

1. Summarize the five phases of the design process.
2. How does a letter of agreement and the retainer protect both designer and client?
3. Contrast the information a designer gathers for a residential profile with a commercial client profile.
4. What factors about a client's living space provide clues for a successful design plan?
5. Contrast an adjacency matrix with a criteria matrix.
6. Why are careful measurements important for a successful design plan?
7. Contrast measurements for inside mount shades and blinds with measurements for outside mount shades and blinds.
8. Summarize the following ways interior designers establish fees: (A) fixed, (B) hourly, (C) cost plus, (D) retail, and (E) per square foot.
9. What types of drawings might an interior designer use during the schematic phase of the design process?
10. What is the benefit of using CADD software when developing a design plan?
11. What three factors influence furniture arrangements for a design plan?
12. How do a bid and a change order differ?
13. What items are included on a professional presentation board?
14. Summarize the differences between contracts for residential projects and commercial projects.
15. Name at least four activities that occur during project completion.
16. What is the interior designer's responsibility for project and time management?

Think Critically

17. **Recognize values.** Suppose a client has hired you to create a design plan for a kitchen and family room renovation. How can creating profiles for all household members help you recognize what they value most about the space and how they use it? How might this recognition help you create a realistic design plan?

18. **Assess details.** What details should you assess about a client's environment? How can this assessment lead to a better interior design?

19. **Analyze pros and cons.** Make a list of all the possible ways clients may decide to approach setting a project budget. Analyze the pros and cons of each approach. How can analyzing and understanding both sides of all approaches help you better guide clients in establishing project budgets?

Community Links

20. **Services and suppliers.** Presume you are starting your own interior design business. You need to establish business relationships with various service providers (such as upholstery and drapery workrooms, builders, and painters) and product suppliers (such as paint, wall covering, textiles, and furnishings). Use the Internet to investigate various service providers and suppliers in your area. What services or products do they provide? What are their fees? Do they offer discounts to other businesses? How can you judge the quality of the services or products?

21. **Job shadow.** Make an appointment to job-shadow an interior designer in your area. Observe tasks the designer performs and how he or she interacts with clients. What aspects of interior design does the designer find most challenging? most rewarding? Share a summary of your observations with the class.

22. **Measurement practice.** Using two rooms in your home or the home of someone you know, measure the room dimensions and create a floor plan for each room (either on graph paper or using a CADD program). Be sure to include measurements for windows, doors, and any other room features. Transfer your measurements to your floor plan.

23. **Schematic design.** Presume you have been hired to design the waiting room for a new doctor's office in your community. All patients are adults, and a calm and comfortable atmosphere is important to your client. Before committing to a design plan, your client wants you to create two visual ideas about how the waiting room might look. Use bubble diagrams, rough sketches and floor plans, and thumbnail perspectives to present your ideas.

Academic Connections

24. **Writing.** Imagine you are creating an interior design plan for relatives who are building a new house. Begin by making a list of questions you will ask your relatives in regard to how they use their space. Use your questions to gather information about your relatives/clients and write a profile outlining their lifestyle, functions of their space, design preferences, and future needs. Keep a copy of your profile as a writing example in your work portfolio.

25. **Math.** Follow text guidelines to calculate the amount of paint to order for a room that measures 14 ft. wide by 18 ft. long by 8 ft. high and requires two coats of paint (A). How much paint would you need if one 14 ft. by 8 ft. wall is an accent color (B)? Assume each gallon of paint covers 350 square feet.

26. **Math.** Create a list of furniture pieces and accessories you need to order for a client's 12 ft. by 14. ft. family room. Use Internet resources to locate prices for each item on your list. You have decided to use a 20 percent markup with the "cost plus" method for your design fees. Calculate the cost of each furniture or accessory piece with a 20 percent markup on price.

Technology Applications

27. **Scale drawings.** Use a CADD software program to create a scale floor plan, elevation drawing, and rendering of a room in your home. What design preferences do you prefer to use in this room? Write a summary of the plans. Present the drawings and your plans to the class.

28. **Cost estimate.** Presume a client wants you to prepare a preliminary cost estimate for three types of flooring for use in a kitchen. The floor measurements are 12 ft. wide by 16 ft. long. Your client wants to compare hardwood (maple), wood laminate, ceramic tile, and sheet vinyl. Use a computer spreadsheet program to create a cost estimate for each flooring type. Be sure to include separate categories for materials and labor. Share your spreadsheet with the class.

Design Practice

29. **Residential design plan.** Select a room in a residential house, such as a living room, kitchen, media room, master bedroom, bath, or a teen's or child's bedroom. Prepare a design presentation board following the phases for planning and presenting a professional design described in this chapter. Presume your class is your "client." Make an oral presentation explaining the design concept displayed on your presentation board and the written schedule.

30. **Commercial design plan.** Presume you have been selected to design a commercial space, such as a bank lobby, high school lobby, hair salon waiting area, or hotel lobby. Prepare a design presentation board following the phases for planning and presenting a professional design described in this chapter. Presume your class is your "client." Make an oral presentation explaining the design concept displayed on your presentation board and the written schedule.

31. **Portfolio.** Add one or more of your design presentation boards to your work portfolio as an example of your design capabilities. Write a summary about each project to keep in your portfolio.

Teamwork in Interior Design

In a team, use the FCCLA *Planning Process* to plan, carry out, and evaluate a project for the FCCLA *Interior Design* STAR Event. The event conditions and requirements include

- writing a family profile and creating a display board illustrating the family profile

- selecting a floor plan that meets the family's needs

- designing furniture arrangements and color schemes

- selecting background treatments and other items

- creating a design board which includes elevation drawings and materials samples

Use the *STAR Events Manual* on the FCCLA Web site (www.fcclainc.org) to identify specific competition requirements for your project. See your adviser for information as needed.

PART 5

A Safe and Attractive Environment

CHAPTER 20

The Outdoor Living Space and Environment

Terms to Learn

landscape
natural landscape elements
annuals
biennials
perennials
ground cover
hardscape
manufactured landscape elements
enclosure elements
landscape zones
conservation
water conservation
xeriscape
soil conservation
sunroom
landscape architect
American Society of Landscape
    Architects (ASLA)

Chapter Objectives

After studying this chapter, you will be able to

- summarize the goals of landscaping.

- identify natural and manufactured landscape elements.

- determine zones in a landscape site.

- select furnishings for outdoor living.

- summarize conservation measures for landscaping.

- design an outdoor living space.

Reading with Purpose

Locate a magazine article on www.magportal.com that relates to the chapter topic. Read the article and write five questions that you have about the article. Next, read the textbook chapter. Based on your reading, try to answer the questions you had about the magazine article.

The beauty of nature surrounds you. When making housing decisions, you should find ways to enhance and enjoy this beauty. People spend much of their time indoors—in schools, offices, and homes. The **landscape** is the outdoor living space. A beautifully landscaped area or even a small balcony in city housing can draw people outdoors. Everyone can find ways to enjoy the beauty of nature.

When preparing a site for construction, many disruptions occur in the natural surroundings. The construction process often changes the layout of the land.

If you leave the landscape alone after construction, it may never bring you pleasure. On the other hand, if you work in partnership with nature, you can have an outdoor living space that is psychologically rewarding. Note how the landscaping shown in 20-1 enhances the appearance of the home. A pleasing outdoor living space should encourage the positive development of each member of your household.

Planning the Landscape

The basic goal of landscaping is to create outdoor spaces to complement various activities. The landscape should be private, comfortable, attractive, safe, and convenient. If you are like most people, you will also want the area to be easy to maintain. You can achieve any or all of these qualities in a well-planned landscape.

Identify Your Goals

You will have more successful results if you identify your landscaping goals. Some of your goals may include

- recreation and entertainment—including areas for playing and/or socializing

- privacy—attained by enclosures and screens that shield the space from the public

- comfort—which allows you to relax in an inviting space

A

B

20-1
After construction is complete, landscaping can make a site more attractive. Image A shows a swimming pool and landscaping under way. Image B shows the finished pool and landscaping.

New Garden Landscaping & Nursery—Steve Windham

- beauty—which highlights attractive areas and draws attention away from less interesting areas

- safety—which is achieved by installing landscaping elements correctly and providing adequate lighting

- creativity—evident in the ways that you use your landscape to express yourself

- ease of maintenance—which incorporates laborsaving ideas, such as raised planters, watering systems, and ground covers that require no mowing

- conservation—incorporating a "green" element into the landscape through the use of drought-tolerant plants, less turf, and water-conserving recycling methods

Considering everyone's needs and values in the planning process, allows for the creation of a satisfying environment for all household members. Take time to identify your goals before you start your plan. Before designing an outdoor living space, ask yourself the following questions as you formulate your goals:

- What is the lifestyle of your household? Are there children and pets to consider?

- How much time, money, and effort are you willing to spend? See 20-2.

- What is the cost of maintaining the plan?

- If you are concentrating on one area of the site, how will it affect other areas? Will the addition of a patio, deck, or swimming pool reduce the lawn area too much?

- Do you know what types of materials to consider for your plans?

- What activities are likely for the area?

- How much open space do you want to maintain?

- What measures can you take to save water and energy over the long term?

A

B

20-2
Some people prefer to maintain their own landscape (A). A consideration in this attractive brick walk is the cost in time or money for maintaining the edging around the bricks (B).

(B) Photography Courtesy of Ed Pinckney

Landscape Elements

Before planning a landscape, become familiar with various landscape elements. There are two basic types of landscape elements: natural elements and manufactured elements.

Natural Landscape Elements

Natural landscape elements are those found in the natural environment. The terrain and soil are natural elements that are already on the site. Other natural elements include trees, shrubs, flowers, ground covers, boulders, stones, wood, bark, water, sun, and wind. Change is not possible for some elements, such as a natural stream. Alterations to other elements can happen to a certain degree. For instance, you can add or remove trees, shrubs, and large rocks from the landscape.

Topography

The topography, or contour of the land, is basic to the landscape. Level land is the easiest and the least expensive to landscape. The ideal topography is a gentle, rolling terrain with natural drainage.

Soil

Good soil encourages plant growth and provides plants with the right nutrients. It has a proper balance of sand, silt, and clay. The soil must drain well, yet hold enough water to sustain plant life.

Trees and Shrubs

Trees and shrubs range in size from small to large. Trees can provide shade as well as shelter from wind. Evergreen trees and shrubs remain green all year. Deciduous trees and shrubs, on the other hand, lose foliage in the fall and sprout new leaves in spring. Trees and shrubs can also provide privacy, 20-3.

Flowers

Flowers add fragrance and color to the landscape. There are three types of flowers: annuals, biennials, and perennials. **Annuals** and **biennials** last one and two years respectively. Most of these flowers require yearly planting. In contrast, **perennials** last for many years without replanting. Some perennials never need replanting, 20-4. Many gardeners prefer perennials because they require less work than annuals or biennials.

Most flowers grow from seeds or bulbs. If you desire, however, you can plant seedlings. *Seedlings* are young plants started from seeds. You can start the seedlings yourself or purchase them from a nursery. Many home owners start flowers from small starter plants or seedlings they get from a nursery. With the right choices, you can have flowers blooming throughout the growing season. In some geographical areas, it is possible to develop landscape plans that provide year-round color.

Ground Covers

A variety of ground covers are available for use in landscaping. **Ground covers** include grasses and various types of low-growing plants. *Grass* is the most common ground cover, and many types are available for lawns. Some are more appropriate for use in warm climates, while others thrive in cool climates. The

20-3
The hedges behind the fence provide privacy. A major consideration is the eventual height of the hedge.

Photography Courtesy of Ed Pinckney

20-4

This professionally designed landscape combines evergreen and deciduous trees and shrubs with annual and perennial flowers.

The Long Cane Group, Inc. Atlanta, Georgia

growth cycle of grasses varies with the climate. Some grow well in the shade. Others need full sun. Some grasses can stand heavy traffic, while others will tolerate very little.

Other ground covers include *low-growing plants* that are useful in places where grass is not desirable or maintainable. You can purchase ground covers in the form of vines, woody plants, or herblike plants. Some are evergreen and others are deciduous, but all are perennials. Use ground covers when low maintenance is a need or requirement. Also, use ground covers in places that are difficult to maintain. Most ground covers are not suitable for high-traffic areas.

Boulders and Stones

Usage of boulders and stones—available in various sizes—is common in landscaping. Boulders with unusual forms, textures, or colors will add

interest to any landscape. Such additions to the landscape plan are the hardscape of the plan. **Hardscape** is anything in the landscape other than vegetation and outdoor furniture.

Water, Sun, and Wind

Water, sun, and wind will always be a part of the outdoors. They are natural landscape elements. Water is a basic need of any plant life, but high water levels can cause swampy yards, wet basements, and poor plant growth. Orientation to the sun and wind affect the use of outdoor living areas. At times, you need protection from these elements. At other times, you want to take advantage of them.

Manufactured Landscape Elements

Manufactured landscape elements are those elements not found in the natural environment. They are, however, a common sight in most landscapes. These elements include hard surfaces, such as walks, driveways, steps, and various structures such as walls, fences, patios, and decks. These items are also a type of hardscape, 20-5. Numerous other items, such as lighting and outdoor furnishings, are landscape elements.

Hard Surfaces

When hard surfaces are a requirement, you can create them with *brick* or *concrete*. Concrete can form bricklike

20-5

A variety of manufactured landscape elements are used in this setting. Notice the pergola at the right

Photography Courtesy of Ed Pinckney

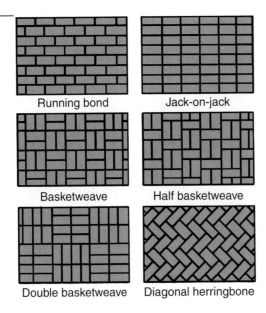

20-6
Bricks can be placed to form a variety of designs.

Running bond

Jack-on-jack

Basketweave

Half basketweave

Double basketweave

Diagonal herringbone

blocks, stepping-stones, and slabs, 20-6. You can purchase these items ready to use, or you can make your own by placing the concrete into forms. *Asphalt paving* produces a hard surface and is relatively inexpensive to apply. In some cases, soil is compact enough to create a hard surface. *Flagstone*, shown in 20-7, is a flat stone found in certain areas of the country. It

20-7
This attractive walk is constructed of flagstone.

can be set in concrete or placed on a bed of sand. Such surfaces are also part of the hardscape in the landscape plan.

Enclosure Elements

Walls and fences are **enclosure elements**, or features that enclose a space. They are useful for keeping children or pets in a secure place. They can also keep out unwanted visitors. Enclosure elements consist of various materials—wood, brick, block, stone, concrete, plastic, metal, or a combination of these. A "green" approach to creating fencing and decking is to use a unique combination of wood and plastic fibers. To make such fence and deck products, manufacturers use wood materials "left over" from other manufacturing, such as wood pellets from furniture manufacture, and recyclable plastic grocery bags, 20-8.

Landscapers and home owners often use *freestanding walls* along property lines. These walls give privacy and serve as boundaries. *Retaining walls* have soil against one side, 20-9. They are useful for terracing and forming boundaries for yards and planting beds.

A *fence* is usually less expensive than a wall and is easy to construct. Fences are available in many styles and several heights. Figure 20-10 shows several styles. Most fences do not provide as much privacy as walls. Some local city, county, or municipalities place restrictions on fences, such as the height of a fence.

Unlike a row of hedges or trees, enclosure elements do not need time to grow. After construction or installation, both walls and fences are available for immediate use. However, there may be times when hiding an unpleasant view or gaining the full privacy is not possible with a fence due to height restrictions. In such instances, planting hedges and trees may provide a screen. Be sure to consider the eventual height of such hedges and trees. What will they look like in five years?

20-8
The fencing provides privacy around the pool. A special "green" bonus is that the manufacturer makes this fencing by combining recycled wood and plastic.

Photography Courtesy of the Trex Company, Inc., Winchester, Virginia

20-9
Retaining walls are used to hold soil in place.

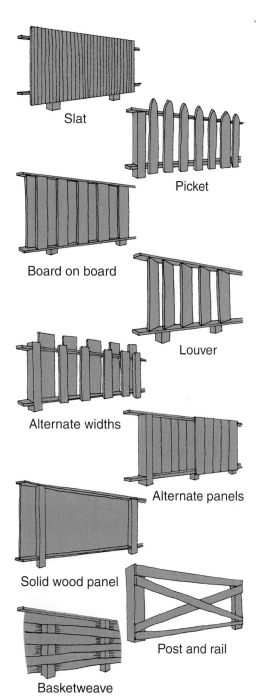

Slat

Picket

Board on board

Louver

Alternate widths

Alternate panels

Solid wood panel

Basketweave

Post and rail

20-10
Fences are available in a variety of designs. Nine popular styles are shown.

Rea-Lynn Gilder

There are many other types of structures used in landscaping. You may build them or buy them ready to put in place. Courtyards, patios, decks, and terraces can enhance and extend an outdoor living space. Other structures to consider include fountains, barbecue pits, gazebos, playhouses, and storage structures. A variety of containers with plants also adds beauty to a landscape.

Outdoor Furniture

Outdoor furniture is another manufactured landscape element. Furniture materials usually include metal, wood, fiberglass, plastic, or glass. Manufacturers often make outdoor furniture from a single material or a combination of materials. Many furniture styles are available to meet most needs. Sometimes enclosure elements and other structures also serve as furniture.

Artificial Lighting

Another important element of the landscape is artificial lighting. Outdoor lighting should be functional and provide safety and security. Lighting allows nighttime work or leisure activities. It can also add beauty to an outdoor setting, 20-11.

Floodlights, spotlights, and underlighting can be useful in accenting a landscape site. *Automatic timers* are available for security lighting. These timers turn lighting on and off at predetermined times. *Photoelectric cells* turn lights on at dusk and off at dawn. *Motion detectors* activate lights when there is movement within a certain area. Some lights conserve energy. For example, many manufacturers produce low-voltage outdoor lighting kits that operate on 12 or 24 volts. Lights that use solar energy store it directly from the sun.

The location of a property predetermines some natural landscape elements. Household members can choose other natural elements, as well as all manufactured elements. Recognizing the elements available can help you design an outdoor living space that meets all needs and goals.

Designing Outdoor Living Spaces

Designing a landscape is similar to designing the interior of a home. You can design the space yourself or you can hire a landscape architect. Designers and landscape architects think of landscape areas as outdoor rooms. As you may recall from Chapter 4, divisions (or zones) inside of a house relate to certain activities. The exterior grounds have three divisions, or **landscape zones**, as well that relate to outdoor activities. Landscape zones include the

- *public zone*—a part of the site that can be seen from the street

- *private zone*—a part of the site for recreation and relaxation that is generally separated from the public zone

- *service zone*—the part of the site that includes sidewalks, driveways, and storage areas for tools, trash cans, lawn equipment, and other items

20-11
The outdoor lighting plan of this home provides excellent safety and security.

Photography Courtesy of Palm Harbor Homes

HEALTH/SAFETY

Monitoring Outdoor Air Quality

The quality of the air you breathe depends on where you live and can vary from one day to the next or one hour to the next. The U.S. Environmental Protection Agency (EPA)—along with state, local, and tribal agencies—monitors and forecasts levels of air pollutants across the country. The Air Quality Index (AQI) alerts the public to dangerous levels of five air pollutants. These are

- *particulate matter*—dirt, dust, ash, soot, pollen, mold spores, chemicals, and acids suspended in the air; comes from vehicle exhaust, power plants, wood burning, wild fires, and other sources
- *carbon monoxide*—a colorless and odorless gas; a by-product of fuel burning, especially vehicle exhaust
- *sulfur dioxide*—a gas released when sulfur-containing coal and oil are burned; mostly produced at power plants and other industrial sites
- *nitrogen oxide*—a gas created by burning such fuels as coal, oil, or natural gas; higher concentration occur near busy roadways
- *ground-level ozone*—a gas formed by chemical reactions of pollutants, including nitrogen oxide, in sunlight

These pollutants, especially ground-level ozone and particulate matter, are most harmful to human health. They can cause and aggravate health problems, especially in children, older adults, and people with asthma and other chronic illnesses.

The AQI is often cited in news and weather reports. You can also check the current and forecasted AQI in your area by going to www.airnow.gov. The higher the index—which runs from 0 to 500—the more unhealthy the air. The index is divided into five color-coded levels for easier reading.

Only the home owner and designer can decide how much landscaping is desirable for each zone. The landscape plan should include backgrounds and accents. Be sure to allow for activities and traffic. Innovation is important to the use of landscape elements when planning the zones of an outdoor living space, 20-12.

Review the elements and principles of design and incorporate them into the zones or area of a landscape. Recall the ways to use color effectively. You can apply what you have learned to the form, line, color, and texture of the landscape elements you choose. The land-scaped space should have unity and balance. Landscape elements should be in proportion to one another and to the structures they surround.

20-12
This family's love of private outdoor meals and relaxation influenced their desire for a beautiful, yet functional, deck.

Photography Courtesy of JELD-WEN Windows and Doors

Landscape Backgrounds

The backgrounds for landscaping include the soil and topography, the hard surfaces, and the ground covers. They provide an important foundation to any landscape plan.

You may not have good soil on the site. If not, with knowledge and effort, you can improve it. The use of compost and mulch can improve soil. *Compost* forms from decomposing or rotting natural material. Working compost into the soil replenishes nutrients. *Mulch* is an organic material, such as straw, peat moss, bark, or leaves. Landscapers and gardeners use it to cover the soil, usually around plants, to prevent weed growth. Both compost and mulch are important to building soil. They increase the penetration of water and air, help the soil hold water, and control soil temperatures. If you plan to include grass or any other plants in your landscape, the condition of the soil is important.

Grass is one of the most appealing parts of the landscape. It creates a pleasing floor covering for the landscape site and can provide recreational areas for household members. It also prevents soil erosion and supplies oxygen to the air. After mowing the grass, use the clippings to produce organic matter (compost or mulch) to replenish the soil. Grass unifies or connects all parts of the landscape.

Use a variety of plants other than grass as ground cover in areas where there is no traffic. These plantings typically do not need as much care as grass, 20-13. Local factors may limit choices since some plants will grow only in certain soil, temperature, and sunlight conditions.

Loose aggregate, such as sand, gravel, cinders, wood chips, and bark, is suitable for sections of the site that have poor soil or are difficult to water. Use loose aggregate when low maintenance is

20-13
Native plants with colorful flowers or foliage can create a beautiful front yard requiring less care than grass.

desirable or water is scarce. Sometimes it serves as mulch in planting areas.

Sections of the landscape's floor will have pavement or other coverings consisting of hard materials. For example, common surfaces include driveways and sidewalks. Hard surfaces on a lot should slope away from the house to provide proper water drainage. Standing or freezing water on a driveway and sidewalk is a hazard.

Walks are one of the easiest landscape elements to construct. They can consist of any durable material and often serve as borders. Walks divide the landscape site into separate areas and act as pathways to these areas, 20-14. You should choose an attractive pattern for the walk. If the ground level varies, include steps in the route. Most walks are long-lasting. However, changes are sometimes necessary when plant life matures and becomes larger. If you anticipate changing the route at some point in the future, use stepping-stones to form a walkway. They are easier to move than most other materials used for walk construction.

20-14
A walk does not have to be placed in a straight line. This walk was designed to complement the landscape.

Trees, shrubs, walls, and fences create the boundaries of the landscape. Walls can act as a screen, giving visual privacy, 20-15. They also curb noise and serve as windbreaks. You must decide which areas to enclose with walls. If there is a good view in one direction, consider taking advantage of it by leaving it open.

Consider planting suitable shrubs or evergreens close together to form a wall. For a dense grouping, combine trees with shrubs. For example, plant short shrubs among the tall trees. Also consider planting two rows of trees, staggering the plantings to make a continuous barrier.

The original function of property walls was to keep enemies away. Today, they serve different functions. Walls may separate one property from another, provide privacy, and block wind. Many walls are decorative, using such materials as wood, stone, or concrete.

Fences often serve the same purposes as walls. Some are solid, while others have openings. Fences that allow others to see into a private space often have coverings of vines for more privacy.

Gates are part of the landscape's wall. They can add an interesting touch to the enclosure. Gates must blend with the walls of the landscape.

Trees not only create shade, but also create interesting shadows and patterns as the sun shines through. The spreading branches of some trees give a canopy effect. For this reason, some landscape

20-15
A wrought iron gate can be attractive and functional.

Photo Courtesy of California Redwood Association

A

B

20-16
The trees along this walk create a pleasing design as the sun shines on and through the trees (A). A pergola as part of the landscape background provides partial shade (B).

(A) Photography Courtesy of Ed Pinckney; (B) The Long Cane Group, Inc. Atlanta, Georgia

architects put trees in specific locations for the shade they produce. Outdoor structures, such as *pergolas,* can also add partial shade, 20-16. Overhead structures can also provide necessary shade. Such materials as canvas, bamboo, fiberglass, louvers, or lath can form ceilings or overhead structures.

Accents

Landscape accents form the finishing touches. They are the colorful flowers, the interesting boulders, and the other special features home owners choose. Some accents become background elements for smaller accents. For example, a boulder may serve as a background for a cluster of flowering plants. You should include a variety of accents in every landscape plan.

Flowers are not a permanent landscape element. Because they die in dormant seasons, flowers generally serve as an accent. When in bloom, they are spectacular in their color and showiness. There are many forms, heights, and colors of flowers from which to choose, 20-17.

Flower plantings should be simple. Too many types or colors in a single bed will produce a disorganized appearance. Some flowers need full sunlight. Others do well in the shade or partial sunlight. Find out which flowers will do best in your landscaping project.

Planting beds are good choices for flowers. These beds are the spaces that are set aside for plants. Raised beds or planters are effective. They are ideal for older people or people who use wheelchairs. Home owners can move portable planters from one outside area to another, and then move them inside during the cold season.

Choices of materials for planters include wood, plastic, glass, metal, concrete, and glazed ceramics. Look for planters that are durable and decorative.

20-17
The potted red, yellow, white, and purple flowers create a splash of color as an accent on this terrace.

Photography Courtesy of Ed Pinckney

In areas with freezing temperatures, avoid planters containing glass, ceramic, and other materials that shatter when the moisture in soil freezes.

Landscape architects and home owners often choose boulders and stones as accent pieces. Informal placement of these items in the landscape creates a casual look, 20-18. They have a more formal appearance when they serve as borders along paths and flowerbeds. Place boulders and stones to show off their interesting features. Rock gardens are popular in landscaping.

Sculptures, murals, and mosaics can enhance a landscape design. The selection of these accents is very personal. They express household member's tastes, and consider form, color, and texture. A landscape will have a cluttered appearance with the use of too many accents. Place most accents at eye level. Sculpture fits well against a background of foliage. You may, however, want to combine it with some type of structure.

Other Landscape Features

Throughout a landscape, you can use many different features. You can have fun planning them and may even enjoy building some of them.

Some home owners might want a *gazebo* in the landscape. A gazebo is a raised platform that has four, six, or eight open sides. Relaxing in a gazebo is a wonderful way to enjoy the landscape. A gazebo can also double as a playhouse. Some gazebos have a protective roof. Others have lattice or vine-covered roofs. Gazebos are easy to adapt to fit the home owner's desires.

Water features are other popular landscape items. Water projects can be very enjoyable. The sound and sight of running water has a soothing effect, 20-19. Having water fall from a high level produces pleasing sounds. Jets, bubbles, and sprays can also make soothing water sounds.

20-18
The boulders in this flowerbed serve as both an accent and a background.

Water in motion has a special attraction. Installation of a small, inexpensive circulating pump in the water feature can move water. Be sure to recycle water that you use in a landscape element. Use it again in the landscape or to water plant life.

20-19
A water feature can add a soothing effect to any landscape.

Some people want to attract birds to their property. To do this, include a pool or pond in the landscape. The pool can be small or large. Small pools work best if they are near a group of plantings.

Hanging feeders and birdhouses will also attract birds to a yard. For those who enjoy watching birds, plan the landscape to attract them. The local cooperative extension service provides information about what plants in a given area attract birds. Be sure there are good places for nests in the landscape.

Furnishing Outdoor Living Spaces

Outdoor furnishings can extend the living space since they invite people outside. The furnishings can help make the landscape site enjoyable and functional for the entire household.

Outdoor furnishings generally include tables, chairs, accessories, and cooking equipment. Furnishings that are durable and weather resistant are best for outdoor use. They should have high-quality construction. Choose furnishings that resist the deterioration caused by temperature extremes, sunlight, wind, and water. Furnishings should also be soil resistant. Figure 20-20 describes materials commonly used in outdoor furniture and other outdoor accessories.

If you plan to move the outdoor furniture frequently, it should not be too heavy. When selecting furnishings, use what you have learned about organizing space and traffic patterns. The principles apply to outdoor living spaces as well as indoor spaces.

You may want to store the furniture during the off-season or use it in another location. Some furniture is appropriate for both indoor and outdoor use. If you want furniture for dual-purpose use, keep this in mind when making your selection, 20-21.

Carpeting is sometimes part of the outdoor furnishings. It is best if outdoor carpeting consists of 100 percent synthetic fiber. Olefin, acrylic, and nylon are suitable fibers for outdoor use. The best outdoor carpeting uses needlepunched or tufted construction. The needlepunch process produces felt-like carpeting. Tufting produces loops. The loops may or may not be cut. Glue or tape either type of carpeting securely to a hard surface. For more information on carpet construction, see Chapter 13.

Additional furnishings include decorative and functional accessories. Accessories add the finishing touches to the furnished area. Common examples of decorative accessories include wind chimes, sculpture, driftwood, and urns. Examples of functional accessories include pillows and cushions, cooking equipment, and waste containers.

Fabrics for outdoor pillows and cushions usually consist of woven or knitted synthetic fibers. The fillers for pillows and cushions must be weather-resistant. These materials can usually withstand moisture. Nevertheless, protect pillows and cushions from standing water.

Accessories often set the mood for the landscape area. There is no end to the choices you have when you select accessories. Coordinate the style and color of your outdoor furnishings and accessories. Consider accessory needs and determine where and how to use them. When selecting furnishings and accessories, consider the comfort, convenience, durability, portability, storability, quality, design, and maintenance of these items.

Materials for Outdoor Furniture		
Materials	**Types**	**Descriptions**
Metal	Aluminum	• Lightweight and rustproof • Sometimes has a finish to prevent corrosion
	Wrought Iron	• Heavy and not very portable • Rusts without the proper finish
	Molded Cast Iron	• Heavier than wrought iron • Brittle • Rust, cracks, and breaks easily
	Steel	• Strong and durable • Weather resistant
Wood and Woody Plants	Cedar, Cypress, and Redwood	• Needs a protective coating to prevent deterioration
	Rattan, Wicker, and Bamboo	• Cannot be finished to withstand continuous outdoor conditions • Works well for sunroom furnishings
Plastics	Urethane	• Durable • Requires minimal maintenance • Used for molded items
	Polyester and Acrylic	• Used for furniture tops
Glass	Fiberglass	• Lightweight • Strong and durable • Weather resistant • Can be designed to fit contours
	Glass	• Common for tabletops • Must be high quality

20-20
Outdoor furniture is made from a variety of materials.

20-21
This attractive, lightweight furniture can be used for both exteriors and interiors.

Brown Jordan International Company, Designs by Rich Frinier

Outdoor living spaces may not seem complete without the addition of cooking equipment, 20-22. Portable or stationary units are available. Position a portable unit so it does not interfere with the landscape. Locate it in an area that provides protection from strong winds and hot sun. Users will not want the smoke from the unit to be a bother. Keep portable equipment in outdoor storage when not in use.

20-22
The addition of an outdoor kitchen enhances the usability of the exterior space.

20-23
Well-planned outdoor lighting can help extend the use of outdoor living spaces.

Photo Courtesy of Lindal Cedar Homes, Seattle, Washington

If you choose stationary cooking equipment, place it in a convenient spot. However, do not allow it to detract from its surroundings. A well-planned unit can add pleasure to the landscape. Fuels for cooking equipment include charcoal, natural gas, or propane. Cooking equipment that uses propane or natural gas is generally more convenient than equipment using charcoal as fuel.

Lighting the Outdoor Living Space

Lighting can create a type of magic in the landscape. It can extend the use of the outdoor living space and invite you outside at night. Lights also enhance the view from inside the house, 20-23.

Appropriate lighting is important for each area of a property. Outside lighting should illuminate the sidewalks and driveways. It should provide a clear view to and from the house. At the same time, lighting should discourage intruders. Lighting at entryways can help home dwellers see who is approaching.

While spotlights are good for lighting specific features, floodlights are useful for large areas. You can highlight a garden sculpture or flowing water with a spotlight. Uplighting is especially appropriate for small areas. *Uplighting* is the practice of directing the light upward from the ground level into plants or other landscape features. Uplighting a large tree, for example, can create a spectacular focal point in a night landscape plan.

If possible, situate light fixtures to hide them from view. Place ground-level lights behind plants or structures. Install higher fixtures under eaves or on rooftops.

Landscaping for Conservation

Conservation is the process of protecting or saving something. Your landscaping decisions can help to conserve soil, water, and energy.

Efforts at conservation should begin when a house is under construction, 20-24. Disturbances to the soil occur during construction. Planting ground covers at this time, helps prevent erosion of the topsoil. In steep areas, building terraces can prevent erosion, too. Builders should be encouraged to employ these and other conservation measures.

Once construction is complete, permanent conservation efforts can begin. Even if you or a client have been in a home for some time, it is possible to make significant contributions to conservation. The lifestyle of a household is probably the most important factor in conservation. Environmentally conscious households want to conserve natural resources.

Home owners want their outdoor space to be comfortable and attractive. They can accomplish this and still conserve natural resources through landscaping.

Water and Soil Conservation

Awareness is the first step in conserving water. **Water conservation** includes reducing water use and eliminating water waste. If you live in a dry part of the country, you realize how important it is to conserve water. People throughout the United States are becoming more aware of the need to conserve water. In many places, water prices have increased substantially while available water supplies have decreased. This is

20-24
The orange fencing material is used to prevent soil erosion during the construction of a new home.

Photography by Carolyn S. Turner

GREEN CHOICES

GreenScaping: What Is It?

According to the U. S. Environmental Protection Agency (EPA), GreenScaping is a set of landscaping practices that can improve the health and appearance of your lawn and garden while protecting and preserving natural resources. The practices focus on the "4 Rs"—reduce, reuse, recycle, and rebuy.

By adopting simple landscape changes, it is possible to create a GreenScape—that over time—can save time and money while protecting the environment. Here are some simple steps for effective GreenScaping:

- Eliminate unnecessary water and chemical use.
- Use landscaping plants that require less care.
- Conserve water supplies by choosing plants native to your area and those that use less water.
- Use chemicals properly and only when necessary to keep waterways and drinking water clean.
- Reduce yard waste by recycling yard trimmings into free fertilizer, compost, and mulch.

forcing consumers to review their water use habits.

Planning a water-efficient landscape design is one answer. **Xeriscape** is a landscaping method that utilizes water-conserving techniques. Originally developed for arid or semiarid climates, xeriscaping is becoming more prevalent in other climates, too. Xeriscaping involves choosing and grouping plants native to an area according to the amount of water and sunlight they need. Watering deeply and less often encourages plants to develop deep roots. Using mulches and adding more trees and grass promotes water retention.

Plan to use the most water in areas that receive the most use. These areas often include the lawn, play areas, and gardens. Using runoff water from roofs and gutters can reduce water costs.

Patios and similar areas need water only for accent plants. Areas near the property boundary may require little or no watering. If you use native plants, you should have low water use. Native plants are better adapted to the climate and usually need less watering than other plants, 20-25.

Watering, if needed, should supply plants with enough moisture to live. Too much water can lead to plant disease. Excess water also prevents plants from developing properly. It is better to water less often but deeply. Deep watering can help roots grow better and make plants more drought resistant.

The most effective watering method is trickle irrigation, or *drip irrigation*. This technique involves delivering water directly to the base of the plants, reducing evaporation and runoff. Some trickle irrigation systems use narrow tubing routed under the ground. Other systems deliver water to plants through a porous hose aboveground.

The most common watering method involves the use of sprinklers. Sprinklers spray plants with water droplets or a fine mist. You can move portable sprinklers to various positions in the landscape. Built-in sprinkler systems have several stationary sprinkler heads in various locations throughout the landscape. Because they require no moving, built-in systems are generally more convenient than portable sprinklers. A considerable amount of water is lost to evaporation when using sprinklers, particularly those that spray fine mists. If sprinklers are not controlled, water runoff can be excessive, 20-26.

Irrigating at night saves water. However, with night watering, some plants are susceptible to certain diseases. Know the characteristics of your plants. Irrigating when the wind is calm will help reduce evaporation. A system controlled by a timer will also help save water. If possible, try to recycle water. You can use water from a pond to water grass or plants. Can you think of other ways to recycle water?

Soil conservation includes improving and maintaining the soil. Organic matter is the result of decaying plant or animal material. For example, leaves and manure are organic matter. Analyzing the soil is a very important part of soil conservation. Home owners can send soil samples away for testing or analyze them on-site. The results of these tests will determine what to do to improve the soil. Usually, soil improvement is a project most home owners can handle with advice from an expert. However,

20-25
The native plants in this landscape require very little water.

20-26
The sprinklers in this built-in system are controlled to conserve water.

for large or complex projects, a garden center or yard maintenance service can handle the job.

Mixing organic matter with the native soil can improve the soil. The organic matter creates air space in the soil. It also retains moisture and requires less watering. Improved soil increases the chances for good plant growth.

Soil conservation also includes taking steps to avoid erosion. The topography of the yard must encourage a natural drain pattern so water drains away from the house slowly. This gives moving water enough time to penetrate the earth, instead of eroding it. Improper grading and leveling of the lot encourages water to form streams, carry dirt off the lot, and create gullies.

Give special care to installing perforated plastic pipes to the ends of the downspouts. Burying these pipes underground to direct the water away from the foundation of the house has several benefits. One benefit of channeling water underground is soil conservation since water won't run off the downspouts to cause erosion and gullies. Another benefit reduces the risk of basement flooding since underground piping directs the water away from the house's foundation.

The plants you select for planting and the plan you develop for their placement can further prevent erosion and conserve the soil. To accomplish this, select plants and trees with good root systems and give careful consideration to their placement in the landscape plan. When planning a landscape, it is important to consider both water and soil conservation.

Energy Conservation

Home owner interest in conserving energy through landscaping continues to increase. The proper use of landscape elements helps modify the climate in and around a home. For example, good landscaping helps reduce heat gains in the summer and heat losses in the winter. In areas that require the use of air conditioning, effective landscaping can reduce cooling as much as 75 percent. Landscaping that provides plenty of summer shade helps reduce these costs. In regions that do not require the use of air conditioning, landscaping can help make the home interior more comfortable.

Properly placed vegetation and manufactured landscape elements can block prevailing winds. Windbreaks can save enough energy to lower heating bills by 10 to 15 percent.

Trees with high branches and many leaves provide summer cooling by blocking the sunlight. Tall trees provide less shade than those that are widespread. Since deciduous trees lose their leaves in the winter, they provide summer cooling and still allow you to benefit from the warmth of the winter sun. Deciduous trees are a good choice for placement on the south and east sides of buildings. Evergreen trees are good as windbreaks on the north and west sides of buildings because those sides get more sunlight all year long. The types of trees that do best vary from region to region.

Shrubs and vines provide good shade for the walls of a house. Most walls retain heat in the summer sun. Shrubs and vines act as insulation to reduce the heat reaching the walls. Evergreen shrubs and vines will also help prevent heat loss in the winter. If you plan enclosures to collect heat from the winter sun, use deciduous plantings.

Overhangs and roof extensions offer shade, too. Architects and designers can plan them to shut out summer sun and take in winter sun.

A **sunroom**, or garden room, is another structure that can use energy more efficiently. A sunroom structure uses energy from sunlight to heat a living space. Tile floors absorb energy from the sun, and in turn release heat into the room. The room may be part of a house or entirely separate.

To ensure a sunroom conserves energy, it must be in the correct position. For instance, it should face south, away from any shade cast by nearby trees or shrubs. In addition, use window treatments to regulate the amount of sunlight that enters the room during the day. They can act as insulation during the night to contain the heat, as in 20-27.

Conserving natural resources for future generations is everyone's concern. You can do your part, too. Information

is available to help you make decisions about conservation. Before deciding which measures to include in a landscape, learn all you can. Since the role of landscaping varies from region to region and season to season, gather information specific to your area.

Information about conservation measures is available from landscape dealers or the cooperative extension service in your county. Look for publications from the U.S. Department of Agriculture (USDA). Most large communities have at least one garden club. Members of these clubs can guide you to helpful conservation resources in your area. Libraries and the Internet are also excellent sources of information, too.

Completing a Scaled Plan

Awareness of what you have and how you want to use it is essential to developing a good outdoor plan. Be sure to consider the needs, interests, and desires of a household. In addition, consider the site's climate, topography, soil conditions, and orientation to the sun. What is attractive and what is unattractive about your outside environment? Determine the best natural resources on the site. Note the sunny and shady areas, 20-28.

After compiling all the necessary information, you are ready to develop a scaled plan, or *site plan*, for designing a landscaping. The northern edge of the site should be at the top of the plan. It is a good idea to begin a plan for the outdoor space with a map of the entire property. A landscaping plan should include the following information:

• property boundaries

• location of the residence, showing windows and doors

• location of other structures

• orientation to the sun and wind

20-27
The tile floor of this sunroom absorbs energy from the sun during the day and releases the heat during the night.

20-28
Thought was given to this well-designed landscape plan in that it provides enjoyment from the interior as well as the exterior.

Photography Courtesy of JELD-WEN Windows and Doors

- location of the driveway and sidewalks
- position of both underground and aboveground utilities
- location of existing plant life, rocks, and other natural features

Developing the Landscape Design

As with interior design plans, you can produce scaled plans of a landscape site either manually or with a CADD computer program. Whichever method you use, draw the plan to scale. To show the greatest detail, use this scale: *¼ inch equals 1 foot*. When you need less detail, it may be possible to use one of the following scales: *1 inch equals 10 feet* or *1 inch equals 20 feet*.

Drafting

Using graph paper, you can produce a drawing similar to Figure 20-29. You can also create several overlays to decide

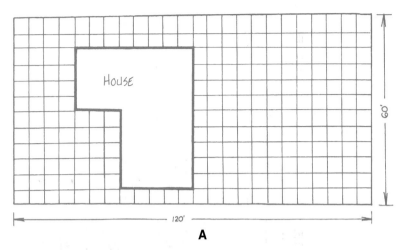

A

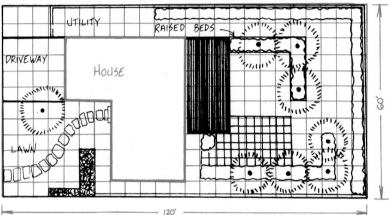

B

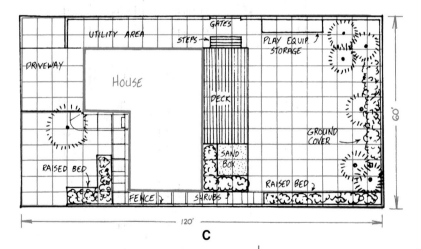

C

20-29
Landscape plans can be drawn on graph paper (A). Two alternate landscape designs are shown for the home site in images B and C.

Rea-Lynn Gilder

MATH MATTERS

Calculating Volume for Landscape Design

Volume is the amount of space occupied by a three-dimensional object. It is measured in cubic units, such as cubic feet (cu. ft.) and cubic yards (cu. yd.). A cu. ft. is a space that is 1 ft. wide by 1 ft. long by 1 ft. deep. A cu. yd. is 3 ft. wide by 3 ft. long by 3 ft. deep, or 27 cu. ft.

The volume of a three-dimensional square or rectangle is calculated by multiplying length times width times height (depth). Other mathematical formulas calculate the volumes of pyramids, cones, spheres, and cylinders.

Landscape architects and other design professionals use volume calculations in their work. For example, suppose a 15 ft. by 20 ft. brick patio is being installed in a grassy yard. The grass and dirt covering the patio site must be dug up and removed. The brick pavers and sand will rest on 6 in. (or .5 ft.) of gravel. A volume calculation gives the amount of gravel needed to install the pavers.

Volume = 15 ft. × 20 ft. × .5 ft. = 150 cu. ft.

Gravel is ordered in cubic yards.

Cu. yd. = cu. ft. ÷ 27
150 cu. ft. ÷ 27 cu. ft. = 5.6 cu. yd. of gravel

---

which plan you prefer. When drawing plans entirely by hand, the drafting process can be very time-consuming. Some landscape planning kits have ready-made symbols that designers can use to mark landscape elements.

Computer-Aided Drafting and Design (CADD)

With a computer and landscaping software, a designer can create scaled plans. A designer can draw the grounds area and all items on the premises with computer graphics. Besides designing the landscape plan, a computer-aided drafting and design (CADD) program can create a realistic view of how a completed design will look, 20-30. Some software programs allow you to view designs for the yard and outdoor living area from a walk-through perspective.

It is possible to learn some landscaping software in several hours. More complicated versions, usually used by landscape architects, will take longer. However, spending the time to learn a CADD program usually results in more designs and more views to help you or a client better visualize possible results.

Regardless of which tool you use to create a design, feel free to experiment. Produce several designs and consider different placements for the features. Clearly mark spaces for specific uses. Complete the design by arranging the outdoor furnishings. Remember to allow for traffic and convenience when planning furnishing arrangements.

Once you have decided on a landscape plan, it is time to roll up your sleeves and go to work. You and other family members may enjoy working

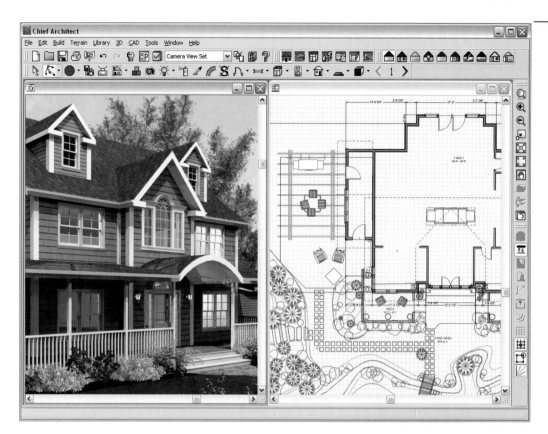

20-30
A CADD computer program used to plan and visualize the landscaping around the home.

Courtesy of Software by Chief Architect

together to create your outdoor living environment. As an alternative, you may choose to hire a landscape firm to carry out your entire plan or just the difficult parts. Many nursery owners have training in landscape design. They are knowledgeable about plants and can help you with the planning.

Another alternative is to hire a landscape architect to design your plan. A **landscape architect** is professionally trained to create designs that function well and are aesthetically pleasing. Members of professional groups such as the **American Society of Landscape Architects (ASLA)** are the most qualified experts in this field. If you desire, you can hire specialists to care for your outdoor living area. Maintenance companies will establish a service contract with you to mow the lawn, keep flower beds free of weeds, and prune shrubbery. They can provide periodic fertilizer applications to your lawn and garden.

CAREER FOCUS

Landscape Architect

Do you like to work with soil and plants? Do you enjoy beautiful outdoor spaces? If you do, perhaps a career as a landscape architect is for you.

Interests/Skills: Do you think about important environment questions and believe it is important to preserve and sustain the environment? Do you enjoy spending time outdoors and sketching drawings? Perhaps you appreciate attractive parks and plazas

and would like to create similar places that provide a balance between people and the environment. People who like this job enjoy working with their hands and being creative and artistic. Landscape architects need good communication skills. They have to explain their ideas to other people and talk to groups. It also helps to have good computer skills along with effective writing skills.

Career Snapshot: Landscape architects make outdoor places more beautiful and useful. They decide where to put flowers, trees, walkways, and other landscape details. They keep sports fields from getting soggy, and work with architects, surveyors, and engineers to find the best place to put roads and buildings. They also work with environmental scientists to find the best way to conserve or restore natural resources.

Education/Training: Most professionals have a four- or five-year college degree in landscape architecture or a related subject. This career requires continuing education and training.

Licensing/Examinations: Nearly all States (49) require landscape architects to be licensed or registered.

Professional Association: The American Society of Landscape Architects (ASLA) (www.asla.org)

Job Outlook: Jobs for landscape architects are expected to grow faster than the average (about 20 percent) for all occupations through the year 2018.

Sources: Occupational Information Network (O*NET) (www.online.onetcenter.org), the Occupational Outlook Handbook, Bureau of Labor Statistics (www.bls.gov), and the American Society of Landscape Architects, (ASLA) (www.asla.org)

Summary

When planning the outdoor living area of a home, first identify household goals. These will depend on the lifestyle, needs, and desires of the household.

Recognizing the types of landscaping elements and their uses will help you make plans. You must determine which natural elements are suitable for the landscaping site. Then choose the manufactured elements that fit the situation.

Planning a landscape is much like planning the rooms inside a house. Just as a house is divided into several areas, the landscape site is divided into three zones—private, public, and service. Each zone requires different treatment. When planning the landscape rooms, consider the floors, walls, ceilings, furnishings, and accents. Also, include lighting in the outdoor living area to make it usable at night.

Knowing the topography and the soil condition of the site is important. This information helps individuals conserve soil and water. Also plan the landscape to conserve energy.

Detailed plans of the outdoor rooms and landscape zones are a requirement for a successful landscape design. For accuracy, draw plans to scale. You can use various resources to help make landscaping decisions and incorporate them into the site.

Review the Facts

1. What is the basic goal of landscaping?
2. Name three examples of natural landscape elements.
3. What are three types of ground cover?
4. List five manufactured landscape elements.
5. How is designing a landscape similar to designing the interior of a home?
6. Name three functions for the "walls" of a landscape design.
7. What are three accents used in landscaping?
8. List five factors to consider when selecting outdoor furniture.
9. List three reasons for including lighting in any landscape plan.
10. What is the benefit of xeriscaping?
11. How does effective landscaping help conserve energy?
12. Name five items to include on a site plan.

Think Critically

13. **Make recommendations.** Assume your neighbor lives in a three-year-old home. The front of the home has a southern exposure. The home has a lawn and a few shrubs, but no mature landscaping. Your neighbor is concerned about how warm the rooms in the front of the home get, especially during the summer. Make some recommendations about how your neighbor might use landscaping to help keep the home cooler in the summer.

14. **Draw conclusions.** Conserving natural resources such as water and energy are important for both present and future generations. Draw conclusions about what could happen if individuals and communities did not use wise conservation practices? What would it be like to live permanently in a drought-stricken environment? How could this become a worldwide problem?

Community Links

15. **Landscape research.** Use Internet or print resources to research newspaper and magazine articles for landscaping and gardening news. Write a report about landscaping ideas that are suitable for your area. Share your report with the class.

16. **Plant purchasing.** Look through the seed catalogs at a local gardening store. Find five annuals and five perennials that grow well in your area. Indicate how they can be purchased (seeds, bulbs, plants). How might you use these plants in a landscape design?

17. **Community beautification.** Consider directing a landscape beautification project in your community. Identify an area needing improvement. (It could be your school grounds, a community park, a government building, an assisted living home, the local library, or another well-known building.) Obtain the assistance of a local nursery to sponsor your project, or create fund-raising projects to meet your goal. Plan the area to be planted with a professional landscape designer serving as a volunteer. Use the principles of design discussed in this chapter along with conservation techniques. Encourage your classmates to roll up their sleeves and help with the planting.

Academic Connections

18. **Writing.** Imagine that you are a reporter for a local newspaper, and there is a water shortage in the area. Your assignment is to write an article on effective water conservation practices. Use Internet and print resources for your research. Also, consider interviewing people in the community who are using good water conservation practices. Write the new article and share it with the class.

19. **Math.** Suppose your client wants to include a backyard playground for the family day care she provides out of her home. Because there will be climbing equipment, your client wants a well-cushioned play surface. The playground area will be 16 ft. by 24 ft. You suggest a rubber-based cushion material. The manufacturer recommends 2 inches of the rubber material over 4 inches of gravel. What is the total volume of the playground site?

Technology Applications

20. **CADD practice.** Use a CADD program to complete the site plan of a house familiar to you. Draw a floor plan of the dwelling's ground level. Divide it into zones. Then design the outdoor living space.

21. **Landscape research.** Search the Internet for two photos of houses that are nicely landscaped. Print a copy of each. Determine the types of manufactured items used in the design and describe how they affect it. Do the items make the design more attractive, safer, more private, easier to maintain, and more conserving of resources? Write a brief report of your findings.

22. **Photo essay.** Use a digital camera to take pictures of the different types of enclosures and fencing used at local schools, child care centers, libraries, and other public buildings. Incorporate your digital photos into presentation software and share your findings with the class. Discuss the likely goal of each type of enclosure and how well the goal for each was achieved. As an alternative, take photos of effective landscape backgrounds to share with the class.

Design Practice

23. **Outdoor design.** Suppose friends asked you to help them develop a private outdoor space around their home. How would you advise them on the following items: where to locate the space, what plants to install to block views from neighbors, and how to make the area easy to maintain? What resources would you use and suggest they review? What special considerations would you make if they lived in an apartment? Then use CADD software to create your design plan to share with your friends.

24. **Portfolio.** Your new client wants you to create a backyard landscape design for his long, narrow backyard. The yard measures 16 ft. wide by 40 ft. long. Your client wants to include an area for entertaining that includes cooking and seating areas along with a small play area for two young children. Use a CADD program to draw the layout of the backyard to scale (¼ in. equals 1 ft.). Select natural and manufactured landscape elements, furniture, cooking equipment, and appropriate play equipment for the children. Save a copy of your landscape design in your portfolio.

Leadership and Teamwork in Outdoor Environments

Do you have passion for preserving the environment? Do you seek ways to increase the beauty of the nature at home and in the community? Many opportunities exist for those who desire to combine their zeal for the outdoor environment with developing leadership and teamwork skills. On the local level, consider volunteering with the community park system. On the national level, think about working with the *Youth Conservation Corps* through the National Park Service.

Link your experience to an FCCLA project through programs such as *Leaders at Work, Community Service,* or *STAR Events*. Use the FCCLA *Planning Process* to plan, carry out, and evaluate your project. See your adviser for information as needed.

CHAPTER 21

Home Safety and Security

Terms to Learn

precautions
electrical shock
toxic
carbon monoxide
radon
mold
lead paint
ventilation
asbestos
noise pollution
decibel (dB)
combustible
asphyxiation
smoke detector
escape plan
deadbolt locks
biometrics
vision disability
hearing disability
hand limitation
mobility limitation

Chapter Objectives

After studying this chapter, you will be able to

- summarize ways to keep a home safe, including accident prevention, safety for children, keeping the air safe and clean, and controlling noise pollution.
- analyze ways to make a home secure from carbon monoxide poisoning, radon, fire, and intruders.
- determine changes that can make a home safe and secure for people with special needs.

Reading with Purpose

On a sheet of paper, write six reasons why the information in this chapter is important to you now and in the future. Think about how this information might help you at home or as an interior designer. When you finish reading the chapter, summarize your six reasons along with the chapter information that supports each.

Photography Courtesy of JELD-WEN Windows and Doors

You face a variety of risks as you go about your daily life. Using common sense and taking preventive measures may avoid other risks. The housing decisions you make for yourself and others can reduce the risk of home accidents. You can also make decisions that will help everyone in the home feel more secure.

A Safe Home

You, and many others, likely think of home as a safe place. Surprisingly, it is not. More injuries take place in home than anywhere else. Home accidents are a major cause of death and serious injury. Each year, accidents around the home hurt more people than traffic and work accidents combined. How safe is your home?

Preventing Accidents

In your own home and in the homes of interior design clients, you should not wait until an accident happens to take safety measures. Survey the home for danger spots. Guard the members of your household or that of a client against accidents that can have painful or even fatal results. Be sure that everyone knows and follows safety rules.

Preventing Falls

Falls are the most common type of home accidents. People of all ages suffer from falls, but the vast majority of those who suffer serious injury are older adults. Children also experience falls, but curiosity is generally the cause of such incidents which usually are less serious.

Taking a few simple **precautions**, preventive actions, can help avoid many falls. Wet floors can cause people to slip and fall. Wipe up water or other spilled liquids immediately. Loose rugs can also cause falls. Choose rugs with a nonskid backing or place a nonskid pad under the rug. Remove tripping hazards by picking up toys, shoes, or other items left on floors or stairs and encourage others to do so, too.

When using a ladder or stepladder, make sure it is securely in place before climbing, 21-1. Whenever possible, a second person should support the ladder. After using a ladder, store it properly so that children will not be tempted to climb.

The bathroom can be especially dangerous because wet surfaces cause many falls. Soap left in the bathtub creates a slippery, hazardous surface. You can reduce the danger of falling in the bathroom by using suction-type nonskid mats or safety strips in the shower and bathtub. Firmly attached grab bars can also help prevent falls.

21-1
Nonskid feet safely keep this ladder in position while in use.

Werner Ladder Co.

The most dangerous room in the home, according to the National Safety Council, is the bedroom. Many falls take place in the bedroom, as do fires. One reason for the high rate of bedroom accidents is that people move around while half-asleep. Placing handy lamps next to the bed will help prevent falls caused by stumbling in the dark.

Stairways should have light switches at both the top and bottom, and a sturdy, secure handrail. When climbing or descending stairs, always keep one hand free to use the rail. Keeping stairs free of clutter will help prevent falls.

Falls also occur on the outside of the home, often as a result of slipping on wet leaves, snow, or ice. Promptly removing snow and ice from sidewalks will help prevent falls. Be sure to remove toys, garden tools, and other possible tripping hazards from walks.

Preventing Burns

Burns are another major type of injury resulting from home accidents. Children under four years of age and elderly people are the most likely victims. A major source of burns and fires results from people smoking in the bedroom.

Hot cooking utensils can cause serious burns, 21-2. Turn panhandles away from the edge of the range when cooking to avoid spills. Open steam-filled pans on the side away from your body. To move hot utensils, use potholders or oven mitts. Be sure the mitt or potholder is not damp because the heat from the cooking utensil could cause steam burns.

Scalding water can cause serious burns, too. Lowering the temperature of your home's hot water supply to 120°F can prevent scalding burns.

Be careful of other household heat sources, such as toasters, hair dryers, steam irons, and portable room heaters.

21-2
Home accidents often occur during busy periods when attention is focused somewhere else.

Preventing Electrical Shock

Electricity in homes is convenient and makes possible a high standard of living. However, proper design, installation, and maintenance of the home's electrical system are crucial to prevent it from becoming a safety hazard. An electrical shock can be fatal. **Electrical shock** is an electric current passing through your body.

Most electrical shocks result from the misuse of household appliances. Since water conducts electricity, do not use electrical appliances near water or with wet hands. Dry your hands before using, connecting, or disconnecting electrical equipment. Do not stand on a damp floor while connecting or disconnecting an appliance's power cord. When disconnecting a power cord, grip the plug, not the cord. Pulling on the cord can weaken wires and eventually result in a shock or fire.

Use heavy-duty extension cords whenever possible. An extension cord should never be lighter than the appliance cord that is plugged into it. To avoid damage to electrical cords, do not tie knots in them or run them under rugs. Replace damaged or frayed cords and defective plugs promptly. Do not plug too many tools or appliances into one outlet. Overloading circuits can cause electrical fires. See 21-3.

The National Electric Code requires safety grounding of all outlets. Kitchens, bathrooms, laundry rooms, and other locations near water require installation of a special type of electrical outlet. The outlet includes a *ground fault circuit interrupter (GFCI)* to prevent shocks. Outlets on the exterior of your home should have weatherproof covers or caps. Circuit breakers and fuses are safety devices. They interrupt electrical power if too much current flows. Always replace a fuse with one having the same rating. Using a fuse with a higher rating could allow wires to overheat, causing a fire.

Preventing Poisonings

Another major cause of home injuries and fatalities is poisoning, 21-4. Swallowing common household products causes most such accidents. Laundry and cleaning aids, medicines, and cosmetics can be **toxic**, or poisonous. So are garden chemicals, materials used in the workshop, and many items found in the garage. The leaves or other parts of

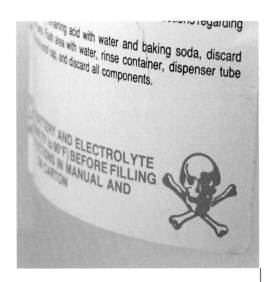

21-4
The skull-and-crossbones symbol is a warning sign for poisonous materials. Many household and gardening products show this symbol on their labels.

some houseplants are poisonous, too, if eaten. The list of dangerous items is long. You can probably think of others.

To help prevent poisoning, always keep products in their original containers. Read and understand the product labels, and follow directions. Then properly dispose the container and any leftover product. Use the safety checklist for hazardous materials in 21-5.

You may wish to use nontoxic alternatives for household products that contain potentially harmful ingredients, 21-6.

Keeping Children Safe at Home

Children are often the victims of home accidents. When they are present, be sure to take extra precautions. To prevent falls, install gates, bars, railings, and other types of barriers. Keep children away from open windows, porches, and stairways. To help prevent falls in the dark, install night-lights.

21-3
In areas where many electrical tools are used, install enough wiring and outlets to safely handle the electrical load.

The Wiremold Company

Safety Checklist for Hazardous Materials
Actions to Take
• Store hazardous materials in locked cabinets that are well ventilated.
• Store hazardous materials in the original, labeled containers.
• Keep hazardous materials beyond the reach of children, pets, and strangers.
• Always read the entire label before using hazardous materials.
• Follow directions carefully and use the materials only in the manner permitted by law.
• Avoid inhaling hazardous materials.
• Wear protective clothing and masks when directions for hazardous materials require it.
• Protect your skin from exposure to accidental spills, and carefully clean spills up.
• Wash your hands thoroughly after handling the hazardous materials and again before eating.
• Wash contaminated clothing immediately after use when directed to do so.
• Cover your pet's food and water containers when using hazardous materials nearby or upwind.
• Dispose the empty containers so they pose no hazards to humans, animals, wildlife, or valuable plants.

21-5
When handling a hazardous material, or any material unfamiliar to you, carefully follow these steps.

Keep children away from electrical appliances and cords. Install safety covers on unused outlets to prevent possible electrical shocks. Guard against fire, and safely store matches and lighters out of sight. It is especially important to involve children in fire drills so they know what to do in case of a fire.

Children can learn to identify symbols that indicate poison, as shown earlier. Many products that can be dangerous to children, however, are not in a poison classification. For example, how many laundry and cleaning products carry a warning label like the one in Figure 21-7? Where do you store these products in your home? Too often, people keep them under the kitchen sink, where children can reach them easily. Be sure to store dangerous products in a safe place, such as behind doors with safety latches or locks.

Keeping dangerous products out of sight is the best safety precaution to use with children. Simply moving them out of reach is no guarantee that children will not try to reach them anyway. Young children cannot judge the distance to an object and the length of their reach. Many serious childhood falls occur when children climb and stretch for distant objects that seem reachable.

A home swimming pool is another potential source of danger for children. For youngsters under five years of age, drowning is the second leading cause of accidental deaths around the home. Local codes usually specify the type and height of fences and other enclosures that home owners must install around pools. In addition, pool owners should observe the following safety precautions:

• Supervise young children at all times.

• Keep a phone and emergency numbers handy, 21-8.

• Learn cardiopulmonary resuscitation (CPR) procedures, a lifesaving tech-nique to use in an emergency.

21-6
The alternatives listed here are less harmful to people and the environment than the well-known products.

Safe Alternatives for Chemical Products

You can substitute vinegar, baking soda, borax, and soap for most of the household products you use. To make an all-purpose cleaner with nontoxic ingredients, combine 1 gallon hot water, ⅔ cup baking soda, and ¼ cup vinegar. For tough cleaning jobs, double the baking soda and vinegar. For specific household needs, use the following mixtures.

Product	Hazardous Chemicals	Safe Alternative
Abrasive Cleaners or Powders	Ammonia, ethanol	Rub area with ½ lemon dipped in borax; rinse and dry.
Ammonia-Based Cleaners	Ammonia, ethanol	Use a mixture of vinegar, salt, and water for most surfaces; for bathrooms, use baking soda and water.
Bleach Cleaners	Sodium or potassium hydroxide, hydrogen peroxide, sodium or calcium hypochlorite	For laundry, use ½ cup white vinegar, baking soda, or borax.
Disinfectants	Diethylene or methylene glycol, sodium hypochlorite, phenols	Mix ½ cup borax in 1 gallon water.
Drain Cleaners	Sodium or potassium hydroxide sodium hypochlorite, hydrochloric acid, petroleum distillates	Flush with ½ cup baking soda, ¼ cup vinegar, and boiling water.
Enamel or Oil-Based Paints	Pigments, ethylene, aliphatic hydrocarbons, mineral spirits	Latex or water-based paints.
Floor and Furniture Polish	Diethylene glycol, petroleum distillates, nitrobenzene	Mix 1 part lemon juice with 2 parts olive or vegetable oil.
House Plant Insecticide	Methoprene, malathion, tetramethrin, carbaryl	Mix a few drops liquid soap and 1 cup water; spray on leaves.
Roach and Ant Killers	Organophosphates, carbamates, pyrethrins	To kill roaches, use traps or a mixture of baking soda and powdered sugar. For ants, use chili powder to hinder entry.

Keeping the Air Safe and Clean

Clean air in the home is more of a concern now than in the past. To save energy used for heating and cooling, houses have become more airtight. Such airtight houses, however, have increased the problem of indoor air pollution.

Few people realize that air pollution can be very bad inside the average home. Indoor pollution comes from many sources. Some insulating materials give off vapors that are pollutants. Tobacco smoke, dust, pet dander, and household cleaning and beauty products all add pollutants to the air in the home. Even stagnant water left in containers like vaporizers and humidifiers pollutes the air.

21-7
This "Mr. Yuk" label was developed to warn children about products that may be dangerous to them.

Permission to use Mr. Yuk was provided by the Pittsburgh Poison Center at the University of Pittsburgh Medical Center.

21-8
Keep emergency numbers directly next to the phone so children can refer to them quickly.

GREEN CHOICES

ENERGY STAR Air Quality Label

Research studies show that air pollution in homes and other buildings is often two to five times that of the outdoors. People have concern about mold, radon, carbon monoxide, and toxic chemicals found in living and working environments. Poor indoor air quality can lead to a number of health problems including allergies, headaches, and such breathing problems as asthma.

One reliable solution is the ENERGY STAR Indoor Air Package. The federal government backs this solution. Homes with this labeling effectively deal with the following problems:

- Moisture control—added protection from mold and other moisture-related challenges
- Pest management—provides defense from pests because there are fewer cracks and other ways for pests to enter the home
- Heating and cooling system and vents—help prevent moisture problems and also filter the air
- Venting of fumes and gases—a ventilation system removes carbon monoxide from the home
- Building materials—selected to reduce the release of gases and other chemicals into the air
- Radon protection—special treatments and designs are used to control radon in the indoor air

When various sources create pollutants in an airtight house, problems may arise. The air can become polluted enough to affect health. People may develop allergies or feel tired and listless. Two pollutants—carbon monoxide and radon—can cause serious illness.

Carbon Monoxide

Perhaps the most dangerous of all indoor pollutants is carbon monoxide. **Carbon monoxide** is a colorless, odorless, tasteless gas that develops from incomplete burning of fossil fuel or wood. Fossil fuels include natural gas, propane, gasoline, coal, and charcoal. Depending on how much gas a person inhales, symptoms can range from temporary headaches to permanent brain damage to even death.

The body's red blood cells readily absorb carbon monoxide. The primary job of red blood cells is carrying oxygen to all parts of the body. When these cells carry carbon monoxide instead, oxygen starvation occurs in the body. The poisonous gas gradually invades every body cell. Nausea, coughing, and dizziness are the first signs of carbon monoxide poisoning. If they suspect such poisoning, people should call 911 or their local fire department immediately—especially if one or more household members, and even pets, show the same flu-like symptoms.

Most cases of carbon monoxide poisoning occur with the onset of cold weather. Restarting furnaces without a proper cleaning from the previous winter's use is a leading cause. Homes that are tightly caulked and weather-stripped prevent indoor air from escaping. These are ideal conditions for the creation and buildup of the poisonous gas. Entire households have been known to die within a few days of starting a poorly maintained gas furnace.

Regular maintenance of fuel-burning appliances is the best way to prevent the creation of carbon monoxide. Venting all fuel-burning appliances to the outdoors is another way.

Radon

Radon is a natural radioactive gas. Radon occurs in high concentrations in soils and rocks containing uranium and some other minerals. Soils with certain types of industrial wastes often contain this substance. Radon can lead to lung cancer. The risk of developing lung cancer from radon depends on the concentration and the length of exposure time to the gas.

You cannot see, smell, or taste radon. Federal and state governments are working to identify high-risk areas and provide information on dealing with the problem. The solution may be as simple as keeping the home well ventilated.

The federal government recommends that you measure the level of radon in your home. A radon test is the only way to know whether radon is present, 21-9.

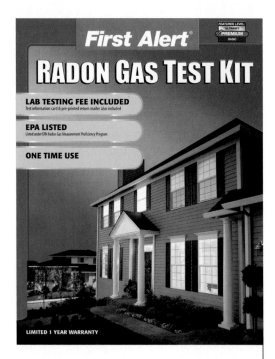

21-9
A radon test kit is available from several companies. Radon detection services are also available.

Photography Courtesy of First Alert®

Mold

Sometimes harmful mold (also commonly called mildew) can begin growing on surfaces in homes. A **mold** is a fungus that grows on damp or decaying matter. Some molds can be harmful to humans. These harmful molds can grow anywhere there is warmth and moisture, particularly in bathrooms, under carpeting, or in the cavities of walls, floors, and ceilings. Whenever flooding or water problems occur in a home, preventing an environment for mold growth requires proper drying and ventilation. Common causes of water problems include leaking pipes and emergencies such as an overflow from a clogged sink.

Health problems, such as allergies and other respiratory conditions, can occur from harmful molds in the air. Continual irritation by harmful airborne mold spores keeps these reactions from going away easily. A house in which household members suffer continuing breathing difficulties and allergic reactions may require a professional inspection for mold. If an inspection finds mold, professional removal is often a requirement.

Lead Paint

Lead paint refers to lead-based paint, which was a common form of paint manufactured before 1978 that contained lead. When the hazards of lead poisoning became clear, the federal government banned the use of lead in paint in 1978. However, homes built or painted prior to that date often have paint that contains lead. Federal law also requires that individuals receive specific information regarding the presence of lead paint before renting, buying, or renovating pre-1978 housing.

The problem occurs when the paint chips, peels, or results in excessive amounts of lead-contaminated dust. For example, opening and closing windows with lead paint creates such chips and dust, thereby allowing the lead to become airborne. Small children sometimes eat paint chips, mistaking them for candy. Lead can also be absorbed by handling of some ceramics and other items containing lead.

Lead can be harmful, especially to young children, pregnant women, and senior citizens. In children, lead poisoning can cause damage to the brain and nervous system, which results in behavior and learning problems. Adults can also suffer many permanent physical difficulties.

A house can be tested for lead paint and airborne lead so the occupants know about any potential hazard. Also, household members can take steps to avoid the harmful effects of the paint. These include professional paint removal from the walls and possibly replacing the windows.

Ventilation

Proper **ventilation**, or air circulation, greatly reduces air pollution levels. The living spaces of the house need ventilation to exchange fresh air for stale air. The attic, basement, or any crawl space under the floor also requires proper ventilation. If a house does not have built-in vents, they can be installed. Home owners can add exhaust fans to increase ventilation. With good ventilation planning, household air exchange occurs at a good rate, 21-10.

Eliminating or controlling the source of the pollutants can reduce air pollution. For example, ventilate the home well whenever painting, staining wood, or using chemicals that release vapors. Always follow manufacturer's instructions when using harsh chemicals. Become familiar with their negative health effects so you can recognize the symptoms if they occur.

Professional sealing or encapsulating for some pollutant types is necessary

21-10
After evaluating your home ventilation, you may be able to correct problems with a few simple steps.

Home Ventilation Checklist

Ask and think about the following questions when evaluating the effectiveness of a home ventilation system. If a home owner answers "no" to any of the following, it may be necessary to make some changes in the home ventilation system.

- Does the home have continuous general ventilation?
- Is there spot ventilation as needed?
- Are windows clear of condensation?
- Are there lingering odors in the home?
- Are exhaust ducts insulated in an unheated space, such as a basement or crawl space?
- Does the exhaust fan over the kitchen range have a vent to the outdoors?
- Is the dryer vented outdoors?
- Does each fuel-burning device (such as a furnace, water heater, or wood-burning stove) have a separate vent to the outdoors?
- Does each bathroom have an exhaust fan vented to the outdoors (and not into a soffit, attic, or crawl space)?
- Is exhaust air free of condensation?
- Has the home been tested for radon? Were the levels high or low?

to prevent polluting the air. Asbestos is a prime example. **Asbestos** is a fireproof, cancer-causing mineral that can easily become airborne and inhaled. Because of its fireproof quality, asbestos was used prior to 1978 in insulation, linoleum flooring, and other building materials. When renovating an older home, any asbestos present requires professional removal or encapsulation.

Two effective solutions for eliminating pollutants in the home are proper ventilation and elimination of their sources. Another solution to consider is the use of an air cleaner. Such devices generally clean the air of particles, not vapors or gases. Before buying an air cleaner, carefully check its *clean air delivery rate (CADR)*. This is the industry measure by which air cleaner manufacturers test the performance of their appliances.

Housecleaning

Housecleaning methods also affect the indoor pollution level. Indoor air quality is a growing concern across the

nation. The federal agency responsible for this issue is the U.S. Environmental Protection Agency (EPA).

Using a feather duster, for instance, merely stirs dust around to later settle on another surface. A central vacuum system helps clean the air by filtering it and exhausting it to the outside. Indoor air cleaners with good airflow and sturdy filters can clean effectively, too. Some vacuum cleaners use a compartment of water to "filter" the air before it returns to the room. Cleaning services are another housecleaning alternative, 21-11. These services will handle any size job at times convenient to the home inhabitants.

Controlling Noise Pollution

Noise is unwanted sound. **Noise pollution** is unwanted sound that spreads through the environment. According to government studies, noise is the leading cause of neighborhood dissatisfaction, which suggests it is a

21-11
Sawdust particles from remodeling settled throughout this house, so a professional cleaning service was called.

Reducing Noise

Listen to your house. Evaluate the noises you hear. Do they interfere with conversation? Are there sounds that invade privacy or cause distractions? See 21-12 for sound levels of some typical household appliances. Compare them to the level of normal conversation.

Solving some noise problems may be a simple matter. Solving others may take more effort. Indoors you can install sound-absorbing materials, such as acoustical ceiling panels. Carpets and draperies also help absorb sound, 21-13. Pleasant sounds, such as music, can muffle unwanted sounds. You may want to consider closing off noisy rooms. When you buy new appliances, you may want to choose those that are designed for quieter operation.

widespread nuisance. Medical research indicates that noise causes physical and psychological stress. It hampers concentration, slows work efficiency, and interferes with sleep. There may even be a link between noise and some harmful effects on unborn babies.

Sound is the sensation the sense of hearing perceives. A **decibel (dB)** is a unit for measuring sound intensity. The quietest sound that people can hear has a rating of 0 dB. Normal conversation is about 60 dB. The loudness of a sound and the length of exposure time to it determine its effect on a person. Continual exposure to loud noise can cause permanent hearing loss.

Household Noisemakers	
Appliance	**Sound Level in Decibels**
Floor fan	38 to 70
Refrigerator	40
Automatic washer	47 to 78
Dishwasher	54 to 85
Clothes dryer	55
Hair dryer	59 to 80
Vacuum cleaner	62 to 85
Sewing machine	64 to 74
Food disposer	67 to 93
Electric shaver	75
Electric lawn edger	81
Home shop tools	85
Gasoline-powered mower	87 to 92
Gasoline-powered riding mower	90 to 95
Chain saw	100
Stereo	up to 120
MP3 Player	100 to 115

21-12
These are the sound levels heard by the person operating the appliance or someone standing nearby. Normal conversation level is about 60 dB.

21-13
The rug on this kitchen floor helps hold down appliance noise and noise from other activities in the kitchen.

Photography Courtesy of Karastan

Insulating exterior walls may control noise from outside the house. Storm windows or multiple-pane glass can keep out some of the noise. Landscaping techniques, such as building berms (earth mounds), erecting walls, and planting shrubs, can also help reduce noise.

A Secure Home

A home should provide security, which is protection from physical harm. It should be a place where people can feel safe and sheltered from the unknown.

If you live in a well-built dwelling located in a relatively crime-free neighborhood, you are likely to feel safe. However, to more fully satisfy the need for security, include some protective devices in the home. Some of these devices monitor the surrounding conditions to make sure the home stays safe and secure.

Security from Carbon Monoxide Poisoning

Any dwelling that burns a fossil fuel or wood indoors should have a carbon monoxide detector. The chemical symbol for carbon monoxide is CO, so this device is a CO detector. Many local building codes require the installation of these detectors in new housing. Some cities require CO detectors in all housing.

This relatively inexpensive device sounds an alarm when low levels of the poisonous gas are present. It provides an early warning to occupants before harmful levels of carbon monoxide develop.

Since most carbon monoxide poisoning occurs when people are sleeping, install CO detectors near bedrooms. The ideal location is on the hallway ceiling outside the rooms. If bedrooms are on a second floor, install the CO detector on the ceiling at the top of the stairs. For greater protection, locate carbon monoxide detectors in the kitchen and at the top of a basement stairway. If battery operated, it is important to check batteries and replace them on a regular basis. See 21-14.

21-14
You can buy a combination carbon monoxide and smoke detector that mounts inconspicuously on the ceiling.

Photography Courtesy of First Alert®

Security from Fire

Home fires are one of the most serious types of accidents, often claiming small children and the elderly as victims. Fires can cause not only bodily injury and death, but also costly damage to property. The leading causes of fire include

- placing **combustible** (burnable) materials too close to a source of fire

- falling asleep while smoking

- carelessness with flammable materials

- operating defective electrical or heating equipment

Fire department officials stress that fire prevention is a matter of common sense. You can help prevent a fire in your home by following these simple rules:

- Choose upholstered furniture constructed to resist a fire caused by smoldering material. Such furniture carries a hangtag from the Upholstered Furniture Action Council (UFAC) certifying that the upholstery is resistant to sources of smoldering heat.

- Store flammable liquids properly, using only approved containers.

- Keep matches in a safe place out of sight where children cannot reach them. Dispose of used matches and lighters in a safe manner.

- Do not overload electrical wires.

- Dispose of trash regularly.

- Have the heating system inspected yearly by a professional.

- Burn only seasoned (dry) wood in wood-burning stoves and fireplaces. Do not use green wood, which can cause the build-up of a dark, flammable tar in the chimney.

- Keep at least three feet of open space around any space heater and never leave one unattended around children. Keep space heaters away from bedding, curtains, papers, and other combustibles.

Some fire deaths result from burns or injuries resulting from panic. However, the deadly smoke and gases a fire releases claim most fire victims through asphyxiation. **Asphyxiation** is the state of unconsciousness or death resulting from inadequate oxygen or some other breathing obstruction. Some simple steps can help you escape injury. The best precaution, however, is having a fire emergency plan, which you will learn about later in this chapter.

Smoke Detectors

An inexpensive **smoke detector** will send a loud warning signal if a fire starts. The detectors are easy to install. Place one on each floor of a building. The diagrams in 21-15 suggest good locations for smoke detectors. Most building codes for new homes require smoke detectors.

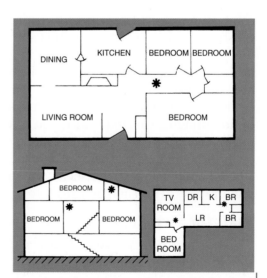

21-15

Smoke detectors should be placed on each floor of a dwelling, especially near bedrooms. They can be mounted on a ceiling or wall.

Honeywell Inc.

There are two basic types of smoke detectors: ionization and photoelectric. The ionization type responds more rapidly to fires where flames are present. The photoelectric detector is quicker to detect a smoldering, slow-burning fire. Both types effectively provide an early fire warning. Most detectors use batteries for operation, but connect directly to the home's electrical wiring. As with other appliances, check for a safety seal before choosing a smoke detector.

If a smoke detector is battery operated, install a fresh battery once a year. Most smoke detectors emit a sharp beep or have a flashing light to indicate that the battery needs replacing. It is a good idea to check smoke detectors for proper operation every month. Most units have a test button for this purpose.

Fire Extinguishers

Fire extinguishers are classified according to the type of burning material they handle. The Class A extinguisher is for fires involving paper, wood, fabric, and other "ordinary combustibles." Utilize Class B extinguishers for liquids that combust into fire, such as overheated cooking oil in a skillet on the range. Class C extinguishers are best for use on electrical fires.

Figure 21-16 describes the three classes of fire extinguishers. In practice, you can use many extinguishers available today on fires of any type. They are marked ABC. Locate fire extinguishers where they are easy to find and use, 21-17.

Plan for Fire Emergencies

The members of your household should have a plan of action, or **escape plan**, in case a fire occurs. Draw a scale floor plan of your home. On it, mark a main escape route and an alternate route from each room. Remember that children and older people will need special assistance in escaping from a fire. Make sure that all members of the household know the sound of the fire detector alarm and any other signal that household members might use. For example, you might use a loud whistle or a bell to awaken and alert everyone in the home.

Everyone must understand that speed in leaving the burning building is essential. There is no time to waste getting dressed or collecting possessions. Be sure each person knows how to make the door test: If the knob or panels of the closed door are warm, do not open the door. Use an alternate escape route. If the doorknob or panels are not warm, open the door slowly. If no smoke or hot air blows in, it is probably safe to use that exit.

If the home has more than one floor or is high off the ground, it is a good idea to provide a fire escape ladder in each bedroom. This allows another exit from the room when other exits are unusable. Conduct a trial practice in using the ladder as part of the household escape plan.

Part of your plan should include deciding on a place to meet once everyone is outside. After everyone is safely outside, go to the nearest telephone and call the fire department. In many areas, dialing 911 will connect you to an emergency services dispatcher. Some areas will have a local emergency number, instead. Report your name and address and describe the situation.

Once everyone knows the emergency plan, hold a practice drill. Repeat the drills periodically. Be sure to practice the use of alternate routes as well as main escape routes.

Fire Extinguishers and Fire Classifications

Fire Class	Extinguisher Type		Use		Operation
Class A Fires Ordinary Combustibles (Materials such as wood, paper, textiles.) **A** **Class B Fires** Flammable Liquids (Liquids such as grease, gasoline, oils, and paints.) **B** **Class C Fires** Electrical Equipment (Motors, switches, TVs, and appliances.) **C**	**Soda-acid** Bicarbonate of soda solution and sulfuric acid. 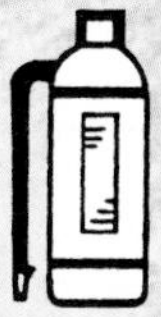		Okay for use on **A**		Direct stream at base of flame.
			Not for use on **B** **C**		
	Pressurized Water Water under pressure. 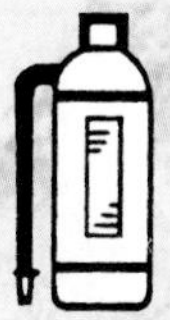		Okay for use on **A**		Direct stream at base of flame.
			Not for use on **B** **C**		
	Carbon Dioxide (CO_2) Carbon dioxide (CO_2) gas under pressure. 		Okay for use on **B** **C**		Direct discharge as close to fire as possible, first at edge of flames and gradually forward and upward.
			Not for use on **A**		
	Foam Solution of aluminum sulfate and bicarbonate of soda. 		Okay for use on **A** **B**		Direct stream into the burning material or liquid. Allow foam to fall lightly on fire.
			Not for use on **C**		
	Dry Chemical 		Multi-purpose type	Ordinary BC type	Direct stream at base of flames. Use rapid left-to-right motion toward flames.
			Okay for **A** **B** **C**	Okay for **B** **C**	
				Not okay for **A**	

21-16

This chart shows fire and fire extinguisher classifications. Use the proper extinguisher effectively to put out fires. Using the wrong extinguisher may lead to electrocution.

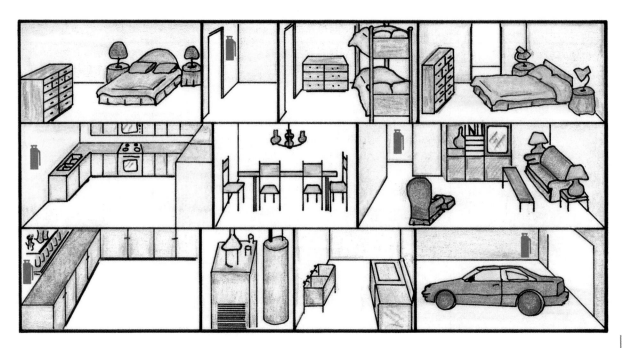

21-17
Install fire extinguishers in the garage, basement, kitchen, and easy-to-reach locations on each floor. Ideally, they should be near exits. No corner of the floor should be more than 75 feet away from an extinguisher.

General Services Administration

Security from Home Intruders

Securing a home from burglary or unwanted intruders is important. Many security measures are merely common sense. For instance, do not publicize the absence of household members when away from home. Most burglaries are committed during the day, while people are away at work or shopping. Take steps to make your home look lived-in, even when you are gone. The following will give a home that lived-in look:

- leaving a vehicle in the driveway
- stopping delivery of newspapers and mail, or having a friend pick them up daily at the normal times
- returning emptied trash cans from the curb
- using a variable timer to turn lights, radio, or TV on and off
- keeping the yard mowed, or snow removed from walks
- opening drapes during the day and closing them at night
- keeping a dog that barks at strange noises

Do not let strangers into your home. You should have some way of knowing who is at the door without opening it. A peephole or a chain lock permits you to see who is there. Monitoring devices are available that permit you to see and hear the person at your door before that person sees you. See 21-18. If a stranger asks to use your telephone, offer to make the call for him or her. Other security precautions include using outside lighting at every entrance to your home and installing secure locks on all doors and windows. You can also install a home security system with an alarm.

HEALTH/SAFETY

Creating a Family Emergency Plan

Hurricanes. Earthquakes. Fires. Power outages. Terrorist attacks. These are a few of the natural and manmade disasters that can suddenly turn lives upside down. You need to identify the potential hazards in your area and know how local authorities will alert you to these dangers. Also, create an emergency plan with members of your household.

Check with the American Red Cross, the U.S. Department of Homeland Security, and local authorities for the most up-to-date and detailed information. Fill out the "Family Emergency Plan" form at the U.S. government's ready.gov Web site. The form prompts you for information about household members' medical issues, an evacuation location, and how members will contact one another if separated.

Put a copy of the emergency plan in your emergency preparedness kit. Make sure everyone knows how and when to dial 911 for emergencies. Following are some general tips.

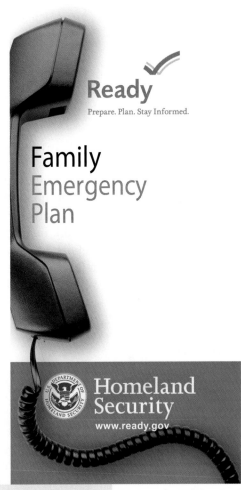

U.S. Department of Homeland Security (www.ready.gov)

- Assemble an emergency preparedness kit. Everyone in the household should know what it contains and where it is located. Keep a copy of your emergency plan in the kit or wherever it will be handy.

- Know the locations of shut-off switches for electricity, gas, and water services, and how to shut them off. (Since improperly turning on the gas is dangerous, get assistance from the utility company to turn it back on.)

- Eliminate in-home hazards. Move heavy items to low shelves; remove items hung over beds. Strap or bolt heavy furniture and appliances, including water heaters, to walls, floors, and secured cabinets.

- Hold an emergency drill several times a year. Rehearse your plan and make changes as necessary.

The American Red Cross says one person in each household should be trained in first aid, CPR, and the operation of an automated external defibrillator (AED).

When home alone, children should observe additional rules. Children should know how to use the phone, and important numbers should be available nearby. When answering the phone, parents should instruct their children give no details. For example, children should not tell a caller they are home alone or what time someone is to return.

Make the exterior of your home as visible as possible. Install a system to light exterior doors and the yard. Use automatic timers so lights are on from dusk to dawn. An alternate method is to use motion-detecting lights that go on when anything moves near the house. Trim all shrubs so that doors and windows are clearly visible from the street. If shrubs are growing under windows, make sure that they are thorny or cannot hide an intruder.

Locks and Other Security Devices

To make doors as secure as possible, install **deadbolt locks**, 21-19. This is a lock bolt that unlocks by turning a knob or key without action of a spring. Use a double-cylinder lock that requires a key to unlock from the inside as well as the outside. When moving to a new residence, change the lock cylinders to prevent entry by anyone who previously had a key to the door. Lock cylinders

A

B

HEALTH/SAFETY

Assembling an Emergency Preparedness Kit

During a natural disaster or other emergency, your home and community may lose power, heat, water, telephone, and Internet services. Emergency responders may be temporarily unavailable. You may have to evacuate your home. Roads, stores, doctor's offices, and other businesses and services may be closed. Hopefully, this will never happen to you. However, if it should, having an emergency preparedness kit in your home will be crucial. The kit should contain at least three days of supplies for each household member. Kit content recommendations vary; however, following are a few basics:

- water (at least 1 gallon of commercially bottled water per person per day)
- non-perishable food (prepackaged or precooked and canned), including infant formula and baby food if needed
- manual can opener, forks, and spoons
- prescription medicines (at least a 7-day supply)
- First aid kit and manual
- household chlorine bleach (not scented, color safe, or bleaches with cleaners)
- hand-crank or battery-powered radio and flashlight or lantern
- extra batteries
- cell phone with charger
- basic tool kit (hammer, wrenches, pliers, screwdrivers)
- blankets or sleeping bags and extra clothing (in cold climates, store warm clothes)
- face masks (N95-type masks are often recommended) to facilitate breathing

Fill a large envelope with the following: a list of emergency numbers and contact information; an area map; cash; copies of identification, credit cards, bank account information, and insurance policies; and copies of car and house keys. Put these items in one or more tightly closed containers in a cool, dry place that is inaccessible to children, pets, or pests. Check the kit several times a year and replace old, expired, or damaged items with fresh supplies.

The American Red Cross (www.redcross.org), the U.S. Department of Homeland Security (www.ready.gov), and the Federal Emergency Management Agency (www.fema.gov) offer more information about preparing for emergencies, including suggestions of other items to include in kits.

are less expensive than complete locks. Be sure to hire a reputable locksmith to make this change.

Keep all windows and exterior doors locked. If there is a door between the garage and the house, keep it locked too. Never leave keys in the locks. Also, do not hide keys near entrances, such as under a mat. Intruders know the usual hiding places and can find them easily. Install extra locks or take other measures to make sliding doors and windows secure.

Install strong exterior doors that are made of metal or have solid wood cores. Many doors are so weak that they can be broken through with a strong kick. Hang the doors so the hinge pins are on the inside. If the pins are on the outside, a burglar can remove them and open the door. If you have a glass pane in the door, installing a rigid transparent panel is a good security measure. A panel of plastic, such as acrylic, is ideal for this purpose.

Another deterrent to burglary is to mark your valuables with an identification number. Marking valuables can deter a thief, since marked items are more difficult to sell for quick cash than unmarked items. If a burglar steals your possessions, these items are easier to trace and identify with an identification number. Keep valuable items, such as jewelry and savings bonds, safely locked away. People may wish to store them in a home safe, a private security vault, or a safe deposit box at the bank.

Home Security Systems

Many people install electronic home security systems in their homes. The newest models use biometrics to determine who belongs in the home and who does not. **Biometrics** is the measurement and analysis of an individual by using a unique physical characteristic. Safe, keyless entry into homes is possible with security systems that use biometric data. Fingerprints, the pattern of an eye's iris, and vein patterns in hands are some of the biometrics that can identify the members of a household.

The typical home security system, however, uses window and door sensors. The sensors trigger an alarm when someone forces open a door or window. Some systems also have sensors that respond to vibrations, body heat, or noise. Some include smoke detectors or water-flow alarms, which signal a plumbing problem. Many home security systems will signal a burglary attempt with flashing lights, a siren, an alarm bell, or a combination. Other systems connect to a monitoring station. If you are away, the monitoring service you hire will know when the alarm goes off. This service will notify the fire department or police. You can expect to pay a monthly fee for the monitoring service in addition to the installation charge.

Often the presence of a home security system will ward off intruders. Placement of signs or stickers around the house and on doors and windows of the home indicate the presence of the home security system. A barking dog may serve the same purpose. Some owners train their dogs to protect them. People who live on the same street may form a Neighborhood Watch program. People in such a program report any suspicious activities on their street to police. Some people prefer to live in a place that has security guards in stations or gatehouses.

Personal needs and beliefs will affect the way people choose to keep their homes secure. For instance, some people feel safe with a security guard nearby. Having a guard may make other people feel restrained or uncomfortable. No matter what your situation, you will probably want to take some security measures. Choose those that make you feel comfortable and safe within your home.

Whether you own or rent, take measures to prevent home accidents and safeguard your home against intruders. You will also want your home to be safe and secure for the other household members.

Equipping a Home for People with Special Needs

Sometimes physical disabilities may make it necessary for a person to move from his or her home. However, if modifying the present home is possible, a move may be unnecessary. There are many ways to equip a home to meet the special needs of people.

Using Universal Design

Housing features that are nuisances or inconveniences to the average person can be significant barriers to people with physical disabilities. One example is having no bathroom on the main level. Another example is a house with steps at every entrance.

As you recall from Chapter 4, universal design refers to structural and nonstructural features that make a house easier for everyone to use. For example, a bathroom on the main level and a no-step entrance are *structural features*. These must be included in design plans during building or remodeling. Pull-out cabinet shelves, appliance lifts, easy-to-grasp handles, and cold water dispensers on refrigerators are examples of nonstructural features, 21-20. *Nonstructural features* are items that interior designers and home owners can easily add to an existing house to make it more usable.

Universal design addresses the needs of everyone, not just one segment of the population. Its main purpose is to make a house and all its components more usable. The design concept considers all household members, from the tallest to the shortest and the weakest to the strongest. Universal design addresses all the different stages in a person's life and the different personal needs they pose. With universal design, people can "age in place." Consequently, they do not need to find other housing during periods of temporary or permanent physical disability.

Features for Special Needs

Few, if any, consumer products are designed specifically for people with physical disabilities. Consequently, the challenge for these consumers is finding products with features that complement their abilities. For example, various models of ranges are available with side, back, or front controls. People who can see objects close-up but not far away would benefit from an appliance with front controls, as shown in 21-21.

A person with a **vision disability** may have any degree of vision loss. For

21-20
A refrigerator with through-the-door ice and water service was chosen for this home because family members include small children and adults with disabilities.

Photography Courtesy of Whirlpool Home Appliances

21-21
Front controls on the range are easier for people with physical disabilities to reach and operate.

Whirlpool Appliances

21-22
A Braille cookbook and Braille controls on the microwave help this visually impaired person make meals.

Whirlpool Appliances

most people, changes in vision begin after the age of 40. These changes often become more severe after age 65. One of 20 people over the age of 85 is legally blind. People with a vision disability live most comfortably and safely in familiar surroundings. Adapt living areas to the needs of a person with a vision disability with the following measures:

- Prominently mark changes in floor levels and countertop levels. Refer again to 20-21.

- Place furniture away from traffic lanes.

- Increase the amount of lighting and make sure it is evenly distributed.

- Use highly visible colors, such as yellow-orange and red.

- Avoid using similar colors together. Instead, use contrasting colors to visually separate items.

- Keep a consistent light level in bedrooms and halls. Use night-lights.

- Where appropriate, use Braille or tactile markings in cookbooks and on controls, as in 21-22.

The checklist in 21-23 will help you analyze how well a home is adapted for the needs of people with vision disability.

The most common disability among older people is hearing loss. Hearing ability declines gradually, so a person with a **hearing disability** may have any degree of hearing loss. Hearing-impaired people need a communication system that complements their hearing ability. Amplifying devices on doorbells and phones may be sufficient. People with a total hearing loss will need visual signals, such as a flashing light.

Meeting the Needs of People with Visual Impairments	21-23

Meeting the Needs of People with Visual Impairments

✓ Are raised numbers or letters used on entrance doors, especially in apartment dwellings? (Note: They should be at least 3 feet above the floor.)

✓ Are hanging objects higher than the person with poor vision?

✓ Are obstructions removed from major traffic areas?

✓ Are sliding doors used on closets and elsewhere to eliminate walking into an edge of an opened door?

✓ Are handles treated with knurling (or a special adhesive) on doors that lead directly to steps or other potentially dangerous areas?

✓ Are push-button controls identifiable by touch?

✓ Are all control dials marked or shaped so fingers can feel different positions and know what settings they are? (In some cases, click stops may be substituted.) The important controls to mark are

   ✓ range

   ✓ oven

   ✓ mixer

   ✓ faucets

   ✓ washer

   ✓ dryer

✓ Is storage adequate so items can be stored separately on adjustable shelves or similar items can be stacked without piling too high?

✓ Do water faucets always have hot water on the left and cold water on the right of the user?

21-23 This checklist helps people adapt living spaces for people with vision loss.

Hand limitations result from arthritis and other conditions limiting movement and gripping ability. These individuals need large lever-type controls on doors and faucets. Special faucets are also available with proximity sensors or electric eyes that turn them on and off. Electronic touch controls on appliances are often easier to use than knobs, which require grasping and turning. Light switches that an individual can press are easier to use than those that move up and down. On outside doors, keyless push-button locks are good.

A person who has a **mobility limitation** has difficulty walking. Living spaces that are all on one level will eliminate the need for using stairs. For climbing and descending stairs well, they must be easy to use. The stairway must have secure handrails and a nonskid surface on each step. Ideally, people with limited mobility should use stairways with shorter, wider steps.

Some people with mobility impairments move well with the use of a walker. Other people require a wheelchair. Accessibility requirements change drastically when interior designers take the needs of a person using a walker or wheelchair into account. Determine if your house can provide a comfortable and convenient environment to a person with limited physical ability.

CAREER FOCUS

Security Management Specialists and Systems Installers

Can you imagine yourself in a career in public safety? If you can, perhaps a job as a security management specialist or a security and fire alarm systems installer is for you.

Interests/Skills: Do you have an interest in helping people and keeping them safe? Are you a hands-on person who likes to work with systems and tools? Do you have an interest in electricity and electronics? Along with knowledge and skills about equipment, wiring, computer program applications, and ability to monitor such systems and those who design and install them, security management specialists and security and fire alarm systems installers need to have excellent communication skills. Meeting with clients and understanding their security needs is crucial to the work of the security management specialist and the installer. Effective problem solving, manual dexterity, and precision are also key skills.

Career Snapshot: Along with knowledge about computers and electronics, customer service, and public safety, management specialists and installers of security equipment must also understand building and construction and the tools involved in repair or construction of houses and buildings. In-depth knowledge of telecommunications systems is key. Installers of security equipment need to think critically and solve complex problems. In addition, installers must determine whether certain systems comply with laws, regulations, and standards. In addition, security management specialists must have strong organizational skills and effective written communication skills.

Courtesy of ADT Security Services

Education/Training: Most of these occupations require an associate's degree or training at vocational schools. Along with schooling, security management specialists and installers of security equipment may receive informal on-the-job training with experienced workers or participate in a recognized apprenticeship program.

Licensing/Examinations: Most states require licensing for any firm or individual that installs, monitors, or maintains fire and burglar alarm systems.

Professional Associations: Central Station Alarm Association (CSAA) (www.csaaul.org); Electronic Security Association (ESA) (www.alarm.org)

Job Outlook: Jobs in this area are expected to grow much faster than average through 2018 (20 percent or higher).

Source: Information from the Occupational Outlook Handbook (OOH) (www.bls.gov/OCO); Occupational Information Network (O*Net) (www.onetcenter.org)

Summary

A safe home provides freedom from accidents and offers security. Home accidents can occur to people of all ages. To assure safety for older people, children, and people with disabilities take special precautions. Preventive measures can eliminate many falls and other accidents. They can also lessen the possibility of injury as a result of fire, burns, and electrical shock.

A healthy home environment is free of air and noise pollution. Develop awareness about pollutants and how to reduce them or control their sources. Proper ventilation and wise use of cleaning methods and materials are steps toward having a healthy home. There are various ways to control noise inside a home.

Make a home more secure by using protection and warning devices. Reduce the possibility of injury or death from fire by installing monitoring devices and fire extinguishers. An emergency plan is important in case of the need to evacuate. Good locks and an alarm system will help make any home more secure. Mark valuables to help to deter theft and make stolen items easier to recover. Adjusting structural and adding certain nonstructural features can make a home safe and secure for those with special needs.

Review the Facts

1. Summarize three types of home accidents. Give a possible cause for each and a precaution that could prevent it.

2. What two people groups are the most likely victims of home accidents?

3. Name three health problems that may result from inside air pollution.

4. How is sound measured?

5. What is the difference between noise and sound? Name two ways noise can impact people.

6. What is the best way to keep household members secure from carbon monoxide poisoning?

7. List four ways to prevent fire in a home.

8. Name three essentials every household should have to prevent fire injury.

9. What are five ways to make a home appear occupied when household members are away?

10. List two guidelines children who are home alone should follow.

11. What type of locks should be used on exterior doors?

12. How do biometric security systems differ from typical home security systems?

13. What is the difference between structural and nonstructural features in universal design? Give an example of each.

14. Who in the household benefits when a home incorporates universal design?

15. What are three adaptations a home owner or interior designer could make to adapt a home to the needs of a person with a vision disability?

16. Name one way to adapt a home for a person with a hand limitation and a person with a mobility limitation.

Think Critically

17. **Analyze responsibility.** How important is it to be aware of harmful molds in residences? Can people unknowingly experience exposure to harmful indoor air quality? Who is responsible for investigating the presence of harmful mold: the current homeowner, the previous owner, or some government agency? Explain your position.

18. **Identify evidence.** Use Internet and print resources to research the severity of lead poisoning among small children. Identify evidence to support ways to prevent lead poisoning in children. Should government agencies require the testing of older homes to determine lead-paint presence before households with young children are allowed to move into the units? Why or why not?

19. **Draw conclusions.** Instead of moving to a group-living arrangement, many older adults want to continue living in their own homes as long as possible. Yet, in their older years, getting around their homes grows more difficult. Draw conclusions about whether or not local building codes should require universal design features in new homes. Consider cost, aesthetics, and the benefits of such requirements.

Community Links

20. **Fire extinguisher know-how.** Visit a local hardware store or home improvement store that sells fire extinguishers. Note the different models available and their prices. Learn how to use a fire extinguisher. Explain its features and operation to the class.

21. **Article review.** Read an article about a household accident in your local newspaper. Write a summary of the article and identify ways the accident could have been prevented.

22. **Resource list.** Create a resource list of companies that specialize in detecting and abating radon, carbon monoxide, mold, lead paint, and asbestos in residences in your community. Call or e-mail the companies to confirm the services they offer. Share the list with your class.

23. **Security interview.** Investigate various types of home security services available in your community. Select one service provider and make an appointment to interview a manager about the security services this company provides. What types of systems does it use? How does home design influence the security system? Share your findings with the class.

Academic Connections

24. **Reading.** Read two or more articles about childproofing a home on such Web sites as *Kids Health* or *BabyCenter.* Presume you are an interior designer who has been asked to make home safety recommendations to a young couple with two children under age 3. The couple has a three-bedroom ranch style home. The back entry has a sliding glass door off the deck. Based on the information you have read, write a summary of recommendations you have for this couple.

25. **Science.** Use Internet sites, such as the Environmental Protection Agency (EPA) Web site, to investigate more about the impact of radon in homes and its impact on human health. What is the difference between short-term and long-term testing for radon? What recommendations exist for lowering radon levels in the home? Write a report summarizing your findings.

Technology Applications

26. **Fire escape plan.** Use CADD software to create a floor plan showing each floor of your home or the home of someone you know. Draw the escape routes for each floor on the plan and note the locations of smoke detectors, carbon monoxide detectors, and fire extinguishers throughout the home. Share your plan with the class.

27. **Mold prevention.** Search the Internet for information on mold and mildew prevention in the home. Identify ways people can prevent mold or mildew and how to eliminate it once mold or mildew occurs. Develop a report on your findings using presentation software. If possible, locate photos of different types of mold to enhance your report. Share the report with your class.

Design Practice

28. **Design for safety.** You have been asked to assess and design an indoor and outdoor environment for a young couple with two children. One of the children uses a wheelchair. Use Internet or magazine resources to locate a floor plan for a home on one level. Evaluate the floor plan and determine features to add or remove to make this home safe and secure for the family. What design features might need to be added to the kitchen, bathroom, and child's bedroom? What outdoor features would ensure safety and a place for both children to play outdoors? Locate photographs of items you think are essential for the safety and security of your client's family. Prepare a visual and written summary to present to your clients. Save a copy as an example in your portfolio.

29. **Portfolio.** Develop a storyboard, photo essay, or an electronic report using presentation software on safety and security recommendations in the home from an interior designer's perspective. Use a digital camera to take pictures to accompany your report. Keep a copy of your presentation in your portfolio.

Active Citizenship—Lead Paint Removal

Lead poisoning from paint dust and paint chips is very harmful to human health—especially for children. In many communities, older housing in low-income areas poses a risk for people with few resources to stop the problem.

As an active citizen, investigate community organizations that work with lead paint removal for low-income housing. How can volunteers get involved? Is there an age requirement for volunteers who work with lead paint removal? If an age requirement exists, how can you support the organization if you are under age?

Use the FCCLA *Planning Process* and the guidelines for an FCCLA *Community Service* project to plan, carry out, and evaluate your project related to lead paint removal in low-income housing. See your adviser for information as needed.

CHAPTER 22

Maintaining a Home

Terms to Learn

disinfectant
plumbing plunger
closet auger
finish nail
box nail
short circuit
redecorate
remodeling

Chapter Objectives

After studying this chapter, you will be able to

- evaluate and select the cleaning tools, products, and schedule needed to maintain a home.

- summarize how to properly maintain the landscape.

- explain how to use basic tools for common home repairs.

- summarize ways to improve storage and organize space.

- assess redecorating choices.

- evaluate the pros and cons of remodeling.

- summarize resources for home maintenance.

Reading with Purpose

Before reading the chapter, make a list of everything you already know about the chapter topic. As you read the chapter, check off the items that are covered. Take notes on the items that are not on your list.

Maintaining a home involves keeping it clean, safe, and in good repair. It also involves making sure that equipment, electrical and plumbing systems, and other parts of the home are in proper working order. Regular home maintenance keeps the home environment secure and comfortable. You will use the decision-making process to choose how and to what level you maintain your home.

Cleaning and Maintaining a Home

Every house is different, and everyone has different standards of cleanliness. One person wants every part of a room spotless and each object in its place, 22-1. In contrast, another person may not mind some clutter. When people share a home, they should come to an agreement on acceptable cleaning standards. The standards should be realistic. Everyone should be able to work together to meet the standards.

Keeping family members healthy and safe requires a certain minimum standard of cleanliness. Inhabitants of a home must contain and remove garbage from the dwelling regularly. If garbage is uncovered or left for a period of time, it can attract animals and insects. In addition, remove or properly store any items that cause odors. This helps to keep the air fresh.

22-1
Cleanup is much quicker and easier when household members help keep the home tidy.

Interior Home Maintenance and Cleaning

It is important to decide how much time you can devote to cleaning. Your decision affects your choices in home furnishings and accessories. For instance, if you want to devote as little time as possible to cleaning, choose furnishings that do not show soil readily or contain fine woods. Also, avoid furniture and accessories that require frequent care. These include items that must be polished, shined, or frequently dusted.

Cleaning is easier if there is little or no clutter to maneuver around. You can eliminate clutter in a number of ways. You can recycle items such as newspapers and cans and other items your community designates. Discard items that are obviously old, broken, or unusable. If you are like most people, you will keep some items that you treasure, even though they produce clutter.

Cleaning Tools

Cleaning the home is easier if you have the right equipment or cleaning tools. There are two main types of cleaning tools. The first type removes loose dust and dirt. These tools include

- a dust mop for picking up dust on hard floors
- a broom and dustpan for sweeping hard-surface floors and steps
- a vacuum cleaner with attachments for carpets, hard floors, woodwork, furniture, upholstery, and window treatments
- cloths for dusting and polishing

The second type of cleaning tool removes soil that is stuck to surfaces. These cleaning tools include

- sponges for washing walls, woodwork, and appliances
- a pail to hold cleaning solutions
- a wet mop for cleaning floors
- a toilet bowl brush

A stepladder or stool for reaching high places, whether loosening dust and dirt or removing it, is necessary for safety. See 22-2 for a variety of cleaning tools.

Cleaning Products

Cleaning products include the chemicals that aid you in your cleaning tasks. The basic cleaning products you should always have include

- glass cleaner for mirrors, bathroom fixtures, and the surfaces of kitchen appliances

- grease-cutting liquid for fingerprints, oily stains, or soap residue

- mild abrasive powder for stubborn stains on countertops and work surfaces

22-2
These are some tools used to get surfaces clean.

GREEN CHOICES

Eco-Friendly Cleaning Products and Tips

Some on-the-shelf cleaning products are "greener" than others. Products that are more kind to the environment are labeled with "green" on the label or product description. Using these products can help reduce strain on the environment.

Another option is to use common household pantry items: this could save money and be environmentally friendly. See the items below:

Cleaning Need	Eco-Friendly Homemade Solution
Oven	Table salt. Cover the area with baked on food with salt while the oven is still warm. When oven is cool, scrape away food and wipe with damp sponge.
Windows	White vinegar and water. Using a spray bottle, spray glass with a solution of 3 tablespoons white vinegar and 1 gallon cool water. Avoid streaks by wiping panes with newsprint.
Floors	Liquid soap, white vinegar and water. Damp mop once a week with 1 gallon of water mixed with ⅛ cup liquid soap and ⅛ cup white vinegar.
Countertops	Baking soda and water. Add 4 tablespoons baking soda to 1 quart warm water for a nontoxic all purpose cleaner.
Clothes Drying	Clothesline. Hang clothes on an outdoor clothesline for fresh-smelling clothes. Let the sunshine dry the clothes.
Stains on White Clothing	Borax and water. Remove stains from whites by dabbing spots with a mixture of one part borax and six parts water.
Mold and Mildew in Bathroom	Tea-tree oil and water. Prevent mold and mildew by spraying stains with a spray bottle filled with 1 cup water and 1 drop tea-tree oil.

Figure 22-3 shows a list of some useful cleaning agents, waxes, and polishes. Many cleaning products also contain a **disinfectant**, which is a cleaning agent that destroys bacteria and viruses. Before you purchase any cleaning product, check your supplies. You may already have what you need. Look for those that serve more than one purpose. There are many multipurpose cleaning products. Most are available in dry and liquid forms.

22-3

Using the proper cleaning agent for the job is important.

Cleaning Products	
Cleaning Agents	**Method of Action**
Water	Dilutes and flushes dirt away
Alkalies • Soaps • Washing soda • Some general purpose cleaner • Ammonia	Breaks down surface tension of water, allowing the cleaning agent to penetrate dirt better
Synthetic Detergent	Relieves surface tension to clean and cut grease better than soaps; does not react with minerals to form scum deposits as soap does
Acid • Vinegar • Lemon juice	Cuts grease and acts as a mild bleach
Fat Solvent	Dissolves soil held by grease
Fat Absorbent • Fuller's earth • Talcum • Bentonite • Cornmeal	Absorbs oils in a dry form, then brushed away with the soil
Abrasive • Silver polish • Scouring powder • Steel wool • Soap pads	Rubs dirt away in dry form or with water (depending on type)
Waxes and Polishes	**Method of Action**
Solvent-Base Cleaning Wax • Liquid wax • Paste wax	Loosens soil on hard floors, removes old wax, and forms a new wax coating
Water-Base Cleaning Wax • Emulsion wax • Solution wax	Loosens soil on hard floors other than wood and cork, and forms a new wax coating; won't remove old wax, which must be stripped with remover
Furniture Polish • Aerosol and pump spray • Creamy liquid • Paste polishes	Lifts soil, removes old wax, and forms a new wax coating
Multipurpose Cleaner Wax	Lifts soil from countertops, tiles, appliances, cabinets, and furniture; removes old wax and forms a new wax coating

You must also be aware of dangers associated with many cleaning products. Check labels to see if the products are toxic. Many cleaning compounds are poisonous or flammable. In addition, always read labels on cleaning products to make sure they will not damage the surface you are cleaning. Follow directions carefully. Finally, do not mix different cleaning products. Some products create toxic gases when mixed with other cleaning agents.

To help make cleaning easier, keep all cleaning items in an organized area, 22-4. Always store cleaning products in locked cabinets out of children's reach. Keep cleaning products away from heat sources.

Cleaning Schedule

Some people prefer to get their work done early in the day. Others like to sleep late and work at night. Some people like housework, while others do not. Whatever your energy level or your work pattern is, scheduling your cleaning tasks allows you to better use your cleaning time. Figure 22-5 shows a list of common tasks.

22-4

Storing cleaning supplies in one place helps make cleaning easier.

Kraftmaid

Checklist for Cleaning Tasks
Daily Tasks
✓ Make bed
✓ Straighten bedroom, bathroom, living area, and eating area
✓ Wash dishes
✓ Wipe kitchen counters and range top or other cooking surface
✓ Sweep or vacuum kitchen floor
✓ Empty wastebaskets and other garbage containers
Weekly Tasks
✓ Change bed linens
✓ Do laundry and mending
✓ Wash kitchen garbage can or change liner
✓ Wash kitchen floor
✓ Clean bathroom sink, tub, and toilet
✓ Wash bathroom floor
✓ Dust accessories
✓ Dust and polish furniture
✓ Vacuum lamp shades
✓ Vacuum carpet
✓ Shake out small rugs
Monthly Tasks
✓ Vacuum and turn mattress
✓ Wash mattress pad
✓ Vacuum drapes and wipe blinds
✓ Vacuum upholstered furniture
✓ Clean kitchen shelves
✓ Clean refrigerator
✓ Clean oven
✓ Clean woodwork
Semiannual Tasks
✓ Clean closets
✓ Dry-clean or wash bedding (comforter, bedspread, pillow shams, bed skirt, blankets)
✓ Clean drapes thoroughly (wash or dry-clean as appropriate) and wash curtains
✓ Wash seldom-used glassware and dinnerware
✓ Clean silverware (if silver and not stainless)
✓ Replace shelf liners
✓ Wash walls, including bathroom

22-5

A checklist for cleaning tasks will help keep you on schedule.

Your cleaning schedule may vary from day to day or week to week. It depends on the use of your facilities. The more often facilities are used, the greater the need for cleaning. Less use usually means less cleaning. The larger the household is, the greater the cleaning task. When making a cleaning schedule, include the name of the person responsible for each task. Divide the tasks among household members.

Weekly cleaning tasks are easier if each household member helps with daily maintenance. For example, each person can be responsible for cleaning the bathtub or shower after bathing. An immediate wipe-down should leave it clean. Supply a sponge, brush, or towel. You may also need to use a glass cleaner. Keep everything needed for the task in the bathroom.

Techniques and procedures for regular and special cleaning of household items depend on their individual characteristics. There are many different types of furnishings on the market, requiring different cleaning approaches. See 22-6 for guidelines for furniture care and maintenance.

Over time, walls and woodwork will need more than cleaning. If the paint begins to chip or fade, you will want to repaint the surface. If wall covering was installed, you may need to periodically re-paste corners that begin to peel. If wall coverings fade or become damaged, you will need to strip the walls and select a new wall treatment, 22-7.

Exterior Home Maintenance and Cleaning

Just as it is necessary to clean and maintain the interior of a home, home owners also need to establish a schedule for the house's exterior. A house represents one of the biggest lifetime investments. It is extremely important to keep the structure in good condition,

to avoid costly repairs, and preserve its economic value. You will need to monitor all exterior areas.

Roof, Gutters, and Downspouts

Often home owners do not realize the importance of keeping the roof, gutters, and downspouts free of debris, such as leaves and branches. For roof construction that includes shingles or metal, it is important to protect it from moving branches that may scrape and damage the roof during a windstorm. Also, do not permit leaves and twigs to accumulate on the roof as they contribute excess moisture that eventually causes damage.

Proper maintenance of gutters and downspouts also is essential. Keep gutters and downspouts clear of anything that may block the proper flow of water off the roof. Routine cleaning and special attention after storms and in autumn after heavy leaf-fall keeps water flowing in gutters and downspouts, 22-8. If rainwater cannot flow off the roof, it will back up into the attic space and wall cavities. Water can cause extreme damage and eventually contribute to problems from mold, rot, and termites.

Exterior Walls

The exterior walls of a house can be made of wood siding, manufactured siding, or masonry, such as brick or stucco. It is important to monitor wood siding for rot and replace siding as needed. Regular painting or staining is necessary to protect wood siding from the eroding effects of weather. Between paintings, pressure-wash the exterior siding to remove stains caused by mildew, 22-9. Also wash and paint manufactured siding, such as fiberboard and fiber cement siding, on a regular basis.

If a house is of brick construction, routine inspection of the mortar is

Furniture Care and Maintenance	
Always observe the following general cautions: • Save care labels that come with new furniture and follow instructions. • When using commercial cleaning products, read and follow the manufacturer's label instructions. • When using chemicals, protect your eyes with safety goggles or glasses.	
Furniture Materials	**Cleaning Procedures**
Wood • Used indoors	Regular cleaning: Vacuum and/or dust with a soft, dry cloth; do not use oil or treated cloth. Special cleaning: • Use a liquid furniture wax or cream polish that gives the desired gloss. • If dirty, clean with a cleaning or polishing furniture wax according to label directions. Moisten a soft cloth with the cleaner and rub briskly, changing the cloth when soiled.
Upholstery • May be on furniture with or without springs • Generally used indoors • May have a stain-repellent finish	Regular cleaning: Vacuum and check for any objects lodged in the folds of fabric or under cushions. Special cleaning: If heavily soiled, clean with a solution of two teaspoons of detergent to one pint of water. Test a small area on the back or underside for fading before proceeding with cleaning. Dip a brush or cloth in the solution and clean only small areas at a time. Rinse the cleaned area before moving to another and avoid wetting the furniture too much.
Aluminum • Generally used outdoors	Regular cleaning: Wash painted frames with mild soap and water. Coat the finish with auto wax to add protection. Do not use abrasive material or strong detergents. Special cleaning: • To brighten mildly discolored surfaces, wash with a solution of soap and water, and a small amount of a mild household acid, such as lemon juice, vinegar, or cream of tarter. (Aluminum used outdoors may darken.) • If the finish is pitted, polish with a soap-filled steel wool pan cleaner and rinse dry. All steel wool must be removed or it will rust and stain the aluminum.
Painted Metal Furniture • Often used outdoors • Also used indoors in children's rooms or casual settings	Regular cleaning: Wash surface with warm water and a heavy-duty liquid detergent. Rinse thoroughly with clean water to remove any detergent residue. Wipe dry or allow to air dry in a sunny or heated room. Apply automobile liquid or paste wax and polish.
Wicker, Rattan, and Bamboo • Can be used throughout the home • Is often used on enclosed porches • Is not recommended for regular outdoor use	Regular cleaning: Vacuum, then wipe with a rag soaked in a mild detergent and warm water solution. Use a small brush to remove stubborn dirt. Special cleaning: If mildew is a problem, wash the furniture with a solution of ¾ cup of chlorine bleach and one quart of water. Since bleach may lighten the surface, apply it to the entire piece of furniture.
Plastic Resin • Used most often outdoors • Also used in children's rooms	Regular cleaning: • Use a nonabrasive all-purpose cleaner or a cleaner-polish and follow package directions. • Wipe the surface with a solution made of hand dishwashing liquid and warm water. Rinse thoroughly and dry with a clean, soft cloth.
Slipcover • Adds a new look to old furniture • Protects new furniture	Regular cleaning: Vacuum while still on furniture, remove, and shake out loose dirt outdoors. Special cleaning: If washable, wash in warm water and laundry detergent. Do not overcrowd the washer. Smooth over furniture while still a little damp. Straighten seams and cording. Do not use furniture until the covers are completely dry.
Cane • Used in the seats of dining room or occasional chairs	Regular cleaning: Vacuum or dust regularly. Occasionally wipe with a damp cloth.
Redwood • Used outdoors because of natural resistance to weathering and rot	Regular cleaning: Maintain a coating with a sealer to keep out moisture and thus retard cracks. Scrub with detergent and water. Rinse and dry thoroughly before sealing. Special cleaning: Colored sealers restore redness to grayed redwood.

22-6
For best results, always use the right cleaning agent and technique for each type of furniture surface.

22-7
Wall covering a room can add depth and dimension. This fresh and crisp wall covering provides a soft tranquil atmosphere. The border shown, in a larger scale pattern, is placed at the baseboard for an unexpected visual interest. Over time, home owners may need to repair or replace wall coverings.

©2009 Sherwin Williams Company

22-8
One storm or windy fall day can fill gutters with enough leaves and twigs to prevent rainwater from reaching the downspouts.

22-9
Pressure washing this siding helps keep it free of dirt and mildew.

important. Over time, the mortar between the bricks deteriorates and requires replacement. The term for this replacement procedure is *repointing* the brick.

Stucco walls also require washing to eliminate the growth of mildew. However, use special care because it is easy to damage the walls by a high-pressure washing.

Regardless of your home's exterior, it is important to have the home inspected annually for termites. Termites are pale-colored insects that feed on wood, particularly wood that is holding moisture. Termites can destroy the structure of a house. Many companies offer service contracts that provide annual inspections and effective treatments, should any termites appear.

Windows and Doors

Windows and doors are expensive investments in a house and require special attention. They need regular cleaning and careful inspections to make sure they stay properly caulked and sealed. Use caulk and sealants to fill cracks and gaps that may appear over time. Caulking prevents air leakage, which is a cause of higher heating and cooling costs. Replace weather stripping that wears out over time. Inspect windows and doors made of wood for rot, too, and replace them as needed. Wash windows regularly to keep them looking good. See *Green Choices: Eco-Friendly Cleaning Products and Tips* for an eco-friendly way to clean windows.

Driveways and Outdoor Living Spaces

Driveways and outdoor living spaces, such as patios, terraces, decks, and porches, represent expensive components of the home's exterior environment. They, too, require routine inspection and maintenance.

Driveway materials consist of concrete, asphalt, brick, or a variety of other products. All are subject to heavy traffic, which eventually results in the need for repair. Periodically check driveway surfaces for cracks and other signs of deterioration. Then make timely repairs by filling cracks with a compatible product. When repairs become extensive, the home owner may need to resurface or replace the driveway.

Periodic pressure washing keeps the areas free of excess dirt and algae growth. You can also apply water-sealant products to the surface to repel moisture. Likewise, take these same steps to properly maintain patios and terraces.

Inspect decks and porches for any signs of damage or rot. They, too, benefit from routine pressure washing and occasional painting or staining. Careful inspection of handrails, steps, and railings is important to make sure they are safe and secure for use.

Outdoor and Lawn Care

After you have spent time, money, and energy in making the outdoor living space attractive and inviting, you need to maintain it. Make a maintenance schedule for your outdoor living environment. Maintaining the outdoor living space requires some special tools.

Tools for Outdoor Tasks

If you have a lawn, a lawn mower is probably the most expensive and necessary outdoor tool. Most lawn mowers use gasoline or electricity. The mower shown in 22-10 not only cuts grass, but also shreds it for mulch. Since landfills are filling up, communities are encouraging people to use clippings as mulch throughout the landscape. Many communities charge extra to accept yard waste. Some areas will not accept it at all.

Many yard tasks involve the use of tools that cut through plants or soil. This is true of all the tools mentioned thus far. The more frequently you sharpen these tools, the easier they are to use. In addition, sharp tools are safer and less likely to damage plants. You may want to sharpen your tools yourself, or you can have them sharpened professionally.

Yard Maintenance

Schedule yard maintenance tasks according to the season of the year. The specific outdoor tasks will vary depending upon where you live. Plant life may need special care to withstand extremely hot or cold weather. During such periods, watering continues but fertilizing stops. Applying mulch around the bases of trees, shrubs, and bushes helps insulate the roots. In addition, mulch helps to retain moisture and maintain a more moderate temperature. Home owners may need to wrap sensitive plants for protection from extreme cold or wind.

Some summer-flowering bulbs, such as gladiolus, need to be dug up after the leaves have dried. Replant these bulbs in the spring. Bulbs that bloom in the spring, such as tulips, require fall planting. Bulbs that bloom in the spring generally do not require digging up and replanting.

For people who live in an area where the ground freezes during winter, it is important to begin watering and fertilizing landscape plants when the ground thaws. At the first sign of sprouting in the spring, uncover roses and other plants that require covering during the winter. Wait until the last frost to plant summer-blooming bulbs and flower seeds. You can divide perennials into smaller clumps at this time, and trim most trees and shrubs. Long-handled lopping shears are the best tool for shaping trees and shrubs and removing dead limbs.

22-10
Many mowers shred the cut grass into fine pieces that sift to the soil and serve as mulch for the lawn.

Other powered outdoor tools commonly used around a home are leaf blowers, lawn trimmers, and weed cutters. Outdoor hand tools include pruning and lopping shears, shovels, rakes, and hoes, 22-11.

Keeping mulch around plants inhibits weed growth and helps retain the moisture in the ground. If plants begin to wilt, it is usually an indication that the plants need watering. The age of the plants, the soil characteristics, and the weather are all factors in determining the watering schedule. Drip irrigation is especially useful for directing water straight to a plant's roots.

A lawn requires regular care during the growing season. When watering a lawn, it is better to water thoroughly and less often than to underwater often. Thorough watering encourages deeper root growth. The soil should remain moist between 8 and 12 inches under the ground. Weeds compete for space, moisture, and nutrients in the lawn. Eliminate these unsightly plants by hand weeding or by chemical methods. Handle any products you apply to the yard carefully. Like household cleaning products, yard care products may be poisonous. Check to see how long after treatment it is safe for children and pets to play on the lawn. Use and store them according to directions.

Mowing the grass is a critical part of lawn care. If you mow the grass in a diagonal direction, you will prevent a striped look. Change directions each time you mow. Mowing the lawn too closely will prevent the development of a healthy root system. A general rule is to cut only the top third of the grass with each mowing, 22-12. Your mowing schedule will depend on the rate your grass grows.

Making Common Home Repairs

Keeping a home safe and comfortable requires regular care and maintenance. Home-owner maintenance includes the inspection and repairs needed to keep the home safe and

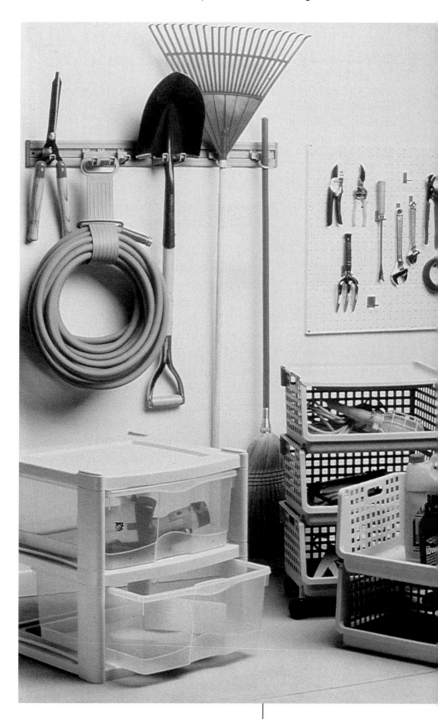

22-11
Keeping the landscape well maintained often involves enough tools to merit their own storage center in the garage.

Rubbermaid

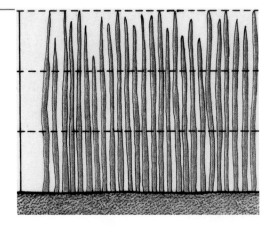

22-12
Green grass is usually brown near its base. For a green lawn after mowing, never cut more than one-third off the top.

prolong its life. Often you can make the repairs yourself with the right tools and some basic knowledge of what to do.

When knowledge and experience is limited, you may want to hire a professional to do the work. This is especially important when safety is involved. Some utility companies have professional service people to handle electrical or gas repairs. Even the best do-it-yourself home owner needs to call on a skilled professional from time to time.

The Basic Tools

Tools can be expensive, so buy quality tools because they last longer. Consider shopping around or buying from discount stores. Build your supply of tools by buying only what you need. To get the right tool for your job, ask for advice from people with experience. Figure 22-13 shows some basic home-maintenance tools.

Hammer

Use a general purpose 16-ounce model hammer with a curved claw primarily for driving and pulling nails. The curved claw provides leverage when pulling nails. The medium-weight head performs finish work as well as rough work.

Screwdriver

Use a screwdriver for driving and removing screws. A straight-blade screwdriver and a Phillips tip screwdriver are typical for most household repairs. Both come in various sizes. The blade of the screwdriver must fit the slot(s) in the head of the screw to work.

Adjustable Wrench

A wrench is useful for tightening and loosening nuts and bolts. This tool is adjustable to fit nuts of different sizes. If a nut is hard to turn, apply a few drops of a lubricant. Let it soak for the recommended time period. If the wrench slips off the nut, turn the wrench over.

Side-Cutting Pliers

This tool is useful for cutting wire and stripping the insulation and plastic coating from electrical wire. Take care to not cut into the wire when removing the insulation.

Long-Nose Pliers

These pliers are appropriate for bending wire and positioning small components into close and difficult work areas. This tool is not a substitute for a wrench. Do not use it when objects must be securely gripped and tightened.

Channel-Lock Pliers

Another name for channel-lock pliers is *slip-joint pliers*. Use this handy tool to tighten nuts and bolts. This basic plumbing tool provides a secure grip on many common materials.

Pipe Wrench

The pipe wrench is a holding tool for assembling fittings on pipe. Teeth are set at an angle in one direction. The teeth are designed to grip a curved surface firmly and produce a ratchet effect. This effect forces a tight grip and prevents the grip from loosening.

Basic Home Maintenance Tools

Slip-Joint Pliers

Side-Cutting Pliers

Long-Nose Pliers

Pliers: Used for gripping and cutting.

Standard Screwdriver

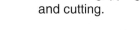

Phillips Screwdriver

Screwdrivers: Standard is used for a screw with a slot on the head. Phillips fits a screw with a T-shaped slot.

Pipe Wrench

Adjustable Wrench

Wrenches: Used for loosening and tightening pipes, pipe fittings, and nuts.

Portable Cordless Drill

Hand or Power Drill: Used to make holes in various surfaces.

Steel Tape Measure: Used to measure long distances.

Folding Rule: Can be used by one person to measure long distances.

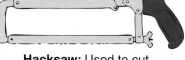

Drill Bits

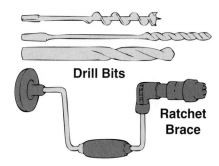

Ratchet Brace

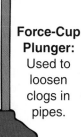

Force-Cup Plunger: Used to loosen clogs in pipes.

Claw Hammer: Used to hammer and remove nails.

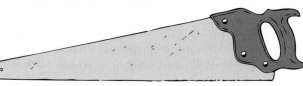

Hacksaw: Used to cut through metal.

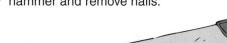

Crosscut Saw: Used to cut wood.

22-13
These basic tools will help you handle many household maintenance tasks.

Plumbing Plunger

A **plumbing plunger** is a device that creates a suction motion to clear a blocked drain. Another name for a plunger is a *force cup*. There are two types. Use a molded plunger for curved surfaces, such as the toilet bowl. The flat plunger is for level surfaces, such as sinks, showers, and tubs.

Tape Measure

Choose a retractable tape measure that is at least 16 feet long and ¾-inch wide. There are many types of measuring tapes on the market. Some have a thumb lock to prevent the tape from retracting when in use.

Hacksaw

The hacksaw is a general-purpose tool for cutting metal. The teeth of the hacksaw cut pipe when pushing the tool forward. A hacksaw has no cutting action when pulling it toward the body.

Crosscut Saw

This saw, used to cut across the grain of wood, can also serve as a general purpose saw for sheet materials such as plywood. Many types work well for a variety of purposes. A ten-point crosscut, for example, has 10 teeth per inch of saw blade.

Power Drill

A power drill is a light-duty tool to drill holes and drive or loosen nuts and screws. Both corded and cordless models are available. With a special attachment, it becomes a lightweight buffer or grinder. The drill chuck determines the size of a drill. The chuck is the clamping device that holds the drill bit. Common sizes are ¼-inch and ⅜-inch. For versatility, you need a ⅜-inch chuck, variable speed, and a reversible motor. You need a variety of drill bits, which are sized by diameter in one of three systems: fractional, decimal, letters, and metrics. Straight-shank drill bits will drill holes in metal and wood.

Closet Auger

When there is blockage in the toilet caused by a washcloth or some item that is retrievable, the closet auger is a useful tool. A **closet auger** is a device used to bore through items with a twisting and turning motion to free blocked plumbing or wastewater lines. In some cases, a comb, pencil, or other object causes a blockage that is not retrievable. By alternately using the closet auger and plumbing plunger, a person usually can force the object through the pipe.

Electricity Tester

Electrical circuits can be tested safely with an electrical tester, called a *neon tester*. Most hardware stores sell this item inexpensively. The tester is designed to light up in the presence of 110 volts and 220 volts. To use, firmly press each lead against the terminals. If the circuit has electricity, the light will go on.

Flashlight

A two-cell unit is sufficient for most household needs. An industrial rated flashlight is brighter and more durable.

Toolbox

One of the most overlooked yet vital components of a tool collection is a toolbox to hold tools. Metal or plastic toolboxes are affordable and come in a variety of sizes and shapes. The main purpose of a toolbox is to keep tools in the same location for use when repairs are necessary. See 22-14.

Plumbing Repairs

Plumbing problems can occur in any home at any time. Some problems appear suddenly, such as when someone accidentally drops an item into a toilet. Other problems develop over time.

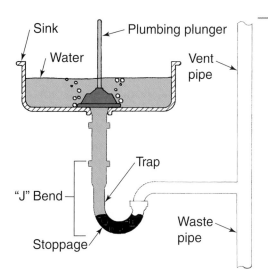

22-14

When shopping for toolboxes, buy one that holds all the tools you use regularly.

Lasko Products

Drains become sluggish or faucets and pipes begin to leak. Certain problems can result in water damage to parts of the home, adding to the repair costs.

If home owners can handle minor plumbing repairs themselves, they can save the expense and inconvenience of hiring a plumber. One of the most common problems is a clogged drain. Pipes tend to clog when foreign matter finds its way into waste lines and accumulates.

Clogged Drains

The most common cause of a clogged drain is foreign matter, such as grease and hair, in the drainage system.

Stoppages in the drainage system rarely occur in straight, horizontal, or vertical runs of piping. They usually occur where two pipes join together with a fitting, creating a change of direction. Stoppages may also occur in the trap, 22-15. Chemical drain cleaners or plumbing plungers and closet augers are most often useful for clearing these stoppages.

If a drain is partially clogged, one cleaning method uses a chemical drain cleaner. Drain cleaners are available in liquid or crystal forms. Liquid drain cleaners are heavier than water and settle into the trap to dissolve grease, food, soap, and hair. Crystal cleaners in granular form begin the chemical cleaning process when they come in contact with the water in the trap.

Use these chemicals with caution because they are poisonous and caustic. Many contain sodium hydroxide—or lye—which is a caustic manmade chemical. A *caustic* substance will burn your skin. Wear protective gloves and keep your face away from the drain opening. Carefully read the directions on each container. Use acid drain cleaners to dissolve soap and hair. Alkalies cut grease. Never mix chemical cleaners because toxic gas may form. Some of these products are combustible.

A more environmentally friendly option is to use a commercial enzymatic biological drain cleaner. These products are not caustic and will not combust. Another simple home remedy for the drain is to put a handful of baking soda with ½-cup vinegar in the drain and follow it with a flush of boiling water.

If a drain is completely clogged, chemical cleaners may not work. The tool to use in this case is a flat plumbing plunger, 22-16. First remove the basket strainer in the sink waste outlet. If it is a double compartment sink, plug the other waste outlet with a rag to prevent loss of pressure in the drain. Place the flat force cup of the plunger directly over the drain opening. Two inches of standing water will provide the necessary seal for the force cup to take hold. Grip the plunger handle firmly with both hands and push down with a slow, even pressure. Pull up quickly and repeat the process several times. This will unstop most sink drains.

If the stoppage still exists, try an auger with a flexible spring cable. Place a container under the trap. Loosen two nuts on the trap and remove the J-bend. Use a small auger with a ¼-inch spring

cable. Feed the cable slowly into the drainpipe. Rotate the cable as you feed it. Turn the handle until the obstruction is broken up, 22-17. When finished, remove the cable, replace the J-bend, and tighten the nuts. Flush the drain with hot water and check for leaks.

When a toilet has a clog, try to determine the cause of the stoppage. If the substance will not cause additional blockage when forced into the drainage system, use the molded plunger. If material such as a diaper caused the stoppage, use the closet auger. Since an auger has a flexible spring cable, it can make sharp turns in a drain.

For some items, you may need to use the plunger and auger in alternating sequence. Compare the two methods in 22-18. Should these methods fail, the only solution is to shut off the water to the toilet, disconnect the toilet from the floor, and retrieve the object from the toilet's underside. Whenever the seal between the toilet and floor is broken, you must replace the rubber or wax ring that serves as the seal. As you can see, this repair can become extensive. You

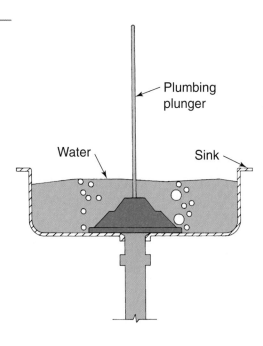

22-16
A plunger is pumped up and down to form a suction and surge in the drain.

Plumbing plunger

Water

Sink

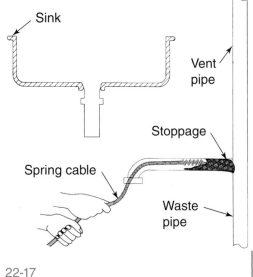

Sink

Vent pipe

Stoppage

Spring cable

Waste pipe

22-17
The auger, which has a flexible spring cable, may need to be placed near the blockage to remove it.

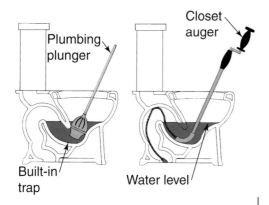

22-18
Both the plumbing plunger and the auger may be needed for toilet blockage.

22-19
Studs that are used to form walls are often placed 16 inches apart. Use a stud finder to locate wall studs before inserting fasteners to support heavy objects that are hung on a wall.

may wish to hire a professional plumber to do this job.

Tree roots and debris growing into the lines can also block the sewer lines. When this occurs, professional help is required to clean out or open the lines.

Installing Nails and Screws

Nails and screws are fastening devices. Each has special uses in household repairs. Nails can be easy to drive, but may be difficult to remove. Screws can be easy to remove.

Nails come in two basic shapes. A **finish nail** has a very small head. You can drive it below the surface by using another nail or a nail set tool. Fill holes with wood filler or putty. Use finish nails when appearance is important. Installing paneling or shelves are two examples. A **box nail** has a large, flat head. Use it for rough work when appearance is less important.

When driving a nail, hammer the head until it is seated on the surface, but leaves no mark on the surface.

If you are placing nails or screws in walls, location is important. To secure heavy objects, place fasteners in line with a stud behind the wall surface. This allows you to drive the fastener into the

wood of the stud for additional support. You can find studs by tapping along the walls lightly. You will hear a lower tone when you tap the walls bordering hollow spaces between studs. When you tap a stud, you will hear a noticeably higher tone. You can also purchase inexpensive stud-sensing devices at hardware stores and home improvement centers. See 22-19. After you find one stud, you can usually find adjacent studs by measuring 16-inch intervals to the left or right.

To install a wood screw, drill a pilot hole. Use the proper type of screwdriver, either a Phillips or a straight screwdriver. Try to match the size of the screwdriver to the head of the screw. Using an undersized screwdriver makes the task more difficult and can damage the screw head.

Electrical Repairs

When electricity enters a house, the wires connect into the service entrance panel. Service entrance panels contain either circuit breakers or fuses. Circuit breaker entrance panels are more common than panels with fuses, 22-20. Overloading a circuit in a house with appliances or other electrical items, the fuses or circuit breakers cut off the power. This prevents damage to wiring and possible electrical fires.

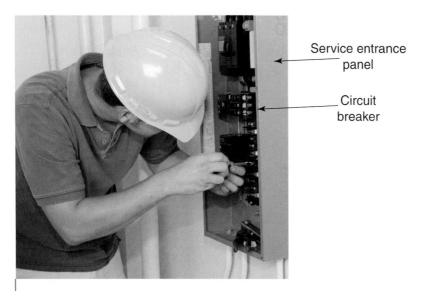

22-20
The service entrance panel monitors the electrical system for the house.

The most common cause of electrical problems is likely a short circuit. A **short circuit** is an undesirable current path that allows the electrical current to bypass the load of the circuit. Sometimes the short circuit occurs between two wires due to faulty insulation. It can also occur between a wire and a grounded object, such as a metal frame on an appliance. Sometimes a black carbon deposit indicates where the short occurred. A short circuit requires repair before resetting a breaker or replacing a fuse. If you are unfamiliar with making such repairs, call an electrician.

Circuit Breakers

Usually a circuit breaker trips when the circuit is overloaded. This happens when too many electrical appliances are in use on a circuit at one time. The switch on each breaker switches to the *off* position when a problem occurs. This interrupts the power.

Disconnect some appliances before restoring electricity to the circuit. Large appliances—such as refrigerators, ranges, or dishwashers—generally require their own circuit. To restore the electricity, move the handle of the circuit to the *reset* position, then to the *on* position. The reset position is usually on the opposite side of the on position.

Fuses

You must replace a blown fuse to restore power. There are two types of fuses—plugs and cartridges. Plug fuses screw into the entrance panel like light-bulbs. A plug fuse has a clear window with a metal strip—or fuse link—across it. When current level exceeds the rating of the fuse, the link melts and a gap forms. The result is a broken circuit with no flow of current.

To replace a plug fuse, remove the main fuse or turn off the connection switch. This will disconnect all power. Use a flashlight, if necessary, to locate the blown fuse. The window of a blown fuse is black or the fuse link is broken.

Spring clips hold cartridge fuses in place. These fuses often show no sign of being blown. If the power is off, follow the same steps as in replacing a plug fuse. Always replace the blown fuse with a new one of the exact size. To avoid electrical shock, stand on a dry surface and be sure your hands are dry.

Wall Switches

All types of electrical switches can wear out as they get older. Do not attempt to replace a wall switch unless you know how to work with electrical wiring. Fatal electric shocks can occur. The illustration in 22-21 shows the black wires to disconnect to remove a faulty switch.

Power Cord Plugs

For the safety of members of the household, replace damaged or worn electric plugs before using them. When replacing a plug on a flat two-wire cord, use a snap-down plug.

To attach the snap-down plug, lift the top clamp. Slit the cord apart to ¼-inch from the end of the cord. Push the cord into the plug and tightly close the clamp. Test the cord to see that it works. Feel the plug to make sure it is not over-heating.

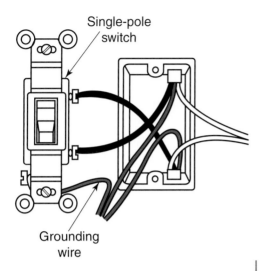

Single-pole switch

Grounding wire

22-21
Use extra precaution when repairing electrical switches.

Making Replacements

Home maintenance includes more than making repairs. It includes replacing the parts of your house that wear out or become obsolete. It also includes replacing appliances that are no longer worth repairing.

When purchasing a quality item, it should perform well for many years before replacement becomes necessary. However, nothing lasts forever. A wise consumer, therefore, budgets for the repair and replacement costs that are certain to come. When repair parts become unavailable or costs become too high, it probably is time to make a replacement.

Meeting Storage Needs

Whether a home is large or small, the inhabitants need to make the most of their space. Organized storage helps to keep clutter out of the living spaces. Finding items is easier, too, when storage space is organized.

Organize for Storage

There are many ways to reorganize closets using a variety of storage devices. Various types of storage components are available to help tailor the space to the storage needs. Many of these organizers do not require nailing to a structure, so a person can easily move them. Another option for organizing is to hire a professional organizer or purchase a custom closet organization system. See 22-22.

Durable cardboard or plastic storage boxes come in many sizes, colors, and styles. Many have drawers or doors. Some fit under beds; others will fit in small spaces throughout the house. Consider using these items to organize closet storage. Boxes can be painted, papered, or covered with fabric to match room decor.

Often utility rooms and garages have poorly organized storage space. Shelves and storage containers can make

22-22
Closet organizers can be customized to fit any closet.

California Closets Organizational Solutions for the Whole Home. ©California Closet Co. All Rights Reserved. (www.californiaclosets.com)

22-23
The coat storage in this hallway utilizes hooks, seating space, and storage drawers and cubbies.

Many home owners and designers choose to convert space under a stairway or at the end of a hall or room to storage. You can buy ready-to-use shelves or other storage items for this space. Purchase them in components and adapt them to the space that exists. You can also build your own storage units.

Hooks and poles are useful types of storage that are popular for hanging coats, 22-23. You can also use them in bathrooms to hang towels and bathroom supplies. Also, consider attractively placing supplies in baskets or decorated buckets with handles.

Space Savers

The design of many furniture pieces helps save space. A sofa bed and a daybed are two such pieces. They double as sofas and beds. This saves room if you do not have space for both.

You can replace your regular bed frame with a platform that has drawers. This provides storage and sleeping space in the same area. You can also use stacking beds in a children's room to save space.

Stacking chairs and folding chairs are other types of space-saving furniture. Multipurpose storage and organizer units can double as small tables in the bedroom, living room, or home office. Padded chests or window seats used for seating, with storage underneath, also save space, 22-24.

storage in these areas more efficient. Attach some types of shelves to the ceiling for off-the-floor storage.

Consider placing shelves in window nooks and over radiators. Shelf arrangements on bare walls provide open storage for displays. Attach racks to doors or walls to hold magazines, books, or supplies.

22-24
These built-in window seats are attractive and offer hidden storage in the family room.

A drop-leaf table takes up little space when the leaves are down. Expanding it is easy when extra tabletop space is necessary. Consider building a hinged table surface or desk that attaches to the wall. It can have legs that fold out or a hinged support that swings out from the wall. The table lies flat against the wall when it is not in use. To save space, mount other household furniture and equipment to the wall.

In the kitchen, mounting small appliances on the wall or under kitchen cabinets can free valuable shelf space for other uses. Drawer trays, adjustable racks, hooks, and other shelving components keep food supplies, cooking equipment, and dinnerware orderly, 22-25.

Well-organized storage helps make living easier. It keeps clutter out of living spaces. Having enough storage helps you make the most of your housing.

Redecorating

Eventually you will probably want to change or update your decorating scheme, or **redecorate**. Parts of a home may look out of fashion. Some furnishings may show wear. Perhaps you may simply want a new look. As life situations change, so do needs and values. In turn, you may redecorate part or your entire home accordingly.

Redecorating is different from decorating because there is already a base from which to start. When home owners decorate wisely the first time, there should be several items to keep when redecorating. Old and new items do not need to match. They only need to complement each other.

Use the same process in planning the redecoration that you used before decorating. Planning is important when blending the old with the new. Determine what you want to keep and what you want to replace. Evaluate why you want to eliminate certain items. Can you change any of them to fit your plan?

22-25
Storage drawers for plates and cups are convenient for all household members, even those with special needs.

Sometimes redoing what you already have can meet your needs. For instance, a sofa may be sturdy, but you may not like its color or pattern. Reupholstering may satisfy your decorating needs at a lower cost than replacing the sofa. This is especially true if you can do the work yourself.

You may redecorate in a single stage, or you redecorate in a series of steps. Limited time and money may convince you to take the step approach. After deciding what you want to change, divide your project into phases. For instance, the process in redecorating the living room may include painting the walls, replacing the carpet, and changing the window treatment. If you decide to repaint, do that step first since the room's new color may affect other redecorating decisions, 22-26. As sales occur, replace some furniture and accessories. Your priorities and budget help determine the sequence.

Professional services are available to help you decorate. As you recall, an interior designer is a person who specializes in applying the principles and elements of design to interiors. An interior designer can plan a decorating scheme, make purchases, and supervise the work

22-26
Here, the room's color stayed the same, but the home owner chose to change window treatments and bedding as her first redecorating step.

Calico Corners—Calico Home Stores

to make sure it is correct. A designer will save you time and help you avoid costly mistakes. A designer also has contacts that you cannot make on your own, such as sources for the furnishings you want.

Only you can decide how much help you want from a designer and how much you want to do on your own. Most designers expect to do the bulk of the planning and let the client do some of the purchasing. Determine your needs, and then identify the work you want the designer to do.

Some furniture stores employ designers or decorators that you can hire. There are generally no charges for

this service, but store personnel expect that you will purchase some furniture.

Knowing what you want will help you communicate your desires to a professional. You will be the one living with the decisions, so make your wishes known.

Remodeling

Remodeling is usually more expensive than redecorating. This is because it involves changes to the structure, such as adding a wall or a room. There are times when remodeling is more of a bargain than moving or trying to live with the house's flaws.

Remodeling can extend livable space to existing areas, such as finishing a basement, 22-27. Some people choose to add usable space to a structure, such as a family room addition or an attached garage. Others choose to enclose a porch or build a patio. Some remodeling jobs—such as creating a more spacious and convenient kitchen—increase the market value of a home, 22-28. Other projects may not increase the value of a home, but provide great comfort and satisfaction to the household.

There are many ways to measure the cost of remodeling. Home owners who are considering remodeling need to ask themselves the following questions:

- Is the cost of remodeling a better value than moving or keeping the living space the same?

- Will remodeling increase the quality of life in the home?

- Will the remodeling process cause too many inconveniences for household members? Adding a room is not likely to be as inconvenient as remodeling the kitchen or bathroom.

- Will there be a need to move shortly after remodeling?

22-27

This remodeled basement adds more living space in the home.

Photography Courtesy of the National Association of the Remodeling Industry, Basements and Beyond, Regional Winner, Northwest, Residential Interior over $100,000.

22-28

A more spacious and modern kitchen significantly increases a home's value.

Photography Courtesy of the National Association of the Remodeling Industry, DiApice Remodeling Inc., Regional Winner, Northeast, Residential Kitchen under $30,000.

Home owners also need to decide whether to use professionals or do the work themselves. People who do their own remodeling can save about half the cost of hiring the work out. However, the work could take twice as long or longer for people who choose to do their own work. If a project is simple and the home owner knows what to do, handling the remodeling may be worthwhile. When tasks involve rewiring and adding plumbing, hiring a professional is generally best. In fact, local building codes may require it. Home owners may do some tasks themselves and hire professionals for others, or they may hire a remodeling service to do the whole job.

GREEN CHOICES

Remodel with REGREEN

If you are thinking about remodeling your home then you should consider REGREEN. This is the nation's first program for remodeling homes with "green" changes.

The American Society of Interior Designers (ASID) and the United States Green Building Council (USGBC) developed REGREEN. It is a series of guidelines that include the best ways to remodel a home using "green" ideas. The guidelines are for either room-by-room or the entire house.

REGREEN is also under development as a curriculum for school programs. Also, the program includes a website to assist consumers and professionals in green house remodeling.

Information courtesy of the American Society of Interior Designers (ASID) (www.asid.org/regreen).

Getting the Best Value for the Money

It pays to do some homework before starting a remodeling project. This helps avoid making changes that cost more than they are worth. Start by researching information about remodeling products, trends in design, and financing. Get estimates on how much a remodeling project will cost. If you (or a client) need a home improvement loan, shop to find the best rate. Will it be possible to regain the costs of remodeling when selling your house? See 22-29.

Some contractors specialize in remodeling projects. When home owners do not want to do the work themselves, they should use a licensed contractor who will guarantee the work. Before choosing a contractor, learn the answers to the following questions:

- Is the contractor licensed? by whom?

- How long has the contractor been in business?

- Do former clients express satisfaction with the contractor's work? Ask the contractor for references or find names of clients at the local building department.

- Will the contractor show you a similar completed project?

- Does the contractor have insurance coverage for all workers?

- Will the contractor provide lien waivers to show payment for supplies and subcontractors used for the project? A *lien waiver* protects the home owner from liability if the contractor does not pay for items used to remodel a house.

Do not pay for the entire remodeling project until all the work is finished to your satisfaction. The best arrangement is to pay 25 percent of the total fee before work starts and the rest upon completion. Contractors are more likely to complete a project the way a home owner wants it if they are waiting for payment.

Home Improvements and Increased Home Value	
Projects that make a home more desirable often increase its value. A higher value means a better sales price when the owner sells the home. Sometimes the sales price is high enough to offset part or all of the improvement costs. The following figures show the average percentages of home improvement costs that are offset by a higher sales price.	
Project	**Percentage of Costs Offset by Higher Sales Price**
Fireplace addition	100–125%
Kitchen remodeling	75–125%
Solar greenhouse addition	90–100%
Garage or patio addition	75–100%
Bathroom remodeling	75–100%
Bathroom addition	50–100%
Room addition	40–75%
Addition of energy saving measures (such as storm windows or more insulation)	40–50%
Maintenance-free siding	40–45%

22-29
Remodeling improves the usefulness and appearance of a home and often increases its resale value.

When making a remodeling plan, keep the neighborhood in mind. Keep improvements in line with nearby houses. Try not to raise the value of a home more than 20 percent over the value of neighboring homes. Raising the home's value by more than 20 percent may mean the home owner will not get the full value selling the house.

Consider adding features that conserve energy when remodeling. Such features are bargains because they lower monthly energy bills. They also increase the resale value of a home. Removing a drafty window and replacing it with a wall or with an insulating window add value. Insulating windows provide a good view and insulate better than standard windows. Add insulation to walls or replace old doors with insulating doors. Also consider replacing older appliances with energy-efficient models.

Resources for Home Care

There are resources for home owners to use if they need help in maintaining their homes. Resource people can offer advice, or they can do the work. Consider seeking both advice and help with the work.

Help with Home Maintenance

If you don't have the help you need in your family, or the time, hire people to do cleaning and maintenance for you. Service companies have employees who work by the hour, the day, or the job. You contract with the service, not with individuals. In contrast, you can hire an individual who provides a specific service. Individuals set their own rates. See 22-30.

22-30
Before hiring self-employed individuals, check their references and talk with former clients. Be sure the individual does good work and upholds his or her contracts.

The cost of the services varies with the job as well as the size and location of the house. When hiring a cleaning service, it is important to learn what specific tasks are done at what costs. You may need to hire someone else or pay more for certain cleaning tasks. For instance, window washing is not usually part of a weekly cleaning service.

It is also possible to hire someone to help with outside maintenance. You may have someone mow the lawn and trim the trees and shrubs. Employing the services of a landscaping or yard maintenance company on a regular basis is also possible. They will provide complete maintenance or just do the specific projects the home owner requests.

Other Resources

Many home owners learn more about how to do their own home maintenance. Home improvement centers offer free workshops and helpful literature. Many community colleges and technical schools offer free or inexpensive courses on home maintenance. Decorating, remodeling, and home maintenance programs are common on TV stations. Explore Internet sites by using *home improvement, landscaping,* and *gardening* as search words. You can buy DVDs and books, or borrow them from the local library. Newspapers and magazines often feature articles on home maintenance techniques and new products. Clip the articles and start your own resource file.

CAREER FOCUS

Professional Organizer

Can you imagine yourself in a career as a professional organizer? If you share some of the following interests and skills, you may consider exploring a career as a professional organizer.

Interests/Skills: Does organizing items and finding the right place for them excite you? When you walk into a friend's room that is cluttered, do you immediately want to help organize and straighten the space? Does clutter often distract you from the task at hand? Skills include problem solving and organizing material. A professional organizer can help individuals and businesses take control over their surroundings. The ability to communicate with a client is essential in this career. Other important skills include: having a good understanding of space and volume; ability to take measurements and plan space; strong ability in math and computer programs; and effective drawing and sketching skills.

Career Snapshot: Professional organizers help people in many ways. Organized people save time and money. They also have reduced stress and frustration levels. Professional organizers can help deal with everything from paper to professional responsibilities. They can give parameters on what to keep, what to toss, and where to take action. Professional organizers can consult on interior spaces. For example, kitchen and bathroom cabinets, closets, and garages need order. Professional organizers are especially helpful when homes or offices have been taken over by clutter and junk. They teach their clients valuable techniques and conduct workshops and seminars. Their goal is to teach people how to organize their belongings.

Education/Training: No specific requirements are mandatory except for knowledge in the area of expertise. A high school diploma is recommended. Courses in computer programs, psychology, business management, accounting, and interior design are helpful.

California Closets Organizational Solutions for the Whole Home. ©California Closet Co. All rights reserved. (www.californiaclosets.com)

Examination/License: Voluntary certification is available through the Board of Certified Professional Organizers (BCPO) (www.certifiedprofessionalorganizers.org)

Professional Organizations: The National Association of Professional Organizers (NAPO) (www.napo.net)

Job Outlook: Business opportunities for professional organizers are rapidly growing. Due to demands placed on individuals, more people are turning to professionals to help get their personal and professional lives in order. The job outlook for the future is good.

Source: The National Association of Professional Organizers (NAPO) (www.napo.net)

Summary

The first step in maintaining a home is to keep it clean. The proper tools and cleaning products are important. A cleaning schedule for the household helps accomplish tasks.

Yard maintenance also requires certain tools and products. Make a schedule for outdoor maintenance by the seasons. Maintenance needs are greatest in the fall and spring. Do other tasks on a regular basis during the growing season.

The right tools can speed up home repairs. Basic tools and knowledge of their use can help home owners make simple repairs. A professional should do repairs that pose safety risks or require expert knowledge. Repairs and replacements are part of home maintenance.

Creating and organizing storage space can simplify home maintenance. It can also increase living space. Many storage ideas are very affordable and easy to incorporate.

Redecorating and remodeling have their place in home maintenance. Both require careful planning. Many helpful resources exist for redecorating and remodeling as well as home maintenance. Home owners can do the work themselves or hire a specialist.

Review the Facts

1. What cleaning tools are basic for cleaning a home?
2. What three basic cleaning products should every home have?
3. What are two advantages of a cleaning schedule?
4. Summarize maintenance and cleaning tasks for two exterior areas of a home.
5. Identify outdoor power and hand tools necessary for lawn-care tasks.
6. What is the danger in mowing a lawn too low?
7. Why are watering, mulching, and fertilizing necessary elements of yard maintenance?
8. Name five basic tools needed for home repairs and summarize their uses.
9. List five common home repairs.
10. Contrast cleaning a clogged drain with chemical cleaners and mechanical methods. Which is most likely to work?
11. When would you use a finish nail and a box nail?
12. What are two causes of an electrical short circuit?
13. Contrast plug fuses with cartridge fuses.
14. Why is remodeling usually more expensive and complex than redecorating?
15. What questions should home owners ask themselves when considering a remodeling project?
16. Name three resources that help home owners maintain their homes.

Think Critically

17. **Analyze features.** The idea of "easy maintenance" usually appeals to home buyers looking for a home. Analyze types of features to seek in a home for it to deserve the title of "easy to maintain." Make a list of both interior and exterior features. What features would be at the top of your list? Why?

18. **Evaluate resources.** Suppose you have been hired to help a young professional set up his or her first apartment. Using $125 to get started, evaluate what cleaning tools, cleaning products, and basic repair tools would you recommend this young professional buy. Check prices at a local hardware store or home improvement center to identify current costs, or check out their Web sites to save a trip. What items would be on the list and why? What is the cost of each?

19. **Make recommendations.** Evaluate properties in your neighborhood for exterior maintenance problems. Make a general list of problems you see, but do not record the properties by name or address. As you identify each problem, recommend solutions or repairs that you think could remedy the problems.

20. **Draw conclusions.** Cleaning and maintaining a home require human energy. Some people, particularly some older adults, are not physically able to complete heavy housework. They may hire someone to clean their homes or do their yard maintenance. Draw conclusions about whether you think this represents a growing service because of the increasing number of older adults. Give evidence to support your thinking.

Community Links

21. **Tool demonstration.** Visit a hardware store. Have the manager or a knowledgeable salesperson describe some of the tools and supplies. Ask the manager to demonstrate how to use some basic tools.

22. **Cleaning schedule.** Use the checklist in 22-5 to develop a cleaning schedule for your home. List the cleaning tools and supplies needed to perform the tasks on the schedule. Visit the Web site of a local hardware and home improvement store and determine the price of these items. What would be the range of cost for all these items new? Could most persons setting up a household be able to afford these items? As an alternative project, develop a schedule for outdoor maintenance of your home.

23. **Kitchen remodel.** Visit a home improvement center that offers design assistance in remodeling kitchens and baths. Determine the square footage of the kitchen in your home (width by length) and ask a salesperson how much it usually costs to remodel a kitchen of that size. Does it cost a lot of money to remodel a kitchen? What steps are required to remodel a kitchen?

Academic Connections

24. **Reading.** Read a book on home maintenance or lawn and garden care from a reputable source. Talk with the reference librarian at your local library for recommendations. Write a report summarizing the five best ideas you learned from the book.

25. **Science.** Mix together one or more of the alternative cleaning solutions described in *Green Choices: Eco-Friendly Cleaning Products and Tips.* Use each solution to clean the appropriate surface. How well did each product work? Use Internet or print resources to investigate how these eco-friendly solutions function and how they benefit the environment. Give an oral report to the class about your findings.

Technology Applications

26. **Bedroom redecoration.** Using a CADD software program, create a redecorating plan for a bedroom, including a rendering of the final design. Develop a preliminary budget for the project. Create a presentation board showing samples of colors and designs you plan to use. Put the items together in a binder and share the decorating plan with the class.

27. **Lawn-mower technology.** Use Internet or print resources to investigate several types of eco-friendly lawn mowers, such as solar-powered lawn mowers, battery-powered lawn mowers, or programmable robotic lawn mowers. What technology makes these mowers unique? What are the pros and cons of the mower(s)? If you were a landscape designer, would you recommend one of these mowers to a client? Why or why not? Write a summary of your findings.

Design Practice

28. **Family room remodel.** Your new clients want to remodel their basement for family room space. The family requires space for watching movies and playing video games along with space for playing games and storing toys for their children ages 3 and 5. Easy maintenance is a requirement. The current basement has two small semi-finished rooms that each measure 12 ft. by 14 ft. The family prefers to have one large open room that uses furnishings to designate the space usage. Create a workable floor plan for an open-concept family room using CADD software. Research various attractive, but durable, materials for walls, floors, furnishings, and storage suitable for the client's needs. Create a presentation board to show all materials and furnishings you recommend for this project. Write a summary outlining your recommendations for the family room and indicate how this plan meets the client's requirements.

29. **Portfolio.** Presume you have been hired to develop a plan for organizing bedroom closet space for a three bedroom home. One walk-in closet measures 8 ft. wide by 10 ft. long by 8 ft. high. The other two closets measure 8 ft. wide by 3 ft. deep by 8 ft. high. Use Internet or print resources to help develop the plan and locate photos of organizer examples. Use CADD software to provide scale floor plan drawings (1 in. equals 1 ft.) and elevations of the closets. Make printouts or save your design plans to a CD. Be sure to note placement and dimensions of new storage system components. Write a summary explaining your choices for each closet to include in your portfolio.

Building Teamwork Skills by Helping Others

Keeping up with cleaning and home maintenance requires a lot of human energy. Some people, including older adults and those with physical challenges, find it difficult to keep up with many home maintenance tasks—especially outdoors. Although some may hire the help they need, many others have limited resources. They may opt to forgo outdoor cleanup and maintenance or rely on the kindness of others for help.

As an FCCLA chapter, use the FCCLA *Planning Process* to organize one or more fall or spring cleanup days for neighborhood citizens in need around your school. Consider preparing a flyer about the service (including a list of items chapter members can do) and distributing it to neighborhood homes. Include a contact phone number to schedule your service days. Be sure to take photos of your work and the people you serve.

Use your fall or spring cleanup project for one of the *Chapter Service* STAR Events—*Chapter Service Project Display* or *Chapter Service Project Manual*. Follow the guidelines for these events in the FCCLA *STAR Events Manual* on the Web (www.fcclainc.org). See your adviser for information as needed.

CHAPTER 23

Trends in Housing Design and Technology

Terms to Learn

photovoltaic (PV)
geothermal energy
graywater
Zero Energy Home (ZEH)
Earthship
automated houses
renewable energy sources
nuclear energy
hydroelectric power
cogeneration
fuel cell
microturbine
ecology
solid waste
hazardous waste
visual pollution
integrated waste management
compost

Chapter Objectives

After studying this chapter, you will be able to

- analyze design and housing trends, including green and sustainable buildings and technology in housing.

- summarize ways to provide and conserve energy and maintain a clean environment.

- assess feasible and innovative housing solutions for the future.

Reading with Purpose

Find an article on the *Google News* Web site that relates to the topics covered in this chapter. Print the article and read it before you read the chapter. Then, as you read the chapter, highlight sections of the news article that relate to the text.

How can people have better housing for a sustainable future? No one knows just what the future holds. However, by learning from the past and watching for new developments, people can improve housing now and in the future.

Trends in Housing

As the needs of people change, their housing must change to meet their particular needs. Many factors influence housing designs and construction. Two factors have great influence on housing today and in the future—concerns about the environment and new technologies for use in housing. Specific concerns include

- **Energy costs.** The high cost of energy impacts every aspect of daily living. In homes, the costs for providing heating, cooling, and lighting are of major concern.

- **Water.** Along with energy costs, people also have concern about the quality and availability of pure, clean water. How can people conserve this resource now and for future generations?

- **Waste.** The amount of waste a typical home produces is great. Looking for ways to handle these wastes, along with wastes that result from building homes, is a focus for all those who work with housing.

As a result of these issues, a major trend in the housing field is the focus on incorporating green and sustainable design into housing. The goal of such design is to create self-sufficient housing that uses minimum natural resources. The following passage outlines several ways that green and sustainable design will continue to impact housing.

Green and Sustainable Buildings

As you recall from discussions throughout this text, "green" buildings refer to those structures that use materials and techniques to conserve resources in all aspects of construction and maintenance. The planning of such buildings uses green design or sustainable design. These buildings use one or more green products or measures in the structure. Green products conserve scarce resources, and generally utilize sustainable and recyclable materials. For example, the use of steel in construction more often replaces the use of wood—wood is a limited commodity and thereby is costly. Using bamboo for flooring is sustainable.

Although these homes conserve resources, today's green-built homes are virtually indistinguishable from other homes. The following include some uses of green products and design in today's typical homes:

- **Doors and windows.** Insulation in exterior doors is an energy saver in cold and warm climates. Insulated, low-E glass in windows helps keep homes more comfortable and energy efficient.

- **Siding and decking.** Vinyl and fiber-cement siding reduce the need for cedar, redwood, and other products on exterior walls. Plastic lumber and composite products (made from recycled wood fibers and plastics) are common decking materials.

- **Roofing.** Such roofing materials as metal and fiber-cement are more durable. They reduce the need for frequent roof replacement. Some older-style roofing materials require frequent replacement and are a major source of landfill waste.

- **Heating, cooling, and hot water.** High-efficiency heating, cooling, and water-heating units greatly reduce energy use in most homes. Using passive-solar design takes advantage of the sun's energy to help heat homes through glass features with a southern exposure to the sun. In addition, proper insulation of walls and attics reduces energy loss in homes.

- **Fixtures and appliances.** New energy-efficient dishwashers, refrigerators, and clothes washers require less energy. Look for the ENERGY STAR label. New toilets and faucet aerators use less water to operate, 23-1.

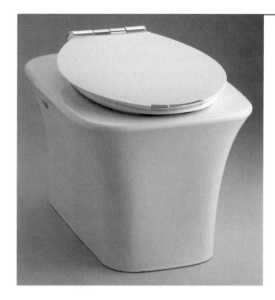

23-1
New plumbing fixtures, such as this toilet, are designed to use less water.

Photo Courtesy of Kohler

GREEN CHOICES

Eco-Friendly Labeling and Certification Programs

Many guides assist consumers or professionals in making decisions in finding green housing solutions. When selecting a new house or products for the home, choose an eco-friendly program to guide your choices.

Each of these programs certify/label green components in different ways and some are highlighted in *Green Choices* features throughout this textbook. Programs that certify or label green housing and products include

- **ENERGYSTAR** (www.energystar.gov)—Identifies products and structures that use at least 30 percent less energy than the standard products and structures.

- **Energy Guide** (www.eere.energy.gov/consumer/tips/energyguide.html)—Relates the approximate energy consumption and utility cost of operating the products.

- **LEED Rating System** (www.usgbc.org)—Certifies structures that have overall sustainable features.

- **FSC—Forestry Stewardship Council** (www.fscus.org)—Identifies companies that follow sustainable practices in wood manufacturing.

- **WaterSense Label** (www.epa.gov/watersense)—Tags products that use less water.

- **Sustainable Furniture Council** (www.sustainablefurniturecouncil.org)—Tags furniture that was manufactured using sustainable practices.

- **REGREEN** (www.asid.org/regreen)—Provides guidelines for incorporating green in remodeling projects.

- **Carpet and Rug Institute (CRI)** (www.carpet-rug.org)—Verifies that a product has low-emission of VOCs (Indoor Air Quality testing).

The steps you take to conserve energy lower your energy costs, reduce pollution resulting from energy production, and save valuable resources. What are some simple steps you can take to start conserving energy now? Continue reading to learn more about special programs that promote green and sustainable buildings.

Examples of Green and Sustainable Buildings

As you have learned in the *Green Choices* features throughout this text, numerous programs and organizations promote green and sustainable housing design. Many provide certification indicating that houses have features that support the environment and sustainability. One such outstanding organization is the *Southface Energy Institute*.

Southface Eco Office and Resource Center

The Southface Energy Institute is a resource for home owners, residential and commercial builders, and people who want to learn more about environmentally friendly design. With a mission to promote sustainable homes, workplaces, and communities, the campus of the Southface Energy Institute headquarters shows many techniques and features of sustainable design. The headquarters—located in Atlanta, Georgia—is a showcase for innovative building designs and techniques. It also has the LEED-Platinum designation, 23-2.

The headquarters consists of a three-story commercial building, the Eco Office, an attached residential building, and the Resource Center. These buildings display many innovative features for homes and commercial structures. The buildings address energy efficiency, thermal comfort, indoor air quality, and accessibility. Also highlighted are ways to reduce waste and use recycled materials. These sustainable designs and technologies include the use of recycled building materials and utility-operating activities (such as energy, water, and waste management).

The headquarters has many energy related features. These include passive solar heating and cooling, and solar water heating and solar-electric systems. A special roof component of the Resource Center includes solar-electric shingles. These shingles are **photovoltaic (PV)**, which means they convert sunlight into electricity. Photovoltaic shingles resemble conventional fiberglass roofing shingles. The electricity they produce supplies part of the facility electrical needs. As in other solar applications, the PV shingles are on a south-facing roof to receive full sun.

The Southface campus utilizes a well-planned passive solar design and daylighting. This office space takes advantage of sunlight as a prominent light source year-round. Exterior shades block direct sunlight while interior light shelves bounce sunlight deep into the office. The use of daylighting strategies offsets the larger need for artificial lighting and is balanced with light-monitoring sensors.

Other energy-saving measures at the Center include energy-efficient ENERGY STAR appliances and a geothermal heat pump. In a practical sense, **geothermal energy** for heating and cooling involves a heat exchange, via a buried liquid-filled pipe designed in a loop. This creates an ultra-efficient heating and cooling system that utilizes the stable temperature of the surrounding earth. This approach is more efficient than conventional air-exchange systems.

The Center's landscape emphasizes the principles of drought-tolerant landscaping. In addition, the Center uses a rainwater catchment irrigation system for watering and flushing toilets. The

A

B

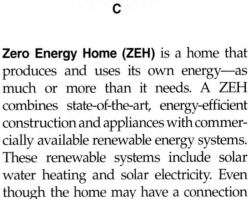

C

23-2
The Southface Eco Office and Resource Center buildings have many innovative features for offices and homes (A). Photovoltaic shingles are installed on the roof of the Southface Resource Center to make electricity from the sun's rays (B). The "light shelf" in the window area helps deliver the sunlight deep into this office space (C).

(A and B) Southface Energy Institute, Atlanta, Georgia; (C) Photo by Jonathan Hillyer

landscaping also uses such recycled materials as wood-chip mulch and concrete rubble for stepping-stones. **Graywater** is wastewater from washing machines, showers, and sinks. It is not contaminated with human waste and can be used for landscape watering.

Zero Energy Homes (ZEH)

An example of a sustainable energy home is a Zero Energy Home (ZEH). The **Zero Energy Home (ZEH)** is a home that produces and uses its own energy—as much or more than it needs. A ZEH combines state-of-the-art, energy-efficient construction and appliances with commercially available renewable energy systems. These renewable systems include solar water heating and solar electricity. Even though the home may have a connection to an electrical grid, it has zero-energy consumption from the utility company.

The U. S. Department of Energy partners with building professionals and organizations to further develop the ZEH concept. Design features of a Zero Energy Home include

- climate-specific design

- passive solar heating and cooling

- energy-efficient construction

- energy-efficient appliances and lighting

- solar water heating system

- small solar electric system

Specific advantages of Zero Energy Homes are many. They include

- improved comfort—because the energy-efficient structure reduces temperature variations in the home

- reliability—because the home will continue to operate even during blackouts

- energy security—because the home produces its own energy and protects the occupant from fluctuation in energy prices

- environmental sustainability—by saving energy and reducing pollution

Earthship Housing

Another example of sustainable building design is Earthship housing. The name of the housing, **Earthship**, suggests the need for housing to be self-sufficient just as a "ship" has to be self-sufficient. This housing uses passive solar and earth-sheltered design along with the use of recycled materials to produce sustainable dwellings. Earthships have the feel you might expect of housing built on another planet. This is because the form of the housing structure does not necessarily follow the angular dimensions people associate with traditional housing, 23-3.

Michael Reynolds, an architect, founded the Earthship concept and the Earthship Biotecture business headquartered in Taos, New Mexico. Near Taos, whole communities of Earthships exist. Earthships have been built in the United States, Canada, Mexico, Honduras, Nicaragua, Bonaire, Jamaica, Bolivia, Scotland, England, France, The Netherlands, Spain, India, and Japan. There are approximately 3,000 Earthships worldwide.

The houses are all different from the outside but share a number of features. Figure 23-4 shows the following features:

- building with recycled materials

- water harvesting

- contained sewage treatment

- solar/thermal heating and cooling

23-3
The Earthship housing has organic and natural shapes not usually found in angular traditional homes.

(A and B) Earthship Biotecture, Taos, New Mexico

A

B

Thermal wrap   Walls of rammed earth and tires   Metal from recycled appliances   Solar panels   Sky lights   Solar hot water

23-4
This diagram shows the features of Earthship housing.

Earthship Biotecture, Taos, New Mexico

- solar and wind electric power

- food production

The southern side of an Earthship house faces the sun and collects the heat of the sun through windows to warm the home. Usually there are two sets of windows. The outer set creates a greenhouse where plants and food are grown. The interior set of windows connects to the living space and controls the amount of heat entering the house from the greenhouse space.

The back wall on the north side of the housing is actually built of earth, called a *berm*. The berm stores heat collected from the sun.

Recycled materials form these homes. For instance, used tires filled with earth form the walls. Then plaster fills in the cracks and forms a smooth surface on the walls. In addition, glass bottles serve as decoration as well as allowing light into the houses. The glass bottles are cut crosswise and the bottoms connect to create cylinders. These cylinders are embedded into walls, 23-5. The bottles appear as round lights in the photo.

Usually owners attend workshops on construction methods and requirements to build the homes. The building of these homes is very labor intensive. In general, all these homes are individualized and reflect the lifestyle and interests of the owner.

Automated Houses

Automated houses are dwellings that have an integrated and centrally controlled system based on computer technology. This system controls all the systems in the home and focuses primarily on one or more of the following areas:

- convenience

- energy management

- entertainment

- safety

23-5
This is the interior of an Earthship bathroom that uses bottles in the walls for decoration and transmission of light. The round "lights" are the bottles.

Earthship Biotecture, Taos, New Mexico

23-6
By looking at its exterior, you cannot identify this SMART HOUSE from any other house.

SMART HOUSE, L.P. 400 Prince George's Blvd., Upper Marlboro, Maryland

Homes built today incorporate many versions and features of "smart" technology. The exteriors of homes with automated systems look like any other homes, 23-6. However, the homes contain advanced systems, components, and materials—all the result of ongoing technological development.

The SMART HOUSE

Historically speaking, electronic houses were something that only appeared in science fiction for much of the twentieth century. In the 1980s, however, the National Research Center of the National Association of Home Builders (NAHB) helped the advancement of home automation by initiating The SMART HOUSE Project. The technology wired the home with a single multiconductor cable that included electric power wires, communications cables for telephone and video, and other connections to appliances and lamps. The multiconductor cable was then linked with electronic devices to control the supply of power throughout the home. The SMART HOUSE was designed to respond to the resident's needs by adjusting lighting, temperature, and even music. Currently,

NAHB is no longer the leader in marketing home automation but instead private companies are leading the way for home automation.

The basic idea of home automation is to employ sensors and control systems to monitor a residence, and adjust the systems according to the user's needs. By doing so, the home becomes a safer, more comfortable, and more economical residence. For example, the system can turn off the lights and lower the thermostat after everyone has gone to bed. It can monitor burglar and fire alarms and optimize the operation of the water heater by anticipating hot water usage.

Home automation technologies require widespread changes to building construction. These organizational changes may impact house wiring and cabling for power and communications. The development of a new information infrastructure offers the possibility of broader participation in civic and community activities, access to educational resources, as well as work and entertainment. Higher-bandwidth communication technologies are available to provide electronic community town meetings, distance learning, home shopping, and video-on-demand.

After meeting technical and organizational challenges, many will find a fine line between an intelligent house that maintains comfort levels and an overbearing house that monitors the inhabitants too closely. Few people object to using a thermostat to control the temperature in a house, but most cherish the power to set and reset the thermostat. As the hardware and software to control home automation systems become increasingly complex, human interface designers must make it easy for inhabitants to program the house and to override preprogrammed settings.

Today, The Home Technology Alliance (HTA) brings together housing industry professionals to create the optimal home experience powered by technology. This program aligns with the vision of NAHB for all Americans having access to the housing of their choice. (See NAHB Web site for more information about the NAHB vision.) HTA strives to create an environment in which residents from every segment of housing have the opportunity to experience an automated and connected home environment.

Housing Concerns

Many housing concerns today revolve around environmental issues. The use of renewable energy sources and conserving natural resources receives attention in the media and by the general public. The sources of energy, energy efficiency, and a clean, healthy environment are key housing concerns.

Energy Sources

Fuel provides heat, and people need heat to live. Like all forms of energy, fuel begins as solar energy derived from the sun. Nature converts solar energy to raw materials such as oil and coal. The conversions take millions of years to complete. The raw materials are then refined and used as fuel for electricity. The chart in 23-7 shows that coal is the nation's main source of energy. Nuclear energy, hydroelectric power, natural

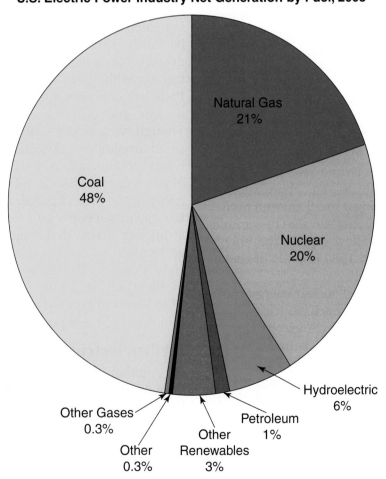

U.S. Electric Power Industry Net Generation by Fuel, 2008

Coal 48%

Natural Gas 21%

Nuclear 20%

Hydroelectric 6%

Petroleum 1%

Other Renewables 3%

Other 0.3%

Other Gases 0.3%

23-7
The United States relies heavily on coal to fuel the generation of electricity for industrial use.

U.S. Energy Information Administration, *Electric Power Annual* (2010)

gas, and petroleum are the other leading energy sources in the country.

There is a depleting supply of such common sources of fuel as oil and coal. These sources of energy are *nonrenewable*. Researchers continually work to find new sources that will supply enough fuel for the future. They are studying **renewable energy sources**, which replenish themselves regularly. Renewable sources of energy include the sun, wind, water, and geothermal energy, all of which can be converted to electricity. Also, many communities are converting solid waste into energy by implementing a controlled burning process known as *combustion*. You can learn more about municipal solid waste management on the EPA Web site.

23-8
The Palo Verde nuclear plant in the Arizona desert is the largest in the world.

Arizona Public Service

Nuclear Energy

The discovery of nuclear energy marked the beginning of the atomic age. This was a monumental breakthrough for scientists and energy experts worldwide.

Nuclear energy production occurs in a nuclear reactor by the breakup of Uranium-235. The release of heat occurs when the nucleus of an atom *fissions*, or splits into two pieces. This process produces an abundance of energy by using a small amount of fuel. One nuclear pellet the size of a miniature marshmallow equals the energy produced from 1,780 pounds of coal or 149 gallons of oil.

More than 100 nuclear energy plants provide nearly as much electricity as oil, natural gas, and hydroelectric power combined. Petroleum, natural gas, and coal produce more electricity than nuclear energy. However, in some states, nuclear energy is the leading source of electrical power. See 23-8. There are over 436 nuclear plants in operation worldwide.

Although fewer new nuclear energy facilities are currently under construction, the current nuclear energy facilities continue to play a major role in providing electric power. Research shows the benefits of nuclear power over the past decades. Nuclear energy does not pollute the air with gases or dust. However, there are concerns about the effects of nuclear energy on the environment. Though nuclear plants produce only a small amount of radioactive waste, the waste remains radioactive for hundreds of years. Careful disposal of this waste is necessary to protect people from potential hazards. People also fear incidents at nuclear plants that might cause the accidental release of radioactive materials. Previous accidents at Chernobyl in the Ukraine in 1986 and at Three Mile Island in Pennsylvania in 1979 are reminders of these potential hazards.

Hydroelectric Power

Another important source of energy is **hydroelectric power**. Water moving through rivers and dams generates this electrical power. Water as a source of energy is not new. Waterpower was first converted into electricity using waterwheels in the late 1800s.

Today's hydroelectric plants use turbines to drive electric generators. A *turbine* is a series of blades that surround a shaft. Flowing water powers the turbine. The swiftness of the water determines the turbine's speed. The higher the speed of the turbine, the greater is the generation of electricity. See 23-9 for an example of a hydroelectric system.

Most of the hydroelectric generating systems are located on major rivers. Dams are the usual location for these plants, but the placement of small plants can be at any point along a river.

Solar Energy

Many people build houses to take advantage of the natural heating effect of solar energy, 23-10. Solar energy could supply a majority of the energy needed to heat and cool buildings throughout the United States. Solar heating systems are expensive to install. A major part of the expense is the high cost of the component parts. Ongoing long-term research and development is necessary to reduce costs, improve reliability, and improve performance of technologies that solar programs use.

Despite the high installation cost, those who use solar energy usually see a great reduction in their utility bills. In the long run, solar heating systems usually cost less than conventional systems. See Chapters 6 and 9 to review the two types of solar heating systems, active and passive.

Active solar systems can heat space, heat water, or produce electricity. An active solar system that converts sunlight into electricity is a *photovoltaic system*. The sun shines on panels (called arrays) and converts this solar energy into electricity.

The downside of photovoltaic systems is they generate electricity only when the sun shines. The system's batteries can store enough electricity to power

23-9
This illustration shows the seven hydroelectric power generators at Hoover Dam.

a house for several days, but persistent overcast weather can deplete it. Deluxe systems can match the reliability of power supplied by utility companies, but they are expensive. As the cost of solar electric systems declines, environmentally conscious home owners will likely invest in this technology.

Some solar energy heating systems supply more energy than a home needs. Home owners can sell the excess to a utility company or store it in the lines until needed by the producer. *Net*

23-10
This house has solar panels on the roof to take advantage of active solar heating.

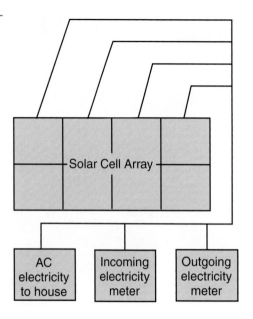

In a photovoltaic system, silicon chips are joined with electrical wires to form solar cell arrays. The arrays collect different amounts of solar energy, depending on the season, time of day, and degree of cloudiness.

metering programs also provide consumer investment in renewable energy generation. The plan allows customers to use their own generation to balance their consumption. The electric meters turn backwards when they generate electricity in excess of their demand, 23-11.

Geothermal Energy

The geothermal energy that comes from the Earth's core creates volcanoes, natural hot springs, and geysers. In certain locations, the heat is present near the surface. In other locations, it is possible to reach the heat source by drilling deep holes through lava, a type of volcanic rock. Reykjavik, Iceland, is the first city in the world to become almost entirely heated by geothermal energy. Approximately half a million people in California, Mexico's Baja Peninsula, and the Mexicali Valley meet their fuel needs with geothermal energy. The United States generates more geothermal electricity than any other country. For example, California has 35 geothermal power plants that produce almost 90 percent of the nation's geothermal electricity. Other geothermal projects are under development in the United States.

Geothermal heat pumps use the Earth's constant temperatures to heat and cool buildings. While temperatures above ground are unstable, temperatures in the upper 10 feet of the Earth's surface remain constant. The soil temperatures are usually warmer than the air in winter and cooler than the air in summer. The heat pumps transfer heat from the ground (or water) into buildings in winter and reverse the process in the summer. Although most homes still use traditional furnaces and air conditioners, geothermal heat pumps are becoming more popular. In recent years, the U.S. Department of Energy (DOE) along with the Environmental Protection Agency (EPA) have partnered with industry to promote the use of geothermal heat pumps.

Geothermal energy has advantages and disadvantages. One advantage is its low cost in comparison to other fuels. It also is a source of heat that does not emit harmful pollutants into the environment. A third advantage is that geothermal energy is a renewable resource.

There are some drawbacks, however, to using an open-loop geothermal energy pump and pulling directly from the groundwater. Some geothermal waters contain chemicals that require responsible disposal. A second disadvantage is the direct use of geothermal energy can only occur near the production sites. Transportation of hot water over long distances cannot occur without losing heat and turning cold. Closed-loop systems address these problems. The geothermal loop is made of a tough plastic that is extremely durable and buried underground to allow heat to pass through efficiently. The fluid in the loop is water or an environmentally safe antifreeze solution that circulates through the pipes in a closed system.

Wind as Energy

The use of wind as energy dates back to early civilizations with the use of windmills to pump water and grind grain. Wind is gaining popularity as an energy source. Most wind machines today are the horizontal-axis type. They have blades like airplane propellers. A typical horizontal wind machine stands as tall as a 20-story building and has three blades that span 200 feet across. Wind machines stand tall and wide to capture more wind. A minimum average annual wind speed of 10 miles per hour is necessary to run a wind generator. An average above 12 miles per hour allows the development of an excellent wind system.

Some regions of the United States have strong, shifting winds that are useful for power generation. Wind turbine generators grouped together to form wind farms can convert air motion to electrical current, 23-12. The electrical current that wind machines produce feeds into utility lines or storage systems. The systems keep the power flowing even when the air is still.

Cogeneration in Residences

Cogeneration—also known as combined heat and power (CHP), and total energy—is an efficient, clean, and reliable approach to generating power and thermal energy from a single fuel source. CHP uses heat that is otherwise waste from conventional power generation to produce thermal energy. This energy provides cooling or heating for industrial facilities, district energy systems, and commercial buildings. The development of new technologies that produce electricity make this system possible. These developments include photovoltaics, fuel cells, and microturbines.

- A **fuel cell** is an equipment system that produces electricity from the use of chemicals. Research is underway to handle the waste products of heat and water.

23-12
This wind system converts the power from constant breezes to create electricity for nearby residents.

- A **microturbine** is a small turbine engine that produces electricity.

Cogeneration systems are available to small-scale users of electricity. Currently, modular systems are useful for commercial and light industrial applications. Several factors could affect CHP growth to more residences. They include the initial cost of buying a cogeneration system, maintenance costs, and environmental control requirements. CHP in residences makes the occupants less dependent on electrical utility companies to provide electricity. This can be helpful especially in blackouts and during natural disasters when electric power may not be available.

Energy Efficiency

In the 1970s and 1980s when oil prices rose rapidly, came the passage of laws to encourage energy conservation. The interest in energy efficiency involves not only using less energy, but also making better use of used energy. Research on alternative energy sources, such as wind and solar power, was encouraged. Many home owners and home builders were recipients of tax credits for using energy-saving features and appliances in new homes. Many people took advantage of these laws by adding energy-saving features to their houses. In the 1990s and the early 2000s, there was less emphasis on energy efficiency. With escalating energy costs by 2009, came a renewal of interest in increasing energy efficiency with the promotion of tax credits for making such changes in the home.

The purpose of tax laws is to encourage people to buy energy-efficient products for their homes. This advice applies to items as small as appliances or as large as a house. Every household has many opportunities each day to save energy and lower its utility bills. Using energy wisely and preserving it for the future is an increasing public concern.

One of the biggest decisions that will affect how much energy you use is the type of home you buy. Some houses have more energy-efficient features than others. These features not only save money in the long run, but also help make the house more comfortable. The checklist in 23-13 can help you choose an energy-efficient house.

A Clean Environment

Ecology is the relationship between all living things and their surroundings. People harm the environment each time they put undesirable items into their surroundings. This results in pollution. Look around you to see the many types of pollution that can harm your surroundings.

People make many demands on the environment. Often they use it without regard to protecting and preserving it for future use. If the environment is to continue to satisfy so many needs, people must actively preserve it, 23-14. Researchers must continue to find solutions for the growing pollution problem. Pollution not only destroys the environment, but also affects human health.

Environmental scientists study the impact of housing and other development on the environment. These scientists recommend ways for building and development that have little to no impact on the environment.

Solid Waste

Every year people throw away tons of solid waste materials. **Solid waste** is any waste material that is not a liquid or a gas. Much of the waste comes from homes in the form of garbage. The *solid waste stream* is the total output of garbage. Dumping solid waste into sanitary landfills or incinerating it occurs most often. Both methods have drawbacks.

Nearly 73 percent of solid waste is buried, but solid-waste experts project that landfill space is filling up fast. Suitable sites are difficult to find because of the toxic substances that seep from landfills into groundwater despite safeguards.

As you recall, with landfills filling up local governments or private operators are implementing *combustion*, which is a controlled burning process or incineration to reduce waste volume. More than 14 percent of solid waste goes through this process. Incinerators do not pollute the groundwater, and they can generate energy. A variety of pollution control technologies significantly reduce the gases emitted into the air during this process. Also, burning waste at extremely high temperatures destroys chemical compounds and disease-causing bacteria. Regular testing ensures that residual ash is nonhazardous before going to the landfill.

Checklist for an Energy-Efficient House

Notice and evaluate these features for home energy efficiency.

Orientation and Landscaping
- Orientation of long side of house (N, S, E, or W)
- Windows facing east (Note number and compute area in square feet.)
- Windows facing west (Note number and compute area in square feet.)
- Shade from landscape features on east or west sides
- Southern exposure unobstructed or shaded by deciduous trees

Thermal Resistance
- Attic insulation (Note the type and thickness.)
- Wall insulation
- Under-floor insulation, especially in homes with crawl spaces, cold basements, and garages under living areas
- Insulated ducts
- Insulated hot water pipes
- Insulated hot water heater
- Double- or triple-glazed (paned) windows with low-E glass
- Solid-core wood or insulated metal door
- Storm doors

Lighting and Windows
- Fluorescent lighting in work areas
- Windows or skylights over work areas
- Windows occupying less than 10 percent of the total wall area (Measure the window area and calculate its percentage of total wall area.)

Appliances
- Refrigerator located away from range, dishwasher, and direct sunlight

Ventilation
- Ceiling fans
- Whole-house fan
- Window/door placement appropriate for cross-ventilation
- Attic vents near the roof ridge
- Attic vents beneath the eaves
- Air infiltration
- Weather-stripping around doors
- Weather-stripping around windows
- Weather-stripping around attic entry door
- Caulking around door frames
- Caulking around window fames
- Caulking around penetrations for pipes and wires
- Tightly fitted windows

23-13
Use this checklist to compare houses for energy efficiency.

Texas Energy Extension Service

A

B

22-14
Maintaining a beautiful view of the environment such as this requires all people to care for the environment (A). Many communities sponsor "community cleanup" days, when residents help remove trash to restore their environment (B).

(B) Keep America Beautiful Association

Certain waste is particularly harmful. **Hazardous waste** is poisonous waste material that damages the environment and causes illness. The U.S. Environmental Protection Agency's (EPA's) definition of hazardous wastes includes all corrosive, ignitable, reactive, or toxic substances.

Modern industry produces many toxic substances that are hazardous to the environment. However, the average household also contains a variety of hazardous materials that require special disposal methods. Among the most common chemical hazards in the home are batteries, bleach, disinfectants, drain cleaners, insect sprays, medicines, and metal polishes. Certain lawn and home workshop products are also hazardous. Special methods and requirements exist for disposing of these toxic wastes. Most communities have waste-management procedures for the disposal of household hazardous wastes.

Water Pollution

Half of all Americans use groundwater for drinking water, but it can become contaminated. This contamination occurs when hazardous chemical wastes, pesticides, or other agricultural chemicals seep down through the soil into underground water supplies.

Few people know the origin of their drinking water. Many people believe that municipal water systems remove all toxins from drinking water before it reaches their homes. Generally, water receives proper treatment at municipal treatment plants. Federal and state laws require water suppliers to periodically sample and test their water supply. If tests show water standards in violation of the law, the supplier must correct the situation. Home owners with private wells should test their water periodically.

Even if the water that enters a home is pure, a house can contribute to its pollution. Many homes built prior to 1988 contain plumbing systems that use lead-based solder (SAH-duhr) in pipe connections. Older homes may even have lead pipes. In such systems, lead can enter drinking water as a corrosion byproduct. Some galvanized and plastic pipes may give off harmful chemicals to the water supply.

Modern technology can make a water supply safe. However, be sure to check you are not drinking polluted water. Samples of water from a home are easy to test.

Other Types of Pollution

Air and noise pollutants exist outdoors as well as indoors. Review

Chapter 20 for safety and health issues related to air and noise pollution. **Visual pollution** is the harm done to the appearance of the environment as a result of human activities. Signboards, debris along roadsides, and the destruction of natural surroundings are examples of visual pollution, 23-15.

Researchers continue to learn more about the effects of various pollutants on people. All pollutants are harmful in one way or another. People should welcome research and technology that helps them have a healthy environment. A healthy environment will help make future housing better.

Solving Environmental Concerns

The need for energy and the desire for a clean environment pose challenges for housing. **Integrated waste management** is one approach that tries to address all areas. A hierarchy of preferable waste handling options developed by the EPA is the basis for this approach, 23-16. The EPA encourages every community to use this approach when deciding how to handle their trash. Beginning with the most preferable option, the hierarchy includes the following choices:

- **Source reduction.** This choice avoids the excess that quickly becomes trash through the careful planning of a product or package from the very first step in development.

- **Recycling, reusing, and composting.** This option involves finding useful roles for discarded materials.

- **Waste combustion with resource recovery.** Using incineration to handle solid waste and making use of the energy released by such incineration is another option.

- **Waste combustion and landfilling.** With this option, combustion helps reduce the bulk of the waste before it is buried.

23-15
Most of the litter polluting roadsides consists of materials that can be recycled and reused.

Slowing the expanding volume of waste—the first option—offers the greatest opportunity for controlling environmental problems. Finding useful roles for trash, and the energy that incineration releases, also offer opportunities. The most wasteful method of handling trash is dumping it in a landfill. In this case, there is nothing to gain but something is lost—either energy or land.

Source Reduction

As you can see, careful planning is the best approach to waste management. Though industry plays the major role at this step, you can also play an important role.

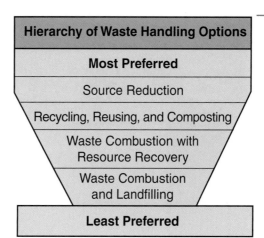

Hierarchy of Waste Handling Options

Most Preferred

Source Reduction

Recycling, Reusing, and Composting

Waste Combustion with Resource Recovery

Waste Combustion and Landfilling

Least Preferred

23-16
This illustration shows the five options for handling waste, ranked from most to least preferred.

Think about some of the ways your buying decisions can help the environment. Buy only those items that are the least environmentally harmful to produce. Also, buy those that are safe to use and less of a burden to dispose. Consider the amount and kind of packaging each item you buy uses. Some packaging is necessary for the protection and safety of the product. However, some packaging is excessive, adding to the solid waste problem. Finally, decide not to buy unneeded items or those with excessive packaging. This has the greatest environmental impact of all.

Recycling, Reusing, and Composting

The second level in the hierarchy is to recycle, reuse, and compost. Recycling means to reprocess resources for another use. The EPA's goal is to increase the level of recycling in the United States. Many communities have recycling programs and waste disposal restrictions. You play a very important role in the total recycling effort.

Paper, cardboard, aluminum, glass, and many plastics are all recyclable products, 23-17. Manufacturers can make newspapers into many other products, such as newsprint, molded-fiber packaging, home insulation, cereal boxes, and roofing felt. Aluminum is recycled into new beverage containers,

storm doors, and gutters. Manufacturers can also make glass containers by crushing and melting recycled glass. Crushing some recycled glass is useful for asphalt pavement mixes or permeable media in foundation drains.

When plastic products are disposed, they take hundreds of years to decompose. Thus, plastic recycling is becoming more important. A type of plastic that is successfully recycled from soda bottles is polyethylene terephthalate, or PET. Manufacturers use PET as a fiber in carpeting. A similar type of plastic is recycled into a material to make outdoor items, such as fences, decks, picnic tables, benches, and trash containers.

Another form of recycling the EPA promotes is *composting*. **Compost**—the end result of composting—is biologically decomposed organic material that can enrich soil and grow plants. Mix yard trimmings, such as leaves and grass, with food scraps (such as vegetable and fruit peelings, but no protein or meat) and other organic materials to produce compost. Large-scale composting can occur at the municipal level, or you can compost yard wastes in your backyard. See the EPA Web site for more information on composting.

Many people believe the United States can recycle on a large scale. For example, many people use recycled materials to build new homes. Making products from recycled materials can often be more expensive than using customary materials. However, with the increasing costs of natural materials recycling becomes more affordable. Recycling also saves natural resources and landfill space.

Waste Combustion with Resource Recovery

In this level of the hierarchy, some of the waste combustion undergoes conversion to energy. Properly equipped combustors can convert water into

23-17
Recycling is just one way to protect the environment. What other ways are effective?

steam to fuel heating systems or generate electricity. Incineration facilities can also remove materials for recycling. The creation of energy from garbage incineration can provide heat and electrical power for homes, schools, and businesses.

Innovative Housing Solutions

Shifting populations, lifestyle changes, and longer lifespan dictate attention to new alternatives. Housing designs of the future will reflect these and other considerations, such as the needs and values of people.

Home owners are continually seeking new solutions to meet their changing lifestyles, such as redesigning the space within a home. Recent research indicates that most new home owners have less interest in a separate living room that gets little use in comparison to home owners in the past. Instead, many current house plans include great rooms. Will homes of the future eliminate separate living rooms? Will they instead have the increasingly popular entertainment rooms or home theaters? Lifestyle changes dictate the future direction for housing design.

Housing must accommodate the physical changes in people that take place naturally as they age. Housing should also take advantage of new technologies. Protecting the environment is another important goal of future housing. A discussion of housing designs that improve the quality of life of individuals and families while protecting the environment follow in this section.

Universal Design for Future Generations

As you recall from Chapter 4, *universal design* (UD) is the design of products and environments to be usable by all people without the need for adaptation or specialized design. The design of a universal home is convenient, safe, and comfortable for persons of all ages, physical characteristics, and abilities. Because of this design, people who have very different needs can all enjoy the same home. This home will continue to be there even when needs change. Some common universal design features include no-step entries, one-story living, extra floor space, and wider doorways. Floors and bathtubs with nonslip surfaces can prevent accidental falls. Thresholds that are flush with the floor make it easy for wheelchair access. Finally, adequate lighting helps improve vision for those who have low vision or are blind. Newer universal design innovations include adjustable-height bathroom cabinets and counters as well as adjustable-height sinks and cooktops in the kitchen.

Planned Communities— the Future

Planned communities are one answer to today's housing problems, and the expectation is they will continue to grow with sustainability as a goal. Instead of growing by one building at a time, the design of these communities will meet present and future needs. Urban planners and designers give careful consideration to the use of resources and the needs and values of the residents. Community associations govern planned communities. Well-run associations can raise the quality of life as well as property values for residents.

"One-stop living" is the description people often use for planned communities. They are as self-sufficient as possible. Businesses, shops, recreation, and schools are included in the planning. Homes in these communities are an escape from the usually congested suburbs and high commuter traffic.

Columbia, Maryland is an example of a planned community. This is one of several communities planned by architect James W. Rouse. It is located on 14,000 acres of land between Baltimore and Washington, DC. About 3,200 acres are set aside for parks, lakes, and a golf course. The city of Columbia consists of a cluster of nine residential villages—or *satellite communities*—that surround an urban downtown. Columbia is a culturally diverse community. Homes are available in a wide range of prices and styles, for purchase or rent.

Included in the planning of Columbia were specialists from many fields: architects, sociologists, educators, religious leaders, and doctors. They tried to answer the question, "What should be included in a well-planned community?" See Figure 23-18 for planning factors they considered.

As an example of a planned community with a goal of sustaining the environment, Columbia continues to attract new businesses, employees, and home owners to live, work, and invest in the downtown area. Community members and leaders are working toward making Columbia and Howard County a model green community. In addition to Green Building standards, the Columbia Town Center will soon implement a *Sustainability Program*. Redevelopment of the Columbia Town Center has the potential to be the single largest effort toward green technologies and sustainability countywide.

New Urbanism

As you recall from Chapter 2, *new urbanism* is a type of planned community. However, it has a different focus—houses in which people both live and work. For example, a person may have an art gallery on the first floor and live on the second and third floors. In many of these communities, planning makes better use of land, especially near the central business district or community area that needs extensive renovation.

The Congress for the New Urbanism (CNU) is the leading organization promoting neighborhood-based developments as an alternative to *urban sprawl*—the spreading of urban developments such as housing and shopping centers on undeveloped land near a city. Active members include planners, developers, architects, engineers, public officials, investors, and community activists who create and influence the built environment. Their work brings restorative plans to hurricane-battered communities, turns

23-18 These factors were considered when the planned community of Columbia, Maryland, was designed.	**Factors for Designing a Planned Community**
	• The lifestyles desired by the occupants
	• Affordable housing
	• Easy access to schools, health facilities, places of worship, stores, and government offices
	• Recreational facilities that appeal to individuals and groups of all ages
	• The use of parks, playgrounds, and green belts to separate space and create neighborhood zones
	• Affordable public transportation
	• Employment opportunities at all levels
	• Education opportunities at all levels
	• Effective and affordable health care facilities
	• Effective communications about community events and activities

around failing shopping centers, and reconnects isolated public housing projects back to the community. Followers of New Urbanism are striving to become leaders in community building.

New Living Spaces

Many of today's housing problems relate to space. About 75 percent of the people in the United States are living on less than 10 percent of the land, yet space for housing is difficult to find. It is also expensive. In just 40 years, the cost of land has risen dramatically from about 10 to 25 percent of a home's purchase price. In some areas, the cost will be as much as 50 percent. To solve this problem, some forward-thinking individuals are exploring new sources of living space.

One expanding "frontier" is outer space. Although you may not be able to imagine it, living in a space colony is not impossible. For humans to exist for periods in outer space, extensive testing is a requirement to guide the development of life-support systems as well as new methods of food production and waste management. Ongoing climate

research is happening under controlled conditions that simulate outer space.

From 1991 to 1993, the Biosphere 2 project in Arizona investigated ways to grow and harvest plants in climate conditions similar to outer space as well as human reactions to the controlled environment, 23-19. This project's unique ecosystem echoes a community of organisms living in nature and their reaction to changed environments. Currently, the Biosphere is an adaptive tool for Earth education and outreach to industry, government, and the public.

The University of Arizona (UA) assumed management of Biosphere 2 in June 2007, with a leasing agreement, from owners CDO Ranching and Development. The 3.14 acre enclosed facility now serves as a tool to support research already underway by UA scientists. As a laboratory for big-scale projects, the university's stewardship of Biosphere 2 will allow the UA to perform key experiments with the aim of quantifying some of the consequences of global climate change.

Some people think living space could extend downward into the earth.

Earth-sheltered housing, caves, cellars, and basements all have their place in the story of housing. However, the idea of building whole, modern communities underground has not attracted any interest.

Floating Houses—Living on the Water

Throughout the world, as many as 200 million people live in coastal areas prone to flooding. Many scientists predict an increase in coastal flooding as a consequence of changing climate conditions. Such changes are causing a rise in sea levels and the number of flood-producing storms. From the Netherlands to New Orleans, architects and other experts are designing and developing new types of flood-safe housing for a sustainable way of living.

With the goal of helping provide safe, affordable, and sustainable housing, the *Make It Right Foundation* is funding such developments in the Lower Ninth Ward of New Orleans. When Hurricane Katrina hit the southern coast of the United States in 2005, much of this community was destroyed by flooding. Katrina was one of the costliest natural disasters in U.S. history, killing more than 1500 people and causing more than $81 billion in damages.

The Make It Right Foundation spearheaded the building of 150 single-family homes in a neighborhood heavily damaged by a levee breach. Various architects and design firms are designing the homes. These homes must be able to withstand flooding and be sustainable. Many of the homes rise off the ground on piers or stilts. They are only accessible by flights of stairs that are difficult for some people to climb.

Morphosis Architects and a team of UCLA architecture graduate students came up with a solution to this accessibility problem. They designed a raft-like house that can float in up to 12 feet of water, 23-20. The two-bedroom, 1,000 square foot "FLOAT House" is suitable for affordable housing because its components can be mass-produced and assembled on-site. Energy- and water-conserving elements include

- solar-powered panels that generate power for the house

- a concaved roof that collects rainwater and funnels it to a cistern in the base of the house

- highly insulated structural panels for walls

- energy-efficient appliances and fixtures

- geothermal heating and cooling

The long narrow house, which can have a front porch, resembles the local architectural style (similar in look to a Louisiana shotgun house). Secured to two steel guideposts (that are anchored to two 45-foot deep piles in the ground) the house floats, or rises vertically on the guideposts, only when the water level rises during severe flooding. The home design aims to protect a home owner's investment and limit catastrophic damage. However, the home occupants must still evacuate during a hurricane or flood.

Although the concept of floating houses is not new in the world, the New Orleans FLOAT House is the first of its kind in the United States. Because of its design and the prefabrication of its component parts, this house is affordable and adaptable for use in many regions in the U.S. and beyond.

A

23-20
Development of the FLOAT House began to help supply housing that is flood-safe, affordable, and sustainable in the Lower Ninth Ward of New Orleans (A). This drawing shows the components and layout of the FLOAT House (B).

(A) Courtesy of Morphosis Architects. Photography by Iwan Baan. (B) Drawing Courtesy of Morphosis Architects.

FLOAT HOUSE: PARTS

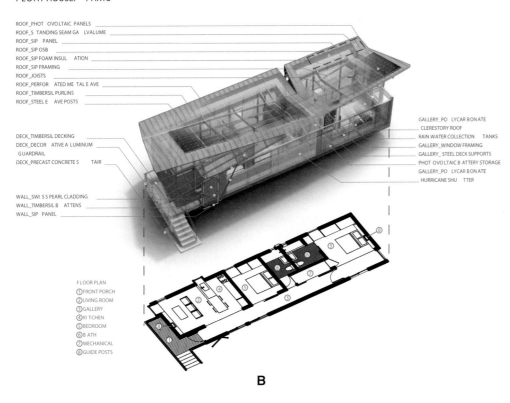

ROOF_PHOT OVOLTAIC PANELS
ROOF_S TANDING SEAM GA LVALUME
ROOF_SIP PANEL
ROOF_SIP OSB
ROOF_SIP FOAM INSUL ATION
ROOF_SIP FRAMING
ROOF_JOISTS
ROOF_PERFOR ATED ME TAL E AVE
ROOF_TIMBERSIL PURLINS
ROOF_STEEL E AVE POSTS

GALLERY_PO LYCAR BON ATE
CLERESTORY ROOF
RAIN WATER COLLECTION TANKS
GALLERY_WINDOW FRAMING
GALLERY_ STEEL DECK SUPPORTS
PHOT OVOLTAIC B ATTERY STORAGE
GALLERY_PO LYCAR BON ATE
HURRICANE SHU TTER

DECK_TIMBERSIL DECKING
DECK_DECOR ATIVE A LUMINUM
 GUARDRAIL
DECK_PRECAST CONCRETE S TAIR

WALL_SWI S S PEARL CLADDING
WALL_TIMBERSIL B ATTENS
WALL_SIP PANEL

FLOOR PLAN
① FRONT PORCH
② LIVING ROOM
③ GALLERY
④ KI TCHEN
⑤ BEDROOM
⑥ B ATH
⑦ MECHANICAL
⑧ GUIDE POSTS

B

CAREER FOCUS

Environmental Scientist

Can you imagine yourself as an environmental scientist? If you can, read more about this challenging and exciting career.

Interests/Skills: If you share any of the following interests you may choose to explore a course of study that would lead to a career as an environmental scientist. Are you investigative and realistic? Do you enjoy working with ideas and do you like to search for facts and figure out problems mentally? Do you prefer practical, hands-on problems and solutions? Do you appreciate the outdoors along with plants, animals, and real-world materials like wood, tools, and machinery? Environmental scientists typically have skills in the sciences, have critical-thinking ability, can express themselves to others in writing and speaking, and work well with people.

Career Snapshot: Environmental scientists find and fix pollution and other environmental problems. They figure out what is in the air, water, and soil to make sure that the environment is safe. They also give advice on how to clean the environment. For example, they might design a safe way to get rid of trash. Some environmental scientists help to make laws about protecting the environment. They also help companies follow the laws. Environmental scientists work in laboratories and offices. They also work outside, taking measurements.

Education/Training: All of these workers need a college degree. Most need an advanced degree—either a master's, which takes 1 or 2 more years after finishing college, or a doctoral degree, which takes longer.

Licensing/Examinations: (none currently)

Professional Associations: National Association of Environmental Professionals (NAEP) (www.naep.org)

Job Outlook: The number of jobs for environmental scientists is expected to grow much faster than the average for all occupations through 2018. This is because people want the environment to be cleaner, and more businesses and governments will hire these scientists to help do that.

Sources: Occupational Information Network (O*NET) (www.online.onetcenter.org), the Occupational Outlook Handbook (www.bls.gov/OCO/), and the Bureau of Labor Statistics (www.bls.gov)

Summary

Some of the greatest trends in housing relate to the environment and new technology. Green and sustainable buildings utilize materials and techniques that conserve resources. Examples of green and sustainable buildings include the Southface Eco Office and Resource Center, Zero Energy Homes, and Earthship housing.

Producing and conserving energy and energy efficiency are present-day concerns that relate to housing. All forms of energy begin as energy from the sun. Nature converts it to raw materials that can be refined for fuel. Nuclear energy is a form of energy that occurs through fission. It produces an abundance of energy from a small amount of fuel. Generating power from the sun's rays, wind, and moving water is also possible.

An unhealthy environment affects housing and human health. Land, water, and air pollution are major concerns. Some communities simply burn or bury their garbage. Other communities recycle and sort their garbage. They use combustible materials from trash as fuel for operating power plants or for heating. Metal cans, plastic, and glass are also reusable. Composting is another form of recycling. Scientists are trying to find more ways of recycling garbage.

Innovative housing solutions help meet people's concerns about their housing. Universal design makes housing more useful and comfortable to more people. It affects the housing structure as well as the interior components used in everyday life. Planned communities create a pleasant balance between housing and the surrounding environment. Planned communities now exist only on land, but future communities may exist below ground, in space, or on the water. Floating houses offer a flood-safe housing solution to meet the needs of people who live in flood-prone areas.

Review the Facts

1. What issues impact the trend of incorporating green and sustainable design into housing?
2. Identify four types of green products that help make today's homes sustainable.
3. Name four housing concerns, other than energy use and conservation, addressed by the Southface Eco Office and Resource Center.
4. Contrast the features of a Zero Energy Home (ZEH) with an Earthship home.
5. Summarize the key features of an automated house.
6. Name the five major sources of energy in the U.S. today.
7. Give an example of a renewable energy source.
8. Contrast the advantages and disadvantages of nuclear energy.
9. Compare hydroelectric and geothermal energy.
10. How is wind used as an energy source?
11. List five features to look for when buying an energy-efficient house.
12. List the four waste-handling options for communities, from most preferred to least preferred, as recommended by the Environmental Protection Agency.
13. What is the benefit of compost?
14. Describe a planned community.
15. How does new urbanism help deal with the problem of urban sprawl?
16. Why are floating houses a benefit in flood-prone areas? Give three features of a "FLOAT House."

Think Critically

17. **Analyze recycling.** New uses for recycled materials are continually changing. Make a list of three items that are not currently being recycled in your community. Analyze how recycling these items could benefit new housing. Some examples include converting old auto frames into steel beams and other building materials and recycling plastic water bottles into carpeting. What are your ideas?

18. **Predict consequences.** Environmental scientists and others study the impact of housing on the environment. Predict the consequences of failure to build and renovate housing that has little to no impact on the environment.

Community Links

19. **Construction technology.** Check with a home builder in your city to find out how he or she uses new technology in constructing houses. This should include building materials, construction techniques, and equipment. Ask if he or she has built an automated house or a house utilizing green or sustainable building technology. How is this type of housing becoming more affordable in your community?

20. **Recycling options.** Determine which waste products your community accepts for recycling. Share the findings with your classmates. If your school does not currently have a recycling plan, make it a class project to start one. Work with your instructor and the school administration to develop a workable plan.

21. **Composting project.** Composting can be done at school, in the community, or at home. Investigate the process for developing a worm-composting system for your school or community. What equipment will you need? What types of worms are best for composting? What "menu" do composting worms require for best results? With your classmates, start a worm composting project for your school or community. Use the composting materials to enrich the landscaping area in a community park or surrounding the school.

22. **Household hazardous waste.** Investigate your community's requirements for proper disposal of household hazardous waste that can pollute the environment and negatively impact human health. What products does your community consider household hazardous waste? What are the disposal procedures? Share your findings with the class.

23. **Photo essay.** Check the buildings in your community to see how many have solar heating systems. Using a digital camera, photograph the visible solar collectors. Compile a photo essay with presentation software complete with written photo descriptions, to share with your class. What types of buildings (residential, commercial, or government) seem to use solar power most often?

Academic Connections

24. **Writing.** Presume you are an investigative writer for a building technology magazine. Your assignment is to research and predict the most common trends for housing that has little to no environmental impact 50 years from now. Write an article in which you discuss the top five sustainable items.

25. **Social studies.** In teams, research economic considerations related to sustainability and housing. What are the economic costs to the United States of failure to build and renovate housing that meets sustainability standards? Share your research with the class.

Technology Applications

26. **Photo essay.** Use Internet and print resources to collect photos and descriptions of new housing technology. Select three interesting items. Print images off various Web sites for a photo essay. Develop a one-page, photo essay of the items to share with the class. As an alternative, use presentation software to display photos and descriptions to the class.

27. **Cogeneration for the home.** Investigate the use of cogeneration systems, such as fuel cells and microturbines, for the home. What is the benefit of such systems? How will such systems help home owners become less dependent on energy from other sources outside the home? Write a report about your findings.

28. **Floating house technology.** Research more about the technology used for the "FLOAT House." Use the *Morphopedia* and *Make It Right* Web sites to gather more information about how the house is assembled and functions. If possible, view the house-assembly animation on the FLOAT House. Write a paragraph indicating your views about the usefulness of this technology now and in the future.

Design Practice

29. **Green interior design.** Presume you have been hired to design a "green" kitchen remodel for a home in your community. You have been involved with the client as extensive renovations to most rooms and all the house systems (heating, cooling, and water) have been done over time. The kitchen size is 16 feet by 24 feet. The client desires an eat-in kitchen that makes use of green products and finishes in the design. Consider using the *REGREEN Residential Remodeling Guidelines* (ASID/USBGC) as a resource along with any relevant local building code information. Include the following in your "green" kitchen interior design plan:
    - CADD floor plan drawing that shows the kitchen layout including eating area, food preparation area, and a food storage area with a pantry.
    - CADD elevation drawing to show cabinetry and storage.
    - Sample selections for ceiling, wall, and floor treatments; cabinetry and trim finishes; furnishings (table and chairs); kitchen appliances (range or cooktop/ ovens, refrigerator, dishwasher, and microwave or convection oven).

    Then prepare a design presentation board and a written summary about each of the products and finishes you chose for this "green" kitchen design project to share with the client (the class).

30. **Portfolio.** Create a digital brochure using presentation software that promotes affordable green and sustainable housing design. Illustrate your presentation with photos or drawings cite the source of the images. Share your digital brochure with the class and save a copy on a CD or a USB storage device (such as a thumb drive or flash drive) for your portfolio.

Leading the Way to Green Building with LEED®

The LEED (Leadership in Energy and Environmental Design) Green Building System™ is a certification program through the U.S. Green Building Council. This certification encourages adoption and use of green building practices. To find out more about LEED certified buildings in your community, survey several architects to determine which community buildings have LEED certification.

To learn about sustainable design features and LEED, arrange a tour of one or more LEED buildings for your FCCLA chapter. Use the FCCLA *Planning Process* to plan, carry out, and evaluate your activity. Consider using this tour as part of a project for the FCCLA *Leaders at Work* program. See your adviser for information as needed.

PART 6

Careers in Housing and Interiors

CHAPTER 24

Researching Careers

Terms to Learn

career
occupation
career cluster
lifelong learning
transferable skills
cooperative education
entrepreneur
aptitude
abilities
job shadowing
mentor
internship
apprenticeship
associate's degree
bachelor's degree
master's degree
unskilled labor
semiskilled labor
skilled labor
networking

Chapter Objectives

After studying this chapter, you will be able to

- summarize how career clusters and pathways can help you choose a career.

- distinguish between different career levels.

- determine the significance of lifelong learning and transferable skills to a successful career.

- evaluate important factors involved in considering careers.

- demonstrate how to use sources of career information.

- summarize the relationships between careers and personal and family life.

Reading with Purpose

Read the summary at the end of the chapter before you begin to read the chapter. On a sheet of paper, note the main points outlined in the summary. As you read the chapter, take additional detailed notes for each main point.

The actions you take now will lay the groundwork for the career you will have in the future. Would you like to be an interior designer? Do you see yourself buying and selling real estate? Are you interested in teaching housing and design? See 24-1. Preparing for your career may seem overwhelming at first, but doing a step at a time will make the process easier. If you have not started to think about your future, now is a good time to begin. What would you like to do for a living? Whether your future will be in a housing field or some other, this chapter presents guidelines that are useful for planning your career.

Career Planning

Do not be fooled into thinking the right job will simply "come along." In today's highly competitive workplace, that is most unlikely. People who make no career plans usually find themselves left with jobs no one else wants. Instead, investigate what resources you need to achieve your goal and map out a plan. What can you do now, next semester, next year, and so on to improve your chances of successfully entering the career of your choice?

Having a career means you will hold several occupations related by a common skill, purpose, or interest over your lifetime. A **career** is a series of related occupations that show progression in a field of work. The term *job* is commonly used to mean *occupation*. Strictly speaking, a *job* is a task, while an **occupation** is paid employment that involves handling one or more jobs.

An example of a career is the course followed by some construction workers over a span of several years. They may enter the field doing one job well, learn to do others, and eventually supervise parts or all of various construction projects. As you move from one job to the next, you will gain new skills and knowledge.

Career clusters are groups of occupations or career specialties that are similar or related to one another, 24-2. The occupations within a cluster require a set of common knowledge and skills for career success. These are called *essential knowledge and skills*.

The 16 clusters were developed by state partnerships among educators, employers, and professional groups. The purpose of the clusters is to prepare students to transition from school to a rewarding career in an era of changing workplace demands.

Career Pathways

If one or two job titles in a career cluster appeal to you, it is likely that others will, too. This is because the jobs grouped together share certain similarities. To help you narrow down your options, each career cluster is further divided into *career pathways*. These

24-1
While in high school, this real estate agent took housing-related courses and participated in extracurricular and volunteer activities that allowed her to apply her knowledge.

Sixteen Career Clusters

The Career Clusters icons are being used with permission of the States' Career Clusters Initiative
www.careerclusters.org

24-2
The career clusters can help you determine your career area of interest.

subgroups often require additional and more specialized knowledge and skills.

Knowing the relationship between careers in a given pathway is helpful when researching information about careers. The skills required for different jobs in a similar field may overlap somewhat. Preparing for more than one career in a related field allows more flexibility when you are searching for employment. If you cannot find the exact position you desire, your skills will be needed by other occupations in the same pathway. The more you learn about related careers now, the more easily you will be able to adapt to changes in your occupation later.

The career clusters most closely related to the housing and interior design industries are the Architecture & Construction cluster and the Arts, Audio/Video Technology, & Communications cluster. You can learn more about these clusters, their pathways, and their career options in Appendix D, *Related Careers*. You can also explore the career clusters Web site at www.careerclusters.org.

Programs of Study

Since occupations in a career pathway require similar knowledge and skills, they also require similar programs of study. A *program of study* is the sequence of instruction used to prepare students for occupations in a given career pathway. The program includes classroom instruction, cocurricular activities such as student organizations, and other learning experiences including work-site and service learning.

Customizing a program of study for an individual learner's needs and interests results in a *personal plan of study*. A plan of study will help prepare you for the career direction you choose. You start by taking the appropriate classes in high school and participating in related organizations, 24-3.

24-3
A program of study can guide you to choose classes that are most valuable for your future career.

Once you have laid this foundation, seek out programs that address your career interest. You may even find that some high school classes can count toward college credit. Your plan of study does not expire with high school. Students should update their plans at least yearly, but more often if plans change.

Joining Organizations

Belonging to a student organization can help you reach your career goal. You will find student organizations focused on almost every career topic. They will help you learn more about career options and meet other students and professionals who can help you establish a career. You will learn teamwork skills that are needed in the workplace. Student organizations that may help you in a housing or interior design career include the following:

- *Family, Career and Community Leaders of America (FCCLA)* is an organization for students of family and consumer sciences education. Its goal is develop-ing leadership qualities with an emphasis on personal, family, work, and community activities. This organization has more than 220,000 members in more than 7,000 chapters. National programs include Dynamic Leadership and competitive STAR (Students Taking Action with Recognition) Events. FCCLA's Web site can be found at www.fcclainc.org.

- *SkillsUSA* is an organization for students preparing for technical, trade, and skilled-service occupations. Its goal is to create a strong American workforce. Programs include the Professional Development Program, which builds employability skills such as communication and teamwork. The Work Force Ready System offers assessments for career and technical education, including areas such as technical drafting, residential wiring, and plumbing. Other assessments are being developed and will be available soon. To learn more about SkillsUSA, visit their Web site at www.skillsusa.org.

- *Business Professionals of America (BPA)* is an organization of students planning for careers in business management, office administration, or information technology. Students learn workplace and leadership skills. BPA offers competitive events through its Workplace Skills Assessment program. To learn more, see the BPA Web site at www.bpanet.org.

You may also belong to professional organizations as a student member while you are still in school. Becoming involved in professional organizations now can help you land a job in your chosen field. Your membership shows employers that you are already involved in the organization and serious about a career in this area.

Organizations with student members include the American Society of Interior Designers (ASID), National Society of Professional Engineers (NSPE), and American Association of Family and Consumer Sciences (AAFCS). Student chapters also exist for the National Association of Home Builders (NAHB) and the United States Green Building Council (USGBC). If you eventually plan to become a member of the American Institute of Architects (AIA) or the National Kitchen & Bath Association, you can start by joining the student chapters of these organizations. See 24-4. To be a student member of these organizations, you must be enrolled in a certain number of courses that will lead to a career in the given area. There is also a fee, which is usually less than a professional membership fee.

Lifelong Learning

No matter what career you enter, you will be expected to keep pace with the changes in your field. Continually updating your knowledge and skills is known as **lifelong learning**. The term implies that your need for learning will never end. You cannot assume that the skills you have will be all you ever need during your career. Technology and other advances mean you must continue to learn to keep up with changes in the field. Employers usually provide some training. However, employees are often expected to use time outside the job to stay up-to-date in their field of expertise. People who enjoy their work will view lifelong learning as an exciting challenge.

Possessing **transferable skills** can help you succeed in whatever job you choose, 24-5. The transferable skills useful in all jobs include reading, writing, speaking, and basic math. The essential skills identified for a given career cluster, however, are transferable across the careers within that cluster.

Transferable skills can help employees during career transitions. Many people today do not stay in one career their entire lives. They may change career directions at some point and pursue other interests. If there is a decline in their industry, jobs may be eliminated. These employees may need additional training or education to succeed in a new career area. Having transferable skills can help smooth career transitions.

Career Levels

Career opportunities in housing and interior design are sometimes grouped according to the qualifications and level of responsibility linked to each specific occupation. By these measures, work opportunities can be divided as follows:

- entry-level positions
- midlevel positions
- professional positions

Professional Organizations	
American Society of Interior Designers (ASID)	www.asid.org
American Association of Family and Consumer Sciences (AAFCS)	www.aafcs.org
National Association of Home Builders (NAHB)	www.nahb.org
United States Green Building Council (USGBC)	www.usgbc.org
American Institute of Architects (AIA)	www.aia.org
American Institute of Architecture Students (AIAS)	www.aias.org
National Kitchen & Bath Association (NKBA)	www.nkba.org

24-4
You can investigate professional organizations using these Web sites.

24-5
Transferable skills are valuable in any career and are especially helpful to people who change careers.

Entry Positions

The qualifications for entry-level positions vary widely. People in entry-level positions follow the directions of those in midlevel and professional positions. Although you will be ready to perform many tasks, this is usually a period of learning. Often there is opportunity to move up if you do your job well. Design assistants with two to three years of postsecondary training often qualify for entry-level positions.

Does your school have a program in cooperative education? **Cooperative education** programs offer opportunities to work part-time and attend classes part-time. These programs combine classroom instruction with paid, practical work experience. You may be able to secure a job through this kind of program. It will probably be an entry-level position that provides on-the-job training. You will also receive help from a counselor or career education teacher in your school.

Midlevel Positions

People in midlevel positions often work as *support personnel* to the professionals. They carry out the decisions of

the professionals. Their job assignments often include supervising workers who have less authority and responsibility.

In housing construction, for example, one supervisor oversees the work of many laborers. Supervisors rarely do the wiring, plumbing, or roofing themselves, but know how to do these jobs well. Consequently, they are well qualified to evaluate workmanship and supervise those actually doing the job.

The middle level in a given career field may have sublevels. This is especially true on large or complex projects. As a result, midlevel supervisors report to a head manager with higher authority. The fact that midlevel supervisors are themselves supervised does not make their work any less important. They also need good communication and teamwork skills to effectively manage the work of others.

Professional Positions

Jobholders in professional positions make decisions that affect the lives of individuals, families, and whole communities. Engineers, planners, project managers, and designers are some of the people with professional-level positions. Generally, a bachelor's degree is required for these jobs as well as special training and experience. Some professional positions also require an advanced degree, 24-6.

Another professional position is that of principal designer. The *principal designer* is the interior designer who finalizes all design decisions on a project. In smaller businesses, this is often the owner and perhaps the only interior designer. In larger businesses, it may be the lead designer on a project. Depending on the size of the business, the principal interior designer may also be the project manager. The project manager oversees the implementation of the project design, coordinating all units to deliver the final project.

24-6
An architect is a professional position that requires a degree and additional training.

Entrepreneurship

People who desire to work for themselves can start and run their own business. These people are called **entrepreneurs**. Perhaps you or someone you know mows lawns, shovels snow, provides child care, or makes baked goods for extra spending money. All are examples of entrepreneurs in your community who are working part time. Entrepreneurship allows people to run a money-making venture for several hours a week. This allows them to focus full time on going to school or raising a family. Some ventures become so successful that full-time careers are possible.

Entrepreneurship is a good way to have a successful career that you can control. However, success is not guaranteed. People who want to become entrepreneurs need to be prepared for the risks and responsibilities of running their own businesses. You can read more about entrepreneurship in Appendix B, *Entrepreneurship*.

Considering Career Options

To prepare yourself for a meaningful job in the workplace requires advance planning. This involves setting goals, which are aims or targets a person tries to achieve. Preparing yourself for the future involves setting goals today.

Before you can set career goals, you need to explore the real you. Consider your values, which are beliefs or ideas about what is important. You also need to identify your interests, abilities, and aptitudes. You can then use the career clusters to determine which occupations match your aptitudes, abilities, and interests.

Once you decide which careers interest you, begin to evaluate other important factors. Among these are the kind of wages you might earn and the education or training you would need. Knowing the job duties and responsibilities will also impact your decision.

Examining Career Interests

Few teens know exactly what career they want. Sometimes adults who have prepared for one career decide they want to pursue another. As you grow older, you may notice that your interests change. This is perfectly normal. Active people are constantly developing new interests.

Usually a person's interests parallel his or her likes. If you enjoy mowing the lawn and keeping flowerbeds well maintained, you may enjoy a landscaping career. See 24-7. However, if you dislike that type of work, a job involving these tasks is definitely not for you.

Interests involve people, data, or objects—and sometimes all three. In the case of the landscaping job, the focus was on objects: a beautiful lawn and flowerbed. By shifting the focus to people or data, different landscaping-related jobs come to mind. A person who

likes to focus on data may enjoy designing landscaping plans. In contrast, a person interested in people may enjoy a job teaching landscaping. By reviewing your likes and dislikes, you will get a better picture of the tasks you would enjoy in a career.

Determining Aptitudes and Abilities

Career planning cannot take place until you know what you can do well. What are your aptitudes? An **aptitude**, or natural talent, is an ability to learn something quickly and easily. Are some of your subjects in school much easier than others? Knowing this can help determine some of your talents. You may not be aware of all of your aptitudes if you have never been challenged to use them. A school counselor can give you an aptitude test to help reveal your strengths.

Abilities are skills you develop with practice. As you prepare to handle a new responsibility, you will learn that it requires certain skills. Can you develop those skills with practice? For example,

can a person who is afraid of heights become a good roofer? Can someone lacking finger dexterity learn to manipulate precision tools? It is impossible to excel at every skill, so find out what you can do well.

Considering Earning Levels

You will want to check average earnings before choosing a career. What is the average beginning pay? What does it take to achieve higher earnings? Are additional degrees or training generally required?

When checking pay levels for various careers, you can expect professional positions to get higher pay. Entry level-positions make the least. As you work your way up from entry-level, your pay generally increases. This is because your knowledge and skills also increase, and they are worth more to your employer.

When investigating earning levels, research those of other careers in the same career pathway. You may discover another occupation in the pathway that suits you, yet earns higher pay.

Investigating Education and Training

You will need to consider what educational level is necessary for entering each career you investigate. How much training or experience is needed? Can people enter the field with less training and acquire expertise while working on the job? Are special certificates, licenses, or credentials needed?

Before deciding on a specific career, you may wish to shadow someone who holds the type of job you desire. **Job shadowing** is the process of observing a person in the workplace to learn more about his or her job and its requirements. In addition, you may seek to have a mentor's assistance. A **mentor** is someone with greater experience and knowledge who guides you in your career, 24-8.

You might also consider assisting someone who knows how to do

24-8
A mentor can offer guidance and help you become established in your career.

the job tasks well, such as working in an internship or apprenticeship. An **internship** is an arrangement with an educational institution whereby a student is supervised while working with a more experienced jobholder. An **apprenticeship** involves learning a trade under the direction and guidance of an expert worker.

For example, interior designers with a four-year college degree generally qualify for formal apprenticeship programs. These programs help them gain the work experience needed to take the NCIDQ licensing exam. You also gain valuable experience through working at a part-time job or volunteering at community or charitable organizations.

Perhaps your plan of study leads you to acquire a license or become certified. Other programs may require a college degree. An **associate's degree** is a two-year college degree. A **bachelor's degree** is a college degree usually requiring four years of study. A **master's degree** requires another year or two of study

beyond a bachelor's degree. A master's degree is also called a *graduate degree.*

Learning About Job Duties and Responsibilities

It is important to find out exactly what a job entails. Remember, you will be fulfilling these duties every day for many years. If they do not sound appealing now, it is unlikely that you will enjoy them in a few years' time.

Special skills and training are needed to carry out various tasks. For jobs in the manufacturing cluster, for example, these terms are commonly used: **Unskilled labor** describes workers who fill entry-level jobs that require almost no previous knowledge or experience. **Semiskilled labor** describes workers who have some experience and/or technical training. **Skilled labor** refers to workers who have successfully completed a formal training program beyond high school. When exploring different occupations, look carefully at what each involves and what is expected of the jobholder. Also study the qualifications for entering that field.

Considering Your Personal Traits

Some people have personality traits that are in conflict with the requirements of certain occupations. Choosing one of these occupations would not lead to career satisfaction or success. For instance, if you are outgoing, you may not enjoy work that requires a more reserved person. If you prefer a routine, you may resent a job that involves constant change. Think carefully about your personality while you are exploring career choices and keep your strongest characteristics in mind.

Thinking About Lifestyle

The career you choose affects your lifestyle in many ways. It affects your income, which determines how much you can spend on housing, clothing, food, and luxury items. Your career choice may also affect where you live. You will want to locate where the work is plentiful. If you prefer not to live in a large city, you should be sure to choose work that is available in other areas.

Your friendships are affected by your career choice, too. You are likely to become friends with some of your work associates. You may meet other friends through the people you know from work. Your leisure time is affected by the hours and vacation policies of your job. If you prefer to work weekdays from 9 to 5, you should avoid jobs that require overtime, late shifts, or working weekends.

Researching Employment Outlook

In 10 years, will the need for a certain career increase, stay the same, or decrease compared to average employment trends? Are too many people flocking to a field that is not growing? If the employment outlook for a career is poor, you will have fewer employment choices. It is best to focus on career areas that are growing, 24-9. They will offer you greater employment options when you are ready to begin your career. You can research job trends when investigating other career information.

Weighing Other Factors

There are still more factors to think about when considering your future career. Some of these may be very important to you. Others may not matter if your most important criteria are met.
- **Rewards.** People have different ideas about what constitutes a "reward." For example, does the occupation involve frequent travel? Adventurous people would consider this job factor a reward. However, people who like to stay at home would be annoyed, perhaps irritated and angry, at so much traveling.

Each job situation presents certain conditions that involve personal preferences.
- **Employer.** What companies, government offices, schools, or other workplaces employ people with the expertise? Where are these employers located? Will you be required to move?
- **Workplace.** Is the work environment a quiet office, a noisy factory, or the great outdoors? Is it near public transportation, or will you need a car? Think carefully about your preferences.

Sources of Career Information

When you are ready to find employment, you can get job leads through a variety of sources. Start your search at the placement office of your school. Usually school counselors and teachers can direct you to helpful job information. You can check newspaper want ads and job fairs. Good information is also available in libraries. The professional journals in your career field and the leading professional organizations often announce job openings. Family members and neighbors can provide help, too.

24-9
Interior design careers are expected to grow faster than the overall employment rate, but competition will be keen for most jobs.

Internet Sites

Today, one of the best ways to find jobs is using the Internet, 24-10. You can search for open positions, and many sites also offer tips for job hunting. You can start at the U.S. Department of Labor's Web site. You can also explore the following helpful sources:

- The *Occupational Outlook Handbook* describes the major U.S. jobs and their working conditions, requirements, average salaries, and future outlook. This publication is available in most libraries and on the Internet.

- The O*NET (*the Occupational Information Network*) Web site is replacing the *Dictionary of Occupational Titles* and is the most complete online resource available. It provides tools for exploring careers, examining job

24-10
Internet job-search sites post new job listings every day and often include tips for landing a job.

trends, and assessing personal abilities and interests. It also includes options for finding jobs within a career cluster or searching for jobs related to specific skills.

LINK TO SCIENCE & TECHNOLOGY

Managing Your Online Image

The Internet provides many tools that enable people to market themselves to potential employers and to search for job leads. However, pitfalls abound. Many employers also use the Internet to check job applicants as well as employees. What they are finding posted in cyberspace may cause people to lose job opportunities, promotions, and even their jobs.

A first step in managing your online image is to identify what is currently posted about you. Plug your name into one or more search engines and examine what comes up. Delete anything you wouldn't want a prospective employer to see. However, since you cannot control the flow of information online, be prepared to answer questions employers may ask. Here are some additional pointers.

- Do not say or do anything that is unethical or illegal.

- Do not take photos or videos that show you in a bad light. Images that depict drinking, drugs, gang signs, firearms, and lewd behavior have created problems for those pictured.

- Do not say anything negative about current or former employers, jobs, or coworkers. Negative comments and anything profane, sexist, or racist can result in the rejection of a job application or being named in a lawsuit.

Remember that cybercriminals are trolling the Internet for victims. They collect and piece together data that they use to commit crimes. Avoid posting personal information, especially your address, date of birth, and phone number. Revealing your future whereabouts is also risky. A family was robbed while away on vacation because a teenage son posted their plans on a social networking site.

- The *CareerOneStop* Web site has components for exploring careers, salaries, benefits, education, training, and other resources.

  One part of CareerOneStop is *America's Career InfoNet*. You can use this site for exploring careers, including occupational trends, wage information, and state resources.

  America's Service Locator is another component of Career OneStop. This site helps users find jobs and job-related resources in their local area. These resources include One-Stop Career Centers offering assistance in job-seeking skills, such as résumé writing. They also offer help with various types of job training.

Networking

Many people find employment through networking. **Networking** is the exchange of information or services among individuals or groups. As a newcomer to the career field, the goal of your networking is to learn about possible job leads.

Social networking sites have become popular places to find information on companies and their available positions. Many companies network on these sites because it is an additional source of advertising for them. Users find that these sites expand their job search possibilities. In addition, these sites allow a personal exchange between users and company representatives.

Balancing Family and Work

Your success in a career will affect your satisfaction with your personal and family life. Likewise, your roles and responsibilities related to home life will affect your career. Balancing career and home life is important in any lifestyle, 24-11.

Belonging to a family involves roles and responsibilities. As a son or daughter, your responsibilities at home may involve watching younger siblings, helping with family meals, and keeping your clothes and room clean. Usually these tasks do not interfere with your responsibilities to attend school and perform well. Adding a part-time job can complicate matters, however, and force you to manage your time more carefully.

The roles of spouse, parent, homemaker, and employee are much more demanding and may conflict at times. People with *multiple roles* must balance their responsibilities to fully meet them all. Sometimes family responsibilities will dictate the career decisions you make.

Parents may adjust work responsibilities so they can spend more time with the family. These adjustments might include telecommuting, working less overtime, taking a part-time job, or starting a home-based business. If both parents work away from the home, they must provide *substitute care* for young children.

24-11
Some working couples separate the household tasks into two separate to-do lists, while others like to accomplish tasks together.

Summary

Studying the career clusters can make choosing a career less overwhelming. Within each career cluster are career pathways that are grouped by similar knowledge and skills. Programs of study can help you plan now how to get the education and training you need for the job you want. Belonging to organizations can also help you learn more about a career.

Careers exist at all job levels. No matter what type or level of job a person holds, staying skilled and knowledgeable is important for career success and advancement.

Knowing the real you—your interests, abilities, and aptitudes—is the first step in choosing a career. Other factors to consider include wages and earning levels; education, and training; and job duties and responsibilities. Your personal traits and your lifestyle may impact your decision. You should also research the career outlook, related rewards, employer, and workplace before making a choice. Sources such as O*NET and CareerOneStop can help you thoroughly research career details.

Balancing your career responsibilities with your other roles in life will influence your career satisfaction. How workers feel about their work directly affects their personal and family life. Attitudes about family life also carry over to their workplace roles.

Review the Facts

1. What is the difference between a career and an occupation?
2. What is the purpose of career clusters?
3. Why do careers in a career pathway require similar programs of study?
4. Why is lifelong learning important to a person striving for career success?
5. Give three examples of transferable skills.
6. Why are transferable skills important?
7. In which career level are you most likely to find support personnel?
8. What is the difference between aptitudes and abilities?
9. How many years of study does a bachelor's degree usually require?
10. List five factors you should consider when thinking about a career.
11. Name three sources of career information.

Think Critically

12. **Compare and contrast.** What type of job environment do you think best suits your abilities and interests? Do you think you would be more successful as a member of a team in an established company or as an entrepreneur? Compare and contrast the benefits and challenges each choice offers.

13. **Draw conclusions.** Most workers can no longer expect to work for one employer for an entire lifetime. Occasionally people find themselves out of work through no fault of their own. The ideal, of course, is steady employment. After reviewing this chapter and one or more career Web sites, draw conclusions about which careers appear to have the strongest job outlook. Why? Report your conclusions and your reasoning to the class.

14. **Predict consequences.** Suppose a classmate posted some untrue, inappropriate remarks about you on a social networking site. You are in the process of submitting college applications and waiting for acceptance. You know that your first-choice college examines social networking sites looking for information about their applicants. Predict the potential consequences of these remarks on your pending college acceptance. How could these remarks impact future employment opportunities? What are some ways you safely can deal with such cyberbulling?

Community Links

15. **Career interview.** Conduct an interview with one or more individuals who work in housing and interior design related careers within your community. Ask them how they became interested in their fields, what educational routes they followed, what job duties they enjoy most, and which task they find least enjoyable. What path did their careers follow? Write a summary of your interview(s) to share with the class.

16. **Aptitude assessment.** Ask the school counselor to administer an aptitude assessment and explain your results. Based on your assessment results, determine which types of careers in housing and interior design present the best opportunities for you to succeed. Determine whether any local employers offer these or similar jobs.

17. **Employment options.** Look through a current edition of your local newspaper and online career sites. What employment ads do you find for careers discussed in this chapter? Choose three careers and identify the requirements the ads list for these careers. How can knowing such requirements help you identify your career pathway and develop your program of study?

Academic Connections

18. **Reading.** Obtain a copy of a career-search book (such as the latest edition of *What Color Is Your Parachute?*). Read the book. Then write a book report identifying the important guidelines the author suggests for finding meaningful employment. Select two topics you found most valuable to share with the class. Give evidence to support your reasoning.

19. **Writing.** Select two housing and interior design related careers to research on O*NET (www.onetcenter.org). Read the summary reports for these careers, especially the knowledge, skills, abilities, and interests required to do the work. Analyze whether your personal interests, skills, and abilities are a logical fit with one or both careers. Write a summary explaining why you think you are well suited for either career.

Technology Applications

20. **Online career assessments.** Use such online self-assessments as the *Skills Profiler, Interest Profiler,* or *Work Importance Locator* on the CareerOneStop (www.careerinfonet.org) and O*NET (www.onetcenter.org) Web sites. Take the assessments. Then evaluate how these assessments can help you locate a career that matches your skills and interests.

21. **Contrast career requirements.** Use the Internet to contrast the educational requirements for an interior designer versus an architect. What is different about their job responsibilities and expertise? Find the answers by searching such professional association Web sites as the American Society of Interior Designers (ASID) (www.asid.org) and the American Institute of Architects (AIA) (www.aia.org). Write a summary of your findings to share with the class.

22. **Internet research.** Search the Internet for three sources of information about the job requirements for a housing or interior design position you might pursue. Use one or more references from the U. S. Department of Labor. Investigate the salary potential and job outlook for the profession. Is demand for the career increasing or declining? Summarize your findings and cite your sources.

Design Practice

23. **Class design project.** Presume your school administrator is designating a new 30 ft. by 30 ft. space in the school media center as a career resource center. The administrator has requested that your housing and interior design class submit a proposal for the space arrangement and interior design of the space. Complete all necessary parts of the *design process.* Along with a written description of the program, your class will need to submit a CADD floor plan along with a design presentation board showing photos or samples for the following: wall, floor, and window treatments; furniture and storage options; and equipment required for career research. Once the project design is complete, present it to the school administrator.

24. **Portfolio.** A portfolio showcases your work and abilities and is essential to ultimately finding meaningful employment in your chosen career. An *introduction letter* is an important part of a portfolio. Based on your experiences and accomplishments during this course, write a letter of introduction that offers a short description of who you are and your experiences, abilities, and goals. Use a computer with word-processing software to neatly type and print your letter. Keep your letter to one page or less. Have your instructor or another experienced person proofread your letter. As you gain education and experience, periodically update your letter. Remember, a career portfolio is ever-evolving.

Careers Related to Housing and Interiors

As you have studied the various aspects related to housing and interior design, you may have discovered your interests and skills fall into many career pathways. To narrow your career path and develop a career plan for the future, complete the FCCLA *Career Investigation* STAR Event. See the FCCLA *STAR Events Manual* on the Web (www.fcclainc.org) for event details. See your adviser for information as needed.

CHAPTER 25

Preparing for Career Success

Terms to Learn

résumé
reference
punctual
self-motivation
attitude
verbal communication
nonverbal communication
ethical behavior
team
leadership
conflict
negotiation

Chapter Objectives

- summarize the process of applying for employment, including writing a résumé, preparing an application, and interviewing for a position.

- identify the skills, attitudes, and behaviors important for maintaining a job and attaining career success.

- demonstrate appropriate communication skills to use in the workplace.

- summarize the procedure for leaving a job.

Reading with Purpose

Fold a sheet of notebook paper in half lengthwise before you begin to read the chapter. In the left column, write the chapter headings. In the right column, right a question you have about the topic of each heading. Then read the chapter. Note the answers to your questions while you read.

When you find an employer or specific position that attracts your attention, quickly express your interest. You will need to apply for the job in writing. If the employer wants to learn more about your qualifications, you will receive an invitation for an interview.

Applying for a Position

When you are ready to apply for employment, you will need to know the appropriate steps to take. Having a well-prepared résumé is an important first step. You will need to organize and update your portfolio. Knowing how to write an acceptable letter of application is another goal. Finally, you will want to practice your interviewing techniques.

Your Résumé

A **résumé** is a brief outline of your education, work experience, and other qualifications for work. A well-written résumé can help you get an interview. You will need to include several sections on your résumé. An example appears in 25-1. Make sure that your résumé is precise and without errors. Print your résumé on high-quality, neutral-colored paper (white, gray, or cream colors). Use your printed résumé when an employer requests a résumé sent via traditional mail.

LINK TO SCIENCE & TECHNOLOGY

Tips for Applying Online

Employers and many online job boards have varying requirements for posting résumés to their Web sites. Here are a few general tips for posting your electronic résumé.

- Acquire an e-mail address to use specifically for your job search and use it on your résumé. Choose an appropriate e-mail name. Using an inappropriate or "cutesy" e-mail name may indicate to an employer that you are a less-than-serious job seeker.

- Alter some of the contact information on your résumé to use it electronically. To keep your information out of the hands of cyber criminals, avoid using your home address and telephone number. Instead, acquire a post office box address and buy a prepaid or "pay as you go" cellular phone. Use these numbers on your electronic résumé. Do not put your social security number on your résumé. If an employer shows interest in hiring you, at that time you may need to give your social security number.

- Read the privacy policies of online job boards to which you want to post your résumé. Some reserve the right to sell your personal identifiable information. Others promise never to do so.

- Choose several online job boards that seem to fit your criteria for meaningful employment and post your résumé to them.

- Consider removing your résumé from job-search sites once you find meaningful employment. Some employers may check to see if a résumé is still online once a person is on the job. The employer may want to know why he or she is still "looking" for employment.

Résumé

Sarah H. Johnston
328 Weston Boulevard
Greensboro, North Carolina 27405

EMPLOYMENT OBJECTIVE

A position assisting an interior designer using my computer and art skills in a design studio

EDUCATION

Page High School, graduating June 2011
Followed the Design/Business programs
G.P.A.: 3.5/4.0

RELATED COURSES

- Four years of art classes
- Family and consumer sciences course in housing and interior design
- Computer-aided drafting design (CADD) course from Guilford Technical Community College, Summer 2010 (Received special permission to enroll)

WORK HISTORY

Framing specialist—September 2010 to present
    The Art Shop, Greensboro, NC
Salesclerk—May 2009 to August 2010
    Amy's Upholstery Fabric Shop, Greensboro, NC

HONORS AND ACTIVITIES

Vice President, Family, Career, and Community Leaders of America local
    chapter, 2010-2011
Second place winner in School District's house plans design contest, November 2010
First place winner in School District's still art competition, April 2009

COMMUNITY SERVICE

Habitat for Humanity volunteer, Spring 2011
Arts and Craft Fair for Seniors organizer, Greensboro Community Center,
    February 2010
School Literacy Program volunteer, October 2008 to March 2009
Youth Group soup kitchen volunteer, July 2007 to August 2008

SPECIAL INTERESTS

Interior design (particularly kitchen design), computer design software, sketching

REFERENCES

Available upon request.

25-1
A résumé provides a quick way for employers to learn about the applicant.

Some employers request an electronic résumé that is sent via e-mail or posted to the employer's job site. You can also post an electronic résumé to a number of online job-search sites. To create one, save your résumé as "text only" without any formatting. Then review the text only résumé to make sure lines and headers break properly. Be sure to save this in a separate file from your formatted résumé. Employers may use the electronic file to search for key terms that match their descriptions of an ideal job candidate.

Along with the résumé, you need to develop a list of references. A **reference** is an individual who will provide important information about you to a prospective employer. A reference can be a teacher, school official, previous employer, or any other adult outside your family who knows you well.

You will need at least three references. Always get permission from each person to use his or her name as a reference before actually doing so. Your list of references, along with their titles, phone numbers, and addresses, should be kept private. Share this list only with an employer who has interviewed you and asks for your references.

You can have your references write *letters of recommendation* for you. These give an employer a more in-depth look at your skills. Choose people who know you well. Make sure you choose references who are good writers, since they will be representing you. Ask as many people as possible. Then you can choose the best letters to submit to employers.

Your Portfolio

A well-developed, professional-looking portfolio can help you get a job. A portfolio is a collection of items that show your special achievements and accomplishments. The portfolio includes examples of your work that emphasize your skills, talents, and knowledge.

Items to include in the portfolio are your résumé, samples of your best work, and letters of recommendation. If you have a news article about any of your accomplishments, be sure to highlight your name. Also include reports of special projects you completed and any awards you received. Organize the portfolio logically and place it in an attractive binder.

Letter of Application

The letter of application is often the first contact you have with a potential employer. It can make a lasting impression. It should be neat and follow a standard form for business letters. The paper should be ivory, white, or a neutral color and free of smudges and mistakes. Use a standard font to give the letter a professional look. Be sure to check spelling and punctuation. Have several people read the letter and offer advice for improving it. You should mail your résumé with your letter of application.

A sample letter of application appears in 25-2. It is a good example to use in response to a job ad. The letter should be brief and to the point. It should include the following items:

- title of the job you seek
- where you heard about the job
- your strengths, skills, and abilities for the job
- reasons you should be considered for the job
- when you are available to begin work
- request for an interview

Job Application Forms

A prospective employer may ask you to complete a job application form before having an interview. The job application form highlights the information the employer needs to know about you, your education, and your prior work experience. Employers often use these forms to screen applicants

Letter of Application

328 Weston Boulevard
Greensboro, NC 27405
April 30, 2011

Ms. Cynthia Dawson
Interior Designer
Dawson Design Studio
1359 Lassiter Place
Greensboro, NC 27401

Dear Ms. Dawson:

Mrs. Julia McDowell of The Art Shop told me about your need for part-time employees with computer-aided drafting and design (CADD) skills. I am both qualified and interested in securing a drafting position with your studio.

Having completed a course in housing and interior design at Page High school, I am familiar with floor plan design and arrangement. I also successfully finished a course in computer-aided drafting and design at Guilford Technical Community College during the summer. As a result, I am skilled in using CADD and have a basic understanding of housing and interior design.

Attached is my résumé for your consideration. I will be glad to supply further information and a portfolio of my work in an interview.

Until my graduation on June 5, I am available daily after 4:30 p.m. for an interview. After that, I am available anytime during the day at your convenience. I can be reached at home at (336) 555-2952. I look forward to hearing from you.

Sincerely,

Sarah H. Johnston

Sarah H. Johnston

25-2
Potential employers will know your interests and qualifications from your letter of application.

for the skills needed on the job. You might complete a form in a personnel or employment office. Sometimes you may get the form by mail.

The appearance of the application form can give an employer the first opinion about you. Fill out the form accurately, completely, and neatly. How well you accomplish that can determine whether you get the job. When asked about salary, write *open* or *negotiable*. This means you are willing to consider offers.

Be sure to send or give the form to the correct person. The name of the correct person often appears on the form. Tips for completing the job application appear in 25-3.

Online Application Forms

Many employers now request electronic applications, either through their company Web sites or independent job-search Web sites. When filling out an online application, it is extremely important to include key terms for which the employer may search. This will help you stand out from the many other applications the employer will receive.

When preparing your application, be sure to save it in the appropriate format. If a preferred format is not given, it is best to save the application in document file format or pdf file format. This will enable the employer to find specific search terms in your document. Be sure to complete all the fields of the application. Many job-search sites have sample forms on which you can practice before attempting a real application.

The Job Interview

The interview gives you the opportunity to learn more about a company and to convince the employer that you are the best person for the position. The employer wants to know if you have the skills needed for the job. Adequate preparation is essential for making a lasting, positive impression. Here are some ways to prepare for the interview.

- **Research the employer and the job.** Know the mission of the employer and specifics about the job. Also, try to learn what the company looks for when hiring new employees.

- **Be prepared to answer questions.** Go over the list in 25-4 and prepare answers for each.

- **List questions you want answered.** For example, do you want to know if there is on-the-job training? opportunities for advancement?

25-3
Take your time when you fill out a job application form and follow these tips.

Completing a Job Application Form

- Look over the form to see what information it seeks. How much space is there for writing responses? Which questions pertain to you?

- Read the directions and follow them carefully. Usually applicants are asked to print, using a pen with dark ink.

- Bring your résumé, list of references, and other important data with you so you have all important information at your fingertips. Never write down guesses, only facts.

- Think through your responses first so you can write them concisely.

- When questions do not apply to you, write *N/A*, which means *not applicable*.

- Request a new form if you make a mess. There is no penalty for filling out another form, but you may be rejected if you turn in a sloppy one.

- Review the form one last time to make sure you replied to every question and filled every space.

Interview Questions
• What type of work do you prefer?
• What do you see yourself doing in 10 years?
• What in particular attracted you to this position?
• Why would you like to work for this organization?
• What accomplishments have you had that show your ability to handle this type of job?
• What are your greatest weaknesses?
• Do you believe your grades give a good indication of the type of work you do?
• What did you like most about your last job or work experience? least?
• Why did you leave your previous job?
• Is there any negative information in your past that would affect your employment with this company?
• Why do you feel you are the most qualified person for the job?

25-4
Answer these questions to prepare yourself for a job interview.

- **List the materials you plan to take.** This seems simple enough. However, if you wait to grab items at the last minute, you will likely forget something important.

- **Decide what to wear.** Dress appropriately, usually one step above what is worn by your future coworkers. For instance, casual clothing is acceptable for individuals who will do manual labor or wear a company uniform. If the job involves greeting the public in an office environment, a suit is more appropriate. Always appear neat and clean.

- **Practice the interview.** Have a friend or family member interview you in front of a mirror until you are happy with your responses.

- **Know where to go for the interview.** Verify the address of the interview location by checking the site beforehand, if possible. Plan to arrive ready for the interview at least 10 minutes early.

Good preparation will make you feel more confident and comfortable during the interview. Be polite, friendly, and cheerful during the process. Use a firm handshake. Maintain eye contact at all times. Answer all questions carefully and as completely as you can. Be honest about your abilities. Avoid chewing gum and fidgeting. Also be aware of questions you legally do not have to answer, such as those related to age, marital status, religion, or family background.

A prospective employer may ask you to take employee tests. Some employers administer tests to job candidates to measure their knowledge or skill level under stress. Since all employers support a drug-free workplace, most will likely require you to take a drug test if hired. You can ask those who have completed similar tests what to expect.

After the interview, send a letter to the employer within 24 hours, thanking him or her for the interview. If you get a job offer, respond to it quickly. If you do not receive an offer after several interviews, evaluate your interview techniques and seek ways to improve them.

Evaluating Job Offers

When considering a job offer or comparing two or more positions, you should explore the following work factors:

HEALTH/SAFETY

Discrimination in the Workplace

Federal and state laws protect workers from discrimination because of their race, color, religion, gender (including pregnancy), national origin, age, or disability. Federal laws cover businesses with 15 or more employees. However, the laws in many states cover more businesses and prohibit harassment based on other characteristics.

Federal laws that deal with discrimination and harassment include the following:

- The Fair Labor Standards Act (FLSA) of 1938 regulates minimum wage, overtime pay, and child labor. It is updated each time the minimum wage is raised. This law limits the hours that a child under the age of 16 may work.

- The Equal Pay Act of 1963 requires that men and women receive the same pay for jobs with the same requirements and responsibilities. Exceptions are made if a person gets a pay raise based on seniority or merit.

- The 1964 Civil Rights Act bans employment discrimination based on race, color, religion, sex, or national origin. This law also created the Equal Employment Opportunity Commission (EEOC).

- The Age Discrimination in Employment Act of 1967 bans discrimination against workers age 40 and older. The Older Workers Benefit Protection Act of 1990 allows workers to sue employers over age discrimination. These laws are both important as the aging population continues to grow.

- The Immigration Reform and Control Act of 1986 prohibits the discrimination of U.S. citizens born outside the United States. The Immigration Act of 1990 made it more difficult for noncitizens to get employment in the U.S.

- The Americans with Disabilities Act of 1990 prohibits discrimination against people with disabilities. As long as a person's disability does not interfere with the ability to do the job, he or she must be considered for the position. This law also requires places of employment to be physically accessible to people with disabilities.

Many of these laws also cover issues that do not impact the workplace. To read more about them, check out the EEOC's Web site at www.eeoc.gov or the U.S. Department of Labor's Web site at www.dol.gov.

- **Physical surroundings.** Where is your workspace located? Is the atmosphere conducive to your style of working? Is parking provided? Is public transportation close by?

- **Work schedule.** Will the workdays and work hours mesh with your lifestyle? Is occasional overtime work required?

- **Income and benefits.** Is the proposed salary fair? Will you receive benefits that are just as valuable as extra income? How much sick leave is granted during the year? Is personal or emergency leave available? What is the vacation leave policy? Are there medical and life insurance benefits? Is there a credit union? Will the company pay tuition for college courses or special programs related to your job? See 25-5. Is a cafeteria on the premises? Does it offer food to employees at reduced cost?

25-5
If your goal is to obtain more education while working full-time, look for an employer that reimburses all or part of your higher education costs.

- **Job obligations.** Will you be expected to join a union or other professional organization? If so, what are the costs? Will you be expected to attend meetings after work?

- **Advancement potential.** Is there opportunity for advancement? After demonstrating good performance, how soon can you seek a position with more responsibilities? Before you can advance, are there special expectations such as a higher degree? Are training programs provided?

Talking about advancement requires considerable diplomacy. After all, you should not appear too eager to leave the job for which you are interviewing. Many employers would expect a new employee to remain at least one year at that job. If you place undue emphasis on getting some other job, you will appear uninterested in the current opening.

You may also want to explore the transportation options to and from work. Can you get to work in reasonable time by taking public transportation? Are carpools available? How much effort it takes to get to work will greatly affect your satisfaction with the job.

Succeeding in the Workplace

After securing employment, adjusting to your new duties and responsibilities will occupy your first few weeks. Your supervisor and coworkers will help you learn the routine. An introduction to company policies and procedures as well as the special safety rules that all employees must know is common for new employees.

While your coworkers will be watching what you do, they will also pay attention to "how you work." How to behave in the workplace is an important lesson all employees should learn. Making an effort to do your best will help you succeed.

Health and Hygiene

As an employee, you are a representative of your company. Therefore, your employer expects you to be neat and clean on the job. Taking care of yourself gives the impression that you want people to view you as a professional.

Your daily grooming habits will consist of bathing or showering, using an antiperspirant, and putting on clean clothes. Regularly brushing your teeth and using mouthwash will promote healthy teeth and fresh breath. Keep your hair clean and styled in a way that will not be distracting.

Employers expect workers to dress appropriately. Many places of work have a dress code. If your workplace does not, use common sense and avoid extremes. Refrain from wearing garments that are revealing or have inappropriate pictures or sayings. Some employers have rules requiring that tattoos or piercings beyond pierced ears remain covered. Good appearance is especially important for employees who have frequent face-to-face contact with customers.

Work Habits

Employers want employees who are punctual, dependable, and responsible. They want their employees to be capable of taking initiative and working independently. Other desirable employee qualities include organization, accuracy, and efficiency.

A **punctual** employee is always prompt and on time. This means not only when the workday starts, but also when returning from breaks and lunches. Being dependable means that people can rely on you to fulfill your word and meet your deadlines. If you are not well, be sure to call in and let the employer know right away. If there are reasons you cannot be at work, discuss this with your employer and work out an alternate arrangement. Many people have lost jobs by not checking with their supervisor about time off.

Taking *initiative* means that you start activities on your own without being told. When you finish one task, you do not wait to hear what to do next. Individuals who take initiative need much less supervision. They have **self-motivation**, or an inner urge to perform well. Generally, this motivation will drive you to set goals and accomplish them. All these qualities together show that you are capable of working *independently*.

You are expected to be as accurate and error-free as possible in all that you do. This is why you were hired. Complete your work with precision and double-check it to assure accuracy. See 25-6. Your coworkers depend on the careful completion of your tasks.

Time Management

A good employee knows how to manage time wisely. This includes ability to prioritize assignments and complete them in a timely fashion. It also involves not wasting time. Time-wasting behaviors include visiting with coworkers, making personal phone calls, texting, sending e-mails, or doing other nonwork activities during work hours.

While it is important to complete all your work thoroughly, you must also be able to gauge which assignments are most important. Avoid putting excessive efforts into minor assignments when crucial matters require your attention. Even though you are still accomplishing work, this is another way of wasting of time.

25-6
Expect to have your work carefully scrutinized, especially during your first few months on the job.

Attitude on the Job

Your attitude can often determine the success you have on your job. Your **attitude** is your outlook on life. It is reflected by how you react to the events and people around you. A smile and courteous behavior can make customers and fellow employees feel good about themselves and you. Clients and customers prefer to do business in friendly environments. Being friendly may take some effort on your part, but it does pay off.

Enthusiasm spreads easily from one person to another. Usually, enthusiasm means a person enjoys what he or she is doing. In a sales environment, enthusiasm increases sales. In an office, enthusiasm builds a team spirit for working together.

People who do a good job feel pride in their work. They feel a sense of accomplishment and a desire to achieve more. This attitude can inspire others as well.

Professional Behavior

You will be expected to behave professionally on the job. This includes showing respect for your boss and coworkers. Limit personal conversations and phone calls to break times or lunch. Act courteously; remember that others are focusing on their work. Interruptions can cause them to lose concentration.

Part of behaving professionally is responding appropriately to *constructive criticism*. Every employee, no matter how knowledgeable or experienced, can improve his or her performance. If you receive criticism from a supervisor or coworker, do not be offended. Instead, use the feedback to improve yourself. The more you improve, the more successful you will be in your work.

Decision Making and Problem Solving

Employers value workers who have the ability to make sound decisions. You already read "Using Decision-Making Skills" in an earlier chapter. This process applies in the workplace as well as other aspects of life. The process will help you identify the issue, identify possible solutions, make a decision, implement the decision, and evaluate the results.

Having ability to solve problems on the job shows an employer that you are able to handle more responsibility. Solving problems as a group can strengthen camaraderie and help employees feel more pride in their work.

The ability to make decisions and solve problems requires *critical-thinking skills*. These are higher-level skills that enable you to think beyond the obvious. You learn to interpret information and make judgments. Supervisors appreciate employees who can analyze problems and think of workable solutions.

Communication Skills

Communicating effectively with others is important for job success. Being a good communicator means that you can share information well with others. It also means you are a good listener.

Good communication is central to a smooth operation of any business. Communication is the process of exchanging ideas, thoughts, or information. Poor communications is costly to an employer, as when time is lost because an order was entered incorrectly. Poor communication can result in lost customers, too.

Types of Communication

The primary forms of communications are verbal and nonverbal. **Verbal communication** involves speaking, listening, and writing. **Nonverbal communication** is the sending and receiving of messages without the use of words. It involves *body language*, which includes the expression on your face and your body posture.

Listening is an important part of communication. If you do not understand, be sure to ask questions. Also give feedback to let others know you understand them and are interested in what they have to say. Leaning forward while a person is talking signals interest and keen listening. Slouching back in a chair and yawning give the opposite signal—that you are bored and uninterested.

The message you convey in telephone communication involves your promptness, tone of voice, and attitude. Answering the phone quickly with a pleasant voice conveys a positive image for the company. See 25-7. Learning to obtain accurate information from the caller without interrupting that person's message is important.

Communication tools have advanced with the development of new technologies. To be an effective employee, you need to know how to communicate well with the common tools of your workplace. For example, when sending e-mail communications, remember to think through each message as you would before sending a postal letter. Often messages are sent quickly without thought of how the recipient may interpret them. The same is true of voicemail.

The development of good communication skills is an ongoing process. Attending communication workshops and practicing often can keep your skills sharp. You should periodically give yourself a communications checkup by asking your supervisor to suggest areas that need improvement.

Customer Relations Skills

Working with customers takes special communication skills. The most important aspect of customer relations is always remaining courteous. This may also require patience in some situations. When customers visit your business, you want them to have the best possible service and to leave happy. Remember that your behavior and skills at handling customers can determine if the customer will return to your business. The customer may spread the word about his or her experience with you to other potential customers. Make sure your customers know you appreciate their business.

Customer relations may also involve problem solving. If a customer needs help, you must provide answers as quickly and accurately as possible while remaining pleasant and polite. When a situation becomes stressful, you must be able to control your own level of stress without letting it affect your performance. At the same time, you must be able to lessen the customer's stress and attempt to eliminate its source.

Ethical Workplace Behavior

Ethical behavior on the job means conforming to accepted standards of fairness and good conduct. It is based

25-7
When a caller leaves a message, be sure to repeat that person's request before hanging up to make sure you caught all the information.

on a person's sense of what is right to do. Individuals and society as a whole regard ethical behavior as highly important. Integrity, confidentiality, and honesty are crucial aspects of ethical workplace behavior. *Integrity* is firmly following your moral beliefs. See *Appendix C—ASID Code of Ethics and Professional Conduct* for more information about ethical standards for interior designers.

Unfortunately, employee theft is a major problem at some companies. The theft can range from carrying office supplies home to stealing money or expensive equipment. Company policies are in place to address these concerns. In cases of criminal or serious behavior, people may lose their jobs. If proven, the charge of criminal behavior stays on the employee's record. Such an employee will have a difficult time finding another job.

Interpersonal Skills

Interpersonal skills involve interacting with others. Some workplace activities that involve these skills include teaching others, leading, negotiating, and working as a member of a team. Getting along well with others can require great effort on your part, but it is essential for accomplishing your employer's goals.

Teamwork

Employers seek employees who can effectively serve as good team members. Due to the nature of most work today, teamwork is necessary. A **team** is a small group of people working together for a common purpose. Often cooperation requires flexibility and willingness to try new ways to get things done. See 25-8. If someone is uncooperative, it takes longer to accomplish the tasks. When people do not get along, strained relationships may occur, which get in the way of finishing the tasks.

25-8
When several people pool their ideas, the result is often better than any one person could accomplish.

A big advantage of a team is its ability to develop plans and complete work faster than individuals working alone. In contrast, a team usually takes longer to reach a decision than an individual worker does. Team members need some time before they become comfortable with one another and function as a unit. You will be more desirable as an employee if you know how to be a team player.

Team development goes through various stages. In the beginning, people are excited about being on a team. Later, disagreements may replace harmony. The good result of this is people express themselves and learn to trust the other team members. Eventually leaders emerge and the team develops a unique pattern of interaction and goal attainment. Finally, the team becomes very productive and performs at its highest level. It takes time and a genuine desire to work together to build a strong team.

Creative ideas often develop from building on another person's idea. Honesty and openness are essential. Also, trying to understand the ideas of others before trying to get others to understand your ideas is an effective skill to develop.

Leadership

All careers require leadership skills. **Leadership** is the ability to guide and motivate others to complete tasks or achieve goals. It involves communicating well with others, accepting responsibility, and making decisions with confidence. Those employees with leadership skills are most likely to be promoted to higher levels.

Leaders often seem to carry the most responsibility of a group. Other group members look to them for answers and direction. The most important role of leaders is to keep the team advancing toward its goal. Leaders do this by inspiring their groups and providing the motivation to keep everyone working together.

Good leaders encourage teamwork, because a team that is working together well is more likely to reach goals. They listen to the opinions of others and make sure all team members are included in projects. Leaders also want to set a good example by doing a fair share of the work. In these ways, leaders cultivate a sense of harmony in the group.

Belonging to Organizations

Leading others may not be easy for some people, but everyone can improve their leadership skills with practice. Becoming involved in a school club or organization can help. Taking a role as an officer or a committee chair will give you even more practice.

Belonging to an organization can also help you develop your teamwork skills. You will learn how to work well in a group as you plan events, create projects, and accomplish goals together.

Conflict Management

When you work with others, disagreements are likely to occur. More serious disagreements are called conflict. **Conflict** is a hostile situation resulting from opposing views. It is important to know how to handle conflict to prevent it from becoming a destructive force in the workplace. This is called *conflict management*. A team leader has a special responsibility to prevent conflict among the team members. Several steps can be followed in managing conflict, 25-9.

25-9
These steps can help you manage workplace conflicts.

Conflict Management

Know When to Intervene

The time to intervene is when the team's productivity slows, several members have serious disagreements, and one or more members are obviously unhappy.

Address the Conflict

Acknowledge the conflict with those involved using an "I" approach. "You" statements tend to make people defensive.

Identify the Source of the Conflict

State the problem as clearly as possible, seeking recognition that a problem exists, not a simple misunderstanding.

Identify Possible Solutions

It is important that people involved in the conflict develop ideas for solving it. Individuals who are not involved should not participate in the discussion.

Implement and Evaluate

Make sure everyone understands his and her role in carrying out the agreed-upon solution. Check periodically to monitor the progress and the return to normal teamwork.

Sometimes the cause of a conflict is not so simple or easily understood. Use a positive approach and try to understand the problem from the other's point of view. Avoid jumping to conclusions and making snap judgments. Treat others with respect and in the same way you would like to be treated. Explore positive and negative aspects of each possible solution. If progress falls short of expectations, bring the parties back together and repeat the process. Many disagreements in the workplace can lead to productive change.

Negotiation

Often there are times when employees and employers must negotiate on a task or work-related issue. **Negotiation** is the process of agreeing to an issue that requires all parties to give and take. The goal is a "win-win" solution in which both parties get some or all of what they are seeking.

Negotiation begins with trying to understand the other party's interests.

Possible solutions that meet their mutual concerns can be developed. Often the best solution becomes clear when both parties have ample time to explain what they are trying to accomplish.

Staying Safety Conscious

Safety on the job is everyone's responsibility. Many workplace accidents occur because of careless behavior. Often poor attitudes can cause unsafe behavior, too.

Practicing good safety habits is essential for preventing accidents and injuries on the job. A healthy worker is more alert and less likely to make accident-prone mistakes. Knowing how to use machines and tools and lift properly is the responsibility of both the employer and employees, 25-10. Wearing protective clothing and using safety equipment correctly helps keep workers safe. See 25-11. Your employer will emphasize the safety practices that employees must follow in your workplace.

25-10
Always follow proper lifting procedures to reduce strain on your back.

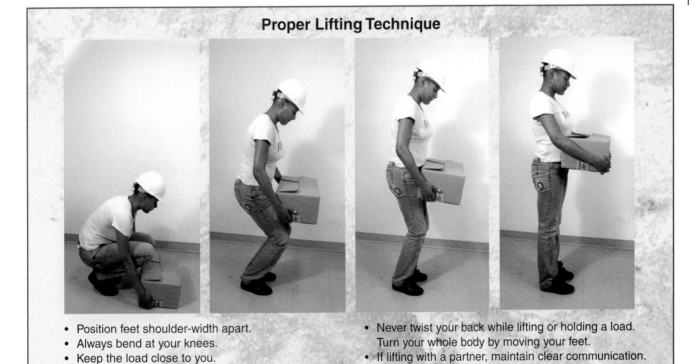

Proper Lifting Technique

- Position feet shoulder-width apart.
- Always bend at your knees.
- Keep the load close to you.
- Lift the load smoothly without any sudden movements.

- Never twist your back while lifting or holding a load. Turn your whole body by moving your feet.
- If lifting with a partner, maintain clear communication.

25-11
Because this surveyor works near construction and traffic, he must wear a hardhat and an orange-colored vest.

The government agency that promotes safety in the workplace is the Occupational Safety and Health Administration (OSHA). You will be required to follow the specific OSHA regulations that apply to your workplace.

Leaving a Job

More money, more responsibility, and better benefits are some of the reasons for leaving a job. There are others, too, but all job departures need to be handled in a way that is considerate of the employer. You should try

HEALTH/SAFETY

Material Safety Data Sheets (MSDS)

About 32 million people work where they may be exposed to potentially hazardous materials and chemicals, according to the U.S. Occupational Safety and Health Administration (OSHA). Short- or long-term exposure to these substances can cause illness, injury, and even death. OSHA's Hazard Communication Standard requires employers to notify employees about these hazards and how to protect themselves. One important element of this standard requires that employees have easy access to a material safety data sheet (MSDS) for any hazardous chemical and material in their workplace.

Included in a MSDS form are the following in English:

- Common names of a substance and name of its hazardous ingredient(s) with the physical and chemical characteristics
- Fire and explosion hazards
- Known health effects and exposure limits
- Signs and symptoms of exposure, medical conditions aggravated by exposure
- Emergency and first-aid procedures to treat those exposed
- Precautions for safe handling and disposal, including use of protective clothing and equipment

More than a half-million products have an MSDS form. The producers of the materials and chemicals usually prepare and distribute these forms to their customers. Employers receiving an MSDS must ensure that employees can access a paper or online copy. If an employer does not receive an MSDS form, the employer must request it from the supplier or importer.

In case of accidents, the forms are given to emergency responders and physicians. The U.S. Environmental Protection Agency and state and local governments also require submission of all MSDS forms to local fire departments and to state and local emergency and response agencies. State and local laws may have stricter requirements.

Although there is no standard format for the MSDS, OSHA provides a sample (Form 174) on its Web site. For an informational booklet about OSHA's Hazard Communication Guidelines, go to the OSHA Web site (www.osha.gov).

not to leave your job with noticeable anger and hostility. Employers know that employees will not stay forever. However, they dislike a too-short notice, especially during a busy season.

When you make the decision to leave a job, let the employer know in writing by giving at least a two-week notice. It would be helpful to give a longer notice if you can. A letter of resignation should state your reason for leaving and the date you expect to leave. See 25-12. The letter allows the employer to begin looking for your replacement. Perhaps there will be enough time to hire someone who can work with you during your final days. Many people have found that a past employer became their greatest ally when they needed a good reference for a future position.

Letter of Resignation

118 Thompson Boulevard
Atlanta, Georgia 30303
June 1, 2011

Mr. John Alston
Alston Home Builders, Inc.
9923 Construction Avenue
Atlanta, Georgia 30303

Dear Mr. Alston:

I plan to leave Alston Home Builders, Inc., effective July 15, 2011. I thoroughly enjoyed my work here and thank you for the excellent training I received. I especially appreciate the opportunity you gave me to work "up the ranks" and demonstrate my ability as an assistant construction manager.

I now plan to further my education and enter the engineering program at Georgia Tech University this fall. Thank you in advance for helping me make a smooth transition in the coming weeks.

Sincerely,

Rick Sampson
Rick Sampson

25-12
A letter of resignation should state your reason for leaving and your last day of work.

Summary

Effective workplace practices are essential for getting and maintaining a job. Getting the job involves developing a résumé, portfolio, and letter of application; completing an application form; and interviewing.

Maintaining the job involves being clean and neat on the job, having good work habits, and using effective time management. A positive attitude and professional behavior on the job are also essential. Developing your decision-making, communication, and interpersonal skills can help you succeed. Having ethics and integrity will help you maintain good conduct. Staying safety conscious will help you prevent workplace accidents.

Terminating the job has procedures to follow, too, including notifying the employer in writing. Leaving a job properly can help guarantee that your employer will give you good references in the future.

Review the Facts

1. Briefly identify the categories of information that a résumé outlines.

2. What is the difference between a résumé and an electronic résumé?

3. List three examples of people who would make good references for a job applicant.

4. What items should be included in a letter of application?

5. What does it mean when an applicant writes *open* or *negotiable* for salary on a job application?

6. List five steps to take to prepare for a successful interview.

7. List five work factors you should explore when evaluating job offers.

8. Why is appearance important to work success?

9. What is the difference between verbal and nonverbal communication?

10. What is leadership?

11. What are the steps of conflict management?

12. What is the goal of negotiation?

13. What is the proper procedure for leaving a job?

Think Critically

14. **Compare and contrast.** Think about how planning and presenting an interior design is similar to and different from preparing yourself for an interview with an interior design firm. Compare and contrast the personal preparations you need to make for the interview with the design process applications you make when preparing a design for a client.

15. **Draw conclusions.** Have you ever had an informal communication experience in which you felt totally misunderstood? How could such experiences impact workplace communication? Draw conclusions about ways to prevent such misunderstandings.

16. **Recognize ethics.** In teams, brainstorm a list of ethical behaviors you have observed in real life. What characteristics help you and your team members recognize these behaviors as ethical? How do ethical behaviors in non-work situations transfer to workplace behaviors?

Community Links

17. **Job shadow.** Select a local employer that offers jobs you might want to pursue as part of your housing and interior design career. Make arrangements with the employer and your school to "shadow" one of the employees. During your job-shadowing experience, be sure to discuss issues the employee feels are essential for career success. Write a summary of your experience.

18. **Application practice.** Obtain an employment application from a local employer or your instructor. Read the application thoroughly. Make a copy of the application. Then practice filling out the application in a neat and precise manner. Have your instructor critique your application for areas that require improvement.

19. **Interview practice.** Invite one or more community employers in the area of housing and interior design to conduct mock interviews with the members of your class. Video-record the interviews. Watch and critique the recording of your personal interview. What were your interview strengths and weaknesses? What are some actions you can take to strengthen your interviewing skills? What advice did the interviewer have for improving your skills? Write a summary of your experience.

20. **Incident reporting.** Talk with the manager of a local interior design firm or home improvement store about company procedures for reporting accident, safety, and security incidents. If possible, obtain samples of forms used for reporting such incidents. Then, with a classmate, role-play a scenario for the class in which an employee is talking with his or her manager about an accident. Demonstrate the procedure to follow when reporting such incidents.

Academic Connections

21. **Reading.** Using the CareerOneStop Web site (www.careeronestop.org) read about *job interviews* and *informational interviews.* What are the similarities and differences between the two types of interviews? Why is preparation for both essential to finding meaningful employment? Write a summary of your findings to share with the class.

22. **Writing.** Review the employment listings in your local newspaper or online job board for jobs related to housing and interior design. Choose one of the listings and write an engaging letter of application for a position you may be qualified to fill. Follow the chapter guidelines for writing such letters. Have your instructor or another trusted adult with experience critique your letter. Make any corrections and save a copy of your letter to use as a guide in the future.

Technology Applications

23. **Résumé research.** Search the Internet for examples of different types of résumés that can be used when applying for a job. Print an example of each. Analyze the similarities and differences among the documents. Then write a summary indicating when you might use each type of résumé in applying for employment related to housing and interior design.

24. **Résumés and references.** Use a computer and word-processing software to create your résumé and reference list. Be sure to include relevant educational, work, and volunteer experiences on your résumé. Print a copy of your résumé and save it on a CD or in a folder on your computer. Make a list of people you would like to serve as references. Contact these individuals to see if they are willing to be your references. Verify their contact information. Then prepare a list to give to potential employers.

25. **Electronic résumés and applications.** Use reliable Internet sources to investigate the proper techniques for posting résumés to online job boards and completing online applications. What changes should you make to your résumé for this application? What key words may be important for an online application for an interior design career? If possible, complete a practice application on a job-search site.

26. **Internet interview quiz.** Search the Internet for opportunities to take free interview quizzes. Take the quizzes and analyze your answers with the recommended responses. Practice until your score reaches at least ninety percent.

27. **Career podcasts.** Locate one or more educational podcasts from a reliable source such as the O*NET Resource Center (www.onetcenter.org). Choose from such topics as career guidance, transferability of skills, creating résumés, or interviewing. Listen to one or more podcasts and write a summary of each to share your findings with the class.

Design Practice

28. **Business card design.** Presume you are an interior designer who is making the transition from working for a design firm to forming your own interior design business. Use your knowledge of the elements and principles of design to create a business card for your new venture.

29. **Presentation interview.** You are a new graduate and have just had your first employment interview with an interior design firm. You have their attention— the interview team liked your enthusiasm and they were impressed with your educational background. They are, however, concerned about your limited client experience. During a second interview, they have asked that you present one of your design projects to the interview team. Practice presenting one of your class projects in preparation for meeting with an interview team.

30. **Portfolio.** Assemble your employment portfolio to use for work-based learning opportunities and post-secondary education applications. Choose an attractive binder or case in which to display your work. Be sure that your portfolio contains the following items: letter of introduction, résumé, references, design project samples (drawings, photos, and materials used) to showcase your abilities to use industry tools. In addition, include any recognition, awards, or honors you have received for your work.

Leadership for Career Success

Do you have the ability to inspire others around you? Do you like to take charge and lead a team toward common goals? Do you strive for new challenges and like learn new things? If you do, you may just have the leadership skills employers look for most.

To further strengthen your leadership abilities, create an FCCLA *Leaders at Work* project that fits your needs in the *Housing and Interior Design* career area. See your adviser for information as needed.

Housing and Related Legislation

Few items affect housing as much as government policy. Even the cost of housing is affected by government controls. Also, the federal government provides supervision and regulation to assure safety in environmental areas. These also affect housing and its occupants, particularly hazardous materials (such as lead-based paint), air and water quality, and conservation of natural resources. Several of the most significant actions that occurred at the federal level are listed here.

1901

The Tenement House Act was passed to improve conditions in tenement houses. It applied to houses already constructed and set standards for building new ones.

1918

The U.S. Housing Corporation was established to provide housing for veterans of war.

1932

The President's Conference on Home Building and Home Ownership discussed the national decline in building and the shrinking availability of mortgage credit. As a result of the Conference, the Federal Home Loan Bank Act of 1932 was passed. This Act established 12 district Federal Home Loan Banks as the framework of a reserve credit organization for home-financing institutions. It failed in its purpose to provide an adequate volume of funds for mortgage credit.

1933

The Home Owners' Loan Act of 1933 established a corporation to refinance the mortgages of distressed home owners. It financed over one million mortgages in three years, investing $3.5 billion in the process. It was considered quite successful.

1934

The Housing Act of 1934 created the Federal Housing Administration (FHA), an agency that still exists today. It also established the Federal Savings and Loan Insurance Corporation to protect deposits. FHA revolutionized home financing methods by making possible lower interest rates and longer amortized mortgage periods. Improvements in housing standards also resulted from the minimum physical property standards set as a basis for FHA participation.

1937

The Housing Act of 1937 started the public housing program with the objective of providing decent, sanitary housing for low-income families. The Act set the principle of basing rental payments on an individual family's ability to pay. It provided for annual subsidy contracts, whereby the federal government pays the difference between costs of managing the project, including debt amortization, and the rental revenues received.

1940

The Lanham Act provided for federal financing of housing for those involved in the war effort. Two million dwelling units were built under this Act during the war.

1942

The National Housing Agency created by executive order was the first attempt to coordinate all federal housing programs.

1946

The Veteran's Emergency Housing Act was passed. It established the VA program for mortgage insurance.

The Farmers Home Administration (now called USDA Rural Development) was created in 1946 in the U.S. Department of Agriculture. This program offers assistance in rural areas to help families obtain housing. Programs include low interest loans and grants to limited-income households and the elderly.

1947

The President's "Reorganization Plan No. 3" created the Housing and Home Finance Agency. The Federal Housing Administration, the Public Housing Administration, and the Home Loan Bank were all brought under the supervision of the Housing Administrator.

1949

Many cities and states tried to deal with run-down, over-populated housing through various renewal efforts. These usually fell short of their goals for lack of money. As a result, the desire for federal assistance to the nation's major cities was posed to Congress. From this experience came the Housing Act of 1949. It developed the now well-known expression of a "decent home and suitable living environment for every American family."

For the first time, the Act permitted land cleared with federal aid to be sold or leased to private developers for residential development. It gave recognition to the fact that private financial resources must be attracted to the housing field to attain the goal of the Act. The 1949 Act became the symbol of the joint effort between public and private interests to decently house the low-income population and to clean and redevelop run-down buildings.

1953

The president established a special committee on government housing policies and programs. This committee's efforts were reflected in the 1954 Housing Act. The objective was to create a total program to prevent housing blight. The committee concluded that federal assistance should be available only to communities willing to undertake a long-range program of slum prevention through sound planning and enforcement of housing and building codes. This became the basis for the "Workable Program."

1954

The Housing Act of 1954 incorporated the many recommendations of the president's special committee, including the "Workable Program." It also established the Urban Planning Assistance Program, sometimes called the 701 Program. It added a great stimulus to public acceptance of the comprehensive plan and the planning process.

The Act also established the concept of rehabilitation, which is the retention and improvement of essentially sound structures in an urban renewal area. It recognized, for the first time, the need for nonresidential urban renewal projects to attack blight in business and industrial areas. This Housing Act also instituted the demonstration grant program, whereby the federal government participated in research-oriented projects.

The 1954 Housing Act was an extremely significant piece of legislation for urban renewal because it focused on the comprehensive goal of urban revitalization rather than the single goal of good housing.

1956

The Housing Act of 1956 established relocation payments for families and businesses, aid for housing for older people, and the General Neighborhood Renewal Program. That program was an urban renewal plan for areas too large for a single project.

1959

The Housing Act of 1959 further extended the urban renewal program and created the Community Renewal Program. This program grew out of the need for comprehensive, long-range planning of a city's renewal activities, both public and private, closely tied to capital financing and land economics. The Act also established special credits for college and university urban renewal projects.

1961

The Housing Act of 1961 shifted more of the financial burden from local communities to the federal government. In cities with populations below 50,000, the federal government paid 75 percent of the net project costs. This reduced the financial burden on cities willing to fight the problems of housing blight. The Act also established the Open-Space Program and the Mass Transportation Program. It greatly liberalized various programs of the Federal Housing Administration.

1964

The Housing Act of 1964 authorized code enforcement of urban renewal projects intended to attack the beginnings of blight in basically sound areas. To reinforce this effort, special low-interest loans for residential rehabilitation were also authorized. The Act also liberalized relocation procedures and aid.

1965

The Housing and Urban Development Act of 1965 authorized the formation of a cabinet-level federal agency, named the U.S. Department of Housing and Urban Development (HUD). The Act approved a variety of new approaches to urban improvement, including grants for the following: neighborhood facilities, public works and facilities, urban beautification, municipal open spaces, and rehabilitation loans to low-income home owners. It set new public housing policies for rent supplements, leased private housing, and the purchase of existing units. The code enforcement "renewal project" of the 1964 Act, having proved unworkable, was revised as an "aid program."

The Older Americans Act of 1965 provided a number of services to aging persons, especially those at risk of losing their independence.

1966

The Demonstration Cities and Metropolitan Development Act of 1966 authorized the Model Cities Program to rebuild or restore extensive blighted areas. The Act stated that physical and social development programs should be coordinated, using local private and governmental resources. The original emphasis on renewal of housing was reasserted.

The Act required the provision of a substantial number of low- and moderate-cost standard housing units in the development of an urban renewal area. This rule did not apply to predominantly nonresidential uses. As incentives for the Model Cities Program and for coordinated metropolitan planning, it authorized supplemental federal funds. Other significant features of the Act included the following:

- "new town" development through FHA financing

- new FHA sales housing program for low-income families

- grants for surveys of structures and sites to determine historical value

- liberalized noncash policy permitting up to 25 percent of the cost of a public building

- authorization of air-rights projects for industrial development

1968

The Housing and Urban Development Act of 1968 was considered the most important piece of housing legislation since the 1949 Act. It added two new programs to house low- and moderate-income families whose incomes were above the level permitted by public housing.

Under the Homeownership for Lower Income Families Program, the government helped pay the home mortgage and mortgage interest of the housing project sponsor. This permitted the sponsor to charge lower rents. Other significant features included the following:

- provisions that relaxed mortgage insurance in urban neighborhoods

- special FHA risk fund for mortgages in deteriorating urban areas

- credit assistance to make low-income families eligible for mortgage insurance

- assistance to private developers of new towns

- creation of a new approach to renewal, known as the Neighborhood Development Program, which provided more flexibility in planning and permitted staged development on a one-year basis

- increased rehabilitation grants from $1,500 to $3,000

- authorization to close out a renewal project when only small parcels of land remain

- aid in alleviating harmful conditions in blighted areas where renewal action was programmed, but immediate action was needed before renewal could be started

The Civil Rights Act of 1968 expanded the Civil Rights Act of 1964 and prohibited discrimination concerning the sale, rental, and financing of housing based on race, religion, national origin, sex, handicap, and family status. Title VIII of the Act is also known as the Fair Housing Act of 1968.

1970

The Housing and Urban Development Act of 1970 extended and amended laws relating to housing and urban development. The Act authorized the establishment of a national urban growth policy to encourage and support orderly growth of populated areas. It gave emphasis to new community and inner city development, encouraging the coordinated effort of state and local governments. Some specific features of the Act include the following:

- provisions for parks, especially in low-income areas

- preservation and restoration of historic and architectural sites

- provisions for curbing urban sprawl and spread of urban blight

700

The Office of Fair Housing and Equal Opportunity established the Federal Equal Housing Opportunity Council. Representatives of 50 federal departments and agencies participated. They coordinated efforts to assure all persons, regardless of race, creed, sex, or national origin, equal and unhindered access to the housing of their choice.

The Clean Air Act was passed to control smoke pollution and provide environmentally sound treatment of solid waste.

1971

The Lead-Based Paint Poisoning Prevention Act was passed in 1971 and amended in 1973. This Act was the first major lead-based legislation and it primarily addressed lead-based paint in federally funded housing. The Act established definitions for lead-based paint and lead poisoning.

1974

The Housing and Community Development Act provided funds that went directly to the general local government. These funds were in the form of community development block grants. They were provided to begin or continue urban renewal or neighborhood development programs. Benefits were directed mainly to low- and moderate-income families. They were assisted in securing decent, safe, and sanitary housing.

The Emergency Housing Act of 1974 authorized HUD to buy $7.75 billion in mortgage loans at below-market interest rates so lenders could offer mortgages at subsidized interest rates. The Act was extended in 1975.

The Real Estate Settlement Procedures Act was designed to give consumers more information about costs related to buying or selling a home.

The Solar Energy Research, Development, and Demonstration Act had two main goals. One was to pursue a vigorous program of research and resource assessment of solar energy as a major source of energy for the nation. The second goal was to provide for the development and demonstration of practical ways of using solar energy on a commercial basis.

The Safe Drinking Water Act of 1974 was enacted to protect public health by regulating the nation's public drinking water supply. Regulations protect against both naturally occurring and man-made contaminants that may be found in drinking water.

1975

The Energy Policy and Conservation Act mandated appliance labeling. The Department of Energy and the Federal Trade Commission jointly oversee the implementation of this Act.

The Emergency Homeowner's Relief Act of 1975 authorized temporary assistance to help defray mortgage payments on homes owned by persons who were temporarily unemployed or underemployed as the result of adverse economic conditions. The Act made it possible for unemployed persons to retain possession of their homes. It was passed because the nation was judged to be in a severe recession with reduced employment opportunities.

The National Housing Act was amended to increase the maximum loan amounts for the purchase of mobile homes.

1976

The Housing Authorization Act of 1976 amended and extended many laws relating to the fields of housing and commercial development.

The Energy Conservation and Production Act required states and localities to adopt Building Energy Performance Standards. Many new energy-saving ideas were encouraged.

An extension of the National Housing Act included $850 million for subsidized housing.

Of that amount, $85 million was reserved for the construction of new public housing. The bill also provided a major increase in funding for a housing program for the elderly.

1977

The Housing and Community Development Act made it easier for people to buy and improve their dwellings. It revised many loan regulations that had become outdated because of inflation. It increased the ceiling for home loans made by federal savings and loan associations. It provided a new system whereby savings and loan associations would have more money available for larger loans. It increased the limit on FHA Title I home improvement loans. It also increased mortgage loan limits for purchases of manufactured houses.

The Department of Energy, the Community Service Act, and the Farmers Home Administration initiated programs for weatherization.

The amended Clean Water Act established a way to regulate discharges of pollutants into U.S. waters. The many important provisions of the Act include the following:

- gave the Environmental Protection Agency (EPA) authority to implement pollution control programs such as setting wastewater standards for industry

- continued EPA's requirement to set water quality standards for all contaminants in surface waters

- made it unlawful for any person to discharge a pollutant into navigable waters, unless a permit was obtained under its provisions

- funded the construction of sewage treatment plants under the construction grants program

- recognized the need for planning to address the critical problems posed by pollution from sources not located at the site

1978

The National Energy Conservation Policy Act was passed to require energy-saving measures nationwide and reduce the country's dependence on oil from other nations. The Act established the following provisions related to housing:

- creation of energy-saving information and services from utility companies to home owners, including the financing of energy-saving improvements

- availability of energy conservation grants and loans for low- to moderate-income families, rural families, the elderly, and people with special needs

- income tax credits through 1984 for home owners on weatherization items and on systems using renewable resources (such as solar, geothermal, and wind energy)

- energy efficiency standards for major home appliances

- increased regulation of electricity and gas rates as well as lower rates during periods of low usage

- The Housing and Community Development Act amended and extended provisions for community projects, especially for people with special needs.

The Consumer Product Safety Commission banned the residential use of lead-based paint.

1979

The Housing and Community Development Act was revised to extend programs and appropriate funds to carry out the initial purpose of the Act. The Act was further revised and extended every year through 1986.

Congress authorized the Office of Technology Assessment to make a detailed study of the potential for conserving energy in homes. The study examined existing and promising technologies and their energy-saving potential.

The Energy Assistance Program provided money for low-income families to help pay winter home-heating bills.

1980

The Household Moving Bill allowed movers to offer binding estimates of what a move would cost. This increased movers' freedom to raise or lower prices. It also established standards for informal dispute settlements. Panels were set up by movers to resolve conflicts.

1981

The president's administration agreed to increase subsidies to builders of low-income housing. The increase was granted in an attempt to revive construction, which had virtually halted due to high-financing costs.

1982

The president presented the following measures to help people buy homes:
- eased regulations on mortgage revenue bonds, making lower-cost mortgage money available to some home buyers
- increased money available for home buyers
- revised Federal Housing Administration rules to permit more first-time home buyers to qualify for loans

- reduced processing time for FHA loan applications
- relaxed government restrictions that limited real estate firms' participation in related businesses, such as providing title insurance

1983

A bill worth $760 million was passed to provide federal loans to home owners facing foreclosure or falling far behind on mortgage payments because of the recession. Loans were made available to home owners who had suffered "substantial loss" of income "through no fault of their own" and who were delinquent for at least 90 days or had received an intent-to-foreclose notice.

1985

The energy crisis laws and policies of the 1970s were dismantled, and tax credits for energy saving measures were stopped.

The Housing and Community Development Act was extended to provide emergency food and shelter to the homeless.

1986

Programs to clean hazardous waste sites were expanded. The EPA was mandated to study problems, set standards, and decide cleanup methods and timetables.

The Safe Drinking Water Act of 1974 was amended to include the protection of the water supply and focus on the prevention of contamination.

1987

Congress authorized funds for community development block grants. A permanent extension was made to insure home mortgage loans.

Inspection for and removal of lead-based paint in federally assisted housing became a requirement. The Federal Omnibus Act included reforms in residents' rights and care standards in nursing homes.

The McKinney Homeless Assistance Act was created to protect and improve the lives and safety of the homeless. Special emphasis was on older people, people with disabilities, and families with children. Grants became available for shelters. Subsidies were provided for low-income renters. Child care programs became available in public housing. The Act was amended in 1988 and 1990 to provide transitional housing as well as permanent housing with supportive services, such as education for homeless children.

1988

The Fair Housing Act gave HUD the authority to penalize those practicing discrimination in housing sales and rentals. Discriminatory practices aimed at home buyers and renters were outlawed in the following cases involving:

- race, color, religion, national origin, or family status
- occupants with physical or mental disabilities
- occupants with children under 18 years of age

The Act also provided architectural accessibility and adaptable design requirements in new multifamily housing.

The Indian Housing Act legally separated the federal government's efforts for Native Americans from other housing programs.

Money from the Community Development Block Grant and the Farmers Home Administration could be used to improve housing conditions along the Mexican border.

A program was begun to determine levels of radon in housing and remove it. Also, there was provision for screening drinking water for lead and for taking measures to reduce lead poisoning.

1990

The Cranston-Gonzalez National Affordable Housing Act was passed to help families purchase homes. Provision was made for the supply of affordable housing to be increased, especially for older people, the homeless, and people with disabilities. Financial assistance was provided for certain first-time home buyers. Rental assistance was available for low-income families.

The Clean Air Act provided measures to reduce pollution for benefit to the health of the general public. These measures contribute to improving air quality both inside and outside the dwellings. Because so many homes have woodstoves and fireplaces, this summary of the Act provides information on how these home-heating systems are affected by the Clean Air Act.

1991

The Cranston-Gonzalez Act was amended to include war veterans and residents of Indian Reservations.

1992

The Residential Lead-Based Paint Hazard Act of 1992 requires sellers, landlords, and agents to warn home buyers and tenants of lead-based paint and its hazards in housing built prior to 1978.

The Energy Policy Act of 1992 required that states adopt a residential building code for energy efficiency that meets or exceeds the Council of American Building Officials (CABO) Model Energy Code. The Act also established thermal insulation and energy efficiency standards for manufactured housing similar to the standards of some site-built housing. In addition, pilot studies were authorized for five states on energy efficient mortgages. Also, energy efficiency labeling for window and window systems was required to assist consumers with making more informed choices.

1995

The Housing for Older Persons Act of 1995 was passed to exempt housing communities of older persons from the Fair Housing Act discrimination charges. In other words, senior housing communities could continue to limit their services to singles or couples age 55 years or older. They are not required by law to open their housing to younger people or those with different family arrangements.

1996

Federal law required regulation regarding the disclosure of lead-based paint in writing to renters and buyers of housing built prior to 1978.

Native Americans Housing Assistance and Self-Determination Act was passed to improve the delivery of housing assistance to Indian tribes in a manner that recognizes the right of tribal self-governance and other priorities.

The federal government amended the Safe Drinking Water Act of 1974 to go beyond just the treatment of water for safety. The law greatly enhanced existing law. It recognized source water protection and provided operator training, funding for water system improvements, and public information as important components of safe drinking-water strategy.

1997

The Housing Opportunity and Responsibility Act of 1997 reformed public housing. The Act provided for the demolition of deteriorating public housing and replacement with mixed-income housing through partnerships with the public sector.

Amendments to the Clean Air Act established air quality standards.

1998

Federal Housing Assistance was increased to Native Hawaiians.

1999

The Federal Omnibus Act of 1987 was amended and expanded to require skilled nursing facilities to provide services to meet the highest practical physical, medical, and psychological well-being of every resident.

2000

American Homeownership and Economic Opportunity Act of 2000 provides for removal of barriers to home ownership, including down payment provisions. Tribal housing, people with special needs, and others benefit from the law.

The federal government expanded the Energy Conservation and Production Act of 1976 to include a model program for weatherizing housing of low-income families. It provides grants for conservation and efficiency for affordable housing. This includes weatherization as a way to reduce energy operating costs and thus lower overall housing costs.

2001

Programs to assist vulnerable older persons are administered through the Administration on the Aging. These programs, federally mandated under various titles of the Older Americans Act of 1965, help vulnerable older persons remain in their own homes by providing support services. Attention was given to assuring these services were equally available to all groups including tribal communities.

2005

The Energy Policy Act of 2005 provided tax breaks for those making energy conservation improvements to their homes. This Act promoted ENERGY STAR compliant technologies for the home and included tax credits for new energy-efficient homes and for energy-efficient appliances.

2008

The Emergency Economic Stabilization Act of 2008 extended many of the consumer tax incentives for energy-efficient existing homes, including renewable energy home applications and systems, such as solar electric and small wind turbines to generate electricity and geothermal heat pumps. The Act also added energy-efficient biomass fuel stoves as eligible for the tax credit. Appliance manufacturers were eligible for tax credits for production of energy-efficient appliances including clothes washers, dishwashers, and refrigerators.

The Housing and Economic Recovery Act of 2008 provided ways to stimulate housing activity to offset conditions that adversely affect consumers and the economy. Major components included a tax credit and increased loan limits to assist first-time home buyers. Provisions of the bill also include

- first-time home buyer tax credit

- reform to Fanny Mae and Freddie Mac (loan limits)

- reform to the Federal Housing Administration (FHA) (increasing loan limits)

- FHA foreclosure rescue (refinancing options for home buyers with problematic subprime loans)

2009

The American Recovery and Reinvestment Act of 2009 (ARRA) intended to provide a stimulus to the U.S. economy due to the recent downturn. It affected many areas of housing including the following:

- extending many consumer tax incentives originally introduced in the Energy Policy Act of 2005 and amended the Emergency Economic Stabilization Act of 2008

- repairing and modernizing public housing, including energy efficiency

- providing assistance in the Section 8 rental program

- helping communities purchase and repair foreclosed housing

- rehabilitating Native American housing

- helping rural Americans buy homes

- providing Assistance to remove lead paint from public housing

The Worker, Homeownership, and Business Assistance Act of 2009 extended the AARA tax credit up to $8000.00 for qualified first-time home buyers purchasing a principal residence. It also authorized a tax credit of up to $6500.00 for qualified repeat home buyers.

APPENDIX B

Entrepreneurship

Entrepreneurs are people who start and run their own business. Like most careers, entrepreneurship has both advantages and disadvantages. There are many issues to research when you are starting your own business. Consider all aspects carefully before deciding that entrepreneurship is for you.

Advantages and Disadvantages of Entrepreneurship

Many people become entrepreneurs so they can be their own boss. They enjoy being able to make all the decisions and work whatever hours they choose.

Some people start a business for the satisfaction of working with subjects they understand or enjoy. Starting a business may also provide a sense of accomplishment. However, many people become entrepreneurs for monetary reasons. If a business is successful, the owner can make a sizable profit.

Chief among the disadvantages to becoming an entrepreneur is the hard work. At first, you may have to work nonstop just to get the business started. During this period, very little money—if any—is coming in. You may have to put most of your savings into the business since affordable loans for an unproven business are rare. If the business fails, you could lose everything. About 30 percent of new businesses do not last two years. Fifty percent close within 5 years. All these factors add to a heightened sense of stress. Too much stress could even affect your health.

Common Characteristics of Entrepreneurs

Certain characteristics are vital for a person to succeed as an entrepreneur. First, entrepreneurs must be optimistic. They have to believe their business will succeed. Entrepreneurs must be self-starters who can recognize when they need to initiate action. They should be hard workers who are willing to put extreme effort into the business. They must be innovative, having interesting new ideas about doing or providing something that is not available anywhere else. Usually, a business succeeds by fulfilling a consumer need. A perceptive entrepreneur will be able to recognize a need that could become a money-making opportunity.

An entrepreneur needs to be committed to the business. This involves using his or her personal money, time, or other resources to make the business succeed. Entrepreneurs must be energetic and in good health to handle long workdays. An entrepreneur must also be willing to take risks. It is a huge risk to give up a steady paycheck for a business that may not succeed.

Common Skills Needed by Entrepreneurs

Entrepreneurs need to be capable of running all aspects of a business. First, they must be good managers. They must have some business acumen so they understand what is happening in the business. They may hire others to handle certain jobs, but they must be able to evaluate their employees' performance. They must be good at decision making, since the final decision on all matters lies with them. Problem-solving skills are also essential and include developing creative solutions that work.

In addition, entrepreneurs need basic skills. Communication skills are important for dealing with employees as well as clients. These skills are also important for communicating with other businesses, such as suppliers. In business, it is essential that written communications are clear because miscommunication can cost money.

Interpersonal skills go hand-in-hand with oral communication skills. You must be courteous in your communications with customers if you want repeat business. You should also be aware of how to best relate to employees. You will want to have cordial relationships with them, yet still remind them at all times that you are the boss.

It is important to have good math skills. Entrepreneurs use them to keep track of their business's profits, losses, assets, and liabilities. Without math skills, you could be cheated by a supplier or underpay your taxes. More importantly, you could lose everything by making a bad deal.

Entrepreneurs also need computer skills. Most procedures today, from inventory to billing, require computers. You must have good knowledge of computers and their uses, or the wisdom to seek an expert's advice.

Demonstrate Understanding

Locate three magazine articles on www.magportal.com (or at the library) about successful entrepreneurs in residential and nonresidential housing and interior design careers. Before reading the articles, divide a sheet of notebook paper in four columns. At the top of the first three columns, write the name of each entrepreneur you selected. In the last column, write your name. Read the articles and note in the appropriate column what personal traits, skills, behaviors, and abilities helped make each entrepreneur successful. Review the characteristics noted for each entrepreneur. In the last column, note which traits, skills, behaviors, and abilities you have that might help you become a successful entrepreneur.

Values and Goals of Entrepreneurs

Many entrepreneurs have similar values and goals. They may value success, especially succeeding through their own hard work. They may value career satisfaction and want this to be a goal for their work. They may value the freedom of creativity.

It is likely that an entrepreneur will value profit. The profit motive is a big incentive for starting a business. The success of a business is based on its ability to make a profit and grow.

Importance of Entrepreneurship

Entrepreneurship is important to a *free market economy*. This is an economic system in which government control is limited and citizens are allowed to privately own and operate businesses. A free market economy is also called *capitalism*, a *market economy*, or *free enterprise*.

Over 95 percent of businesses in the U.S. are considered "small businesses." These businesses each have less than 500 employees. About half the people employed in the United States work for small businesses. Of the people who do not work in government jobs, more than half are employed by small businesses.

Small businesses help create jobs. More jobs help keep the economy strong. A strong economy creates more demand for goods and services, which raises the standard of living. This, in turn, spurs the growth of small businesses that offer the goods and services desired.

Because small businesses usually produce highly specialized products, they may fulfill a focused need. However, to fill this need, they may require employees who are highly trained or experienced in one specialty. Many small businesses employ workers who are just starting their careers. This helps workers gain employment experience.

Types of Small Businesses

There are three types of business ownership or structure. A *sole proprietorship* is a business owned by only one person who has full responsibility. He or she makes all decisions, pays all the costs, and receives 100 percent of the profits.

A *partnership* is a business owned by two or more owners. Usually this is no more than a small group of people. A partner gives an owner someone to share responsibilities and costs. However, all decisions must be made jointly and the profits must be shared. Also, all partners are held responsible for one partner's actions.

A *corporation* is formed to represent the legal aspects of the business. This entity is separate from the individual people who own the corporation or work for it, which offers the individuals some protection. Individual *shareholders* have partial ownership in the company as a result of buying its stock. If the business fails, the shareholders may only lose their initial investment.

Instead of starting a new business, an entrepreneur may choose to buy into an existing business. One type of business is a *franchise*. A franchise is an agreement to sell another company's products or services. The person who buys the franchise, the *franchisee*, then has the exclusive right to sell the product or service in that area. A franchise can make a lot of money for an entrepreneur, but often the license can be very expensive. There may be additional ongoing fees. Also, the franchisee is legally bound to follow all the rules and guidelines of the company. For example, the owner may be required to buy supplies from a specific vendor rather than make his or her own decisions.

A *chain* is different from a franchise. A chain is a business that has many locations. Its owner is generally a corporation or partnership. The owner makes the decisions for all stores in the chain, which are run by managers.

A business option becomes a *joint venture* when an established interior design business joins with one or more companies. All companies share in the initial investment, profits, and losses. For example, suppose an interior design firm joins with an architectural/engineering firm to deliver final interior and exterior products. Each firm contributes to the investment to produce or acquire the products. Jointly, the firms handle the losses and enjoy the profits.

Starting a Business

If starting your own business, you will have many decisions to make and questions to answer. Answering these questions requires careful research.

Select a Product or Service

The first thing you must decide is what type of business is best. It is wise to pick something you already know that can use your abilities and aptitudes. Many experts also suggest sticking with something you enjoy, such as a hobby. You are more likely to put your all into making the business succeed if you enjoy the work.

Entrepreneurial Careers in Housing and Interior Design		
Interior Designer	Upholsterer	Painter
Color Designer	Landscape Architect	Wallcovering Hanger
Ergonomic Designer	Architect	Plaster/Drywall Installer
Historical Preservationist	Drafter	Floor Covering Installer
Professional Organizer	Model Maker	HVAC Installer
Real Estate Appraiser	Building Contractor	Plumber
Real Estate Broker	Carpenter	Roofer
Land Surveyor	Electrician	Bricklayer/Stonemason

You may choose to enter an area that is already established. For instance, you may open the hardware store your neighborhood wants. You may provide a service, such as housecleaning. You may come up with an entirely new product or idea that presents good sales potential. See the following chart for common entrepreneurs in the housing and interior design industry.

Analyze Potential Markets

Once you decide on a product or service, you identify your *target market*. This is the specific group of people who needs your product or service. By narrowing your target market, you have a greater chance of identifying potential buyers. This information will help you plan how to best promote your business.

Study the Competition

Find out if anyone is already making or providing your product or service. If so, how can you make your product better than the competition? Research the details of the competition. Record important facts about your competitors and update them frequently. What do they charge for their product? Where are they located? Include any other facts that will help you plan your business.

Do Market Research

Research the market to find useable data. Data may include your own observations, surveys, or interviews with potential customers. Talking with people directly is known as *primary data*.

Secondary data comes from sources other than direct interaction with consumers. You may research business records, government information, and private databases. You may use the Internet and libraries to do much of your research.

Watching trends is very important. *Product trends* relate to features of the

Career Applications

Suppose you and a team of three friends want to open an interior design business with a focus on green and sustainable design. As an initial step, you need to collect some primary data in your community as well as some secondary data. Here are some questions to guide your research.

- What form(s) of primary data will you use? Develop interview questions or a survey for potential clients.

- What secondary data will your team use? Research several secondary sources of information such as government databases, private databases, and the Internet regarding the interior design market in your community. Write a summary of the information you find.

products themselves. For instance, a current product trend is to make sure products are "green," or environmentally safe. Social trends relate to the consumers, but may also affect your product. For example, social networking sites are now popular and may be an ideal advertising channel for your product. Demographic trends reflect changes to parts of the population, such as the growing population of older adults. Because of this trend, perhaps demand for a housecleaning business for older adults would continually increase.

Understand Your Product Life Cycle

Whether you plan to offer a product or service, you should understand its life cycle phases. These phases cover the life of a product or service from beginning to end. The phases of a *product life cycle* include

- **Introduction.** When you introduce the product or service to the market,

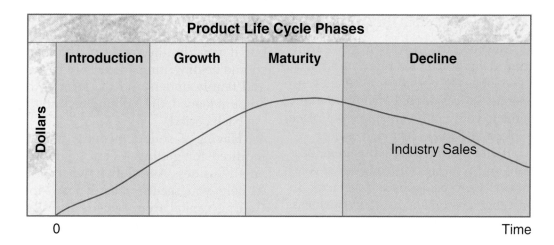

the introduction phase begins. The goals of this phase include informing customers about the product or service and outlining the key benefits. Prices or fees are generally the highest during this phase.

- **Growth.** Once a product or service catches on with customers, the growth phase begins. During this phase, sales and profits for products and services rise rapidly. See the chart that follows.

- **Maturity.** When a product or service reaches the maturity phase, the sales begin to level off. At this point, the market is saturated—or the point at which customers who need, want, and can afford to buy the product or service have done so. Competition among brands is also intense at the maturity phase. Prices or fees are often lower at this phase.

- **Decline.** During the decline phase, sales begin to fall for the product or service. The prices or fees are generally their lowest during this phase. When a product or service begins to decline, business owners and marketers must decide what to do. They may choose one of two options—either discontinue the product or service or develop new marketing strategies to increase sales.

Prepare Market Surveys

If you do a survey to compile market data, be sure to ask the right questions. Your questions should not influence people to answer a certain way. If the questions do not really address what you need to know, the answers will not be useful to you. Use a small group as a sample, and then apply the results to a larger group. Make sure the answers to the questions can be quickly analyzed. For example, it is easy to compile data from multiple choice options for responses.

Choose a Name

The name for your business should appeal both to you and your target market. However, there may also be legal requirements. For instance, your state may require business names to reflect the business structure. You will also want to make sure the name is not trademarked by another business in your area. You may check for trademarks with the Secretary of State office in your state.

Choose the Location

Maybe you will want to work from your own home. Keep in mind that some cities do not allow a business to operate in residential neighborhoods. Perhaps you will be moving from place to place, such as a cleaning service.

If you must choose a business location, you will need to consider several factors. Easy access is a key factor in bringing customers to your business. Also, you will need to consider the location of your competition. You do not want to be so close that customers go to your competition. You do not want to be too far away to be considered competition. How can you improve on your competition's location?

Consider the neighborhood. Is it safe? inviting? Are the people who live there likely to give your business a try? Are they likely to spend money? Check out the neighboring businesses. Will they attract customers similar to those you are targeting? Will the customer base of neighboring businesses alienate your target market?

Once you choose a neighborhood, you can start looking for a store or office space. You will want to consider the actual features of the building. Does it have the utilities you need? What is the lease or rental fee? Make sure your business is easily accessible to traffic. Also check to make sure there is adequate parking for customers.

Find Sources of Capital

You may have the best idea for a new product or service, but you need money to start the business. Where does the money come from?

Hopefully, you will put just a portion of your own savings toward your business. (Enough savings should be preserved for possible emergencies outside the business.) You may plan to borrow money from friends and family, but if you do, the terms of the loans should be in writing. Make sure friends and family understand the terms—the amount loaned, the lending fee, and the payback period.

Having a sound business plan is required for getting a bank loan. The Small Business Association may be able to help you secure a bank loan, too. Getting capital from outside investors is another way to obtain startup money, but the business plan must be sound.

When pulling together capital, be sure you have a little extra. You want to be sure you have enough to cover any unexpected expenses.

Establish the Price or Fee

To decide how to price your product or service, consider the cost of your materials and tools. Deciding the value of your own time or skills is usually more difficult.

- *Demand-based pricing* is determined by what customers are prepared to pay. You may also be able to charge more if your product, service, or business is seasonal.

- *Cost-based pricing* is determined by figuring how much it costs you to buy or produce the item. You then add a certain percentage to that price for profit.

- Checking the prices of similar businesses in your area can help you set *competition-based pricing*. If you have no real competition, you can charge a bit more. However, you do not want to add so much that customers will not buy your product or service.

Develop a Business Plan

The *business plan* documents how you propose to start and run your business. The business plan will also help you think through any unanswered questions about your business.

If you need a bank loan to start your business, your business plan will help you secure it. The business plan shows the bank that you have carefully considered every aspect needed to help your business succeed.

A business plan includes the following sections:

- An executive summary—a short overview

- The description of the business—gives details on your product, service, business structure, how the company will be run, and the company's goals

- Industry analysis—an overview of the market, how it fits into the economy, and detailed information about your competition as well as how you plan to beat them

- The target market—who will be buying your product or service, how many customers you might have, and how much they might spend

- Organization and operations—the structure of the company, staff members and their positions, and the way the company will be run

- Marketing strategy—how you plan to sell the product or service

- Financial plan—includes the startup costs, how much of your own money you will use, who will supply loans and how much you will need, and how you expect to pay the money back; also includes budgets, cash flow statements, and balance sheets measuring net worth

For more information on business plans, review the Small Business Administration's Web site.

Career Applications

Presume that you and your teammates completed your market research and have decided that there is a local market for your "green" interior design business. In order to get financial backing, your team needs to write a business plan. Write a business plan covering the details in all specific parts of the plan. For additional help in writing your business plan, review the *Small Business Planner* tools on the Small Business Administration Web site (www.sba.gov).

Legal Requirements for Starting a Business

Before you start a business, you are responsible for researching the legal requirements you need to fulfill. For example, there may be zoning laws for your home or location. If you plan to work out of your home, make sure a zoning law does not restrict you from doing this in a residential neighborhood. Some laws prevent certain businesses from operating in some areas.

Some businesses need a permit, while other businesses may need a license. For instance, landscape architects, land surveyors, and real estate agents must all be licensed. You will probably have to pay a fee for both permits and licenses.

Check with the Department of Commerce for your state. This office can help inform you of any permits or licenses you will need.

Insurance and Taxes

You will want to limit the amount of risk to your business by getting various types of insurance coverage. You will want to

- protect your business from losses due to fire or theft
- have liability insurance in case your product or service causes injury
- carry disability insurance for yourself and your employees to avoid losses if unable to work due to injury or illness

Navigating the information necessary for tax purposes can seem daunting. However, each state's Department of Commerce has assistance programs that can help you. Also check with the Small Business Administration's Web site.

First, you will need a tax identification number for your business. This is because you will be paying taxes for any profit your business makes. You must also find out how much sales tax you need to charge for a product. Most personal services are not taxed, although some states are considering adding a tax.

Startup Expenses

The most expensive part of being an entrepreneur can be your startup costs. This is because it will take a while for the business to start earning money. You may feel at first that everything is a "loss."

You may spend a lot of money to start the business, but some of this will cover one-time fees. For instance, you may need to buy machines that will last for several years. In contrast, you may need to buy supplies every few months. Your operating fees will be ongoing, but you may never have the need for all the beginning costs again.

Demonstrate Understanding

As a team, research the role of ethics in business practices and procedures. Why is ethical behavior important to a profitable and successful business? How do ethics impact the legal responsibilities of a business owner? For information about legal responsibilities, see the Small Business Administration Web site (www.sba.gov).

Sources of Help

It is unlikely that you are an expert in all areas of entrepreneurship. Where can you go for support?

First, consult the Small Business Administration. Its Web site has helpful answers to many common questions. It also links to the state Departments of Commerce. Many of the regulations that affect small businesses are set by the states. You would be wise to investigate these regulations before starting a business. Your local chamber of commerce may also be able to help you check for local regulations. These sources may be free or require a small fee.

From time to time, you will also need support in these business areas:

- A lawyer will make sure you fulfill all legal requirements.
- An accountant can handle or check your bookkeeping and tax-related records.
- An insurance agent will determine the amount and types of insurance you need.

These professionals can be expensive, but they limit your business risk and provide peace of mind.

Managing for Profit

For a company to succeed, it must make enough money to pay employees, purchase materials, cover other costs,

---

Copyright, Trademark, and Patent Basics

As an entrepreneur, you should know about others' rights related to copyrights, trademarks, and patents. All of these rights fall under the umbrella of *intellectual property*. Intellectual property usually refers to ideas, inventions, or processes that derive from work of the mind or intellect. What are these rights? The following briefly describes each:

- *copyright:* the exclusive legal right to reproduce, publish, sell, or distribute the matter and form of something (literary, musical, or artistic work)

- *trademark:* a device (such as a word) pointing distinctly to the origin or ownership of merchandise to which it is applied and legally reserved to the exclusive use of the owner as maker or seller

- *patent:* an official document giving the exclusive right to make, use, or sell an invention for a term of years

Infringing on someone else's copyright, trademark, or patent can lead to severe legal penalties and fines. The best way to protect yourself and your business from unintentional infringement on the intellectual property of others is to do a search. You will not want to infringe on the designs or products created by others.

You can conduct a preliminary search yourself using the Internet and such sources as the U.S. Patent and Trademark Office or the Library of Congress's Copyright Office. However, it is best to hire an attorney who specializes in doing copyright, trademark, and patent searches.

---

and have some left over to maintain and improve the business. The costs of doing business are called *expenses.* The money that results from customers purchasing the company's product or service is called *revenues,* or *sales.* A business calculates its *income* by subtracting its expenses from its revenues. When the revenues are greater than expenses, the company is said to make a *profit.* When a company's expenses are greater than its revenues, it is called a *loss.* The equation for calculating income is

$$\text{Income} = \text{Revenues} - \text{Expenses}$$

Financial Statements

The preceding formula is the basis for one of three fundamental financial statements used to manage a business— the *income statement.* The income statement is sometimes referred to as the *profit and loss (P&L) statement.* The income statement communicates the results of the company's operations for a given period of time such as one month or one year. See the income statement for Ina's Interiors that follows.

Ina's Interiors Income Statement For Month Ending September 30, 2011		
Revenue		
Interior design services	$5,350	
Designer consultation fees	800	
Total Revenues		**$6,150**
Expenses		
Designer salary	$3,210	
Rent	1,250	
Utilities (heat, electric, water/sewer)	325	
Office supplies	78	
Total Expenses		**4,863**
Income		**$1,287**

The second financial statement used by a business is the *balance sheet*. The balance sheet shows the businesses assets, liabilities, and equity on a given date. *Assets* are items a company owns that have value, such as cash, physical inventory, buildings, and equipment. *Liabilities* are debts, or what a company owes such as bills payable to suppliers, mortgage loans, or various taxes it must pay to state or federal governments. *Equity* represents the owner's rights to the assets of the company. For example, if an owner invests $100,000 in a business to start it, he or she has $100,000 in equity in the business. A business' assets are equal to the sum of its liabilities and equity

$$Assets = Liabilities + Equity$$

The *statement of cash flow (SCF)* is the third fundamental financial statement. The SCF shows how cash came into the business and how it left, or was used by the business. This is different from profit or loss because only *cash* received or paid out is analyzed. The cash flow in and out of business is categorized as either from *operating activities* (for example cash received from customers or paid to suppliers), *investing activities* (for example cash received from the sale of equipment or paid on a vehicle loan), or *financing activities* (for example cash received from an investor or paid to stockholders as dividends).

Managing Revenues and Expenses

The equation for calculating profit demonstrates how either increasing or decreasing the revenues, expenses, or both can impact a business' income. To achieve a planned profit, both revenues and expenses must be managed. Key factors that must be addressed are marketing plans, production, inventory control, and performance analysis.

Marketing Plan

How will your customers learn that your product or service is available? You need to get the message out to them through marketing. You will need to choose which type of advertising to use. The goal is to acquaint customers with the merits of your product or service so they are persuaded to buy it. You may have to explain its value and importance. Sometimes this is accomplished by explaining how it is better than the competition.

You will need to set up a timetable for your advertising. When will you introduce the product? How often will you advertise? This may depend on your advertising budget, too.

Career Applications

When developing a marketing plan, it is important to use creative tools to capture client interest. For your team's "green" interior design firm, create one or more of the following that emphasizes your business identity: logo for business cards and stationary, Web site or page with attractive photography, brochure about the business, a newspaper or Web ad about design services, a newsletter, or a press release.

Channels of Distribution A *channel of distribution* is the route a product takes from the manufacturer and to the customer. For example, the manufacturer may sell the product to a store, which then sells to the customer. In other cases, the manufacturer may sell to a wholesaler, who sells to retailers, who then sell to the customer. Adding businesses to the channel of distribution increases price and production time. As an entrepreneur, you will want to investigate the most cost-effective channel of distribution for your product.

Marketing Strategies for Housing and Interior Design

To effectively market your housing or interior design related business, try the following:

- **Develop a logo or brand.** Having a logo or brand helps create your "business identity." It should be something that your clients and potential clients can easily identify. You can use your brand for your Web site, business cards, stationary, and other documents.

- **Create a Web site.** Developing a Web site is key for marketing your business. Make sure your Web site is attractive and accurately reflects your business and specialty. Include images that show your work. Highlight your educational achievements, awards, and any testimonials you receive from satisfied clients. Be sure to frequently update images and testimonials.

- **Use high-quality photography.** Effective photography skillfully highlights your completed projects to display in your professional portfolio or use on your Web site or in printed materials.

- **Prepare printed materials.** Brochures, post cards, and newsletters can be great marketing tools for your business. Well-designed print materials should be brief and highlight your skills. Distribute these materials to real estate agents, builders, property developers, and others who can help get the word out about your business.

- **Maintain good public relations.** Share your business talents at conferences and workshops or volunteer to use your skills through such community-service organizations as Habitat for Humanity or United Way.

Production Process

No matter how the production is accomplished, you should have two goals for production. First, your product should have quality. If your customers do not believe the item is worth its cost, you will not be able to sell the item. The other factor to consider is efficiency. You will want to be able to make your product quickly so you can sell as many as possible. However, sacrificing quality for speed will probably cost you sales in the long run.

Inventory Records

Keeping track of your inventory is very important. Having too much inventory has a few drawbacks. First, having too much inventory means you probably ordered or manufactured too much to sell at its current price. Lowering the price may not cover your expenses. Second, you may not have enough storage for your entire inventory. If you buy more space, you may have more expenses. Finally, your stock may become dated or damaged over time.

The longer you keep it in inventory, the less you will be able to eventually sell.

If you have too little inventory, you can sell out your product. Getting more product available takes time. Customers will be unhappy if they cannot have the product they want when they are ready to buy. They may shop elsewhere. They may spread the word that your products are appealing, but unavailable.

Some businesses keep a minimal amount of stock on hand at any given time. Some businesses, especially in the interior design industry, stock only samples. Products such as drapery and upholstered furniture are not manufactured until customers place customized orders. Carrying too much inventory can affect cash flow.

Demonstrate Understanding

In teams, investigate the elements of an effective marketing plan. Assign each team member one element to thoroughly research. Combine your research data and prepare an electronic presentation of your findings to share with the class.

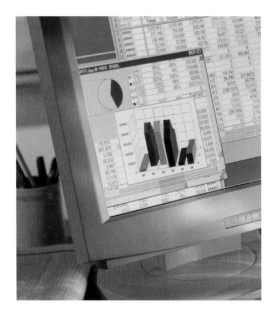

Businesses may keep track of inventory by hand, also known as *physical inventory.* This means visually checking and physically counting the number of items you have available.

Today, it is most common for inventory systems to be computerized. Bar code scanners can "read" special labels and automatically update your inventory in the computer system. You may have a system that keeps constant inventory. That means whenever you add or remove stock, your needed supplies are automatically ordered. Other systems take inventory at set intervals, such as once a month.

Analyzing the Income Statement

Ratios are commonly used to analyze information on the income statement. Ratios express how one number relates to another. For example, a company might find it useful to understand how many dollars in sales are received for every dollar spent on wages (labor cost). This ratio is called the *labor cost percentage.*

$$\frac{\text{(Wages + benefits)}}{\text{Sales}} \times 100 = \text{Labor cost \%}$$

For example, in April 2011, suppose a business paid $2,800 in wages and $420 in benefits to its employees. Total sales for the month were $8,300. The labor cost percentage for April was 38.8 percent.

$$\frac{(\$2,800 + \$420)}{\$8,300} \times 100 = 38.8\%$$

Is a labor cost percentage of 38.8 good or bad? To understand that, this number must be compared to other numbers such as a budgeted labor cost percentage or the labor cost percentages from prior months or years. If a business has planned, or budgeted, for 32 percent labor cost, 38.8 percent would not be good. If labor cost was 40 percent in March of 2011, why did it decrease? This ratio can be used to analyze expenses other than labor as well.

Another ratio is commonly used to measure a company's profitability. This ratio is called the *profit margin.* The profit-margin ratio compares a business' income (profit or loss) to its sales.

$$\frac{\text{Income}}{\text{Sales}} \times 100 = \text{Profit margin}$$

The income statement for Ina's Interiors shows that the business generated sales of $6,150 and a profit of $1,287 for the month of September 2011. The profit margin for Ina's Interiors can be calculated as follows:

$$\frac{\$1,287}{\$6,150} \times 100 = 21\%$$

Another way of stating Ina's profit margin is for every one dollar in sales, the business makes a profit of 21 cents.

Career Applications

Many factors impact loss prevention and business profits. Research various inventory control strategies, laws, and workplace policies that can help entrepreneurs limit business losses and maintain profitability. As part of your research, review articles about how successful entrepreneurs keep losses down and profits up. Share your findings with the class.

APPENDIX C

ASID Code of Ethics and Professional Conduct

1.0   PREAMBLE

Members of the American Society of Interior Designers are required to conduct their professional practice in a manner that will inspire the respect of clients, suppliers of goods and services to the profession and fellow professional designers, as well as the general public. It is the individual responsibility of every member of ASID to uphold this code and bylaws of the Society.

2.0   RESPONSIBILITY TO THE PUBLIC

2.1   Members shall comply with all existing laws, regulations and codes governing business procedures and the practice of interior design as established by the state or other jurisdiction in which they practice.

2.2   Members shall not seal or sign drawings, specifications or other interior design documents except where the member or the member's firm has prepared, supervised or professionally reviewed and approved such documents, as allowed by applicable laws, rules and regulations.

2.3   Members shall at all times consider the health, safety and welfare of the public in spaces they design. Members agree, whenever possible, to notify property managers, landlords, and/or public officials of conditions within a built environment that endanger the health, safety and/or welfare of occupants. If, during the course of a project, a Member becomes aware of an action to be taken by, or on behalf of the Member's client, which in the Member's reasonable opinion is likely to result in a material adverse effect on the health, safety and welfare of persons occupying or using the space, the Member shall refuse to consent to, or participate in that action, and if required by law and/or under circumstances the Member deems reasonably prudent to do so, the Member shall report such action to the governmental agency having jurisdiction over the project.

2.4   Members shall not engage in any form of false or misleading advertising or promotional activities.

2.5   Members shall neither offer, nor make any payments or gifts to any public official, nor take any other action, with the intent of unduly influencing the official's judgment in connection with an existing or prospective project in which the members are interested.

2.6   Members shall not assist or abet improper or illegal conduct of anyone in connection with any project.

3.0 RESPONSIBILITY TO THE CLIENT

3.1 Members' contracts with clients shall clearly set forth the scope and nature of the projects involved, the services to be performed and the methods of compensation for those services.

3.2 Members shall not undertake any professional responsibility unless they are, by training and experience, competent to adequately perform the work required.

3.3 Members shall fully disclose to a client all compensation that the member shall receive in connection with the project and shall not accept any form of undisclosed compensation from any person or firm with whom the member deals in connection with the project.

3.4 Members shall not divulge any confidential information about the client or the client's project, or utilize photographs of the client's project, without the permission of the client.

3.5 Members shall be candid and truthful in all their professional communications.

3.6 Members shall act with fiscal responsibility in the best interest of their clients and shall maintain sound business relationships with suppliers, industry and trades.

4.0 RESPONSIBILITY TO OTHER INTERIOR DESIGNERS AND COLLEAGUES

4.1 Members shall not interfere with the performance of another interior designer's contractual or professional relationship with a client.

4.2 Members shall not initiate, or participate in, any discussion or activity which might result in an unjust injury to another interior designer's reputation or business relationships.

4.3 Members may, when requested and it does not present a conflict of interest, render a second opinion to a client or serve as an expert witness in a judicial or arbitration proceeding.

4.4 Members shall not endorse the application for ASID membership and/or certification, registration or licensing of an individual known to be unqualified with respect to education, training, experien ce or character, nor shall a member knowingly misrepresent the experience, professional expertise of that individual.

4.5 Members shall only take credit for work that has actually been created by that member or the member's firm, and under the member's supervision.

4.6 Members should respect the confidentiality of sensitive information obtained in the course of their professional activities.

5.0 RESPONSIBILITY TO THE PROFESSION

5.1   Members agree to maintain standards of professional and personal conduct that will reflect in a responsible manner on the Society and the profession.

5.2   Members shall seek to continually upgrade their professional knowledge and competency with respect to the interior design profession.

5.3   Members agree, whenever possible, to encourage and contribute to the sharing of knowledge and information between interior designers and other allied professional disciplines, industry and the public.

6.0   RESPONSIBILITY TO THE EMPLOYER

6.1   Members leaving an employer's service shall not take drawings, designs, data, reports, notes, client lists or other materials relating to work performed in the employer's service except with permission of the employer.

6.2   A member shall not unreasonably withhold permission from departing employees to take copies of material relating to their work while employed at the member's firm, which are not proprietary and confidential in nature.

6.3   Members shall not divulge any confidential information obtained during the course of their employment about the client or the client's project or utilize photographs of the project, without the permission of both client and employer.

7.0   ENFORCEMENT

7.1   The Society shall follow standard procedures for the enforcement of this code as approved by the ASID Board of Directors.

7.2   Members having a reasonable belief, based upon substantial information, that another member has acted in violation of this code, shall report such information in accordance with accepted procedures.

7.3   Any violation of this code, or any action taken by a member which is detrimental to the Society and the profession as a whole, shall be deemed unprofessional conduct subject to discipline by the ASID Board of Directors.

7.4   If the Disciplinary Committee decides the concerned Member did not violate the Society's Code of Ethics and Professional Conduct, it shall dismiss the complaint and at the concerned Member's request, a notice of exoneration from the complaint shall be made public. If the Disciplinary Committee decides that the concerned Member violated one or more provisions of the Society's Code of Ethics and Professional Conduct, it shall discipline the concerned Member by reprimand, censure, suspension or termination of membership. The Disciplinary Committee may, in its discretion, make public its decision and the penalty imposed. The Disciplinary Committee does not impose any other form of penalty. The Disciplinary Committee cannot require payment of any monies or mandate certain action to be taken by the concerned Member.

APPENDIX D

Related Careers

In addition to interior design careers, a number of other careers relate to and are necessary components to providing attractive housing for people from all walks of life. The following passages include a number of careers that fall into the *Architecture & Construction* and the *Arts, Audio/Video Technology, & Communications* career clusters. To complete more in-depth career research, use the following career Web sites:

- O*Net (www.onetcenter.org)
- CareerOneStop (www.careeronestop.org)
- U.S. Bureau of Labor Statistics, *Occupational Outlook Handbook* (www.bls.gov/OOH/)

Architectural Drafters

Career Description: Architectural drafters help prepare architectural designs and plans for buildings following the specifications an architect provides. Tasks include, but are not limited to, analyzing building codes, planning interior room arrangements, and preparing rough and detailed scale plans. These drafters must have excellent communication, critical-thinking, math, and problem-solving skills. Many of these positions focus on green and sustainable design.

Technical Skills: Architectural drafters must be able to use CADD software and equipment and traditional drafting equipment, graphics- and photo-imaging software, and project management software.

Education/Training: Most positions require an associate's degree and related on-the-job experience.

Job Outlook: Employment growth for drafters is expected to increase through 2018. However, growth for architectural drafters is expected to be about as fast as average in this same period.

Model Makers

Career Description: With knowledge about blueprints and drawings, model makers are able to construct scale-size mock-ups of buildings and structures. Ability to use woodworking tools to cut shapes and patterns is essential along with strong math (algebra, geometry, calculus), critical-thinking, and problem-solving skills. Model makers must have good finger dexterity to make precise movements and manipulate small objects.

Technical Skills: Model makers must know how to use design tools and techniques and know how to apply principles of engineering science and technology.

Education/Training: Positions may require vocational training, on-the-job-training, or an associate's degree.

Job Outlook: Job growth for model makers will have little or no change through 2018.

Real Estate Agent

Career Description: A real estate agent works with clients to rent, buy, or sell property. Job-related tasks include acquiring property listings, showing clients various sites, and drawing up contracts. Real estate agents also determine competitive market prices for property, work as an intermediary in buyer/seller negotiations, and coordinate property closings. These agents must have strong sales and marketing skills, effective communication skills, and strong ethics and organizational skills.

Technical Skills: Ability to use a computer and a personal digital assistant and competency with software for photo imaging, customer relationship management, and financial analysis is essential. Competency with digital photography and measuring equipment is also necessary.

Education/Training: Most positions require vocational training, on-the-job training, or an associate's degree. Licensing is necessary for real estate agents, generally through the state in which they work.

Job Outlook: Job growth for real estate agents is expected to be must faster than average through 2018.

Construction Manager

Career Description: Construction managers work with building projects from the conceptual stage through implementation and completion of a project. They are involved with planning, budgeting, and time management, interpreting plans, and comparing job specifications and construction methods. In addition, construction managers select, contract, and supervise workers who complete specific parts of a project. It is essential that construction managers have a solid understanding of building materials and

Group 3. Architecture. Interiors. Planning. Hilton Head, South Carolina. (www.group3arch.com) Photography Courtesy of John McManus.

construction methods. Effective design knowledge, communication, problem solving, and ability to establish and maintain interpersonal relationships are requirements.

Technical Skills: Construction managers must have superior computer skills and ability to use software for project management, scheduling, document management, and presentations.

Education/Training: Most positions require a bachelor's degree.

Job Outlook: Employment growth for these positions is expected to be faster than average through 2018.

Cost Estimator

Career Description: People who work in these positions prepare cost estimates for construction projects and services to assist in the bidding process. They may compare vendors and subcontractors; talk with architects, builders, engineers and other project members; and analyze the cost effectiveness of certain products and services. In addition, cost estimators must have exceptional math skills, accounting background, design knowledge, and effective oral and written communication skills. Complex problem solving and critical thinking are also important.

Technical Skills: Use of computers and software for accounting, construction management, project management, and spreadsheets is necessary for this occupation.

Education/Training: Most positions require a bachelor's degree.

Job Outlook: Employment growth for cost estimators is expected to be much faster than average through 2018.

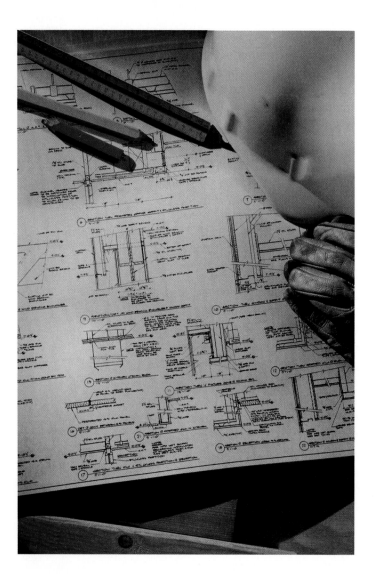

Operating Engineers/ Construction Equipment Operators

Career Description: Operating engineers and equipment operators may work with one or more pieces of such heavy equipment as bulldozers, compressors, and front-end-loaders for excavation. Some of these employees also repair and maintain this equipment. Emphasis on personal safety and the safety of others is key in these jobs. Ability to coordinate machine actions with other work activities is important. Workers need strong knowledge of building materials and methods, mechanical ability, and effective communication skills.

Technical Skills: Operating engineers and equipment operators must be able to drive and manipulate equipment. Ability to use a computer with facilities-management and time-accounting software is essential.

Education/Training: Most of these jobs require vocational or on-the-job training or an associate's degree.

Job Outlook: The job growth for these positions is expected to be about average through 2018.

Brick Mason/Block Mason

Career Description: Brick and block masons focus on laying and binding such building materials as brick, concrete block, or structural tiles with mortar. Workers in these positions must be able to measure, calculate angles, and use levels and plumb bobs. Physical fitness and manual dexterity are important for these positions. Ability to interpret blueprints and drawings is essential. Strong math, critical-thinking, and communication skills are also important.

Technical Skills: Along with ability to use tools such as power saws, welders, and hammers, brick and block masons must be able to use a computer with accounting, analytical, and project management software.

Education/Training: These positions require a high school diploma.

Job Outlook: Employment growth for these positions is expected to be about average through 2018.

Construction Carpenter

Career Description: Construction carpenters must have ability to use hand and power tools to construct structures of wood, plywood, and drywall sheets. Design knowledge and ability to read and follow blueprints and building plans is important. Carpenters use their math skills (arithmetic, algebra, geometry, and calculus) in measuring, cutting, and installing materials. Following safety standards is essential.

Technical Skills: Construction carpenters must be able to calibrate and utilize electronic levels. They must also be able to use a computer with software for accounting, project management, and word processing.

Education/Training: These positions require a high school diploma. Some require additional training at a vocational school or community college. Some employers also offer apprenticeships which provide on-the-job training combined with some classroom instruction.

Job Outlook: Employment growth for construction carpenters is expected to be about average through 2018.

Cabinetmaker

Career Description: With a solid background in math and geometric concepts, cabinetmakers use power tools to cut, shape, and assemble lumber for cabinets and furniture. These individuals must be able to set up and operate such machinery as power saws and jointers to shape wood. Ability to follow specifications on blueprints and drawings is essential. Paying attention to details and having solid critical thinking and communication skills are needed. Physical fitness along with manual and finger dexterity is important.

Technical Skills: Cabinetmakers must be able to use a computer with CADD software and software for project management.

Education/Training: A high school diploma and training on-the-job, at vocational schools, or an associate's degree from a community college are typical for these occupations.

Job Outlook: Employment growth for cabinetmakers will remain about average through 2018. Highly qualified candidates will have excellent opportunities.

Drywall Installer

Career Description: Drywall installers secure drywall or other types of wallboard to interior walls and ceilings of structures. They must be able to read blueprints and drawings in order to measure and mark drywall layouts. They utilize nails and screws along with appropriate hand and power tools for fastening drywall to the framing structure. Math, critical thinking, and good management skills are essentials. Drywall installers must also have physical strength and good manual dexterity.

Technical Skills: Along with tools of the trade (trowels, saws, lifts, and utility knives), drywall installers must also be able to use a computer with software for accounting, word processing, and project management.

Education/Training: A high school diploma is necessary for entry-level positions. Employers provide on-the-job training and may send employees to vocational schools or community colleges for further training. Apprenticeships are possible.

Job Outlook: Employment growth is expected to be about as fast as average through 2018.

HVAC Mechanic/Installer

Career Description: HVAC mechanics and installers service, install, and repair residential and commercial heating and cooling systems. This includes ability to inspect and test systems while complying with acceptable standards, practices, and safety requirements. Because of the complexity of HVAC and refrigeration systems, mechanics and installers must have solid knowledge of machines and tools, such as pressure indicators, thermocouples, and voltage meters. Critical thinking and troubleshooting abilities are needed. Knowledge of design and superior communication skills are essential.

Technical Skills: People who work in these occupations must be able to use a computer and software programs for customer relationship management, word processing, building automation, and CADD.

Education/Training: Many installers begin their training in secondary and postsecondary technical or trade schools. Others receive on-the-job training, vocational training, an associate's degree, or training through formal apprenticeships. Licensure is a requirement for HVAC mechanics and installers.

Job Outlook: Employment growth is expected to be much faster than average through 2018.

Electrician

Career Description: While installing, maintaining, or repairing electrical wires, fixtures, and equipment, electricians must make sure all work meets relevant codes. In their work, electricians may install and connect wires and transformers. In addition, they test electrical systems, plan electrical layouts and installations, and diagnose problems with malfunctioning systems. Practical knowledge of math, machines and tools, design, engineering science, and physics is desirable. Electricians must also have good manual dexterity, vision, and problem-solving ability. Communicating effectively with clients is also important.

Technical Skills: Along with ability to use hand tools and voltage meters, electricians must be able to use a computer with such software as analytical, CADD, word processing, and project management.

Education/Training: Many electricians receive training through apprenticeship programs that combine on-the-job training with classroom instruction. These apprenticeships generally last 4 years. Because most state governments require licensure for electricians, taking an exam that tests knowledge of the

National Electric Code, electrical theory, and state and local building codes is necessary.

Job Outlook: Employment growth for electricians is expected to be about average through 2018.

Plasterer/Stucco Mason

Career Description: Plasterers and stucco masons focus on applying coats of plaster or stucco to walls in residential or commercial structures. They use such equipment as trowels, floats, brushes, spray guns, and utility knives to create decorative finishes to finish coats. These workers need good skills in managing material resources, using good judgment, and time management. Physical fitness and good manual dexterity and coordination are important.

Technical Skills: Plasterers and stucco masons must be able to use a computer with accounting and project management software.

Education/Training: Courses in math, mechanical drawing, and blueprint reading along with a high school diploma are needed for entry-level jobs. Many employers send new employees for courses at vocational schools or community colleges. Some offer apprenticeships that combine on-the-job training with classroom instruction.

Job Outlook: Employment growth for plasterers and stucco masons is expected to be about as fast as average through 2018.

Painter

Career Description: Painters apply paint to walls, buildings, and other structures using brushes, rollers, and paint spray guns. They must be meticulous about preparations before painting, such as covering other surfaces with drop cloths and painter's tape, repairing cracks, filling holes, and applying sealers and primers or other surface preparation. They may also construct scaffolding for working at higher levels. Painters must have good customer relationship skills, know how to work safely, and have good strength and flexibility. They must have ability to mix and match paints, stains, and finishes with oil and thinning or drying agents for desired effects. Excellent communication skills are important for customer relationships.

Technical Skills: Painters must be able to use hand and power tools of the trade. They also must be able to use a computer with software for customer relationship management, project management, accounting, and word processing.

Education/Training: A high school diploma is required to enter apprenticeship programs. Many painters learn the trade through on-the-job training.

Job Outlook: Employment outlook for painters is about as fast as average through 2018.

Carpet/Flooring Installers and Finishers

Career Description: Carpet and flooring installers and finishers lay carpeting and/or finish other types of flooring in residential and commercial buildings. These installers and finishers must be able to precisely measure, plan layouts, and cut and align flooring materials. Installers and finishers must have good math skills, knowledge about safety procedures, and good customer relationship skills. Effective time management, physical fitness and flexibility, and ability to solve complex problems are also necessary skills.

Technical Skills: Carpet installers use such equipment as hammers, drills, staple guns, carpet knives, power stretchers, knee kickers, tensioners, and heat irons. Carpet and flooring installers must be able to use a computer with software for analyzing yardages, making schedules, and project management.

Education/Training: Most of these occupations require a high school diploma and on-the-job training.

Job Outlook: There will be little or no change in employment growth for carpet installers through 2018.

Tile/Marble Setter

Career Description: Tile and marble installers apply hard tile and marble to walls, floors, and ceilings in residential and commercial structures. These installers may prearrange or "dry fit" tiles on a dry floor to figure the layout and where tile cuts may need to be made. Careful attention to detail, physical fitness and flexibility, along with effective critical thinking and math skills are important.

Technical Skills: Tile installers use measuring devices, levels, and spacers along with trowels for spreading adhesive or thin set and rubber mallets for setting tiles evenly. They must be able to follow blueprints and make precise measurements and cuts. Using a computer with CADD and project management software is also a skill for this occupation.

Education/Training: Most positions require a high school diploma and on-the-job training. Some apprenticeships may be available.

Job Outlook: The employment growth for tile and marble setters is expected to be faster than average through 2018.

Roofer

Career Description: Roofers cover residential and commercial structures with such roofing materials as shingles, slate, and metal. They must be able to analyze problems with roofs and identify the best way to repair them. Precision with measuring, cutting, and aligning roofing materials is important. Roofing requires much physical strength, dexterity, and stamina. Strong math ability and critical thinking skills are essential for analyzing and solving roofing problems.

Technical Skills: Roofers must be proficient in using such equipment as blow torches, hammers, and shears. Ability to use a computer with such software as CADD, project management, word processing, and roofing software is essential.

Education/Training: Most positions require a high school diploma with some previous work-related skill and training.

Job Outlook: Employment is expected to grow about 4 percent, or slower than average for all occupations through 2018.

APPENDIX E

Practical Math Review

Math skills are essential to the housing or interior design professional's success on the job. For example, a designer or builder uses computational skills when taking measurements or creating a bid. When a designer works from a set of plans, math is used to obtain distances or to extrapolate actual dimensions.

Could you calculate the areas of ceilings or walls, or estimate the amount of wall covering or fabric a job requires? Could you estimate how much paint is needed to cover a structure's exterior or a room's walls? What if the area to be covered is not rectangular, but a triangular- or circular-shaped space? What if measurements are given in meters instead of feet?

You learned many of these skills throughout this text. This appendix reviews some basic mathematical operations a housing and interior design professional may use.

Place Values of Whole Numbers

A *whole number* (0, 1, 2, 3, etc.) is any positive number with no fractional parts. The position of a digit (number) determines its *place value.* The positions never change, but the digits may.

The number farthest to the right occupies the *ones* place value, or ones position. The digit immediately to the left is in the tens position, followed by the next digit to the left that is in the hundreds position. Moving left, there are the thousands position, the ten-thousands position, and so forth.

> **Example**
> **2, 542, 908**
>
> 8 has a place value of *ones*
>
> 0 has a place value of *tens*
>
> 9 has a place value of *hundreds*
>
> 2 has a place value of *thousands*
>
> 4 has a place value of *ten-thousands*
>
> 5 has a place value of *hundred-thousands*
>
> 2 has a place value of *millions*

Addition

Addition is the combining of at least two numbers to result in a new figure, or *sum.* When adding, align numbers by place value. For instance, line up the numbers that are in the ones column beneath each other. Numbers occupying each of the other place values should also line up in columns.

> **Example**
> Use the format that follows to add these numbers: 799 + 1205 + 2237
>
>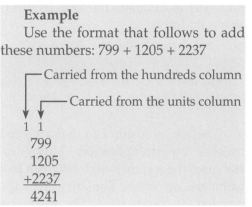

Adapted with permission from *Painting & Decorating* by E. Keith Blankenbaker. Available through Goodheart-Willcox Publisher (www.g-w.com).

Subtraction

This mathematical process involves finding the *difference* between two numbers. You generally write the larger number (*minuend*) first, and write the smaller number (*subtrahend*) beneath it. The result of subtracting the subtrahend from the minuend is the difference. Maintain the place-value columns as in addition. For example, ones-place values should line up in a column, tens-place values in another, and so forth.

Sometimes, it is necessary to *borrow* in subtraction. If a digit borrows, it takes from the next higher place value column. The column borrowed from is reduced by 1 and 10 is added to the digit that required the borrow.

The following example shows how borrowing occurs when subtracting 15 from 43. When borrowing, note a "1" is borrowed from the tens column (the number 4 here). This reduces the number "4" to "3". The number "3" in the ones column now becomes "13."

Example

$$\begin{array}{r} \overset{3}{\cancel{4}}\overset{1}{3} \\ -15 \\ \hline 28 \end{array}$$

Multiplication

Suppose an interior designer has 6 lengths of baseboard trim, each measuring 8 ft. in length. What is the total length of baseboard trim available? One way to calculate the total length is to use addition:

Example

$8 + 8 + 8 + 8 + 8 + 8 = 48$ ft. (of baseboard trim)

The same result can be achieved quicker by multiplication. Multiplication uses the × (times) sign between two numbers, or *factors*. The answer to the problem is the *product*. The following example shows how to achieve the same answer for the baseboard trim with multiplication:

Example

8 ft. $\times 6 = 48$ ft. (of baseboard trim)

Division

If you have 12 sets of house plans and want to give each of four interior designers an equal number of these house plans, division is a useful process. Division is the opposite of multiplication. The *dividend* is the number being divided. The *divisor* is the number dividing the dividend. The answer to the problem is the *quotient*. The following example reads as *12 divided by 4 equals 3*.

Example

$12 \div 4 = 3$

Because you can divide the number 12 into equal parts, each of the four interior designers will receive three sets of house plans. Some division problems do not yield equal parts. For example, 13 divided by 4 equals 3 with 1 left over. The left-over number is called the *remainder*.

Fractions

A fraction is a number that represents a part of something. For example, when making calculations for wall treatments, fractions are often part of the measurements or calculations. A ¾ in. mark on a measuring tape indicates a fraction (part) of a whole inch.

The bottom number, or *denominator*, shows how many parts make up the whole. The denominator cannot be 0. The top number, or *numerator*, specifies some number of those parts. The more parts there are in the whole, the smaller the size of each part. For instance, ½ gal.

of paint is more than ¼ gal. of paint. The parts created by breaking a unit into two are larger than the parts created by breaking it into four.

Proper Fractions

In a *proper fraction,* the numerator is less than the denominator.

Examples

$$\frac{1}{2}, \frac{2}{5}, \frac{3}{4}, \frac{1}{5}, \text{and } \frac{5}{8}$$

Improper Fractions

In an *improper fraction,* the numerator is greater than or equal to the denominator.

Examples

$$\frac{4}{4}, \frac{7}{3}, \frac{8}{6}, \frac{12}{9}, \text{and } \frac{11}{8}$$

If the numerator and denominator are equal, as in (⁴⁄₄), the fraction is *equivalent* (equal) to the whole number 1.

Mixed Numbers

An improper fraction can be written in the form of a *mixed number.* A mixed number consists of a whole number and a fraction.

Examples

$$2\frac{3}{4}, 5\frac{7}{8}, \text{and } 7\frac{2}{3}$$

To convert an improper fraction into a mixed number, divide the numerator by the denominator. The quotient is either a whole number or a whole number with a remainder. The remainder can be written as a fraction. How is the improper fraction ¹⁴⁄₅ converted into a mixed number?

Example

$$\frac{14}{5} = 14 \div 5 = 2 \text{ with a remainder of}$$

$$4, \text{or } 2\frac{4}{5} \text{ (mixed number)}$$

Reducing Fractions

Fractions are usually expressed in their *lowest terms,* or an equivalent fraction in which the numerator and denominator are the lowest possible numbers. To calculate the lowest terms of a fraction, find the largest number that divides evenly into *both* the numerator and denominator. Note how the fraction in the following example is reduced to its lowest terms.

Example

$$\frac{25}{100}$$

Find a number that is a factor of both 25 and 100. For example, both 25 and 100 can be divided by 5. This reduces the fraction to ⁵⁄₂₀.

However, ⁵⁄₂₀ is not in lowest terms since it can be further reduced by dividing its numerator and denominator by 5. The lowest term is ¼; this fraction cannot be reduced any further. The quickest way to reduce ²⁵⁄₁₀₀ to its lowest terms is to use their largest common factor, or 25. Dividing the numerator and denominator by 25 yields

$$\frac{25}{100} = \frac{5}{20} = \frac{1}{4}$$

Adding Fractions

Adding fractions that share the same denominator is simple: add the numerators together and use the same denominator.

Example

$$\frac{2}{6} + \frac{3}{6} = \frac{5}{6}$$

However, fractions with different denominators require another step before the addition. You must find a *common denominator* of the fractions. One way to find a common denominator

732

is to multiply the two denominators together.

Example

$$\frac{1}{2} + \frac{6}{8}$$

Find the common denominator. Multiplying the denominator 8 by 2 gives a denominator 16. Convert each fraction to an equivalent fraction with the denominator of 16.

Example

$$\frac{1}{2} = \frac{8}{16}$$

$$\frac{6}{8} = \frac{12}{16}$$

$$\frac{8}{16} + \frac{12}{16} = \frac{20}{16} = 1\frac{4}{16}$$

$$1\frac{4}{16} = 1\frac{1}{4} \text{ (reduced to lowest terms)}$$

Fractions are easier to read when using the smallest common denominator, or *lowest common denominator (LCD)*. Here is another example showing how to add and reduce fractions. First find the LCD. In this case, the LCD is 24. Convert ⅙ to ⁴⁄₂₄. Then add the numerators and keep the same denominator (24). Check to see if the answer is in lowest terms. If it is not, reduce the answer to its lowest terms. In the following example, the answer is in its lowest terms.

Example

$$\frac{1}{6} + \frac{3}{24}$$

$$\frac{1}{6} = \frac{4}{24}$$

$$\frac{4}{24} + \frac{3}{24} = \frac{7}{24}$$

Subtracting Fractions

Subtracting fractions is a lot like adding fractions. First, convert the fractions so they have a common denominator.

Second, subtract the numerators but keep the denominator the same. Finally, reduce your answer to lowest terms.

In the following example, note the LCD is 40. When you subtract the numerators (20 − 15), the difference is 5. Keep the denominator at 40. Then you must reduce the answer, ⁵⁄₄₀, to its lowest terms. The largest whole number that divides evenly into the numerator and denominator is 5. The final answer is ⅛.

Example

$$\frac{5}{10} - \frac{3}{8}$$

$$\frac{5}{10} = \frac{20}{40}$$

$$\frac{3}{8} = \frac{15}{40}$$

$$\frac{20}{40} - \frac{15}{40} = \frac{5}{40} = \frac{1}{8} \text{ (in lowest terms)}$$

$$\frac{5}{40} = \frac{1}{8} \text{ (reduced to lowest terms)}$$

Multiplying Fractions

It is not necessary to find a common denominator when you are multiplying fractions. Simply multiply the numerators and then multiply the denominators.

Example

$$\frac{2}{7} \times \frac{3}{11}$$

$$\frac{2}{7} \times \frac{3}{11} = \frac{6}{77}$$

If the answer needs to be reduced to lowest terms, do so. In this case, you cannot reduce it any further.

Dividing Fractions

In division of fractions, the *dividend* (number being divided) is multiplied by the *reciprocal* of the *divisor* (the number dividing the dividend). The reciprocal of a number is determined by simply switching the number's numerator and denominator. A number multiplied by its reciprocal equals 1. For example, the reciprocal of 2 is ½ because

$$\frac{2}{1} \times \frac{1}{2} = \frac{2}{2} \text{ or } 1$$

The numerators and the denominators of the fractions are then multiplied and reduced to the lowest terms.

In the following example, find the reciprocal of the divisor by inverting the divisor. Then multiply and reduce to the lowest terms.

Example

$$\frac{9}{12} \div \frac{3}{4}$$

$(\frac{3}{4})$ to $\frac{4}{3}$ (reciprocal)

$$\frac{9}{12} \times \frac{4}{3} = \frac{36}{36} = 1$$

Decimals

Interior designers, builders, and painters may use decimals during estimating—while determining job costs or tracking hours or parts of hours for payroll. A decimal is another way of representing a fraction, or part of a unit. A decimal is made up of digits with each one representing a multiple of ten. A point (.), called a *decimal point,* is used in the decimal system. To read decimal numbers, say them out loud like fractions (0.7 = seven-tenths) or say the word point with the numbers (0.028 = zero point zero twenty-eight).

Place Values

The place value determines the value of the digit. The number written to the left of a decimal point represents the whole number. For example, in the number 487, the digit 4 has a place value of hundreds.

Digits to the right of the decimal show the number of parts required to make a whole. This is the fraction, and its value is less than 1. Read decimal numbers from left to right. For example, 0.591 would be read $^{591}\!/_{1000}$. Zeros are used as placeholders to keep remaining digits in their proper places, as in 0.031 = thirty-one *thousandths.* Place values are multiples of 10.

Example
0.72138 (72138/100,000)

0 has a place value of zero *ones*

. *decimal point*

   7 has a place value of *seven tenths* (7/10)

      2 has a place value of *two hundredths* (2/100)

         1 has a place value of *one thousandths* (1/1000)

            3 has a place value of *three ten thousandths* (3/10,000)

               8 has a place value of *eight hundred thousandths* (8/100,000)

Adding and Subtracting Decimals

When you are adding or subtracting decimal numbers, align the decimal points before performing the operation. The decimal point in the answer drops down and into the same location.

Example
Add:

```
        0.57
       21.678
    +   0.38
       22.628
```

Subtract:

```
   89.538            89.5380
 −  7.2913          −  7.2913
   82.2467           82.2467
```

Note: The preceding subtraction problem requires a zero in the blank space to the right of 8 to allow the completion of the problem.

Multiplying and Dividing Decimals

When multiplying decimal numbers, disregard the decimal points when you perform this operation. Then count the number of places to the right of the decimal point in each factor. The sum of these numbers is the number of decimal places required in the product (the answer). Starting to the right of the product, place the decimal point by moving left by this sum. Review the following problem to multiply decimals.

Example

$$
\begin{array}{r}
0.59 \\
\times\ 12.8 \\
\hline
7.552
\end{array}
$$

0.59 (2 places right of the decimal point)

× 12.8 (1 place right of the decimal point)

7.552 (2 + 1 = 3, count back 3 places from the right to the left and insert the decimal point)

If there are fewer digits to the left than you need, add zeros to the left to maintain the required decimal place values.

Example

$$6\overline{)45} = 6\overline{)45.0}\quad\frac{7.5}{}$$

When dividing decimal numbers, if there is a decimal in the divisor, change it to a whole number by moving the decimal point to the far right. Count the places moved to the right, and then move the decimal point in the dividend the same number of places to the right. You may need to add zeros to keep the place values. Perform the division operation. Align the decimal point in the quotient with the position of the decimal point in the dividend.

Example

$$1.5\overline{)\,.225}$$

(Move the decimal point one place to the right)

$$15\overline{)2.25}\quad\frac{0.15}{}$$

Converting Inches to Feet

The following chart (Figure A) shows the conversion of inches to feet. Values are expressed as decimals and fractions.

Converting Inches to Feet		
Inches	Feet (decimal)	Feet (fraction)
1	0.08	$\frac{1}{12}$
2	0.17	$\frac{1}{6}$
3	0.25	$\frac{1}{4}$
4	0.33	$\frac{1}{3}$
5	0.42	$\frac{5}{12}$
6	0.50	$\frac{1}{2}$
7	0.58	$\frac{7}{12}$
8	0.67	$\frac{2}{3}$
9	0.75	$\frac{3}{4}$
10	0.83	$\frac{5}{6}$
11	0.92	$\frac{11}{12}$
12	1.00	$\frac{12}{12}$

Figure A
Sometimes a housing and interior design professional must convert inches to feet before performing a calculation.

Squares and Square Roots

The product of a number multiplied by itself is the number's *square*. For example, the square of 3 is 9 because $3 \times 3 = 9$. If one side of a square measures 10 ft., the remaining three sides also measure 10 ft. The area (A) of a square is the length of one side squared. Here is the formula:

$A = S^2$

Example

If one side of the square measures 10 ft., the area of the square is

$A = S^2$

$A = 10^2$

$A = 10 \times 10$

$A = 100$ sq. ft.

Alternately, if the area of a square is given as 100 sq. ft., you could determine the length of a side by taking the square root of 100. A square root is written using the symbol $\sqrt{\ }$.

Example

√100 (square root of 100)

A number's square root is a factor of the number. When you multiply that factor by itself, the product is the number. In the above case, the square root of 100 is 10. You can find the square root of any number by using a calculator.

Metric Measurement

When designers, builders, or painters take measurements, they use the U.S. Conventional or the SI Metric system. In the U.S. Conventional system, commonly used in the U.S., basic units of measure include the *inch, foot,* and *yard.* In the SI Metric system, used in many other countries, measures are described as *millimeter, centimeter,* or *meter.* The metric system gives dimensions as decimal fractions (35.2 mm) instead of mixing units of measurement (3′ 7″).

The following examples are U. S. Conventional system units and their SI Metric system equivalents:

Example

1 inch = 25.40 millimeters (mm)
1 inch = 2.54 centimeters (cm)
1 foot = 0.3048 meter (m)
1 yard = 0.9144 meter
1 mile = 1.6093 kilometers (km)

Length

The metric system is convenient to use because its units can be converted from one to another by multiplying or dividing by multiples of 10, (see Figure B). When a designer or contractor reads a metric measuring tape, for example, the smallest unit is the millimeter. Ten millimeters make a centimeter, and ten centimeters make a decimeter (a decimeter is seldom marked on measuring tapes). Ten decimeters make a meter.

U.S. Conventional with SI Metric Measurement Equivalents for Length

Fractional Inch	Millimeters	Inches	Centimeters	Feet	Meters
1/32	.7938	1	2.54	1	.3048
1/16	1.588	1 1/4	3.175	1 1/2	.4572
3/32	2.381	1 1/2	3.81	2	.6096
1/8	3.175	1 3/4	4.445	2 1/2	.7620
5/32	3.969	2	5.08		
3/16	4.763	2 1/4	5.715	3	.9144
7/32	5.556	2 1/2	6.35	3 1/2	1.067
1/4	6.350	2 3/4	6.985	4	1.219
9/32	7.144	3	7.62	4 1/2	1.372
5/16	7.938	3 1/4	8.255	5	1.524
11/32	8.731	3 1/2	8.89	5 1/2	1.676
3/8	9.525	3 3/4	9.525	6	1.829
13/32	10.32	4	10.16	6 1/2	1.981
7/16	11.11	4 1/4	10.80		
15/32	11.91	4 1/2	11.43	7	2.134
1/2	12.70	4 3/4	12.07	7 1/2	2.286
17/32	13.49	5	12.70	8	2.438
9/16	14.29	5 1/4	13.34	8 1/2	2.591
19/32	15.08	5 1/2	13.97		
5/8	15.88	5 3/4	14.61	9	2.743
21/32	16.67	6	15.24	9 1/2	2.896
11/16	17.46	6 1/2	16.51	10	3.048
23/32	18.26	7	17.78	10 1/2	3.200
3/4	19.05	7 1/2	19.05	11	3.353
25/32	19.84	8	20.32	11 1/2	3.505
13/16	20.64	8 1/2	21.59	12	3.658
27/32	21.43	9	22.86	15	4.572
7/8	22.23	9 1/2	24.13		
29/32	23.02	10	25.40	20	6.096
15/16	23.81	10 1/2	26.67	25	7.620
31/32	24.61	11	27.94	50	15.24
1	25.40	11 1/2	29.21	100	30.48

Figure B
Lengths are calculated using the U.S. Conventional and SI Metric systems.

Finding Areas

Area is a two-dimensional measurement. Calculating the area helps interior designers determine how much paint or wall covering is needed to cover a surface. Area is expressed in *square units,* such as 29 sq. ft. or 3 sq. m. To calculate area, measurements must be in the same (common) unit. For example, if a wall is 12 ft. 6 in. long and 8 ft. 6 in. high, you first convert the measurements to inches.

> **Example**
>
> 12 ft. 6 in. = 144 in. + 6 in. = 150 in.
> 8 ft. 6 in. = 96 in. + 6 in. =102 in.

To find the area of the wall, do the following calculation:

> **Example**
>
> 150 in. × 102 in. = 15,300 sq. in.

To find the area of the wall in square feet, convert square inches into square feet by dividing the answer by 144.

> **Example**
>
> 15,300 sq. in. ÷ 144 = 106.25 sq. ft.

Squares, Rectangles, and Parallelograms

A *square* has four sides that are equal in length and meet at right (90°) angles. A *parallelogram* has four sides; two pairs of parallel sides. A *rectangle* is a type of parallelogram with four sides that meet at right angles. The formulas for the areas for each of these figures follows in Figure C.

Triangles

A *triangle* is a three-sided polygon. The area of a triangle, Figure D, is calculated by taking one-half the *base* times the *height.* Use the following formula:

Area (A) = (B × H) × ½
OR
Area (A) = (B × H) ÷ 2

If the base of a triangle is 14 ft. and the height is 5 ft., the area is calculated in the following ways.

> **Example**
>
> A = (14 ft. × 5 ft.) × ½
> A = 70 sq. ft. × ½
> A = 35 sq. ft.
> *OR*
> A = (14 ft. × 5 ft.) ÷ 2
> A = 70 sq. ft. ÷ 2
> A = 35 sq. ft.

Area of Squares, Rectangles, and Parallelograms

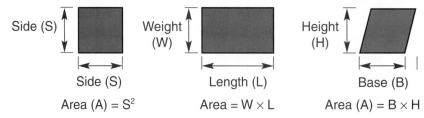

Side (S) / Side (S) / Area (A) = S^2

Weight (W) / Length (L) / Area = W × L

Height (H) / Base (B) / Area (A) = B × H

Figure C
The areas of squares, rectangles, and parallelograms can be found using the formulas shown.

Area of Triangles

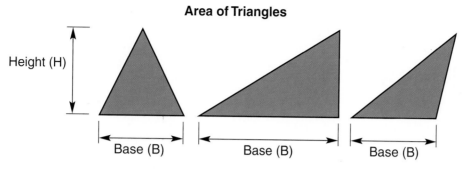

Area (A) = (B × H) ÷ 2
or
Area (A) = (B × H) × $\frac{1}{2}$

Figure D
Triangular areas equal one-half of the base times the height.

Circles and Half-circles

The *diameter* of a circle is a straight line between two points on the circle and passing through the center of the circle. The *radius* of the circle begins at the center and extends to any point in the circumference of the circle. Multiplying the radius by two gives the diameter, Figure E. The formula for finding the area of a circle is

$A = \pi \times r^2$

In the preceding formula, A = area, π (pi) = 3.1416, and r = radius. The radius is squared (^{2}), meaning the radius is multiplied by itself. The following example shows how to calculate the area of a circle with a radius of 4 in.

Example
$A = \pi \times r^2$
$A = 3.1416 \times 4^2$
$A = 3.1416 \times (4 \times 4)$
$A = 3.1416 \times 16$
$A = 50.2656$ sq. in.

The area of a half-circle is half the area of a circle. Use the following formula to calculate the area of a half-circle:

$A = (\pi \times r^2) \times \dfrac{1}{2}$

OR

$A = (\pi \times r^2) \div 2$

Area of Circles and Half-Circles

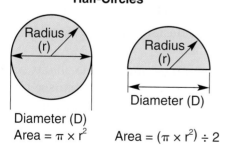

Diameter (D)
Area = $\pi \times r^2$ Area = $(\pi \times r^2) \div 2$

Figure E
Use these formulas when calculating the areas of circles and half-circles.

Glossary

A

abilities. Skills a person develops with practice. (24)

absorbed light. Light that is drawn in by a surface. (17)

abstract form. The physical shape of an object that rearranges or stylizes a recognizable object. (10)

abstract of title. A copy of all public records concerning a property. (5)

accent lighting. A form of lighting that serves as a highlight. (17)

accessories. Items smaller than furnishings that accent the design of a room or area. (17)

acoustical. A common material used for ceilings that reduces or absorbs sound. (14)

Adam style. A style of architecture that emerged during the Federal period. The houses were symmetrical with graceful details. A fanlight over the entrance is characteristic of this style. (6)

adjacency matrix. A diagram that shows the desired relationship of room and space locations. (19)

adjustable rate mortgage (ARM). A mortgage for which the interest rate is periodically adjusted up or down according to a national interest rate index. (5)

adobe. A building material made of sun-dried earth and straw. (1)

aesthetics. Beauty. A pleasing appearance or effect. (10)

agrarian. People who earn their living from the land. (2)

agreement of sale. A document that gives a detailed description of the property and its legal location and all specific terms and conditions of the real estate sale; also called *offer to purchase, contract of purchase, purchase agreement,* or *sales agreement.* (5)

alcove. A small recessed section of a room. (7)

alphabet of lines. Seven different lines commonly used on architectural drawings. (7)

American Society of Landscape Architects (ASLA). Landscape architects that are the most qualified experts in this field. (20)

amortize. To pay off a loan (principal with interest) in monthly installments for a given number of years. (5)

ampere (amp). The measure of the amount of electricity passing through a conductor per unit of time. (9)

analogous color harmony. A color harmony created by combining related hues—those next to each other on the color wheel. (11)

anchor bolts. Bolts set about six feet apart into the concrete of the foundation walls. (8)

annuals. Flowers that must be replanted yearly. (20)

antique. A piece of furniture made over 100 years ago in the style of the period. (15)

appliance. A household device powered by gas or electricity to help people meet their needs. (18)

applied design. A design that is printed onto the surface of the fabric. (13)

appraisal. An expert estimate of the quality and value of a property by a licensed appraiser. (5)

apprenticeship. Learning a trade under the direction and guidance of an expert worker. (24)

aptitude. A natural talent or ability to learn something quickly and easily. (24)

archeologist. Social scientist who studies ancient cultures by unearthing dwelling places of past civilizations. (1)

architect. A person who designs buildings and supervises their construction. (2)

architectural drawings. Drawings that contain information about the size, shape, and locations of all parts of a house or structure. (7)

Arts and Crafts. A style of housing built between 1905 and 1930 based on the Arts and Crafts Movement of the 1880s. Also called *Craftsman,* this style celebrated the use of natural materials worked by hand. (6)

asbestos. A fireproof, cancer-causing mineral that can easily become airborne and inhaled. (21)

asphyxiation. The state of unconsciousness or death resulting from inadequate oxygen or some other breathing obstruction. (21)

assign. To transfer the entire unexpired portion of a lease to someone else; after the transaction, the original renter is not responsible for the lease. (5)

assisted-living facility. A type of life-care housing for older adults who need living assistance with certain daily routines, but not constant care. (4)

associate's degree. A two-year college degree. (24)

asymmetrical. A style in which one side of a center point is different from the other. (6)

attached houses. Housing designed for one household, but shares a common wall with a house on one or both sides. (4)

attitude. A person's outlook on life. (25)

autoclaved aerated concrete (AAC). A mixture of sand, fly ash, cement, and water with aluminum powder (an expansion agent) that is cast into a mold and then cut into blocks after a curing process. (8)

automated houses. Dwellings that have an integrated and centrally controlled system based on computer technology. (23)

B

baby boomers. Members of the adult population born during the period after World War II called the "baby boom," which occurred between 1946 and 1964. (2)

bachelor's degree. A college degree usually requiring four years of study. (24)

balance. The equilibrium among parts of a design. A perception of the way arrangements are seen. (12)

bearing wall. A wall that supports some weight from the ceiling or roof of the structure. (8)

beauty. The quality or qualities that give pleasure to the senses. (1)

bid. A fee contractors charge to build a house; includes both materials and labor costs. (5) A statement that includes the actual costs for products, work, and fees for a project. (19)

biennials. Flowers that require planting every other year. (20)

bill of lading. A receipt listing the goods shipped in a moving van. (5)

biometrics. The measurement and analysis of an individual by using a unique physical characteristic. (21)

blend. A combination of two or more different fibers in making yarn; cotton and polyester is an example. (13)

blinds. Window treatments with slats that can be tilted, raised and lowered, or moved to the side. (17)

bonded fabrics. Fabrics consisting of two layers of fabric that are permanently joined together with an adhesive. (13)

bonded wood. Wood that has been bonded by the application of glue and pressure. (15)

box nail. A nail with a large, flat head. (22)

box springs. A series of coils attached to a base and covered with padding; these springs support the mattress. (15)

breach of contract. A legal term for failure to meet all terms of a contract or agreement. (5)

brick. A block molded from moist clay and hardened with heat. (8)

building codes. Established minimum standards for materials and construction methods. (2)

Building Information Model (BIM). An approach to building that embraces every stage of a building's lifecycle: design, construction, maintenance, and sometimes demolition. (7)

built-in storage. Shelves and drawers that are built into a housing unit. (7)

bungalow. A one-and-one-half story house with a low-pitched roof, horizontal shape, and a covered front porch. (6)

butcher block. A work surface made by fusing a stack of long, thin hardwood strips. (14)

butt joint. A joint formed by gluing or nailing one board flush to another board. (15)

C

Cape Cod. A small, symmetrical, one or one-and-one-half story house with a steep gable roof and side gables. (6)

carbon monoxide. A colorless, odorless, tasteless gas that develops from incomplete burning of fossil fuel. (21)

career. A series of related occupations that show progression in a field of work. (24)

career cluster. A group of occupations or career specialties that are similar or related to one another. (24)

case good. A furniture piece in which wood is the primary construction material. (15)

Casual style. A furniture style that emphasizes comfort and informality. (15)

ceiling treatment. A coating, covering, or building material applied to the ceiling area. (14)

cellulosic natural fiber. Fiber that comes from the cellulose in plants. (13)

census. An official count of the population by the government. (2)

central heat-pump system. An electric refrigeration unit used to either heat or cool a house. (9)

central-satellite decision. A group of decisions consisting of a major decision that is surrounded by related but independent decisions. (3)

ceramic tile. A flat piece of kiln-fired clay coated with a protective glaze. (14)

chain decision. A sequence of decisions in which one decision triggers others. (3)

change order. A document that outlines the details and costs of unexpected plan changes in a bid. (19)

circuit. The path electrons follow from the source of electricity to the device and back to the source. (9)

circuit breaker. A switch that automatically trips and interrupts the flow of electrical current in event of an abnormal condition. (9)

classic. Use of formal architectural elements that have been recognized over time for their enduring design excellence. (6)

clearance space. A measurement term for the amount of space to leave unobstructed around furniture to allow for ease of use and a good traffic pattern. (16)

climate. The combination of weather conditions in a region over a period of years as shown by temperature, wind velocity, and precipitation. (2)

closeout sale. A sale held when a store is moving or going out of business. (16)

closet auger. A device used to bore through items with a twisting and turning motion to free blocked plumbing or wastewater lines. (22)

closing costs. Fees and charges for settling the legal and financial matters for a real estate sale. (5)

cogeneration. An efficient, clean, and reliable approach to generating power and thermal energy from a single fuel source; also known as *combined heat and power* (CHP). (23)

coil springs. Spiral-shaped springs without padding and covering that are used in heavier furniture. (15)

collectible. A highly valuable furnishing less than 100 years old, but no longer made. (15)

color. An element or property of light. (11)

color harmony. A pleasing combination of colors based on their respective positions on the color wheel. (11)

color rendering index (CRI). An indicator of how well light from a source will bring out the true color of an item. (17)

color scheme. The combination of colors selected for the design of a room or house. (11)

color spectrum. The full range of all existing colors. (11)

color temperature. The color of light rated in kelvin (K)—a temperature scale—that impacts how items appear in light. (17)

color wheel. A particular circular arrangement of primary, secondary, and tertiary colors; the basis of all color relationships. (11)

combination yarn. A continuous strand of yarn made from two or more different yarns. (13)

combustible. The quality of being burnable. (21)

comforter. A thick bed covering that consists of two layers of fabric with a filling sandwiched between them. (13)

common-use storage. Storage used by all who live in a house; includes entry storage for outerwear and storage for food, tools, and other shared items. (7)

community. A large city, small village, or rural area. (4)

compact fluorescent bulb. A type of fluorescent lamp that uses 75 percent less energy and operates for nearly 9,000 hours. (17)

comparison shopping. Comparing the qualities, prices, and services linked to similar items in different stores before buying. (16)

complement. A hue that is directly across from another hue on the color wheel. (11)

complementary color harmony. A color harmony made by combining two colors opposite each other on the color wheel; sometimes called contrasting colors. (11)

compost. Biologically decomposed organic material that can enrich soil and grow plants; the end result of composting. (23)

composting toilet. A self-contained, stand-alone toilet; works like a garden compost pile, transforming waste into a stable end product. (9)

computer-aided drafting and design (CADD). Software and hardware that creates designs with a computer. (2)

concrete. A hard building material made by combining cement, sand, gravel, and water. (8)

condominium. A type of ownership in which the buyer owns individual living space and also has an undivided interest in the common areas and facilities of the multiunit project. (4)

condops. A blend of condominium and cooperative ownership in which buyers own their individual living spaces but ownership of the common areas and facilities is cooperative. (4)

conductor. Allows the flow of electricity; usually a wire. (9)

conduit. A metal or plastic pipe that surrounds and protects the wires. (9)

conflict. A hostile situation resulting from opposing views. (25)

coniferous. Evergreen trees that do not shed their leaves. (15)

conservation. The process of protecting something from loss or waste. (20)

construction. A design characteristic that includes materials and structure. (10)

construction drawings. Drawings with detailed instructions to the building to obtain necessary permits and erect the structure. (7)

Contemporary style. A housing style in which the designs are surprising and often controversial; also refers to a twenty-first century furniture style composed of designs that are the very latest introductions to the market. (6)

contractor. A person who contracts, or agrees, to supply certain materials or do certain work for a specific fee. (4)

convection oven. An oven that bakes foods in a stream of heated air. (18)

conventional mortgage. A two-party contract between a borrower and lender; a loan with a long-term fixed rate. (5)

cool colors. Blue, green, and violet and the colors near them on the color wheel; also called *receding colors*. (11)

cooperative. A type of ownership in which people buy shares of stock in a nonprofit housing corporation. These shares entitle them to occupy a unit in the cooperative building. (4)

cooperative education. A program that offers the opportunity to work part-time and attend classes part-time; the program combines classroom instruction with paid practical work experience. (24)

cork. The woody bark tissue of a sustainable plant. (14)

corner block. Small pieces of wood attached between corner boards; they support and reinforce the furniture joints. (15)

countertop. A durable work surface installed on a base cabinet. (14)

Country style. A furniture style that traces its origins to the lifestyles of rural areas. (15)

creativity. The ability to use imaginative skill to make something new. (1)

credit history. A profile of a person's payment record and outstanding debts. (5)

criteria matrix. A matrix that looks at the impact of specific needs on various spaces. (19)

culture. The beliefs, social customs, and traits of a group of people. (2)

curtains. Flat fabric panels that hang to the left and right of a window or may completely cover it. (17)

curved line. A line that is part of a circle or an oval. (10)

D

deadbolt locks. A lock bolt that unlocks by turning a knob or key without action of a spring. (21)

debt-to-income ratio. The division of total debt (debt + housing costs) by gross income. (5)

decibel (dB). A unit for measuring sound intensity. (21)

deciduous. Trees that lose their leaves. (15)

declaration of ownership. The conditions and restrictions of the sale, ownership, and use of the property within a particular group of condominium units. (5)

deed. The legal document that shows the transfer of title from one person to another; describes the property being sold. (5)

dehumidifier. An appliance that removes moisture from the air. (18)

demographics. Statistical facts about the human population. (2)

density. The number of people in a given area. (2)

design. The entire process used to develop a specific project. It also refers to the product or result of the process. (10)

design process. A series of organized phases a designer uses to carry out a project in an orderly manner. (19)

detail view. An enlargement of a construction feature that uses a larger scale than other drawings. (7)

diagonal line. A line that angles between a horizontal and vertical line. (10)

diffused light. Light that scatters over a large area. (17)

direct lighting. Lighting that shines directly toward an object. (17)

disability. An impairment or limit to a person's ability to carry out daily living activities. (2)

disinfectant. A cleaning agent that destroys bacteria. (22)

double-complementary color harmony. A color harmony consisting of two colors and their complements. (11)

double-dowel joint. Glued wooden dowels that fit into drilled holes in two pieces of wood. (15)

dovetail joint. A furniture joint that utilizes flaring tenons and mortises which fit tightly, interlocking two pieces of wood at a corner joint. (15)

down payment. A partial payment made to secure a purchase. (5)

downspout. A vertical pipe that connects the gutter system to the ground to carry rainwater away from the home's foundation. (8)

draperies. Fabric panels with pleats that cover windows completely or are pulled to the side. (17)

dual-career family. A type of family that occurs when both adults in a family are employed outside the home. (2)

duct. A large round tube or rectangular boxlike structure that delivers heated (or air-conditioned) air to distant rooms or spaces. (9)

Dutch Colonial. A housing style with a gambrel roof. (6)

E

Early Classical Revival. A Federal style of architecture that evolved from the classical details of Greek and Italian design. (6)

Early English. An architectural style built by English settlers in North America beginning in the early 1600s. (6)

earnest money. A deposit, or sum of money a home buyer pays to show serious intentions to buy a house; the money is held in a trust until the closing of the deal and is applied to the total payment price. (5)

earth-sheltered. Houses that are partially covered with soil. (6)

Earthship. A type of self-sufficient housing that uses passive solar and earth-sheltered design along with the use of recycled materials. (23)

Eclectic style. Furniture and fabrics that cross over styles and periods. (15)

ecology. The relationship between all living things and their surroundings. (23)

electrical shock. An electric current passing through the human body. (21)

electric current. Another name for electricity. (9)

electricity. The movement of electrons along a conductor. (9)

electric radiant-heating systems. A heating system in which resistance wiring is used to produce heat. (9)

elevation view. Shows the finished exterior appearance of a given side of a house. (7)

emphasis. A center of interest or focal point in a room. (12)

enclosure elements. Items such as fences and walls that enclose a space. (20)

ENERGY STAR label. A label that indicates a product is at least 10 percent more energy efficient than similar products. (18)

EnergyGuide label. A label that states the average yearly energy use and operating cost of an appliance. (18)

engineered quartz. A stonelike countertop material that is a combination of quartz particles with a mixture of binders. (14)

entrepreneur. A person who starts and runs his or her own business. (24)

environment. The total of all conditions, objects, places, and people around you. (2)

equity. The money value of a house beyond what is owed on it. (5)

ergonomics. The design of consumer products and environments to promote user comfort, efficiency, and safety. (16)

escape plan. A plan of action for escaping a home if an emergency such as a fire occurs. (21)

esteem. A feeling of respect, admiration, and high regard of others. (1)

ethical behavior. Conforming to accepted standards of fairness and good conduct, based on a person's sense of what is right to do. (25)

eviction. A legal procedure that forces a renter to leave the property before the rental agreement expires. (5)

exterior elevations. Architectural drawings that show the outside views of the house. (7)

extrusion. A process used to form and shape manufactured fibers. (13)

F

factory-built housing. Housing constructed in a plant and moved to a site. (4)

Fair Housing Act. A law that forbids discrimination in housing and requires multiunits to be accessible to people with disabilities. (4)

family. Two or more people living together who are related by birth, marriage, or adoption. (1)

faux finish. The application of paint in different textures and patterns to create a decorative finish; derives from the French word for *false* or *fictitious*. (14)

Federal. A style of housing that has a boxlike shape. It is at least two stories high and is symmetrical with a flat roof. (6)

FHA-insured mortgage. A three-party contract that involves the borrower, a lender, and the Federal Housing Administration (FHA). (5)

fiber. The raw materials from which yarns and fabrics are made. (13)

fiber optics. A type of heatless light produced by passing an electric current through a cable containing very fine strands of glass. (17)

finance charge. A fee paid for the privilege of using credit. It includes interest and other service fees. (5)

finishes. Substances applied to fabrics to improve their appearance, texture, and performance. (13)

finish nail. A nail with a very small head that can be driven below the surface using another nail or a nail set tool. (22)

fireplace insert. A metal device that fits into an existing fireplace and attaches to the chimney liner. (9)

flammable. Fabrics that burn quickly. (13)

flashing. A water-resistant sheet metal used to help keep the roof watertight. (8)

flat springs. Flat or zigzag springs that are used in lightweight furniture; may have metal support strips banded across them. (15)

float. Long segments of yarn that lie on the surface of a fabric. (13)

floor coverings. Surfaces placed on the structural floor. (14)

flooring materials. Materials that form the top surface of a floor. (14)

floor plan. A simplified drawing that shows the size and arrangement of rooms, hallways, doors, windows, and storage areas on one floor of a home. (7)

floor treatment. Flooring materials and floor coverings. (14)

fluorescent light. Light produced as electricity activates mercury vapor within a sealed tube to create invisible ultraviolet rays. These rays are converted into visible light rays by a fluorescent material on the inside of the glass tube. (17)

foam mattress. A mattress made from latex or polyurethane foam. (15)

folk. House style that originates from the common experiences of a group of people, such as common values and goals. (6)

foot-candle. A measurement of how much light reaches an object or a surface. (17)

footing. The bottom of the foundation which supports the rest of the foundation and the house. (8)

forced warm-air system. A heating system in which a furnace heats and delivers air to rooms through supply ducts. (9)

foreclosure. A legal proceeding in which a lending firm takes possession of the property when the owner fails to make monthly house payments on time or does not fulfill the agreements related to the loan. (5)

form. The physical shape of objects. (10)

formal balance. The identical proportion and arrangement of objects on both sides of a center point; symmetry. (12)

fossil fuel. A fuel that forms in the earth from plant or animal remains. (9)

foundation. The underlying base of the house composed of the footing and the foundation walls. (8)

foundation wall. The walls supporting the load of the house between the footing and the floor. (8)

free form. A shape found in nature that is random and flowing and communicates a feeling of freedom. (10)

freestanding houses. Single-family houses that stand alone and are not connected to another unit. (4)

French Manor. A symmetrically styled home with wings on each side and a Mansard roof on the main part of the house. (6)

French Normandy. Early French homes built by French Huguenot settlers; one-story structures with many narrow door and window openings and steeply pitched roofs. (6)

French Plantation. An architectural style built by French settlers in southern U.S. regions. (6)

French Provincial. A usually symmetrical style of housing that has a delicate, dignified appearance. The windows are a dominant part of the design, and the tops of the windows break into the eave line. (6)

frost line. The depth to which frost penetrates soil in a specific area. (8)

fuel cell. An equipment system that produces electricity from the use of chemicals. (23)

full warranty. A written agreement that provides the consumer with free repair or replacement of a warranted product or part if any defect occurs during the warranty period. (18)

function. How a design works; also it's purpose, usefulness, convenience, and organization. (10)

fuse. A device that includes a wire or strip of fusible metal that melts and interrupts a circuit when an electrical-current overload occurs. (9)

G

gable roof. A roof that comes to a high point in the center and slopes on both sides. (6)

gambrel roof. A roof with a lower steeper slope and an upper less-steep slope on both of its sides. (6)

Garrison. A style of housing in which an overhang allows extra space on the second floor. (6)

general lighting. Lighting that provides a uniform level of light throughout a room; also called *ambient lighting*. (17)

generic name. A name which describes a group of fibers with similar chemical compositions. (13)

geometric form. The physical shape of an object that uses squares, rectangles, circles, and other geometric figures to create form. (10)

Georgian. A style of housing that has simple exterior lines, a dignified appearance, and is symmetrical. Georgian houses have windows with small panes of glass and either gable or hip roofs. (6)

geothermal energy. Energy for heating and cooling—via a buried liquid-filled pipe designed in a loop—that utilizes the stable temperature of the earth's interior. (23)

German. Settler who traveled from the region called Germany today. (6)

girder. A large horizontal member in the floor that takes the load of joists. (8)

golden mean. The division of a line between one-half and one-third of its length, which creates a more pleasing look to the eye than an equal division. (12)

golden rectangle. A rectangle having sides in a ratio of 1:1.618. (12)

golden section. The division of a line or form in such a way that the ratio of the smaller section to the larger section is equal to the ratio of the larger section to the whole. (12)

gradation. A type of rhythm created by a gradual increase or decrease of similar elements of design. (12)

graduated-care facility. A life-care community for older adults in which residents move from their own apartments, to assisted living, or to a nursing-home unit as their needs change. (4)

grain. The direction the threads run in a woven fabric. (13)

graywater. Wastewater from washing machines, showers, and sinks that is not contaminated by human waste. (23)

Greek Revival. Architecture imitating ancient Greece. The main characteristic is a two-story portico. The portico is supported by columns and has a large triangular pediment. (6)

green design. A type of design that strives to have low impact on the environment; a subset of sustainable design. (1)

gross domestic product (GDP). The value of all goods and services produced within a country during a given period of time. (2)

gross income. Income before deductions. (5)

ground cover. Low-growing plants that cover the ground in place of sod. (20)

ground fault circuit interrupter (GFCI). A special electrical device that stops the flow of electrical current in a circuit as a safety precaution. Helps protect people from burns or electrical-shock injuries. (9)

gutter. A horizontal open trough located under the perimeter of the roof to channel away water. (8)

gypsum wallboard. A common building material for interior walls and ceilings; also called *drywall* and *sheet rock*. (14)

H

habitual behavior. An action that is done as a matter of routine without thought. (3)

half-timbered. A type of house in which the wood frame actually formed part of the outside wall. (6)

hand limitation. Limited movement and gripping ability resulting from arthritis or other condition. (21)

hardscape. Anything in the landscape other than vegetation and outdoor furniture. (20)

hardware. The components of a computer system. (18)

harmony. Agreement among the parts. It is created when the elements of design are effectively used according to the principles of design. (12)

hazardous waste. Poisonous waste material that damages the environment and causes illness. (23)

header. Small, built-up beams that carry the load of the structure over door and window openings. (8)

hearing disability. Any degree of hearing loss. (21)

high mass. A space that is visually crowded. (10)

high tech. The latest technology. (2)

hip roof. A roof with sloping ends and sides. (6)

hogan. A building made of logs and mud and inhabited by the Navajo. (2)

home. Any place a person lives. (1)

home generators. An appliance that creates electricity to run household electricity in the event of a power outage. (9)

home inspection. An evaluation of construction and present condition of a house; reveals any defects that may impact home value and sales price. (5)

horizontal line. A line that is parallel to the ground. (10)

house. Any building that serves as living quarters for one or more families. (1)

household. Includes all people who occupy a dwelling. (1)

housing. Any dwelling that provides shelter. (1)

housing market. The transfer of dwellings from the producers to the consumers. (2)

housing-to-income ratio. The division of total housing costs by gross income. (5)

hue. The name of a color in its purest form with no added black, gray, or white. (11)

human ecology. The study of people and their environment. (1)

human resources. Resources available from people. (3)

humidifier. An appliance that adds moisture to the air. (18)

HVAC. Refers to heating, ventilating, and air-conditioning systems that condition the living space for thermal comfort. (9)

hydroelectric power. Electrical power that is generated by water from rivers and dams moving through turbines. (23)

hydronic heating systems. A circulating hot water system in which water is heated to a preset temperature and pumped through pipes to radiators. (9)

I

implement. To put thoughts into action. (3)

impulse decision. A decision made quickly, with little thought of the possible consequences. (3)

incandescent light. Light produced when electric current passes through a fine tungsten filament inside a bulb. (17)

indirect lighting. Lighting that is directed toward a surface that reflects light into a room. (17)

induction cooktop. A cooktop that uses a magnetic field below a glass-ceramic surface to generate heat in the bottom of cookware. The cookware must be magnetic. (18)

informal balance. (asymmetrical) The arrangement of different but equivalent objects on each side of a center point. (12)

infrastructure. The underlying foundation or basic framework. (2)

innerspring mattress. A mattress that contains a series of coil springs that are covered with padding. (15)

installment buying. The process of buying something by making a series of payments during a given length of time. (5)

insulated concrete forms (ICF). Rigid polystyrene foam forms with internal plastic for ties that stack together like building blocks. The forms are reinforced with steel. Concrete is poured into the open middle forming a reinforced concrete wall with insulation on the face. (8)

insulation. A material that restricts the flow of air between a home's interior and the outdoors. (9)

integrated waste management. A waste handling approach that addresses the need for energy and a clean environment. (23)

intensity. The brightness or dullness of a hue. (11)

interest. The price paid for the use of borrowed money. It is usually stated as an annual percentage rate of the amount borrowed. (5)

interior wall elevation. A drawing that shows how a finished wall will look. (19)

International style. A modern style of architecture and furniture design beginning in the 1900s, influenced strongly by the Bauhaus, the German state school of design. (6)

internship. An arrangement with an educational institution whereby a student is supervised while working with a more experienced jobholder. (24)

isometric drawing. Illustrates a space or product in three dimensions and at 30-degree angles. (7)

J

job shadowing. The process of observing a person in the workplace to learn more about a job and its requirements. (24)

joist. Lightweight horizontal support member. (8)

K

kit house. A type of factory-built housing that is shipped to the site in unassembled parts or as a finished shell from the factory. (4)

knitting. The process of looping yarns together. (13)

L

laminate. A product made by uniting one or more different layers, usually a decorative surface to a sturdy core. (14)

landscape. The outdoor living space. (20)

landscape architect. A professional trained to create landscape designs that function well and are aesthetically pleasing. (20)

landscape zones. The ground around a building that is divided into three areas—public zones, private zones, and service zones. (20)

landscaping. Altering the topography and adding decorative plantings to change the appearance of a site. (4)

leadership. The ability to guide and motivate others to complete tasks or achieve goals. (25)

lead paint. A term that refers to lead-based paint which was a common form of paint manufactured before 1978 that contained lead. (21)

lease. A legal document spelling out the conditions of the rental agreement. (5)

lessee. A renter. (5)

lessor. A property owner (landlord). (5)

letter of agreement. A document that spells out the responsibilities of the interior designer and the client for a project. (19)

liaison. A connecting agent (often the interior designer) between the client and other persons involved in a project. (19)

life cycle. A series of stages through which an individual or family passes during a lifetime. (1)

lifelong learning. Continually updating your knowledge and skills. (24)

lifestyle. A living pattern or way of life. (1)

light-emitting diode (LED). Extremely long-lasting bulbs composed of crystals (about the size of a grain of salt) on silicon chips that produce light when a small electric current passes through them. (17)

limited warranty. A warranty that provides service, repairs, and replacements under certain conditions. For example, a warrantor can charge a fee for repairs. (18)

line. The most basic element of design, created by connecting two dots. (10)

log cabin. Originally a one-room, rectangular house made from squared off logs with notches on the top and bottom of each end. (6)

loss leader. An item priced below normal cost to entice people into a store to buy the item plus other items not on sale. (16)

low mass. A space that is simple and sparse. (10)

lumen. A measurement of the amount of light a bulb produces. (17)

M

Mansard roof. A variation of the gambrel roof designed by a French architect named Mansard. The low slopes of the roof encircle the house, and dormers often project from the steeply pitched part of the roof. (6)

manufactured fiber. A type of fiber made from wood cellulose, oil products, and other chemicals. (13)

manufactured housing. Factory built, single-family housing units with wheels built after 1976. (4)

manufactured landscape elements. Landscape components not found in the natural environment. (20)

masonry. A hard building material, such as brick, concrete block, stucco, and natural stone. (8)

mass. The amount of pattern or objects in a space; also the degree of crowding or openness in a space. (10)

master's degree. A degree that requires another year or two of study beyond a bachelor's degree. (24)

memory foam mattress. A foam mattress that supports the body during sleep but returns to its original shape once a person gets out of bed. (15)

mentor. Someone with greater experience and knowledge who guides an individual in his or her career. (24)

meter. A gauge that monitors electrical usage in the house. (9)

microturbine. A small turbine engine that produces electricity. (23)

microwave oven. An appliance that cooks food with high-frequency energy waves. (18)

minimum property standards (MPS). Standards set by the Federal Housing Administration (FHA) that regulate the size of lots. (4)

mobile homes. Factory-built, single-family housing units with wheels built before 1976. (4)

mobility limitation. Conditions that make it difficult for a person to walk from one location to another. (21)

model. A three-dimensional miniature of a design. (7)

Modern style. The housing designs developed in the United States from the early 1900s into the 1980s; also refers to the twenty-first century furniture style that uses simpler lines and abstract forms to result in pieces that can be mass produced from automated machinery. (6)

modular housing. Factory-built housing in a coordinated series of modules. (4)

moisture barrier. A sheet of polyethylene plastic that is spread across the filler before placing plumbing and heating systems and pouring the slab for a slab-on-grade house. (8)

mold. A fungus that grows on damp or decaying matter. (21)

monochromatic color harmony. The simplest color harmony based on tints and shades of a single hue. (11)

mortgage. A pledge of property that a borrower gives to a lender as security for a loan with which to buy the property. (5)

mortise-and-tenon joint. A furniture joint in which the glued tenon fits tightly into the mortise, or hole; one of the strongest wood joints. (15)

multifamily house. A structure that provides housing for more than one household. (4)

multipurpose furniture. Furniture that serves more than one purpose. (16)

multipurpose room. A room used for many types of activities, such as reading, studying, watching TV, listening to music, and working on hobbies. (7)

N

nap. A layer of fiber ends that stand up from the surface of the fabric. (13)

natural landscape elements. Landscape components found in the natural environment. (20)

natural stone. Hardened earth or mineral matter. (8)

near environment. A small and distinct part of the total environment in which you live. (1)

needlepunching. The process of interlocking fibers by using felting needles. (13)

needs. Basic requirements people must fill in order to live. (1)

negotiation. The process of agreeing to an issue that requires all parties to give and take. (25)

neighborhood. A section of a community consisting of a group of houses and people. (4)

networking. The exchange of information or services among individuals or groups. (24)

neutral color harmonies. A color harmony using combinations of black, gray, and white. Brown, tan, and beige can also be used (10).

New England. The region of North American that now includes the states of Maine, New Hampshire, Vermont, Massachusetts, Connecticut, and Rhode Island. (6)

new town. An urban development consisting of a small to midsize city with a broad range of housing and planned industrial, commercial, educational, and recreational facilities. (2)

new urbanism. Refers to communities that are planned to encourage pedestrian traffic, place more emphasis on the environment, and are sustainable. (2)

noise pollution. Unwanted sound that spreads through the environment. (21)

nonbearing wall. A wall that does not support any weight from the structure beyond its own weight. (8)

nonhuman resources. Resources that are not directly supplied by people. (3)

nonstructural lighting. Lighting that is not a structural part of the house. (17)

nonverbal communication. A form of communication that involves sending messages without the use of words; involves *body language.* (25)

nuclear energy. The heat released when Uranium-235 is split in a nuclear reactor. (23)

O

occupation. Paid employment that involves handling one or more jobs. (24)

opposition. Lines that meet to form right angles. (12)

orientation. Placing a structure on a site in consideration of the location of the sun, prevailing winds, water sources, and scenic view. (4)

oriented strand board (OSB). A sheet formed by layering wood chips and fiber in a crosshatch pattern and gluing them together. (8)

outsource. Hiring out product and implementation work to subcontractors who specialize in particular products and tasks. (19)

overcurrent protection device. A device that protects each circuit by stopping the excessive flow of electrical current in the circuit. (9)

owner-built housing. Housing built by the owner, although a contractor may be hired to put up the shell of the house. (4)

P

paint. A mixture of pigment and liquid that thinly coats and covers a surface. (14)

paneling. A building material that is usually made of plywood, but can also be produced from a synthetic material. (14)

panelized housing. Housing that involves panels of walls, floors, ceilings, or roofs that can be ordered separately and assembled at the housing site. (4)

pattern bond. The pattern formed by masonry units and the mortar joints on the face of the wall, creating interesting effects. (8)

pent roof. A small roof ledge between the first and second floors of a house. (6)

perennials. Flowers that bloom for many years without replanting. (20)

photovoltaic (PV). A solar cell that converts sunlight into electricity. (23)

physical needs. Basic survival essentials, including shelter, food, water, and rest. (1)

physical neighborhood. The actual dwellings, buildings, and land that make a neighborhood. (4)

pigment. A coloring agent used in paint and printed materials. (11)

planned neighborhood. Neighborhoods for which developers make decisions regarding the size and layout of individual lots before dwellings are built. (4)

plan view. A view from the top of a building, as with an imaginary glass box. (7)

plaster. A paste used for coating walls and ceilings that hardens as it dries. (14)

plastic wallboard. A building material with a durable decorative finish used for interior walls. (14)

plumbing plunger. A device that creates a suction motion to clear a blocked drain. (22)

plywood sheet. Thin layers of wood veneer that have been glued and pressed together. (8)

points. Fees paid to the lender for the loan (usually one point equals one percent of the loan). (5)

polymer. A chemical compound that forms by joining together a chain of small molecules that contain repeating structural units to form a single-layer molecule. (13)

porcelain tile. The highest quality ceramic tile made of white or light-colored clay; withstands freezing temperatures. (14)

Prairie style. A style of housing designed by Frank Lloyd Wright with strong horizontal design that uses wood, stone, and materials found in the natural environment. (6)

preapproval. A preliminary approval process in which the lender verifies the home buyer's employment and checks tax records, bank references, and the borrower's credit history. (5)

precautions. Preventative actions that can help avoid accidents. (21)

precut housing. Housing components that are cut to exact size in the factory and delivered to the building site. (4)

presentation drawings. Refined drawings or renderings to use for publication or for showing the design to a client. (7)

pressed wood. A board made of shavings, veneer scraps, chips, and other small pieces of wood pressed together. Often used on unseen parts of furniture. (15)

pressure preservative treated (PT). A treatment in which chemical preservatives are forced into the cellular structure of wood under pressure. (8)

primary colors. The colors of yellow, red, and blue from which all other colors are made. (11)

principal. The original sum borrowed for the purchase of a home. (5)

print. A copy of a drawing. (7)

prioritize. To rank goals in order of importance. (16)

private area. The part of a site hidden from view that offers space for recreation and relaxation. (7)

private mortgage insurance (PMI). Insurance that protects the lender if the borrower fails to pay. (5)

private zone. The part of a site hidden from public view. (4)

profile. A concise biographical sketch (or word picture) that portrays the key characteristics about the client. (19)

proportion. The relationship of parts of the same object, or the relationship between different objects in the same group. (12)

protein natural fiber. Fiber that comes from animal sources. (13)

psychological needs. Needs relating to the mind and feelings that people must meet in order to live satisfying lives. (1)

public zone. The part of a site people can see from the street or road. (4)

punctual. A characteristic that shows an individual is always prompt and on time. (25)

Q

quality of life. The degree of satisfaction a person obtains from life. (1)

R

radiation. Lines flowing away from a central point. (12)

radon. A natural radioactive gas. (21)

rafter. A series of beams that support the weight of the roof. (8)

ranch. A style of housing characterized by a one-story structure at ground level that may have a basement. (6)

rational decision. A decision based on reasoning. (3)

realistic form. The design of an object that communicates a lifelike form and traditional feeling. (10)

recycle. To adapt to new use. (16)

redecorate. To change or update a decorating scheme. (22)

reference. An individual who will provide important information about you to a prospective employer. (25)

reflected light. Light that bounces off surfaces. (17)

region. The specific part of the world, country, or state in which you live. (4)

remodeling. Changing a structure, such as adding a wall or room. (22)

rendering. A presentation drawing—usually with color, texture, and shadows—showing a realistic view of the completed house. (7)

renew. To give furniture a new look. (16)

renewable energy sources. Energy sources that replenish themselves regularly. (23)

repetition. Repeating an element of design. It is one of the easiest ways to achieve rhythm in design. (12)

reproduction. A copy of an antique original. (15)

resiliency. The ability to return to the original size or shape. (13)

resilient floor covering. Floor treatments that are generally nonabsorbent, durable, easy to maintain, and fairly inexpensive. (14)

resources. Objects, qualities, and personal strengths that can be used to reach a goal. (2)

restore. To return an item to its original state as much as possible. (16)

résumé. A brief outline of your education, work experience, and other qualifications for work. (25)

retainer. An upfront fee the client pays to engage the services of a designer; usually deducted from the balance due at the end of the project. (19)

reupholster. To update fabric, padding, and springs for a piece of furniture. (19)

reverse mortgage. A payment plan designed for older adults whereby a mortgage company converts the value of the house into income to the residents for as long as they continuously live in the house. Later the mortgage company assumes ownership of the dwelling. (4)

rhythm. A sense of movement that smoothly leads the eyes from one area to another in a design; the cause of an organized pattern. (12)

ridge board. The horizontal member at which the two slopes of the roof meet. It is the highest point of the roof frame. (8)

roles. Patterns of behavior that people display in their homes, the workplace, and their communities. (1)

row houses. A continuous group of dwellings linked by common sidewalls. (2)

R-value. A measure of how well a material insulates, or resists heat movement; the greater the R-value, the more resistant the material to heat movement. (9)

S

Saltbox. A variation of the Cape Cod style of housing created by adding a lean-to section to the back side of the house. (6)

scale. The relative size of an object in relation to other objects. (12)

scale floor plan. A reduced-size drawing that is directly proportional to the actual size and shape of a space or room. (16)

Scandinavian. An immigrant from Sweden, Finland, Norway, and Denmark. (6)

schedule. An organized chart of detailed notes in a ruled enclosure; describes large quantities of information in the drawings. (7)

schematic drawings. Freehand sketches of a proposed plan the designer uses in refining a design. (7)

seasonal sales. A sale held at the end of a selling season to eliminate old stock and make room for new items. (16)

secondary colors. The colors of orange, green, and violet; made by mixing equal amounts of two primary colors. (11)

section view. A view taken from an imaginary cut through a part of a building, such as the walls. (7)

security deposit. A payment that insures the owner against financial loss caused by the renter. (5)

self-actualization. When a person develops his or her full potential as a person. (1)

self-cleaning oven. An oven that operates at extremely high temperatures to burn away spatters and spills. (18)

self-esteem. An awareness and appreciation of your own worth. (1)

self-expression. Showing a person's true personality and taste. (1)

self-motivation. An inner urge to get things completed. (25)

semiskilled labor. Workers who have some experience and/or technical training. (24)

sensory design. The application of design that affects the senses of sight, hearing, smell, and touch. (12)

septic tank. An underground tank that decomposes waste through the action of bacteria. (9)

service drop. The connecting wires from the utility pole transformer to the point of entry to the house. (9)

service entrance panel. A large metal box that receives power from the electric company's service drop or service lateral. It divides the power into individual circuits. (9)

service zone. The part of a site that household members use for necessary activities. (4)

shade. The addition of black to a hue to make it a darker value. (11)

shades. Screens that block unwanted light. (17)

shingles. Thin, protective building materials installed in overlapping rows on roofs. (8)

short circuit. An undesirable current path that allows the electrical current to bypass the load of the circuit. (22)

shutters. Vertical panels that are hinged together to open and close much like folding doors. (17)

siding. The material forming the exposed surface of outside walls of a house. (8)

sill plate. A piece of lumber bolted to the foundation wall with anchor bolts. (8)

single-family house. Housing designed for one family. (4)

site. The piece of land on which a dwelling is built. (4)

site-built housing. Housing built on a lot, piece by piece on a foundation and using few factory-built structural components. (4)

skilled labor. Workers who have successfully completed a formal training program beyond high school. (24)

smoke detector. A device that sends out a loud signal if a fire starts. (21)

social area. An area providing space for daily living, entertaining, and recreation. (7)

soft floor covering. A floor treatment made of fibers, such as carpet and rugs. (14)

software programs. Instructions that tell a computer what to do, such as the operating system. (18)

soil conservation. The act of improving and maintaining the soil. (20)

soil stack. The main vertical pipe that receives waste matter from all plumbing fixtures. (9)

solar energy. Energy derived from the sun. (6)

solid surface. A durable countertop material that contains the color and pattern of the surface throughout. (14)

solid waste. Any waste material that is not a liquid or a gas. (23)

solid wood. Furniture in which all exposed parts are made of whole pieces of wood. (15)

Southern Colonial. A style of housing that features a large two- or three-story frame with a symmetrical design. (6)

space. The area around and inside a form. (10)

space planning. The process of placing furnishings for a well-functioning and visually pleasing area. (16)

Spanish. A housing style from the south and southwest consisting of asymmetrical design with red tile roofs, enclosed patios, arch-shaped windows and doors, wrought iron exterior decor, and stucco walls. (6)

specifications. Documentation that lists types and quality of materials to use and gives directions for their use. (7)

spinneret. A small nozzle with tiny holes (much like a showerhead) through which manufactured fiber solutions are forced to form fibers. (13)

split-complementary color harmony. A color harmony consisting of one hue with the two hues adjacent to its complement. (11)

stenciling. The application of paint by using a cutout form to outline a design or lettering. (14)

structural design. The pattern produced by varying the yarns in woven or knitted fabrics. (13)

structural light fixture. A lighting fixture permanently built into a home. (17)

stucco. A type of plaster applied to the exterior walls of a house. (6)

stud. Vertical 2 × 4-inch or 2 × 6-inch framing member; length varies. (8)

subdivision. The division of a tract of land into two or more parcels that makes it easier to sell and develop. (2)

subflooring. A covering of plywood or oriented strand board (OSB) sheets directly glued and nailed to the floor joists. (8)

sublet. The transfer of part interest of a rental property to someone else; both parties are responsible to the landlord for all terms of the lease. (5)

substandard. Houses that are not up to the quality living standards that are best for people; may be built with inferior workmanship or materials or do not meet local building codes. (2)

Sunbelt. The southern and southwestern regions of the United States. (2)

sunroom. A structure that can use energy more efficiently; also called a *garden room*. (20)

sustainable design. A type of design that strives to have no impact on the environment. (1)

symbols. Icons used on architectural drawings to represent plumbing and electrical fixtures, doors, windows, and other common objects in a house. (7)

symmetrical. A design in which identical objects on both sides of a center point are identical. (6)

synthetic. A manufactured material that imitates or replaces another. (14)

system. An interacting or interdependent group of items forming a unified whole. (9)

T

tactile texture. The way a surface feels to the touch. (10)

tanning. The process of using a complex acid compound, or tannin, to cause leather to become soft and resistant to stains, fading, and cracking. (13)

task lighting. A form of lighting used in areas where specific activities require more light. (17)

team. A small group of people working together for a common purpose. (25)

technology. The practical application of knowledge. (2)

telecommuting. Working at home or at another site through an electronic link to a computer network at a central office. (2)

template. A small piece of paper or plastic scaled to the actual dimensions of the furniture piece it represents. (16)

tenement houses. Early apartments that were built before housing regulations existed. (2)

tertiary colors. Colors made by mixing equal amounts of a primary color with a secondary color adjacent to it on the color wheel; also called *intermediate colors*. (11)

textiles. Any products made from fibers, including fabrics. (13)

texture. The way a surface feels or appears to feel. (10)

thermostat. A device for regulating room temperature. (9)

Tidewater South. An architectural style built by early English settlers in the southern coastal regions of what is now the United States. (6)

tile. A flat piece of kiln-fired clay or natural stone that is available in a wide range of sizes, colors, finishes, and patterns. (14)

tint. The addition of white to a hue to make it a lighter value. (11)

title. A document that gives proof of the rights of ownership and possession of particular property. (5)

tone. The result of adding gray to a hue. (11)

tongue-and-groove joint. A furniture joint made by fitting a tongue cut on one edge of a board into a matching groove cut on the edge of another board. (15)

topography. The arrangement of physical features of the land; the art of representing such features on maps and charts. (2)

toxic. Poisonous. (21)

tract houses. Groups of similarly designed houses built on a tract of land. (2)

trade name. The name a company uses to identify the specific fiber they develop. (13)

Traditional. Houses that reflect the experiences and traditions of past eras. (6)

traffic patterns. The paths people follow from room to room or to the outdoors. (7)

transferable skills. Skills that help a person succeed in a chosen job, including reading, writing, speaking, and basic math. (24)

transition. Drawing attention away from one part of an object to another part. (12)

trap. A bend in a water pipe within or just below a fixture that catches and holds a quantity of water; prevents sewage gases from seeping back into the house. (9)

triadic color harmony. A color harmony created by combining any three colors that are equally distant from each other on a standard color wheel. (11)

truss rafter. A group of framing members forming a rigid-triangular framework for the roof. (8)

tufted. A process of looping yarns into a backing material and securing them with an adhesive compound to form carpets and rugs. (13)

tungsten-halogen lights. The light produced when a gas from the halogen family and tungsten molecules are combined to activate a filament inside a quartz enclosure. (17)

U

unassembled furniture. Furniture that is sold in parts that require assembly; may be finished or unfinished. (16)

unity. Repeating similar elements of design to relate all parts of a design to one idea. (12)

universal design (UD). A design concept that focuses on making living environments, and the products used to create them, without special adaptations. (4)

unskilled labor. Workers who fill entry-level jobs that require almost no previous knowledge or experience. (24)

upholstery. The fabric, padding, or other material manufacturers use to make a soft covering for furniture. (13)

V

VA-guaranteed mortgage. A three-party contract that involves the borrower (who is a veteran of the U.S. Armed Forces), a lending firm, and the Veterans Administration (VA). (5)

value. The relative lightness or darkness of a hue. (11)

values. Strong beliefs or ideas about what is important. (1)

veneered wood. Wood made by bonding three, five, or seven thin layers of wood to one another, to a solid wood core, or to a pressed wood core; often uses fine wood as the top layer. (15)

veneer wall. A nonsupporting wall tied to the wall frame that is covered with sheathing. (8)

ventilation. Air circulation. (21)

vent stack. A vertical pipe that extends through the roof to release gases and odors outdoors. (9)

verbal communication. A form of communication that involves speaking, listening, and writing. (25)

vertical line. A line that is perpendicular to the ground. (10)

Victorian. A style of housing named after Queen Victoria of England that has an abundance of decorative trim. Victorian styles include Italianate, gothic Revival, American Second Empire, Stick, Richardsonian Romanesque, Eastlake Victorian, and Queen Anne. (6)

vision disability. Any degree of vision loss. (21)

visual imagery. A type of nonverbal communication. It is the language of sight and communicates a certain personality or mood. (10)

visual pollution. The harm done to the appearance of the environment as a result of human activities. (23)

visual texture. Texture that you can see, but cannot feel. (10)

visual weight. The perception that an object weighs more or less than it really does. (12)

voltage. A measure of the pressure used to push the electrical current along a conductor. (9)

W

wale. The diagonal rib or cord pattern that forms in a twill-weave fabric. (13)

wall covering. A decorative paper or vinyl applied to a wall with a special paste. (14)

wall treatment. A covering that is applied to an interior wall. (14)

warm colors. Red, yellow, and orange and the colors near them on the color wheel; also called *advancing colors*. (11)

warp yarn. The yarns that run lengthwise in a fabric and form the lengthwise grain. (13)

warranty. A manufacturer's written promise that a product will meet certain performance and quality standards as outlined in the warranty. (18)

waterbed. A mattress consisting of a plastic bag or tubes filled with water. (15)

water conservation. Reducing water use and eliminating water waste. (20)

wattage. The amount of electricity a bulb uses.

watts. A measure of the amount of electrical power used. (9)

weather stripping. A strip of material that covers the edges of a window or door to prevent moisture and air from entering the house. (9)

weaving. The interlacing of two sets of yarns at right angles. (13)

weft yarn. The filling yarns that run in the crosswise direction in fabric and form the crosswise grain. (13)

window treatment. Applications added to window units either for helping control the home environment or for purely decorative purposes. (17)

wood grain. A natural, decorative pattern in wood that forms as a tree grows. How the wood is cut from a log also impacts the pattern. (15)

work area. All parts of the house needed to maintain and service the other areas. (7)

work triangle. The imaginary line connecting the food preparation and storage center, cleanup center, and cooking and serving centers of a kitchen. (7)

X

xeriscape. A landscaping method that utilizes water-conserving techniques and choosing and grouping plants native to an area according to the amount of water and sunlight needed. (20)

Y

yarn. A continuous strand that may consist of staple fibers (short fibers) and/or filaments (long, continuous fibers). (13)

yurt. A portable hut made of several layers of felt covered with canvas. (1)

Z

Zero Energy Home (ZEH). A home that produces and uses its own energy. (23)

zoning regulation. A government requirement that controls land use. (2)

Index